THE IRISH CIVIL WAR IN COLOUR

John O'Byrne

Michael B. Barry

GILL BOOKS

Gill Books
Hume Avenue
Park West
Dublin 12
www.gillbooks.ie

Gill Books is an imprint of M.H. Gill and Co.

THE IRISH CIVIL WAR IN COLOUR
ISBN 9780717195862
© John O'Byrne and Michael B. Barry 2022
John O'Byrne and Michael B. Barry assert the moral right to be identified as the authors of this work.

To the best of our knowledge, this book complies in full with the requirements of the General Product Safety Regulation (GPSR). For further information and help with any safety queries, please contact us at productsafety@gill.ie.

By Michael B. Barry:
Across Deep Waters: Bridges of Ireland
Restoring a Victorian House
Through the Cities: The Revolution in Light Rail
Tales of the Permanent Way: Stories from the Heart of Ireland's Railways
50 Things to Do in Dublin
Dublin's Strangest Tales (with Patrick Sammon)
Bridges of Dublin: The Remarkable Story of Dublin's Liffey Bridges (with Annette Black)
Victorian Dublin Revealed: The Remarkable Legacy of Nineteenth-Century Dublin
Beyond the Chaos: The Remarkable Heritage of Syria
Homage to al-Andalus: The Rise and Fall of Islamic Spain
The Alhambra Revealed: The Remarkable Story of the Kingdom of Granada
Málaga: A Souvenir and Guide
Courage Boys, We are Winning: An Illustrated History of the 1916 Rising
The Fight for Irish Freedom: An Illustrated History of the War of Independence
The Green Divide: An Illustrated History of the Irish Civil War
An Illustrated History of the Irish Revolution 1916-1923
Fake News and the Irish War of Independence

The paper used in this book comes from the wood pulp of sustainably managed forests.

A CIP catalogue record for this book is available from the British Library.

5

Colourising of photographs by John O'Byrne.
Book design by Michael B. Barry.

Printed and bound in India by Replika Press Pvt. Ltd.

Contents

Chronology 1922–23

1922

3 January	Dáil Éireann meets and resumes Treaty debate. On 7 January, the Dáil approves Treaty (64 votes in favour, 57 against).
10 January	De Valera and other supporters leave Dáil. Arthur Griffith is elected President.
14 January	'Southern Parliament' meets and sets up Provisional Government.
31 January	The new Army of the Provisional Government establishes its HQ at Beggars Bush Barracks.
5 March	Stand-off between pro- and anti-Treaty forces at Limerick.
14 March	Public meeting in Cork with Michael Collins disrupted by anti-Treaty supporters.
17 March	De Valera makes a speech warning about the Volunteers having 'to wade through Irish blood' at a meeting in Thurles.
26 March	An IRA Convention at the Mansion House, Dublin, repudiates the Treaty and appoints an Executive.
29 March	Capture of the ship *Upnor* by Cork IRA and seizure of arms.
14 April	Takeover of Four Courts, Dublin, in the early hours, by anti-Treaty forces.
16 April	Despite proclamation banning meeting in Sligo by IRA, Griffith speaks, enabled by the presence of a large number of pro-Treaty troops.
2 May	After several days of jostling for position, firing breaks out between both sides in Kilkenny. Two hundred troops arrive from Beggars Bush and there is an assault on Republicans ensconced in Kilkenny Castle. The castle is captured. A committee representing both sides meets in Dublin and establishes a truce.
20 May	De Valera and Collins announce a pact for the election planned for June.
5 June	British forces shell Provisional Government Army positions in Pettigo, Co. Donegal.
14 June	Collins, at an election meeting in Cork, repudiates the election pact.
16 June	Election in 26 Counties. Results are: 58 pro-Treaty seats; 36 anti-Treaty; 34 Labour and others.
22 June	Sir Henry Wilson is assassinated in London.
26 June	J.J. O'Connell, Deputy Chief of Staff, Provisional Government Army, is kidnapped and held at the Four Courts.
28 June	The Four Courts garrison is issued with a demand to surrender at 3.40 a.m. Artillery bombardment starts shortly afterwards.
29 June	Following continuous shelling, pro-Treaty troops storm breaches in the Four Courts.
30 June	Large explosion at the Four Courts, followed by several others. The garrison surrenders.
30 June	Republicans set up in the Dublin city centre area. Fighting intensifies around the 'Block' in Upper Sackville St.
5 July	After days of fighting, the Block is in ruins. Cathal Brugha emerges fighting, is shot and mortally wounded.
6 July	Republican forces assemble in Blessington but disperse several days later on the approach of large numbers of pro-Treaty forces.
11 July	Following a truce established earlier in Limerick, clashes begin after the arrival of pro-Treaty reinforcements.
12 July	A 'War Council' of three is created by Michael Collins.
20 July	General Prout and his forces take Waterford from the Republicans.
20 July	Anti-Treaty forces withdraw from Limerick after fierce fighting and the shelling of barracks.
24 July	Provisional Government forces land at Westport.
1 August	Harry Boland is shot and mortally wounded during an early-morning raid at a hotel in Skerries where he was staying.
2 August	Pro-Treaty troops land at Fenit and take Tralee.
5 August	Kilmallock is captured by pro-Treaty forces.
8 August	The Provisional Government Army under Major-General Dalton lands at Passage West and advances towards Cork City.
10 August	Cork City is captured by pro-Treaty forces. The anti-Treaty forces regroup at Macroom and then disperse.
11 August	Pro-Treaty forces under Commandant O'Connor 'Scarteen' land at Kenmare and take the town.
12 August	Arthur Griffith dies of a cerebral haemorrhage.

22 August	Michael Collins, on a tour of West Cork, is ambushed and shot dead at Bealnablath.
25 August	W.T. Cosgrave is appointed Chairman of the Provisional Government.
9 September	The Third Dáil meets.
9 September	Republicans attack and retake Kenmare. Commandant O'Connor 'Scarteen' and his brother are shot dead.
16 September	Seven pro-Treaty soldiers (including Colonel Commandant Tom Keogh) are killed by a trap mine near Macroom.
20 September	Pro-Treaty troops mount a sweep through the Sligo area. Six Republicans are captured and shot dead on Benbulben.
Early October	The Railway Protection, Repair and Maintenance Corps is set up to defend the railways and repair damage.
10 October	A pastoral is issued by Irish Roman Catholic Bishops condemning the anti-Treaty side.
15 October	The Public Safety Act becomes effective. It includes powers for military courts to issue death sentences.
17 October	Formation of Republican government in opposition with Éamon de Valera as President of the Republic.
25 October	The Constitution of the Irish Free State is enacted by the Dáil.
10 November	Erskine Childers is arrested at Annamoe, Co. Wicklow, and charged with possession of a revolver.
17 November	Four young Republicans are executed for possession of weapons.
24 November	Childers, sentenced to death, is executed at Beggars Bush Barracks.
30 November	Liam Lynch, IRA Chief of Staff, issues a general order to assassinate those who approved the Public Safety Act.
6 December	The Irish Free State comes into being.
7 December	Seán Hales, pro-Treaty TD, is assassinated in Dublin.
8 December	Four Republican prisoners (O'Connor, Mellows, McKelvey and Barrett) are executed in Mountjoy Prison as a reprisal for the killing of Hales.
10 December	The house of prominent pro-Treaty supporter, Seán McGarry, is burnt at Philipsburgh Avenue in Dublin. His seven-year-old son, Emmet, dies of burns.

1923

13 January	W.T. Cosgrave's house in Rathfarnham is burnt down. During January and February similar action is taken against pro-Treaty supporters.
9 February	After being captured in January, Liam Deasy, Officer Commanding First Southern Division, IRA, issues a call to his comrades for immediate and unconditional surrender.
11 February	Thomas O'Higgins (father of Minister for Justice, Kevin) is shot dead during an attack to set his house on fire.
18 February	IRA leader Dinny Lacy is shot in action at the Glen of Aherlow.
6 March	Six National Army soldiers are killed at Knocknagoshel Co. Kerry, after being lured to a trap mine.
7 March	Nine Republican prisoners are brought to Ballyseedy, near Tralee, tied together and blown up by a mine. Eight die, one escapes.
7 March	Four Republican prisoners are blown up by a mine at Countess Bridge, Killarney.
12 March	Five Republican prisoners are taken from Bahaghs workhouse near Caherciveen and blown up by a mine.
14 March	Republican prisoners (Charlie Daly and three others) are executed in a field near Drumboe Castle, Co. Donegal.
26 March	A meeting of the IRA Executive in the Nire Valley, Co. Waterford, votes narrowly in favour of continuing the war.
10 April	Liam Lynch and party, en route to a reconvened IRA Executive meeting, flee to Crohan West in the Knockmealdowns to escape a sweep by a large force of Free State troops. Lynch is shot and dies that evening.
16 April	The siege of Republicans begins at the Clashmealcon Caves, North Kerry.
24 May	Frank Aiken, the new Chief of Staff of the IRA, issues orders to cease fire and to dump arms.
20 July	The Irish Free State Government sends a request to the British that the Boundary Commission be set up.
15 August	De Valera attends a Sinn Féin meeting in Ennis for the General Election called for later in August and is arrested.
27 August	In the General Election, Sinn Féin (anti-Treaty) win 44 seats; Cumann na nGaedheal (pro-Treaty) win 63; while the Labour Party and others win 46.
13 October	A mass hunger strike in Mountjoy Prison by Republican prisoners spreads to other places of internment. It fizzles out a little over six weeks later. Prisoners are gradually released over the following months, a process that continues up to mid-1924.

In memory of Liam Mellows, who tried to define what an Irish Republic meant, executed in Mountjoy Prison, Dublin, 8 December 1922, and Private John Martin (great-grand-uncle of John O'Byrne), killed in action at Farranfore, Co. Kerry, 27 September 1922.

Acknowledgements

This work benefitted from the help, insights and scholarship of many kind people. Thanks are due especially to: Aoife Torpey, Kilmainham Gaol Archives; Commandant Daniel Ayiotis, Lisa Dolan, Hugh Beckett and Noelle Grothier, Military Archives, Cathal Brugha Barracks; David Power, South Dublin Libraries; Matthew Potter, Limerick Museum; Brenda Malone and Clare MacNamara, National Museum of Ireland; Berni Metcalfe and Glenn Dunne, National Library of Ireland; Daniel Breen and Dara MacGrath, Cork Public Museum; Dee Collins, Mercier Press Archive and Orna Somerville, UCD Archives. Jim Coughlan of the *Irish Examiner* generously furnished images from their historic photographic archive. Exceptional photographs of the Dublin fighting of July 1922 were provided by Pádraig Óg Ó Ruairc. Conor Dullaghan, who maintains a magnificent collection of Irish militaria, kindly made available images from a recently acquired set of early twentieth-century photographs.

The following were very helpful: Tony McCarthy; Suzanne Buckley; Derek Jones; Diarmuid O'Connor; Dennis Kelly; Liam O'Sullivan; Geraldine McCarthy and Donal King; Joe Mooney; Paul Comerford; Gillean Robertson Miller; James Langton; James Osborne; Joe Maxwell; Las Fallon; Marcus Howard; Michael Fewer; Mícheál Ó Doibhilín, www.kilmainhamtales.ie; Philippe Bretagnon, Bibliothèque nationale de France; Proinsias Ó Raithaille; Tim Crowley, Michael Collins Centre; Brian Crowley, Pearse Museum, Rathfarnham; George Morrison; Louise Mulcahy, Patricia Corish, Dún Laoghaire-Rathdown Libraries; Paul Neilan; Peadar Collins; Jonathan Beaumont; Peter Rigney, Mark Merrigan and Ciaran Cooney, Irish Railway Record Society; Professor Frank Imbusch; Tommy Mooney; Paul Clerkin; Colum O'Riordan; John Dorney; Liz Gillis; Gerry White; Jack Kiernan; Gerard Moore; Elaine O'Sullivan; Barry Kenny, Iarnród Éireann and Barry Moore, Waterford Museum.

William Fagan gave valuable advice on the history of photography and colourisation. The authors were privileged to receive exceptional help from Paddy Sammon, and are grateful to have had his kind advice, clarity of view, support and assistance during the preparation of this book. Lastly, and importantly, we, the authors are appreciative of the support of, respectively, Paddy and Patricia O'Byrne, and Veronica Barry.

Introduction

Proverb: *Cogadh carad, caoi namhad* – 'only the common enemy gains when there is a fight among friends'.

The Irish Civil War was indeed a fight among friends and erstwhile comrades. It badly dishonoured and sullied the foundation of the new Irish State and its legacy has distorted Irish politics ever since. It forms a key and extremely painful part of Irish history. This is an illustrated book which tells the story of this war over the period 1922–23. To bring a fresh and vivid perspective to the narrative, the photographs within have been specially colourised.

The origins of the Civil War can be ascribed to a clash between two fundamental beliefs. The first was the extraordinary allure that the Republic, declared in 1916, had for those fighting for Irish independence. The concept of an Irish Republic, with its origins in the times of Wolfe Tone, had been burnished in 1916 by the sacrifices of Easter Week. The other fundamental belief was that of the British negotiators in the excellence, supremacy and inviolability of their British Empire. It was fully evident to Éamon de Valera in July 1921, when he met Lloyd George, that there was no likelihood of the British Government (part of a coalition, always with an eye to keeping their Imperial die-hards at bay) granting total freedom to the neighbouring island to become a 'Republic' outside of the British Empire. And so it transpired, in early December 1921, that the Irish plenipotentiaries had to take what was offered on the negotiating table in Downing Street.

The first six months of 1922 were dominated by arguments between those who accepted the Treaty as the best that could be obtained, and those who held out for a Republic (particularly those who could not stomach the idea of having to take an oath of faithfulness to a British king). These months were taken up by manoeuvrings, the taking over of barracks and efforts to find formulas for compromise. This was against the background of the Provisional Government desperately trying to recruit soldiers for its new Army. Tensions erupted into real conflict at the end of June 1922 when artillery shells were discharged at the Four Courts. As it turned out, strong convictions alone on the anti-Treaty side were no match against a large and growing army, with an abundance of weapons, including armoured cars and artillery, supplied by the British. The issue of Northern Ireland and partition played only a minor part during this time. During the Treaty negotiations, Lloyd George, with his customary resort to 'magical realism', had dangled the prospect of a Boundary Commission in front of the Irish negotiators. They took the bait, anticipating that this process would whittle the northern state down to an unsustainable size.

'Civil wars leave nothing but tombs', wrote a French poet. That was the case in Ireland where the latest estimates hover around a total of 1,400 deaths (thought to approximate to 350 Republicans, 750 National Army and 300 civilians). This figure is small in comparison with other European civil wars of the twentieth century, but a bitter one nonetheless.

This book is laid out in a sequential manner using selected images which tell the story of the Civil War, from A to Z. The granular captions are packed with information, based on years of research by Michael B. Barry. A chronology and glossary have been included to add to understanding. Chapter 1 gives the context of the origins of the war. It begins with the Treaty negotiations and continues up to the end of June 1922. Chapter 2 describes the initial heavy fighting in Dublin. Chapter 3 outlines the amphibious landings by the Provisional Government Army and shows the fighting as it spread across the country. The deaths of Griffith and Collins are detailed in Chapter 4. Chapter 5 describes the end game of the war, including the increasingly bitter reprisals and executions. It narrates how, during the early months of 1923, the war juddered to a halt.

We have endeavoured to achieve balance within these pages and have attempted to stick to the facts (including the portrayal of the cruelties perpetrated by both sides). In addition, we have refrained from using the pejorative term, 'Irregulars' which the Provisional Government instructed the press to use when referring to the anti-Treaty IRA. Instead we have referred here to 'anti-Treaty forces', 'IRA' or 'Republicans'. (In using the latter term we do not imply that those on the pro-Treaty side were not republican; in reality the majority were for the long-term goal of a Republic but they had chosen, in the interim, to take the pragmatic road of accepting the Treaty.) For the pro-Treaty side, nomenclature is a little more confusing, as they also termed themselves the IRA well into 1922. We use, variously, terms such as: 'pro-Treaty forces', 'Provisional Government Army', and the 'National Army' (i.e. that of the Irish Free State which came into being on 6 December 1922).

An illustrated book stands or falls on the quality and scope of its images. Accordingly, we have put a lot of effort into sourcing and searching through a wide range of archives. We succeeded in obtaining, not just what might be termed the 'usual suspects', but also new photographs – gleaned in many cases from private sources. In the search for photographs of the era, we found that it is relatively easy to come up with images of the pro-Treaty side. They had the services of a sophisticated propaganda department which facilitated the embedding of photographers and cinema cameramen within the National Army during big operations. By contrast, the peripatetic life of an anti-Treaty Volunteer was not a place where there were usually cameras – the basic elements of survival, warmth and shelter were more important during guerrilla warfare. Thus, there are few photographs to be had of the anti-Treaty IRA in action. However, we did obtain some. Perhaps one of the most interesting photographs is the impromptu one taken in April 1922 of young anti-Treaty Volunteers outside the Kildare Street Club in Dublin, which they had just seized. They pose by two nondescript trucks while several wear the top hats that they had just appropriated from within the premises. A cautionary note: a few photographs were of poor quality but have still been used, as they were essential in narrating a particular aspect of the story.

This book tells the history of the Civil War using photographs that have been specially colourised. The colour process has been around from the 1840s, when daguerreotypes were hand-coloured. Indeed, one of the earliest colour photographic processes was invented in Dublin during the 1890s by John Joly. There have been arguments on the merits or otherwise of colourisation: one eminent Irish historian was against when he recently wrote that 'colourisation assaults the aura'. On the other hand, an expert from the Royal Photographic Society, in favour of the process, wrote that for him 'colourisation … awoke the magic'. All that one can say in response to these arguments is that taste is very subjective.

In the days of only black-and-white photography, when the photographer pressed the shutter, they would have seen the people or scenes in the photograph in colour. Will the colourised photograph turn out to be an accurate depiction of the historical scene in question? Even modern colour photographs, film or digital, cannot reproduce the exact colours seen by the human eye. All printing, whether black-and-white or colour, is an interpretation of the contents of the original negative, plate or, in modern times, image file. Colourisation is interpretive, but then so is practically everything about photography.

In his colourisation of photographs for this book, John O'Byrne has striven to achieve, as close as possible, an accurate reproduction of colours in a particular scene. Importantly, he works by hand and uses Adobe Photoshop to select every colour segment in a given photograph. This is painstaking work. Think of the complexity of a crowd scene: there could be 50 faces and 100 eyes to select. In other books Artificial Intelligence (AI) software is used, with algorithms to deduce the areas to be coloured and suggest the actual colours. In this book no AI software has been used as in our view it results in a 'pasteurised' or 'waxwork' look.

John O'Byrne's experience is hugely important to the success of this colourisation exercise: he has been professionally working at colourisation since 2015. Crucially, most of his work has focused on early twentieth-century photographs taken in Ireland, many of which have a military theme. He knows the military vehicles and their colours, as well as the detail of uniforms and emblems and the like. In addition, he has studied the clothing (and colours) of that era. To maintain the authenticity of the original photographs, the many cracks, specks, or photographer's inscriptions (or embossing, in the case of the prolific photographer W.D. Hogan) have not been removed.

The intention of this book is to accurately portray the events of the Civil War using a wide collection of well-chosen photographs. As in all eras of human existence, the people at that time lived their lives in colour. In the following pages we have used photographs that have been colourised, in the hope of helping the story of this complicated war to come alive in an accessible and understandable manner.

John O'Byrne
Michael B. Barry
August 2022

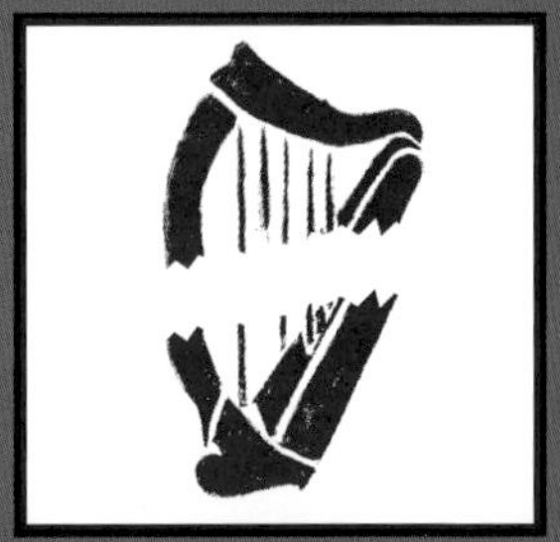

Chapter 1
The Road to Division

The War of Independence ended with the truce of July 1921. In October, a delegation travelled to London for talks which concluded with the signing of the Anglo-Irish Treaty on 6 December. The Dáil debates that followed were punctuated by bitter uproar. The IRA was mainly anti-Treaty. Under the Treaty a Provisional Government was established and a new army formed. As British troops evacuated their barracks, there was friction between both sides. The anti-Treaty IRA met to form an Executive which rejected the authority of the new government. In April 1922 it took over the Four Courts and other prominent buildings in Dublin. An election was held on 16 June 1922 with a resulting majority for those with pro-Treaty views. The assassination of Sir Henry Wilson in London and the kidnapping of a pro-Treaty general proved to be the final triggers for the Civil War.

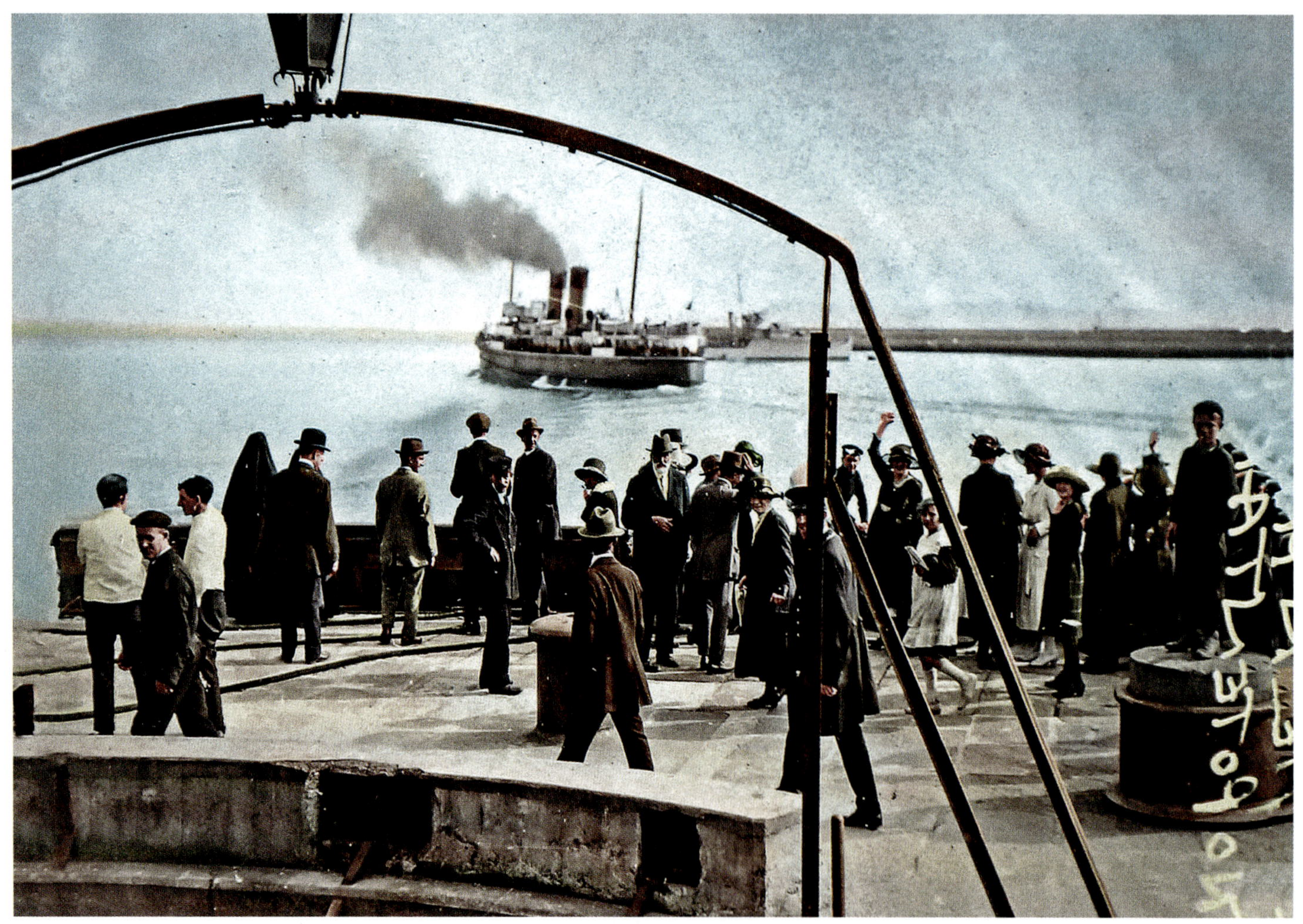

Rendezvous with destiny – the ferry departs Dún Laoghaire. The truce came into effect on 11 July 1921. Éamon de Valera immediately led a delegation to London where he met the British PM, David Lloyd George. There was no meeting of minds. Later correspondence settled on an ambiguous formula to allow negotiations to begin in October.

Right: Arthur Griffith poses for the cameramen. He was a leading member of the plenipotentiaries dispatched in October 1922 to London to negotiate with the British. De Valera chose not to attend and later explained that this was in order to better prepare people for compromise.

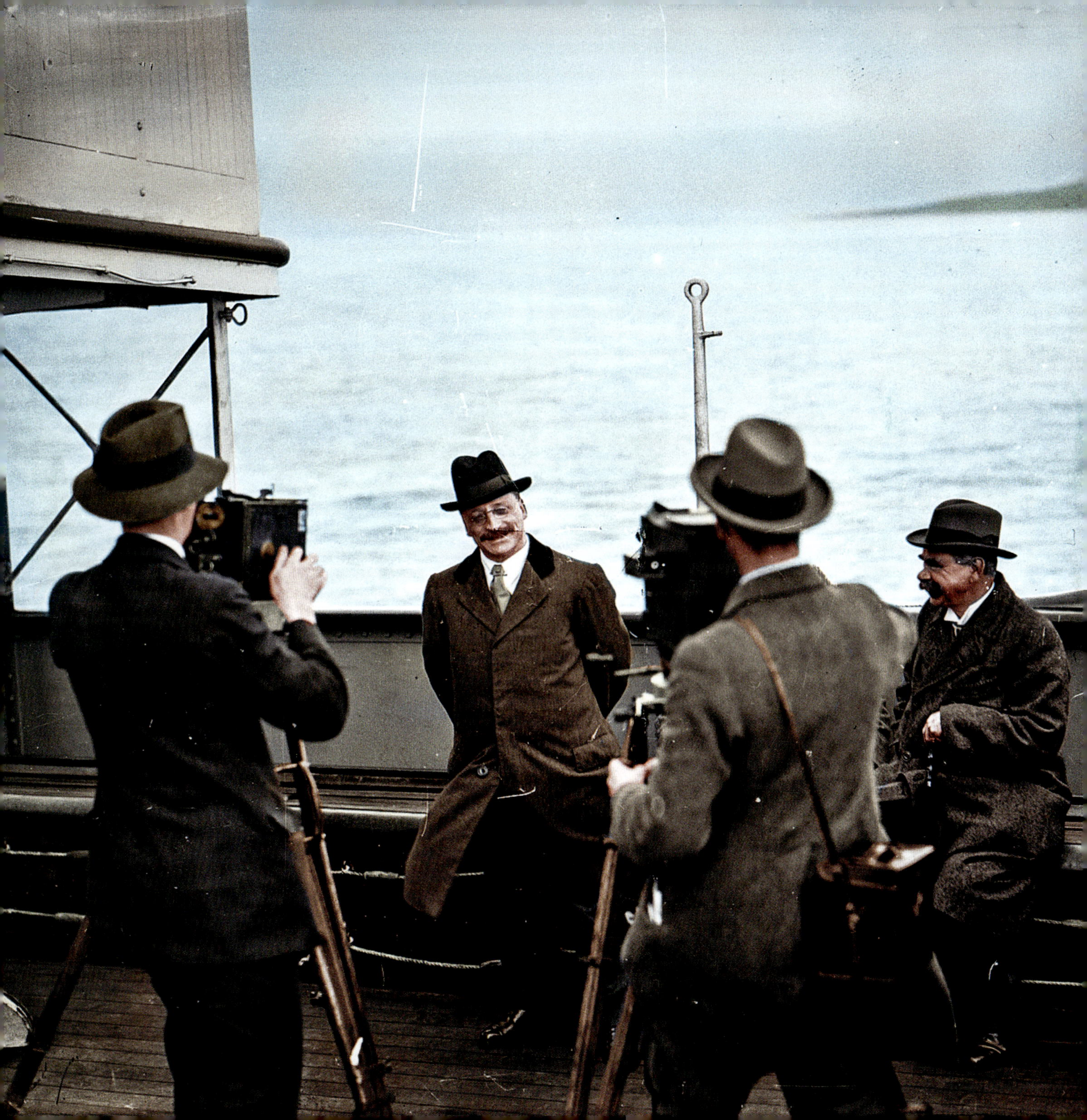

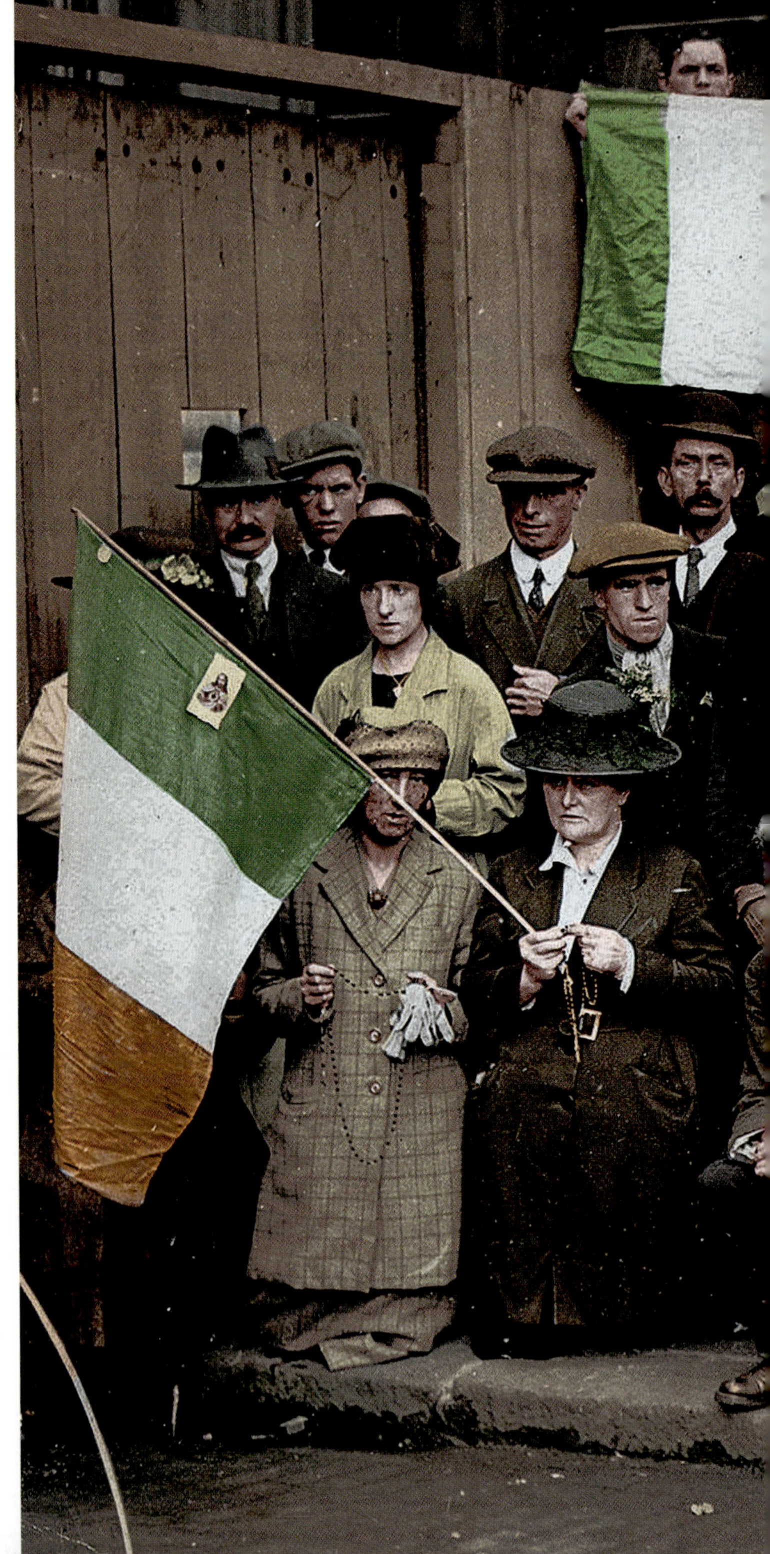

Rosaries and tricolours at Downing Street on 14 July 1921 when de Valera and his delegation meet Lloyd George. With specially constructed barriers in the background, a crowd waits. Some pray on their knees – a woman on the left wields a flag and rosary beads. Similar scenes followed in October 1921 when the plenipotentiaries arrived for the negotiations that led to the Treaty.

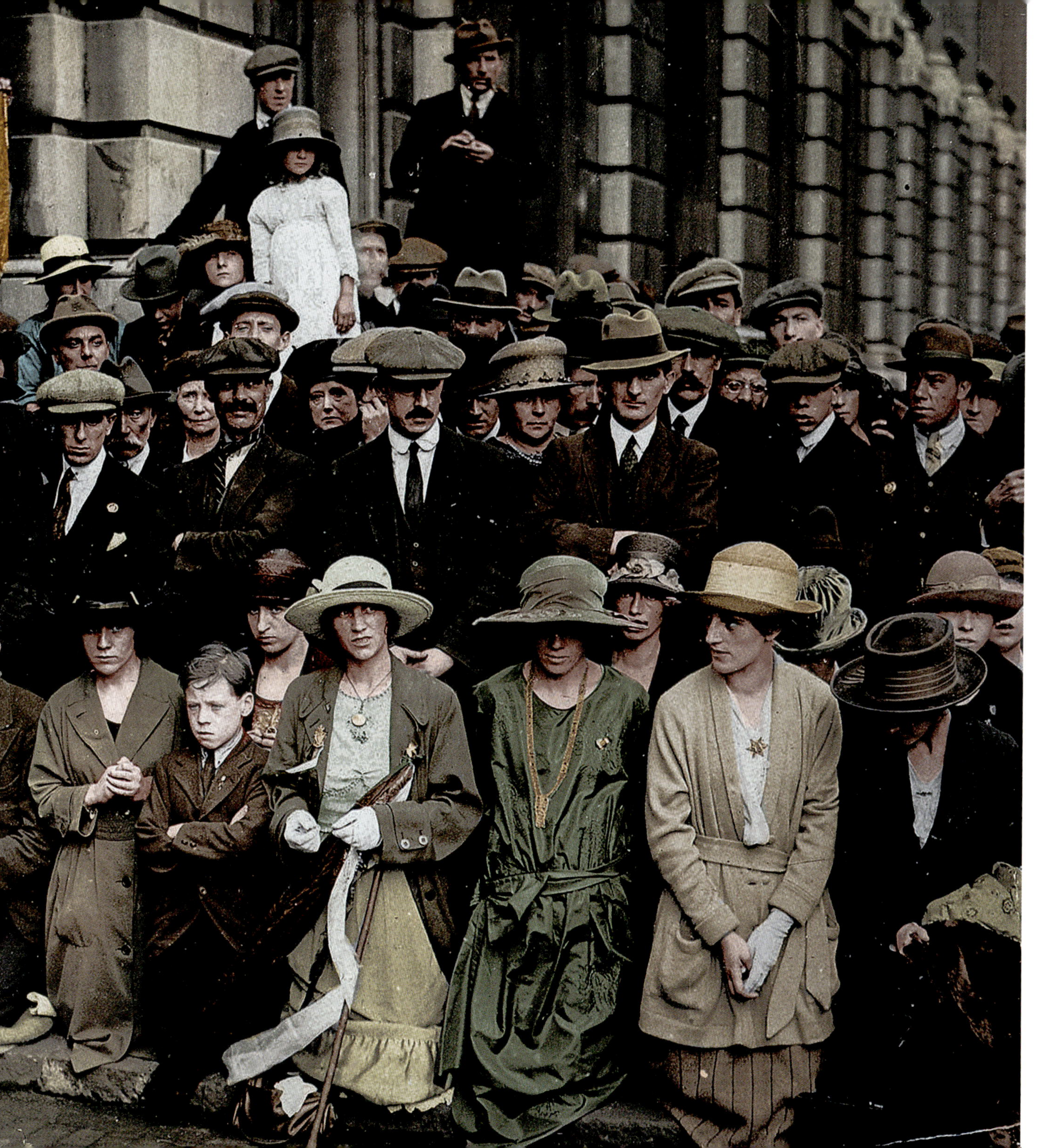

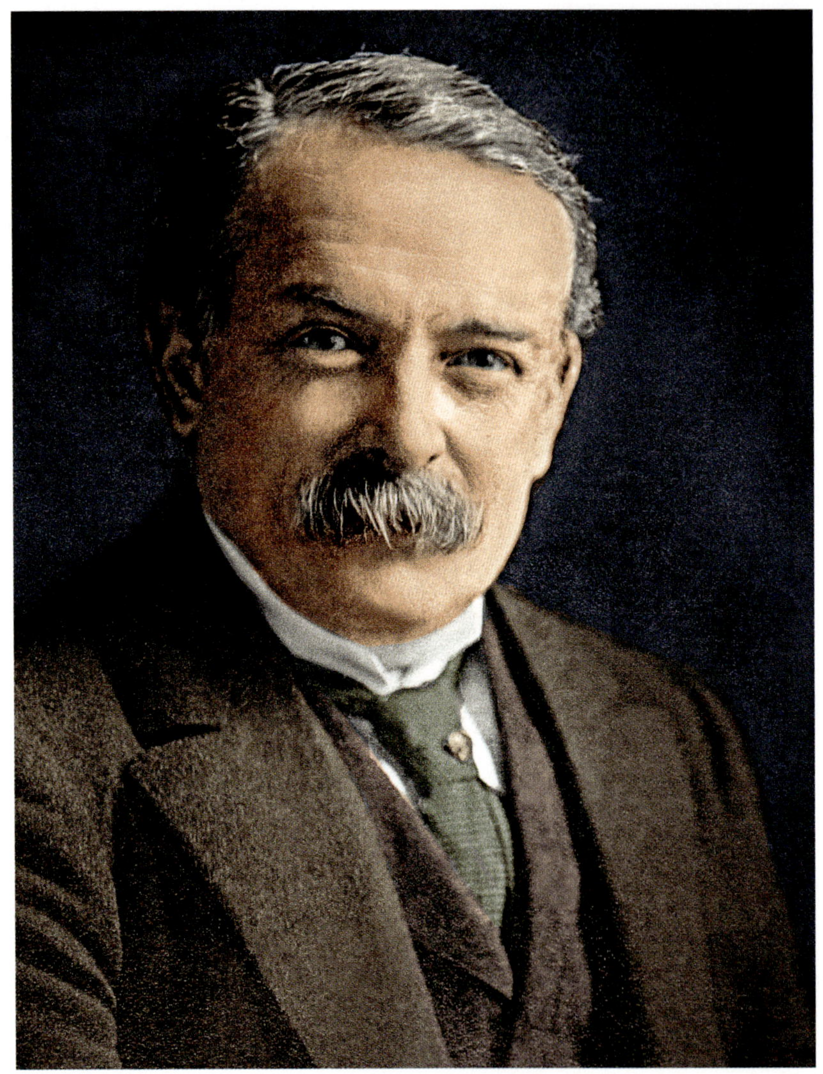

The leading British protagonist at the Treaty negotiations – David Lloyd George.

Right: Michael Collins in London at the end of 1921. The odds were stacked against the Irish delegation. With unclear terms of reference, they were not united and some members like Erskine Childers reported directly back to de Valera.

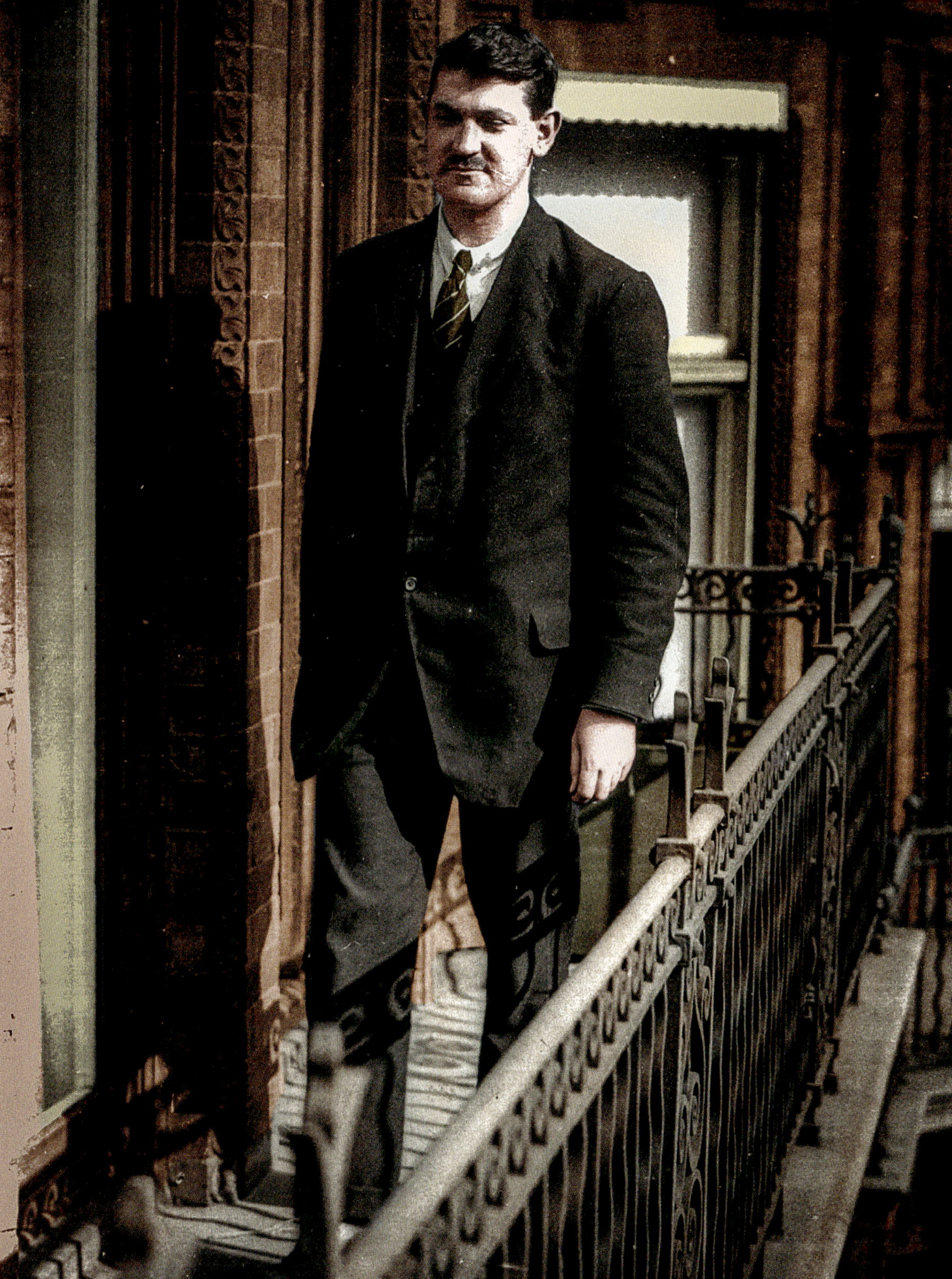

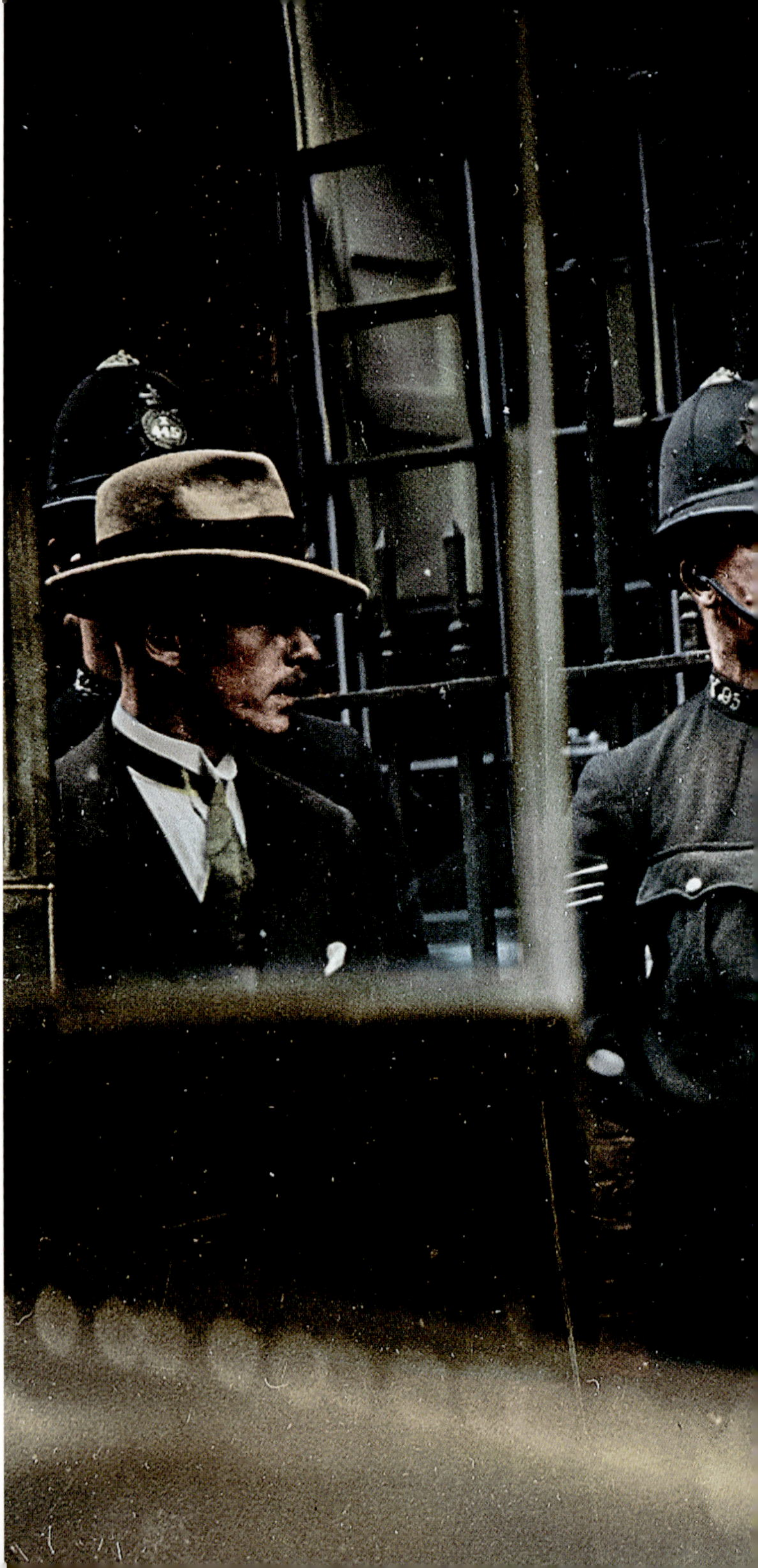

Emmet Dalton warily stands guard (along with, side-on, Harry Boland) as Arthur Griffith and Michael Collins leave No. 10 Downing Street. Lloyd George identified Griffith and Collins as the main movers and had one-to-one meetings with them. Griffith was not in the same league as Lloyd George, a master of manipulation. The negotiations crashed against the rock of British intransigence on the issues of allegiance to the King and membership of the British Empire, fundamental to the imperial mindset. Under pressure from Lloyd George to sign or face renewed war, the delegation did not consult with Dublin and signed the Treaty in London on 6 December 1921.

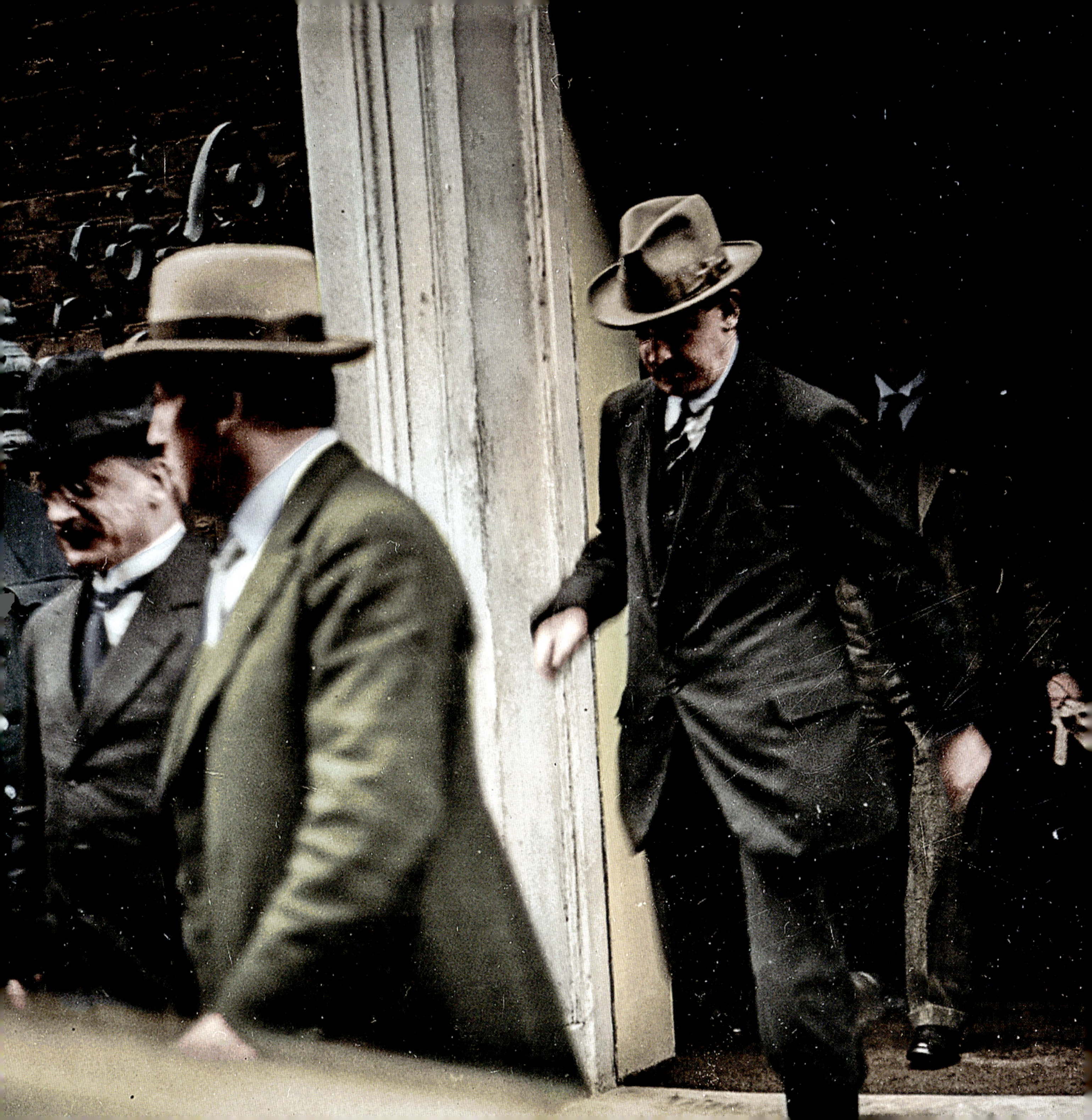

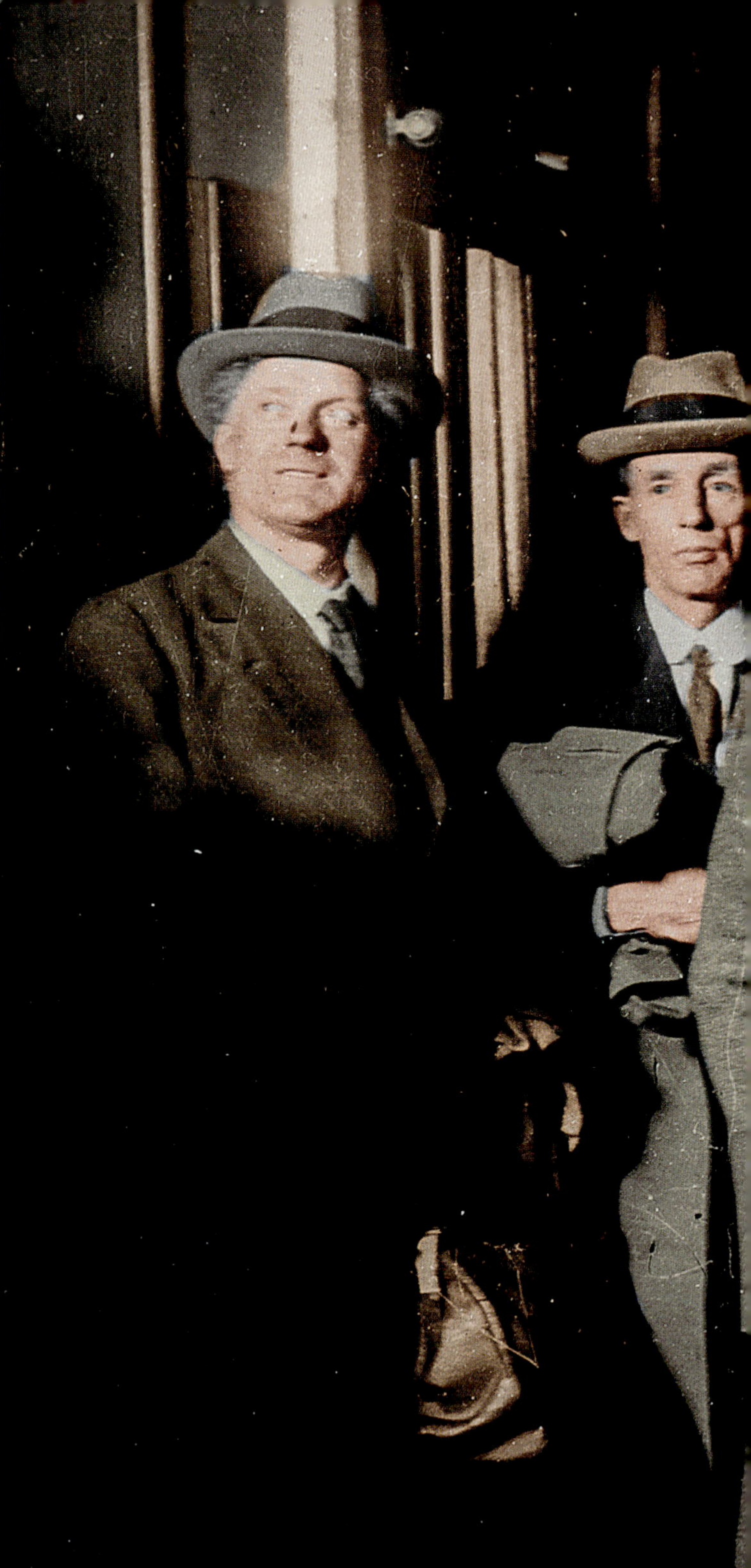

Looking tense and tired, the exhausted plenipotentiaries return to Ireland after signing the Anglo-Irish Treaty. In 18 succinct paragraphs, the Treaty detailed how an Irish Free State would be formed as a self-governing Dominion within 'the Community of Nations known as the British Empire'. Among the provisions, it set out: defence by sea was to be undertaken by the British, who would also retain naval ports; members of the Free State Parliament were to take an oath of allegiance to the Constitution of the Irish Free State and to be 'faithful to HM King George V', the right of the Northern Ireland Parliament to opt out of the Irish Free State (which, to no one's surprise, it promptly did) and for a Boundary Commission to be set up if Northern Ireland did withdraw.

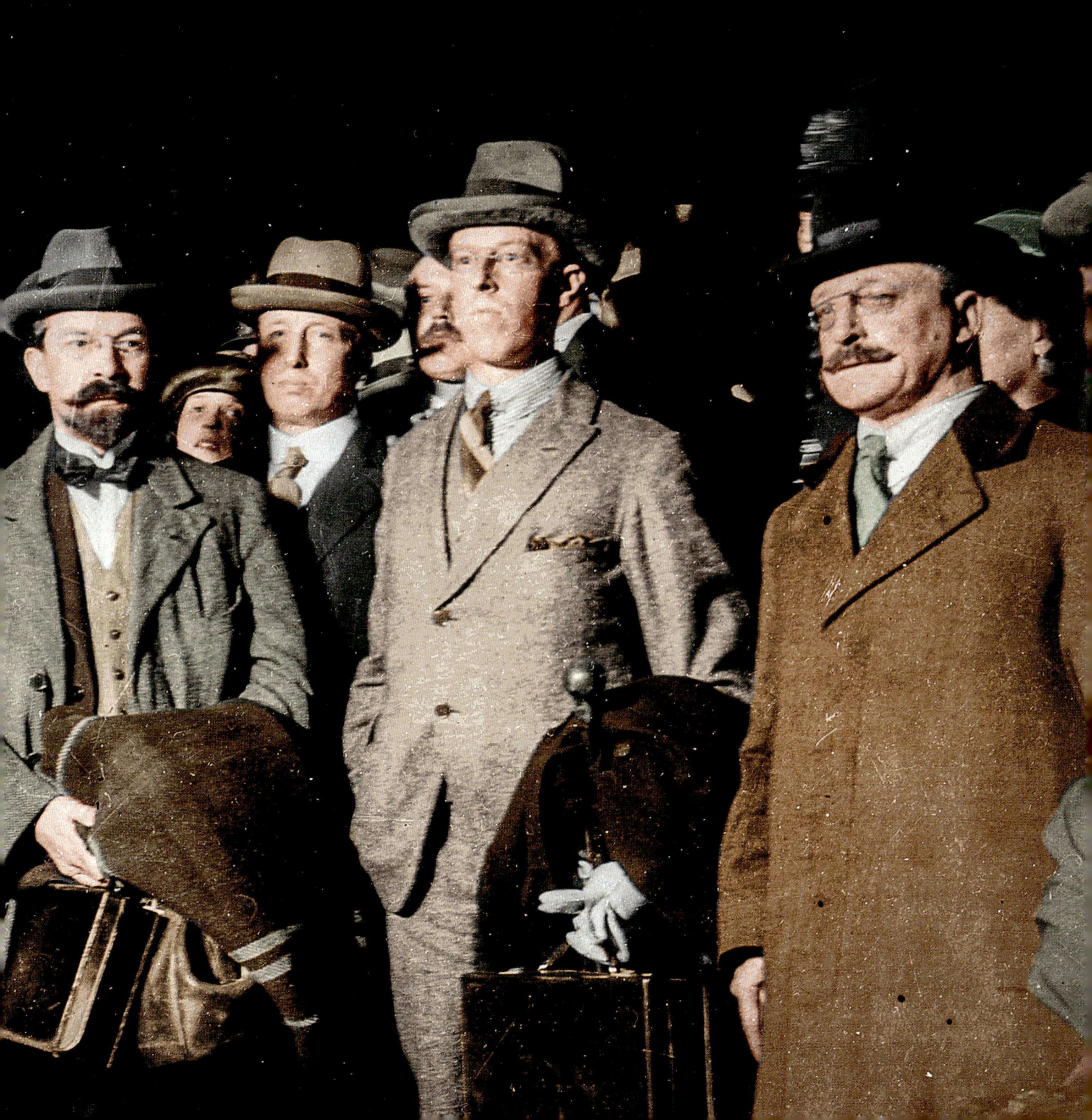

From mid-December 1921 the Dáil met at Earlsfort
Terrace and held heated debates on the Treaty. Giving
up the Republic declared in 1916 and asserted by the
First Dáil in 1919 was the main objection to the pact.
An Irish Republic had been the shining goal in the
struggle for independence since the time of Wolfe Tone.
Pictured are four female TDs: (l-r) Kathleen Clarke
(widow of Thomas), Countess Markievicz, Kathleen
O'Callaghan (widow of the murdered Limerick mayor)
and Margaret Pearse (mother of Patrick). Ultimately, all
six female TDs in the Dáil voted against the Treaty.

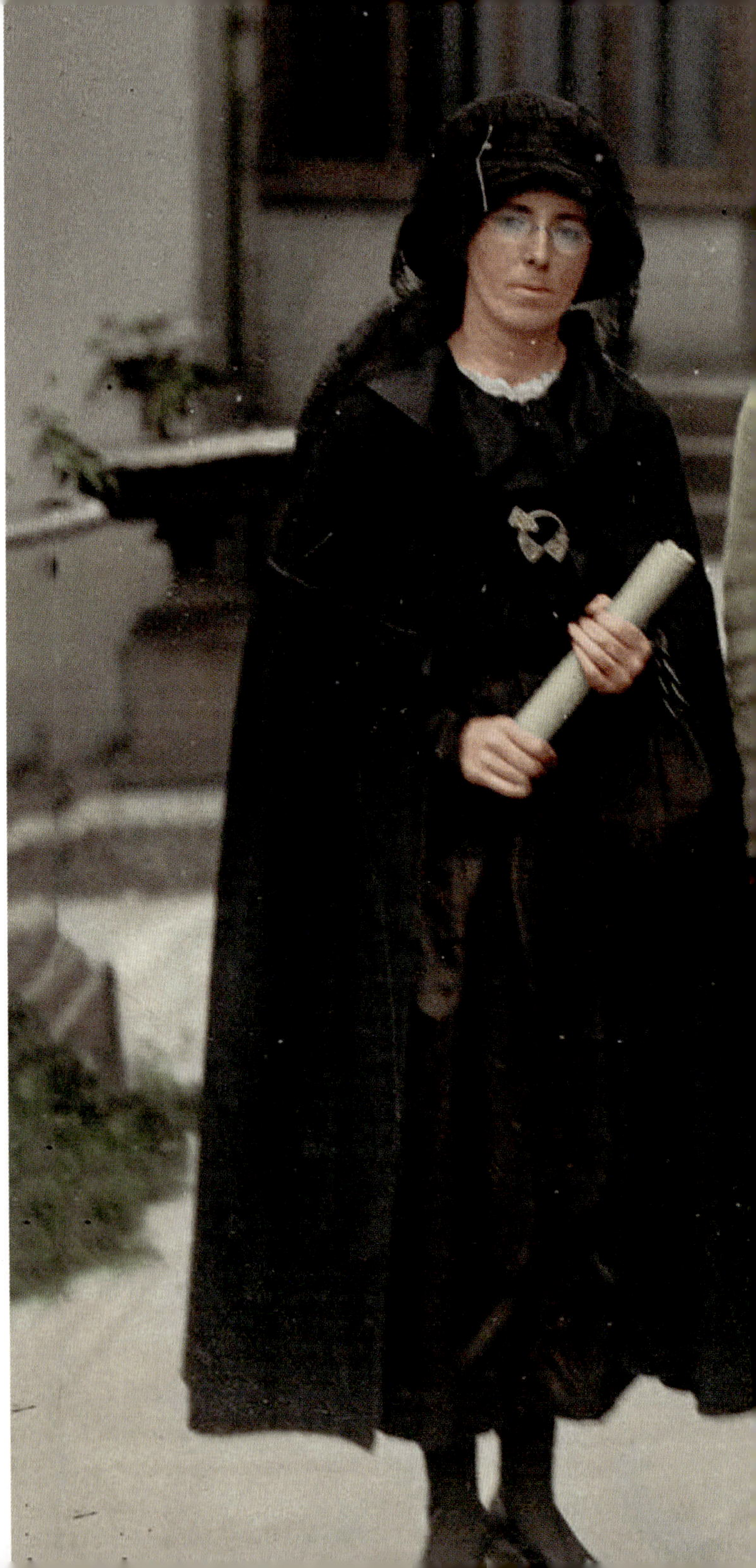

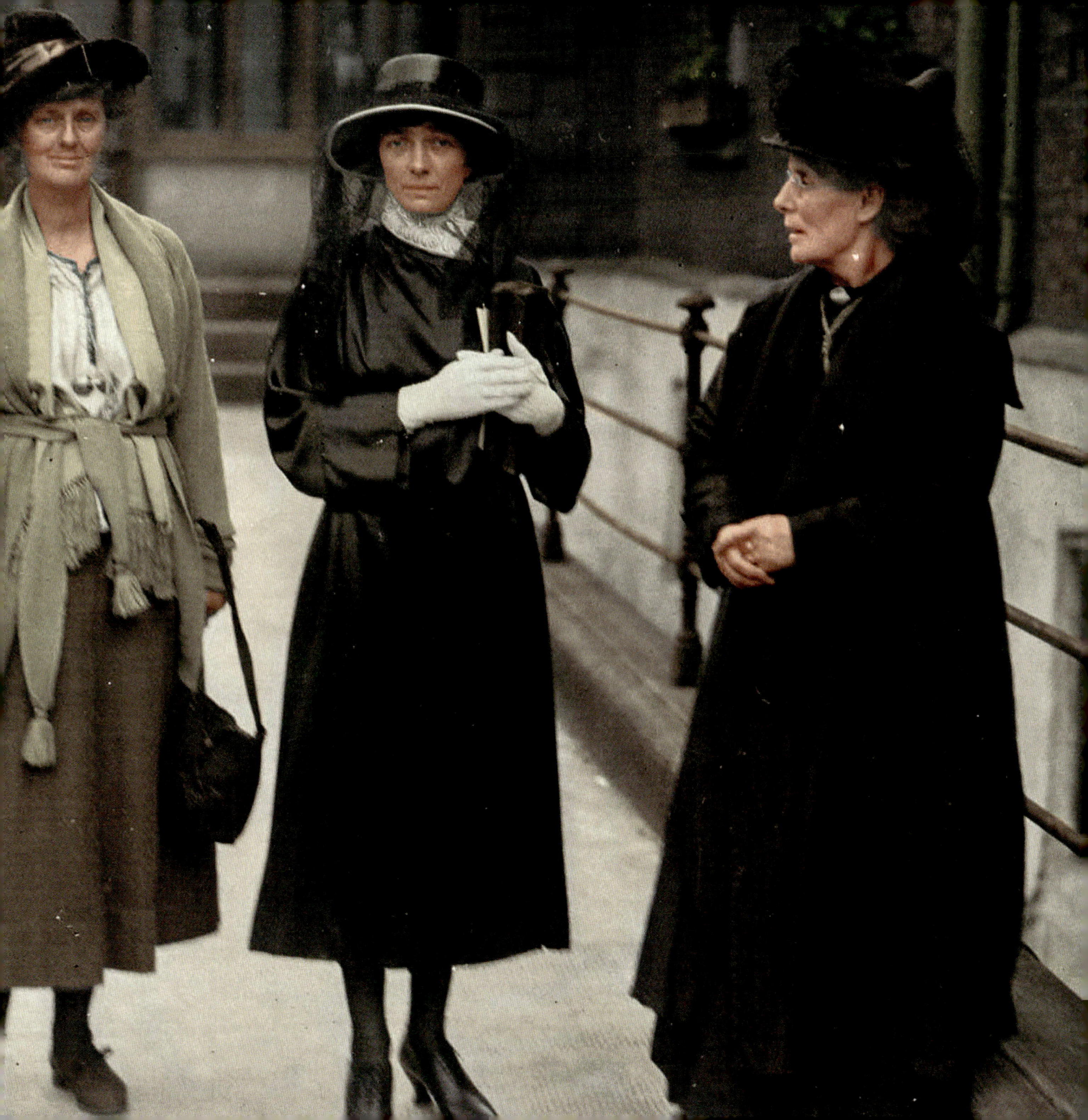

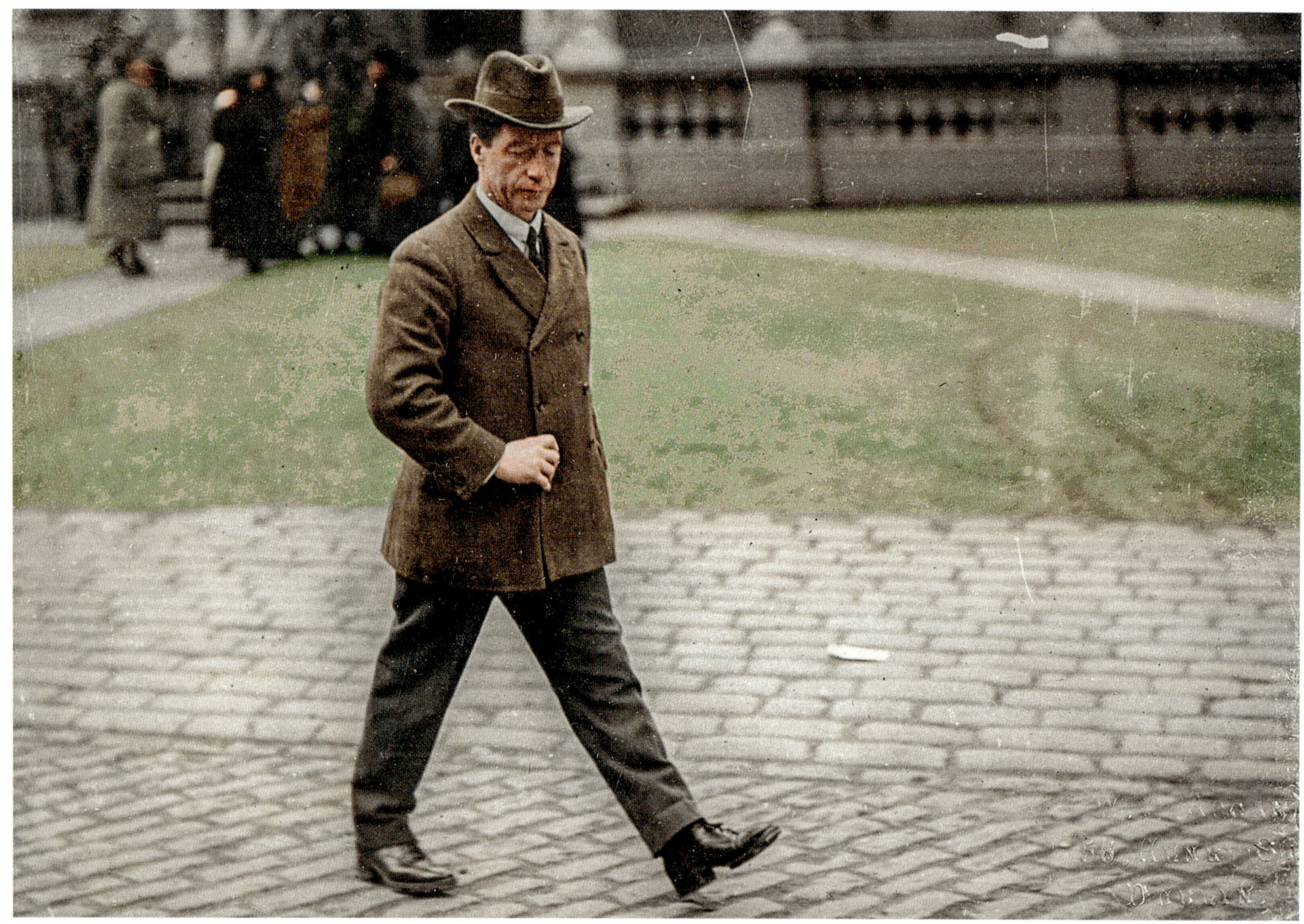

Cathal Brugha was a hero of 1916 – he still bore embedded shrapnel and walked with a limp from the wounds he had received at the South Dublin Union. Brugha, Minister of Defence, was one of the most vocal opponents of the Anglo-Irish Treaty. In his view, it gave up the Republic proclaimed in 1916 for a lesser form of independence.

Right: a dour-looking Richard Mulcahy poses for the cinematographer (camera operator) during the Dáil discussions. It was a difficult time for Mulcahy (then Chief of Staff of the IRA) and his GHQ staff, mainly pro-Treaty. The response to the Treaty varied widely across the IRA. In general, the areas that had been more active during the War of Independence were more strongly anti-Treaty.

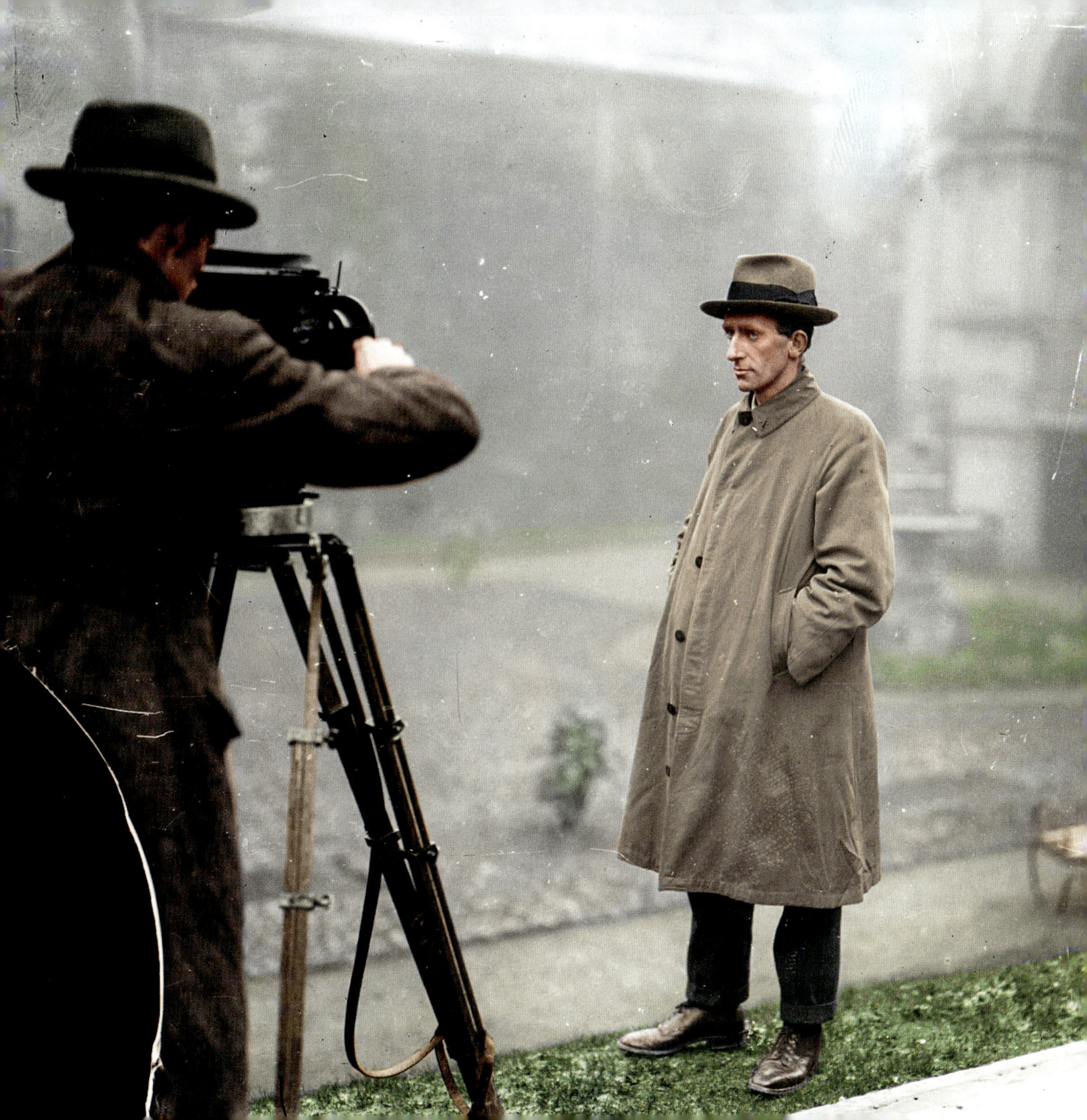

The vote on the Treaty took place on 7 January 1922. It
was narrowly ratified by 64 votes to 57. On 9 January,
Éamon de Valera stepped down as President, saying he
did not have the House's confidence. The following day,
a motion to re-elect him was narrowly defeated. Arthur
Griffith was elected President of the Dáil by the remaining
TDs. De Valera and his anti-Treaty supporters then left the
Dáil. Here they line up for the cinematographer.

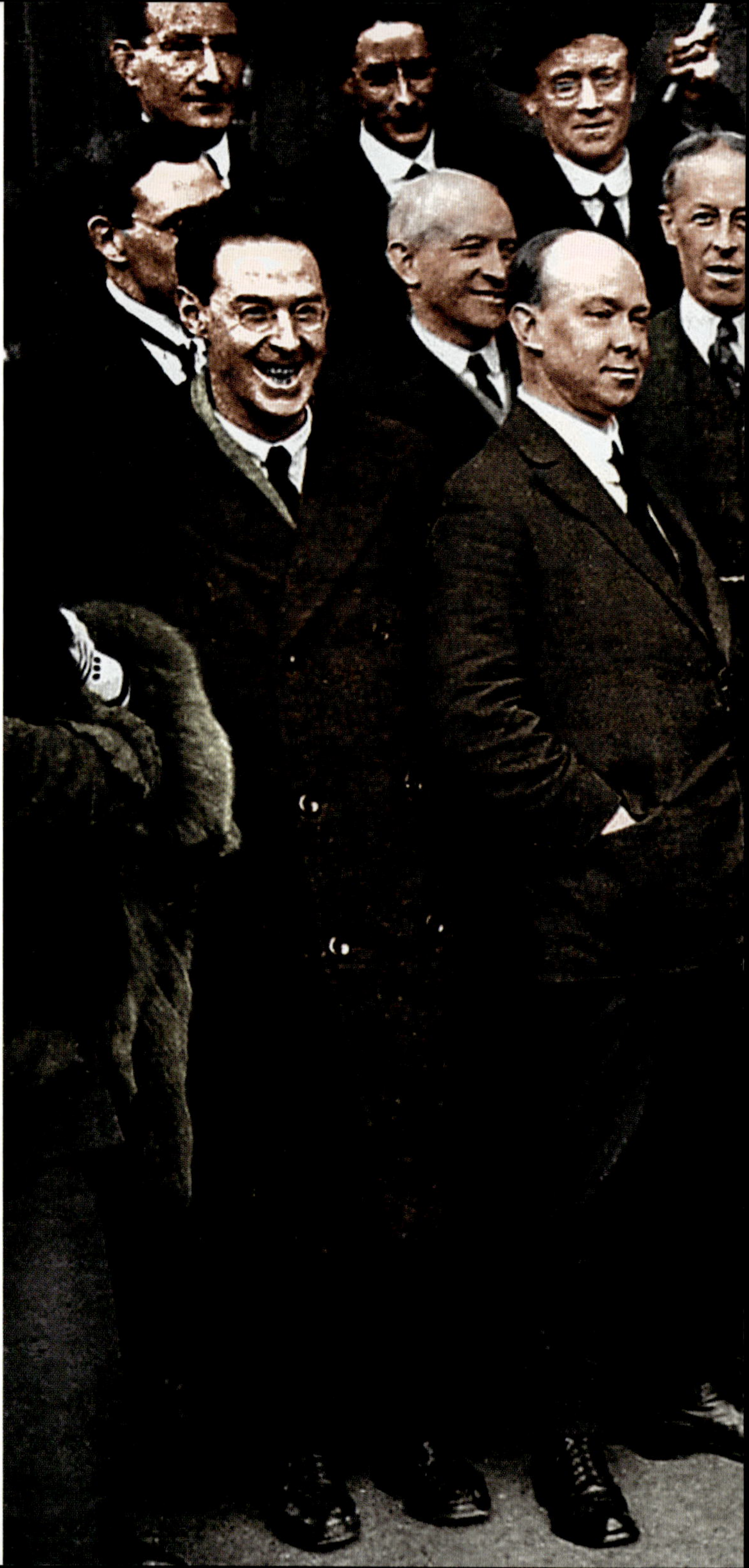

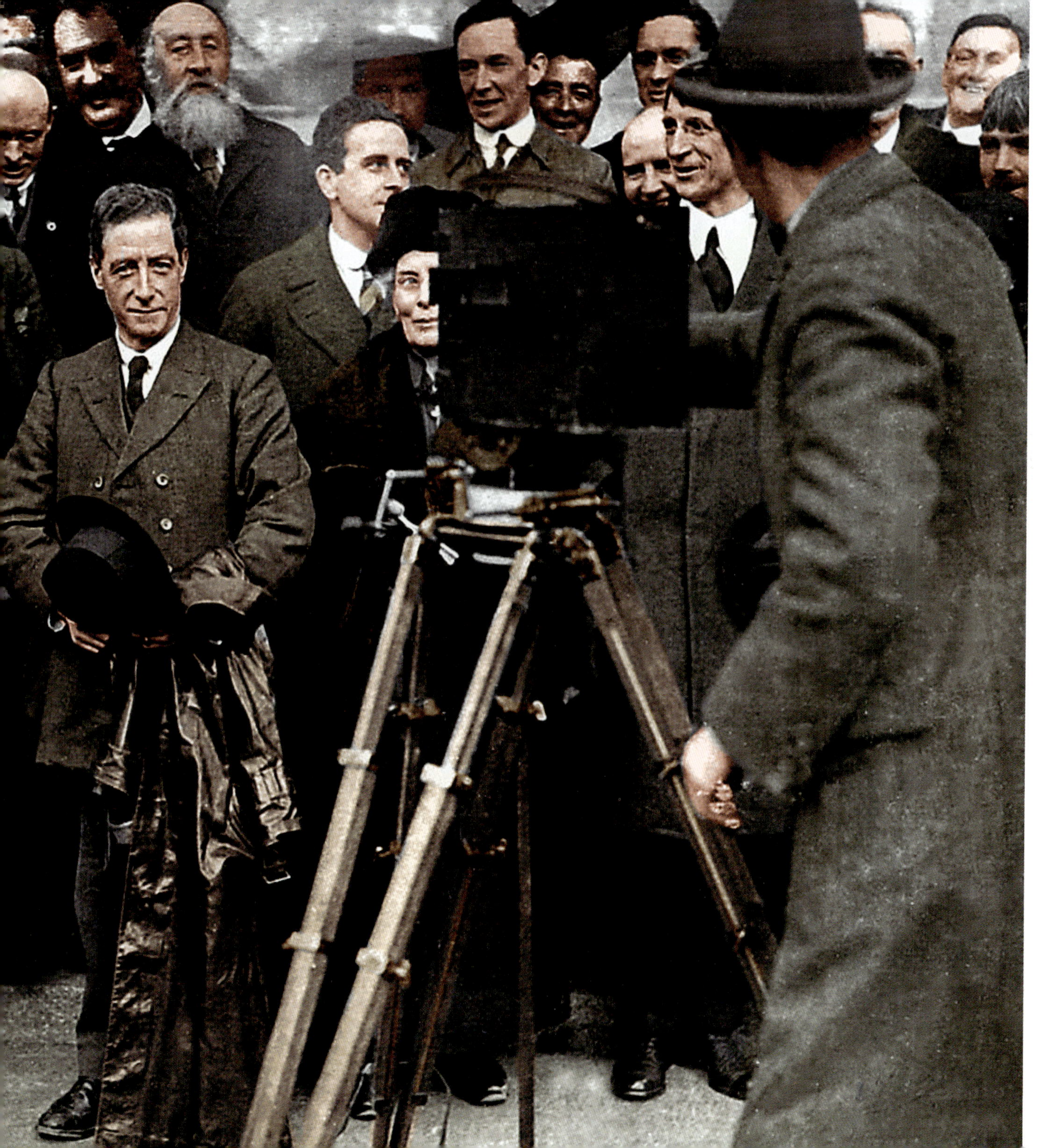

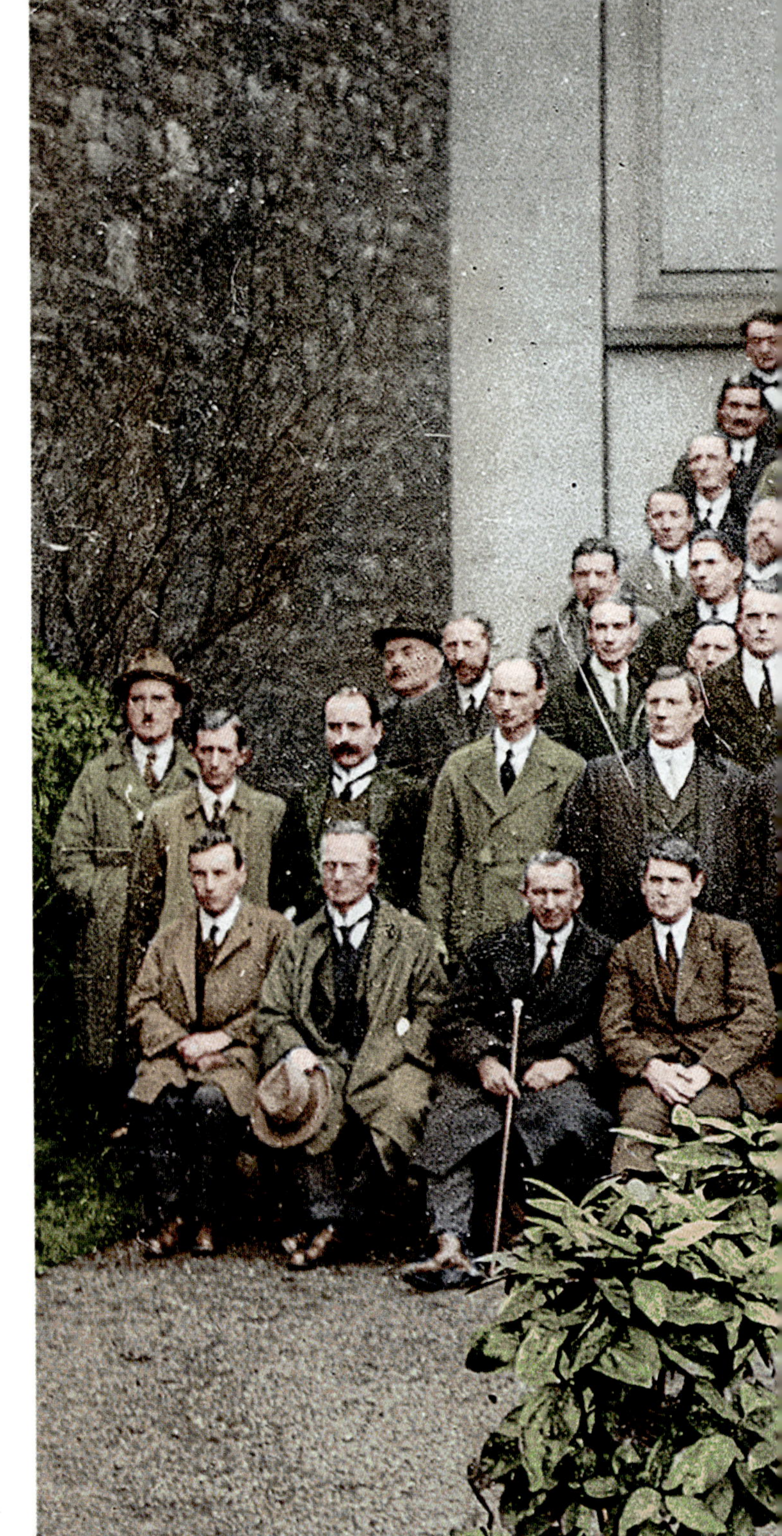

On 14 January 1922, the 'Southern Ireland Parliament'
met in Dublin's Mansion House, in the absence of anti-
Treaty members of the Dáil. In accordance with the terms
of the Treaty, they elected a Provisional Government, with
Michael Collins as Chairman. Here, the new Provisional
Government, along with supporters, assemble for a
photograph.

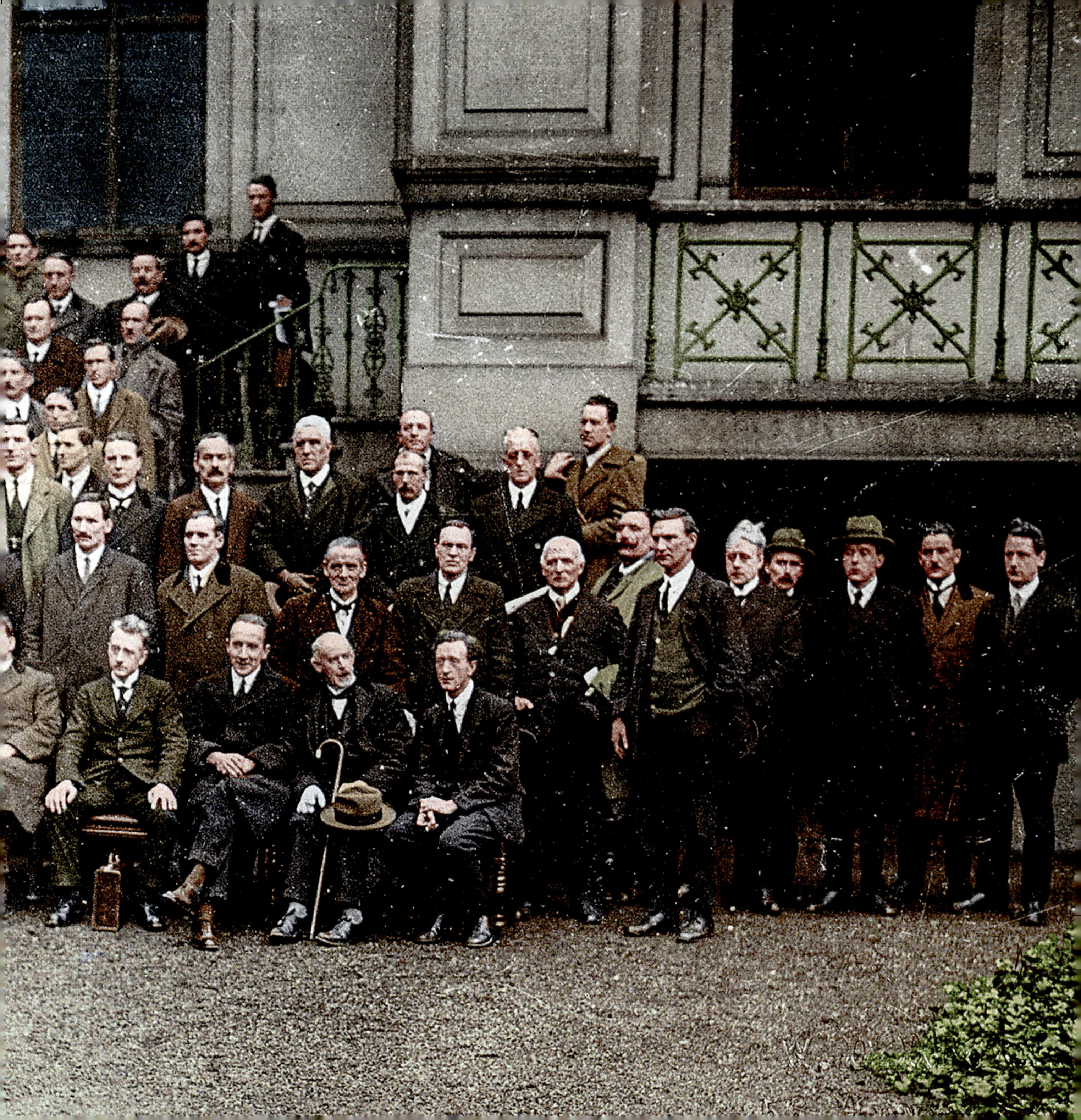

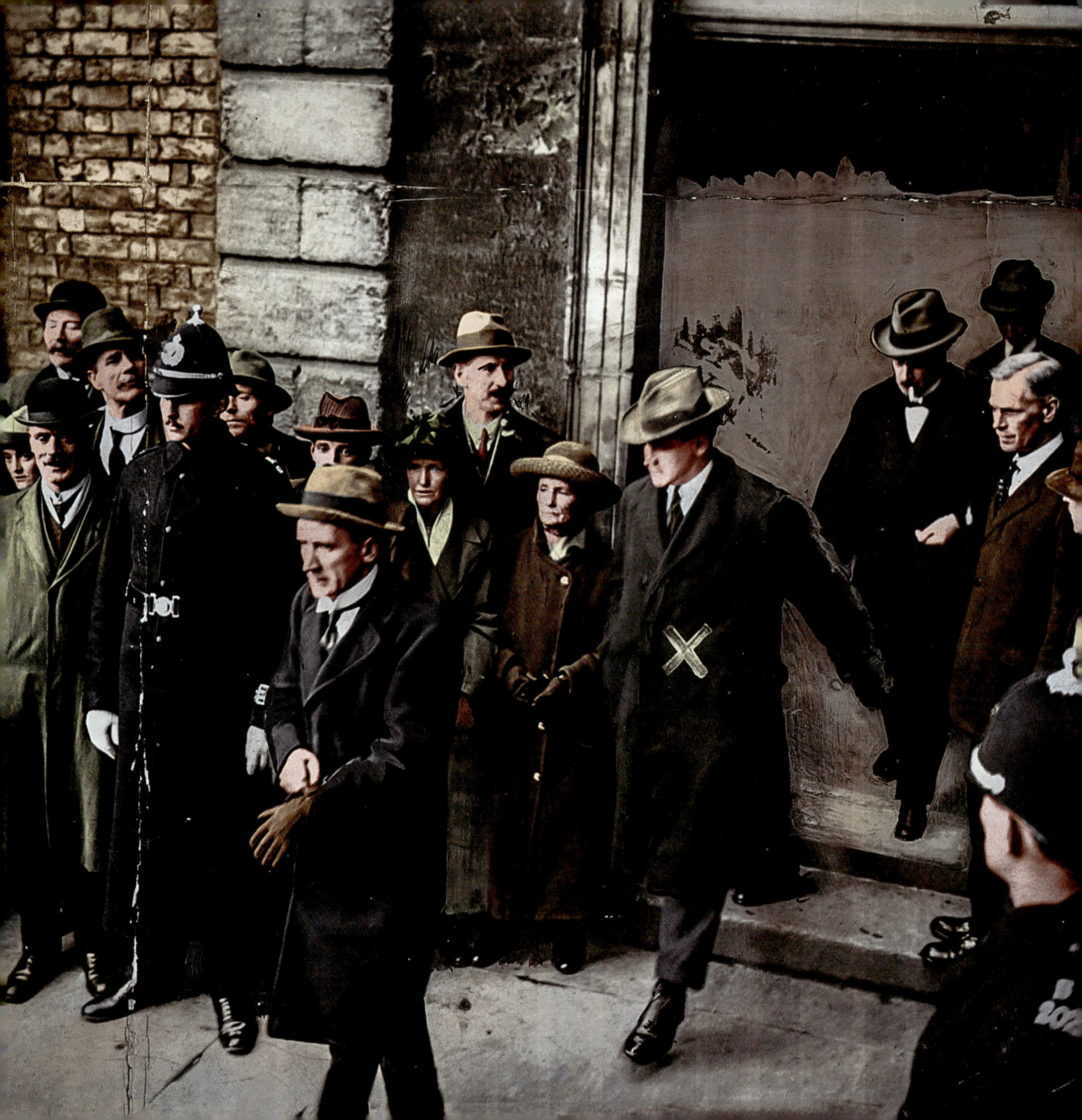

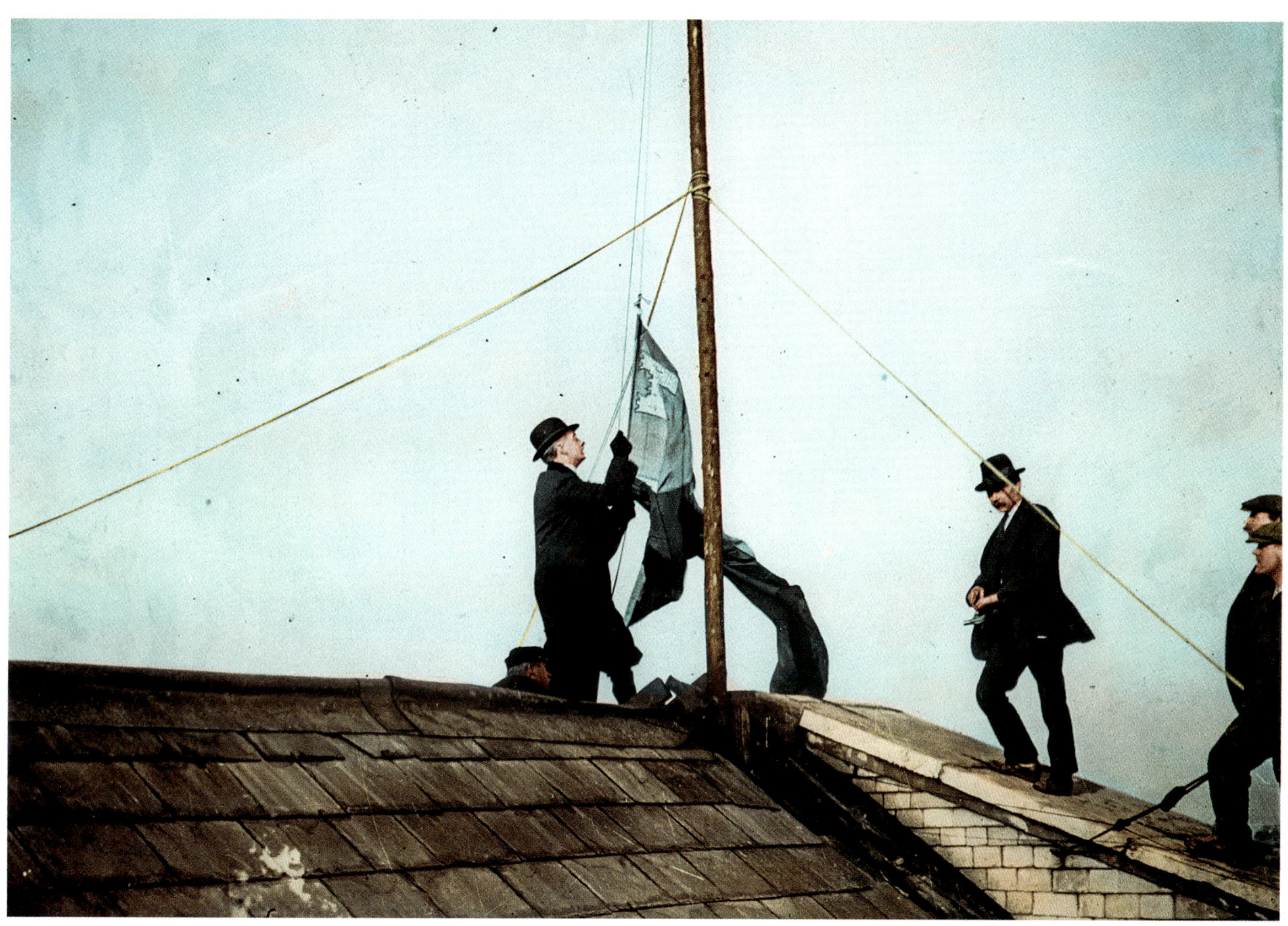

At the end of January 1922, the British Army evacuated the City Hall, adjacent to Dublin Castle. Alderman W.T. Cosgrave (1916 veteran and Minister for Local Government in the 1919 Dáil) hoists the municipal flag.

Left: on 16 January, members of the new government met Lord FitzAlan (the Lord Lieutenant) at Dublin Castle. The Dublin Castle press office recorded that FitzAlan 'informed them [that] they were now duly installed as the Provisional Government'. Another statement, signed by Collins, struck a different tone: 'The members of the Provisional Government received the surrender of Dublin Castle … today. It is now in the hands of the Irish nation'. Here, Kevin O'Higgins and Michael Collins depart after the proceedings.

After the passionate and discordant Dáil debates, the
World Congress of the Irish Race presented a more
harmonious interlude. It was held in Paris from 21 to 28
January 1922, in commemoration of the third anniversary
of the inaugural meeting of Dáil Éireann. Delegates from
the Irish worldwide diaspora assembled in the Hotel
Continental. It was the first manifestation of Irish 'soft
power' and was intended to showcase the sovereignty and
national identity of the new Ireland on a world stage.
There was an exhibition of Irish art and plays and music
were performed. Ten delegates had been chosen by Sinn
Féin to represent Ireland. As it transpired, most of the
delegation were supportive of the Republic – only three
favoured the Treaty. Seen here, relaxing at the Hotel
d'Orsay, amongst others, are from left: Seán T. O'Kelly,
Mary MacSwiney (sister of Terence), Éamon de Valera
and Countess Markievicz. On the right, in a kilt and
about to sample what looks like a dish of escargots, is the
flamboyant 2nd Baron Ashbourne, William Gibson. A
fervent devotee of Irish culture, he was a member of the
Gaelic League, spoke Irish in the British House of Lords
and wore Irish national dress. (In 1926 his sister, Violet
Gibson, who was said to have suffered from mental health
problems, made an attempt to shoot Mussolini in Rome,
grazing Il Duce's nose).

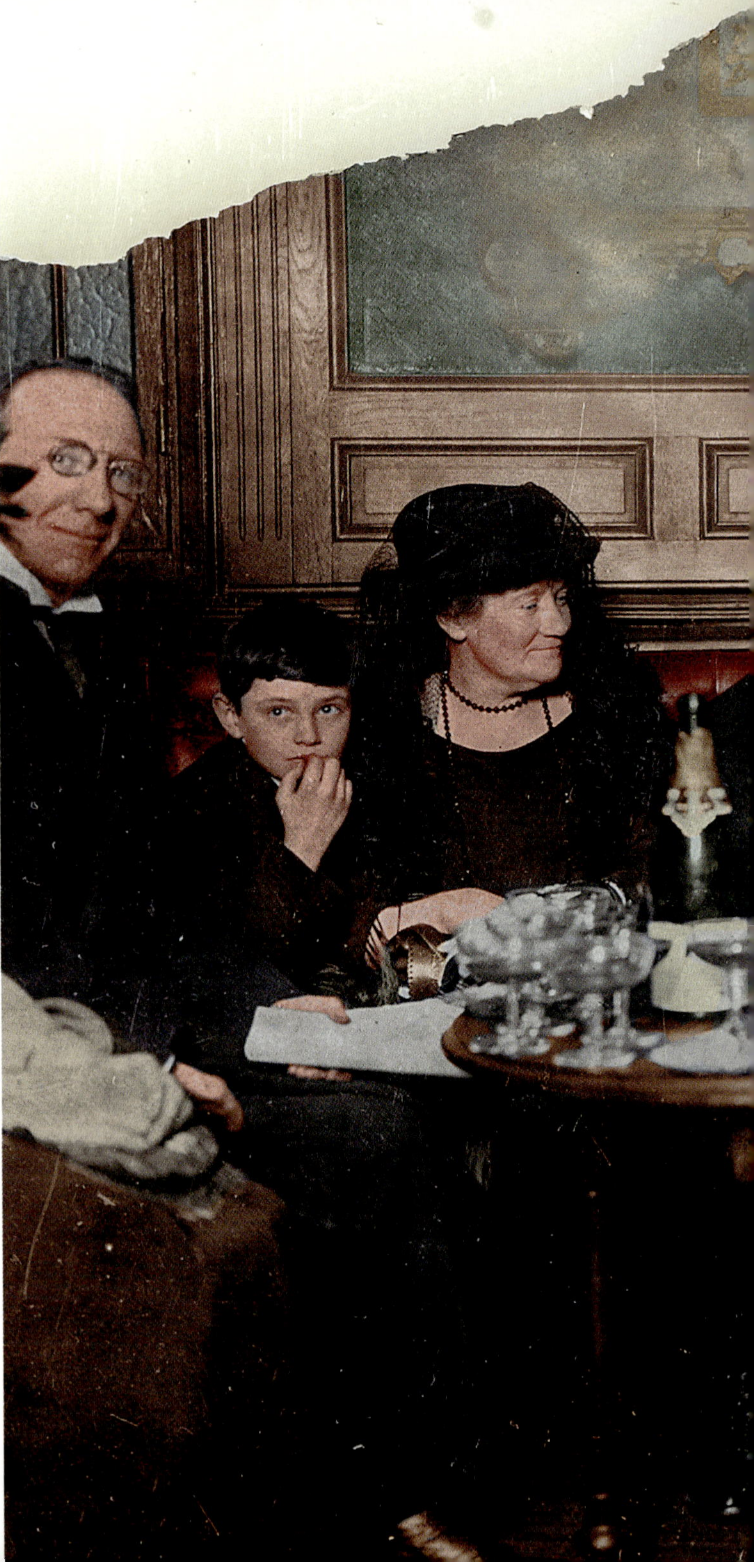

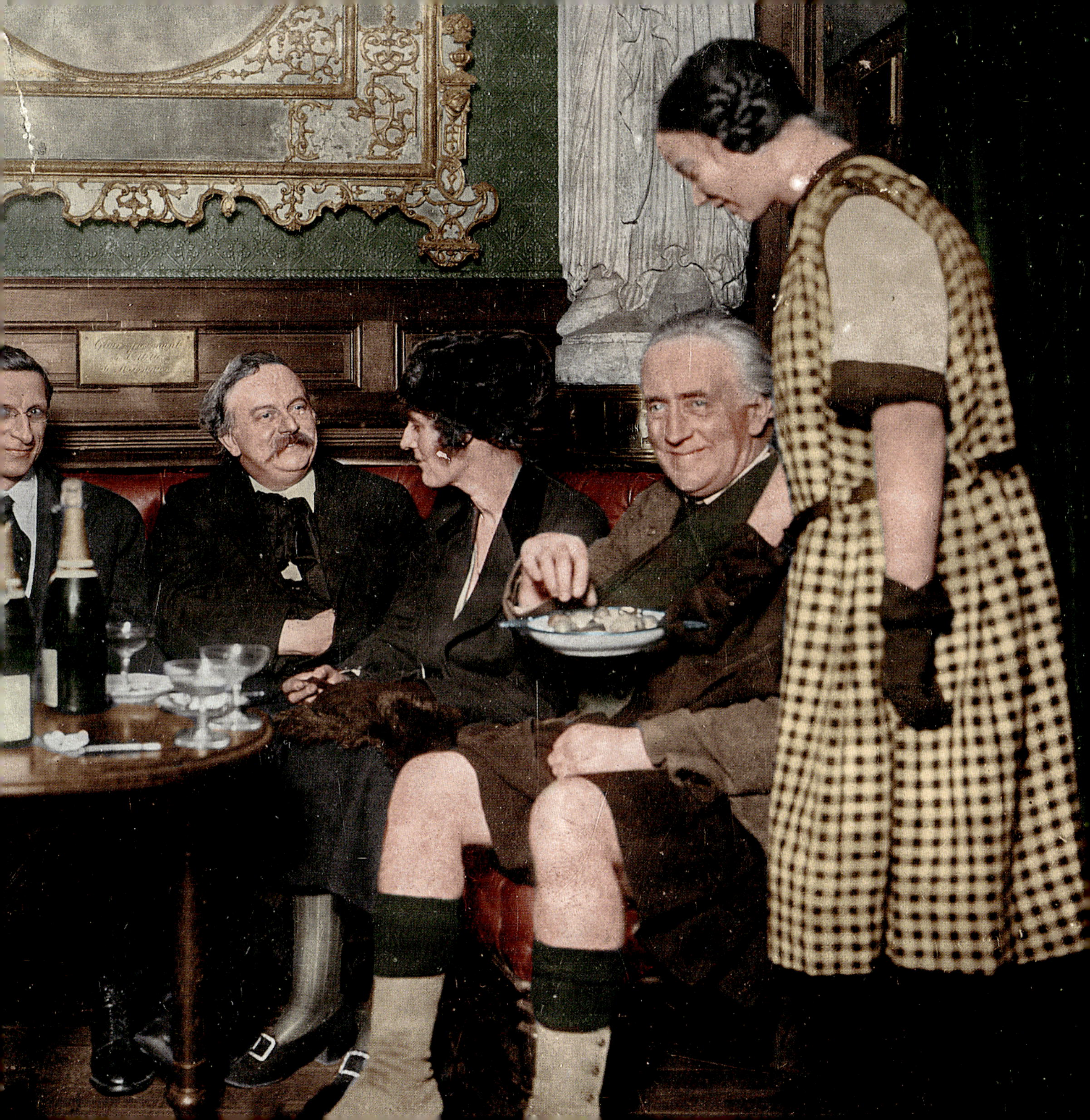

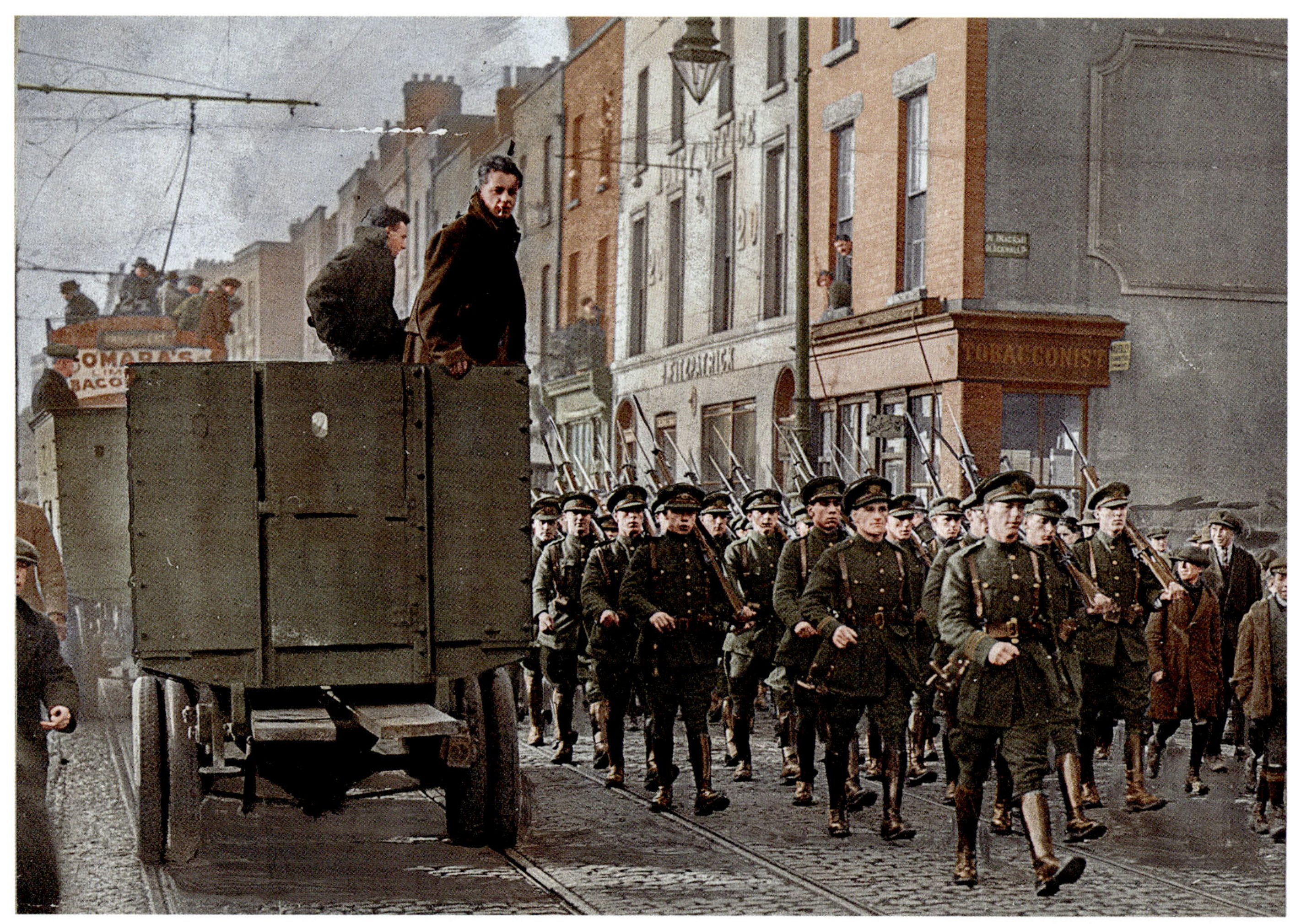

The next big step under the Treaty arrangements was the staged evacuation of the British Army along with the handover of barracks to the army of the Provisional Government. Here Paddy O'Daly marches the newly created Dublin Guard along the Dublin quays on 31 January 1922, on their way to take over Beggars Bush Barracks, former headquarters of the Auxiliaries.

Right: Richard Mulcahy (just appointed Minister for Defence of the Provisional Government), J.J. 'Ginger' O'Connell (Deputy Chief of Staff) and Commandant Tom Ennis observe the arrival of the Dublin Guard at Beggars Bush. The barracks became the initial headquarters of the new army.

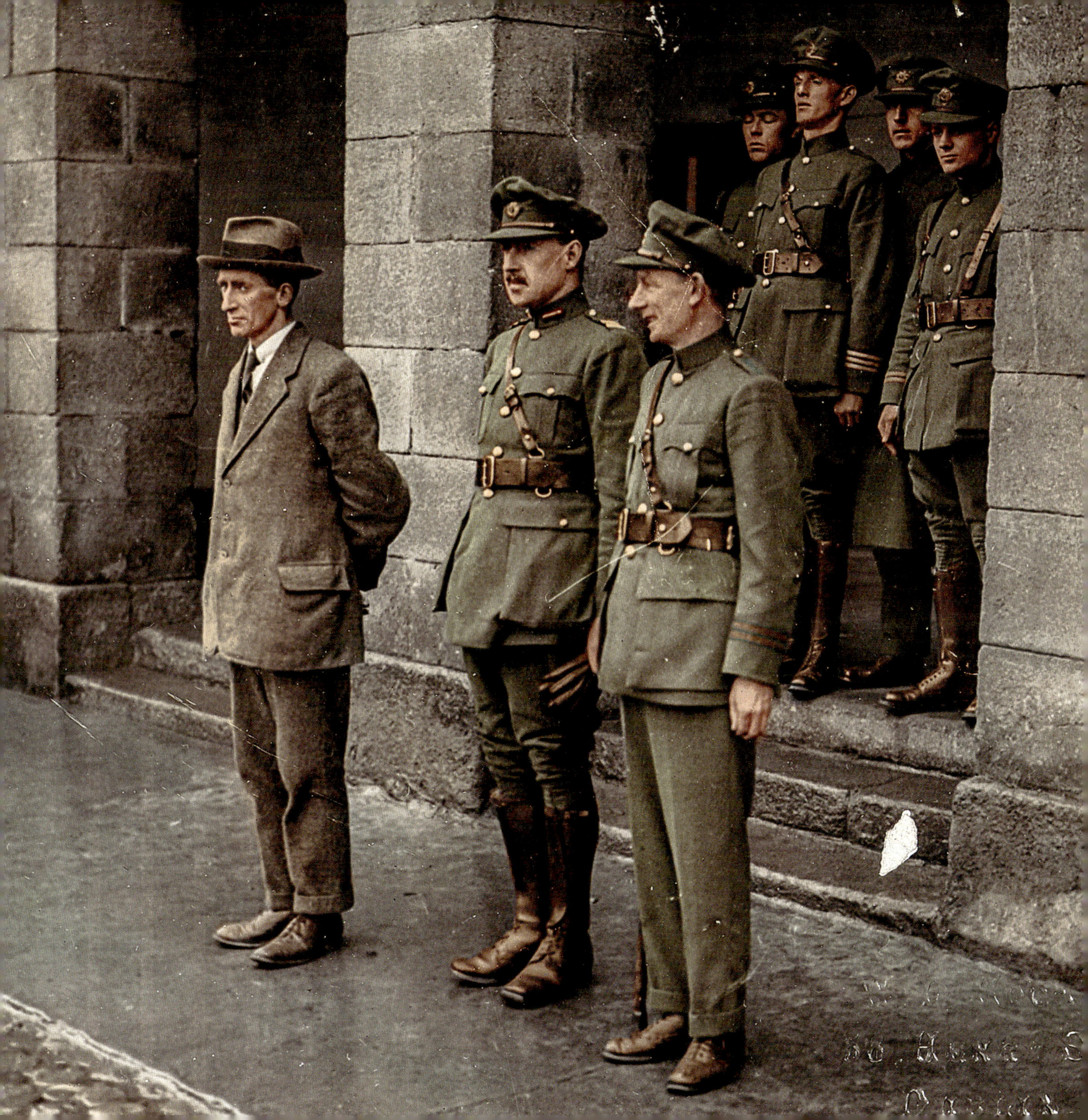

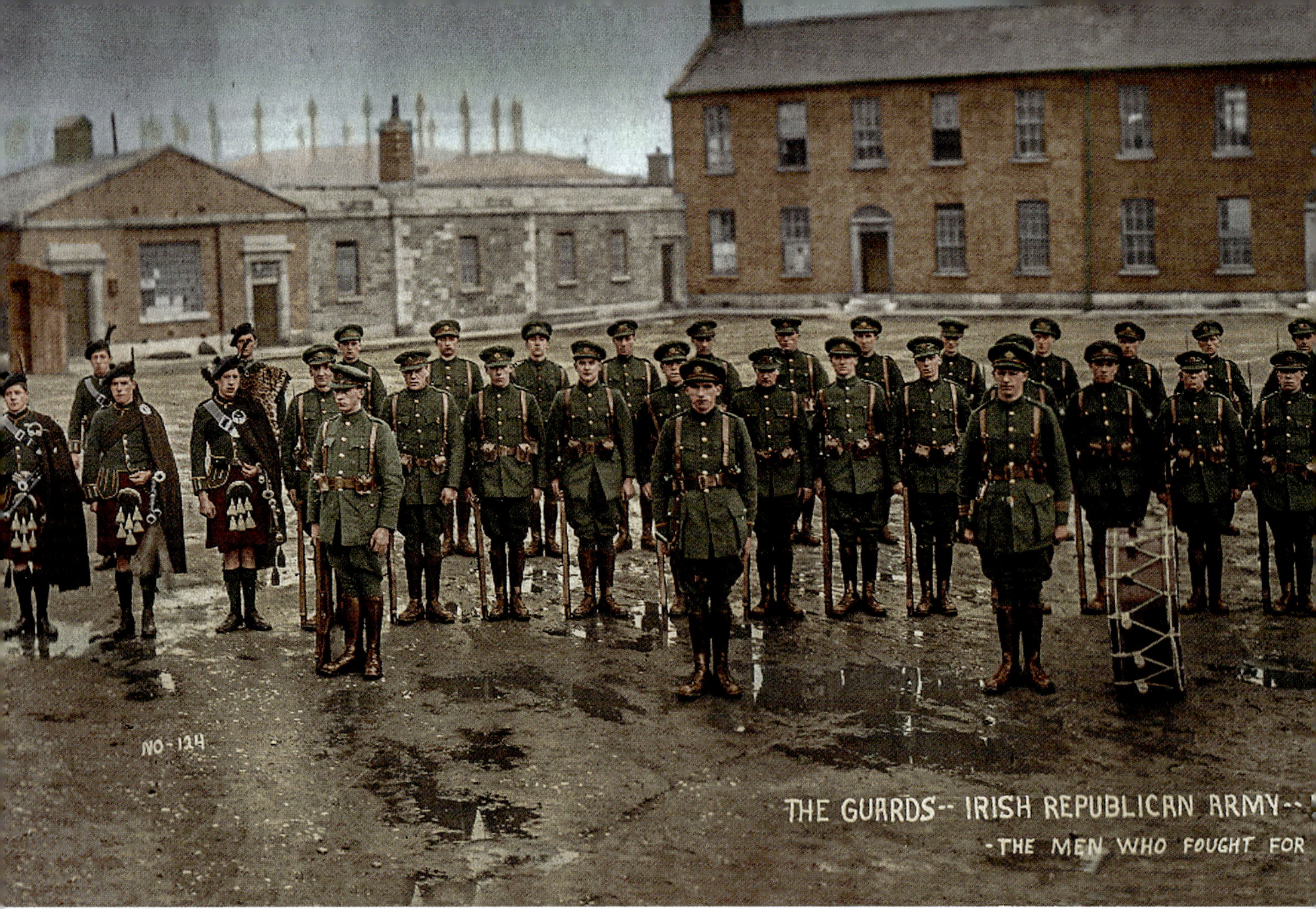

A panoramic photograph taken at Beggars Bush Barracks on 4 February 1922 by the Panograph Photo Company of New York. Flanked by a pipe band, the Dublin Guard line up. In the front, by the drum, is Commandant Paddy O'Daly. Lieutenant Pádraig O'Connor stands to his right.

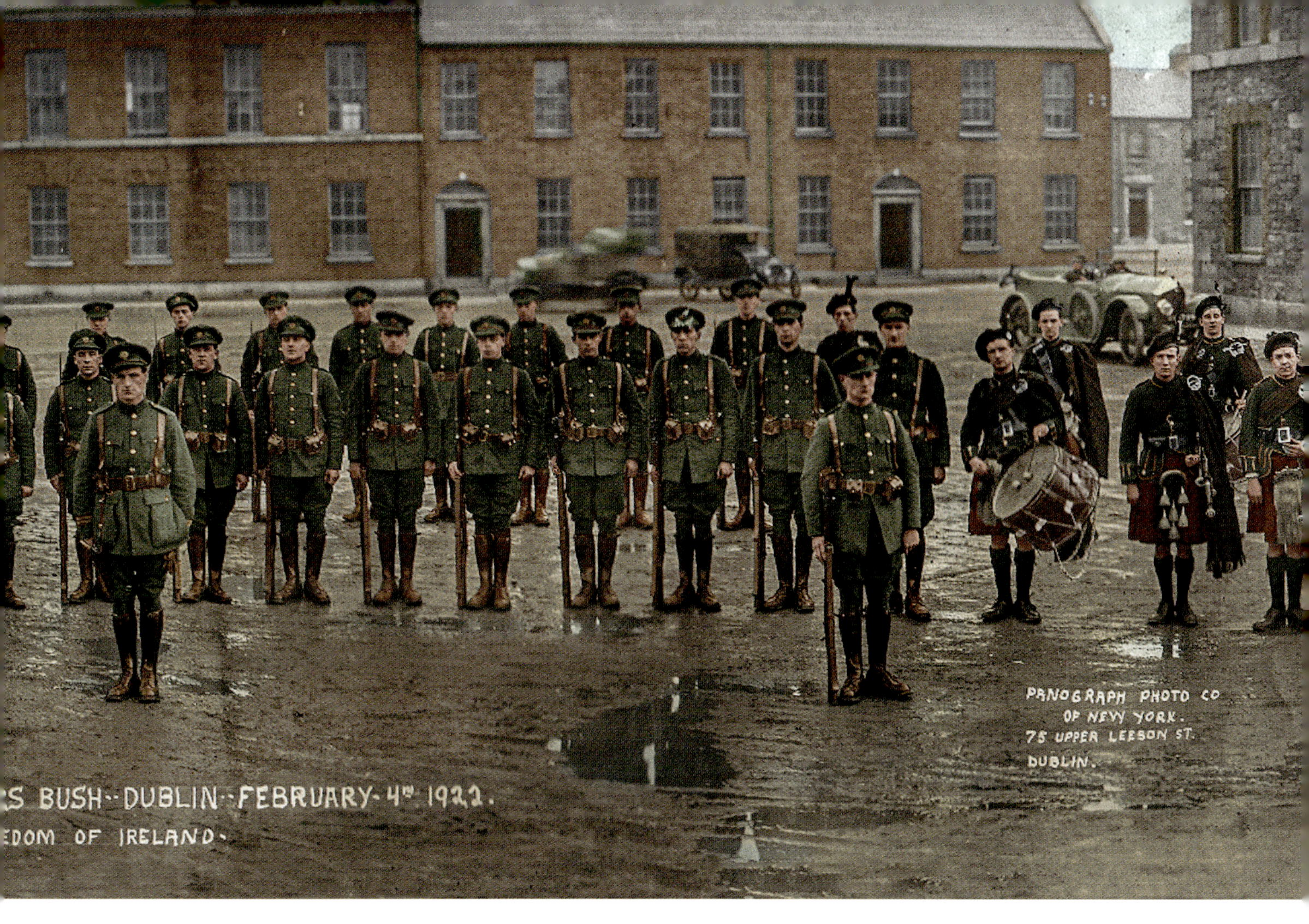
S BUSH--DUBLIN--FEBRUARY--4TH 1922.
EDOM OF IRELAND.
PANOGRAPH PHOTO CO
OF NEW YORK.
75 UPPER LEESON ST.
DUBLIN.

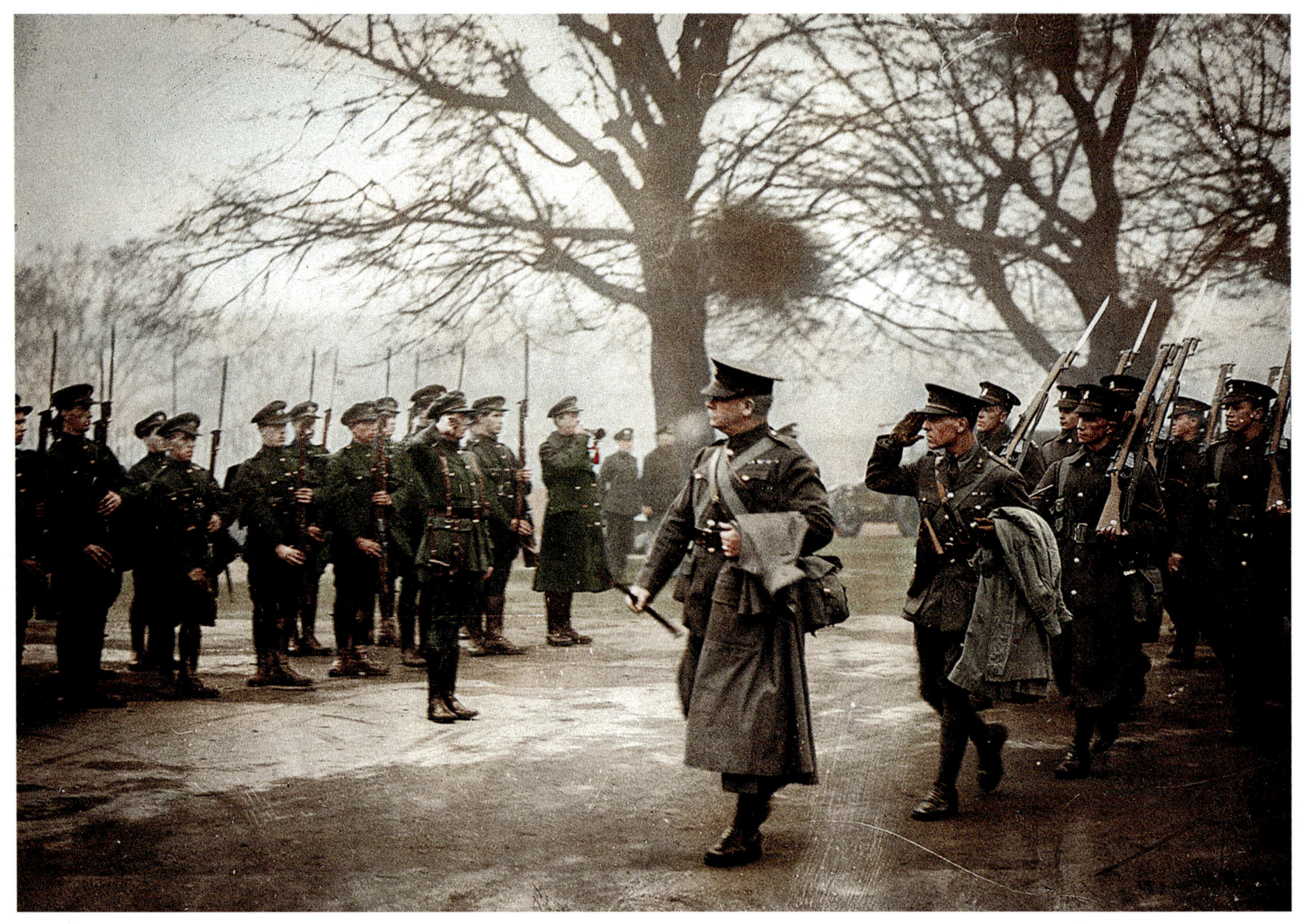

Eyes right at the evacuation – British military march past the new soldiers of the Army of the Provisional Government.

Right: on the boat to Blighty. Temporary cadets of the ADRIC (Auxiliary Division of the RIC) cheer. The Auxiliaries, a comparatively small paramilitary force, had garnered a reputation for widespread brutality during the War of Independence. They were disbanded in January 1922 and a number of them (along with former RIC members) joined another semi-military police force, the Palestine Gendarmerie.

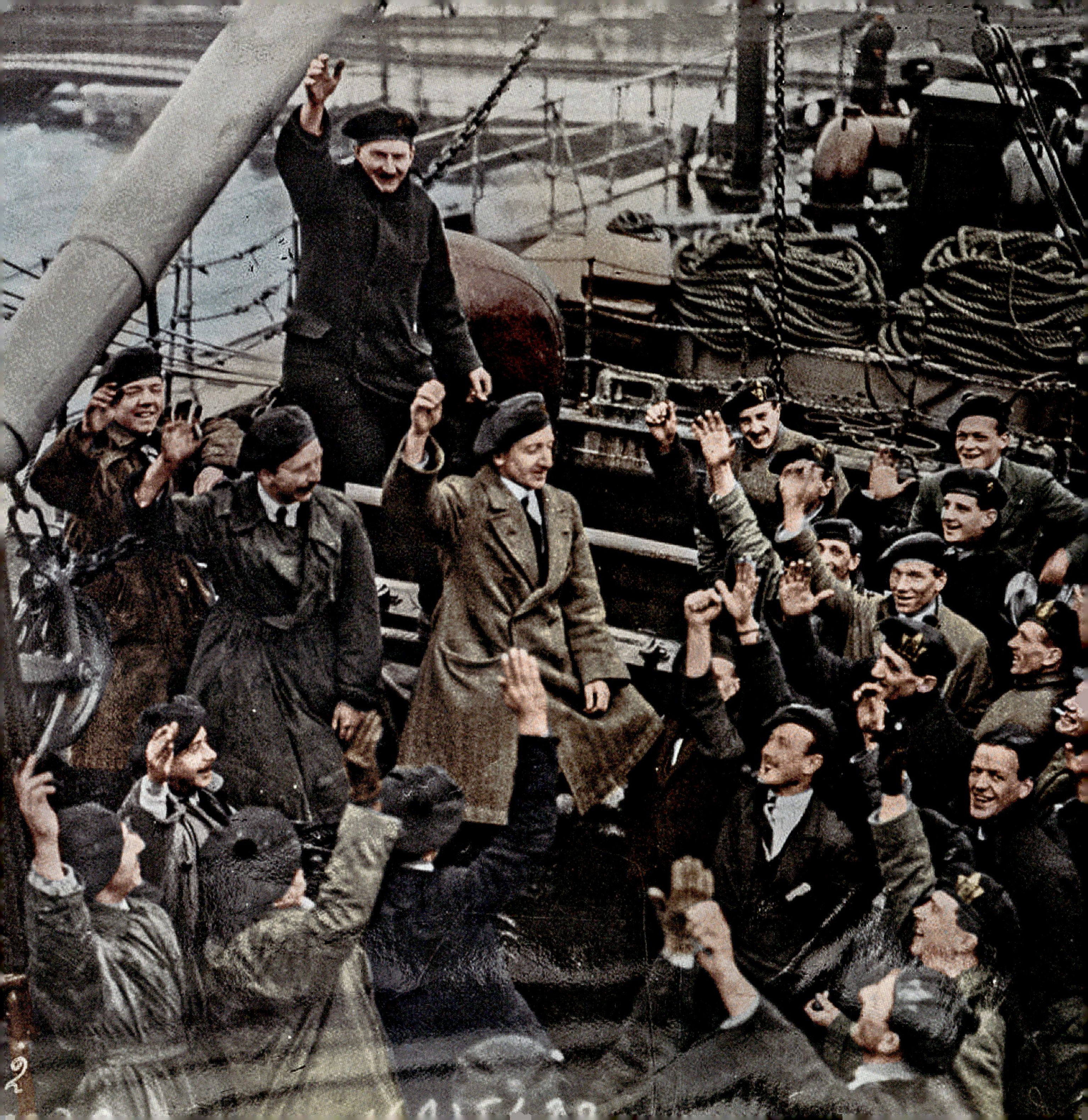

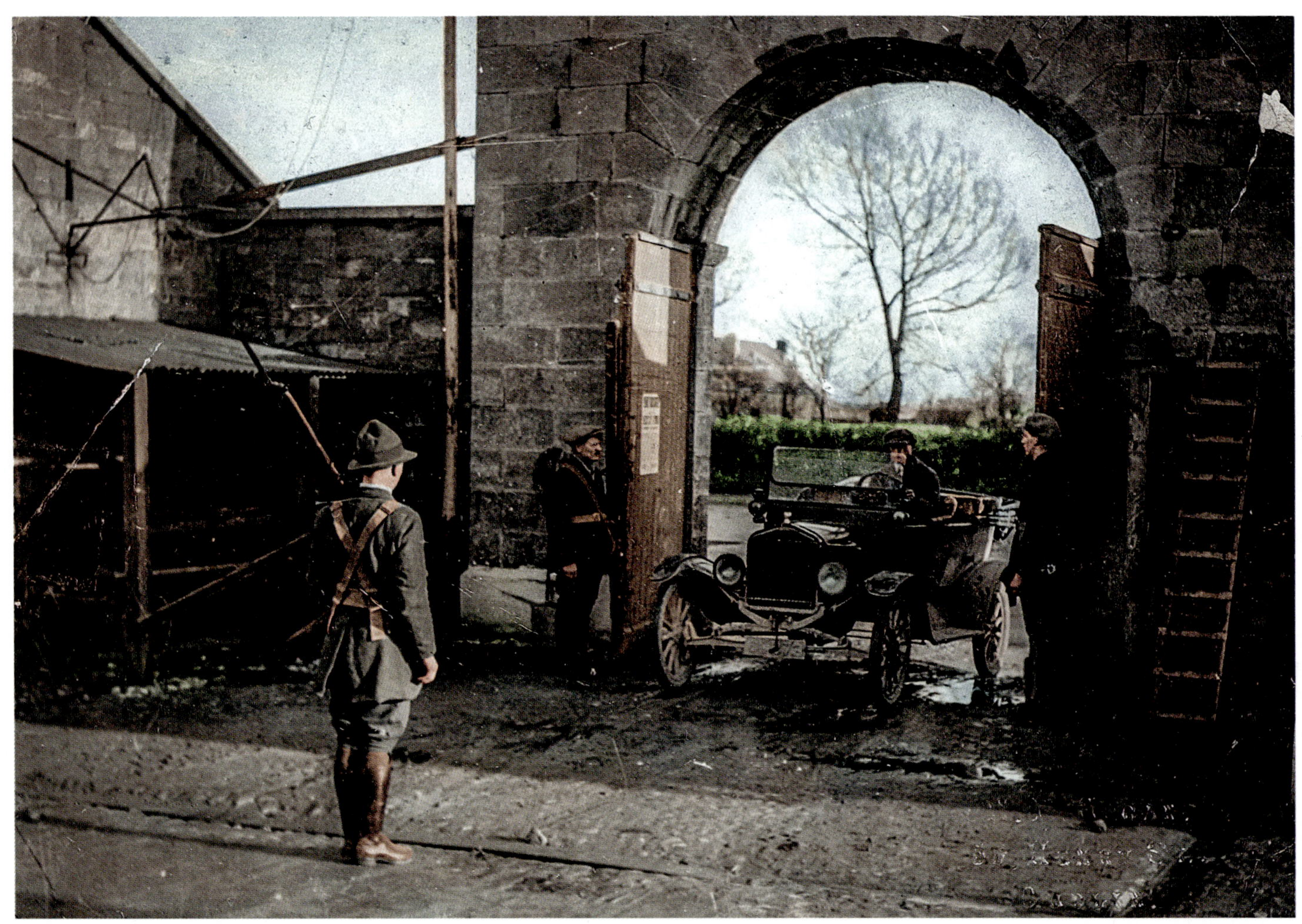

The IRA take over Maryborough (Portlaoise) Barracks in 1922. The British withdrawal was rapid. Barracks were taken over across the regions by local IRA units, irrespective of their attitude to the Treaty. The Provisional Government, accordingly, had difficulty in asserting its authority over large swathes of the country.

Right: as the anti-Treaty IRA flexed their muscles in their local areas, the Provisional Government endeavoured to rapidly build up its forces. At its peak in mid-1923 the Free State Army amounted to around 55,000. Here is the scene as recruits are driven into Wellington (now Griffith) Barracks on South Circular Road, Dublin. It was handed over by the British on 12 April 1922.

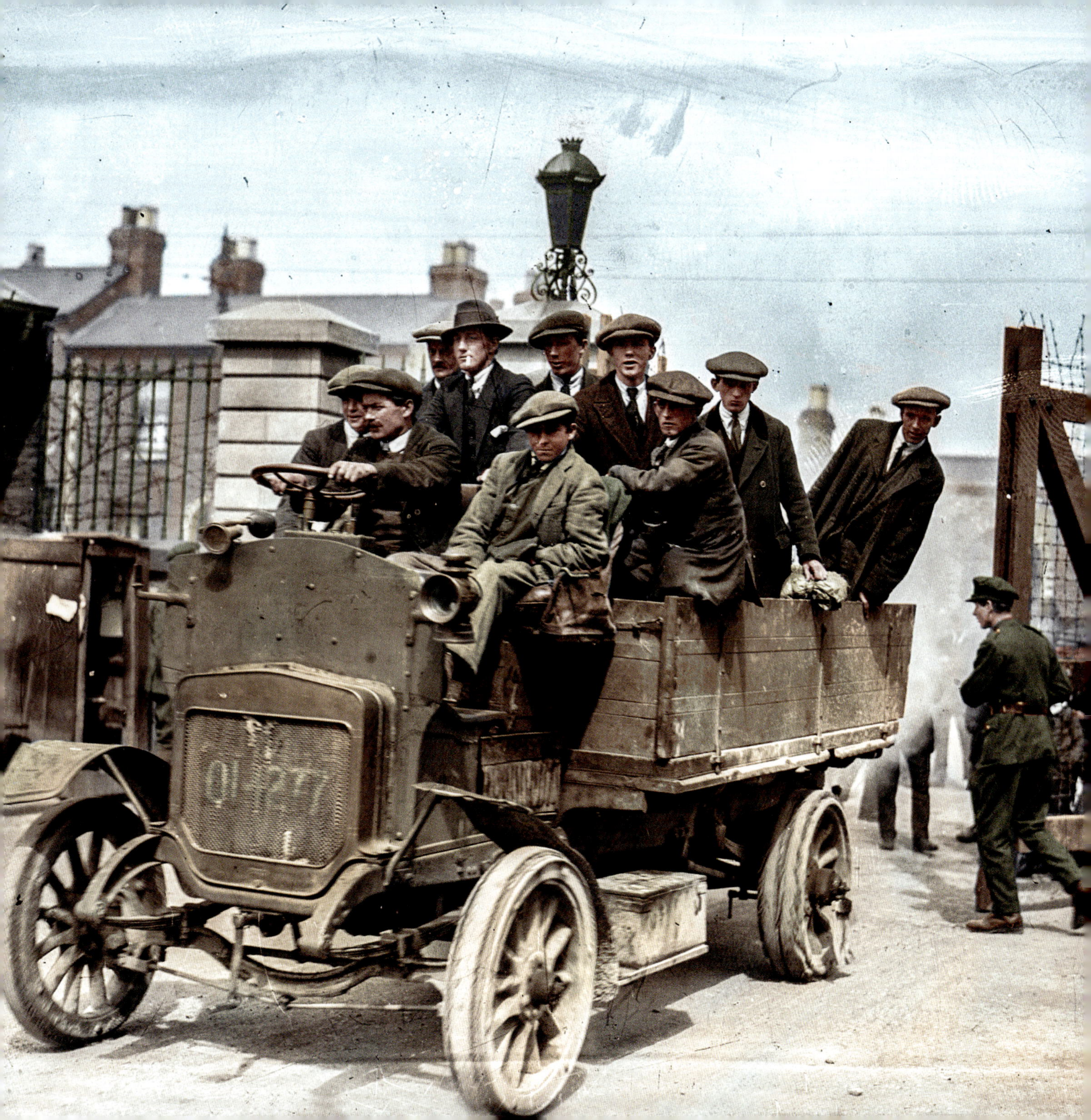

IQ 4277

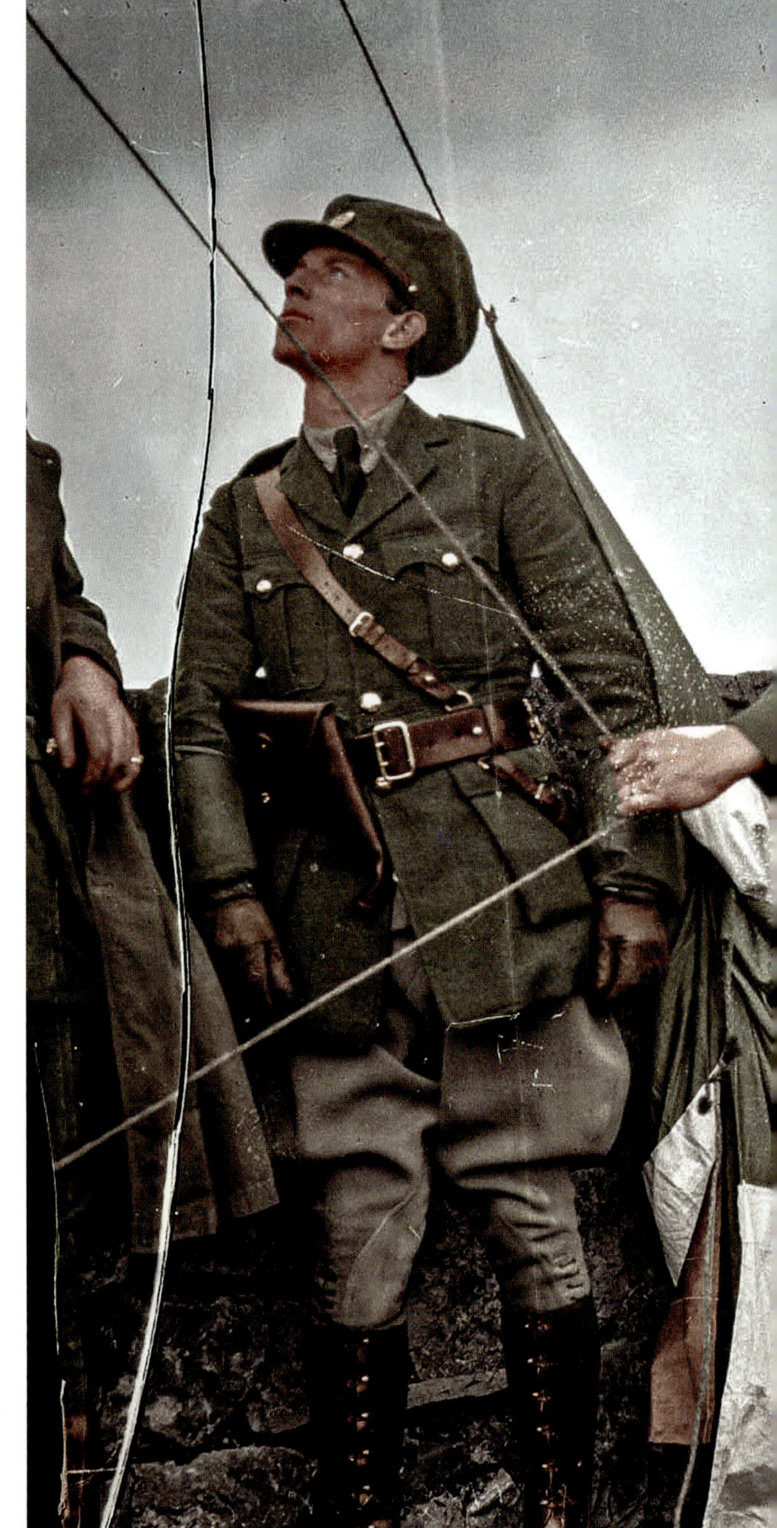

With thousands lining the streets and squares of the town, Commandant-General Seán Mac Eoin raises the tricolour after the handover at Athlone Barracks on 28 February 1922. In a speech, he alluded to Sergeant Custume's heroic defence of the bridge there in 1691 and said that it was over 300 years since an Irish flag had been hauled down — 'the flag of Ireland was being unfurled that day … and they meant to keep it there'.

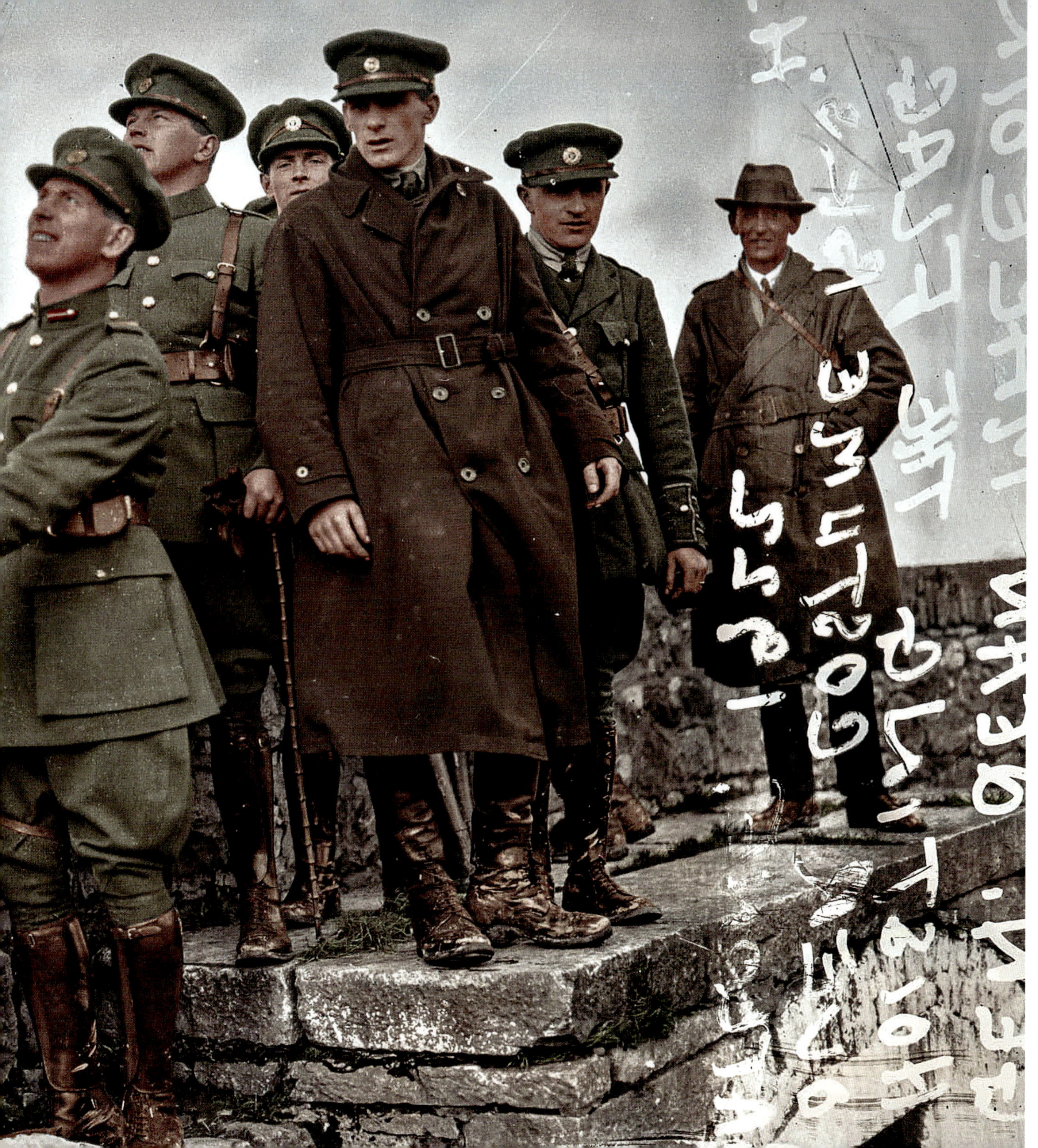

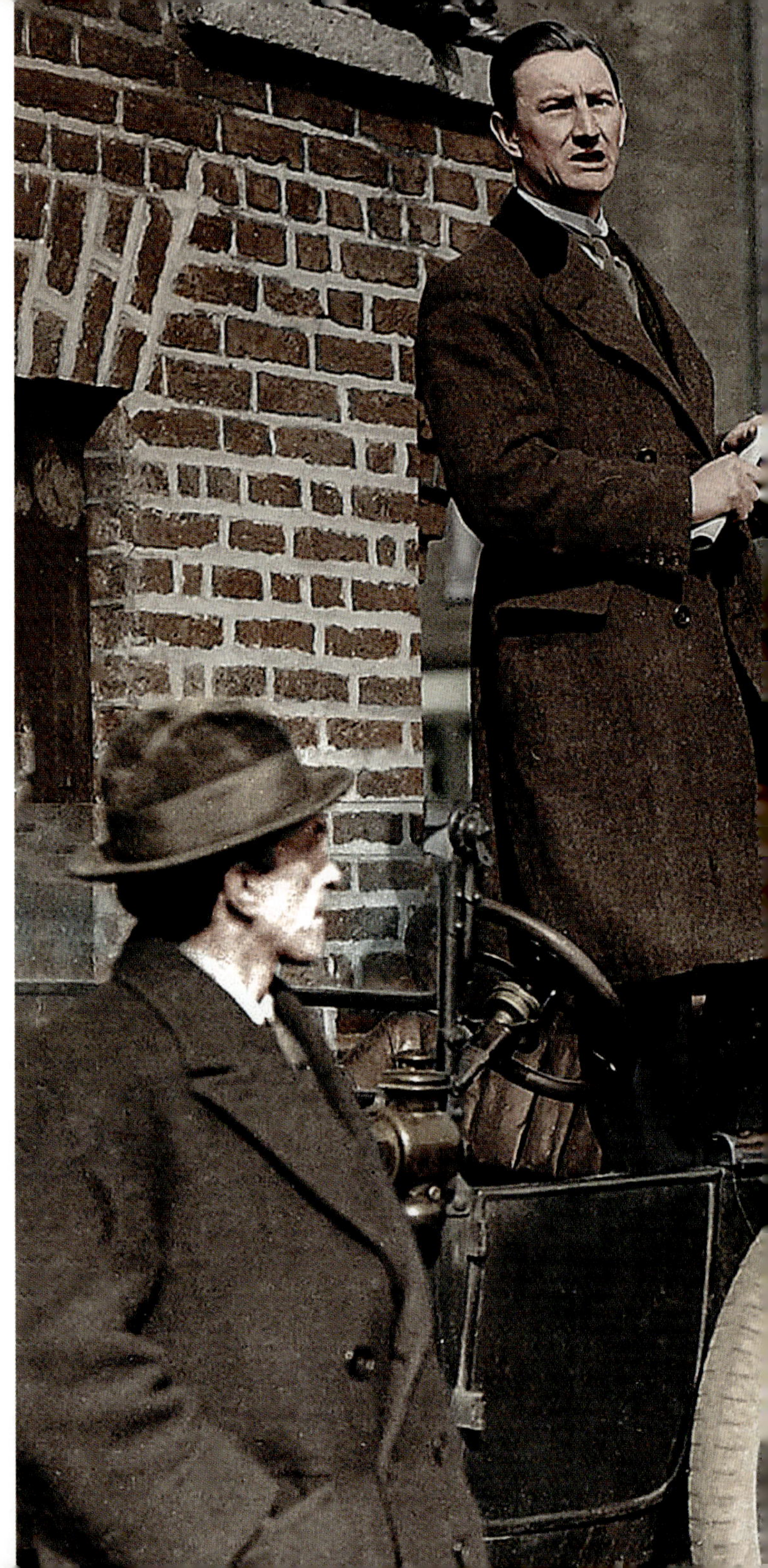

Oscar Traynor, OC Dublin Brigade IRA, speaks at a parade of over 3,000 men at Smithfield in Dublin, on 2 April 1922. They expressed support for the anti-Treaty Executive that had been elected after an IRA Army Convention on 26 March, which had re-affirmed its allegiance to the Republic. Rory O'Connor is on the left. Eleven days later he was one of the leaders of the occupation of the Four Courts.

Overleaf: men of the South. The First Southern Division (Liam Lynch, OC, is in front, fourth from left) at the second IRA Army Convention held in the Mansion House on 9 April. Once again, the Republic was all. The meeting pledged to uphold it and to serve a government that was loyal to the Republic.

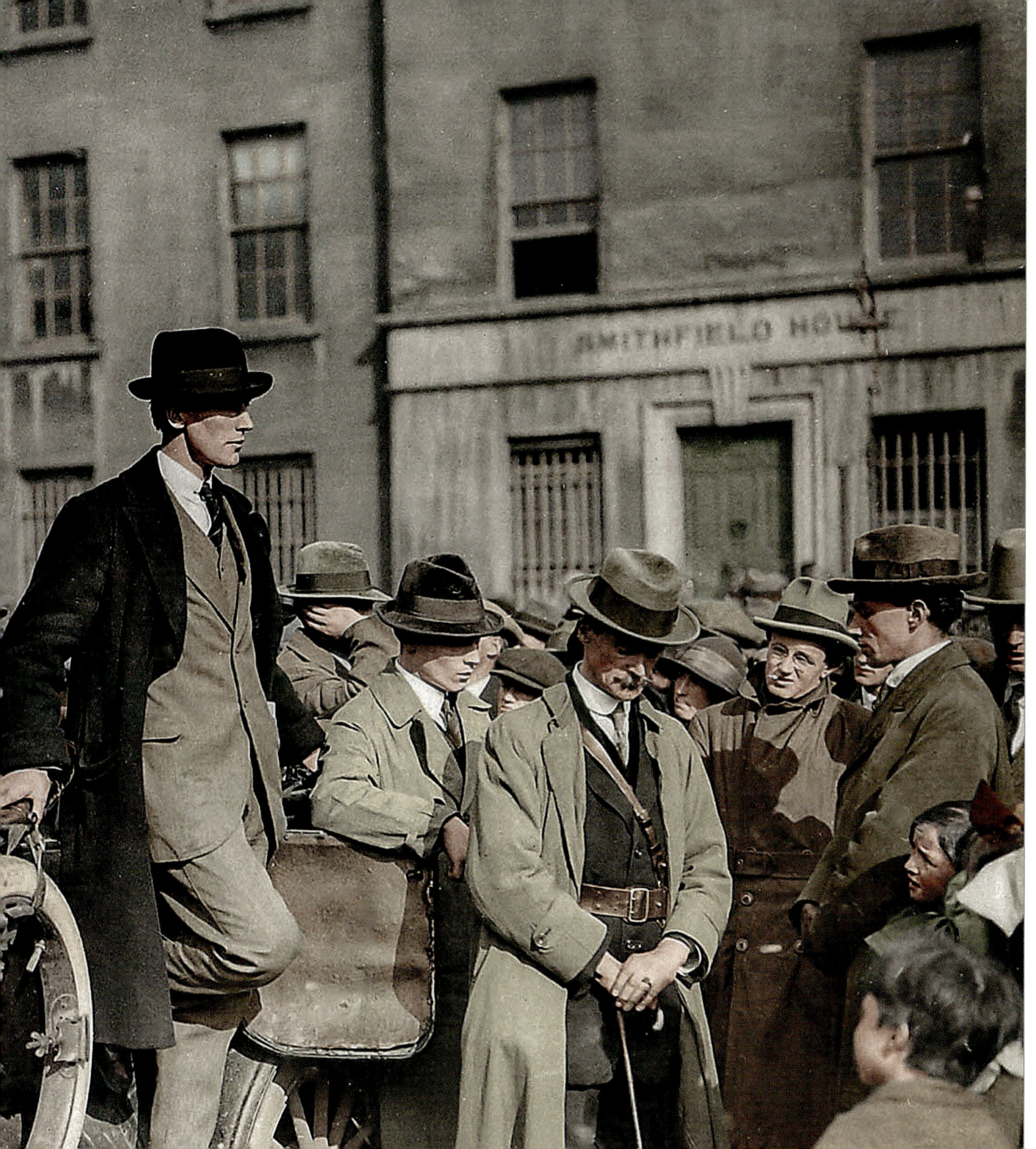
SMITHFIELD HOUSE

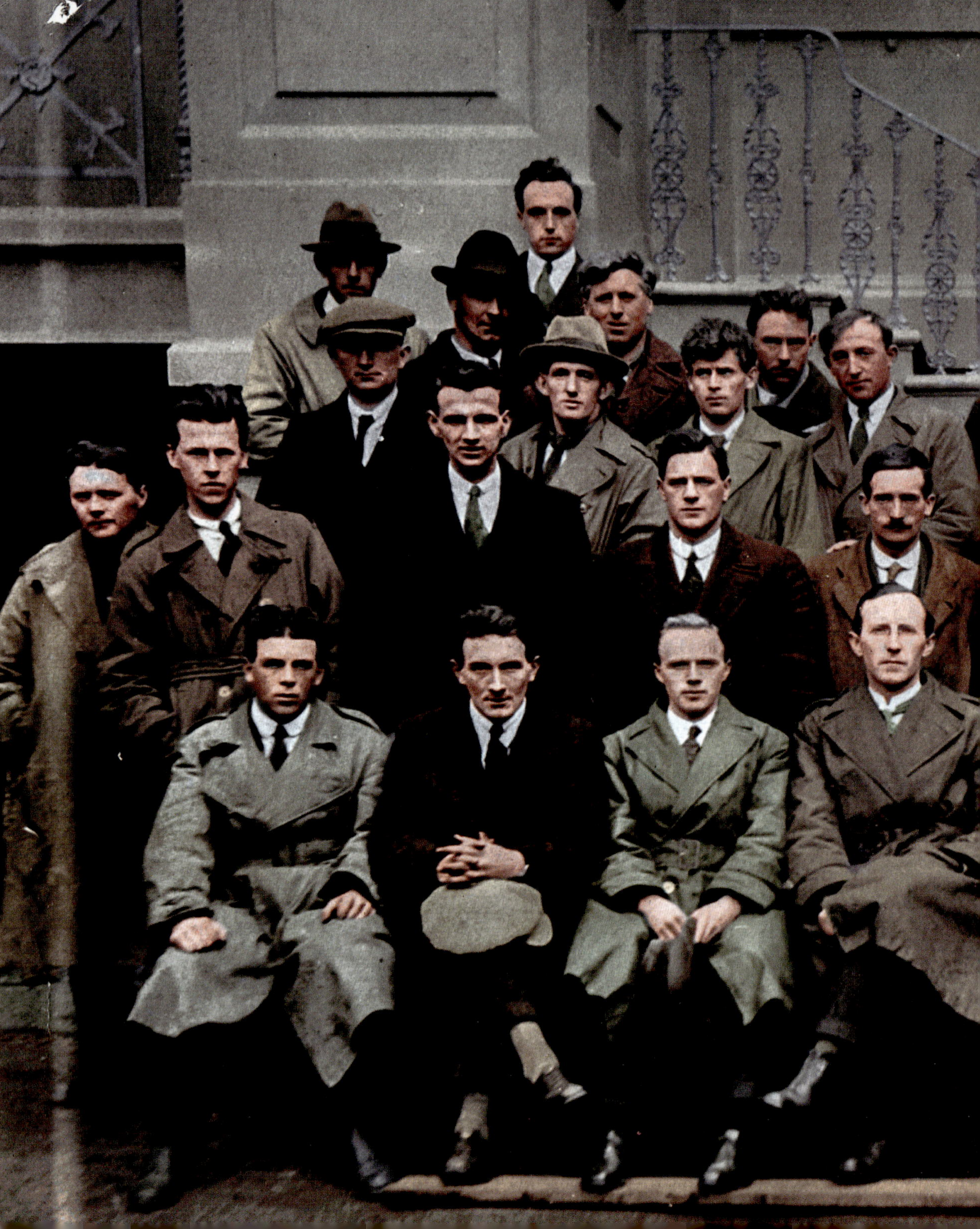

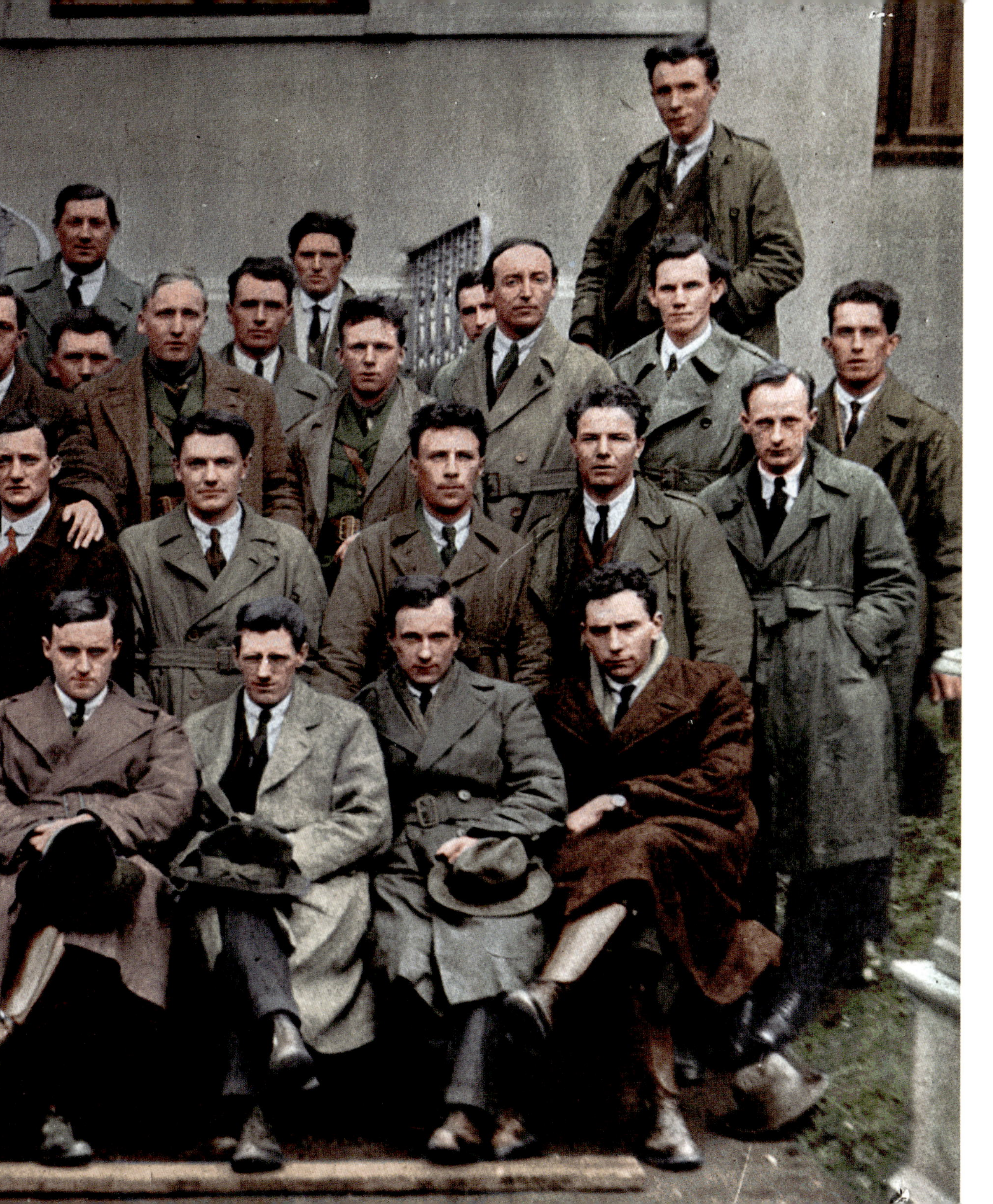

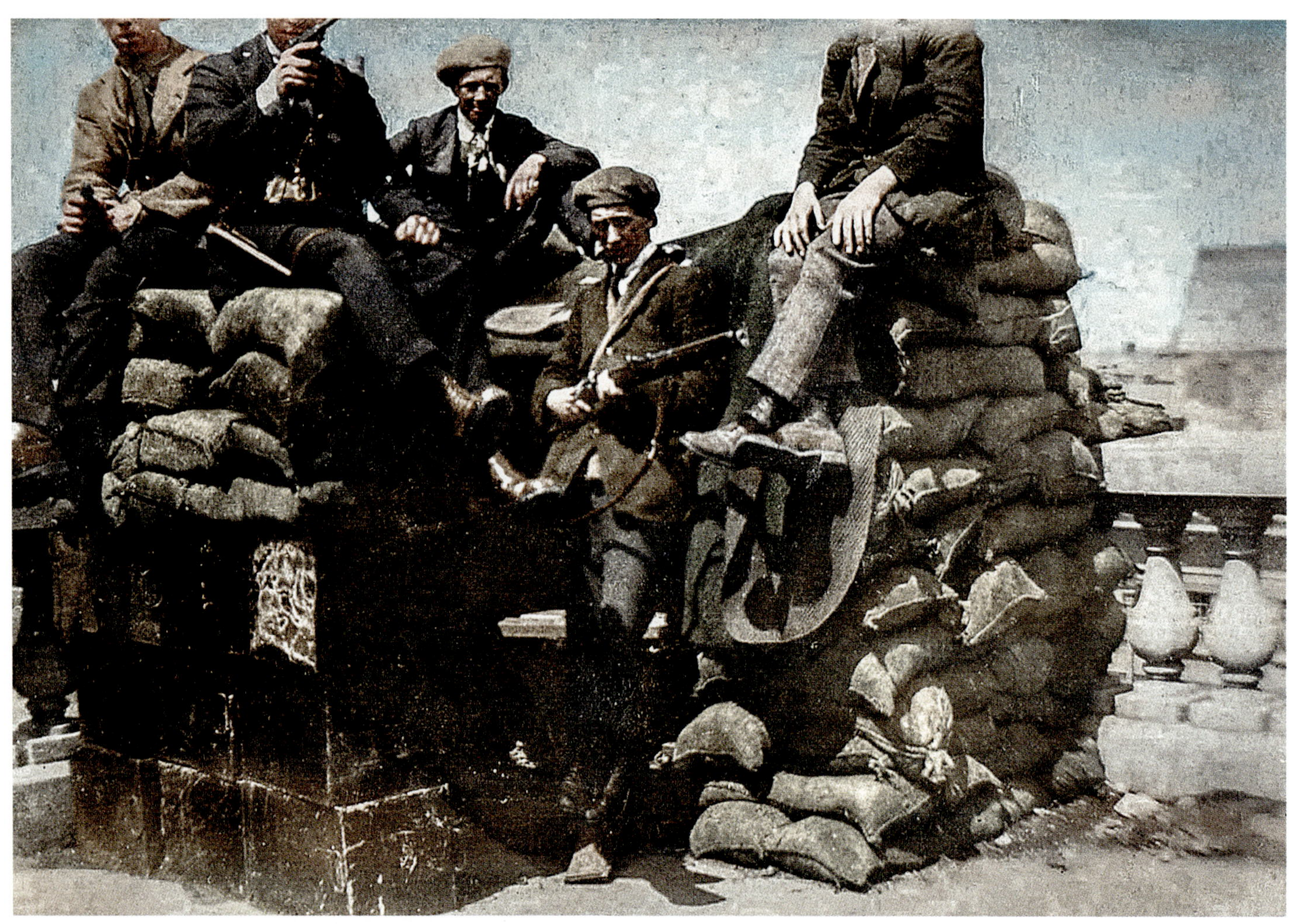

The newly established IRA Executive ordered that strategic buildings in Dublin be occupied. Among these was the Four Courts, which was taken over as their headquarters on the night of 13 April. Here we see IRA men, with sandbags and rifles, on the roof of the Four Courts. After the occupation, the complex was progressively fortified; law books and ledgers were stuffed into windows.

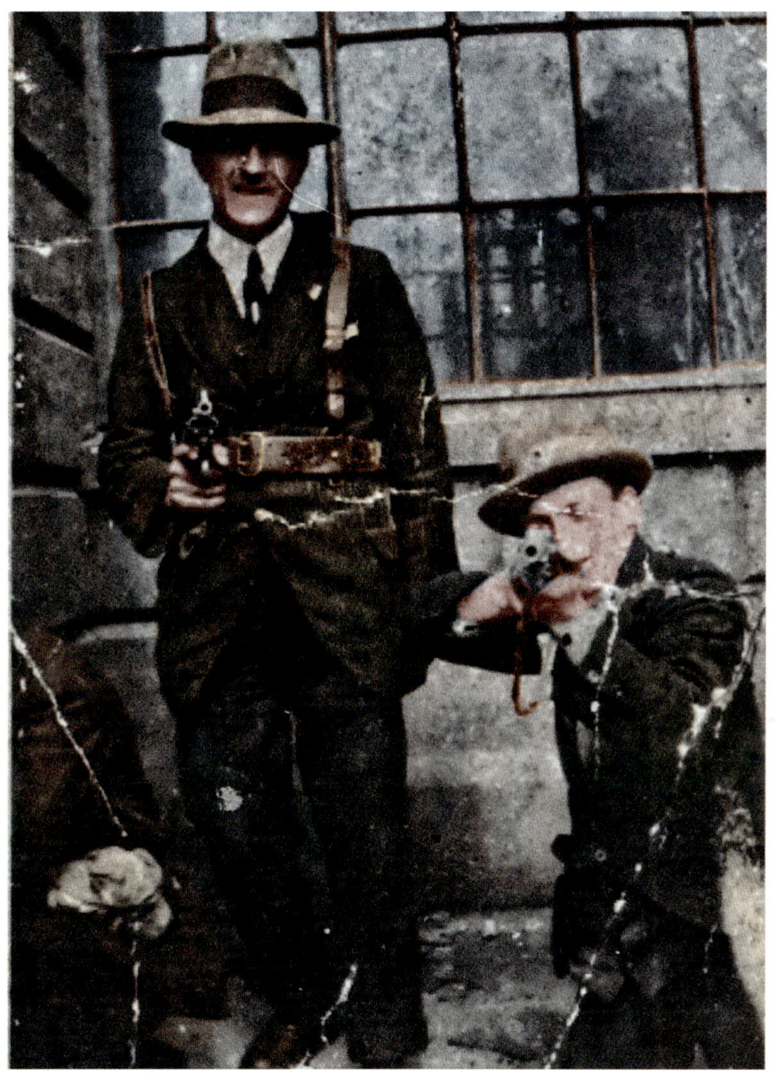

Another scene from the Four Courts. Posing for the camera, the kneeling man aims his rifle. On the left, wearing a semi-military garb of Sam Browne belt with double straps over a suit, William Doyle points his revolver. He was a veteran of the burning of the Custom House during the War of Independence, where he had been arrested. Doyle wavered in his loyalties in the aftermath of the Treaty, but eventually decided to join the anti-Treaty side.

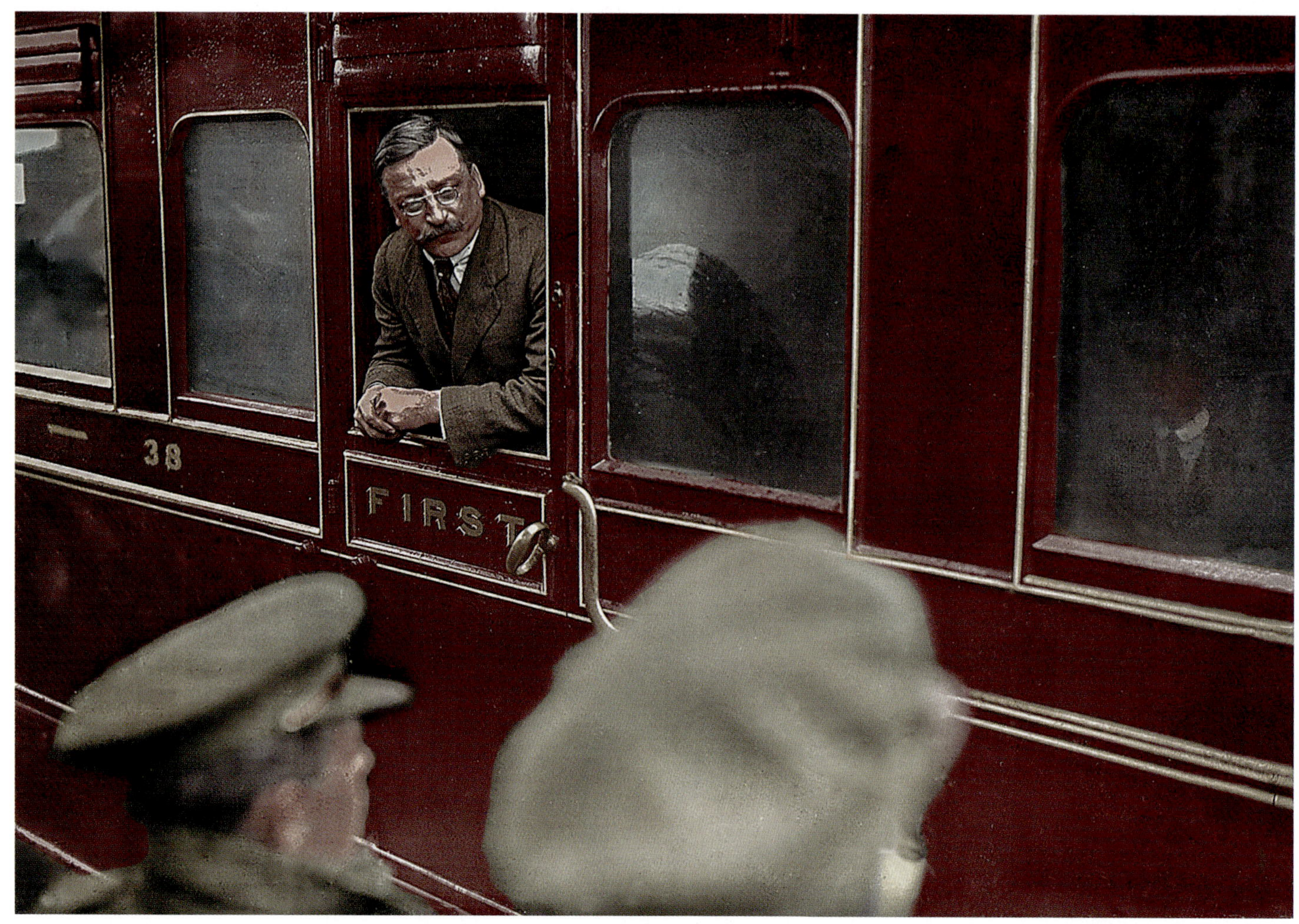

Arthur Griffith at Longford, en route to Sligo for a public meeting there on Easter Sunday, 16 April 1922. Liam Pilkington, of the (anti-Treaty) Third Western IRA, had proscribed the meeting and took over public buildings in the town. In response Seán Mac Eoin led his Provisional Government troops from Athlone.

Right: A watchful Mac Eoin, Webley at the ready, overlooks the meeting in Sligo from a hotel window.

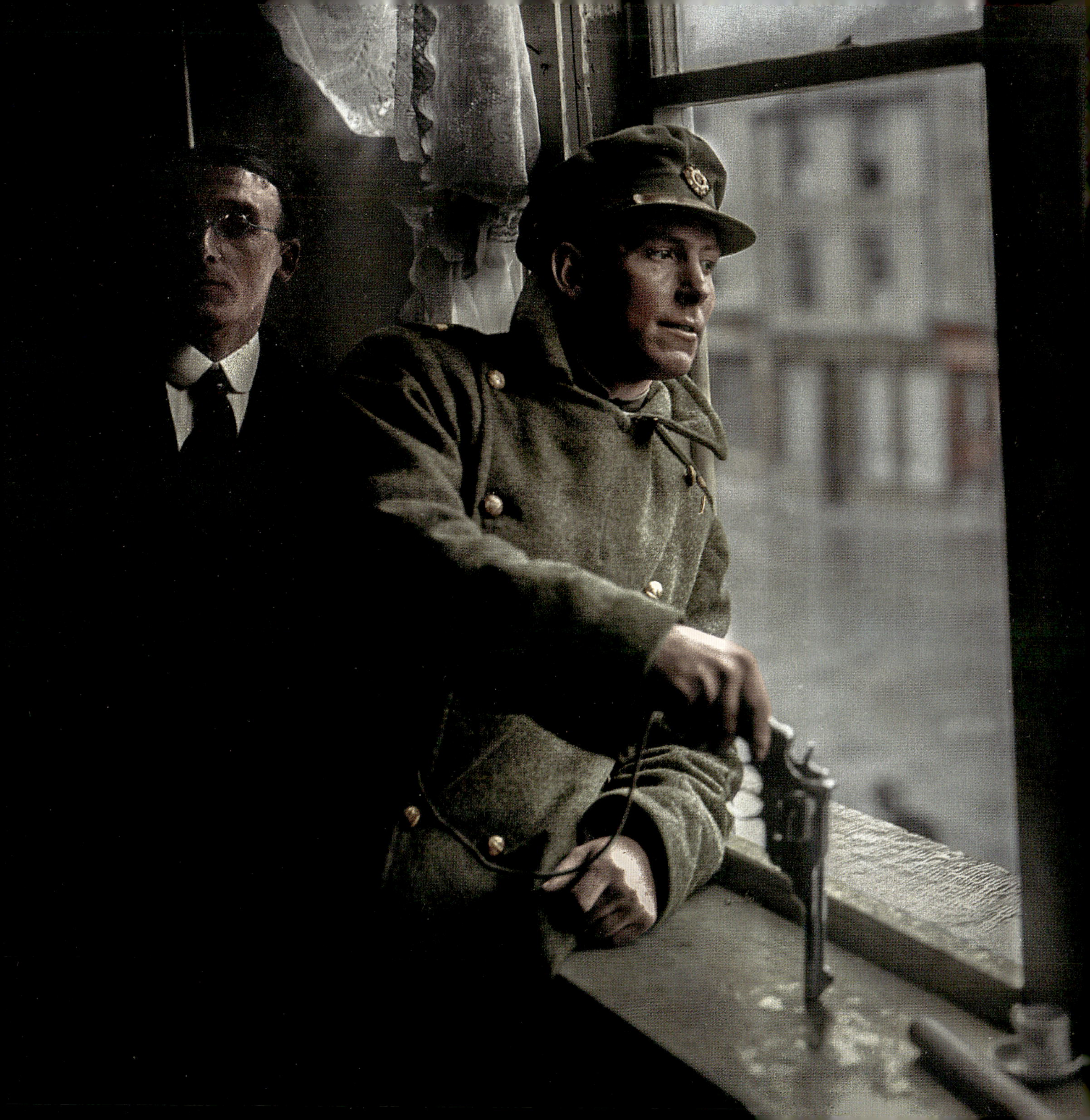

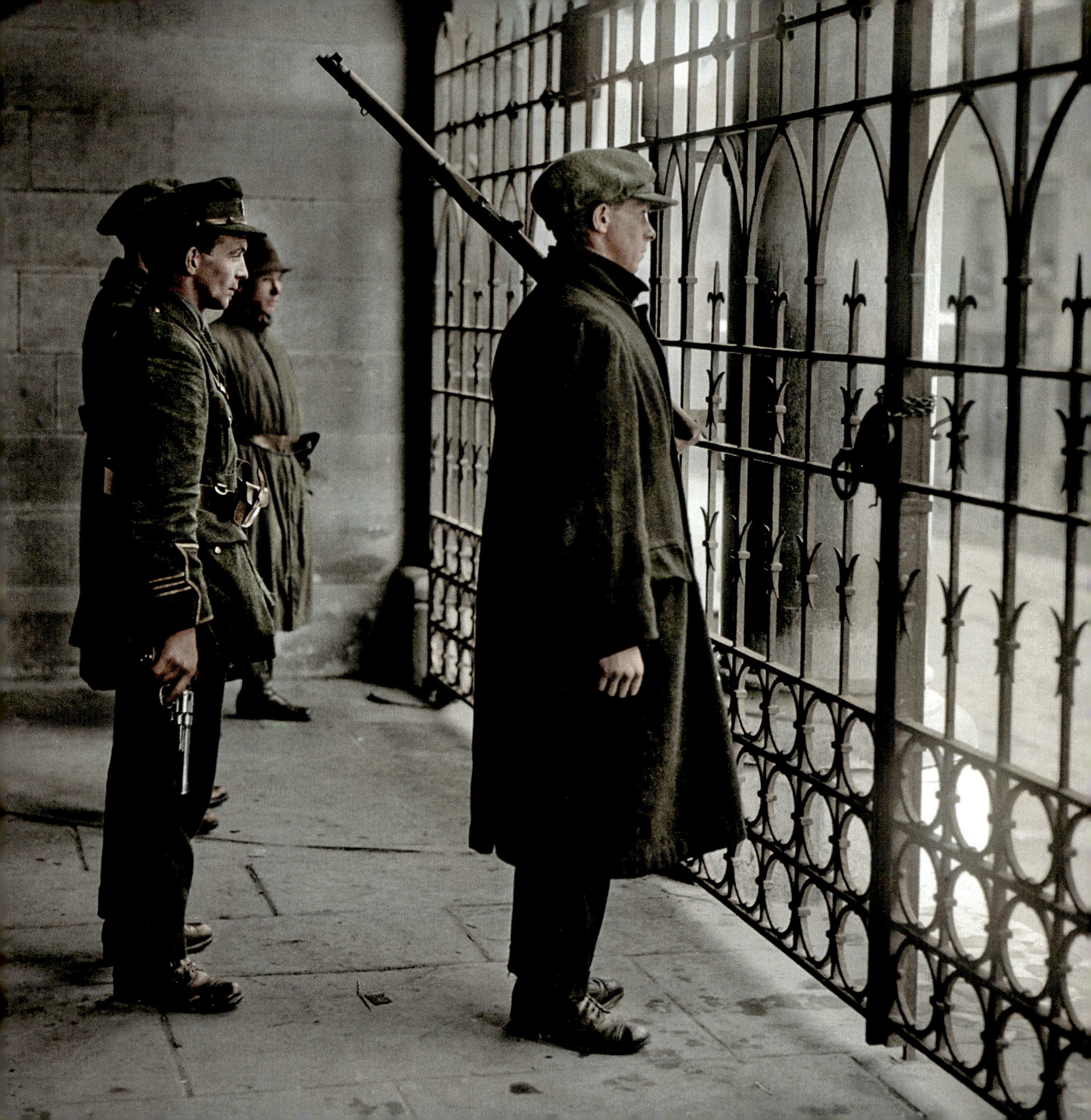

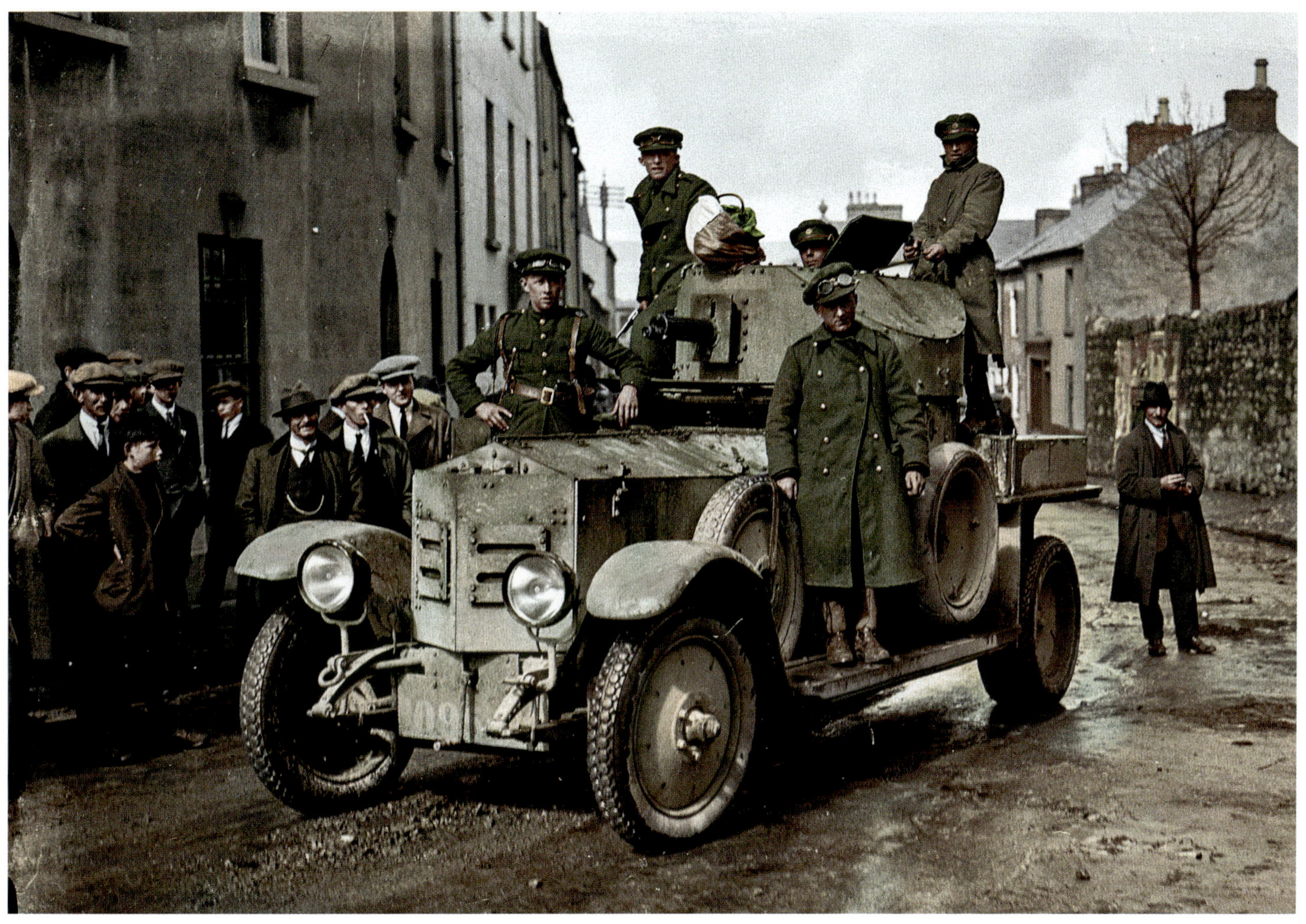

In Sligo, pro-Treaty soldiers stand on a Rolls-Royce armoured car. In line with the tradition of naming these Rolls Royce vehicles during the conflict, this was dubbed *Balinalee* – so named as Seán Mac Eoin had been known as the 'Blacksmith of Ballinalee'. The armoured car was to enjoy a chequered history. On 13 July 1922 it was captured by the anti-Treaty IRA near Lough Gill. It continued (renamed as *Lough Gill*) in anti-Treaty hands until Provisional Government forces put it out of action, near Benbulben, on 19 September.

Left: pro-Treaty men tensely stand at attention as they occupy Sligo Courthouse. With the area flooded by troops, the IRA desisted from interfering with Griffith's meeting.

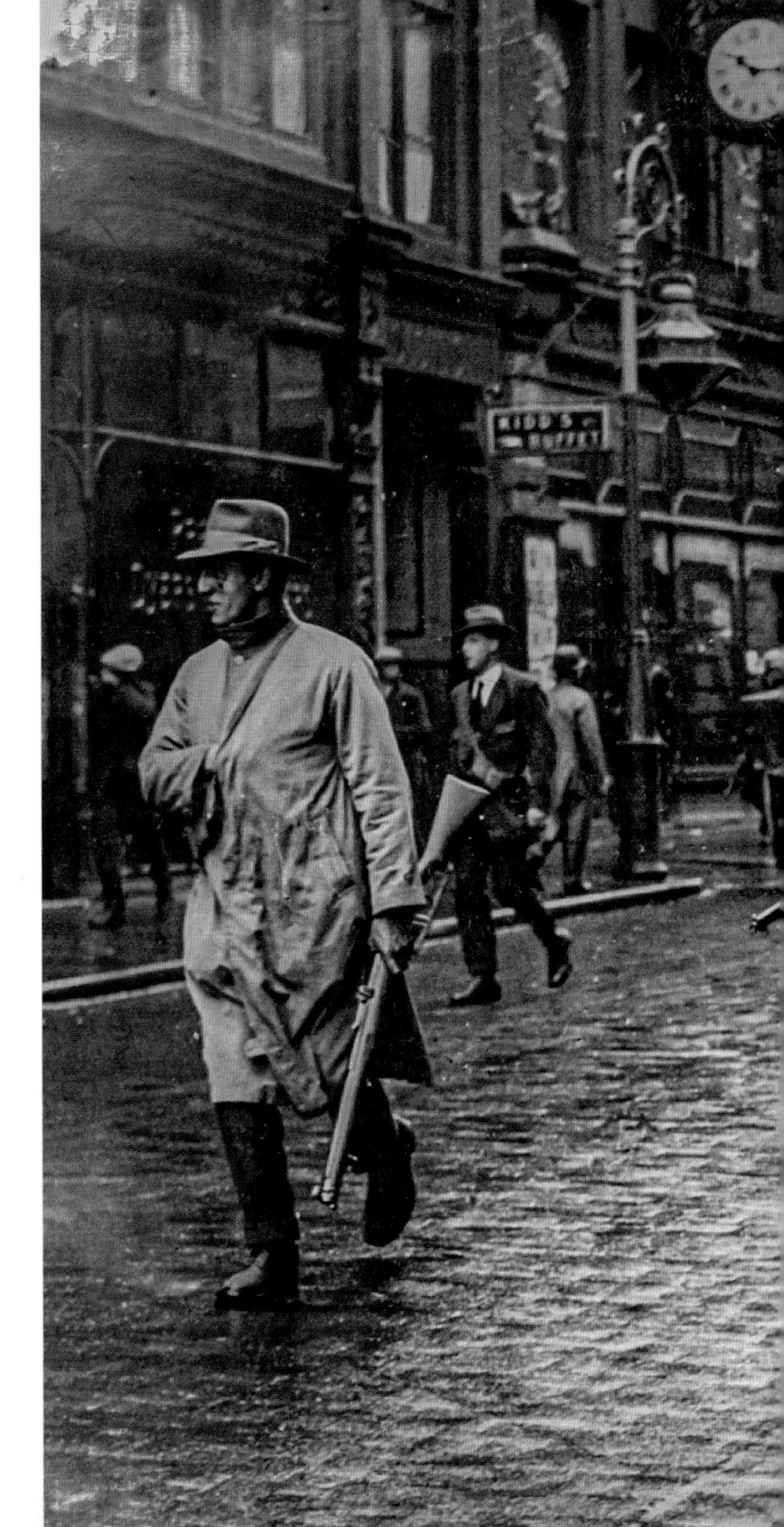

One of the most iconic photos of the Civil War. Asserting their authority (and challenge to the Provisional Government), a unit of the anti-Treaty IRA march along Grafton Street in Dublin.

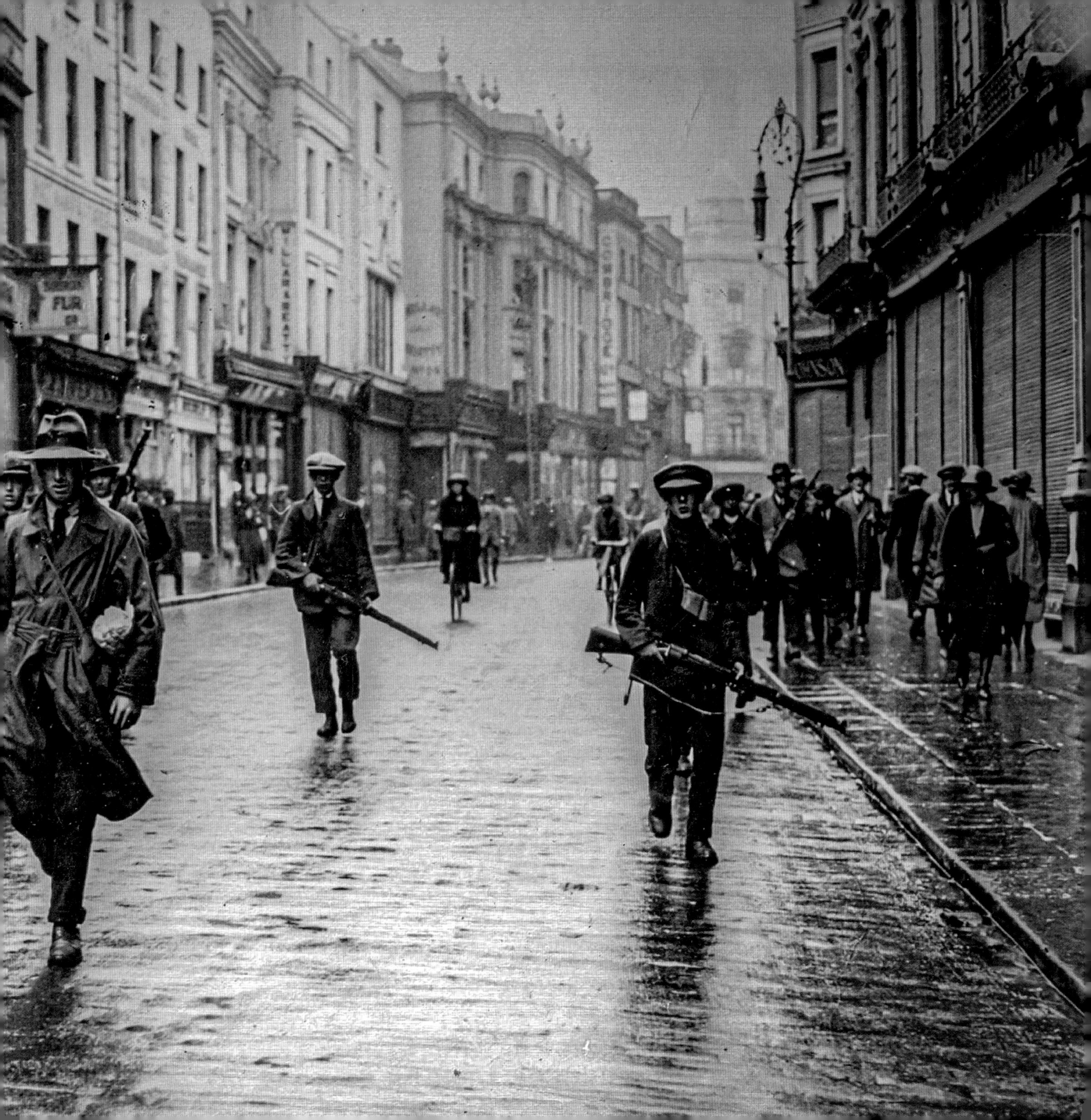

Trucks and top hats. As well as taking the Four Courts in April 1922, the anti-Treaty IRA seized Fowler Hall (in Parnell Square, the Orange Order HQ) and the Kildare Street Club, locations which they regarded as synonymous with Loyalism. Here, Volunteers pose for a photo, at the corner of Nassau Street and Kildare Street outside the eponymous club. One of their trucks has 'Up the Mutineers' chalked on the tailgate (wryly calling themselves 'Mutineers'). The other truck carries what look like sandbags, useful in a time of conflicts and armed clashes. It must have been quite a culture shock when these young men entered the opulent confines of the Kildare Street Club, a sanctum of the upper-class. In a mocking touch, highlighting the incongruity of this luxurious Anglo-Irish bastion in the heart of Dublin, some Volunteers wear the top hats that they had just discovered on the club premises.

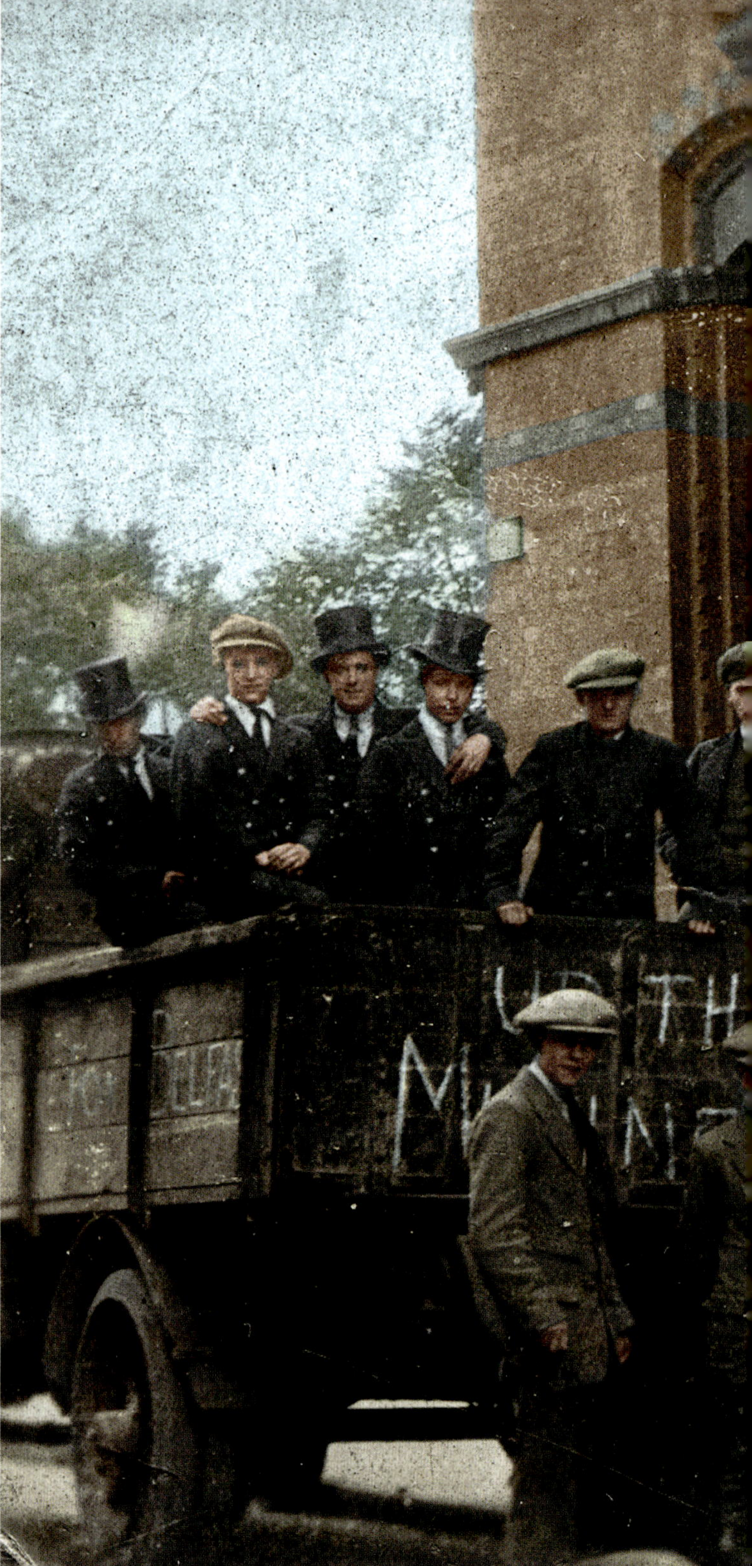

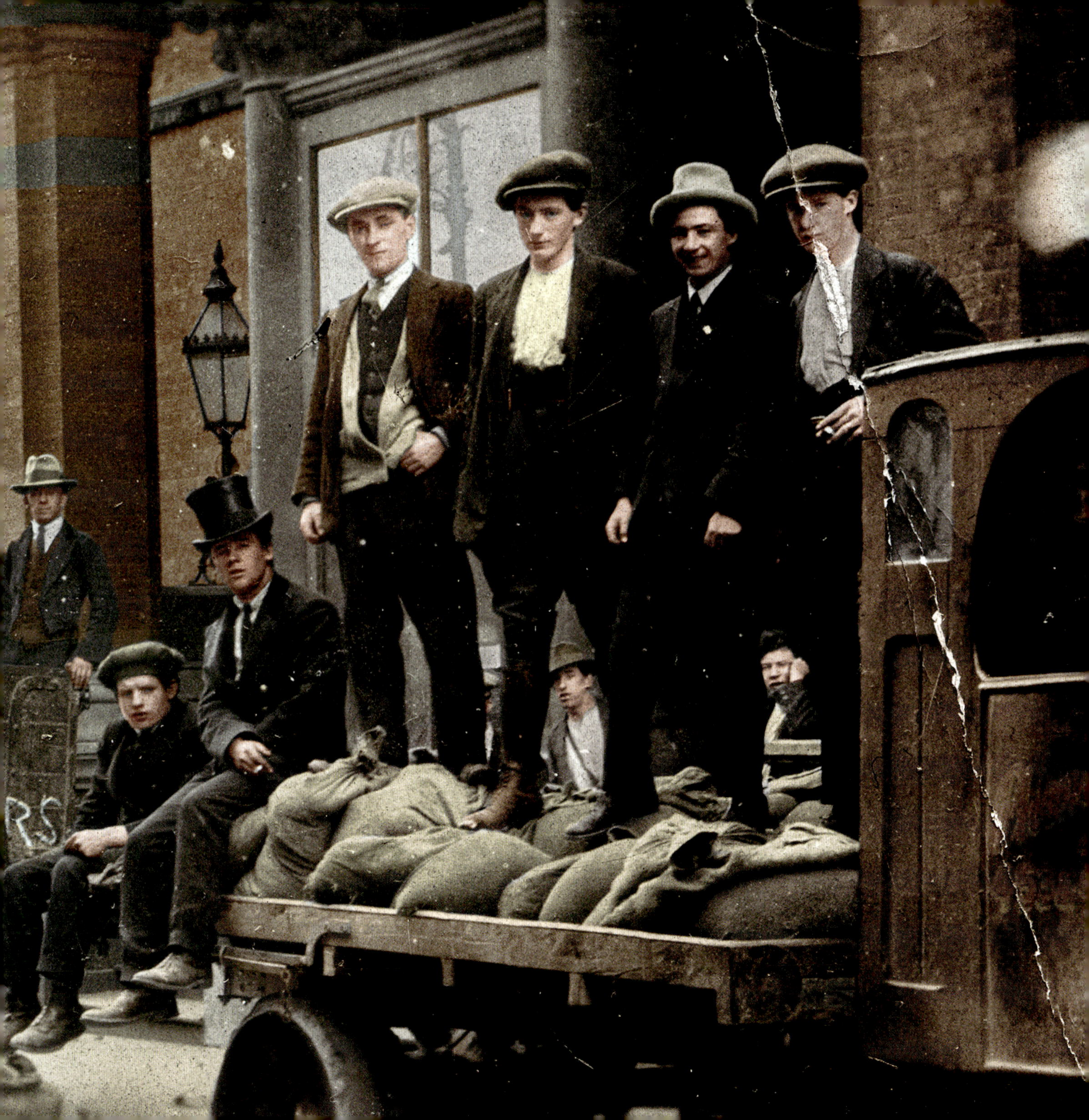

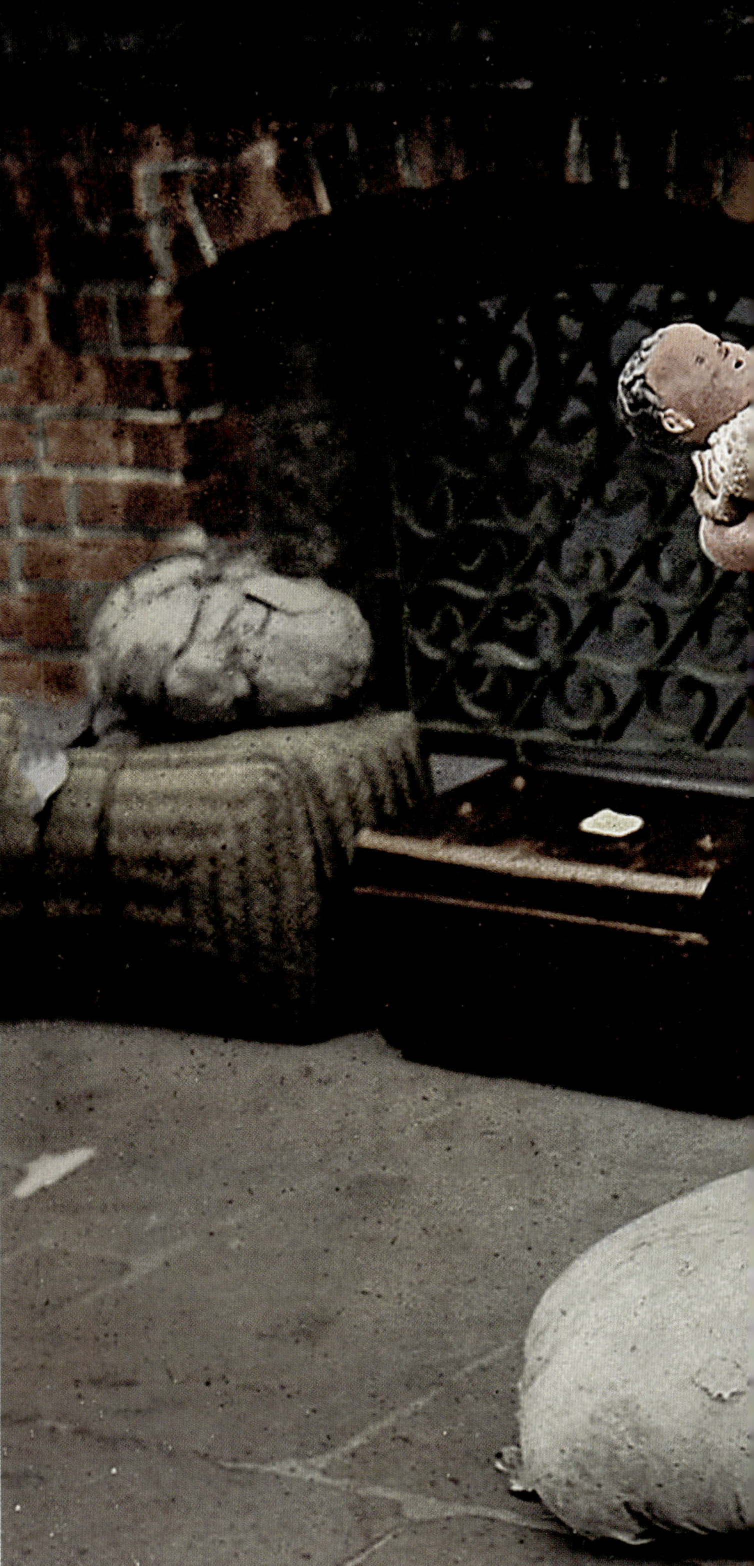

With the opening of the parliament in Belfast in June 1921 the new entity of Northern Ireland had become an established fact, underpinned by the Ulster Special Constabulary and the British Army. Against this reality, the partition of Ireland had not been central in the negotiations in London at the end of 1921. The Treaty included provisions for the Boundary Commission that was to supposedly deal with the issue.

From the beginning of 1922, outbreaks of sectarian violence in the north became more savage and sustained than in previous years. Catholics bore most of the brunt of the violence and thousands of Catholic refugees flooded south. In the photo, Bridie Gallagher, a refugee, stands outside the Kildare Street Club clutching her doll amidst pitiful bundles of possessions. The anti-Treaty IRA used the club and other premises they had seized to house the refugees.

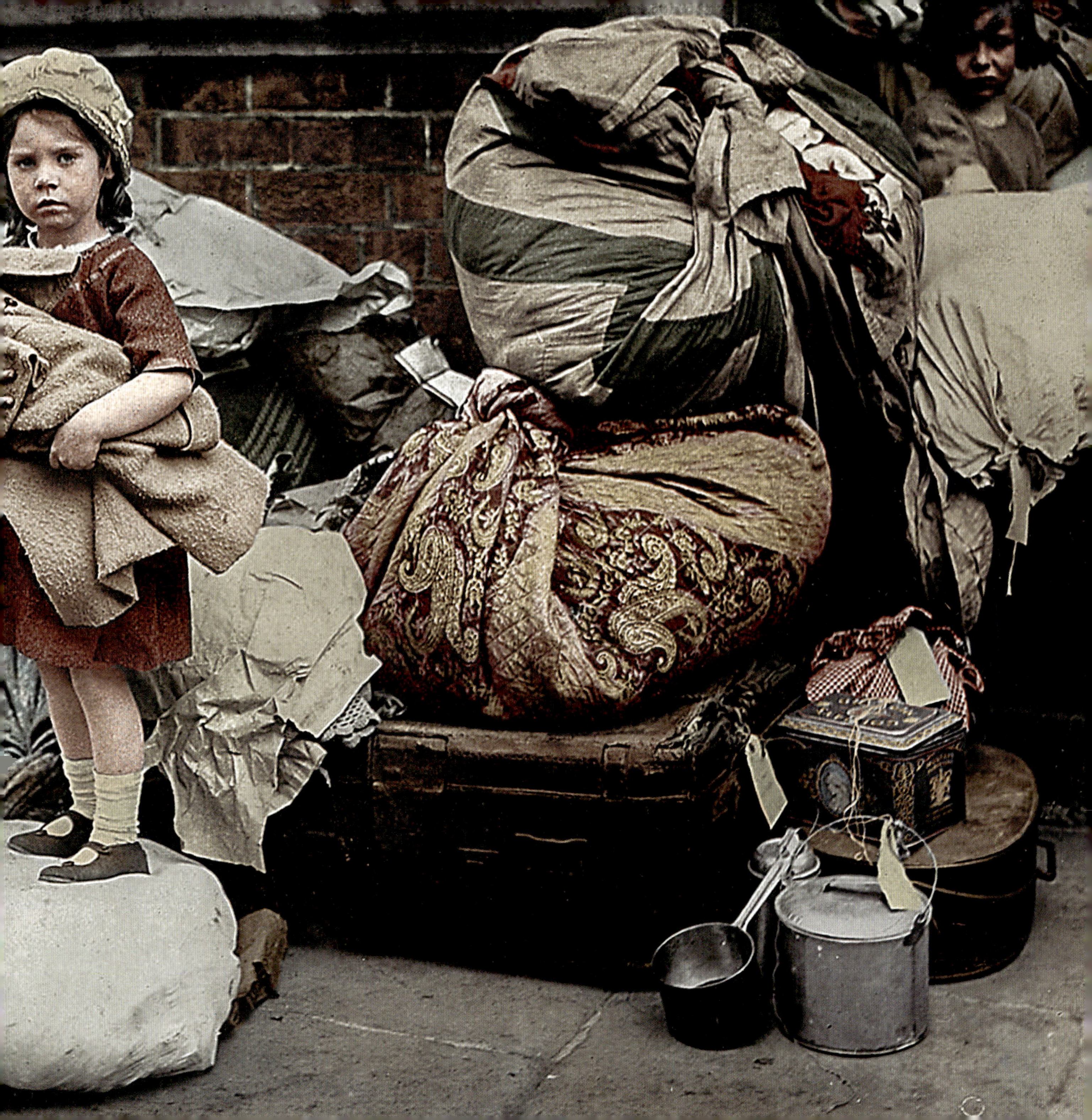

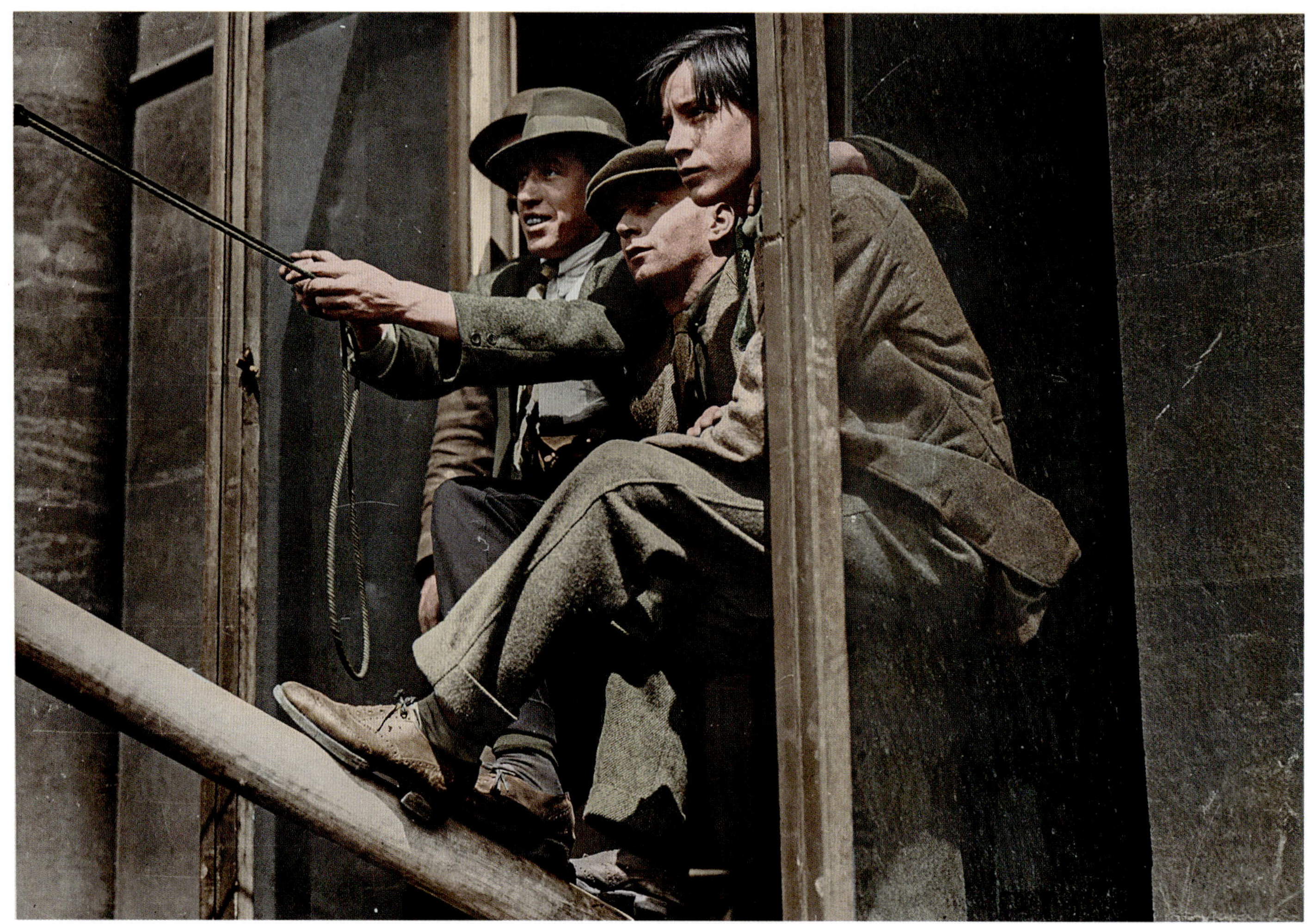

Another building seized by the anti-Treaty IRA to house refugees was the Freemasons' Hall in Molesworth Street, Dublin (housing the Grand Lodge of Ireland, the second-oldest Grand Lodge in the world). Here Volunteers raise the flag. They left in May as part of a peace agreement agreed that month, without having caused any damage to the building.

Right: on 2 May 1922 the IRA took over the Ballast Office in Dublin (strategically located facing O'Connell Bridge). Following negotiations, the building was evacuated later in the month. It was handed over to the Lord Mayor, Lawrence O'Neill (accompanied by associates), photographed here, tapping with his umbrella, seeking admittance.

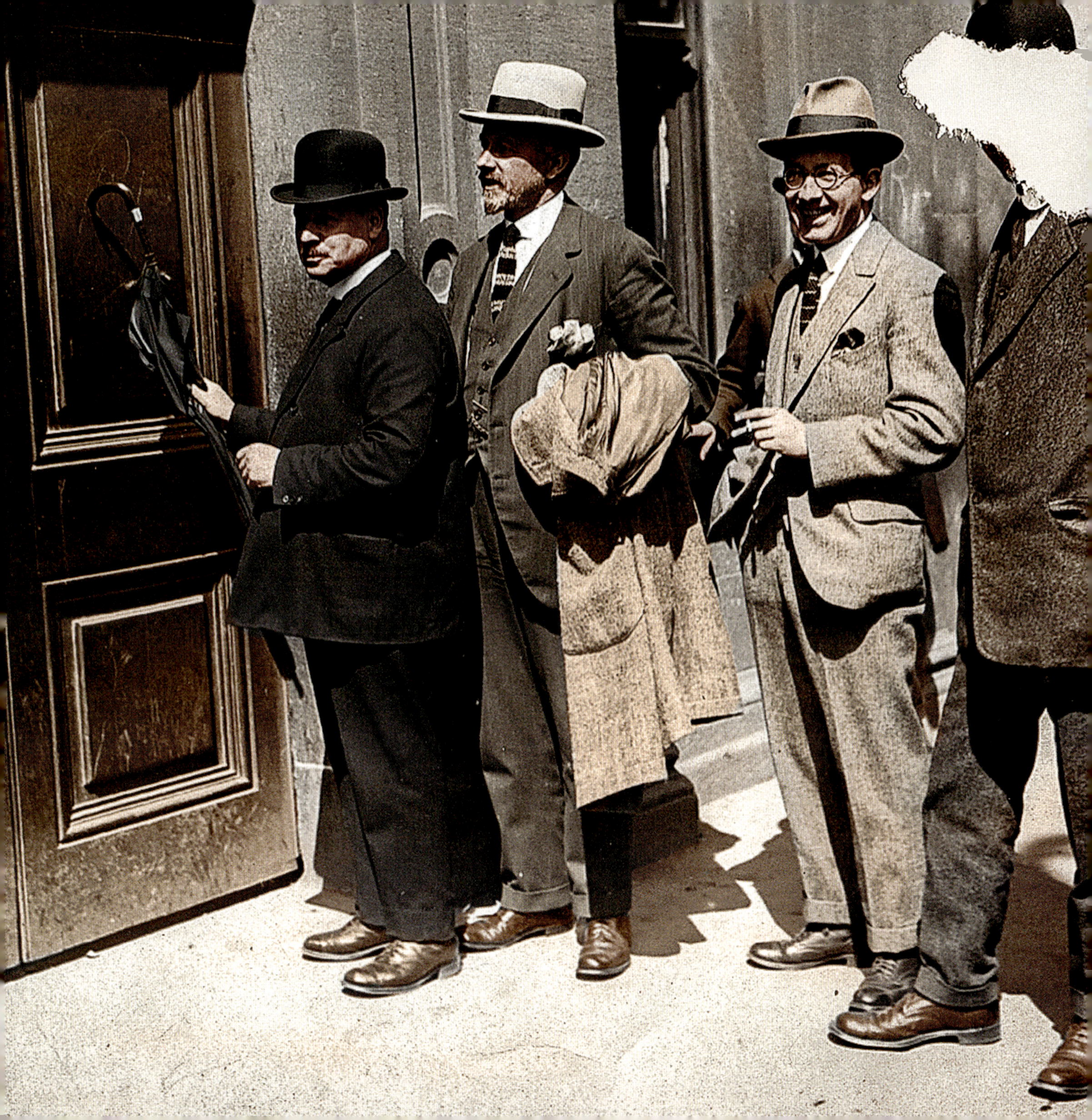

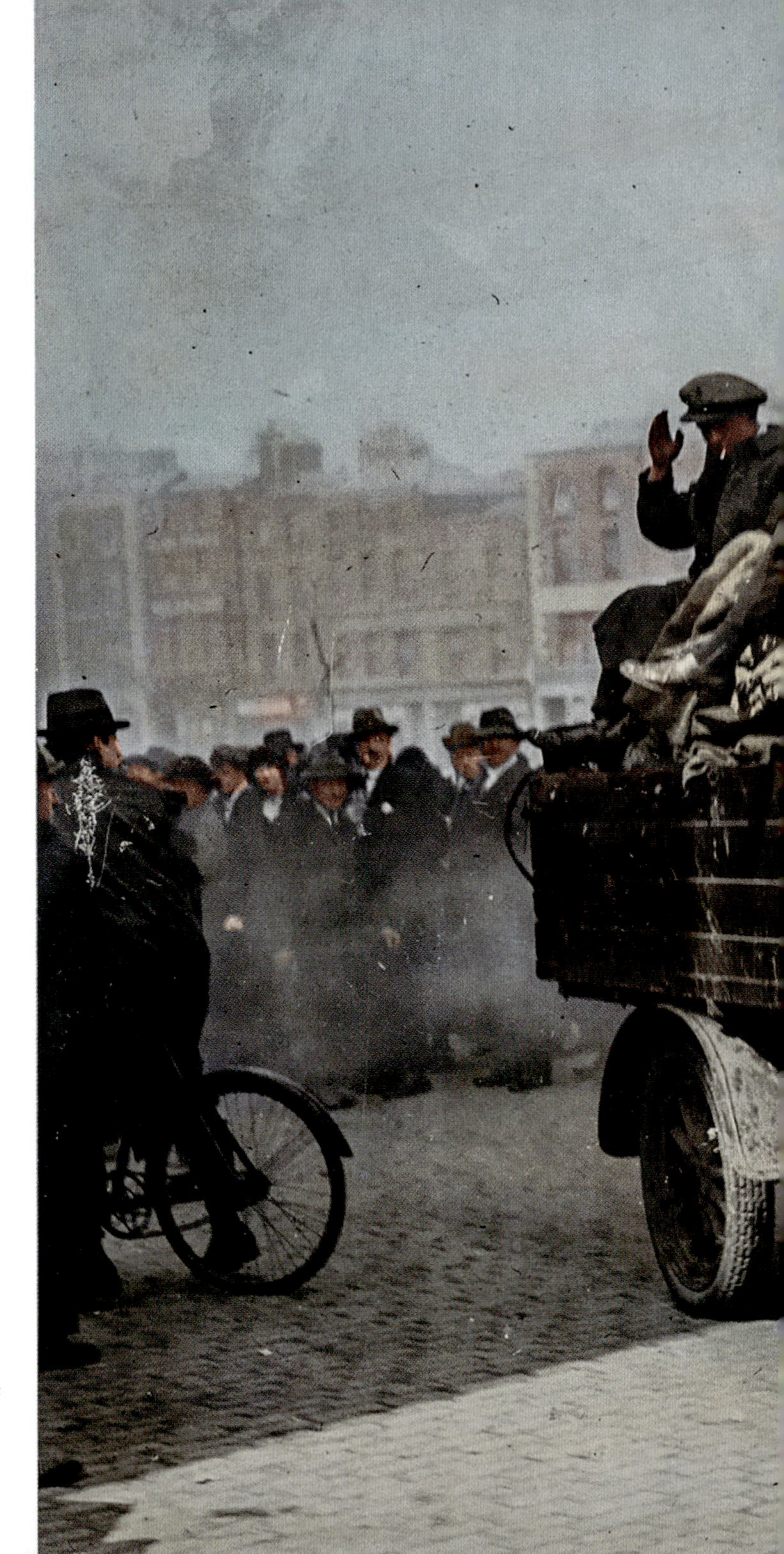

Here we see the IRA unit that had just evacuated the
Ballast Office. In what looks like a crowded and busy scene
on the Dublin quays, they pose in their light truck, packed
with sacks, probably sandbags.

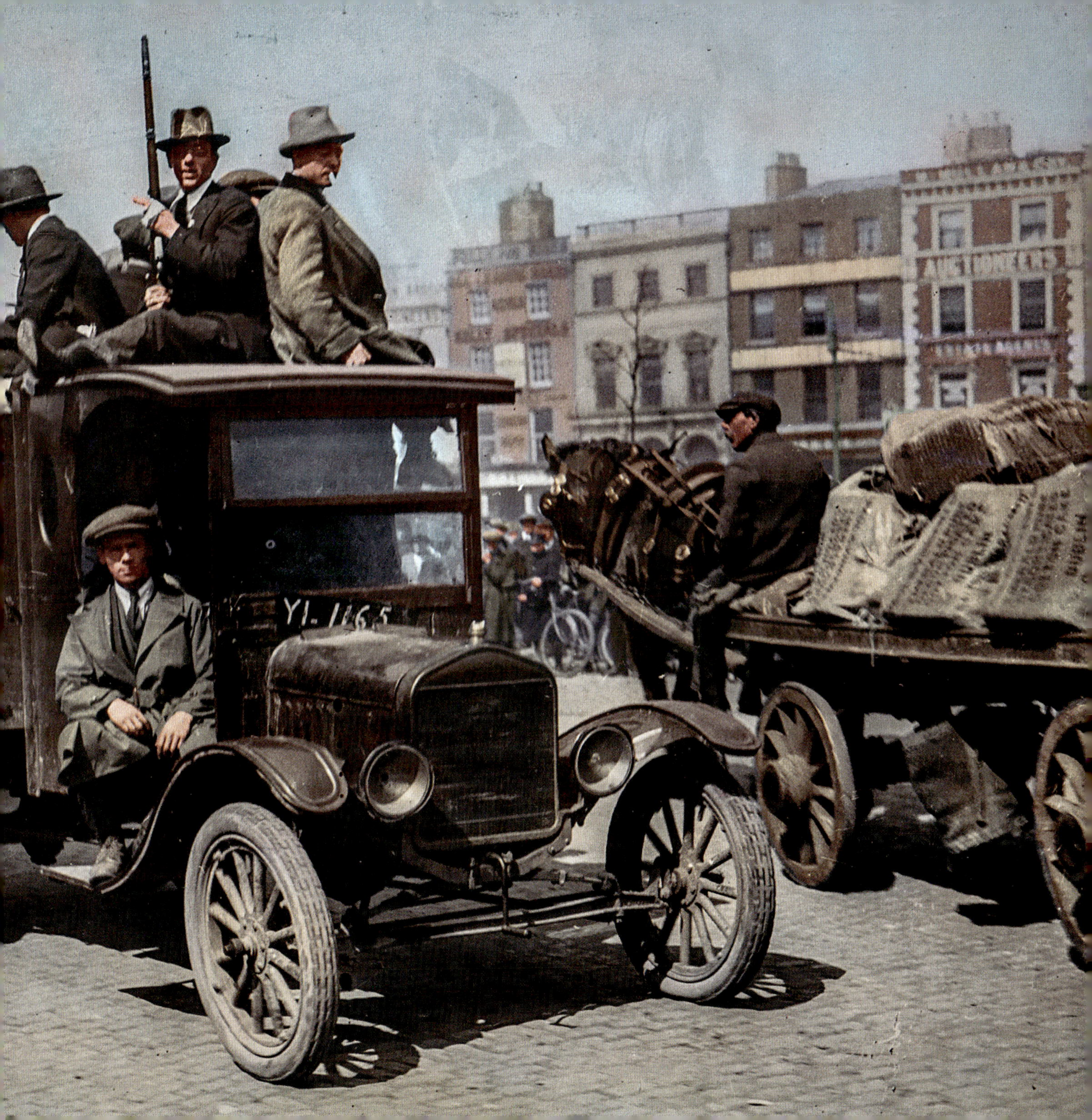

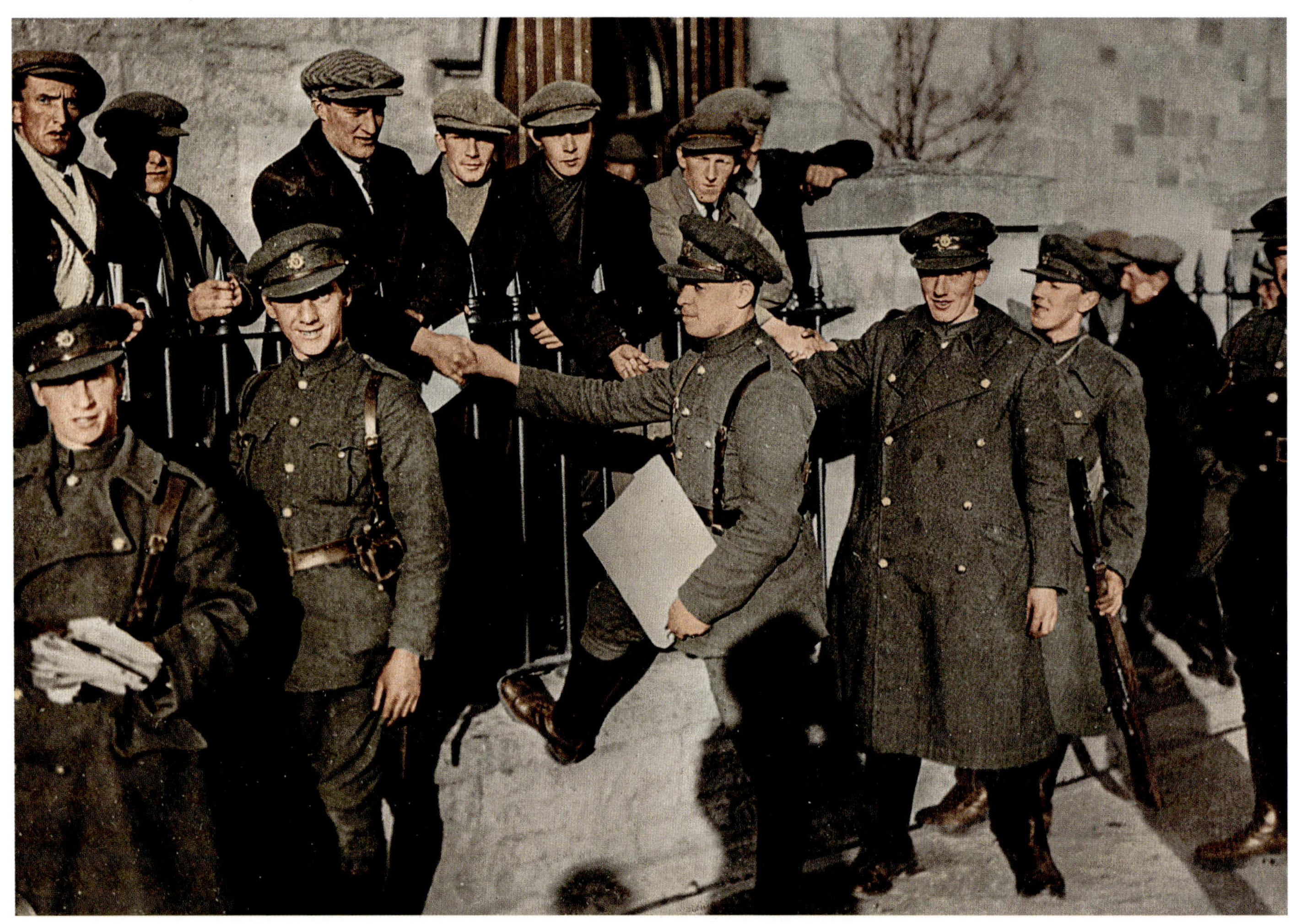

Throughout early 1922 there were skirmishes as both sides jostled for control. A serious incident occurred in early May when anti-Treaty IRA units took over positions in Kilkenny. In response, 200 troops of the Dublin Guard were dispatched by train to the city and there was a day-long confrontation. Initiatives in the Dáil resulted in a joint committee being established in Dublin. It arrived at a compromise: prisoners were released and both sides were to garrison different positions in the city. Here anti-Treaty prisoners, just prior to release, are seen behind the railings at the entrance to the church in the Kilkenny Military (now James Stephens) Barracks. They amicably shake hands with their Provisional Government Army jailers, a few of whom smile for the camera.

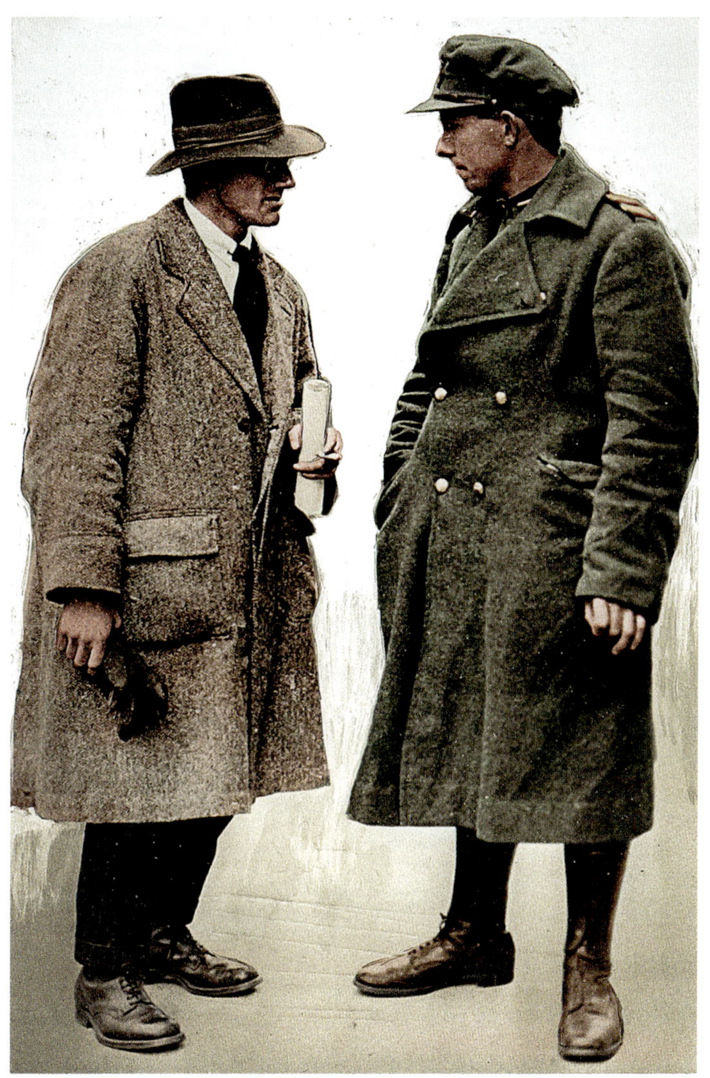

The joint committee met at the Mansion House and on 8 May 1922 decided to extend the agreed truce. Pictured here are, from left, anti-Treaty leader, Seán Moylan and Commandant-General Seán Mac Eoin. During the War of Independence both had been outstanding IRA leaders in their localities. Both had also shared the experience of being captured and having to endure months of imprisonment.

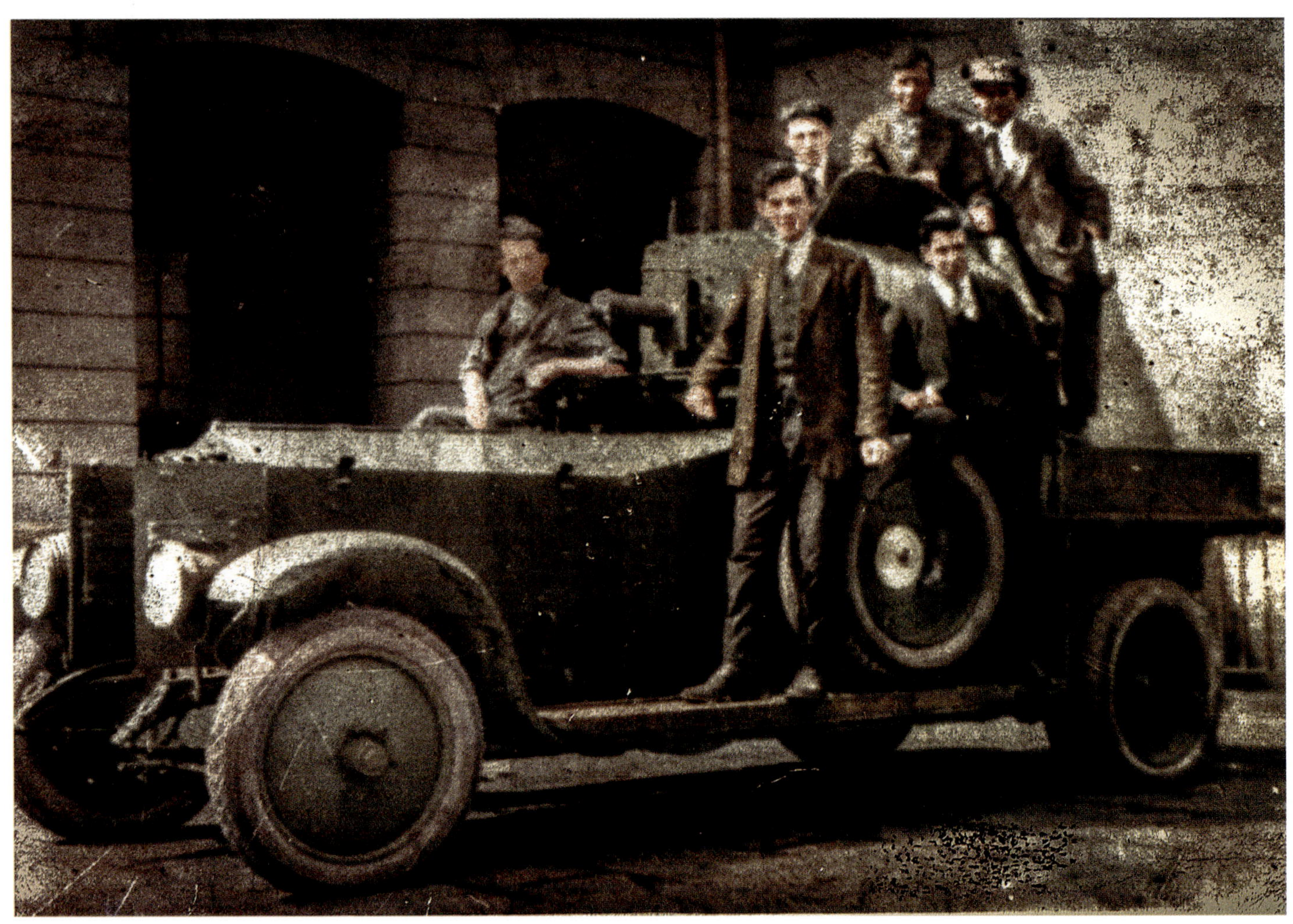

After the local IRA took over the huge Templemore Barracks, Co. Tipperary, a Provisional Government detachment arrived and was refused entry. In April the pro-Treaty GHQ sent a Rolls-Royce armoured car, only for it to be captured by the now openly anti-Treaty occupants. Here is the armoured car at the Four Courts, transferred there by orders of the anti-Treaty leader Ernie O'Malley. It was named the 'Mutineer' – echoing the sardonic term chalked on the lorry at the Kildare Street Club on page 54.

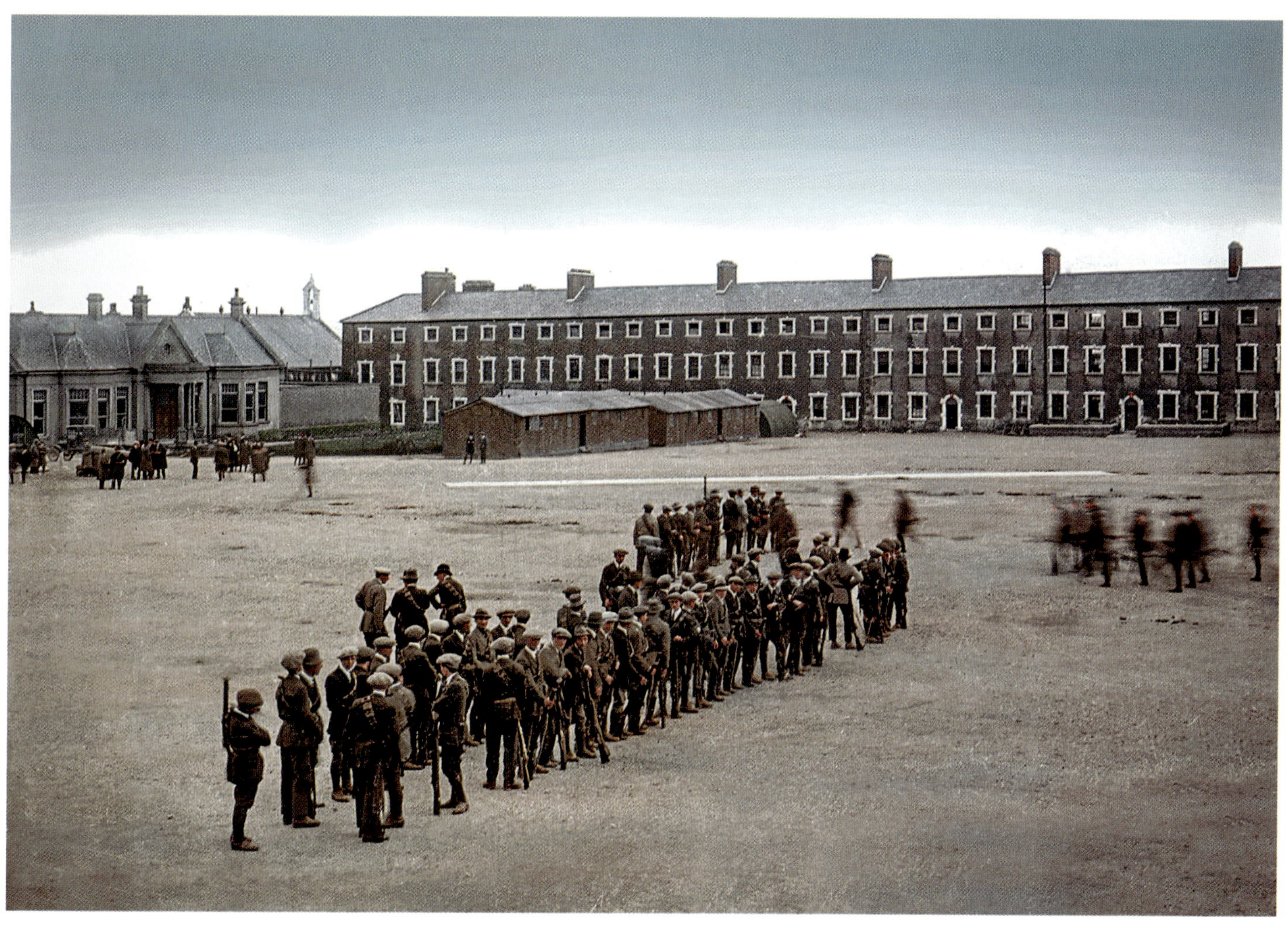

The Cork No. 1 Brigade of the IRA take over Victoria (now Collins) Barracks, Cork, on the evening of 18 May 1922. The British had handed over the keys to a representative of the Provisional Government, Captain Hugh O'Neill. Illustrating the confusion that swirled around, in line with the truce agreement of early May, he handed over control to the Cork No. 1 Brigade, who were anti-Treaty. The British troops had just departed, marching down to the quays to embark on the SS *Classic*, (a cross-channel steamer that was to have the sad task, three months later, of transporting Michael Collins' body to Dublin, page 192). The British troop evacuation had been planned by, amongst others, Major Bernard Montgomery, later the general of El Alamein fame.

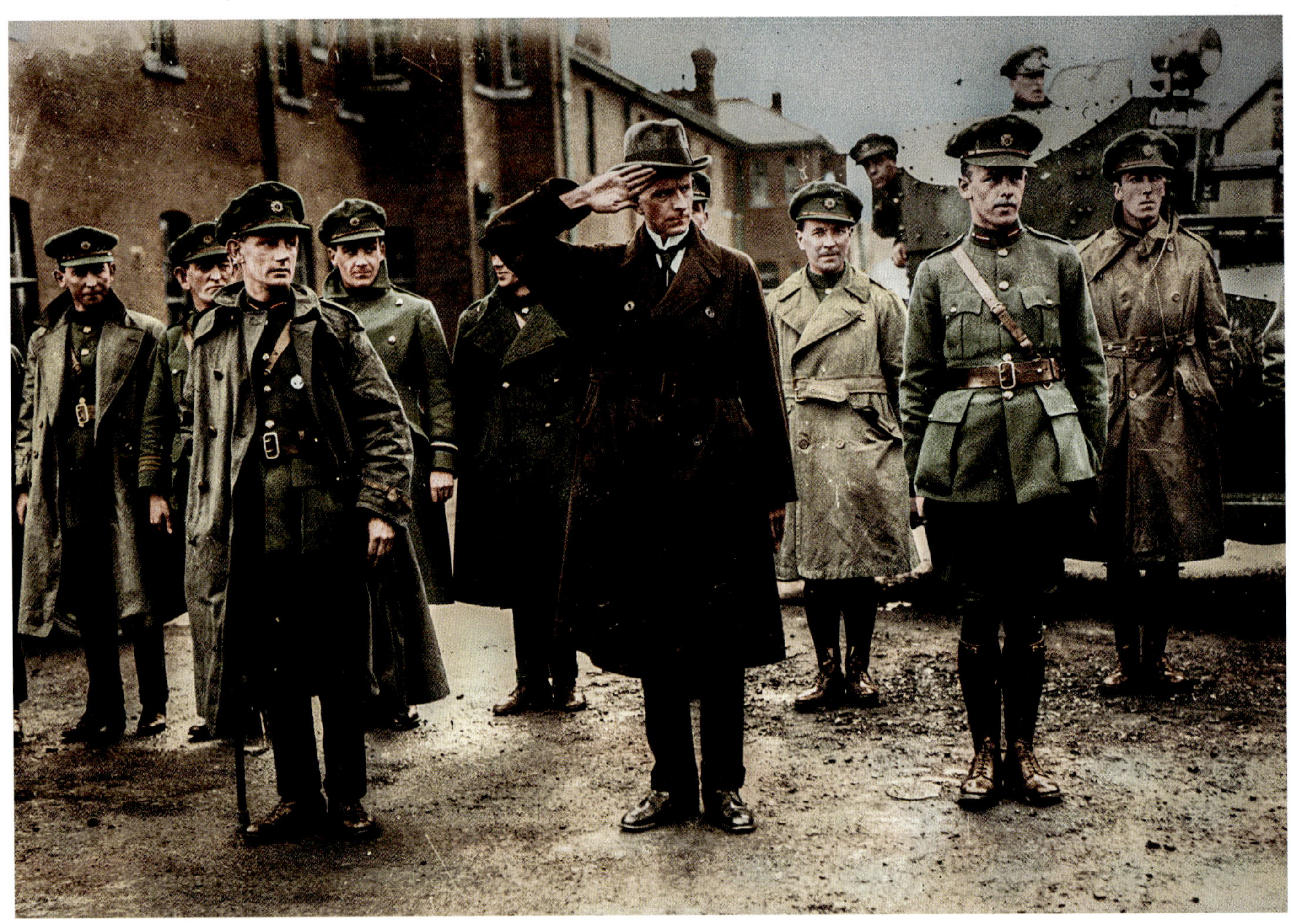

Gradually most of the main military barracks were taken over. An intense-looking General Eoin O'Duffy, Emmet Dalton to his left, takes the salute during the handover of Portobello (now Cathal Brugha) Barracks in Dublin on 17 May. In the background on the right is the armoured car, the 'Custom House', which featured the following July in the fighting in central Dublin (page 96).

Right: wearing a mixture of civilian and military uniforms, pro-Treaty men march through the rainy gloom along the approach road to the Curragh Camp for the handover on 16 May 1922. Lieutenant-General J.J. O'Connell climbed the water tower to erect a giant tricolour, using an improvised flagpole, replacing one cut down by the departing British.

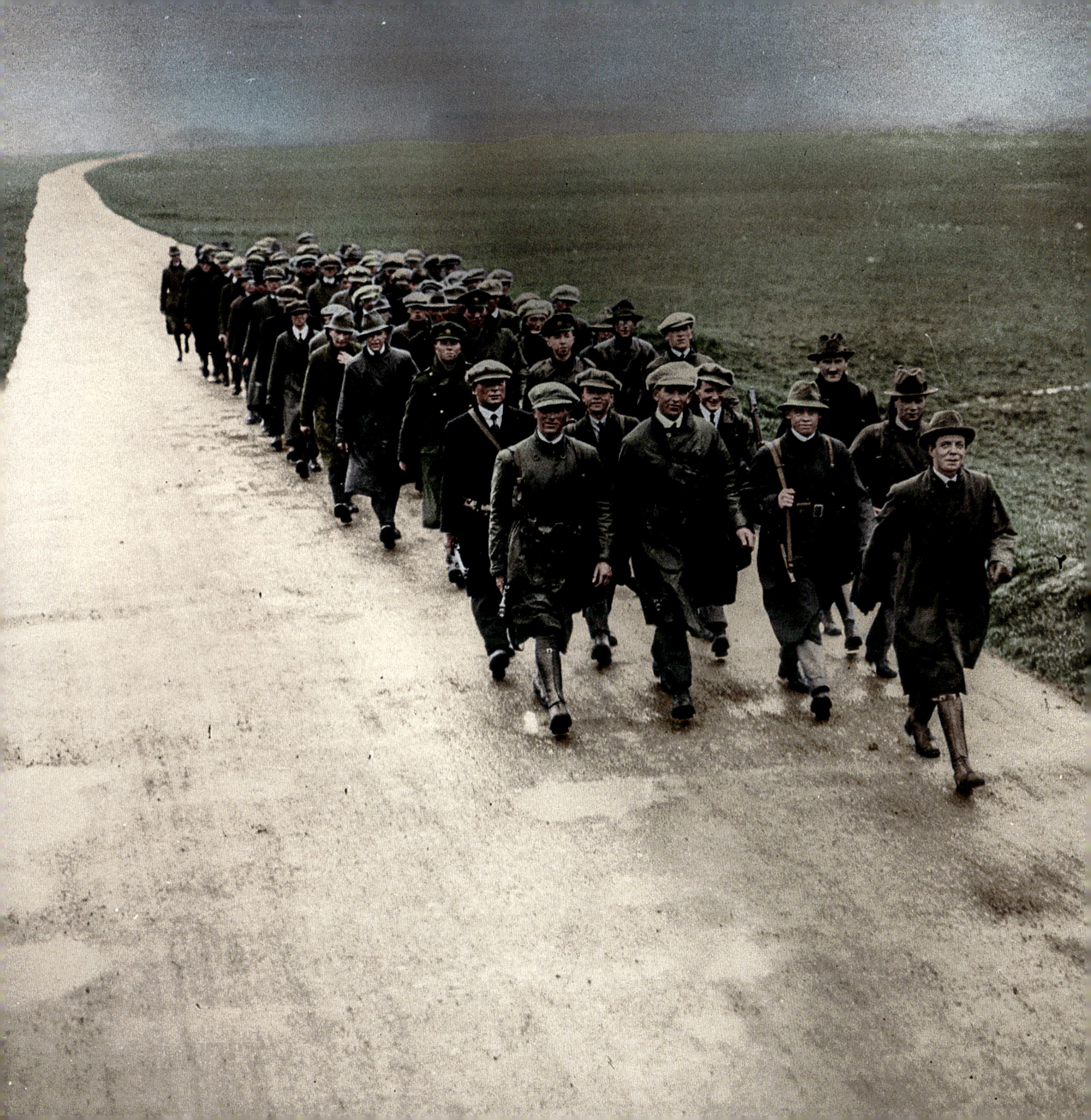

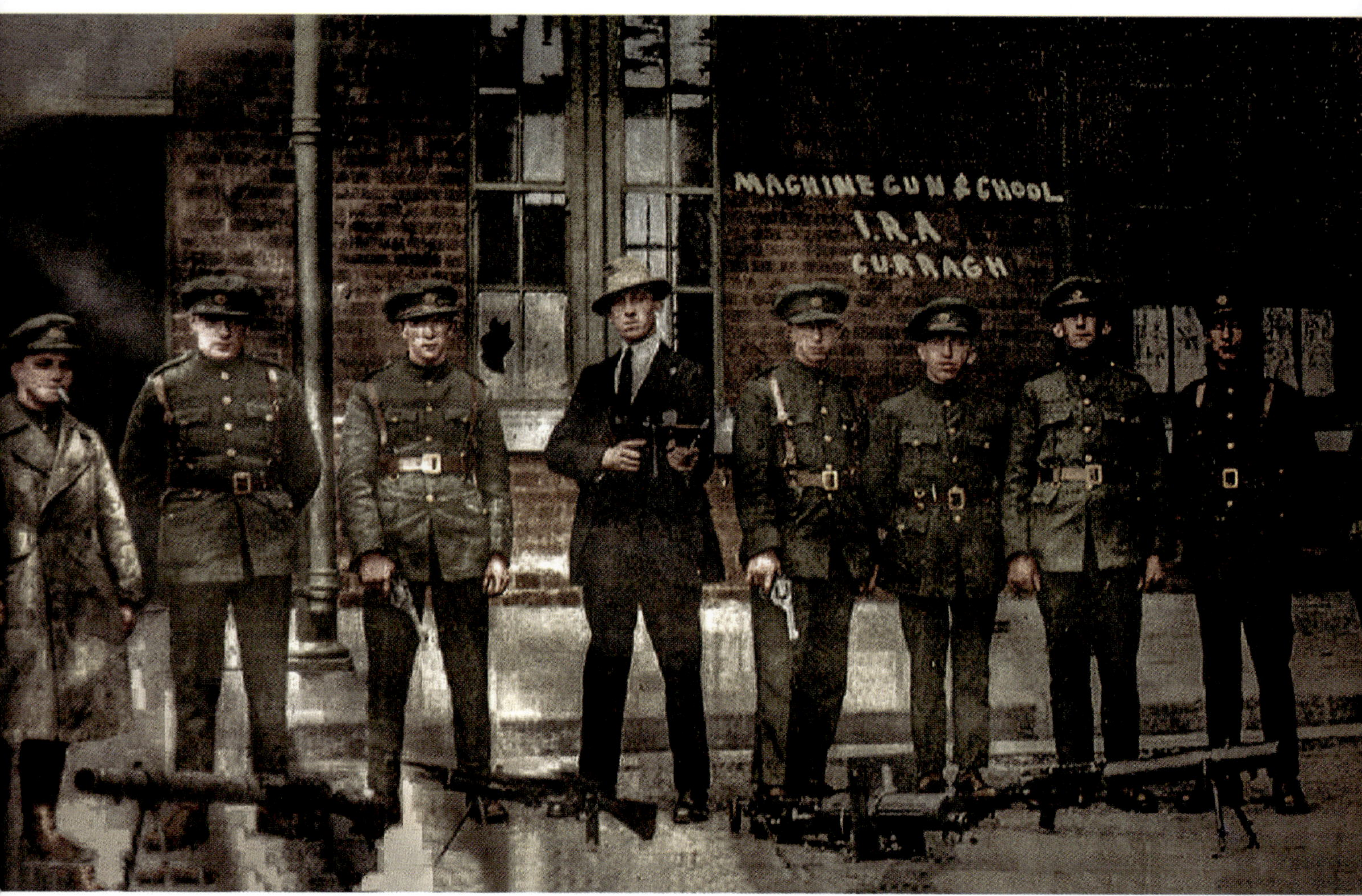

With the takeover of the Curragh Camp, the Provisional Government was able to benefit from the extensive facilities within this large self-contained encampment where large-scale military training had been carried out since the Crimean War in the mid-nineteenth century. Lewis, Hotchkiss and Vickers machine guns feature in this interesting tableau of the 'Machine Gun School' at the Curragh. The central character in civilian attire adopts a menacing pose, brandishing his Thompson sub-machine gun.

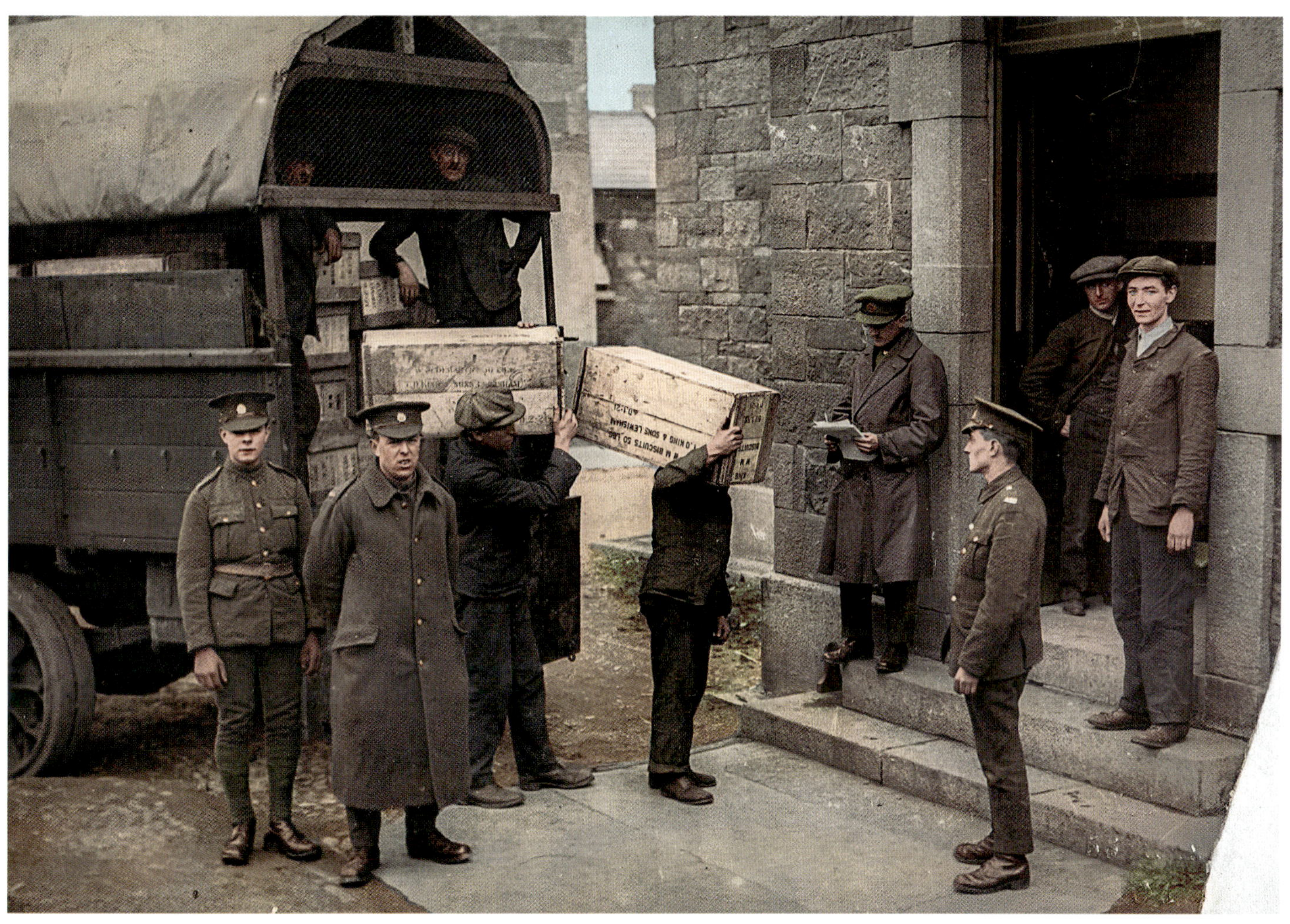

Biscuits from the British Army are delivered at Beggars Bush. The British also supplied more lethal fare to the fledgling Provisional Government Army: armoured cars, rifles and ammunition, as well as the 18-pounder artillery pieces handed over at the end of June which enabled the shelling of the Four Courts at the start of the Civil War. Not all weapons were handed over. At the outbreak of the Civil War a British Cabinet minute noted that they had decided to supply 'ammunition such as gas to the Irish Free State Government for use against the rebels'. SK (lachrymatory) gas grenades were transported by torpedo boat from Holyhead to Kingstown on 5 July 1922 to come under the control of General Sir Nevil Macready. However, nothing further was heard of the gas.

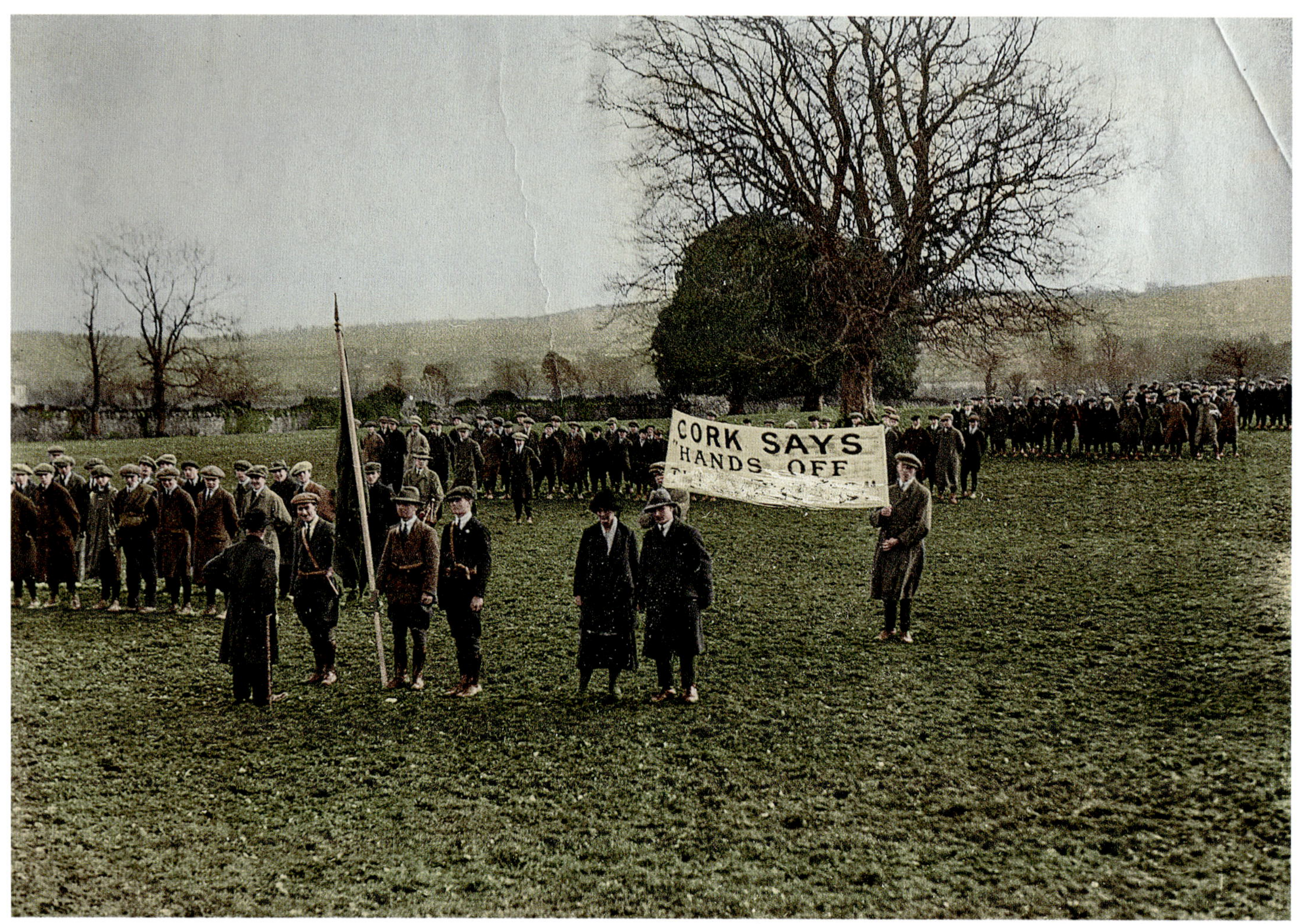

Fianna Éireann, the nationalist youth organisation, took the anti-Treaty side. Here, the Cork Brigade of Fianna Éireann parade at Wilton, on the outskirts of the city, in January 1922. Countess Markievicz stands in the centre. At some stage the bottom line of the banner has been painted over in this photographic print held by Cork Public Museum – a note on the back says that the banner read: 'Cork says hands off the Republic'.

Right: in May 1922 both sides agreed on a candidate list for the elections of 16 June 1922. The result was 36 anti-Treaty candidates elected, while 58 on the pro-Treaty side were successful. Labour and others (who generally supported the Treaty) got 34 seats. Here, Éamon de Valera speaks at a rally. During the Civil War he kept a political flame burning but was sidelined by the IRA leadership.

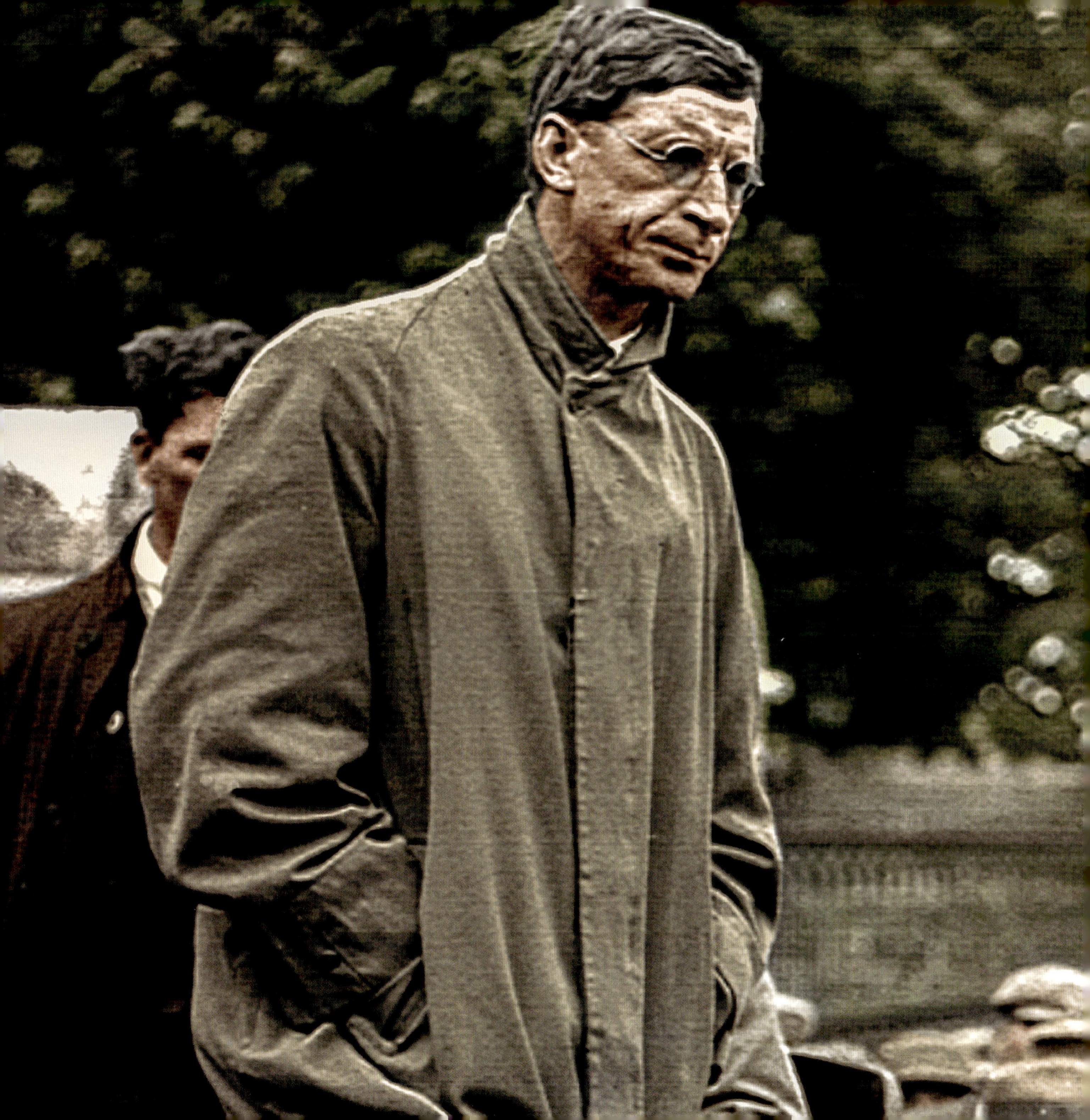

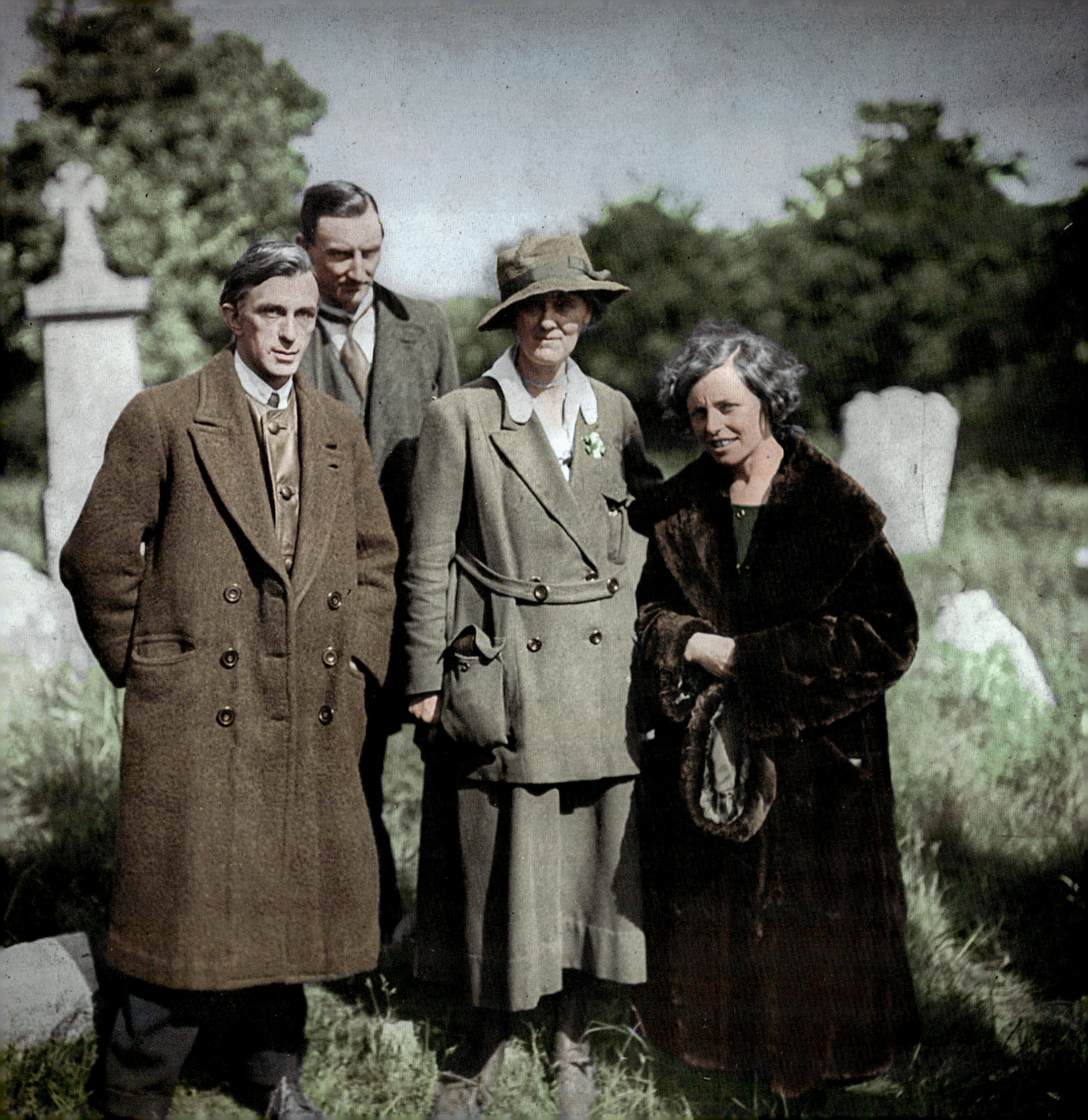

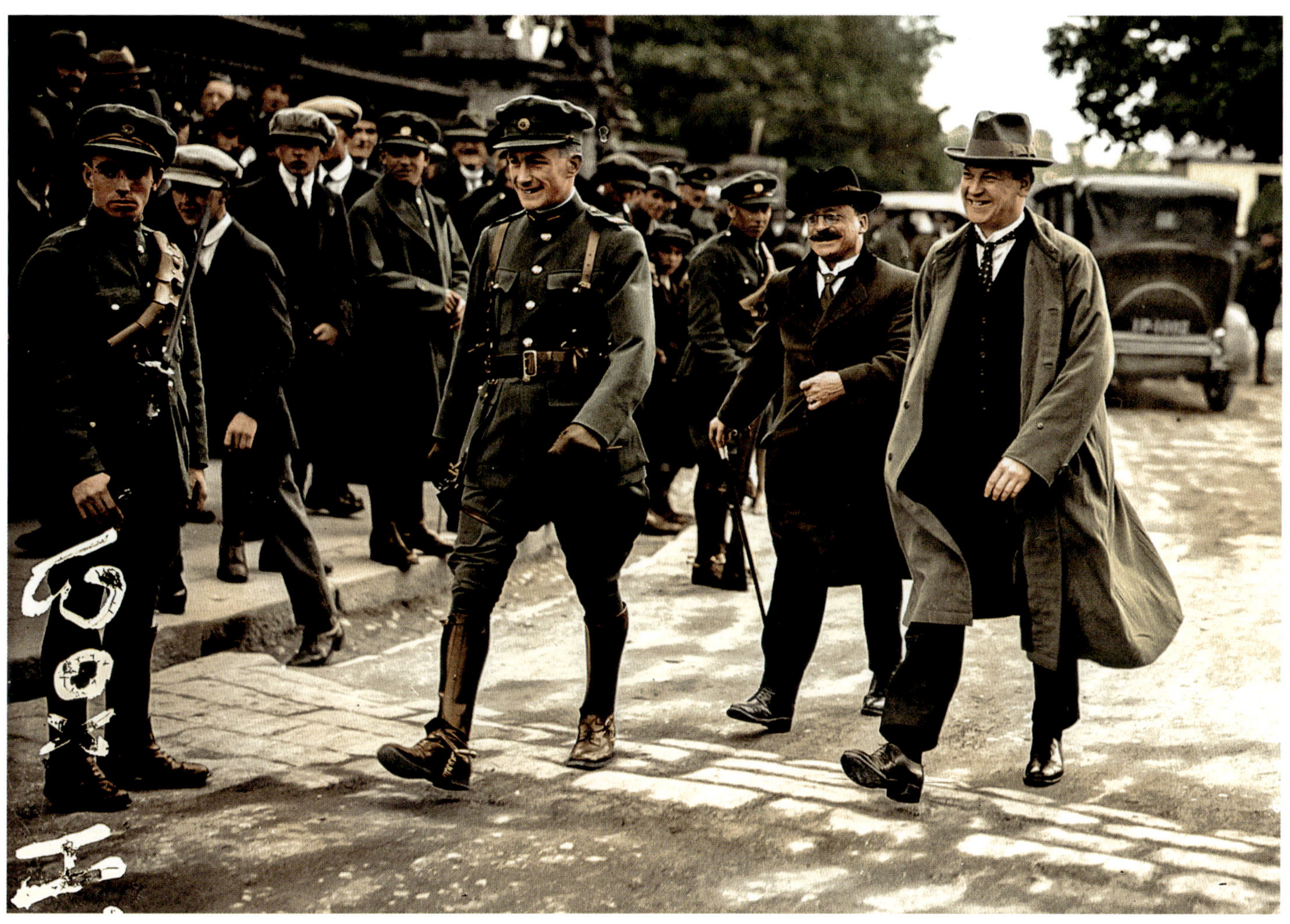

Calm before the storm. Arthur Griffith and Michael Collins stride briskly in Longford on 21 June 1922. Smiling on the happy occasion, they are on the way to attend Seán Mac Eoin's wedding to Alice Cooney at St Mel's Cathedral.

Left: calm before the storm, also on 21 June. At Bodenstown graveyard, Co. Kildare, during the commemoration ceremony for Theobald Wolfe Tone, founder of Irish Republicanism. Seen here are leading lights on the anti-Treaty side: (l-r) Rory O'Connor, Oscar Traynor, Countess Markievicz and Muriel MacSwiney (widow of Terence).

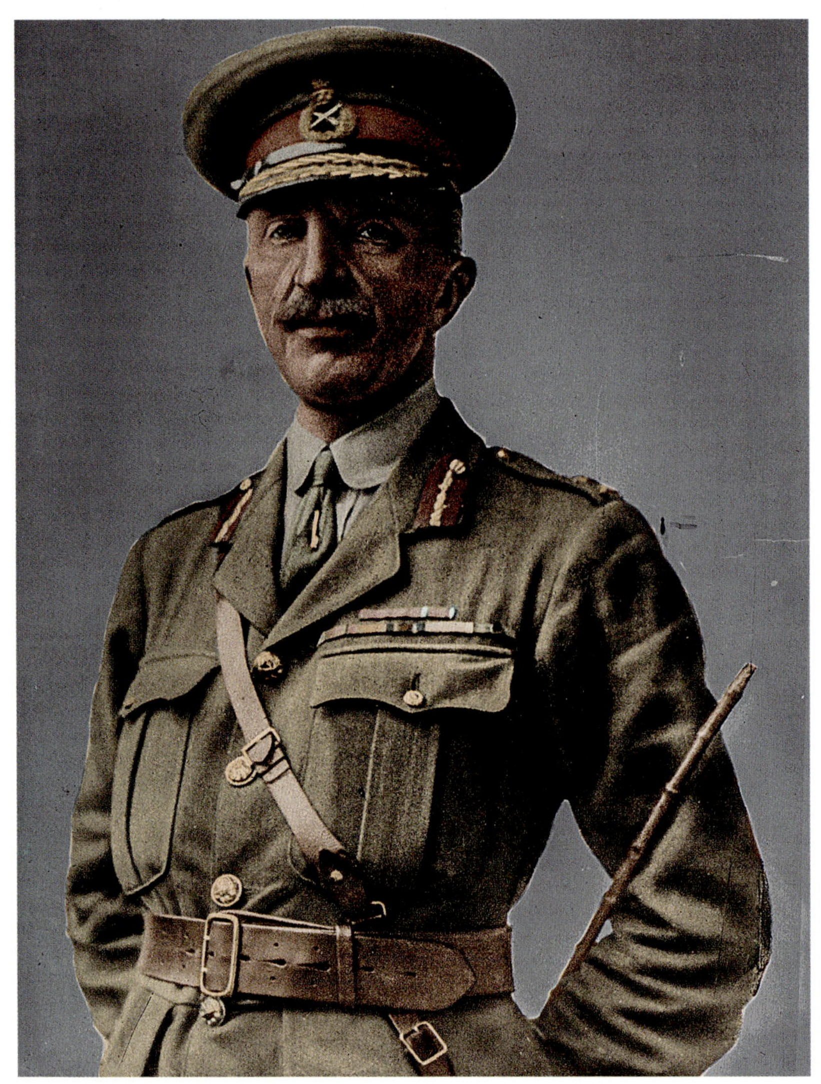

Field Marshal Sir Henry Wilson, a vociferous opponent of the Treaty, had become a figure of hate for Irish nationalists. On 22 June 1922, Wilson was shot in London by two London IRA Volunteers. Lloyd George immediately wrote to Michael Collins stating that the IRA were to blame and that the Four Courts occupation could no longer be tolerated. The British Cabinet ordered an attack on the Four Courts for 25 June 1922. However, the order was rescinded after dissuasion by General Macready.

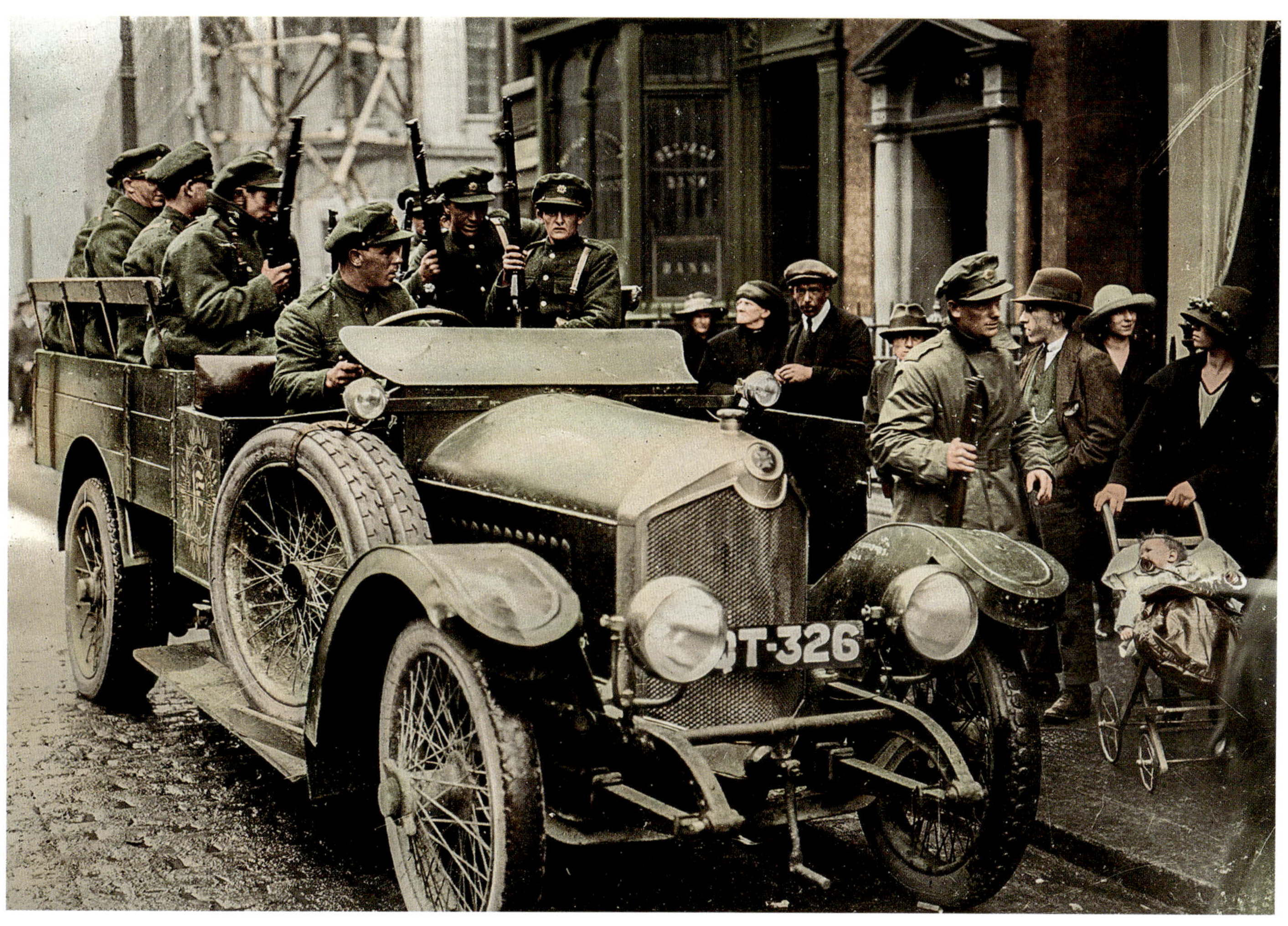

On 26 June 1922 the anti-Treaty IRA raided Ferguson's motor garage on Lower Baggot Street in Dublin and commandeered cars considered to have been imported in defiance of the ongoing Belfast Boycott. Pro-Treaty troops arrived, seen here, and the leader of the raiding party, Commandant Leo Henderson, was arrested and conveyed to Mountjoy Prison.

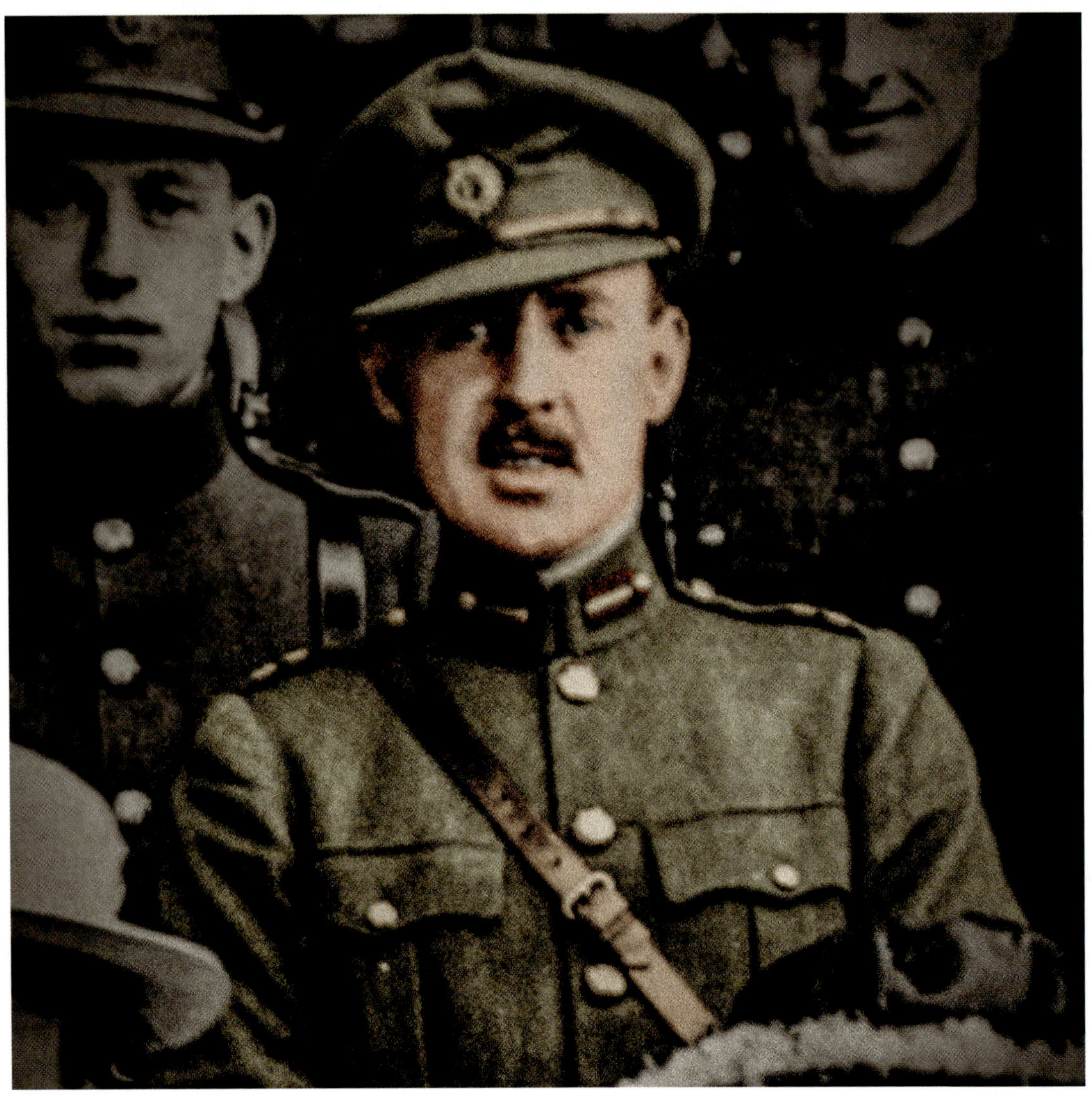

As retaliation for the arrest of Henderson, Lieutenant-General J.J. O'Connell, Deputy Chief of Staff, was kidnapped on the night of 26 June and held captive in the Four Courts. This abduction proved to be the final event which propelled the Provisional Government to decide to assault the Four Courts.

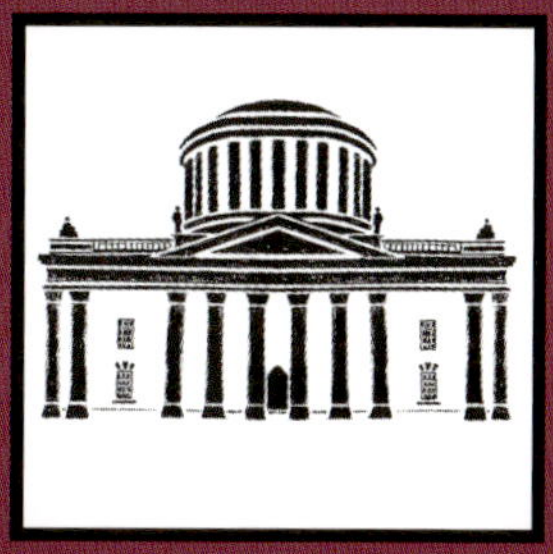

Chapter 2
Fighting in Dublin

Many flare-ups between the opposing sides during the first half of 1922 had increased the likelihood of conflict. Ultimately it was the assassination of Sir Henry Wilson and the kidnap of Lieutenant-General O'Connell that sparked the outbreak of hostilities. Bombardment of the Four Courts, using 18-pounders provided by the British, commenced on 28 June 1922. Days of shelling ended with the storming of the buildings. Fire after a massive explosion destroyed the contents of the Public Record Office. The anti-Treaty IRA took over buildings in central Dublin including the so-called 'Block' on Upper Sackville Street. The street became the scene of bullets, shelling and great buildings on fire. By 5 July the Block, in ruins, was cleared of resistance. Prominent anti-Treaty leader Cathal Brugha was fatally wounded. Republican forces left the city and the war moved to the rest of the country.

On the evening of 27 June 1922, the Dublin Guard,
under Paddy O'Daly, sealed off the area surrounding the
Four Courts. An ultimatum to evacuate the building
was handed in to the anti-Treaty occupants at 3.40 a.m.
the following morning. The first shells were fired from
Winetavern Street shortly after 4 a.m. The Civil War
had begun and the confusion of the previous six months
crystallised into a simple proposition: the 'Free State' or
the 'Republic'.

This photograph shows two 18-pounder guns in operation
at Winetavern Street, shielded by Lancia armoured
personnel carriers. The inexperience of the gunners is
shown by the breaches on the southern quay walls. The
bombardment is well under way as seen by the pockmarks
on the Four Courts buildings opposite. Another Lancia
can be seen jammed against the gates, across the Liffey, to
prevent the exit of the anti-Treaty IRA's captured Rolls-
Royce armoured car.

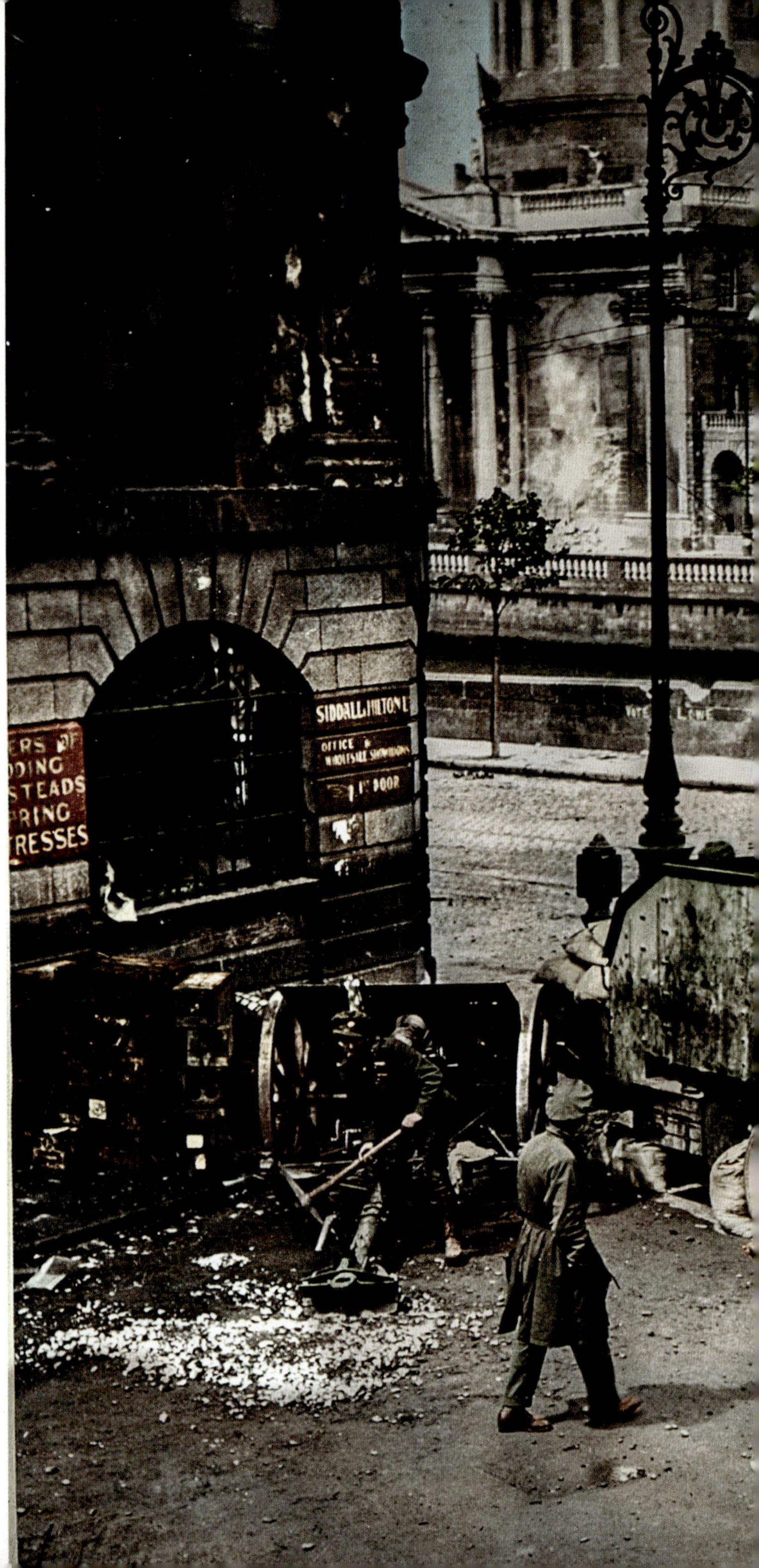

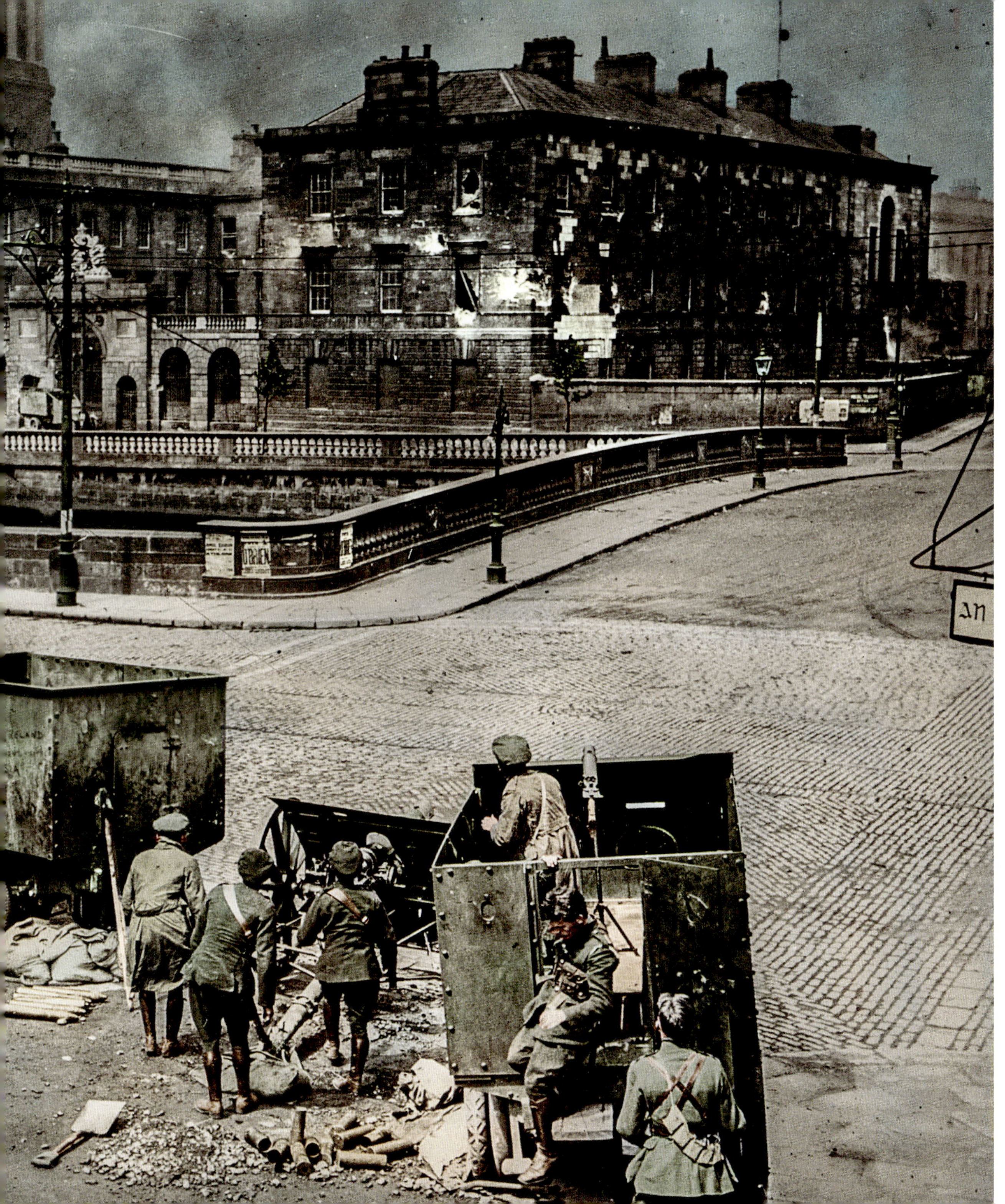

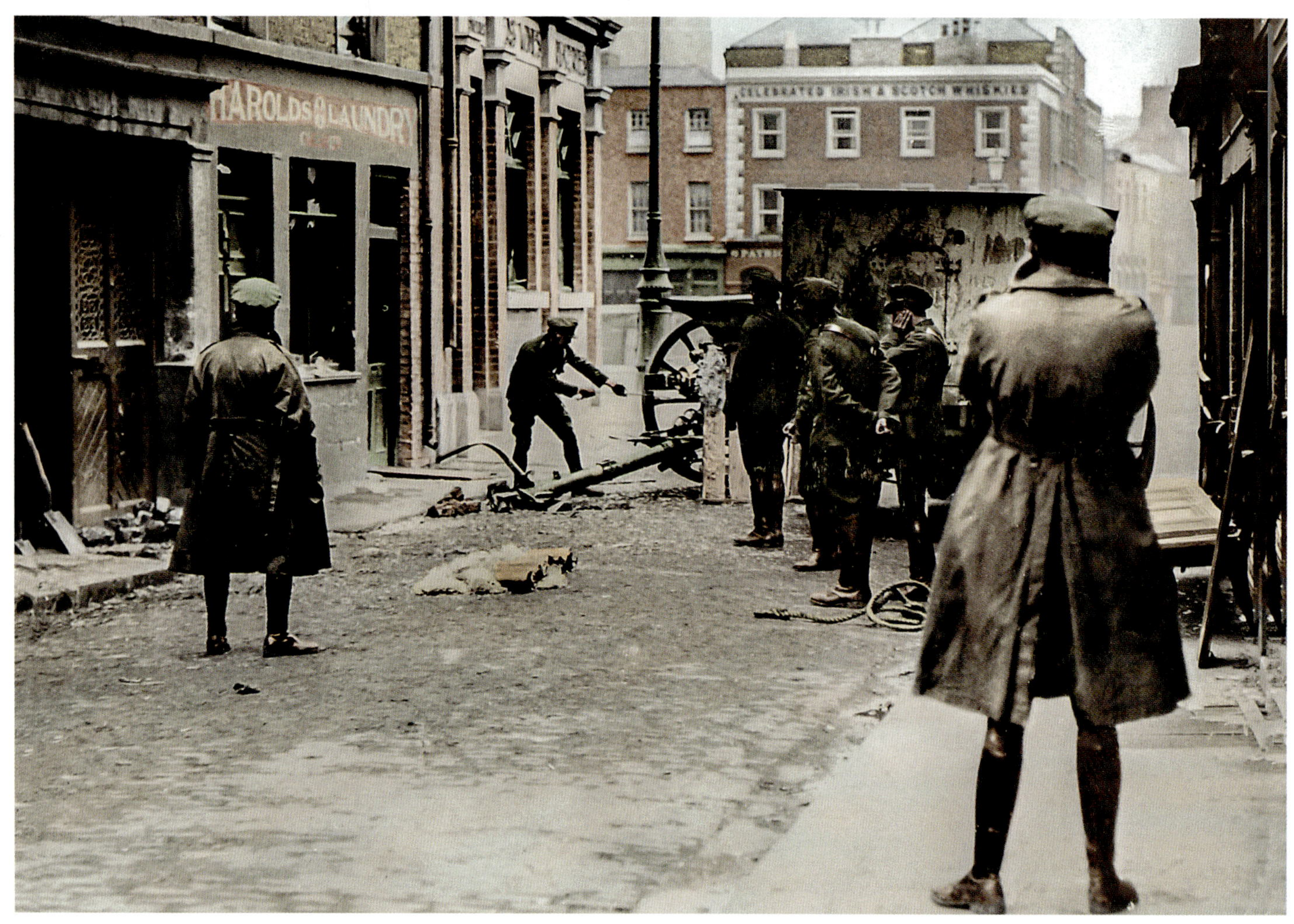

Another 18-pounder, seen here, was situated at Lower Bridge Street and the corner of Merchant's Quay, again shielded by a Lancia. The Provisional Government Army had received two 18-pounders from the British at Marlborough (now McKee) Barracks on the evening of 27 June. Two more field guns were obtained the following day.

Right: shells are prepared, laid out in protective wood wool. High-explosive shells soon ran short. The British had only shrapnel shells, (anti-personnel type, ineffective against the granite walls of the Four Courts) left in stock. These were issued, as General Macready wrote, 'simply to make a noise through the night'. A destroyer was dispatched to Carrickfergus arsenal for the necessary shells.

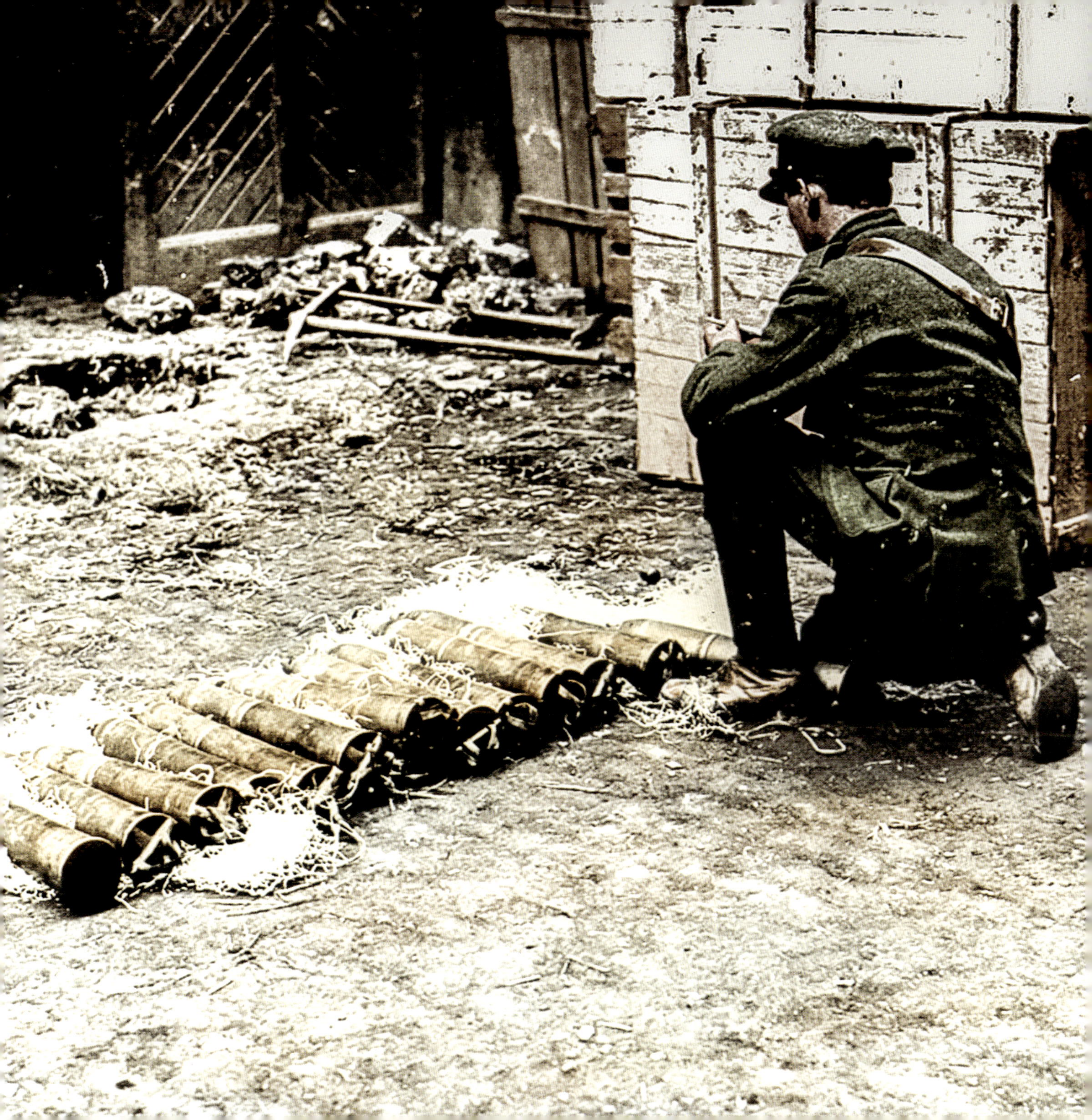

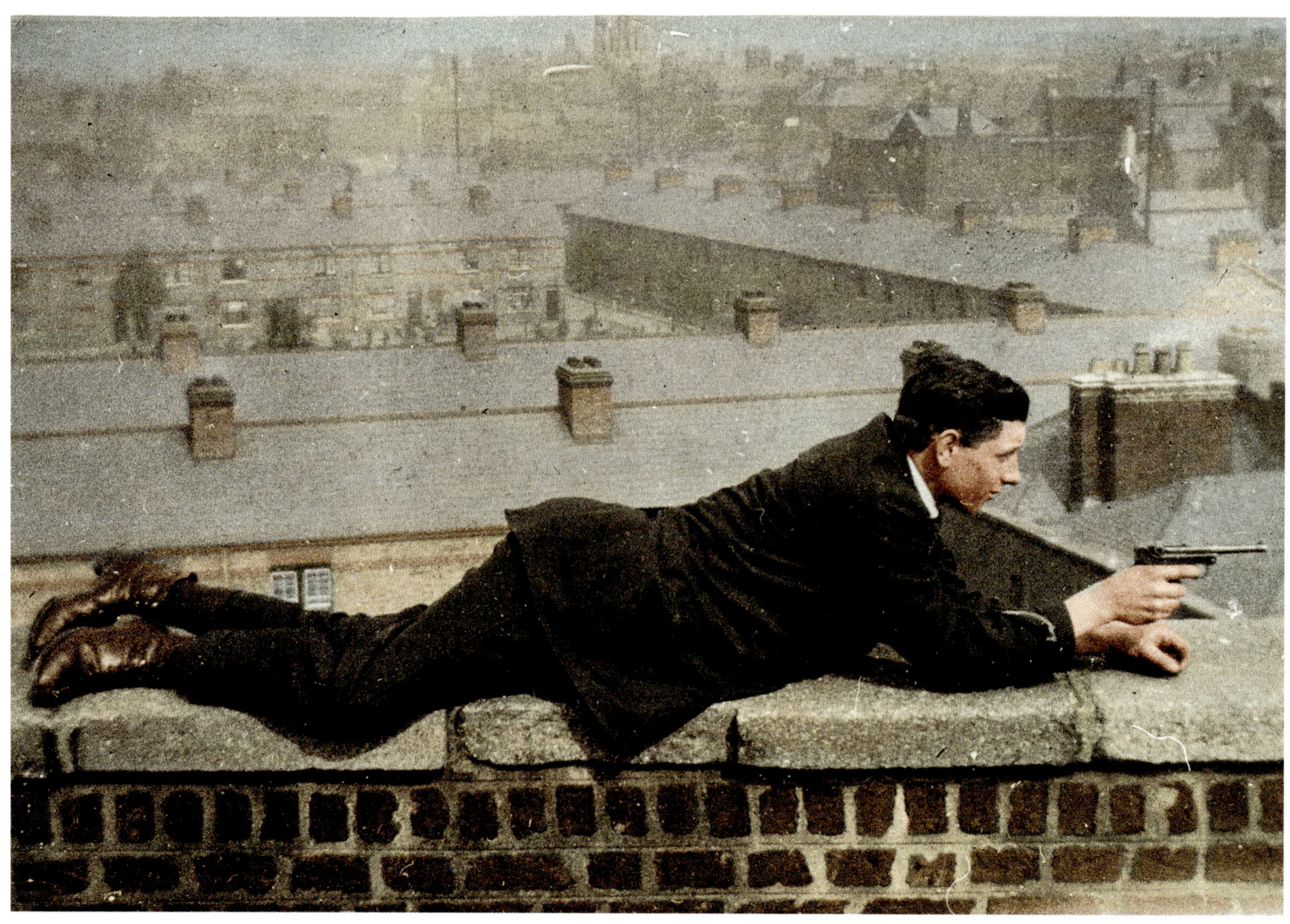

Volunteer Paddy Rigney (veteran of the War of Independence) on the Four Courts roof, during the early days of the occupation. When the assault began at the end of June, the IRA in the Four Courts sniped at the artillery positions from on high. For most of the siege, the defenders could communicate with the outside via messages conveyed by members of Cumann na mBan.

Right: a gunner's view from Lower Bridge Street. A strip of the light-coloured façade of the Four Courts Hotel can be discerned at the left of the red-brick building on Inns Quay. On the eve of the siege the pro-Treaty army had taken over the hotel as their headquarters. In the centre are the breaches created by the shelling at Morgan Place, on the western side of the Four Courts complex.

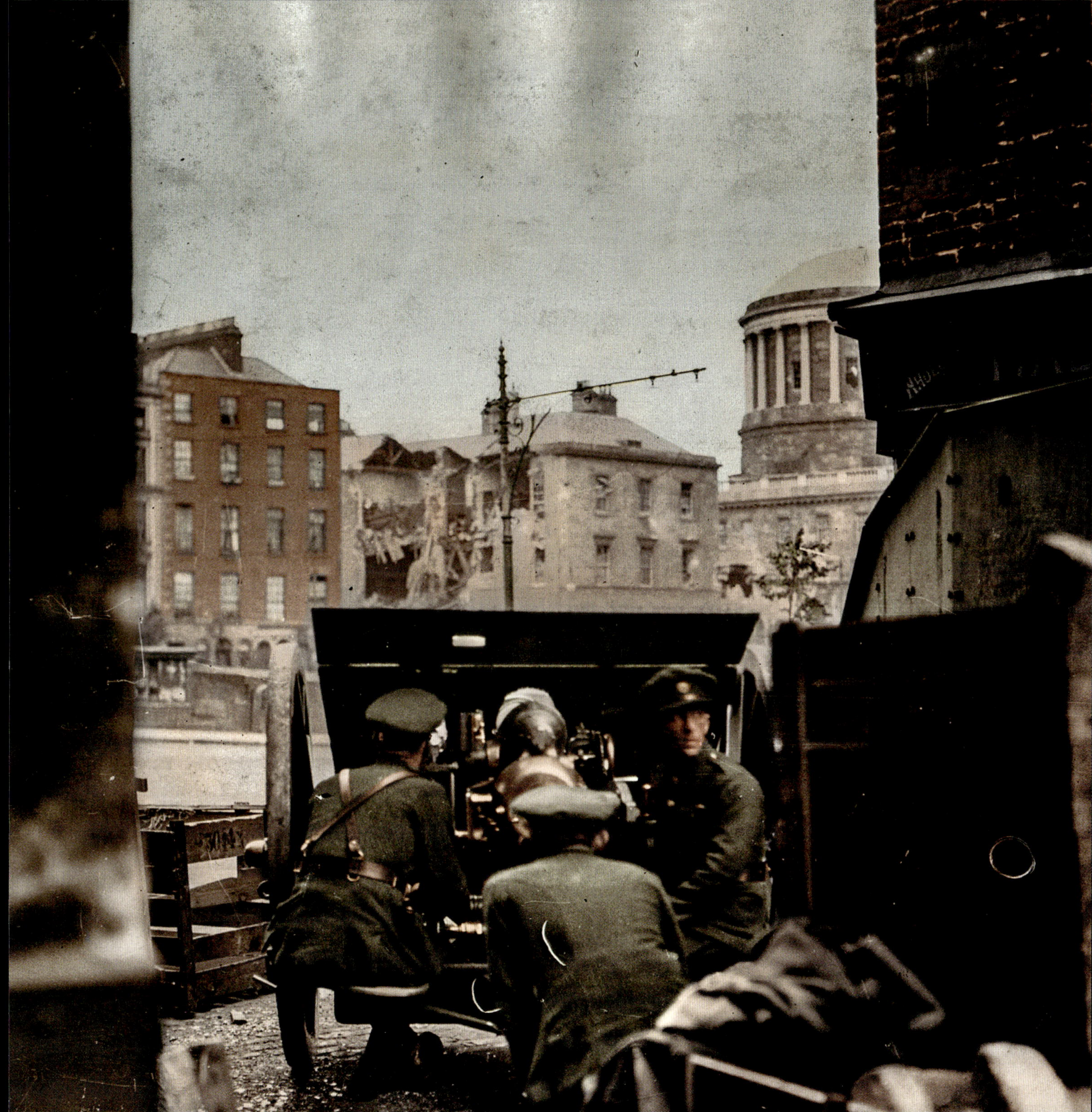

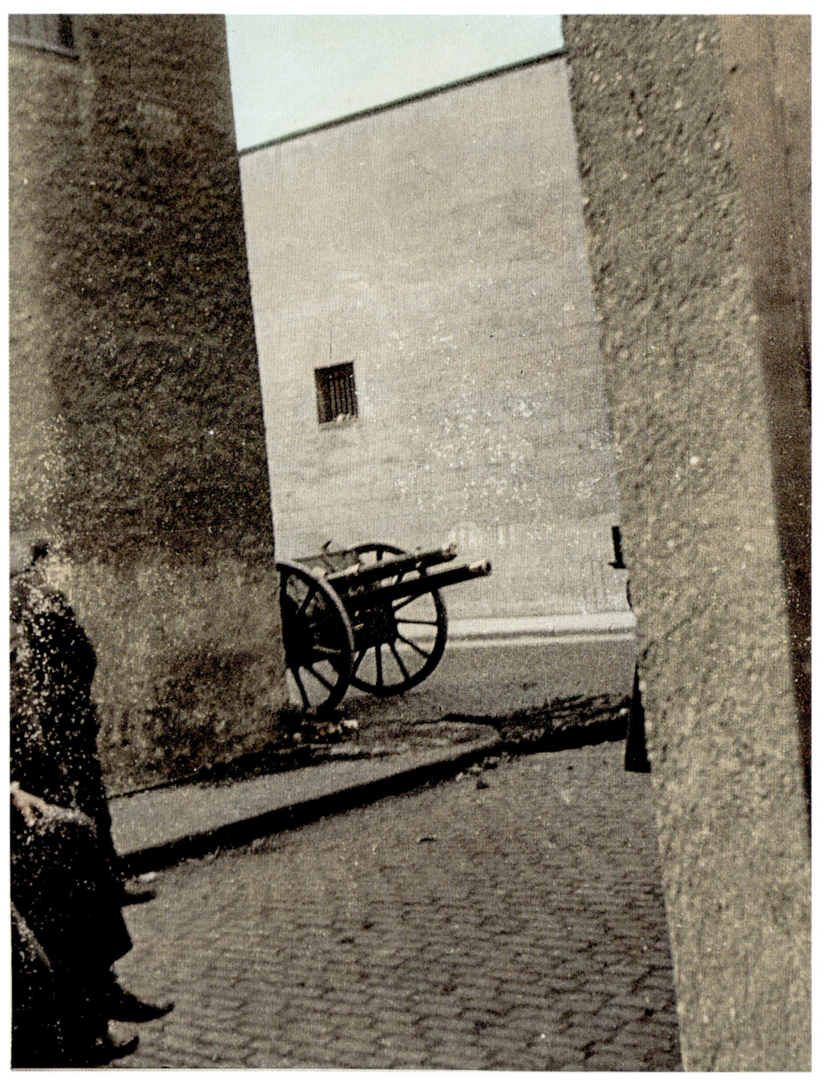

A photograph taken by a local resident (from his own doorway) of the 18-pounder set up in Hammond Lane to the west of the Four Courts. The gun was used to create a breach at the Record House (part of the Public Record Office) on Church Street.

Right: After 3 p.m. on 29 June, Commandant Pádraig O'Connor led troops through the breach, capturing some surprised defenders. Simultaneously, others charged through the breach at Morgan Place.

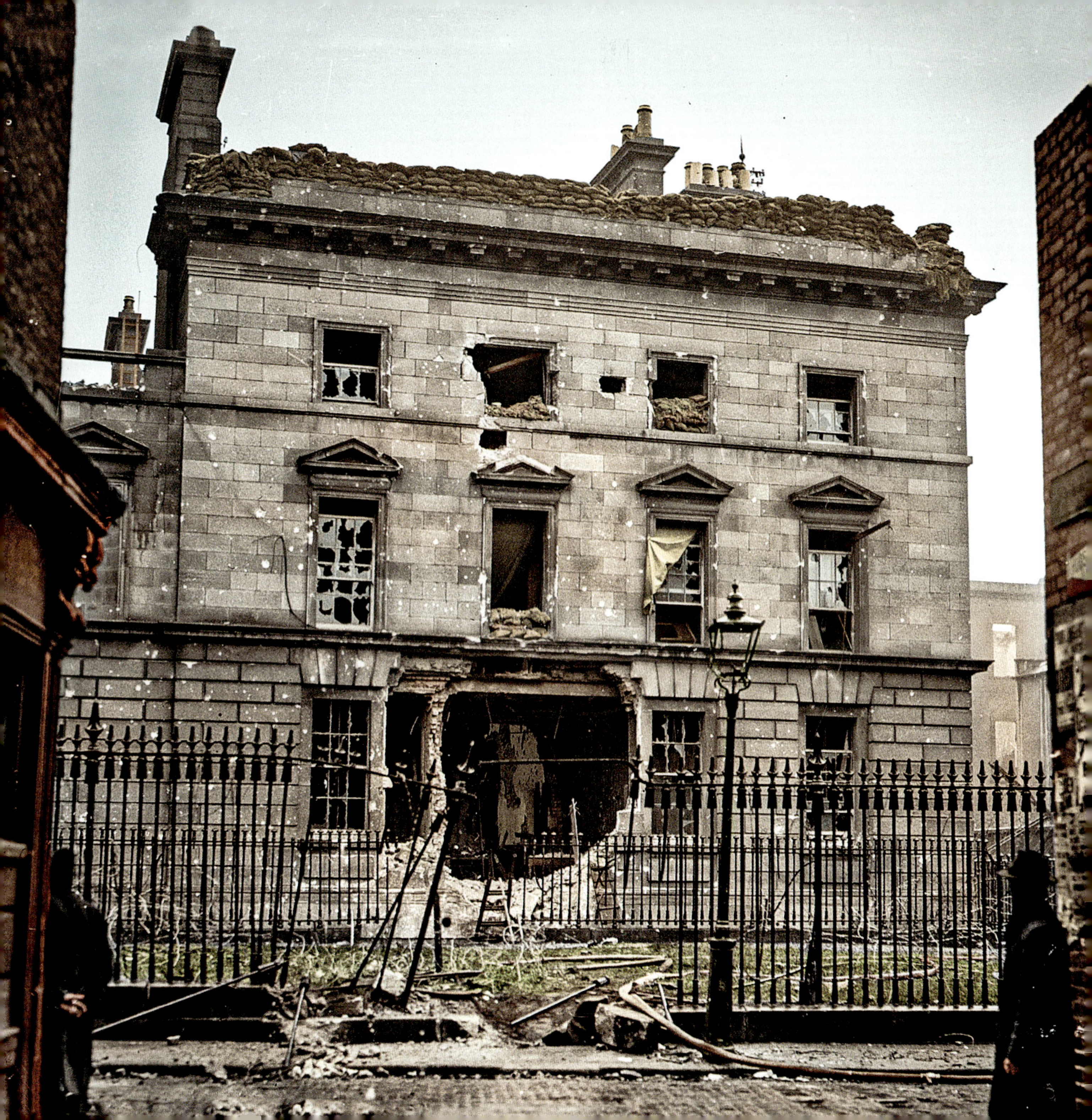

The massive explosion at the Four Courts, the largest
Dublin has ever experienced, resulted in clouds of black
smoke and debris billowing high above the city. On
30 June at around 12.30 p.m. there was an enormous
explosion at the western end of the so-called Headquarters
Block, where munitions had been stored. Many pro-Treaty
troops were injured. Documents (mainly legal), stored in
this building were wafted upwards by fire and blown all
over the city.

The Record Treasury section of the Public Record Office,
adjacent to the centre of the explosion, had its windows
and glazed roof blown out and a section of the wall was
also destroyed. Burning embers from the Headquarters
Block settled and the tightly packed paper documents of
the Records Treasury gradually ignited. The blaze turned
into a firestorm, thick white smoke billowed out and much
evidence of the history of Ireland, made up of medieval
parchments, maps, census, administrative and court
records, was destroyed.

Two more explosions took place in the Round Hall area at
around 2 p.m. on 30 June. The defenders surrendered at
3.45 p.m.

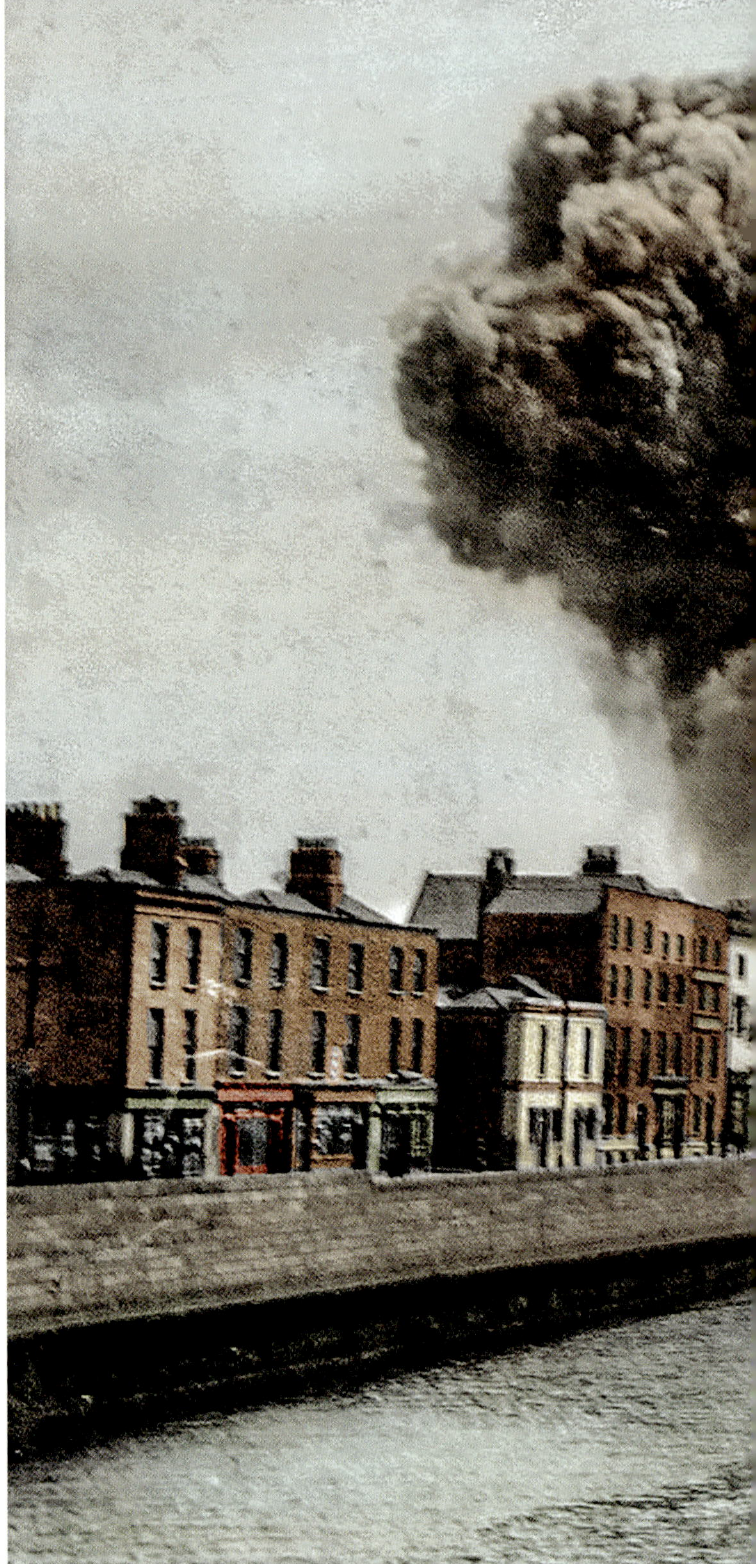

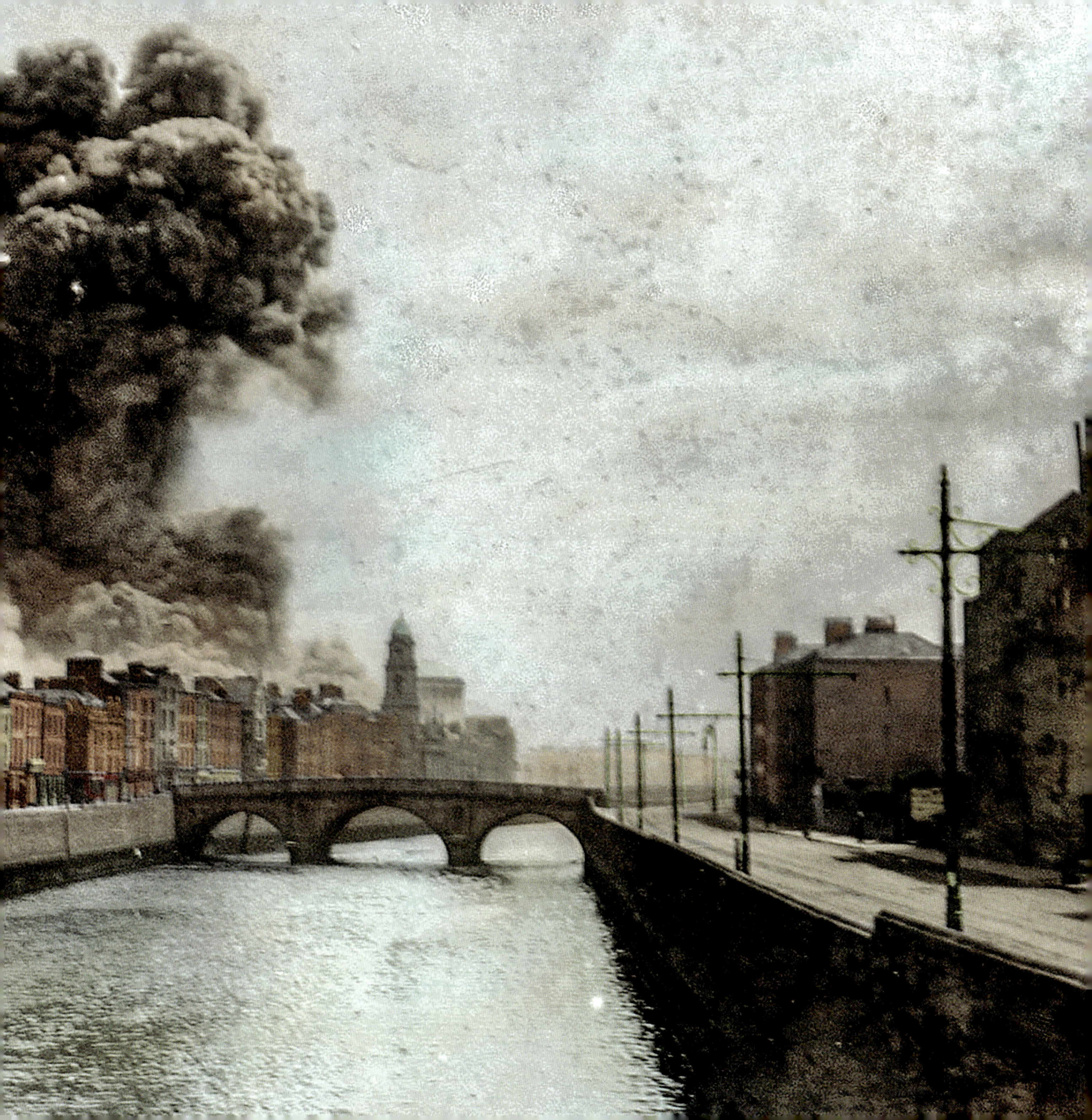

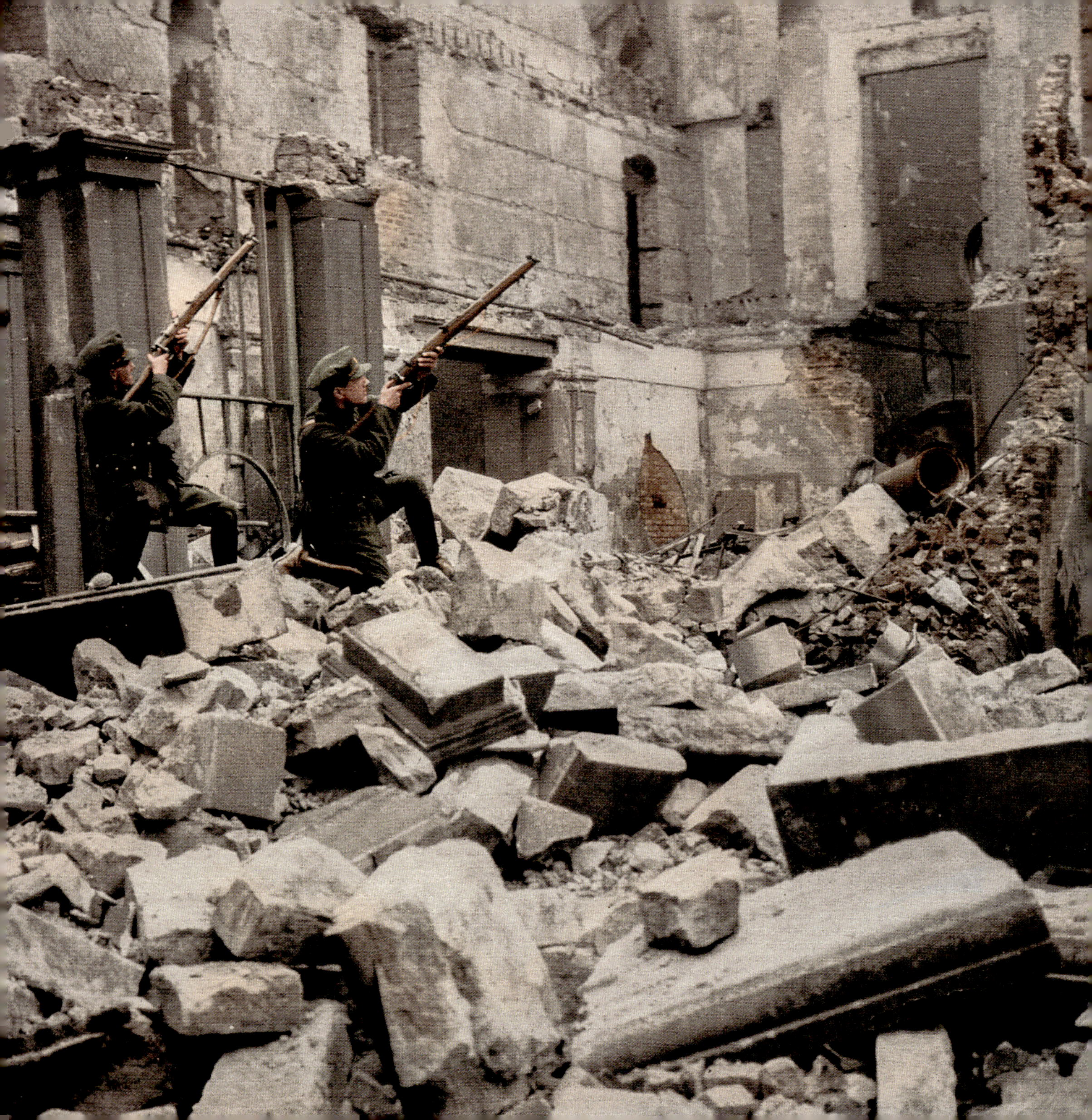

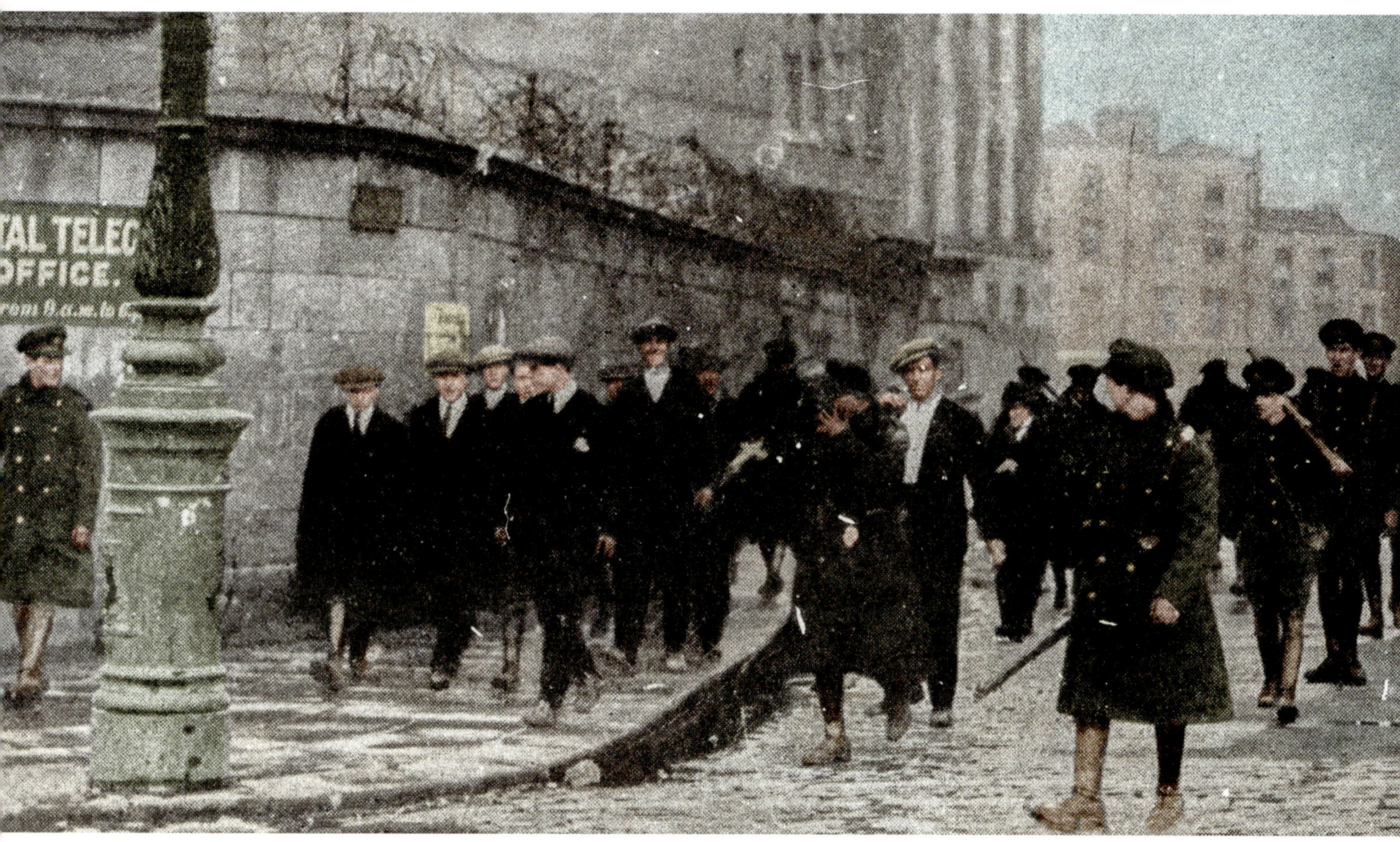

After surrendering on 30 June 1922, the Four Courts garrison are marched to captivity, guarded by Provisional Government soldiers. They are being led to the nearby Jameson's Distillery for temporary detention. Amidst the commotion, the pro-Treaty Commandant Pádraig O'Connor left a door unguarded so that his friend Paddy Rigney (page 82) could escape. Three others, including Seán Lemass and Ernie O'Malley, also took advantage and escaped. To make space for the new influx, civilian inmates of Mountjoy Prison had to be transferred elsewhere and the Four Courts prisoners were conveyed to the prison that evening.

Left: rubble all around, two Provisional Government soldiers pose amongst the ruins at the Four Courts.

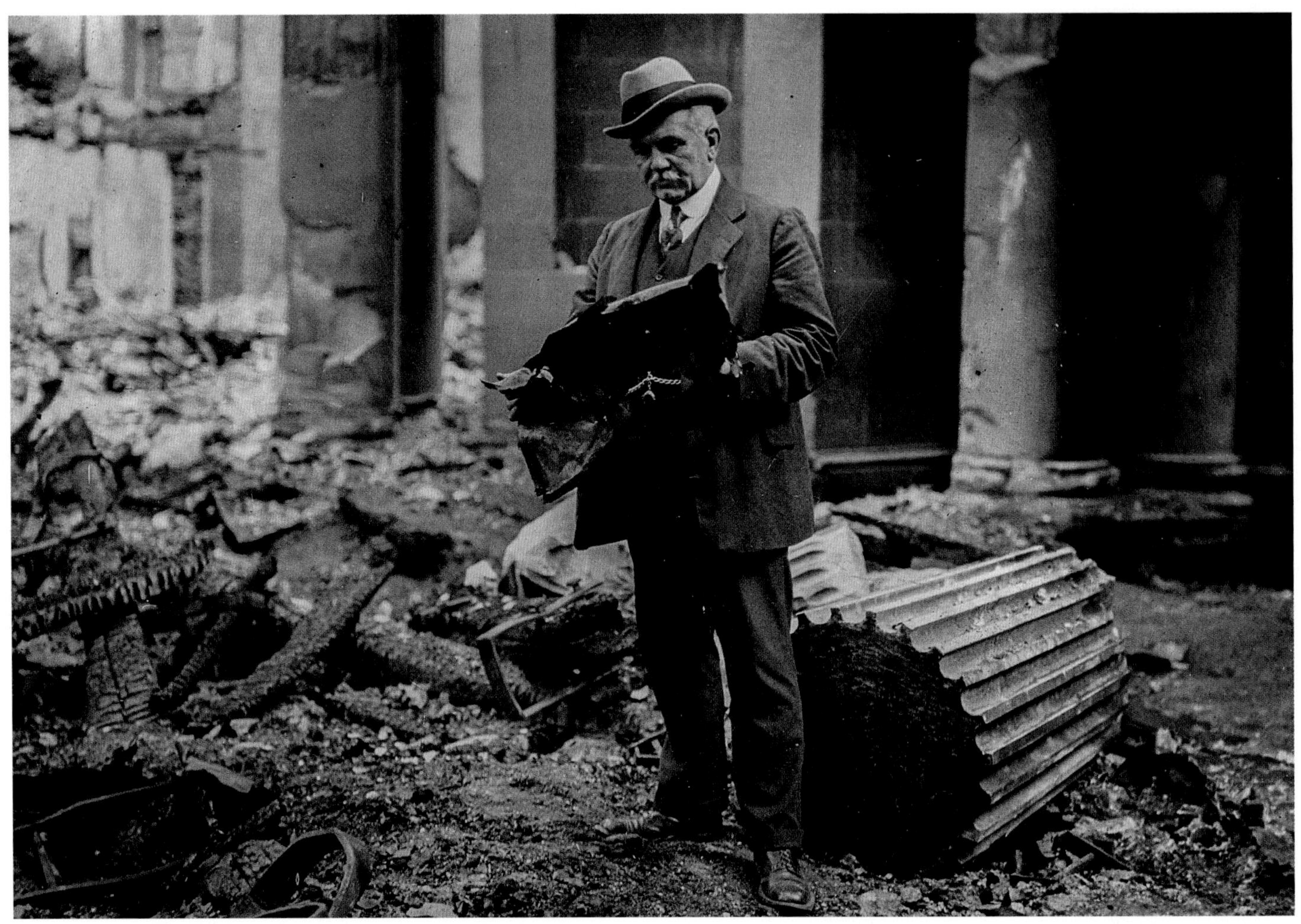

In the Round Hall, once described as the 'physical and spiritual centre' of the Four Courts, the dome had collapsed. Standing amidst charred remains and by a section of a fluted Doric column this gentleman examines what looks like a damaged parchment.

Right: the damaged statue of Henry Joy, Chief Baron of the Irish Exchequer (a cousin of the United Irishman leader, Henry Joy McCracken), casts a ghostly pall over the rubble. This was one of a series of statues depicting Dublin legal luminaries by Edward Smyth (the eighteenth-century sculptor) which had been placed in front of the alcoves dotted around the Round Hall.

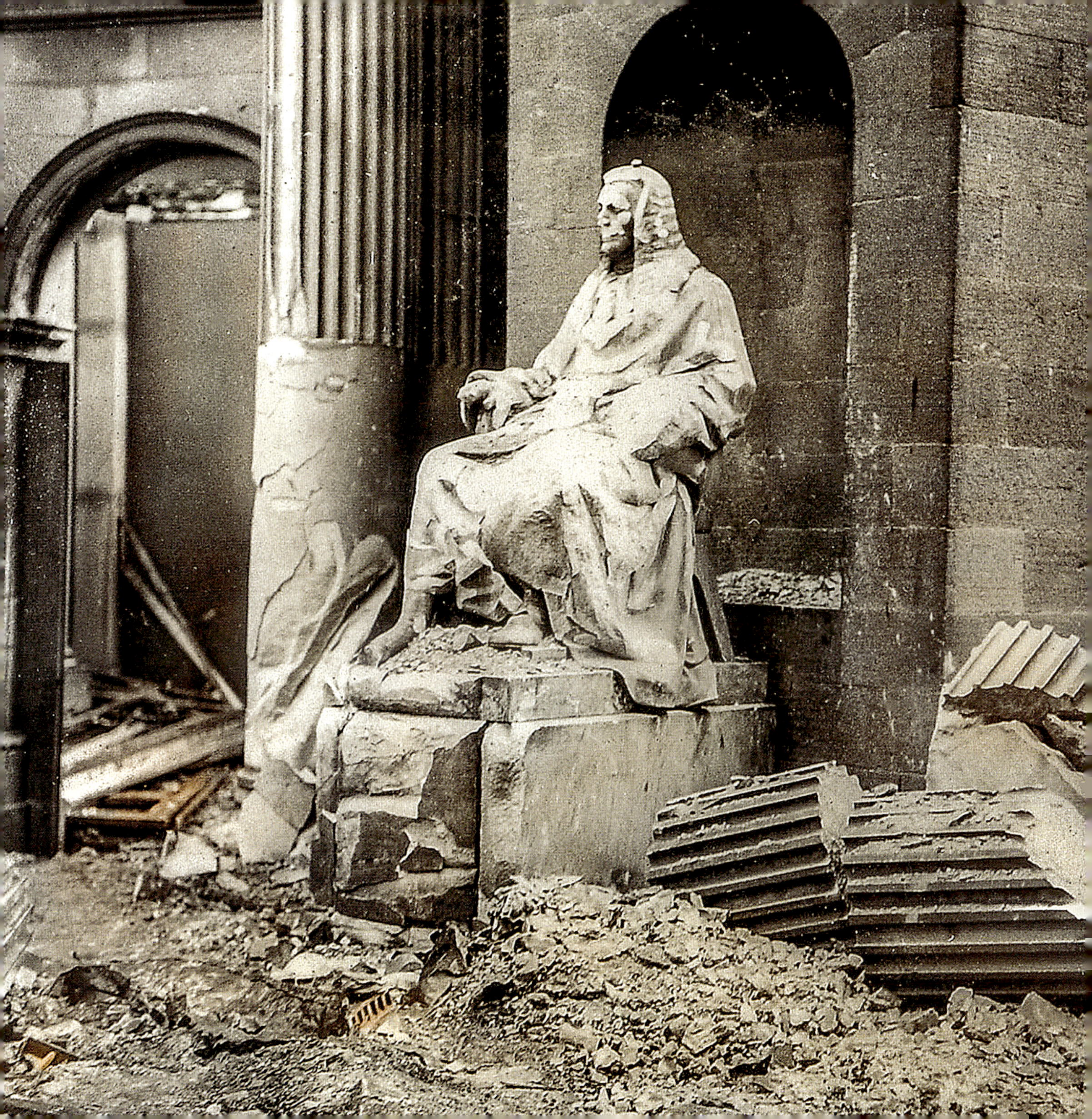

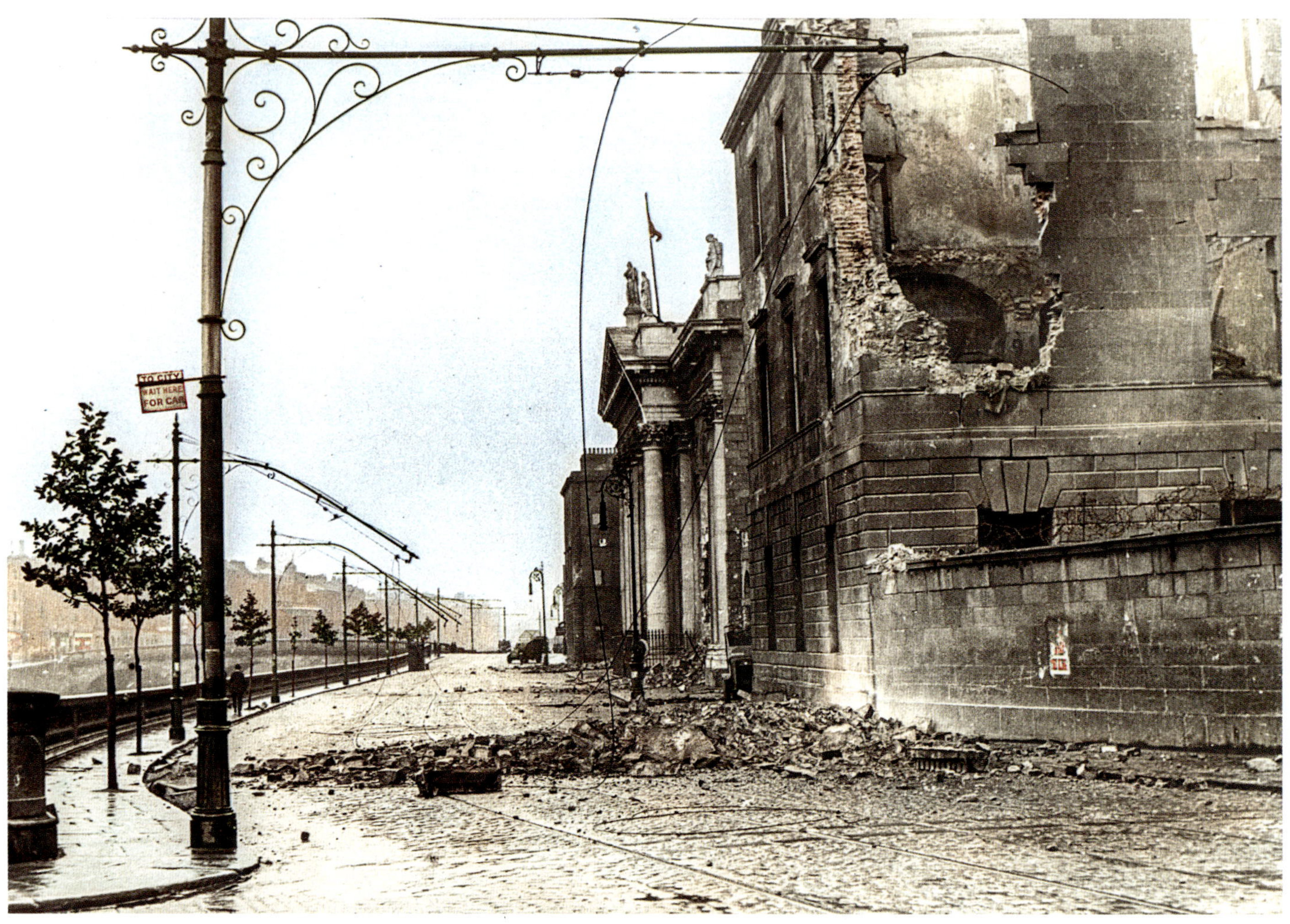

Another view of the Four Courts, looking west along Inns Quay. As rubble lies strewn about, the Lancia armoured personnel carrier is still there, having been moved to the west and now in front of Morgan Place.

Right: looking remarkably unscathed, the *Mutineer* Rolls-Royce armoured car, now back in pro-Treaty hands. Two men of the Dublin Fire Brigade and a soldier pose. During the siege it had patrolled between the buildings of the Four Courts, firing at Free State snipers, but, sensibly, it remained out of sight of the 18-pounders. As the gap in the turret shows, the Vickers machine gun was hit and had to be removed. Renamed the *Ex-Mutineer*, it saw action in Kerry during the Fenit landings on 2 August 1922.

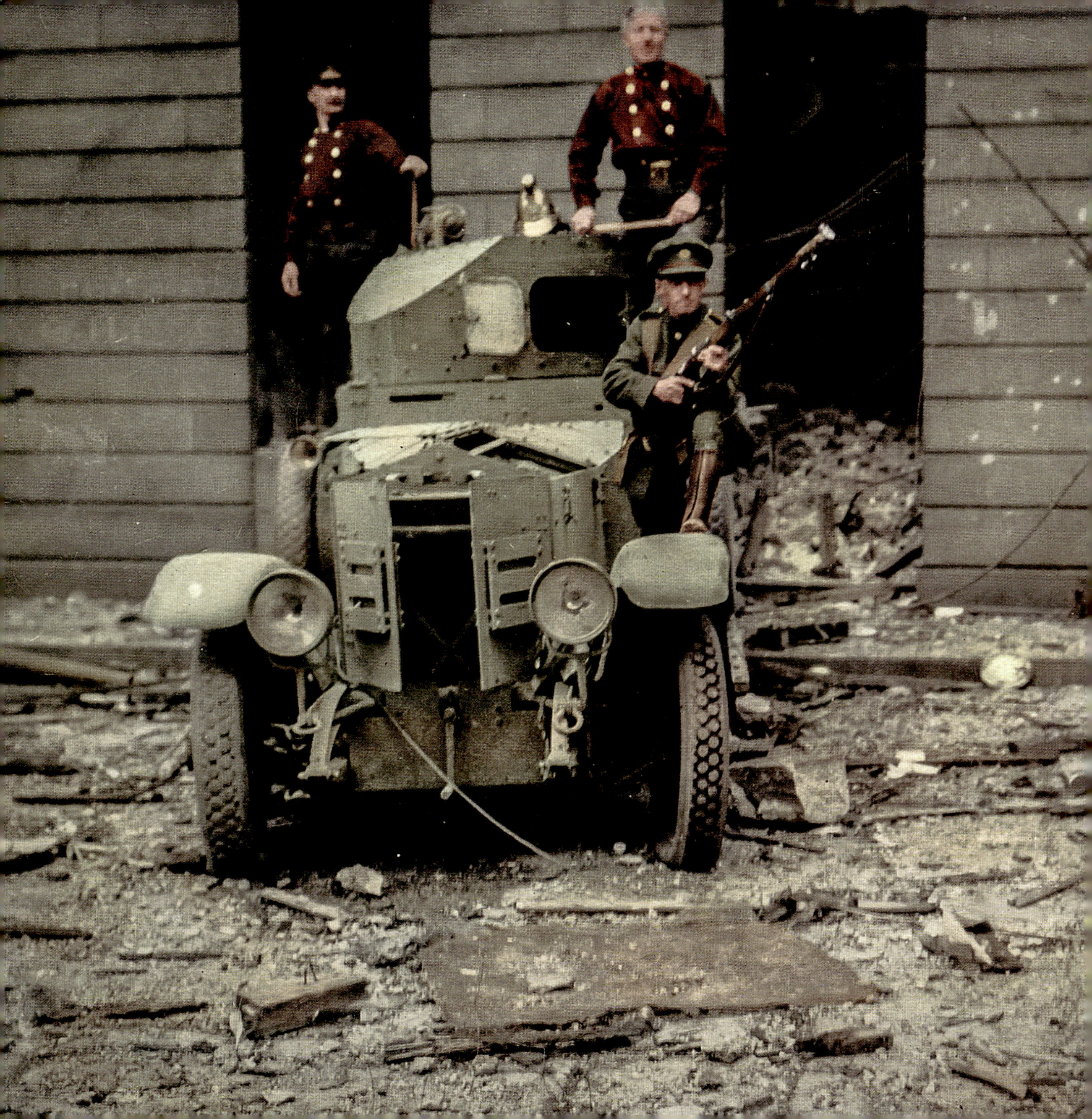

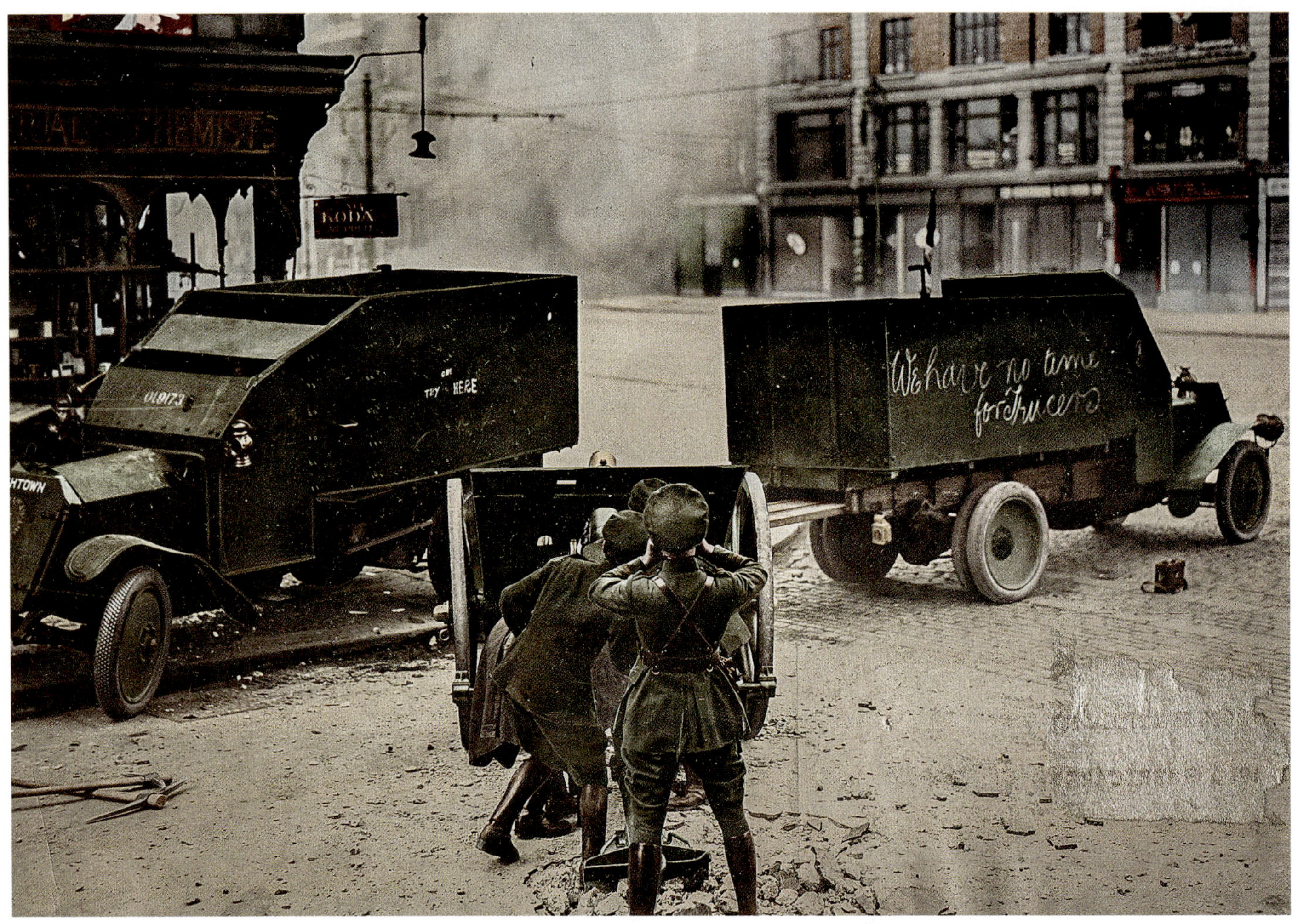

As the siege of the Four Courts entered its final stage on 29 June, the IRA took over buildings around central Dublin to relieve the pressure. This included what became known as the Block on Upper Sackville Street, where Oscar Traynor, OC, set up his headquarters in the Hammam Hotel. As the attack by the pro-Treaty Army intensified, the main IRA force withdrew on 3 July, leaving a small group under Cathal Brugha. On the evening of 4 July, an 18-pounder, seen here protected by two Lancia armoured personnel carriers (note the scrawled message about 'Trucers'), was set up at the corner of Henry Street and proceeded to shell the Block.

Right: a soldier, in the lee of one of the Lancias at Henry Street, with Nelson's Pillar in the background, takes aim at the Block.

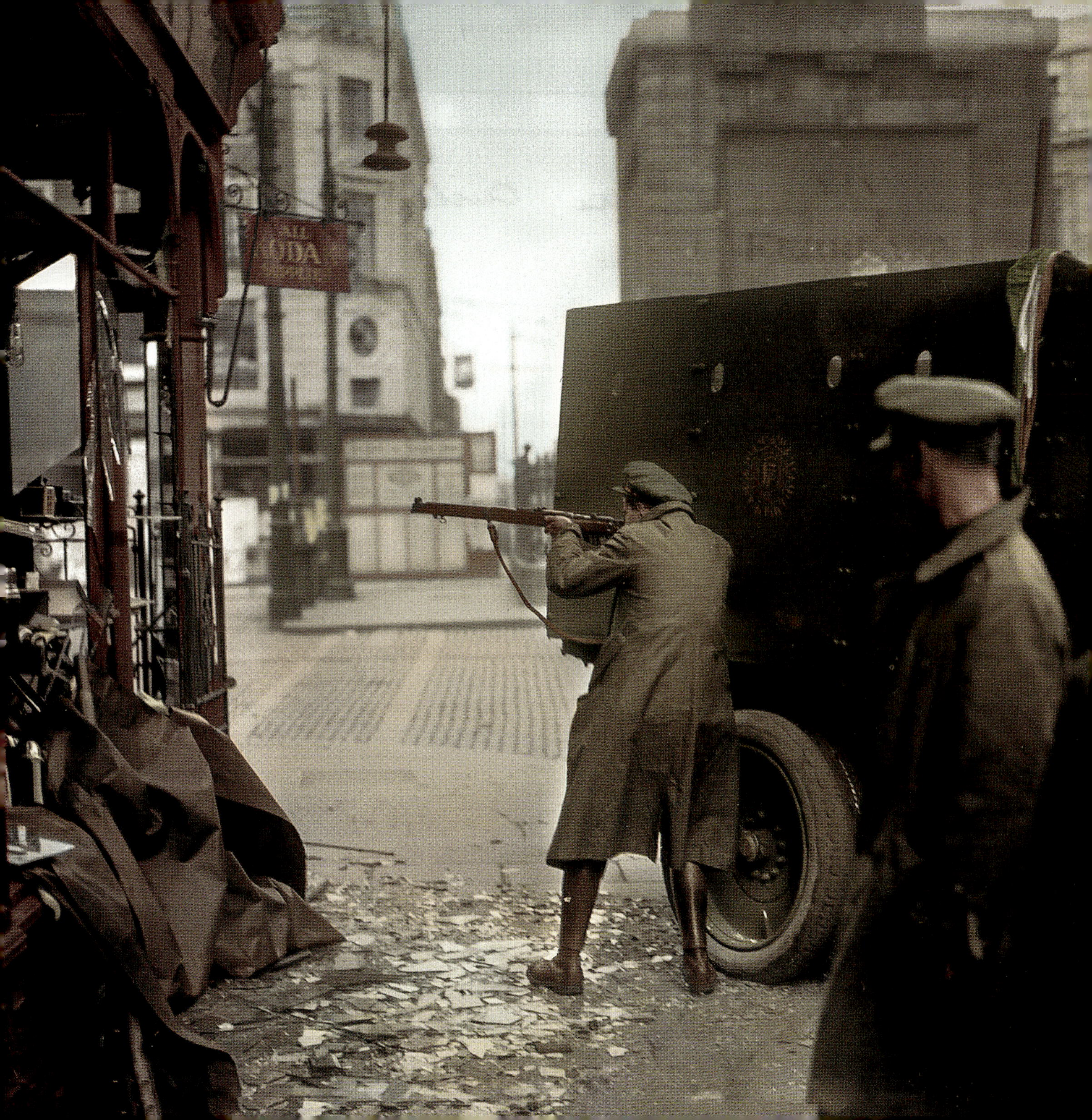
ALL
KODAK
SUPPLIES

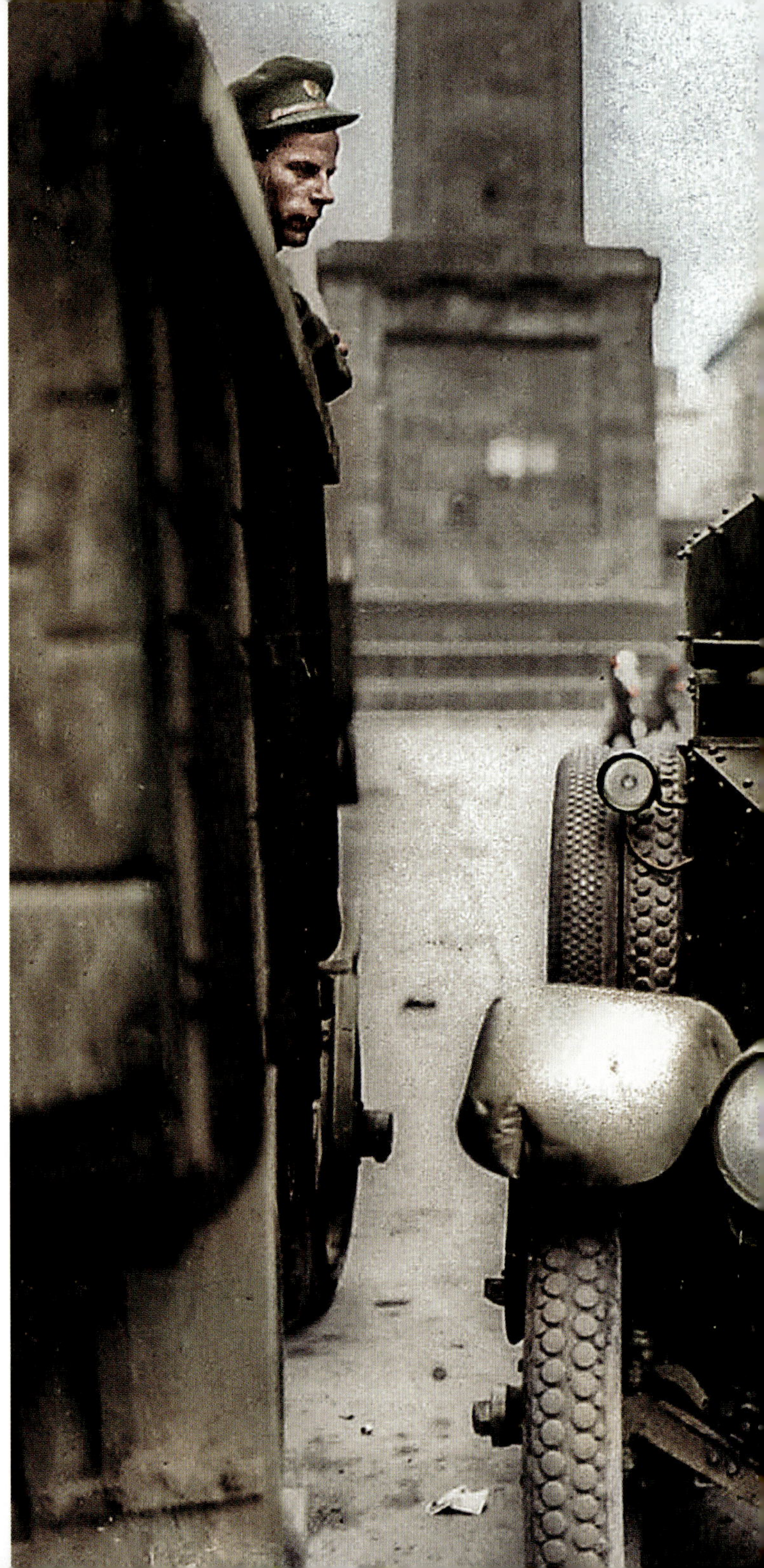

Armoured cars played a major part in the fighting around
Sackville Street. Here, on Henry Street, is the Rolls-Royce
armoured car which had been named *Custom House*.
This was in memory of the IRA action during the War of
Independence which destroyed that building. Bitterness at
the beginning of the Civil War is evident from the figure
of 'Rory Boy' with what looks like a noose around its neck.
The IRA leader, Rory O'Connor, had just been captured
after the surrender of the Four Courts.
Fourteen of these armoured cars, dubbed 'Whippets', were
acquired from the British. These formidable and agile
armoured vehicles were over five metres long and weighed
over four tonnes. Clearly seen are the protective shutters
over the radiator at the front, closed here, during the
fighting.

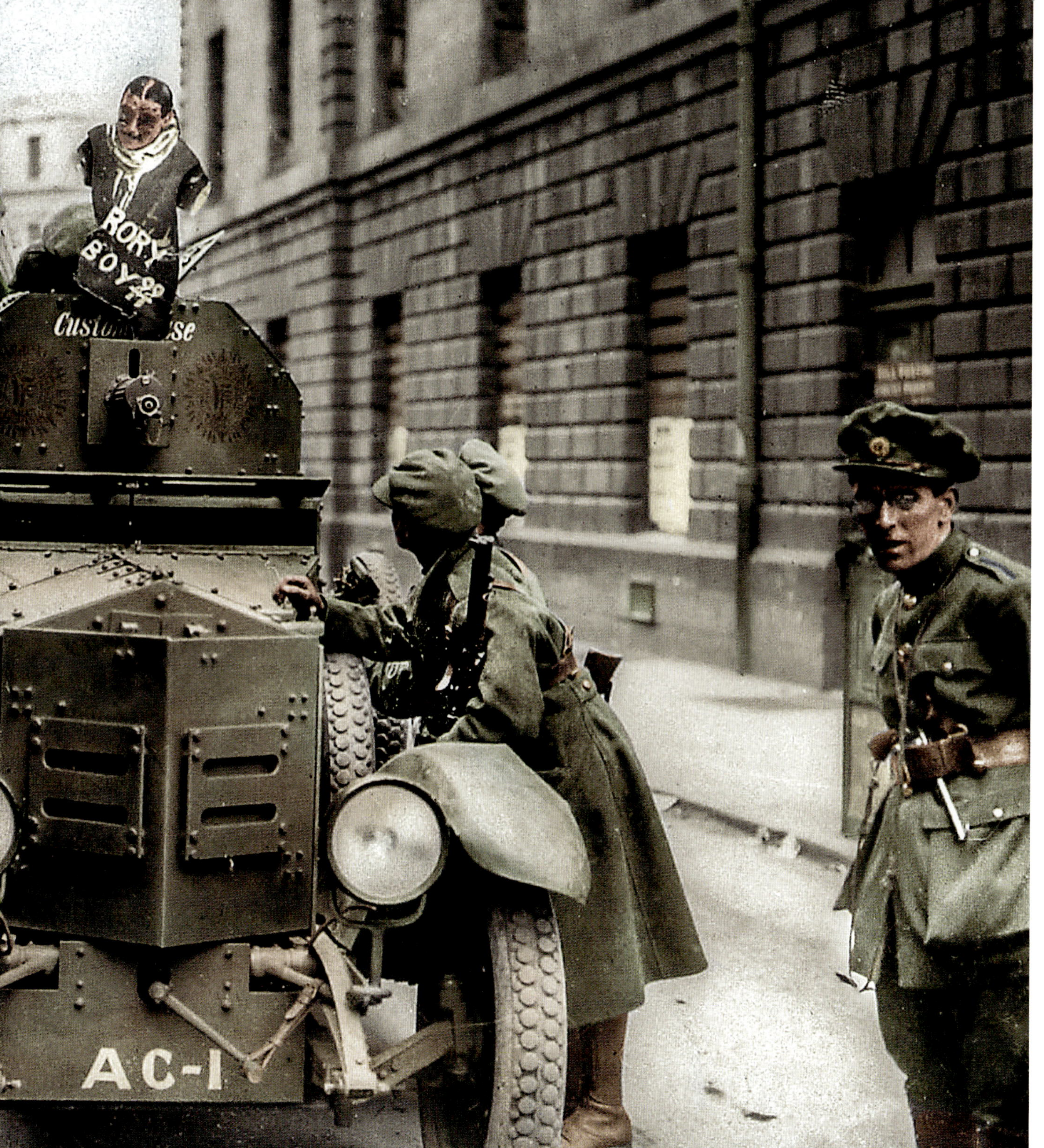

RORY
BOY
Custom ..se
AC-1

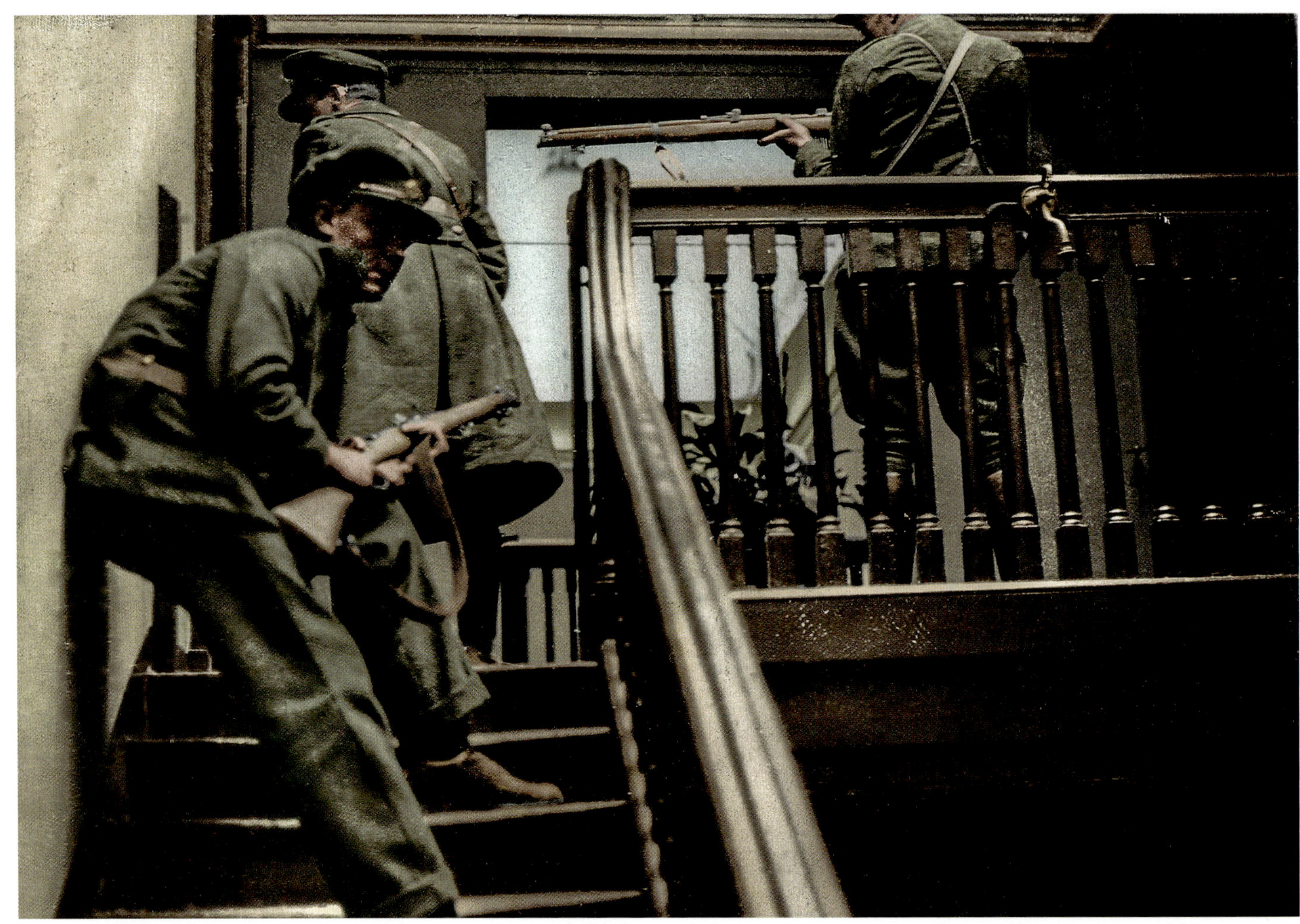

Urban fighting is one of the most difficult forms of combat. Here we see Provisional Government soldiers fanning out inside the Royal Bank of Ireland premises on Upper Sackville Street, across the street from the Block.

Right: kneeling on the Victorian encaustic tiles, a soldier crouches in front of the stained-glass window during the fighting.

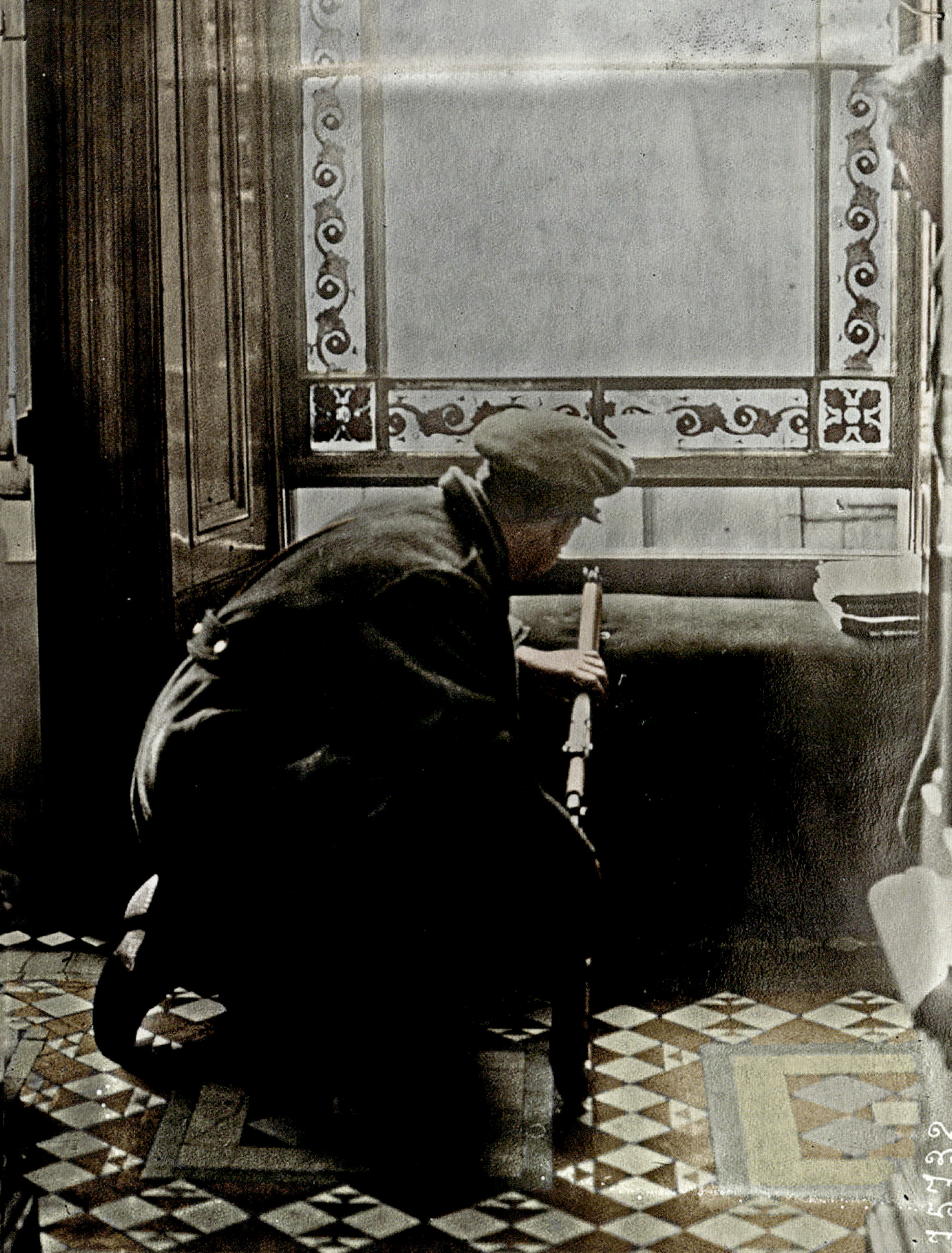

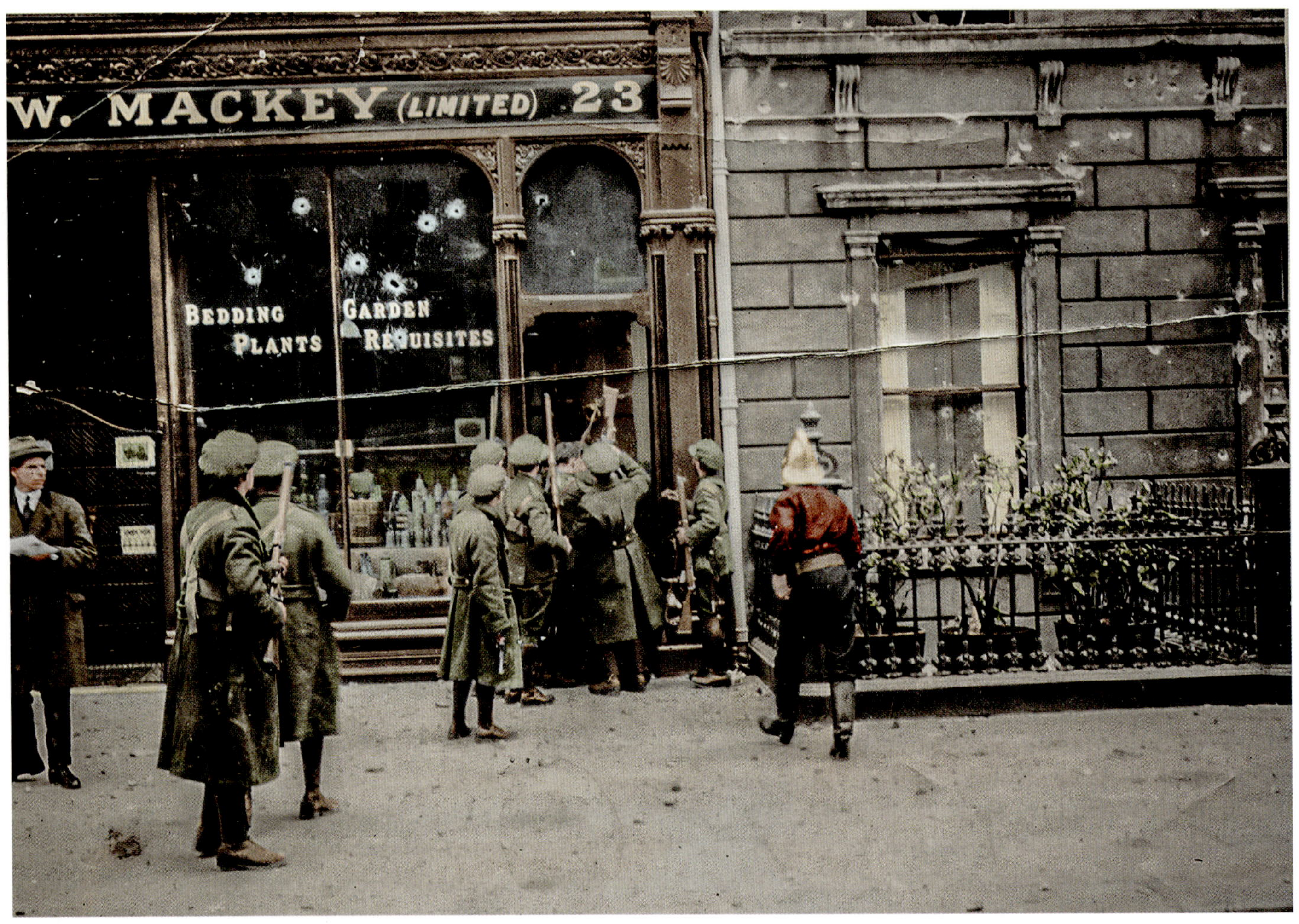

This photograph seems to show soldiers breaking open the door at the side of Mackey's Seeds (whose windows are pock-marked by bullets), as a fireman strides towards them. However, the intention was not to put out fires, as shortly afterwards Provisional Government Army officers broke the windows of the adjacent Gresham Hotel (on the right) and doused it with petrol. Their purpose was to set the building, part of the Block, alight, and thus flush out the anti-Treaty occupiers.

Right: The phrase 'an army marches on its stomach' has been attributed to, amongst others, Napoleon. It certainly had validity in central Dublin in 1922 as evidenced by this soldier bringing a plate of sandwiches to his watchful comrades during the fighting.

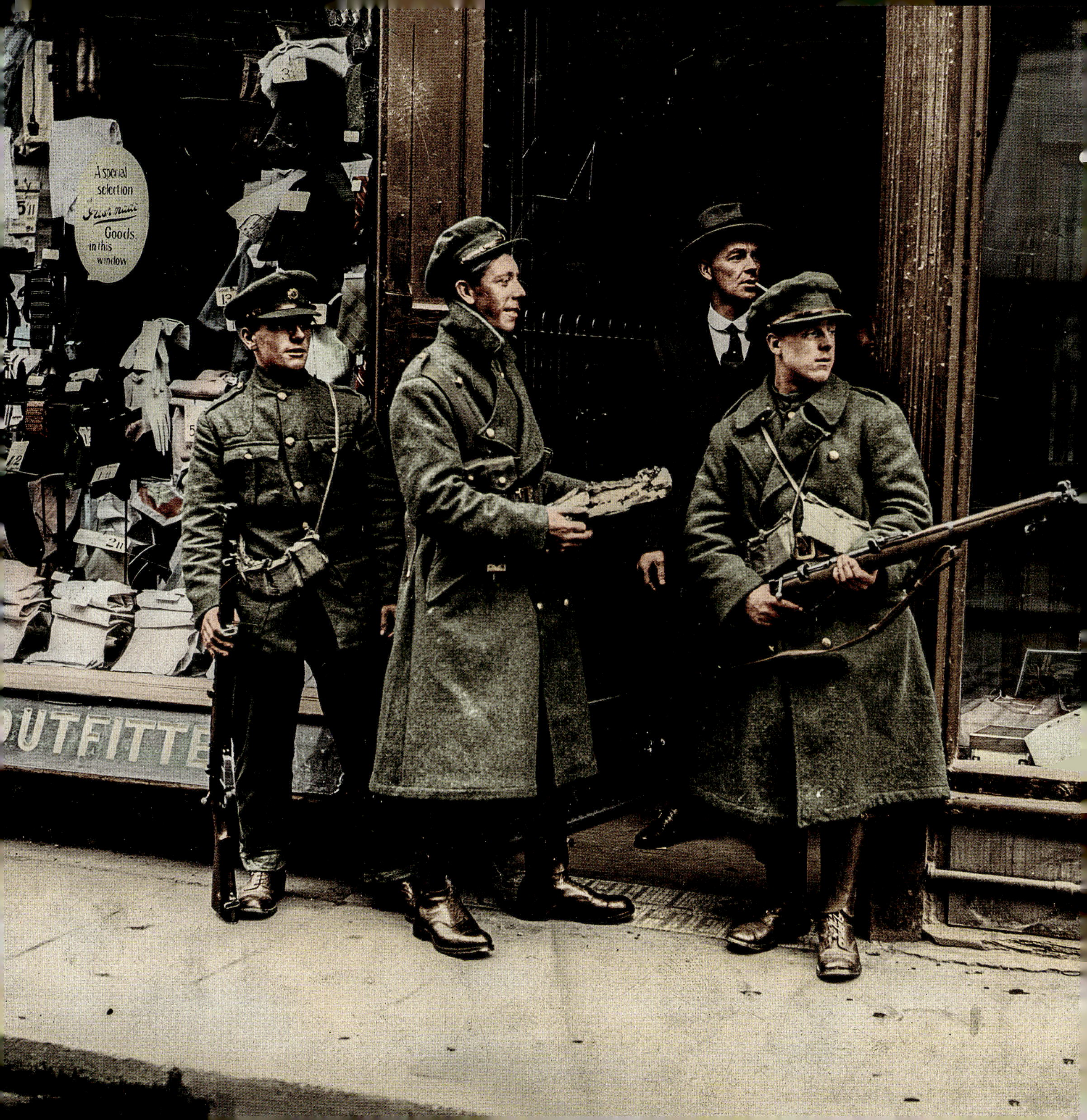

A special
selection
Irish made
Goods
in this
window
5/11
2/11
OUTFITTE

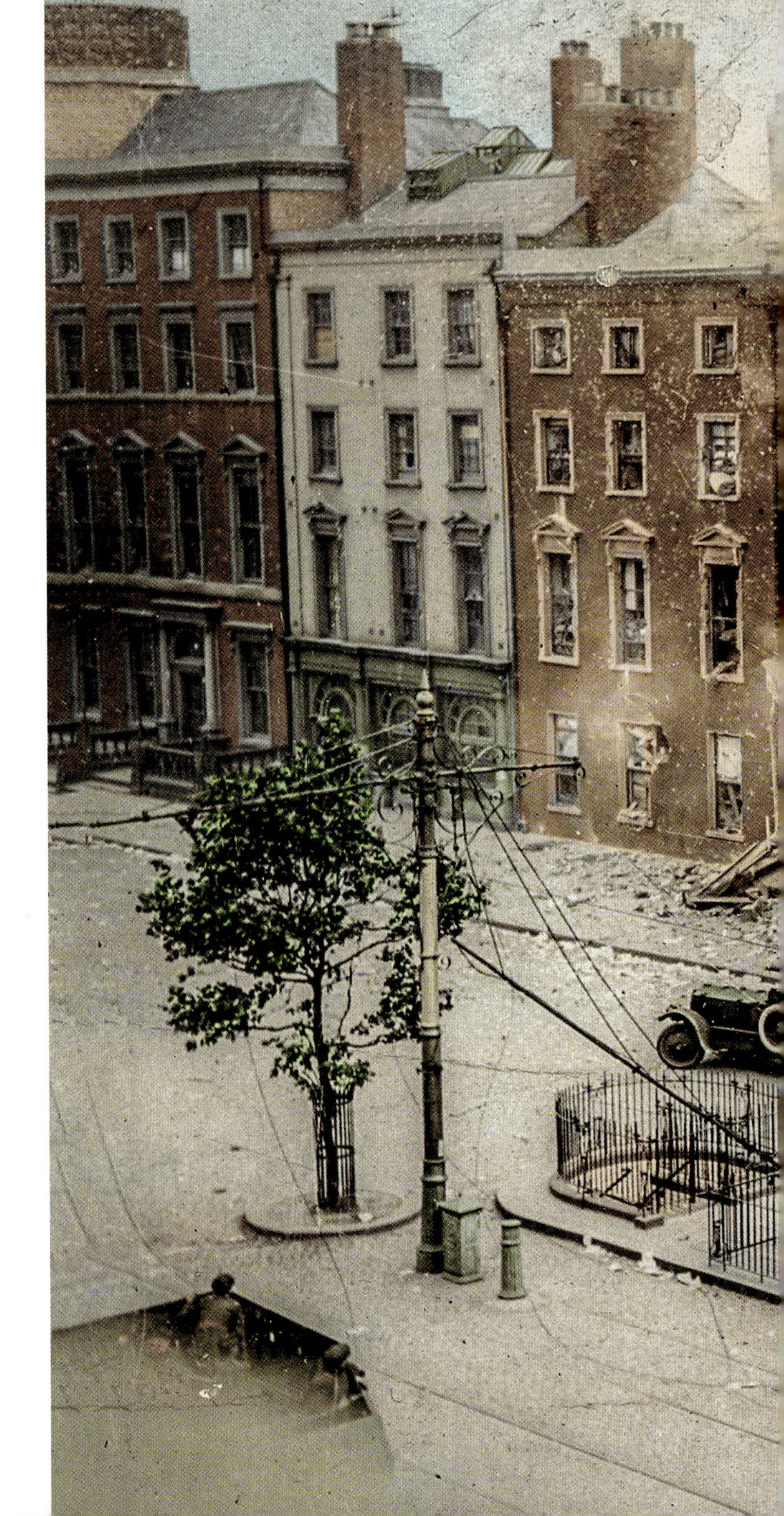

On Upper Sackville Street, a Rolls-Royce armoured car is stationed along the buildings of the Block, some with gaping holes caused by shellfire. Smoke billows from the Hammam Hotel.

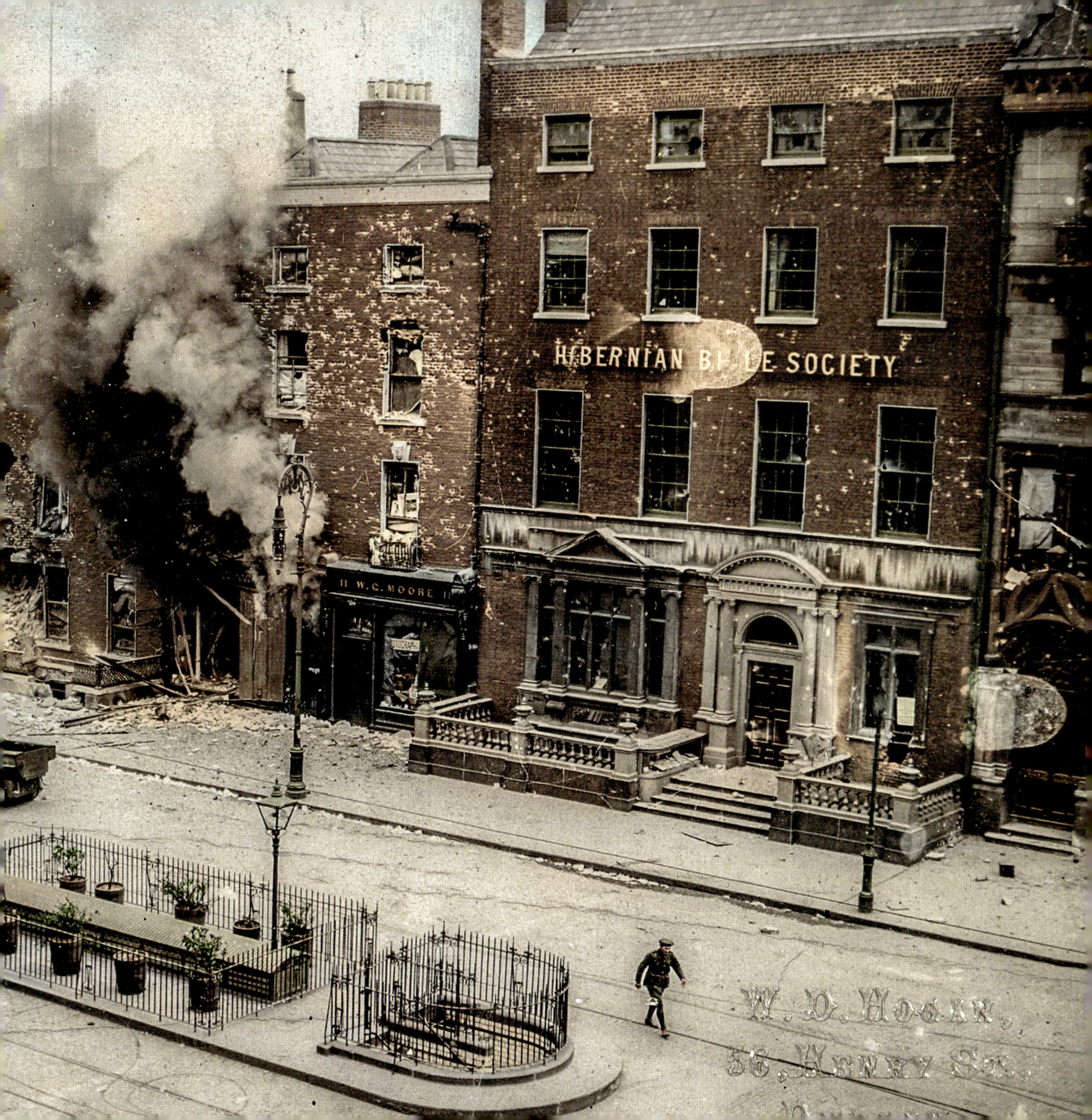

H W. C. MOORE
HIBERNIAN BIBLE SOCIETY
W. D. Hogan,
56, Henry St.,

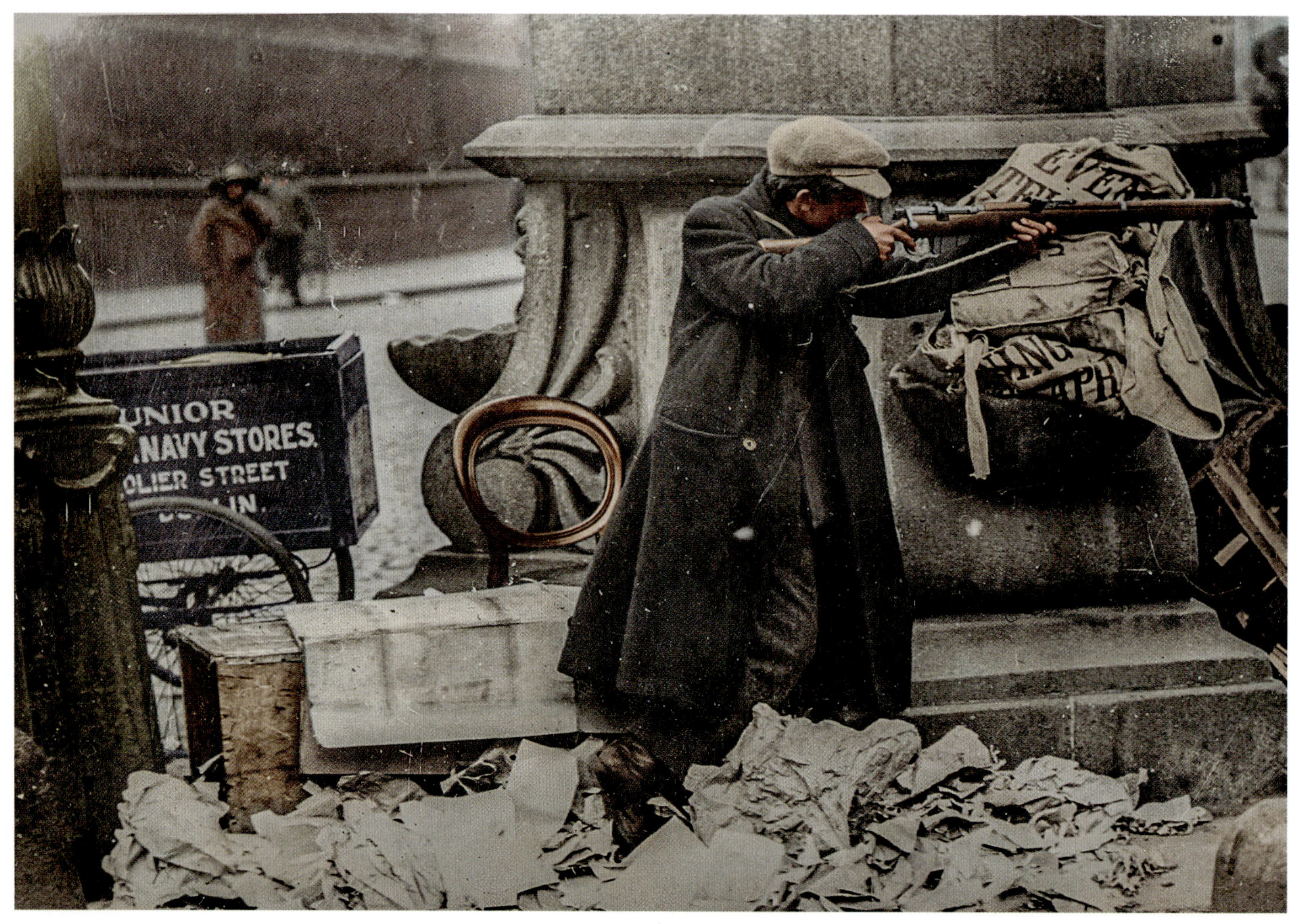

With Trinity College in the background, a pro-Treaty supporter in civilian garb poses with his rifle at a barricade by the granite base of the Crampton Memorial Fountain at the junction of College Street with D'Olier and Pearse Streets (the fountain was removed in 1959). The empty *Evening Telegraph* bags indicate that the litter at the man's feet is trashed copies of the newspaper. As evidenced by the many photographs taken in the College Street area in July 1922, press photographers persuaded pro-Treaty men to strike dramatic poses there (conveniently at a safe distance from the action at the Block).

Right: after being pounded by shells, the Hammam Hotel is now fully ablaze.

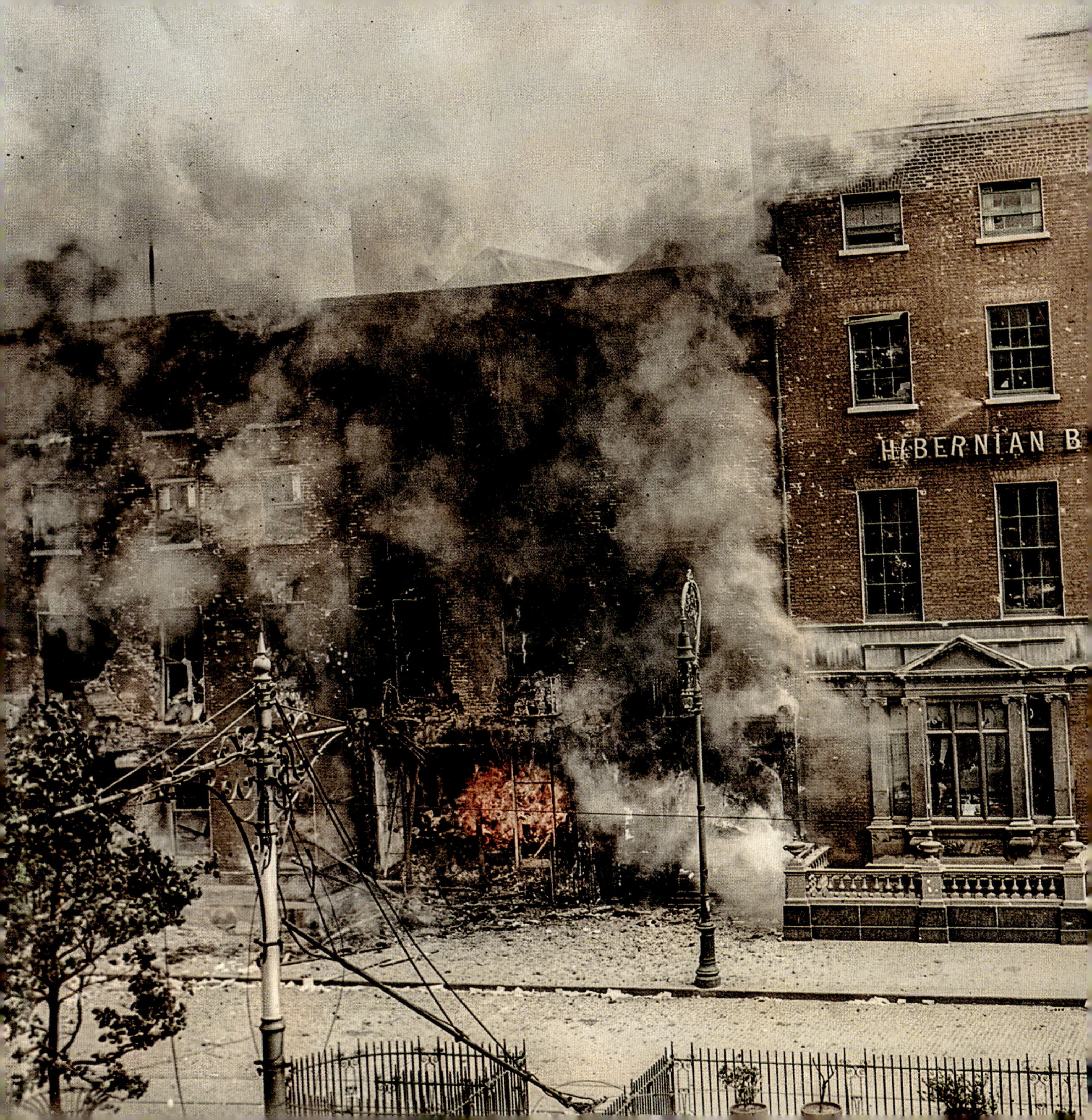
HIBERNIAN B

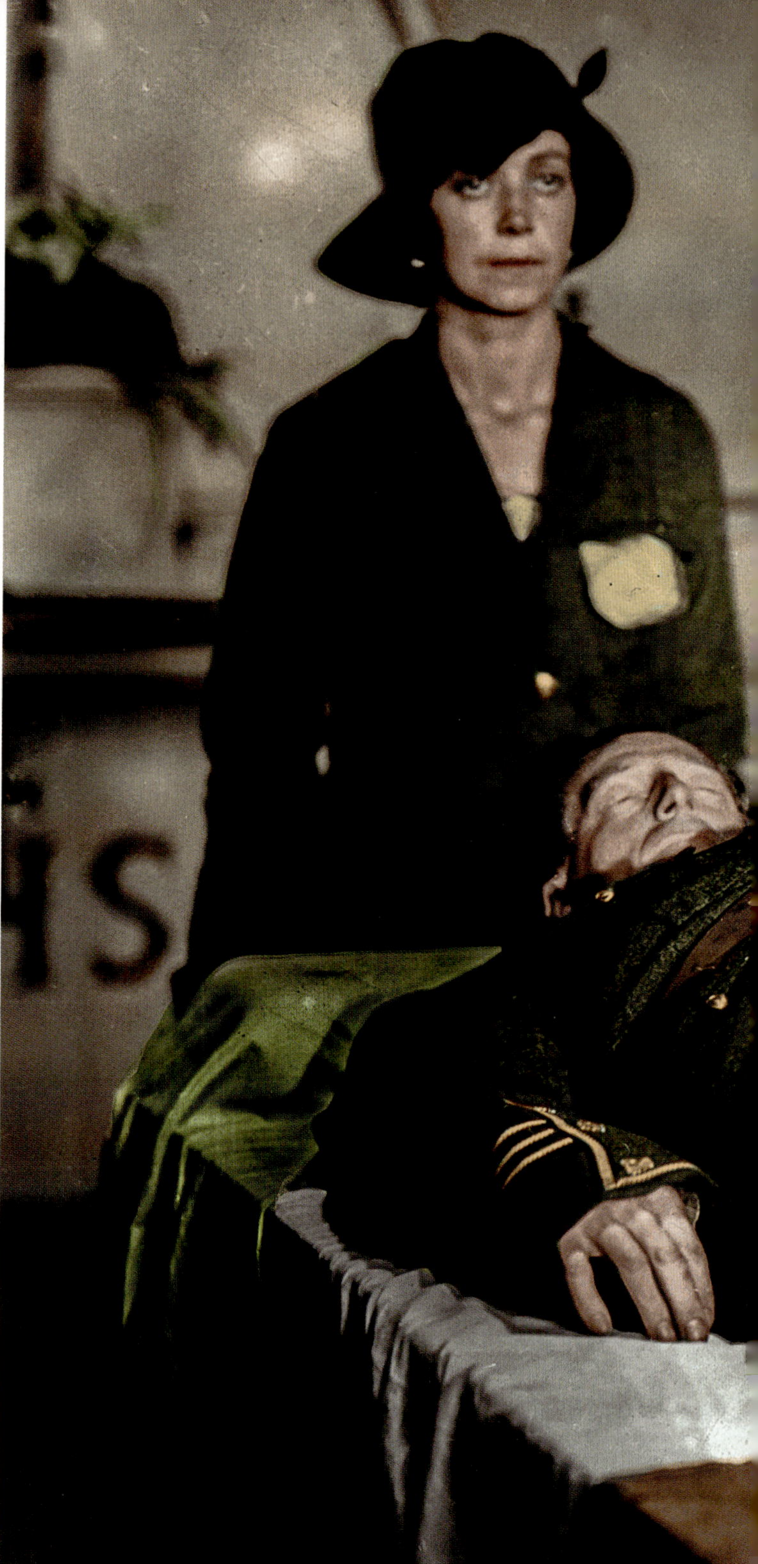

On 5 July 1922, Cathal Brugha was in charge of a small rearguard group, having retreated to the Granville Hotel (a few doors west of the Hammam Hotel) in the central part of the Block. At around 7 p.m., with the hotel in flames, Brugha ordered his men to surrender. Then he emerged into Thomas Lane, behind the hotel, pistol in hand, and ran towards a party of troops. Shots rang out and he was hit by a single bullet, causing a gaping wound in his leg. Wounded in a femoral artery, he died two days later. The photograph shows Brugha laid out in the mortuary of the Mater Hospital, flanked by a Cumann na mBan guard of honour. One account relates, poignantly, that the only volunteer uniform that was available was a little large for Brugha, a small man.

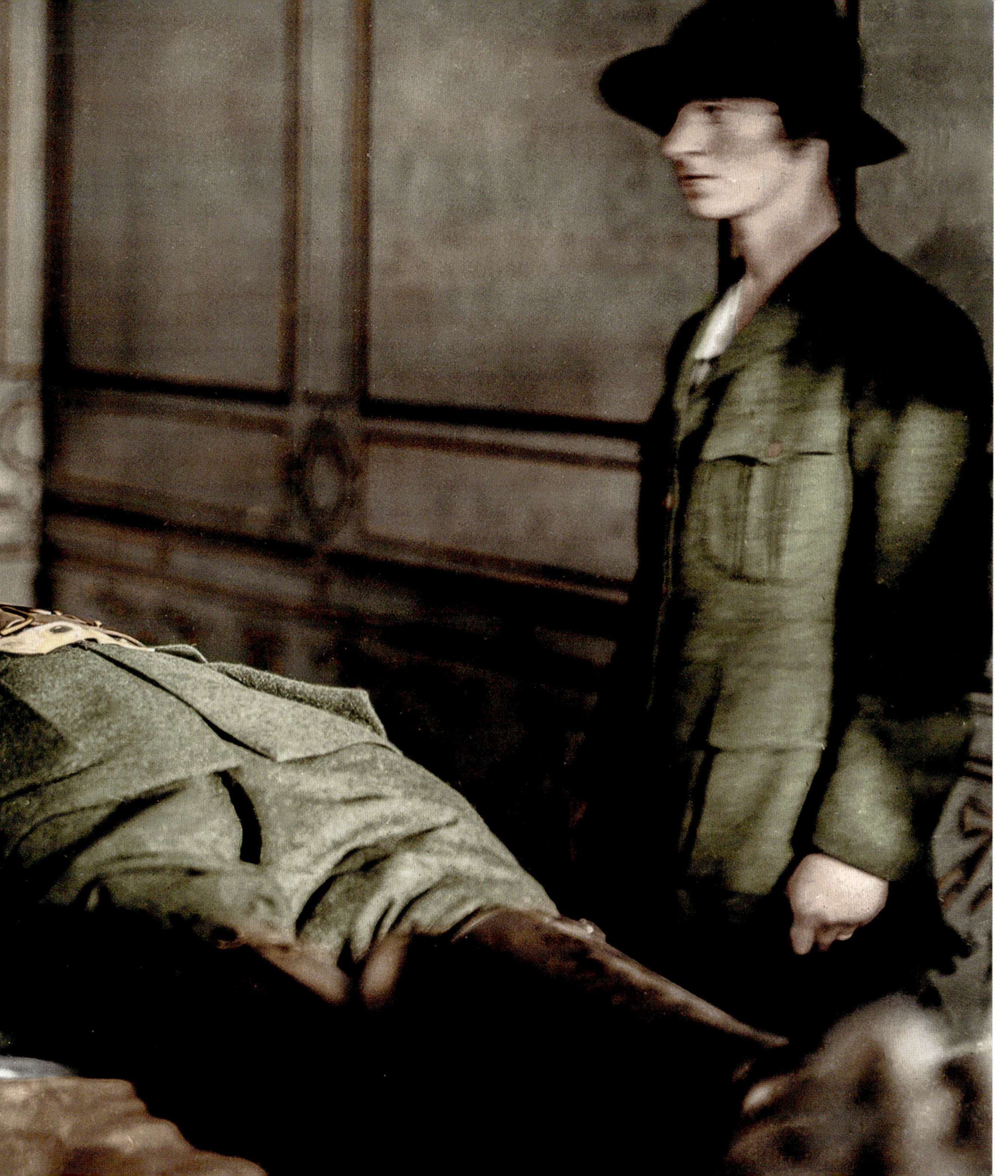

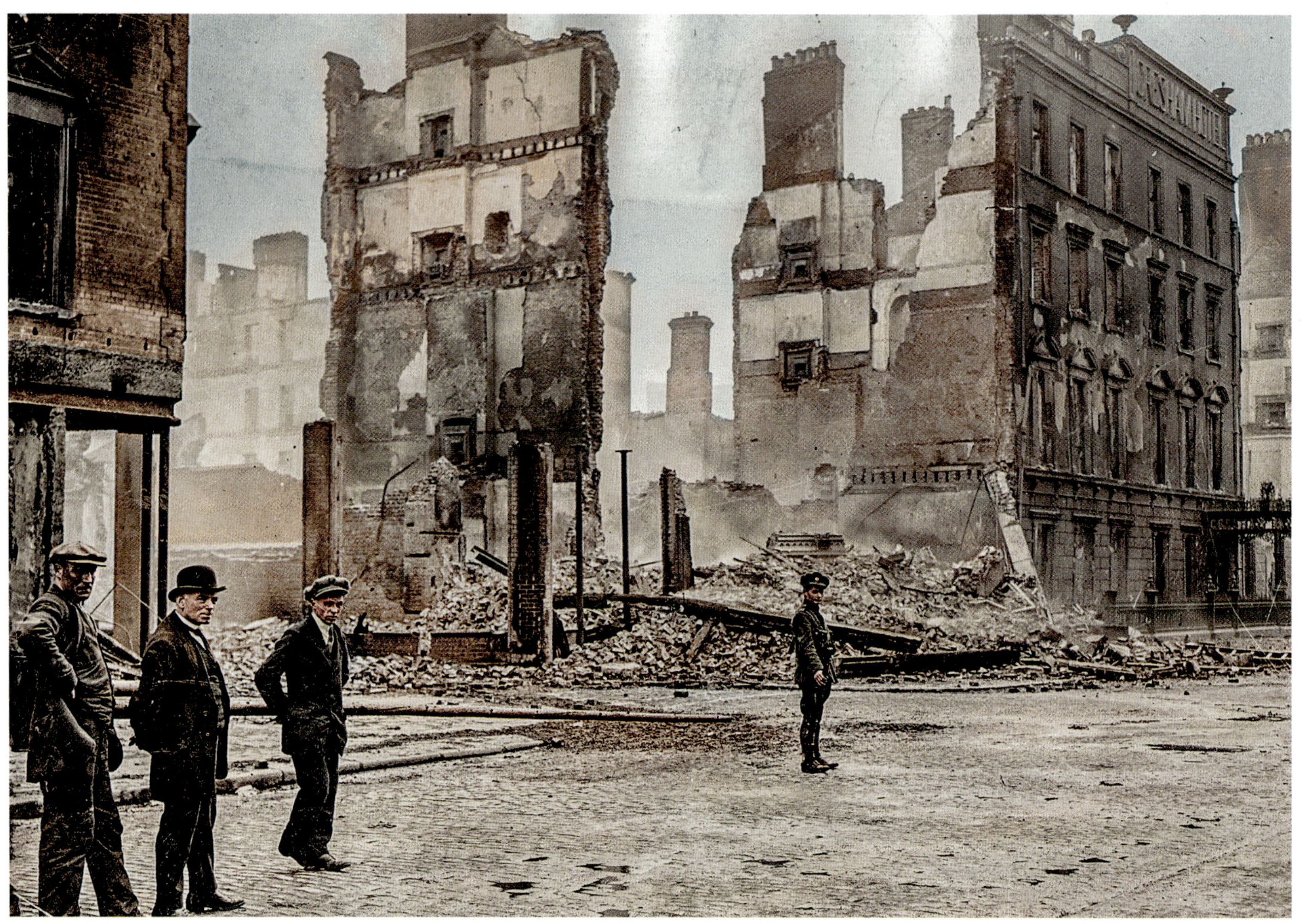

When the fighting ended on 5 July 1922, the Block was in ruins having succumbed to bullets, shells and flames. Some buildings had totally collapsed leaving behind just a few cross walls and rubble. The Gresham Hotel is in the background on the right.

Right: Fr Albert Bibby arrives by car and is seen here conferring with St John Ambulance Brigade personnel by Sackville Street. He, along with his fellow Capuchin, Fr Dominic O'Connor, had been inside the Four Courts during the siege, offering spiritual comfort and helping with evacuation of the wounded. They also assisted in negotiating the surrender of the Republican occupiers.

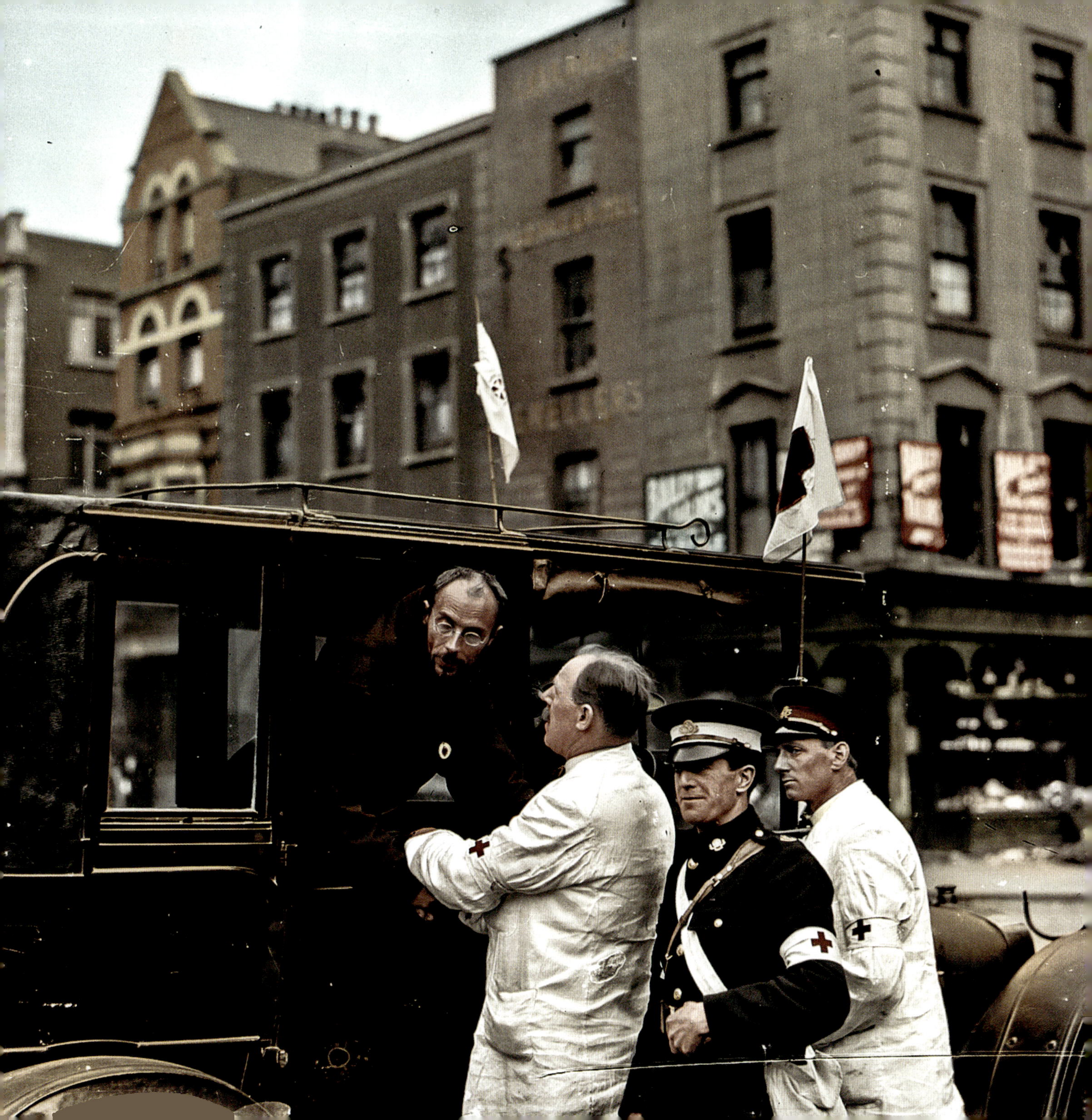

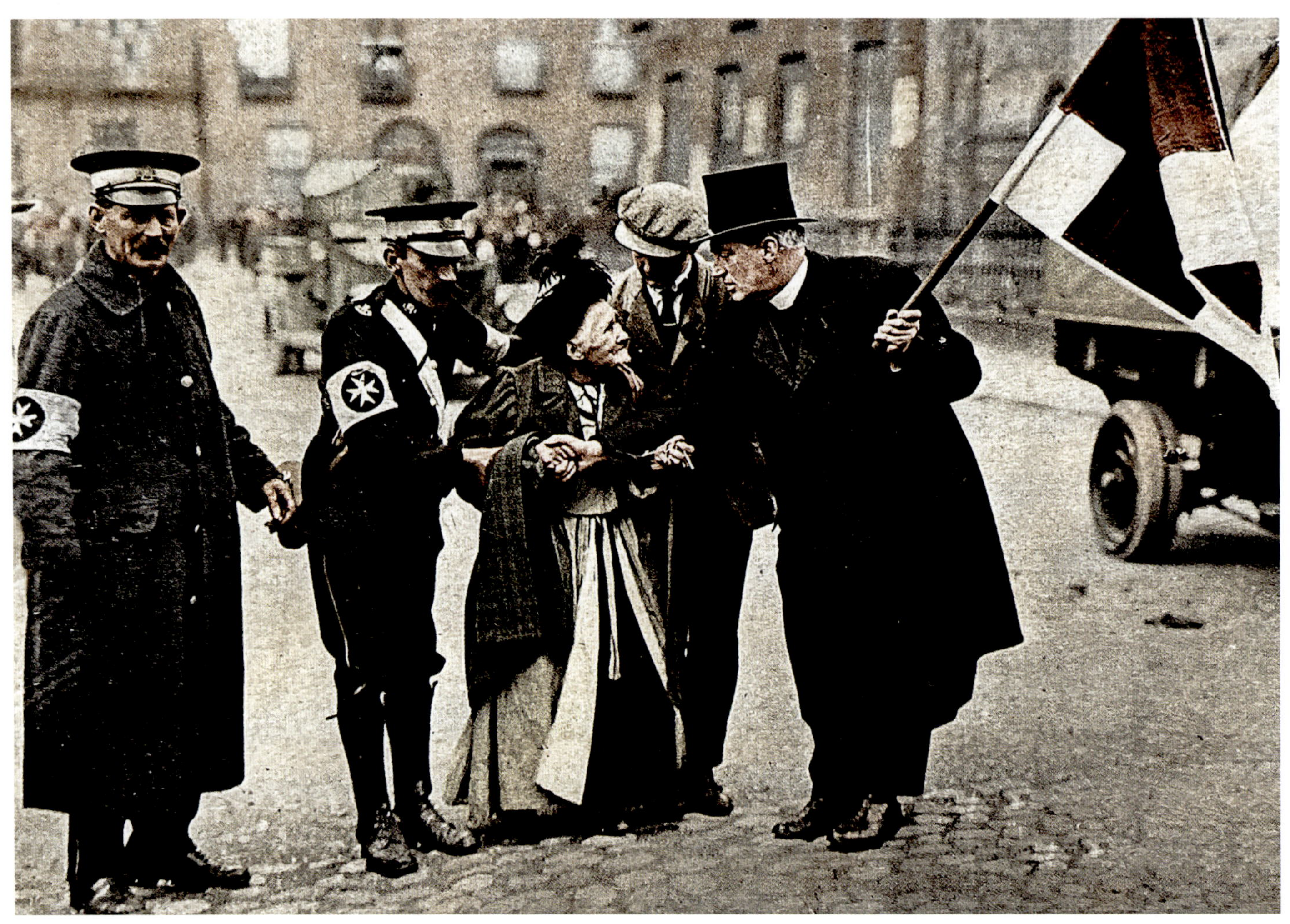

A top-hatted priest waves a flag, as he and St John Ambulance Brigade volunteers give assistance to an elderly lady during the fighting in central Dublin. The brigade had set up two first-aid posts, one at Foster's Place and the other at Sackville Street.

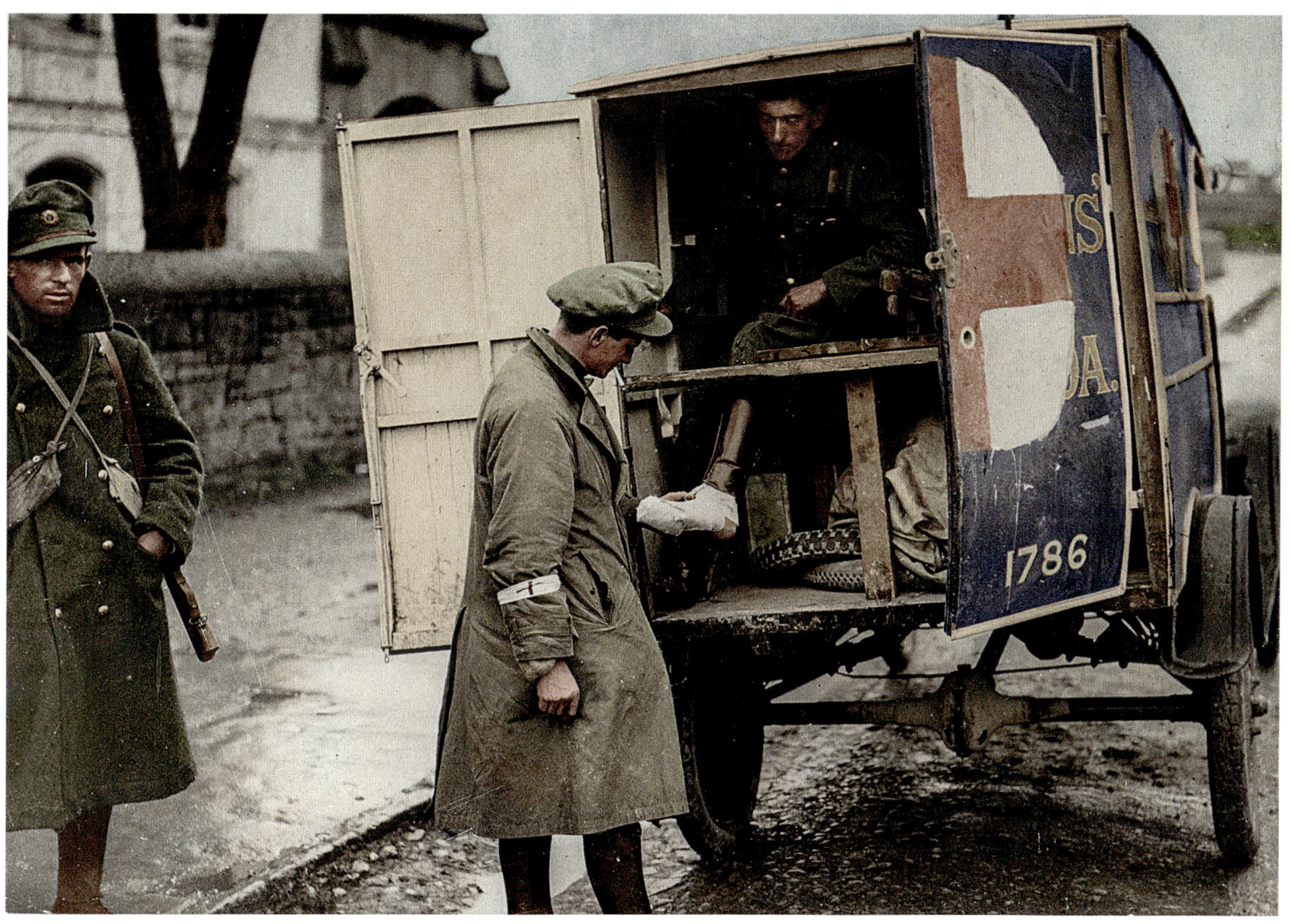

Improvisation was in order after heavy fighting flared up in central Dublin. Pictured here, a recently commandeered delivery van, with a crude Red Cross painted on, is being used as an impromptu ambulance by Provisional Government forces. A medical orderly, cigarette in mouth, casts a cursory look at his colleague's bandaged foot.

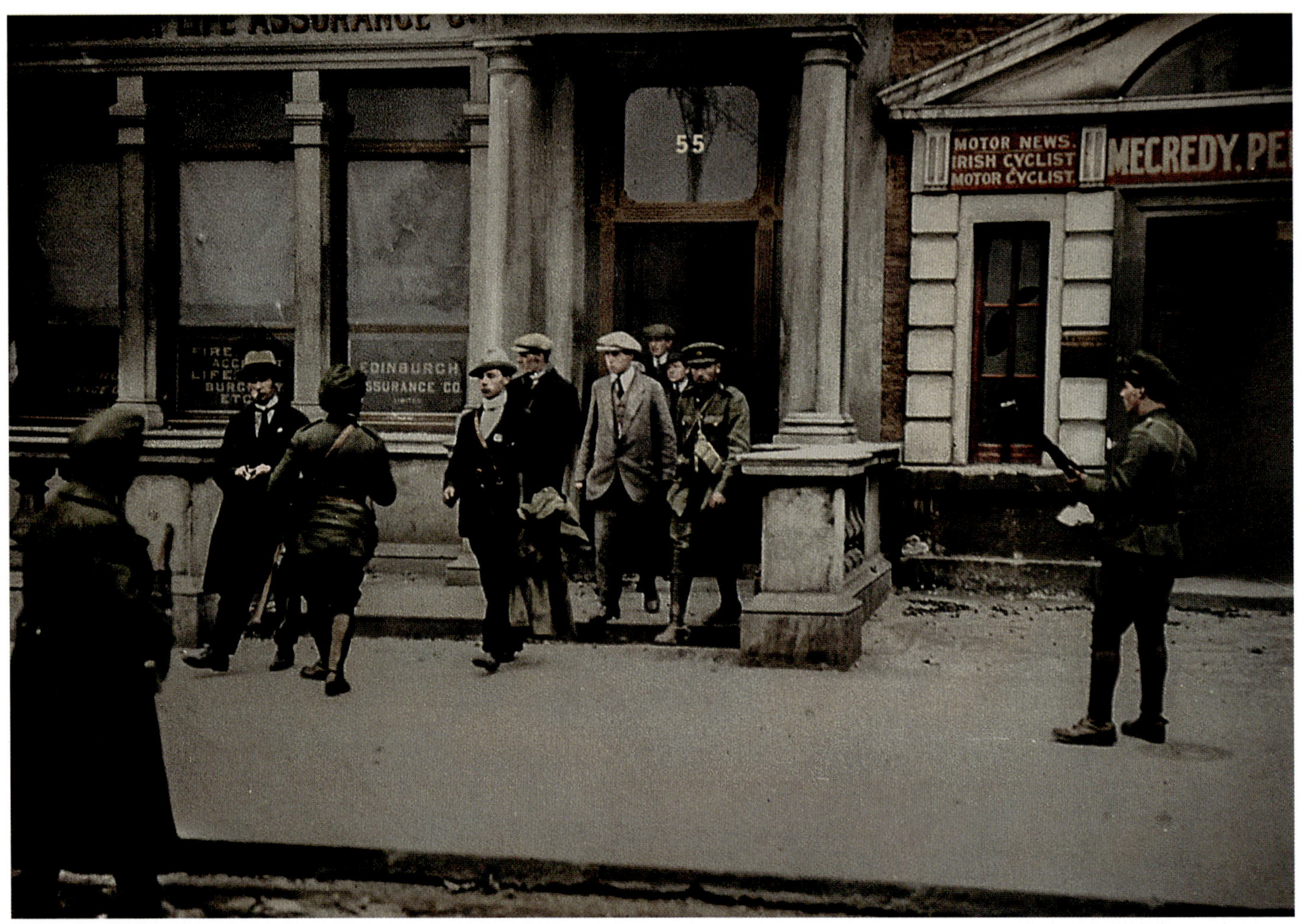

The last to surrender after Brugha was shot; these anti-Treaty men emerge under guard from the Edinburgh Life Assurance building on the west side of Upper Sackville Street. They had tunnelled here from an outpost at the nearby Thwaites Mineral Water Plant.

Right: the caption on this photograph, dated 4 July 1922, by W.D. Hogan says: 'Maude Gonne MacBride on Red Cross Duty'. MacBride (on the right), together with Charlotte Despard (second from the left) and a number of other women, had formed the Women's Peace Committee, which held meetings with both sides of the conflict, urging peace. Her son, Seán MacBride, had been one of the occupiers of the Four Courts and was now in captivity in Mountjoy Prison.

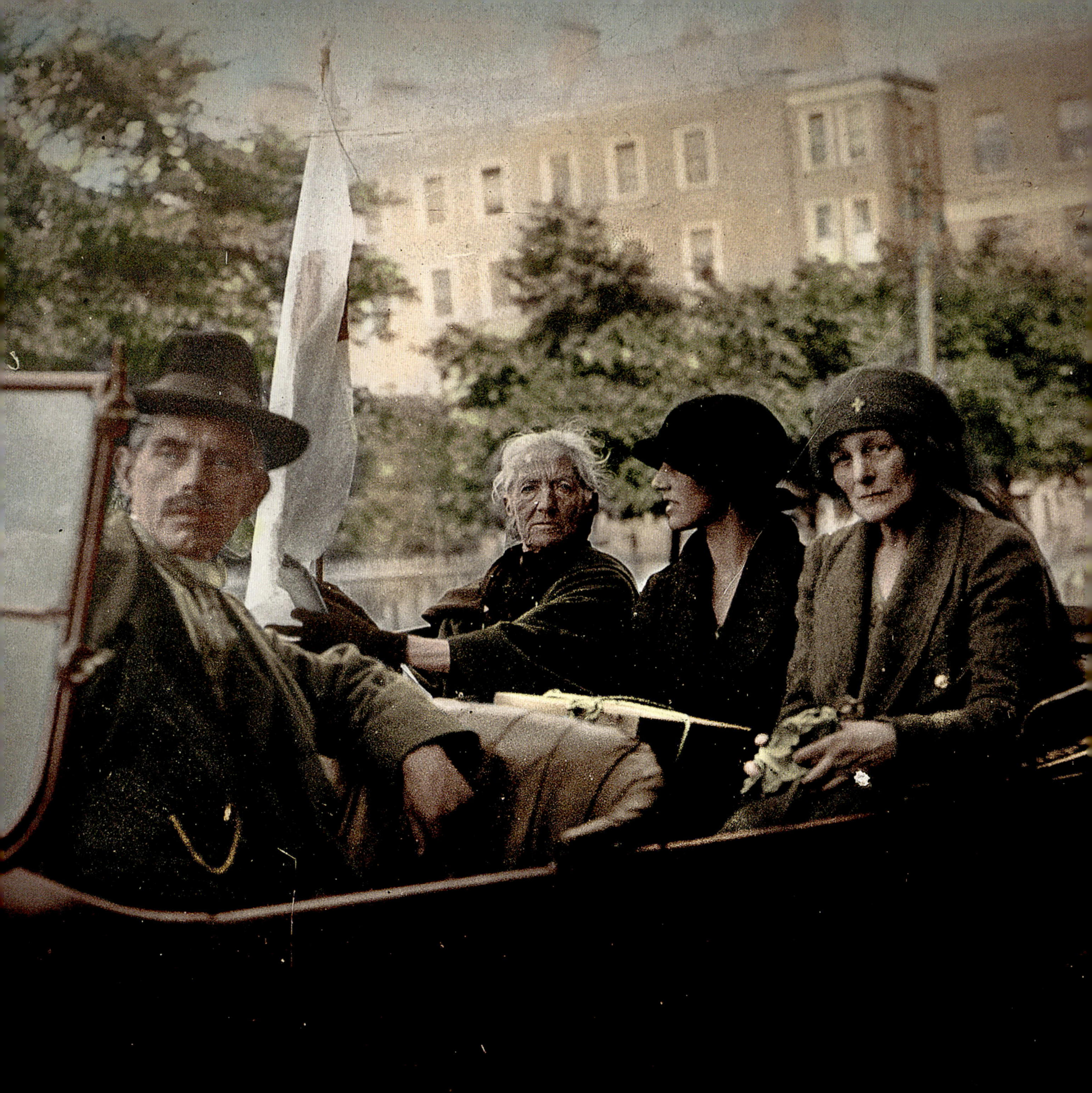

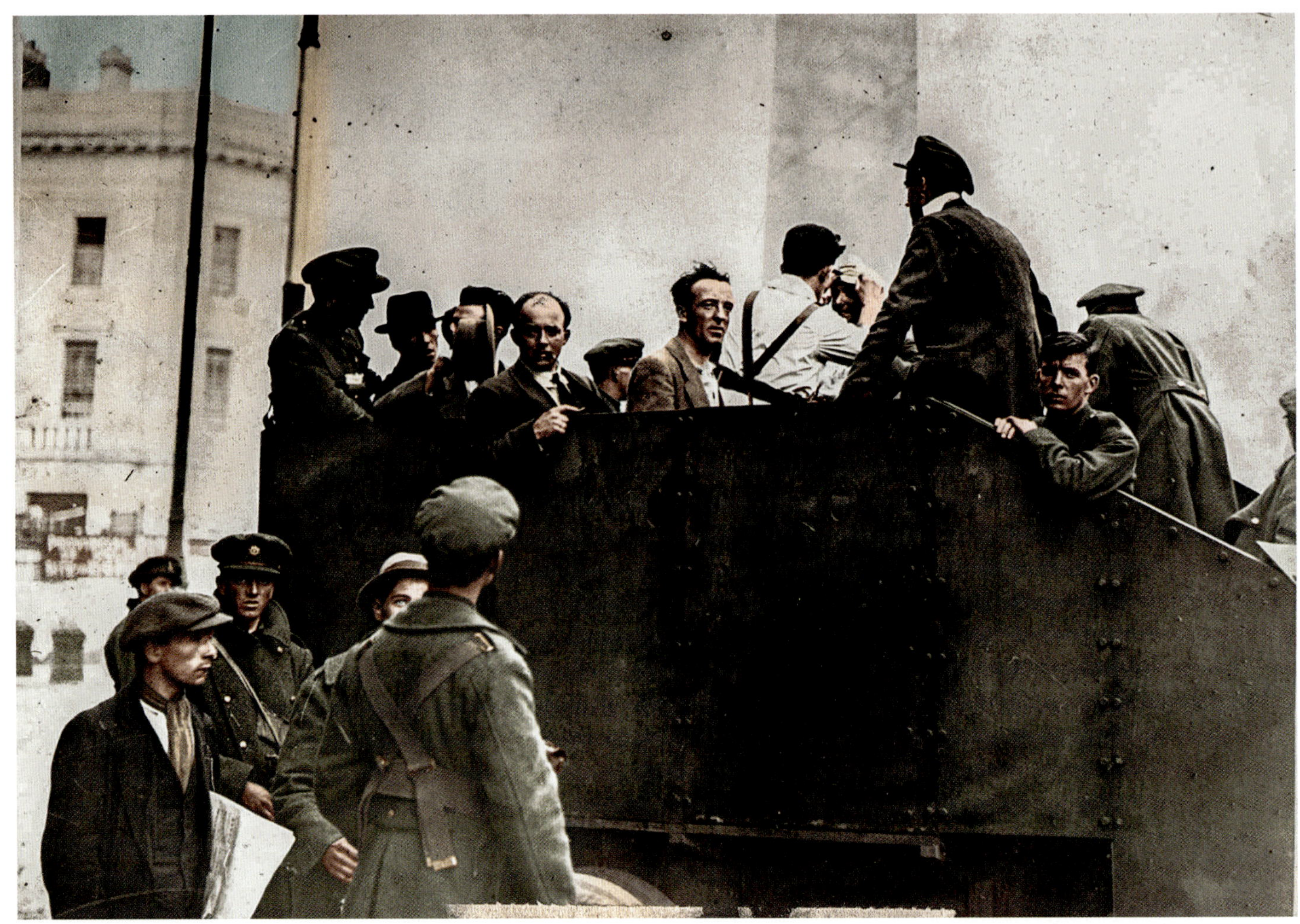

Near O'Connell Bridge, as a paper-seller looks on, anti-Treaty prisoners are loaded into this Lancia armoured personnel carrier. This is a scene towards the end of the Dublin fighting. Some prisoners are bloodied, all look exhausted and apprehensive.

Right: soldiers stand amidst rubble in front of the temporary GPO (note the new 'An Post' branding and 'SÉ', initials for Saorstát Éireann) that had been set up on Upper Sackville Street, while the GPO lay in ruins after the destruction of 1916. As we see here, this post office (in the middle part of what became the Block) also suffered devastation in the course of the fighting in July 1922.

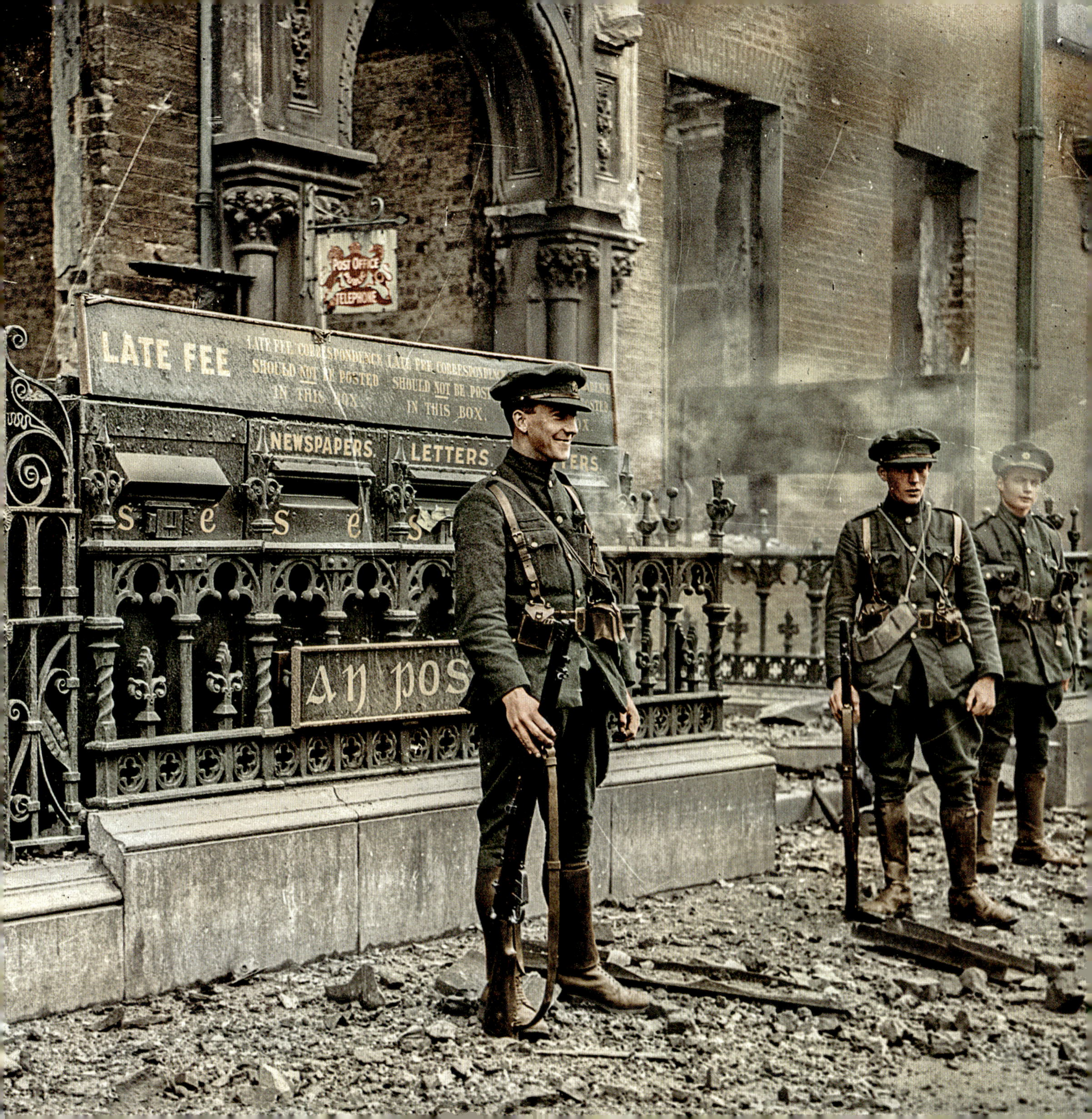
LATE FEE
LATE FEE CORRESPONDENCE LATE FEE CORRESPONDENCE
SHOULD NOT BE POSTED SHOULD NOT BE POSTED
IN THIS BOX. IN THIS BOX.
NEWSPAPERS. LETTERS. LETTERS.
POST OFFICE
TELEPHONE
An pos

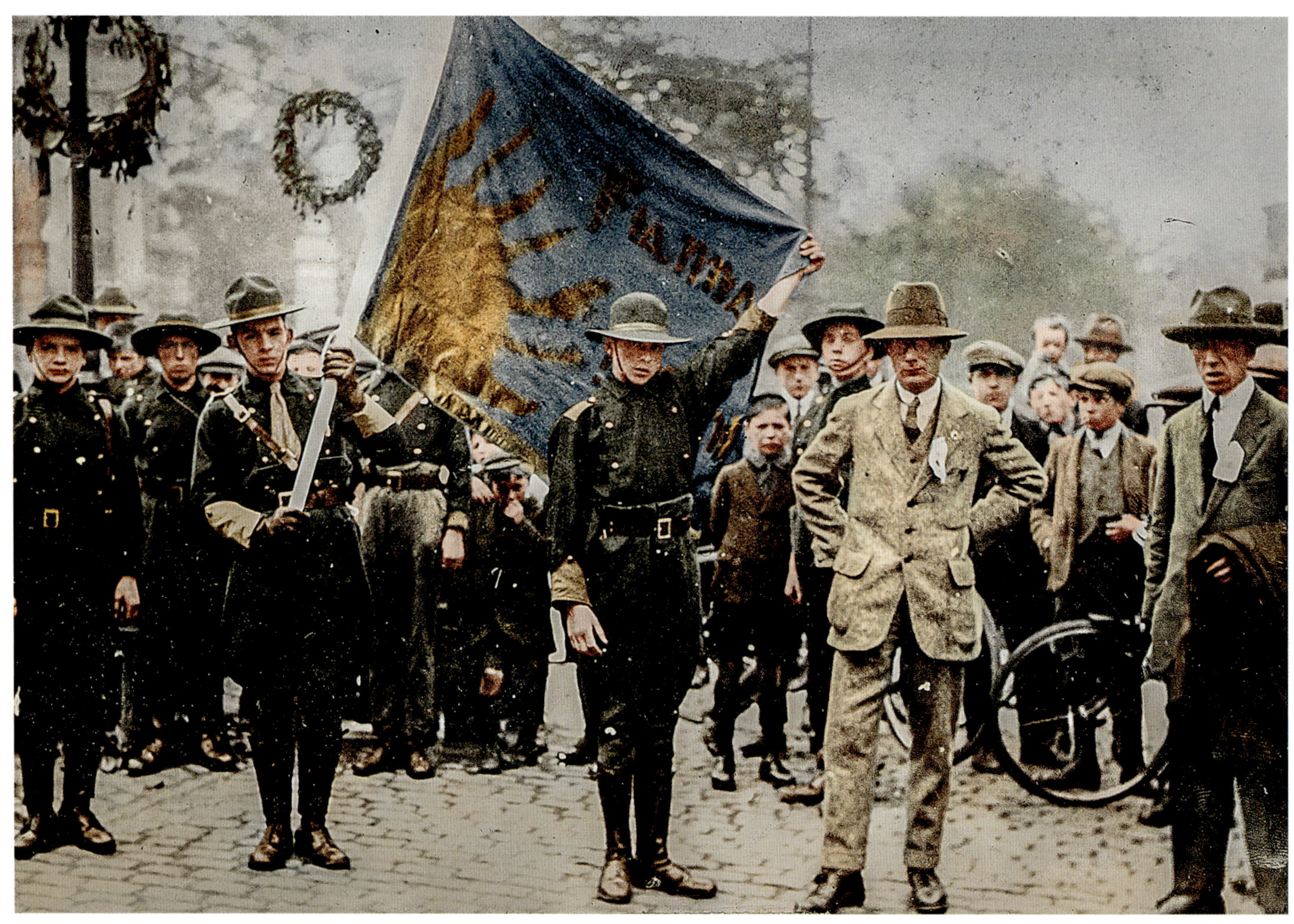

Fianna Éireann at the funeral on 10 July 1922 of Cathal Brugha, who was buried in the Republican Plot at Glasnevin Cemetery. As requested by Brugha's widow, Cumann na mBan provided stewards and the guard of honour during the procession, observed by large crowds. The women's auxiliary movement also later provided military honours at the funeral of Harry Boland, who died on 1 August 1922, after being shot by Provisional Government soldiers at Malahide.

Right: with ambulances racing around and first-aid posts in the city centre, these children, influenced by the pandemonium, rise to the occasion and play at Red Cross, with nurses, flags and a stretcher.

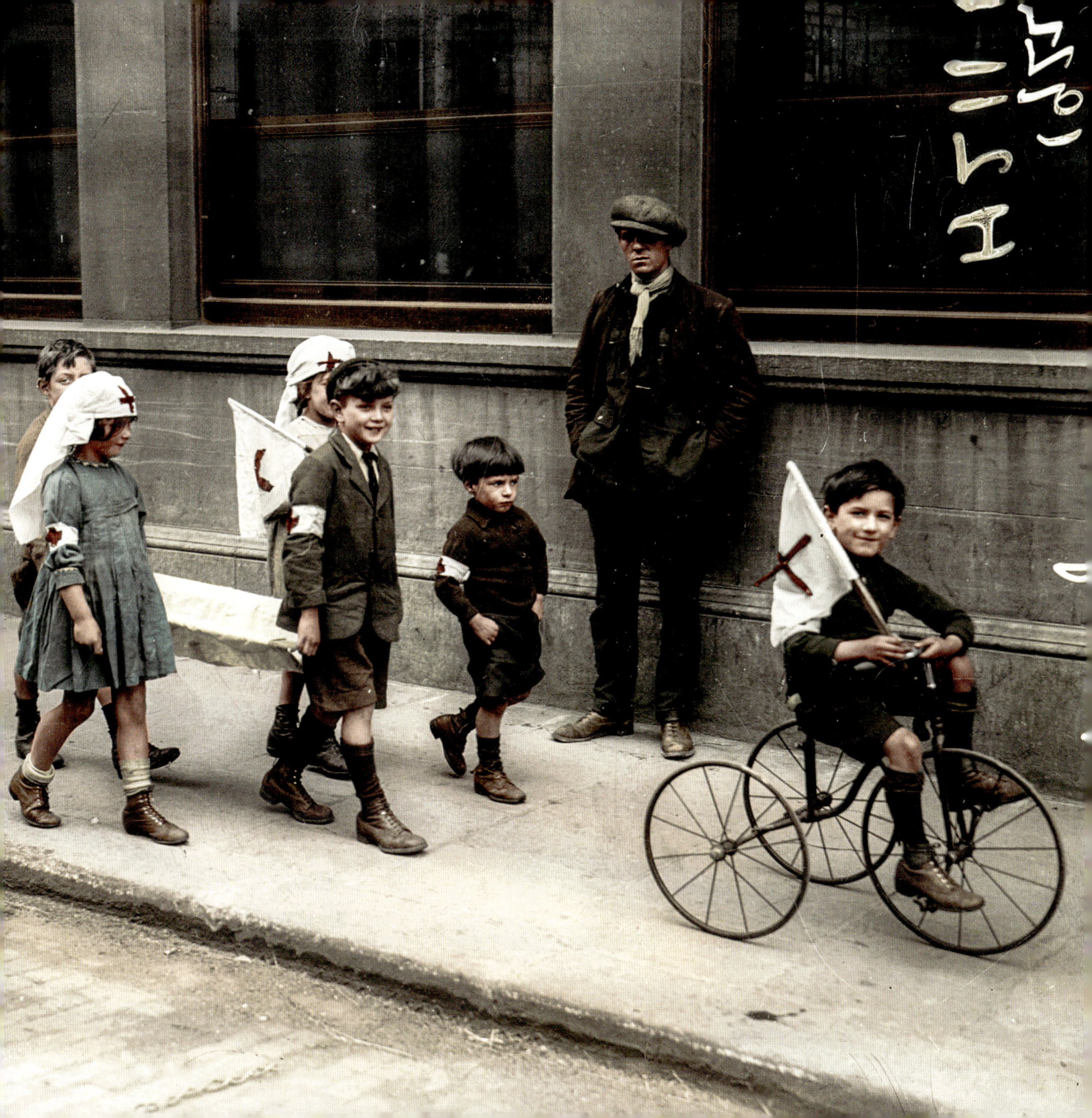

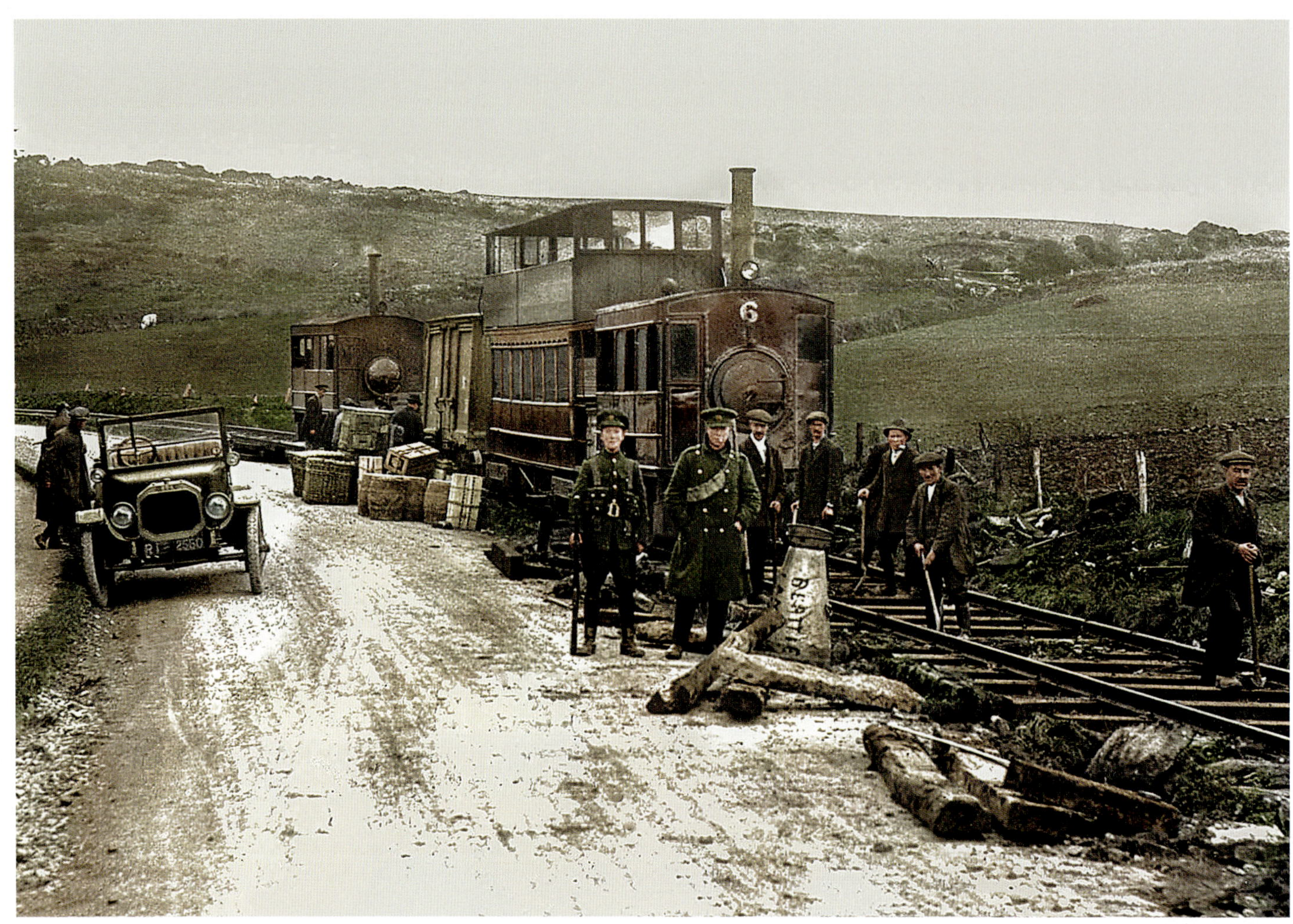

Permanent way men repair the track of the Dublin & Blessington Steam Tramway, damaged by the IRA. When the fighting ended on 5 July 1922, Republican fighters went to assemble at Blessington, where the original plan had been to march on Dublin. When large numbers of Provisional Government troops converged on the town, there was little resistance and they found the Republicans had dispersed. The war now entered a new phase where the fighting was mainly concentrated in the countryside, outside of Dublin.

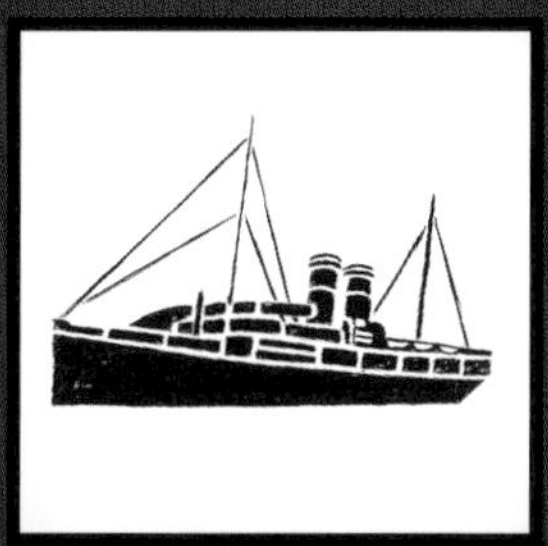

Chapter 3

War Spreads to the Country

As the main conflict moved out of Dublin, there were clashes between pro- and anti-Treaty forces across the country. Limerick, on the Shannon, was a strategic point between Munster and Connacht. In a re-run of the Dublin battles, the Provisional Government Army took control of the city. Using an artillery piece, Waterford was easily captured from the Republicans. With much of Munster and the west under Republican control, the generals of the Provisional Government Army decided in July 1922 to mount a series of amphibious landings on the southern and western coasts. Such landings could be perilous but, by dint of some planning, a poor strategic response from the Republican side and a lot of luck, there was success in Mayo and Kerry. With the taking of Cork on 10 August 1922, the core of the anti-Treaty 'Munster Republic' faded away and the war now entered a guerrilla phase.

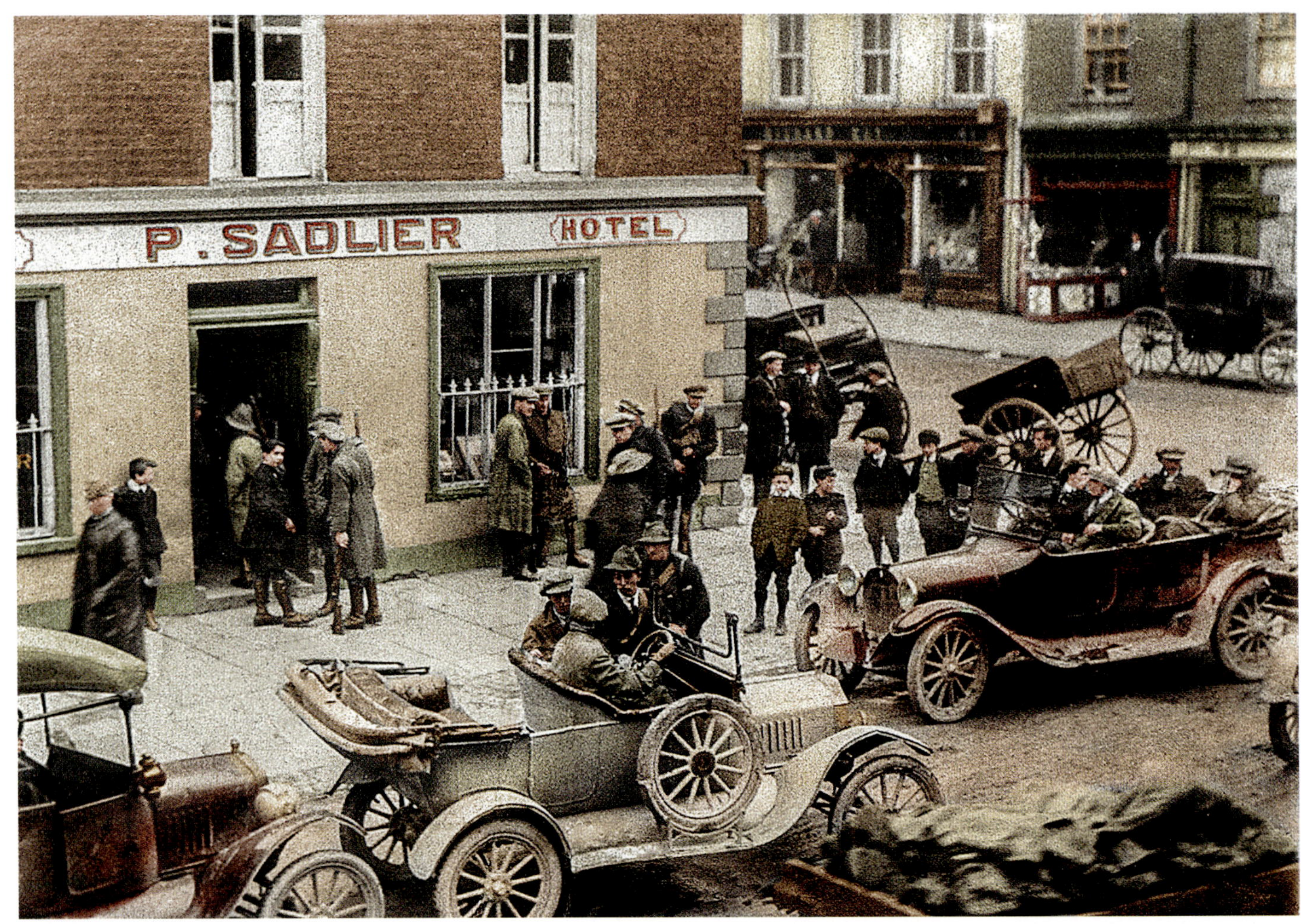

Well-entrenched in their Limerick strongholds, anti-Treaty men park their commandeered cars in front of the Imperial Hotel. Located by the Shannon, and controlling approaches to the south-west and the north-west, the city was strategically important. Pro-Treaty Commandant-General Michael Brennan agreed a truce there on 4 July 1922 with Liam Lynch (Chief of Staff of the anti-Treaty IRA). This bought time for the pro-Treaty side, allowing them to send troops and arms to the city.

Right: Republicans, with rifles and a Lewis gun, in Limerick

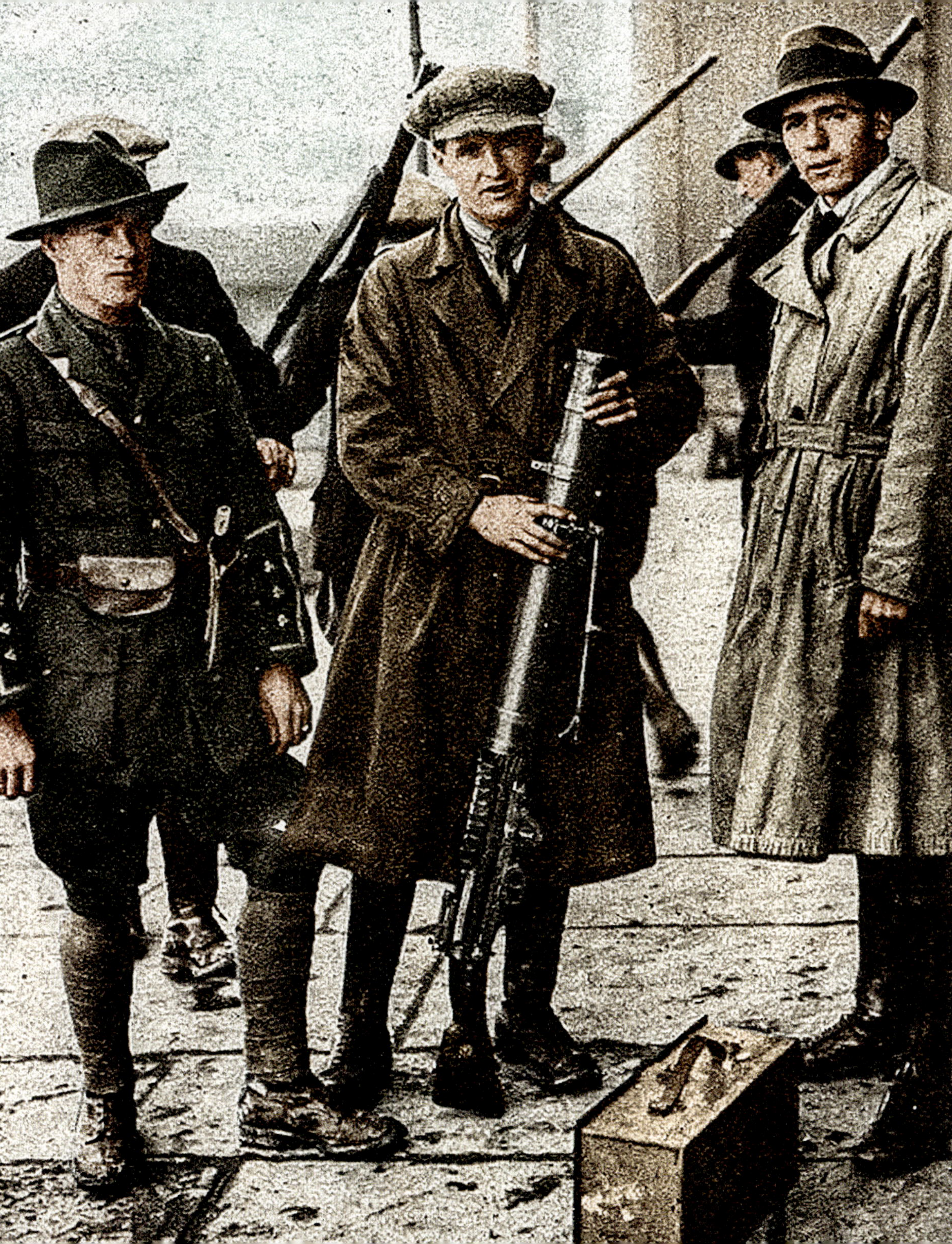

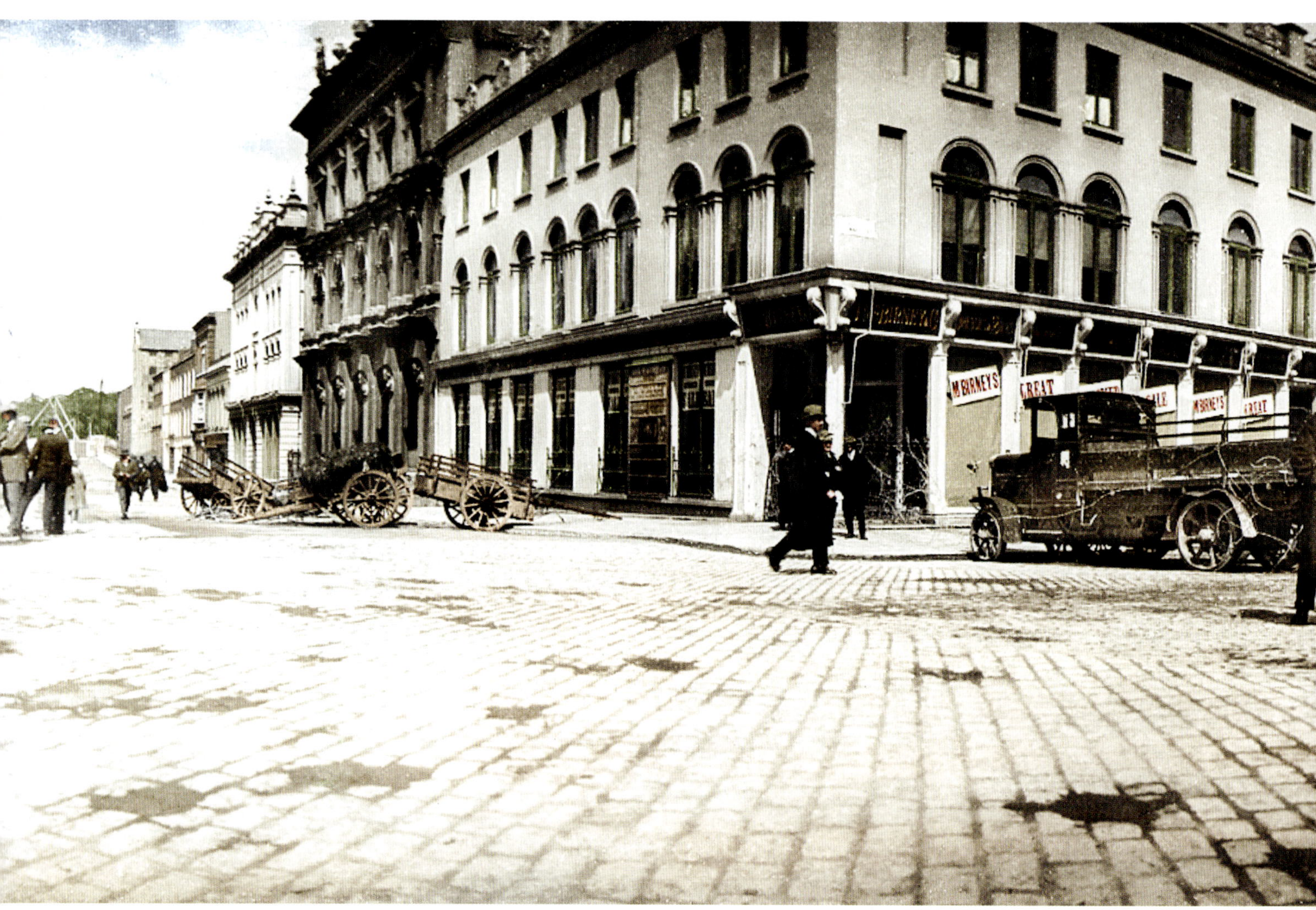

This magnificent photograph by George Imbusch, using a panoramic camera (one of the first in the city), captures the scene of barricades and barbed wire on O'Connell Street, Limerick, then under Republican control. The truce ended on 11 July 1922, when the Provisional Government forces, on the pretext that a soldier had been shot, spread out along the barricaded streets of the city and opened fire on the Ordnance Barracks.

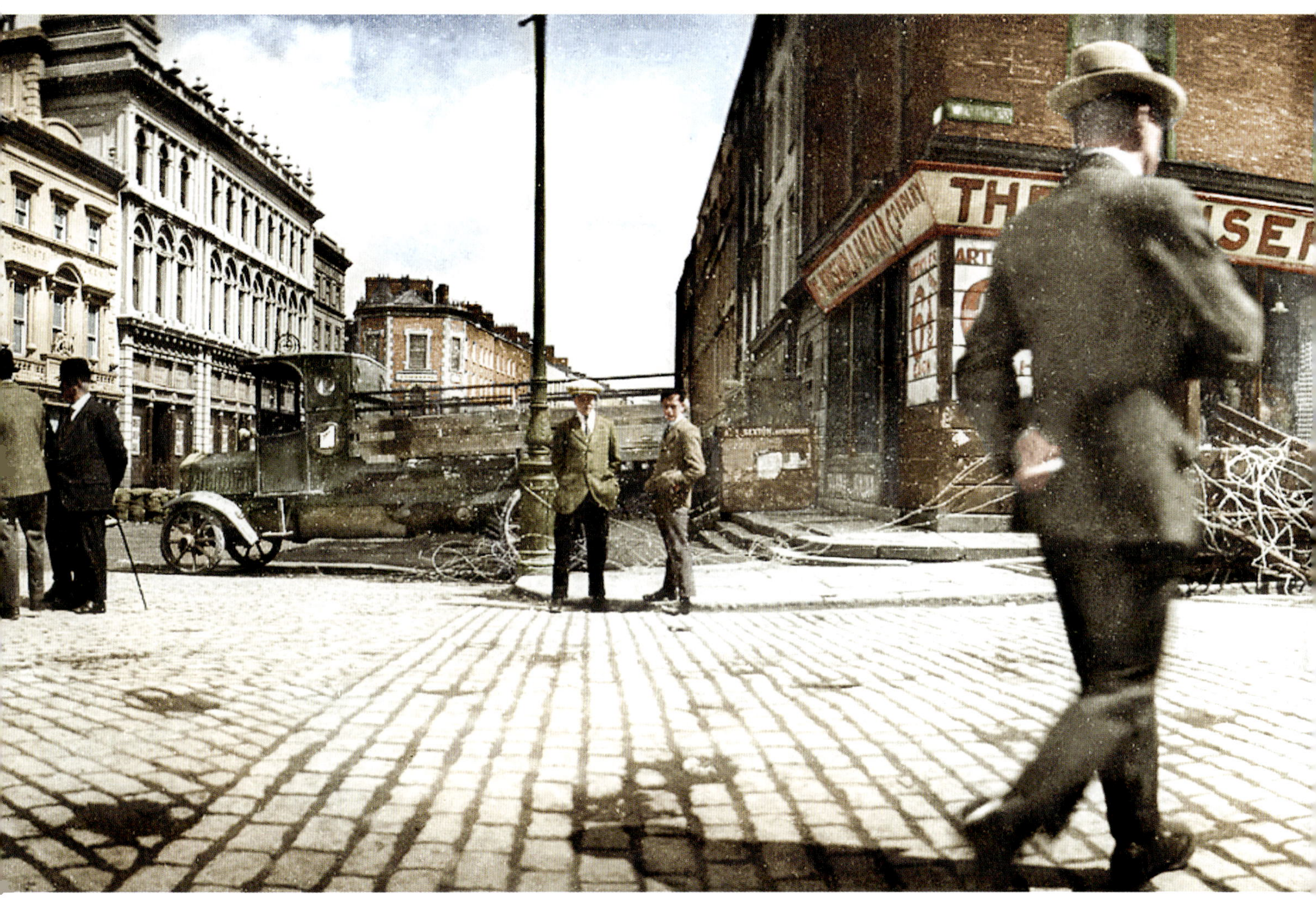

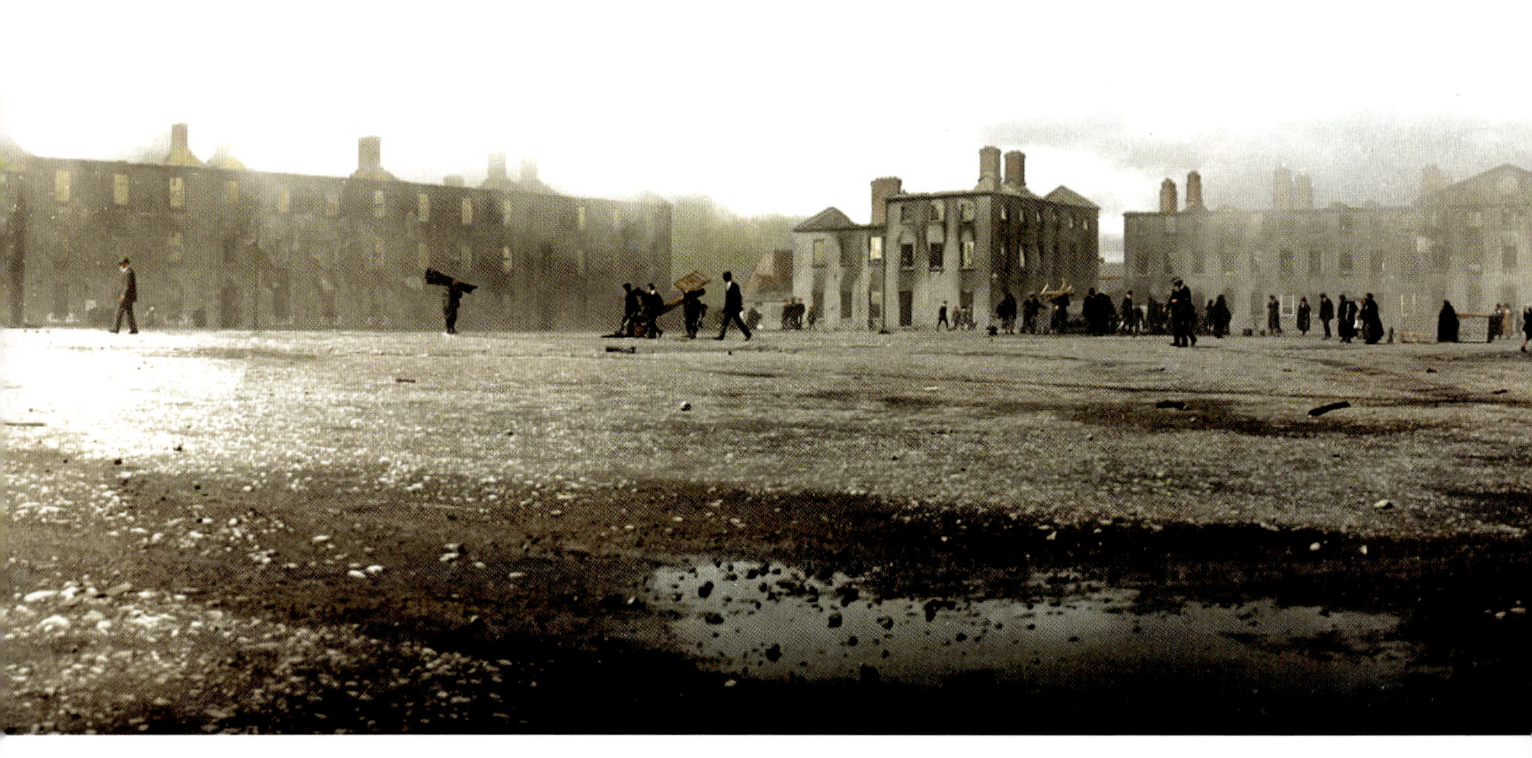

General Eoin O'Duffy fought his way into Limerick on 19 July 1922, bringing troops, an armoured car and, crucially, an 18-pounder. The artillery piece shelled Strand Barracks, which was stormed on 20 July. Next to come under assault was Castle Barracks. In face of the onslaught, Liam Lynch sent an order to the anti-Treaty forces to abandon their now-untenable positions and burn them. Republicans withdrew from the New Barracks and set it on fire. Looting by civilians can be seen in this panorama by the photographer George Imbusch.

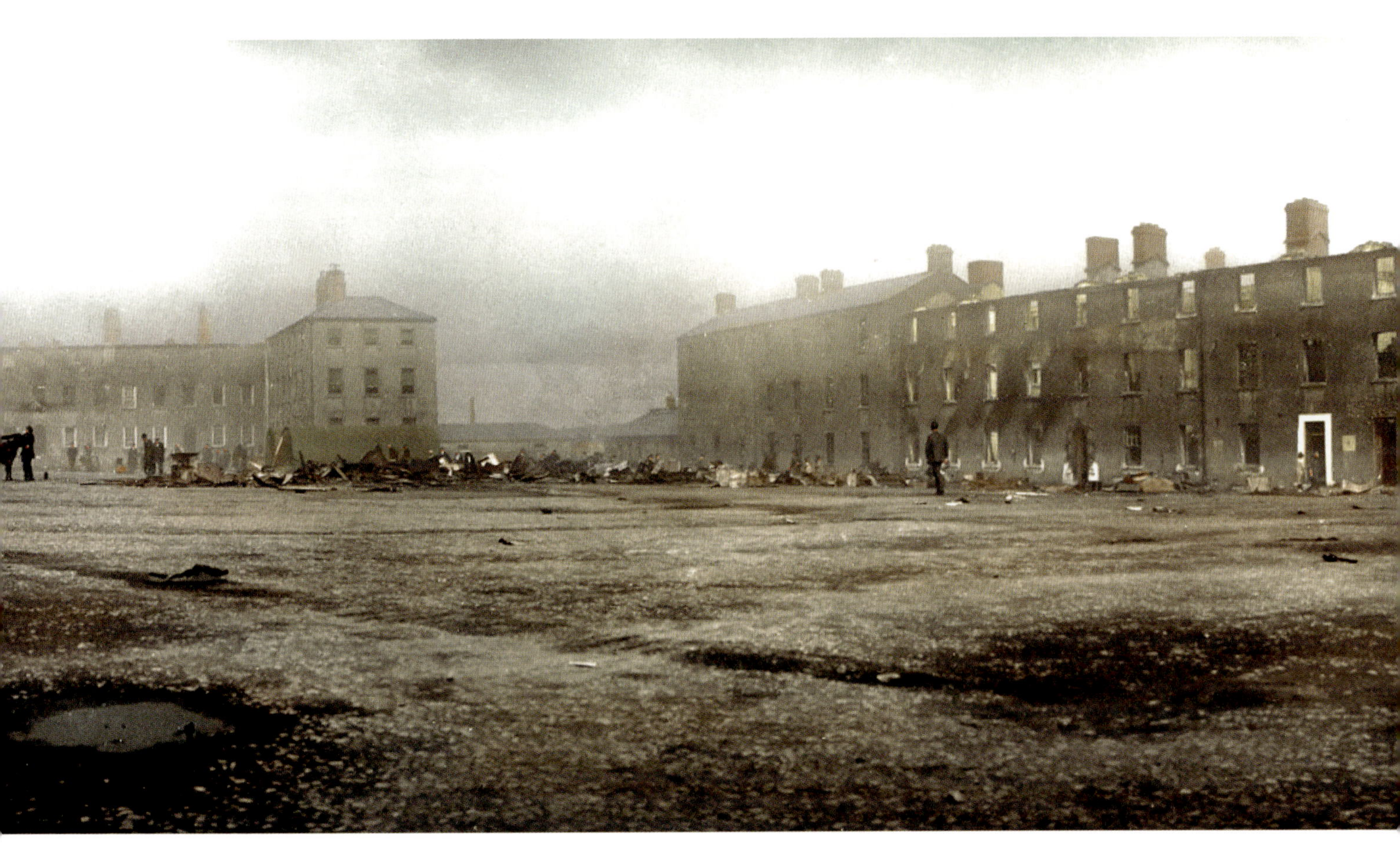

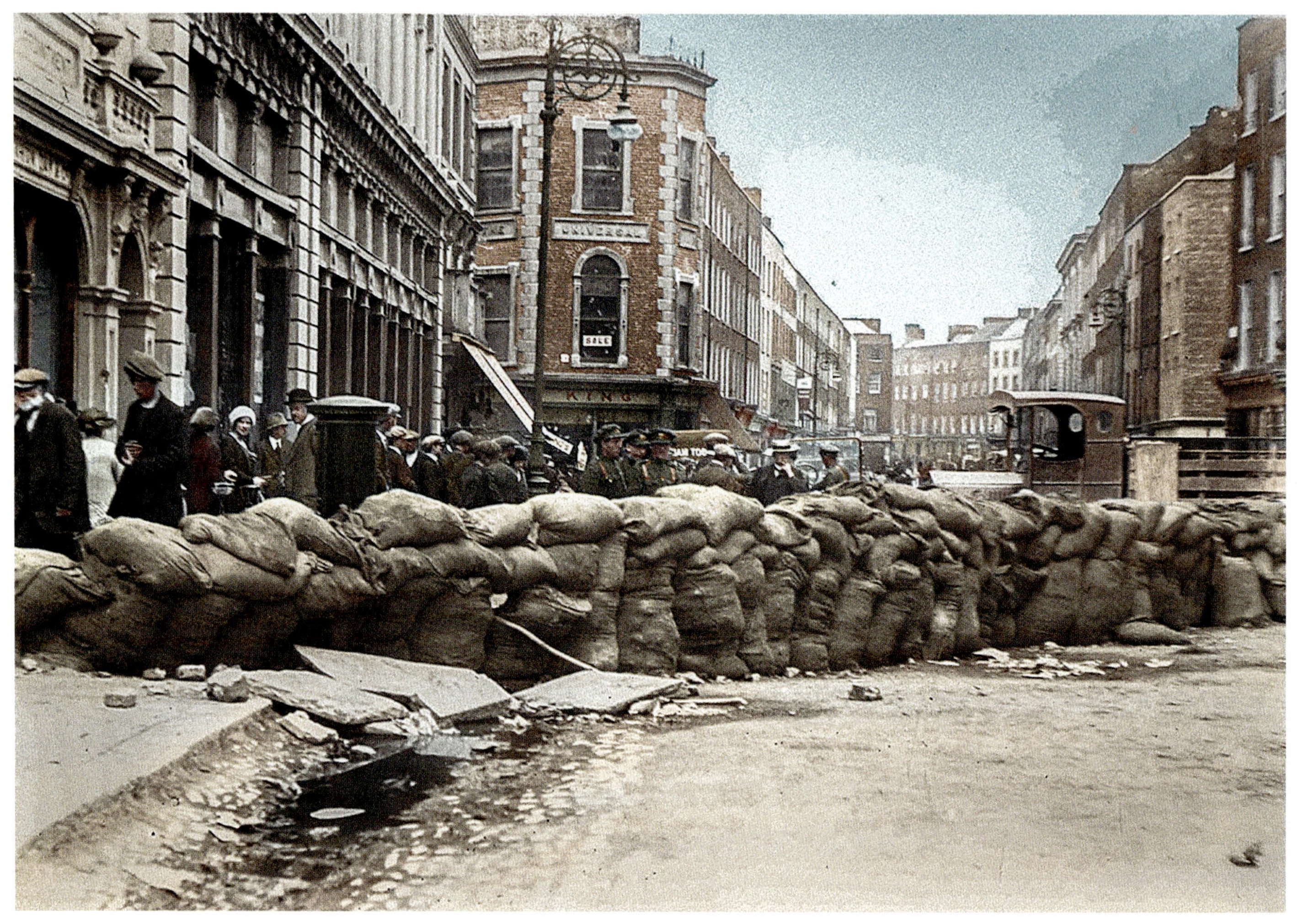

Barricades in Limerick, now under control of Provisional Government forces. The truck to the right, most likely commandeered for pro-Treaty army duties, appears again on page 129.

Right: Strand Barracks after capture. Soldiers and civilians pose for the photographer, neatly framed by the breach in the wall caused by the 18-pounder's shells.

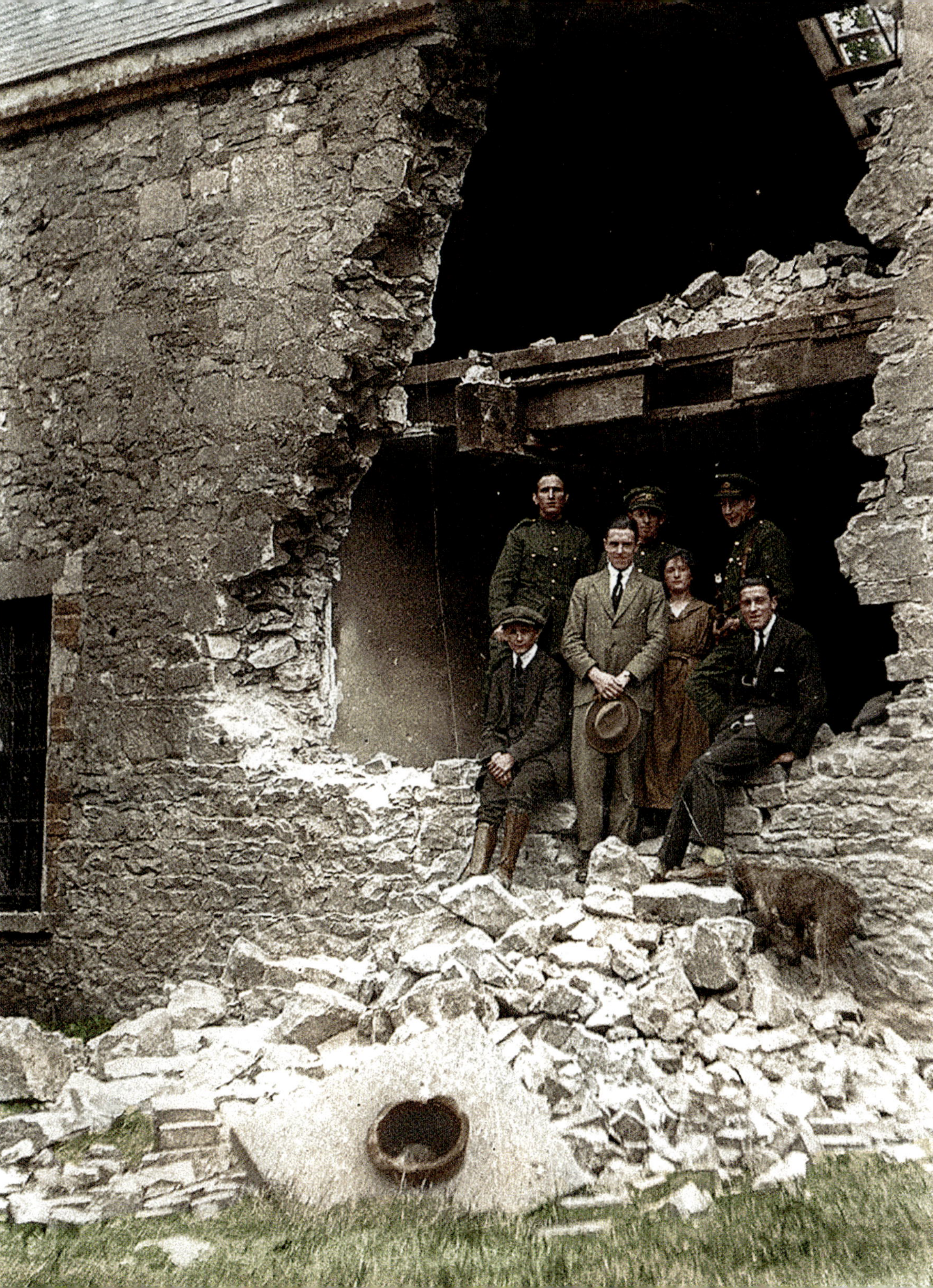

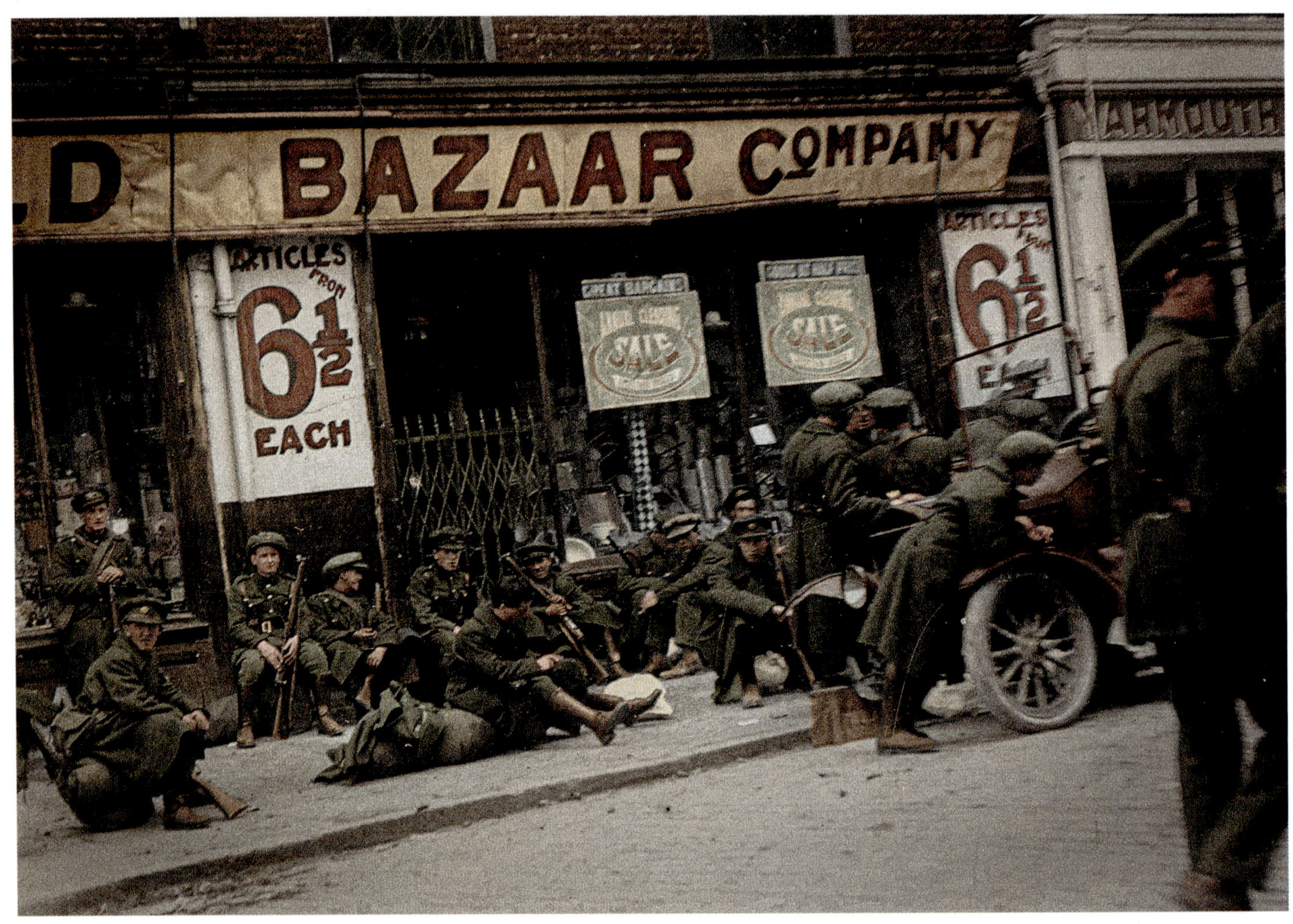

Looking war-weary, Provisional Government troops take a break outside the Household Bazaar Company, William Street, Limerick.

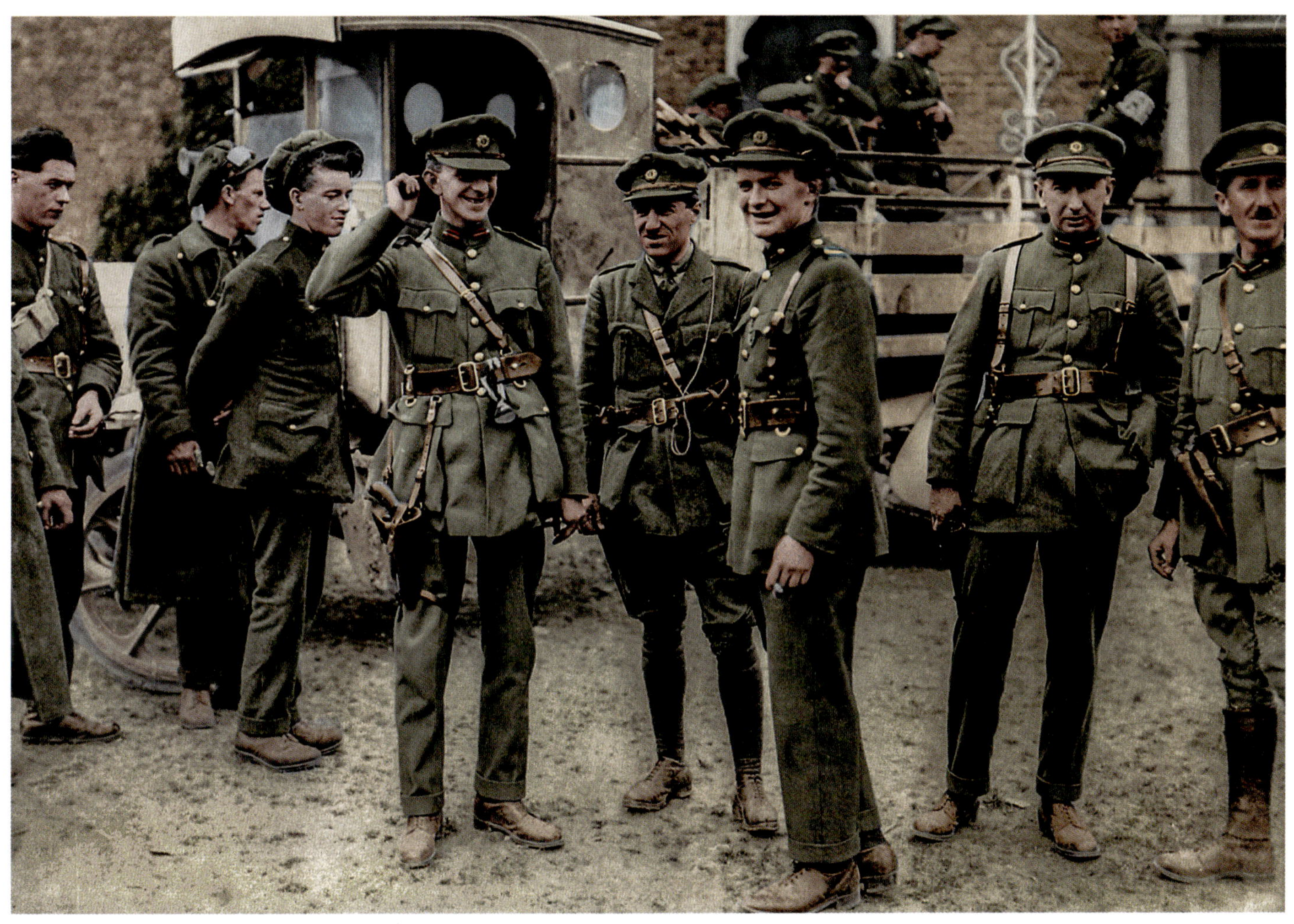

With the city under control, the mood is jovial. With a truck carrying soldiers in the background, the senior Provisional Government Army command in Limerick: General Eoin O'Duffy fourth from the left; centre, cigarette in hand, Commandant-General Michael Brennan; next right, Commandant-General Fionán Lynch, TD; extreme right, just in view, Commandant-General W.R.E. Murphy (formerly a Lieutenant-Colonel in the South Staffordshire Regiment).

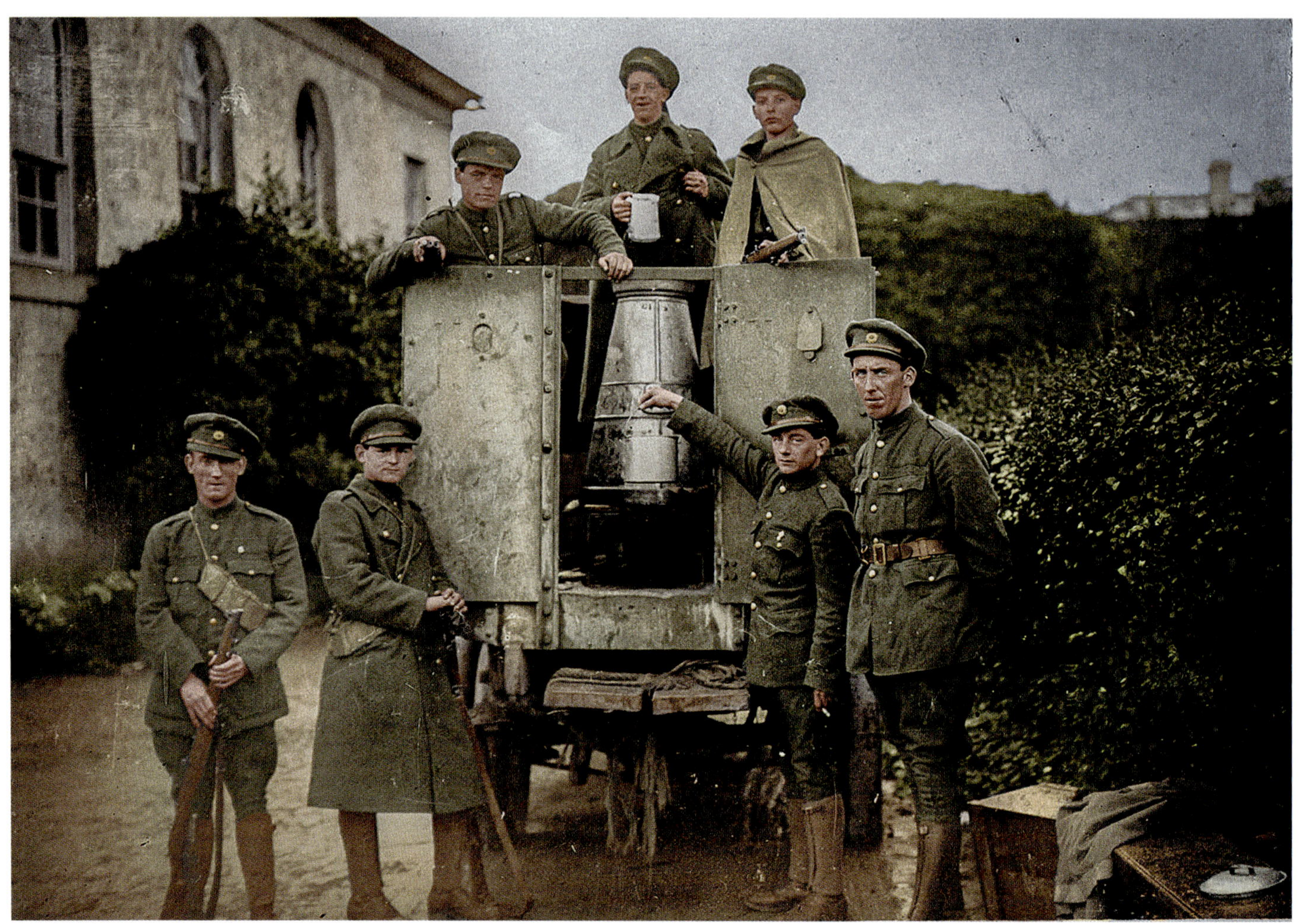

The Republicans withdrew from the city and regrouped in the Kilmallock-Bruree area, close to the border with anti-Treaty Cork. In the last week of July, after consolidating his hold on Limerick, O'Duffy sent Commandant-General W.R.E. Murphy and his troops to the area. Here the photographer portrays the troops at break time, standing around a Lancia armoured personnel carrier, with a milk churn as the centrepiece.

Right: with press photographers and Pathé cameramen embedded with the troops, there are many images to be seen of the Provisional Government Army operating on the 'South-Western Front', as the press dubbed it. Here, a motley assortment of trucks cross a barricaded bridge, carrying troops and an equally motley collection of paraphernalia.

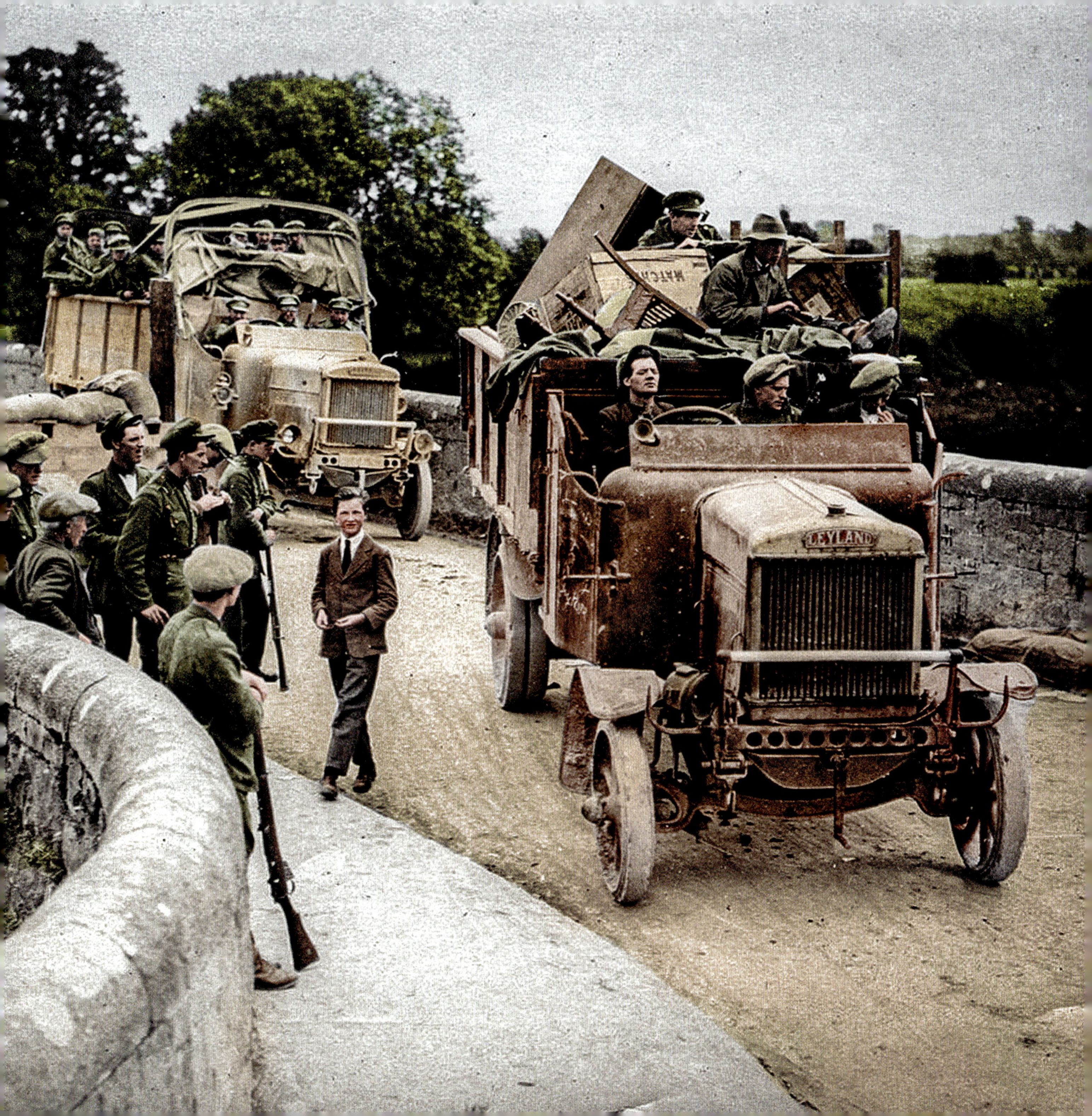

LEYLAND

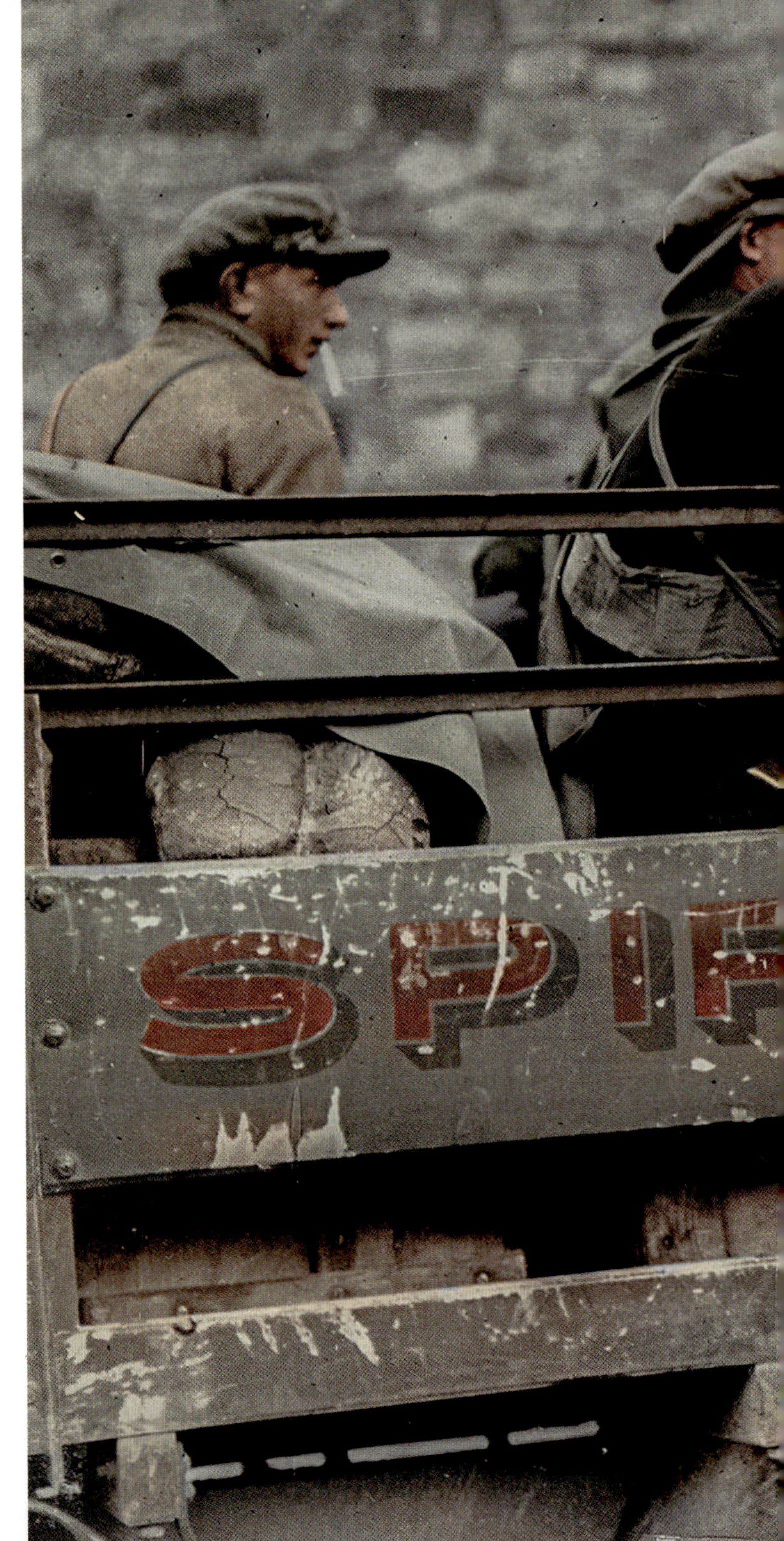

A pro-Treaty convoy passes through a village in the south-west. Improvisation was the order of the day, as seen by the two soldiers in civilian clothing on the commandeered fuel truck, which is followed by an armoured Lancia. The soldiers are offered cigarettes by a local supporter.

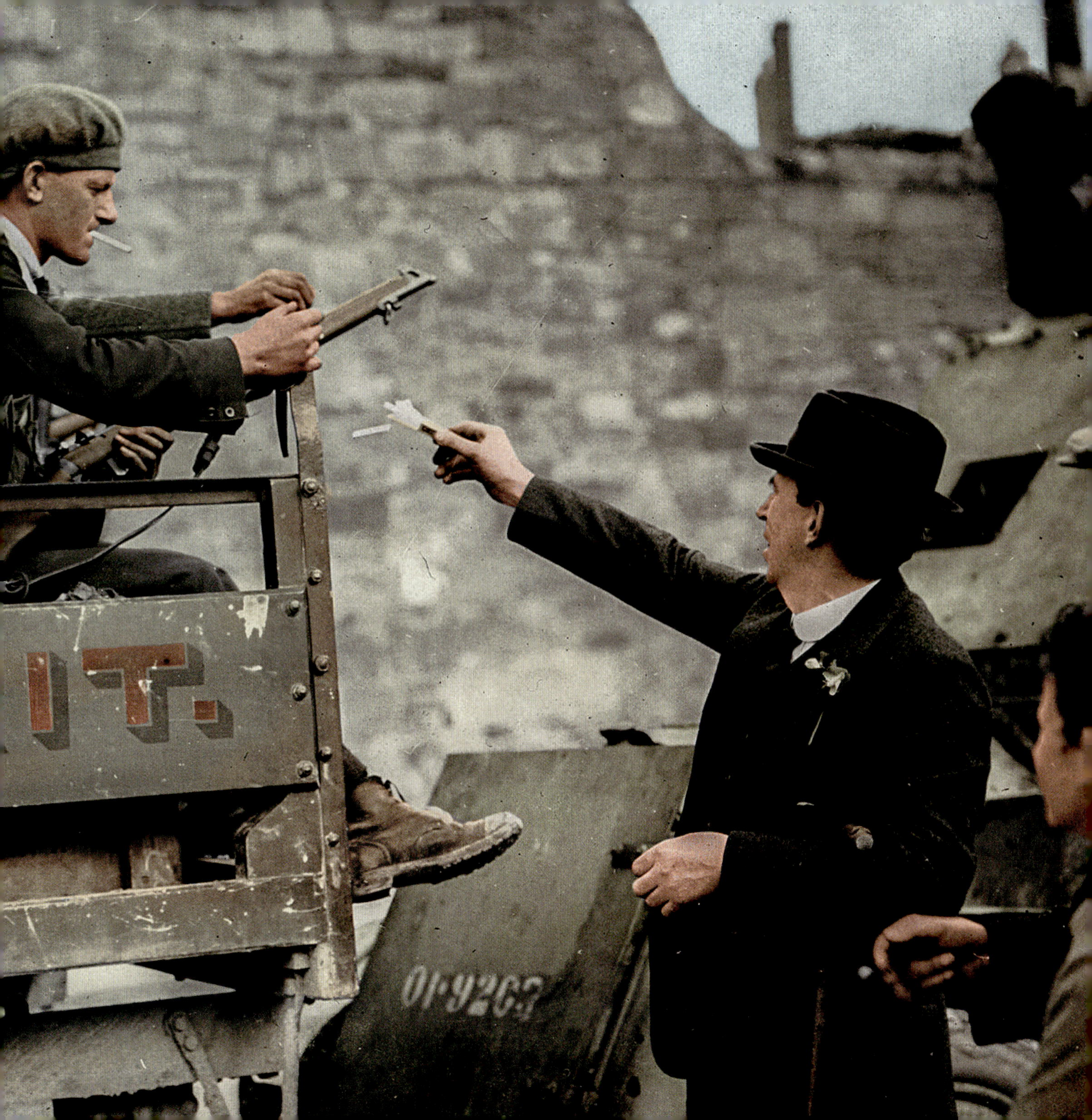
IT.
0Г92СЭ

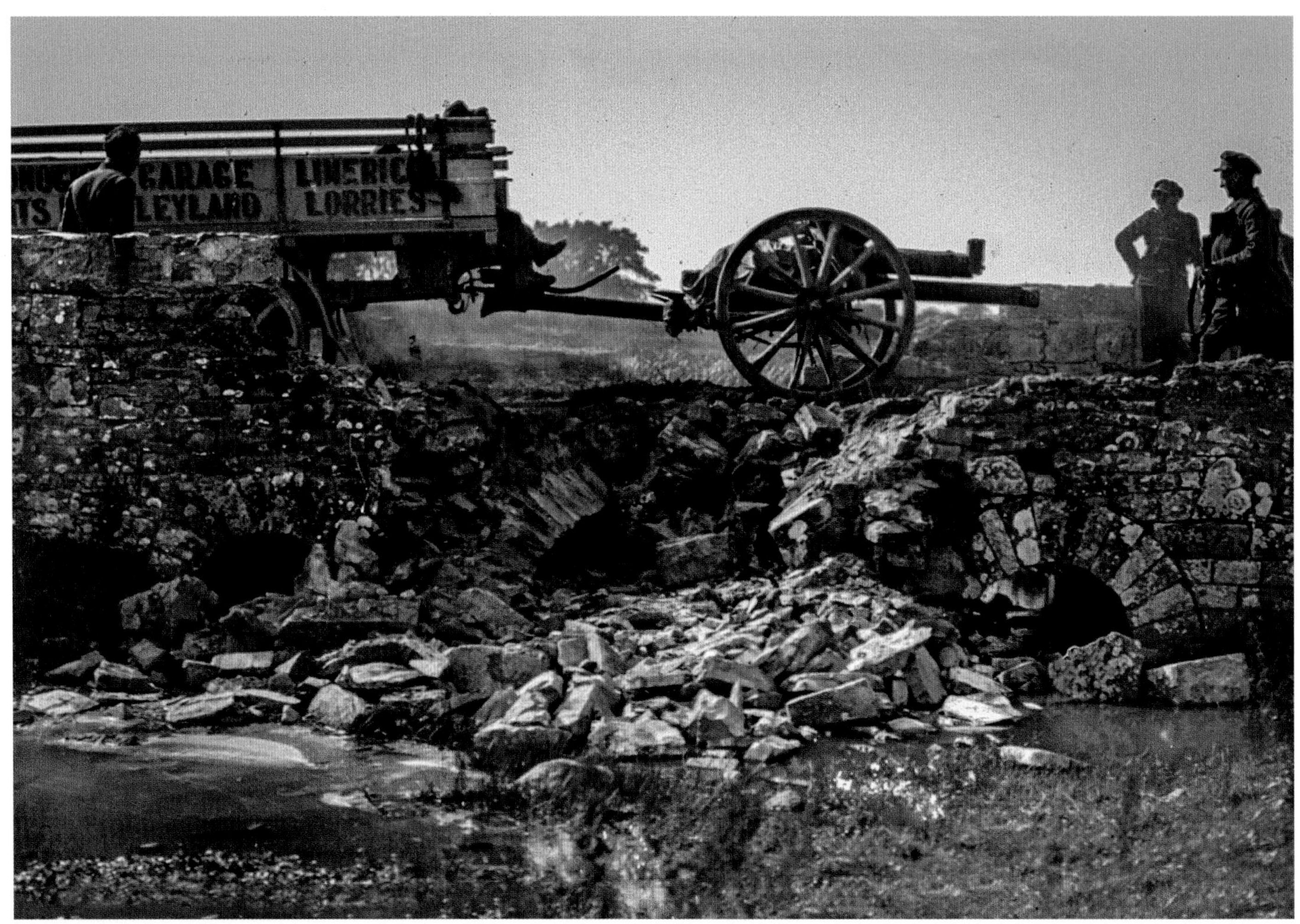

A multi-arch masonry bridge over a tributary of the River Maigue. It was blown up by Republicans hurriedly retreating to Bruree, as the Provisional Government Army advanced. The bridge is partially demolished but the arches are short span, which allowed gaps to be easily filled with rubble to allow passage of this commandeered truck from Limerick that hauls the 18-pounder.

Right: Provisional Government soldiers escort a prisoner. In the early part of the Civil War, relations between both sides were relatively relaxed, and bitterness was not widespread. All was to change over the months that followed. In the photograph, the soldier on the left grins to the camera while the young IRA prisoner looks a little abashed.

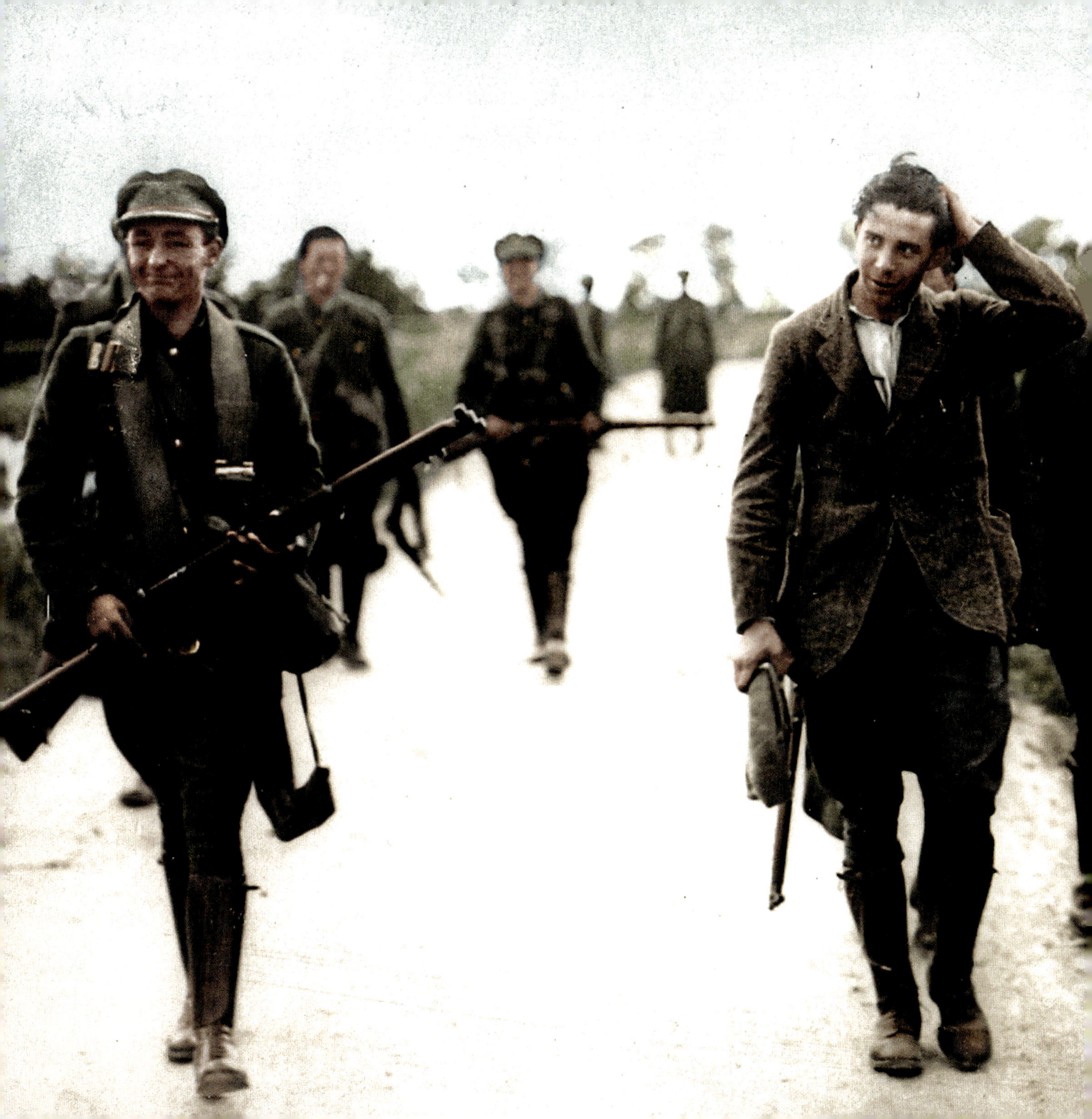

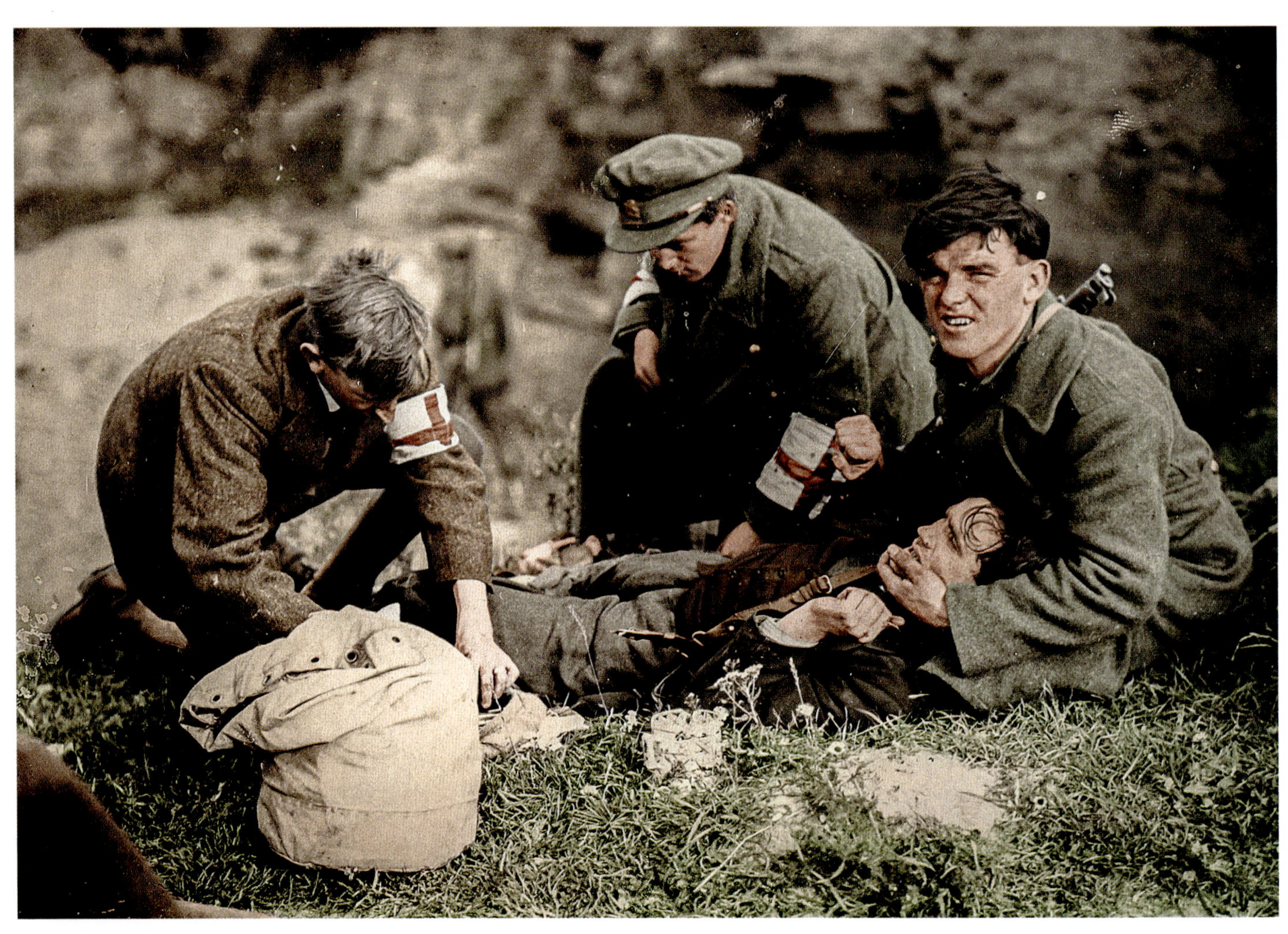

As the fighting rages across the fields of south Co. Limerick, a wounded fighter receives first aid.

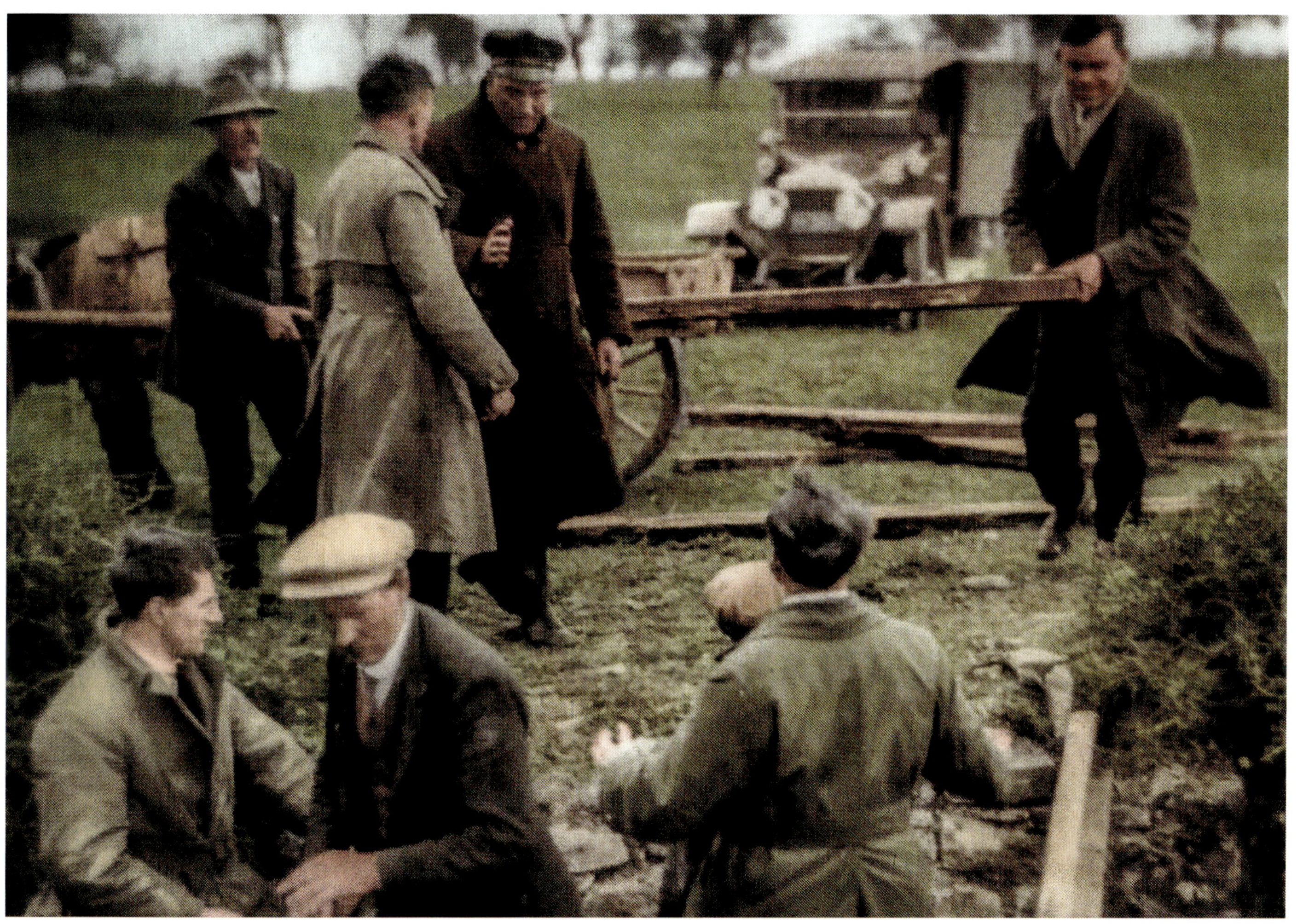

Provisional Government forces moved to encircle Kilmallock in a great arc to the north of the town. It was eventually taken on the morning of 5 August 1922. Most of the defenders had withdrawn. Men of the Kerry IRA had earlier left to face the pro-Treaty forces that landed at Fenit on 2 August. Here is a rare photograph of the anti-Treaty IRA during their retreat from Kilmallock. Dan Breen, top right, carries a plank in an effort to bridge a trench, with Seán Moylan (IRA Director of Operations) lower left-hand corner.

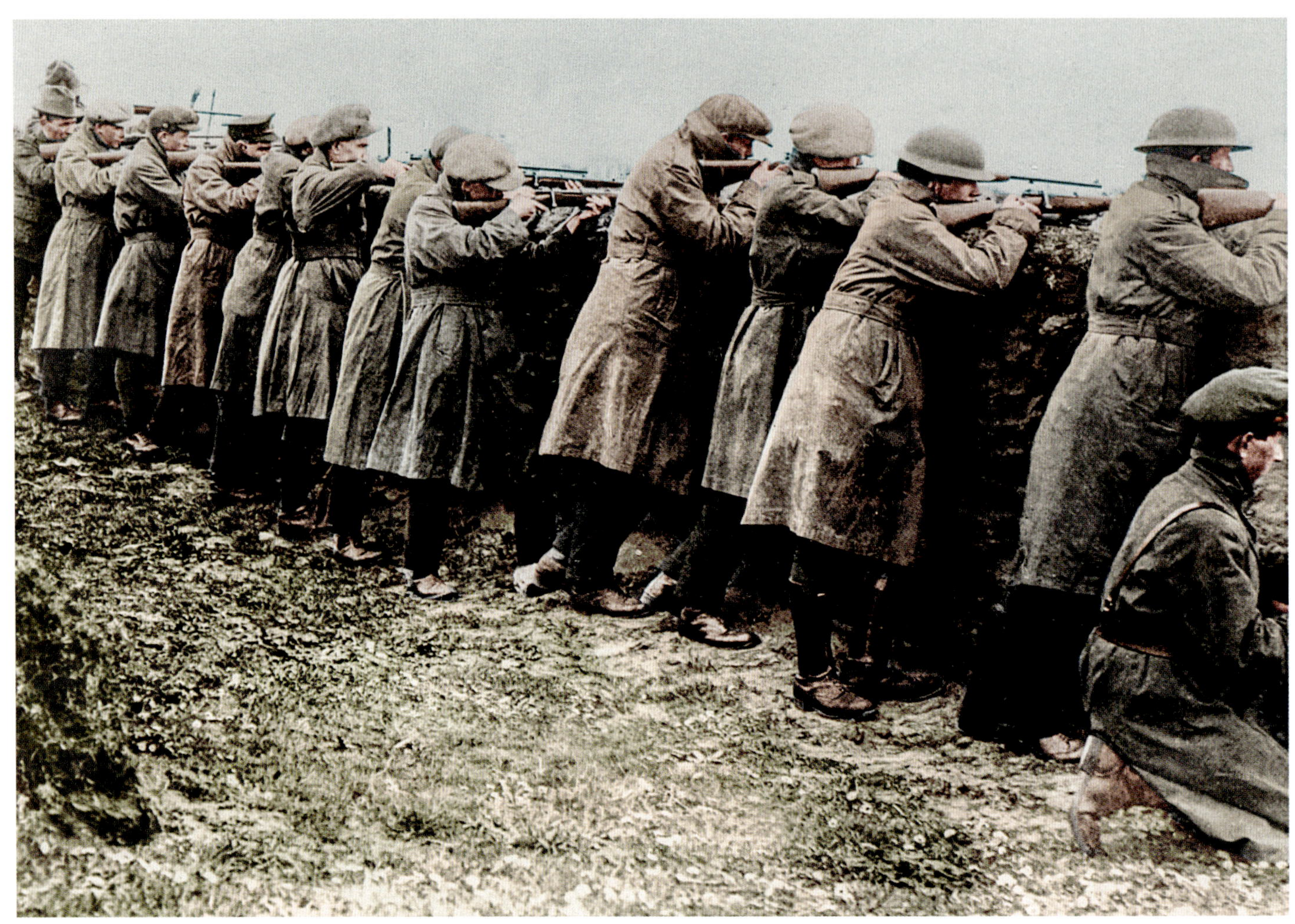

One source has attributed this posed group wearing an assorted collection of helmets and caps to the anti-Treaty IRA. Curiously, the man kneeling on the right has the characteristic soft-topped cap and is wearing the Sam Brown belt of a Provisional Government Army officer. The caption of the *Irish Independent* of 14 July 1922 describes it: 'A war scene in Co. Sligo. Riflemen entrenched behind a wall taking aim'. Practically all of the IRA in Sligo, Mayo and west Galway had taken the anti-Treaty side.

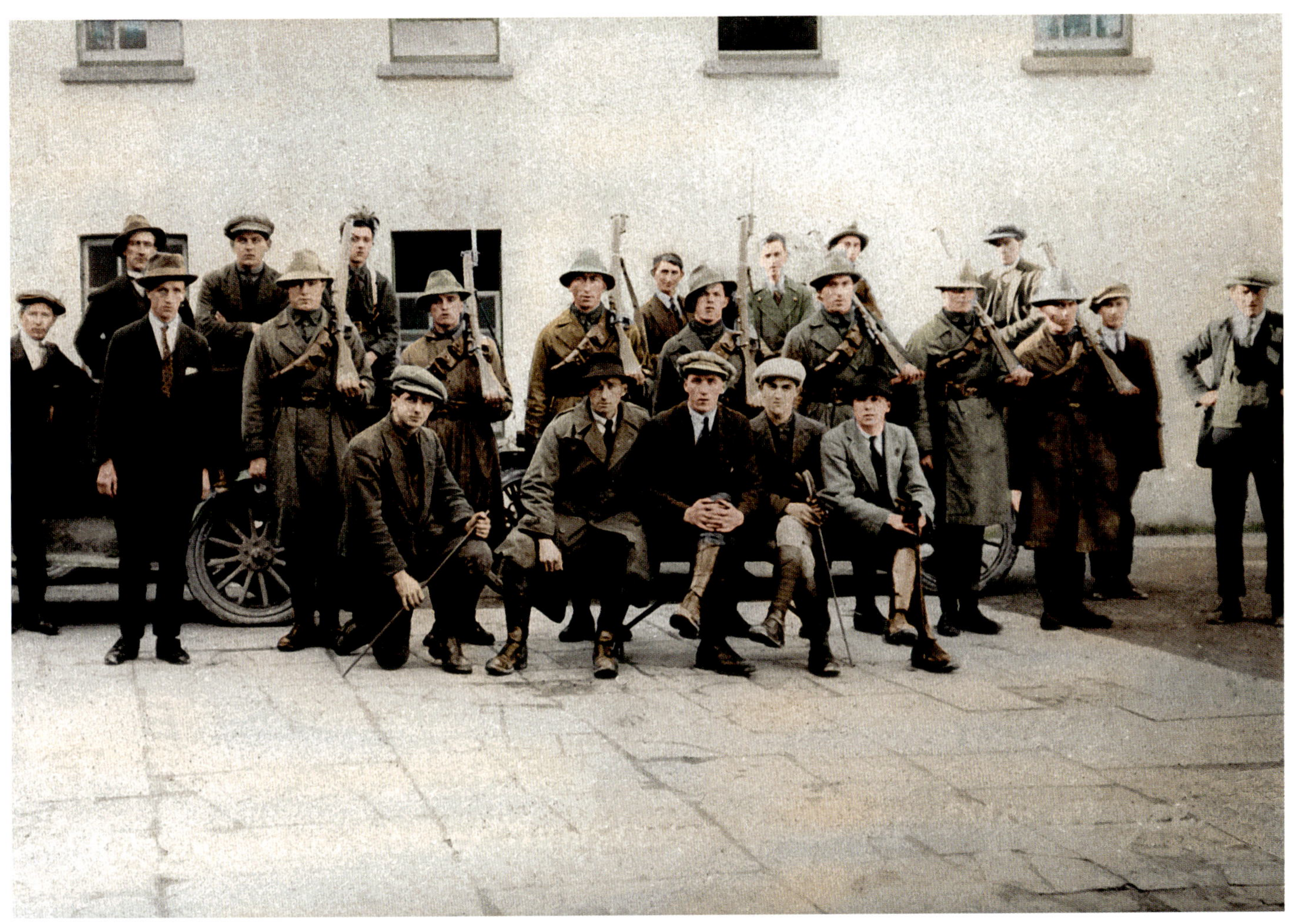

The west Waterford IRA at Dungarvan Barracks, which had been taken over on 4 March 1922. With the taking of Waterford City in July 1922, the Waterford IRA were gradually ejected from the strongholds that they had established here in Dungarvan as well as Ardmore and Kilmacthomas – once more they took to the hills as they had done during the War of Independence.

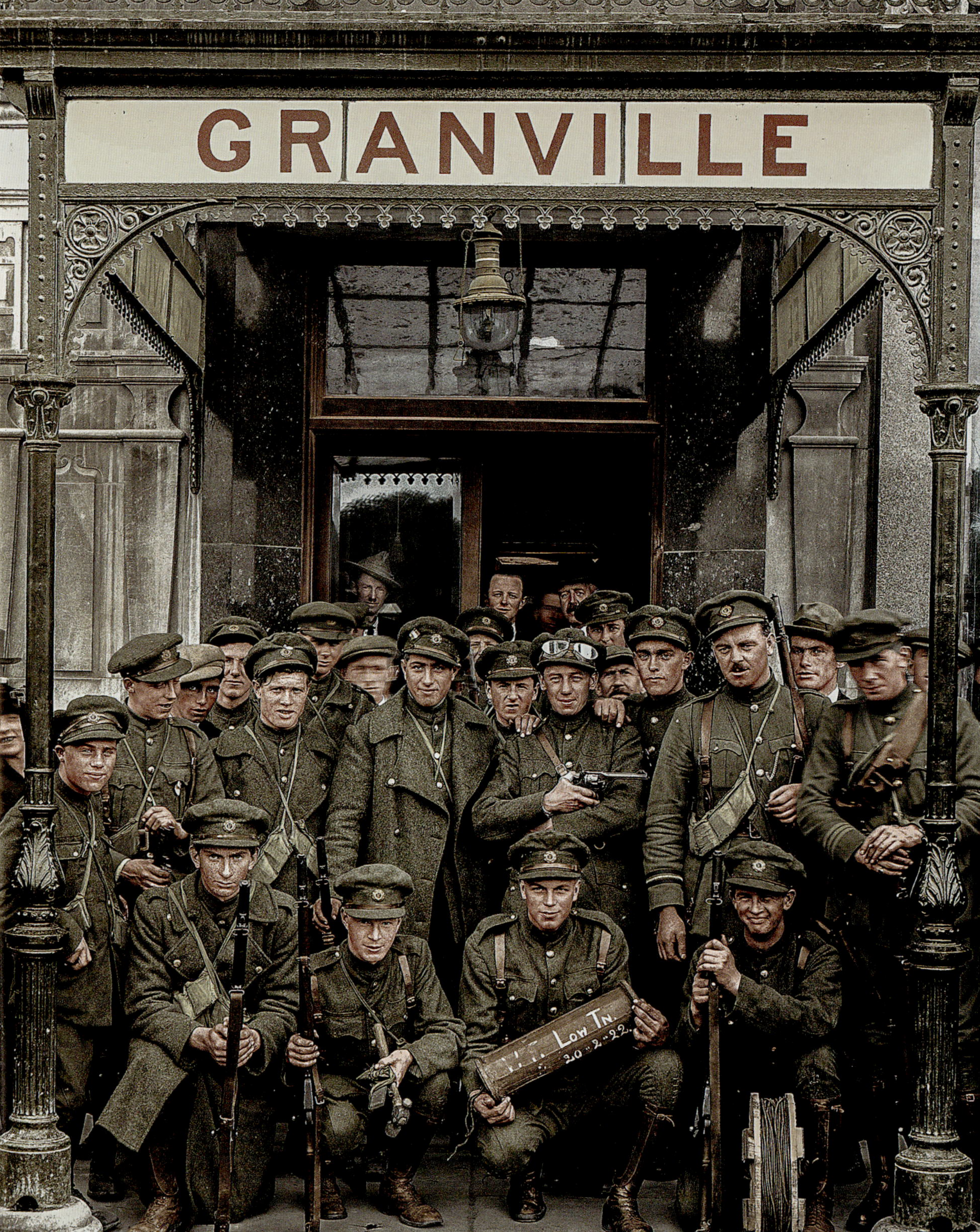
GRANVILLE
Low Tn.
30·2·22

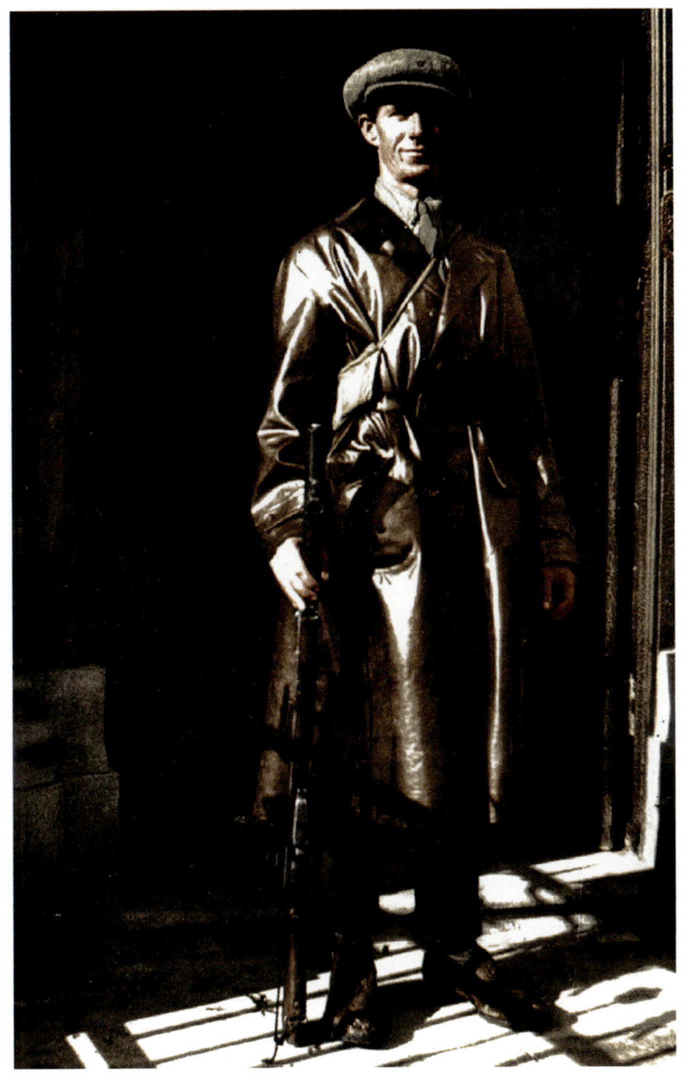

This statuesque anti-Treaty Volunteer stands guard at Carrick-on-Suir in July. Following the taking of Waterford City, pro-Treaty forces captured the town on 2 August. Clonmel was seized seven days later.

Left: on 19 July 1922, Provisional Government troops fought to take Waterford. After seizing the Granville Hotel on the Quays, they discovered a mine. Here they proudly display it in the hotel portico.

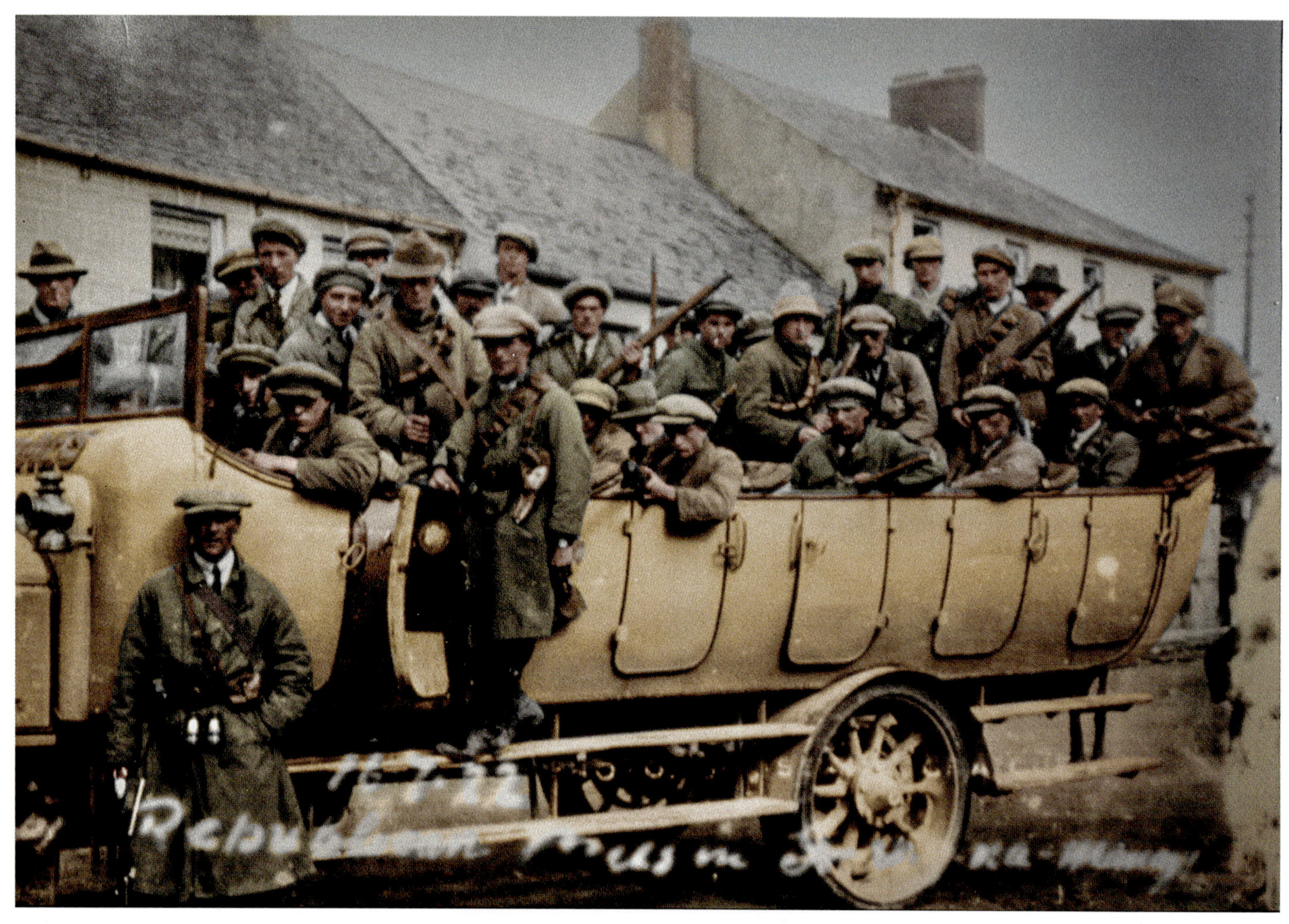

A charabanc-load of the Tipperary IRA poses at Graignamanagh on 11 July 1922.

Right: on horseback in Co. Tipperary, Commandant Pádraig O'Connor (veteran of many actions in Dublin during the War of Independence, and who had led a charge into the Four Courts at the end of June). At the end of July 1922, pro-Treaty forces advanced into the Republican heartland of South Tipperary. O'Connor skilfully led the successful action to capture Tipperary town.

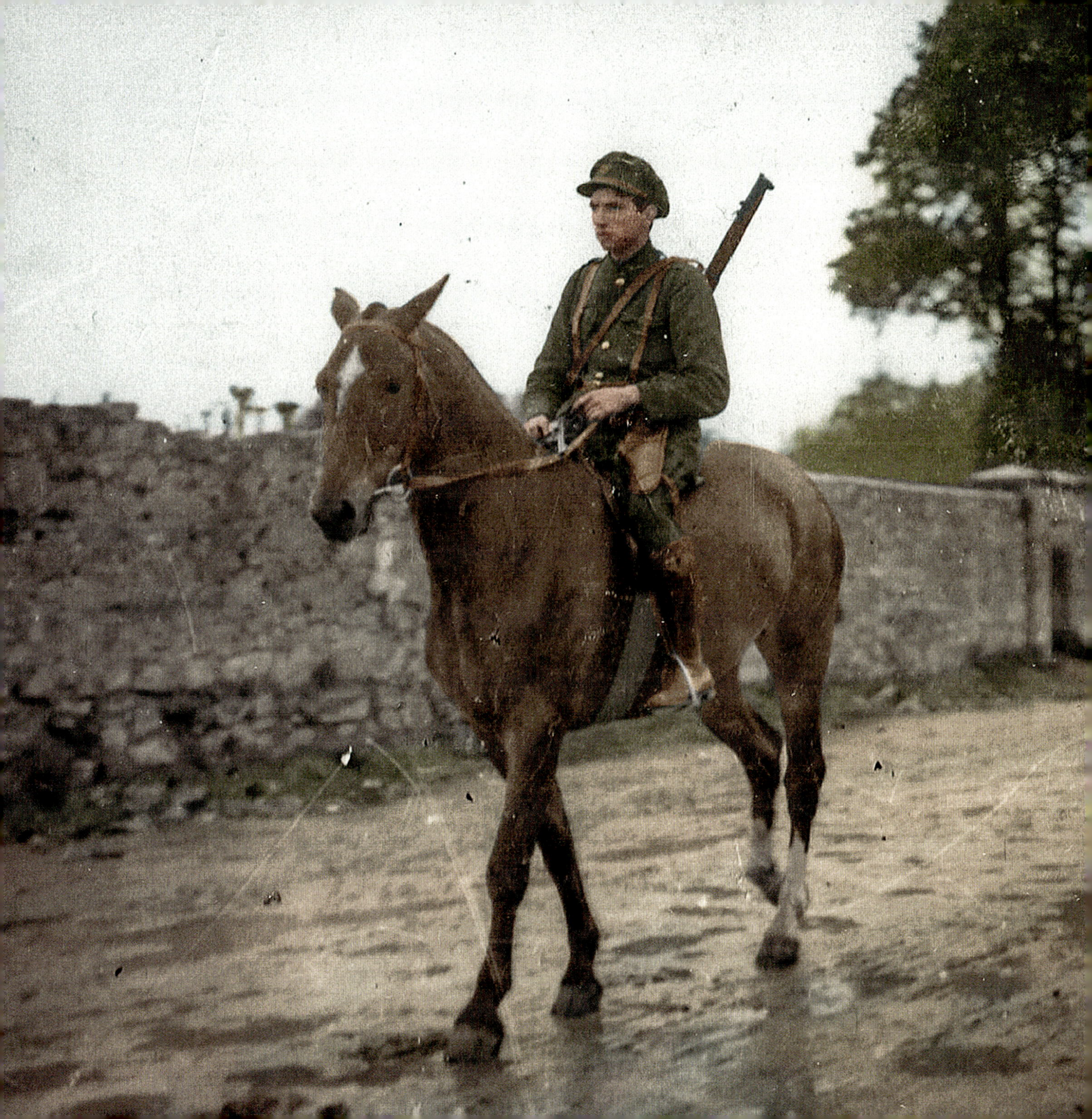

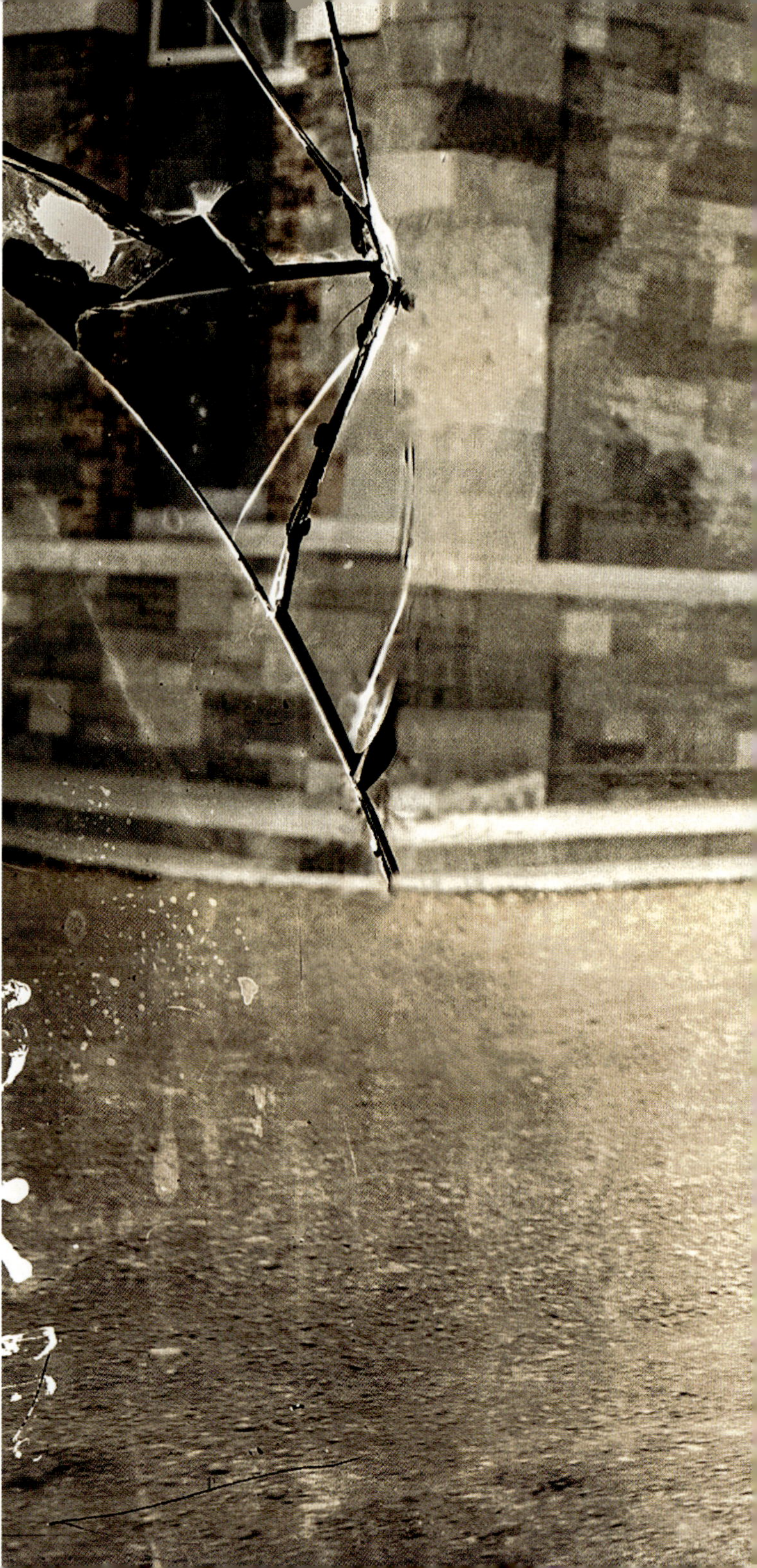

With much of Munster and the west under Republican control, the generals of the Provisional Government Army decided in July 1922 to mount a series of amphibious landings on the southern and western coasts. The first landing was made on 24 July at Westport, Co. Mayo. This successful expedition was followed when *The Lady Wicklow* landed troops at Fenit, Co. Kerry, on 2 August. Following heavy fighting, Tralee was taken later that day.

In this print from a glass-plate negative, Commander-in-Chief General Michael Collins is seen striding through Portobello Barracks, Dublin (now Army GHQ and where he had his quarters) on 8 August 1922. He had just attended a Requiem Mass for soldiers killed in fighting after the landing at Fenit. Behind him is 14-year-old Alphonsus Culliton, adopted as the mascot of the army following his rescue by troops from a skirmish in Co. Wexford.

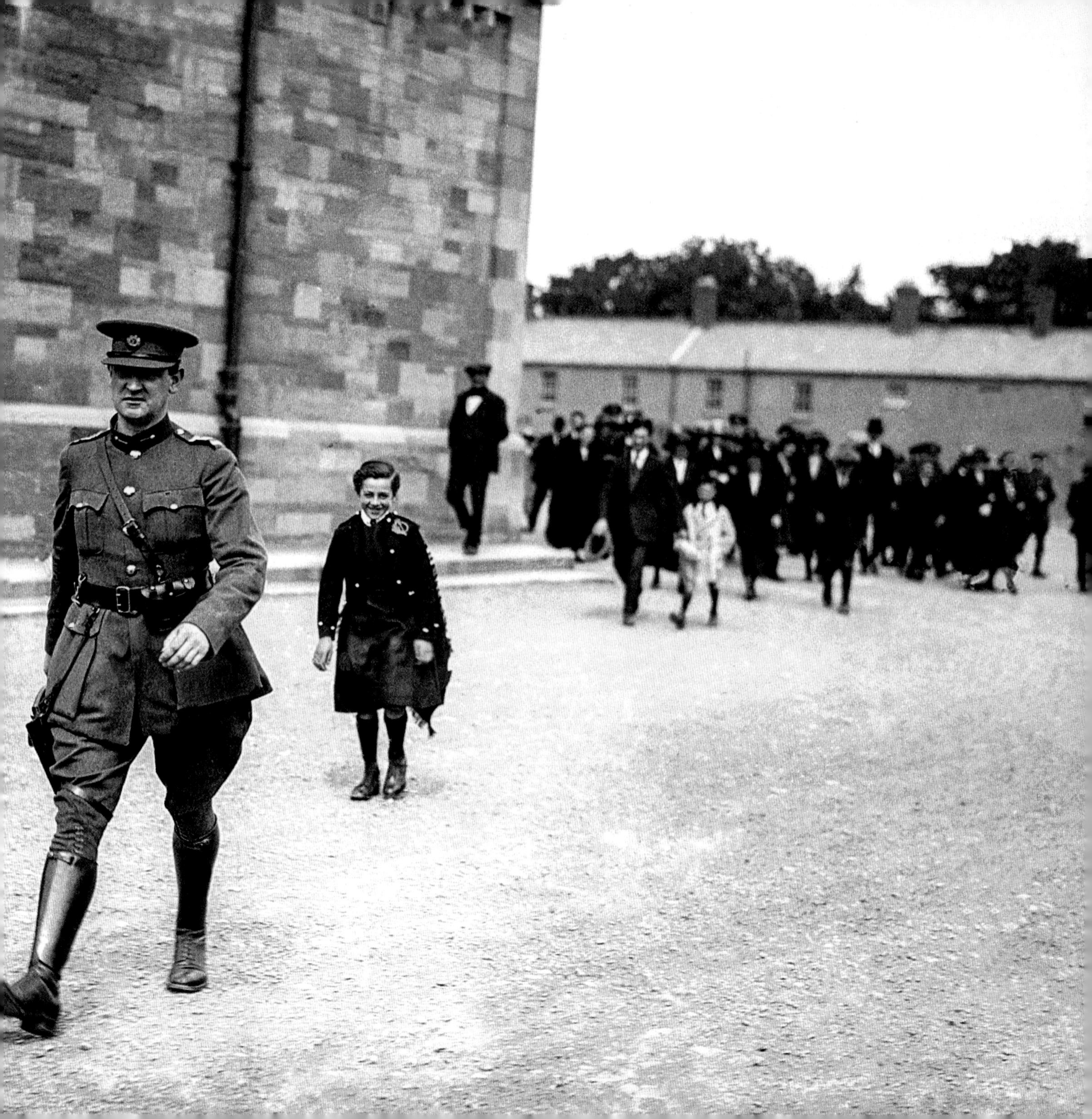

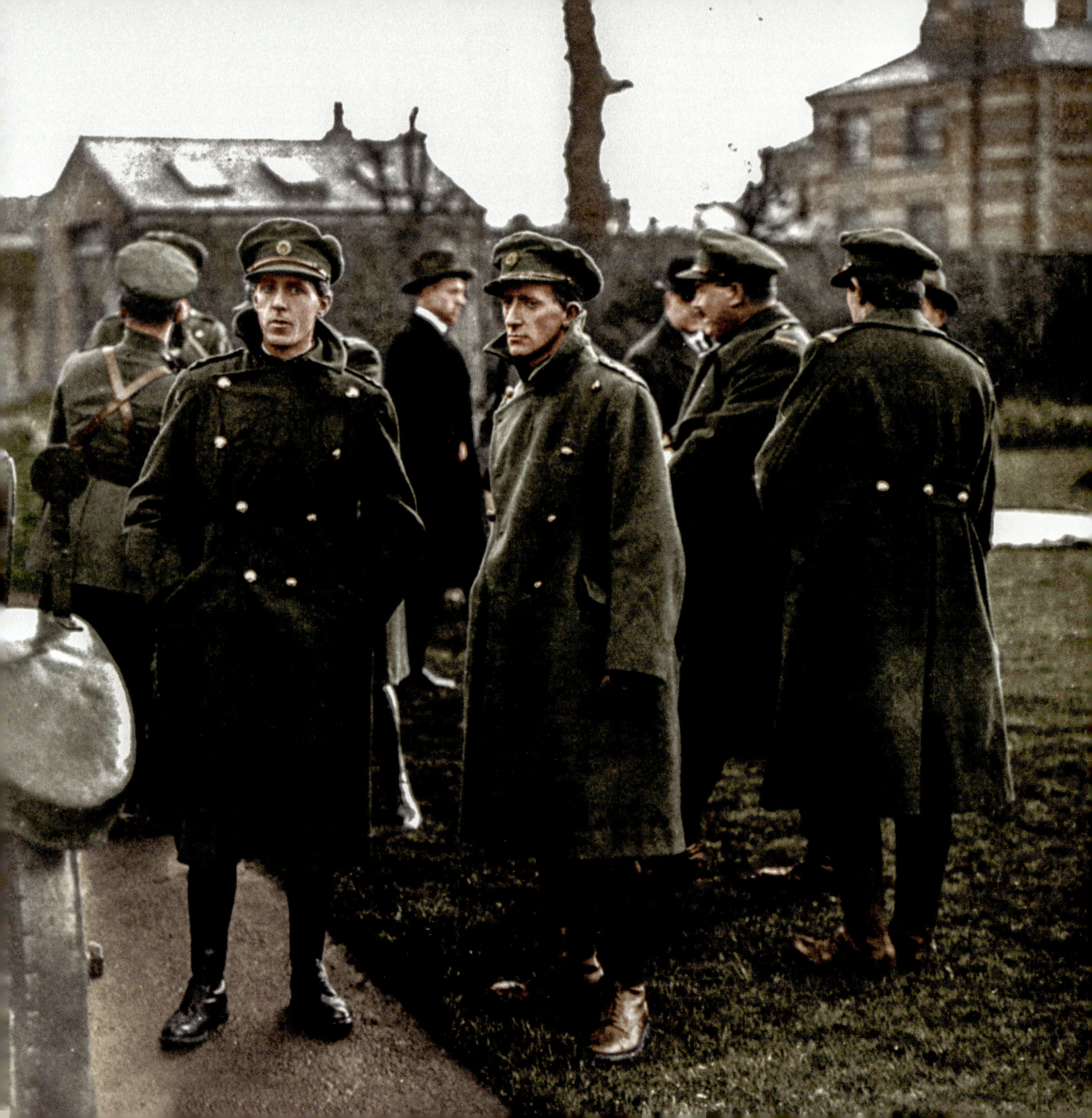

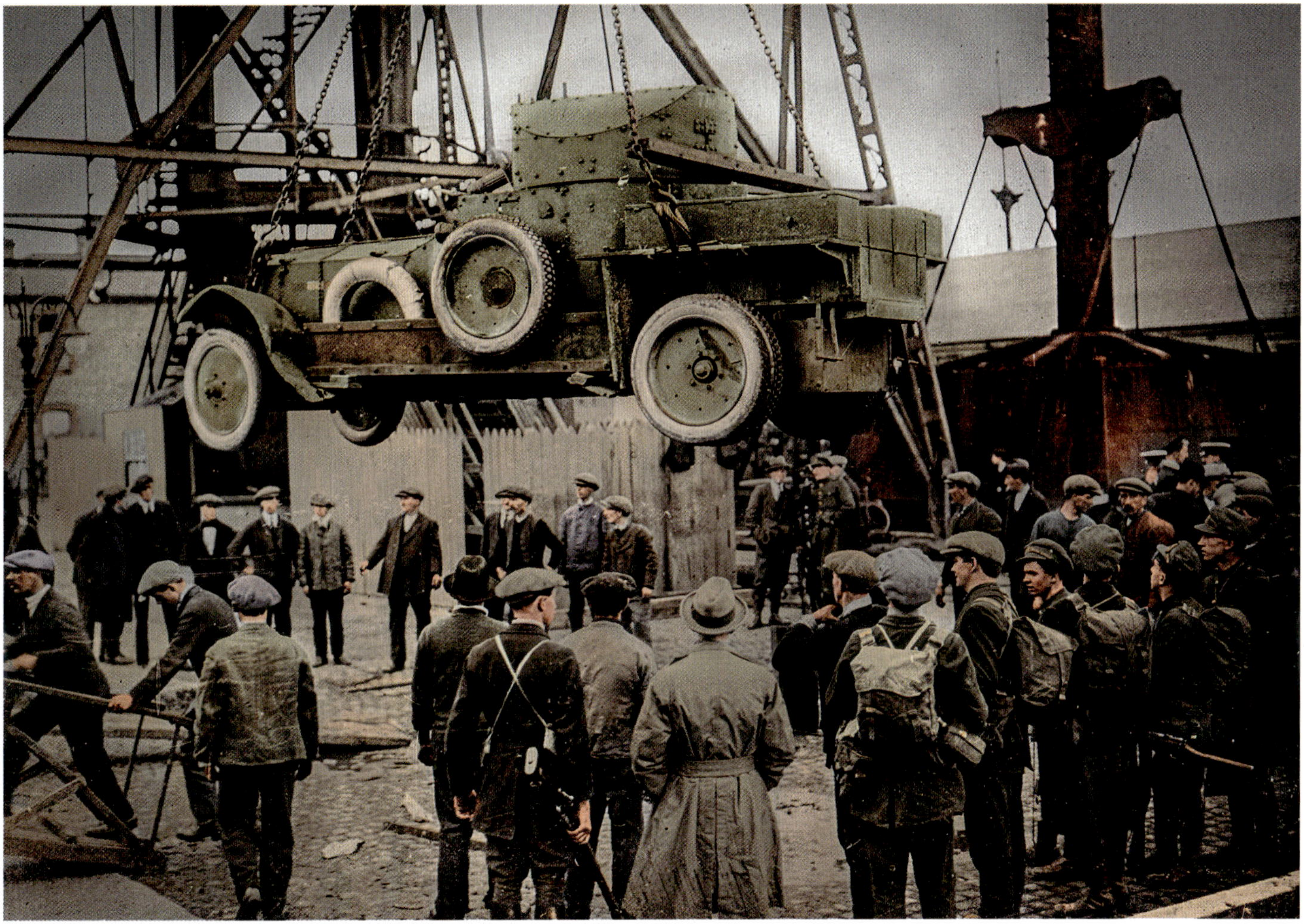

Dublin's North Wall on 7 August 1922. A Rolls-Royce armoured car is being loaded onto the L&NWR steamer *Arvonia*. With a length of 100m there was ample cargo space. Later that day, it and other cross-channel steamers sailed for Co. Cork.

Left: the same day at Portobello Barracks. Tension is evident on the faces of the officers (centre, Generals MacMahon and Mulcahy), as they finalise the arrangements for an amphibious expedition to Cork, a strategy full of risk. With land communications blocked, it was decided to take the county by sea. The successful expeditions to Westport and Fenit had given them the confidence to plan for a large expeditionary force to make a landing in Cork Harbour, with simultaneous landings at Youghal and Union Hall.

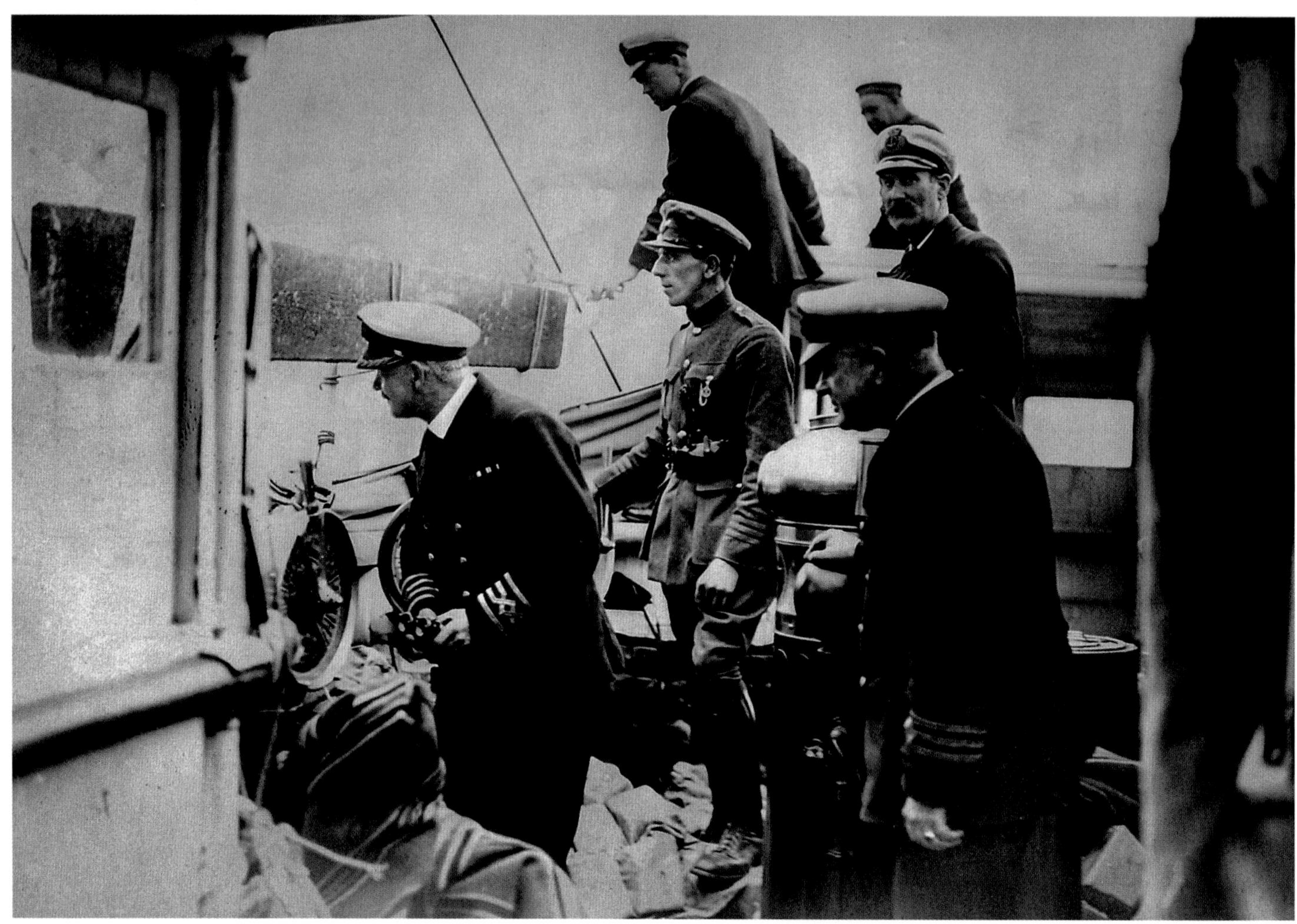

Wariness is the watchword. With a Provisional Government officer in their midst, Captain Roberts (left) and his officers keep a close watch as a baulk of timber swings by during the loading operations. The crew of the *Arvonia* were mostly Welshmen. Understandably, they were not enthusiastic about having to take part in the risky expedition to Cork.

Right: on the *Arvonia*, en route to Cork. Soldiers sit on the *Manager* (named in honour of Tom Ennis who had led the assault on the Custom House in 1921, nicknamed the 'Manager' and now on board the *Arvonia*) Rolls-Royce armoured car. Behind is a Lancia armoured personnel carrier with lettering indicating that it is based at the GHQ Depot at Portobello Barracks.

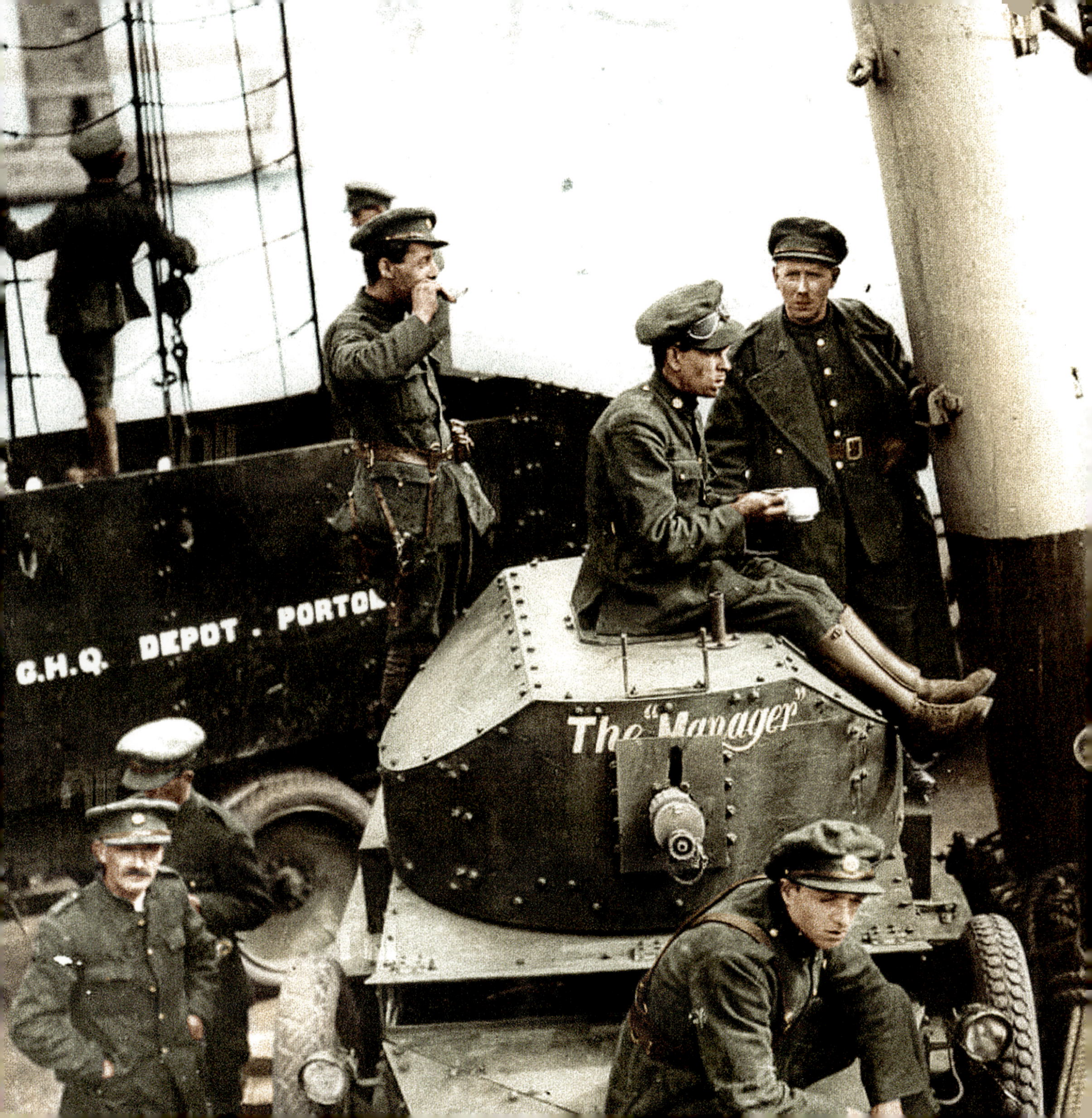

G.H.Q. DEPOT · PORTO
The "Manager"

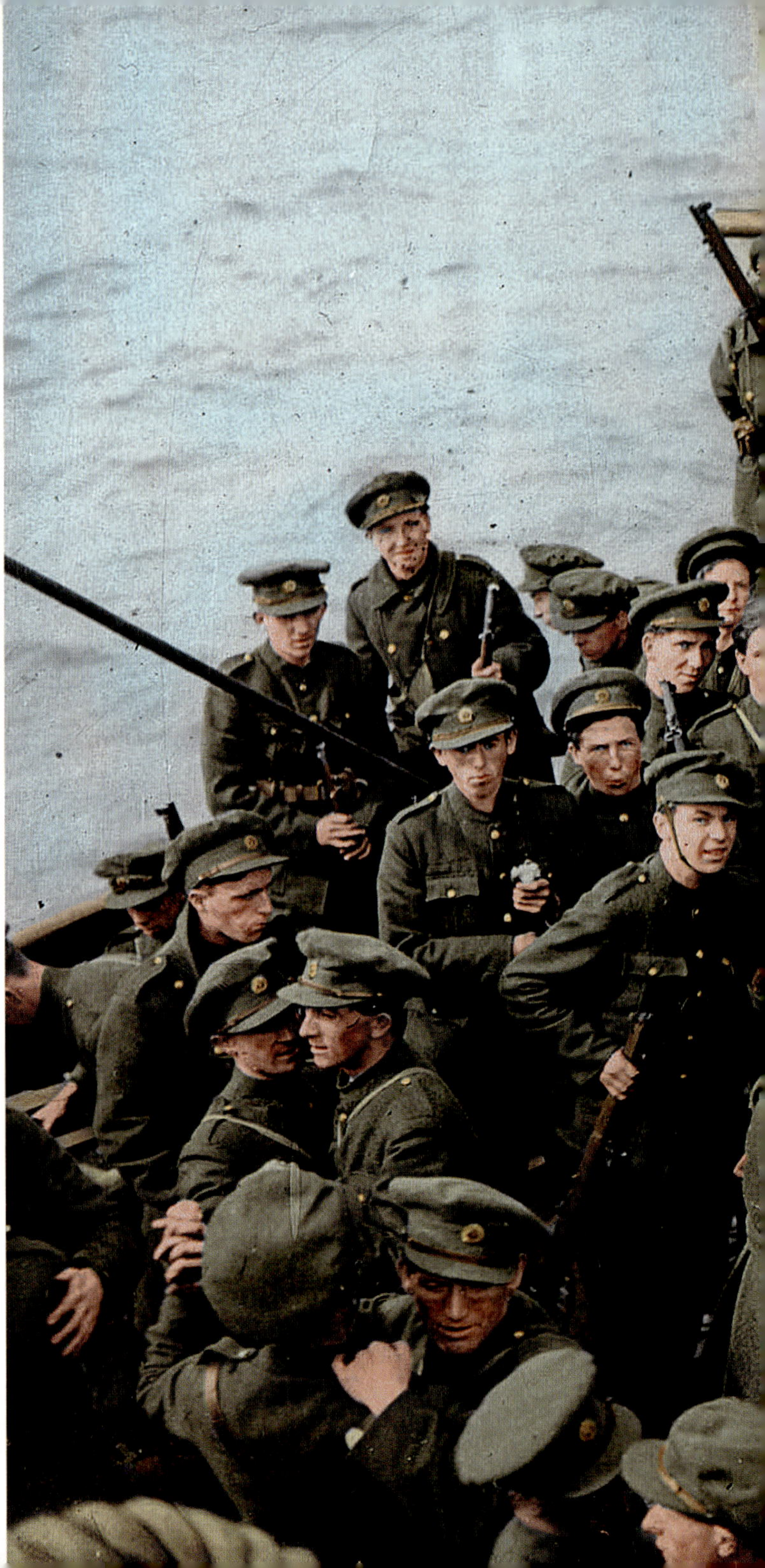

A poignant scene – soldiers dance on the deck of the
Arvonia, to the tune of a melodeon-player, who is perched
on the 18-pounder (just visible on the gun shield is the
chalked legend 'Four Courts', indicating that the gun
was a veteran of the siege at the end of June). To present-
day eyes, the scene of men dancing together may seem
incongruous. However, in a way, it is a touching indication
of the innocence of these (mainly) young men, soldiers
about to face the dangers of war. It was a way to pass the
time on the long voyage south.

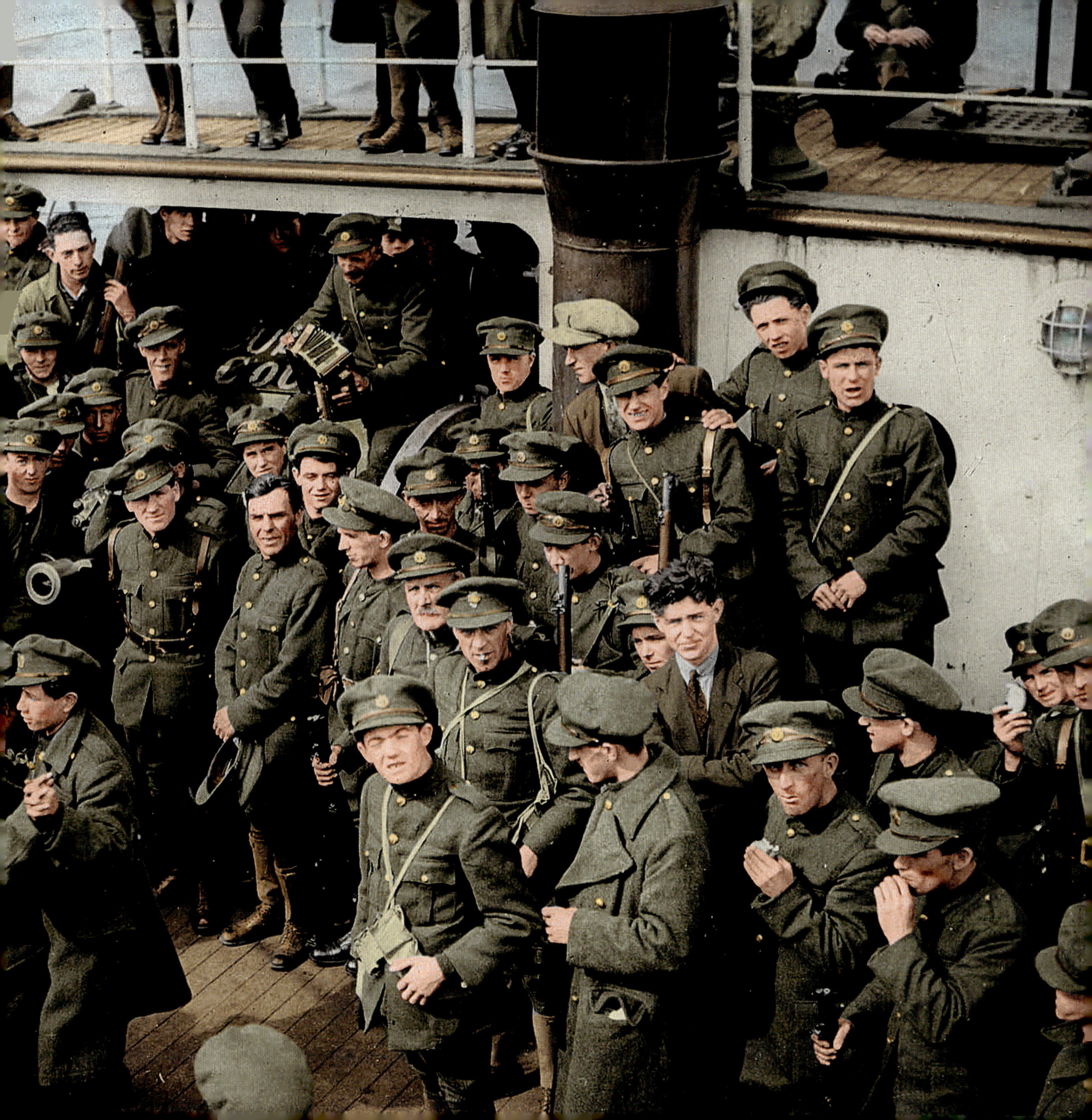

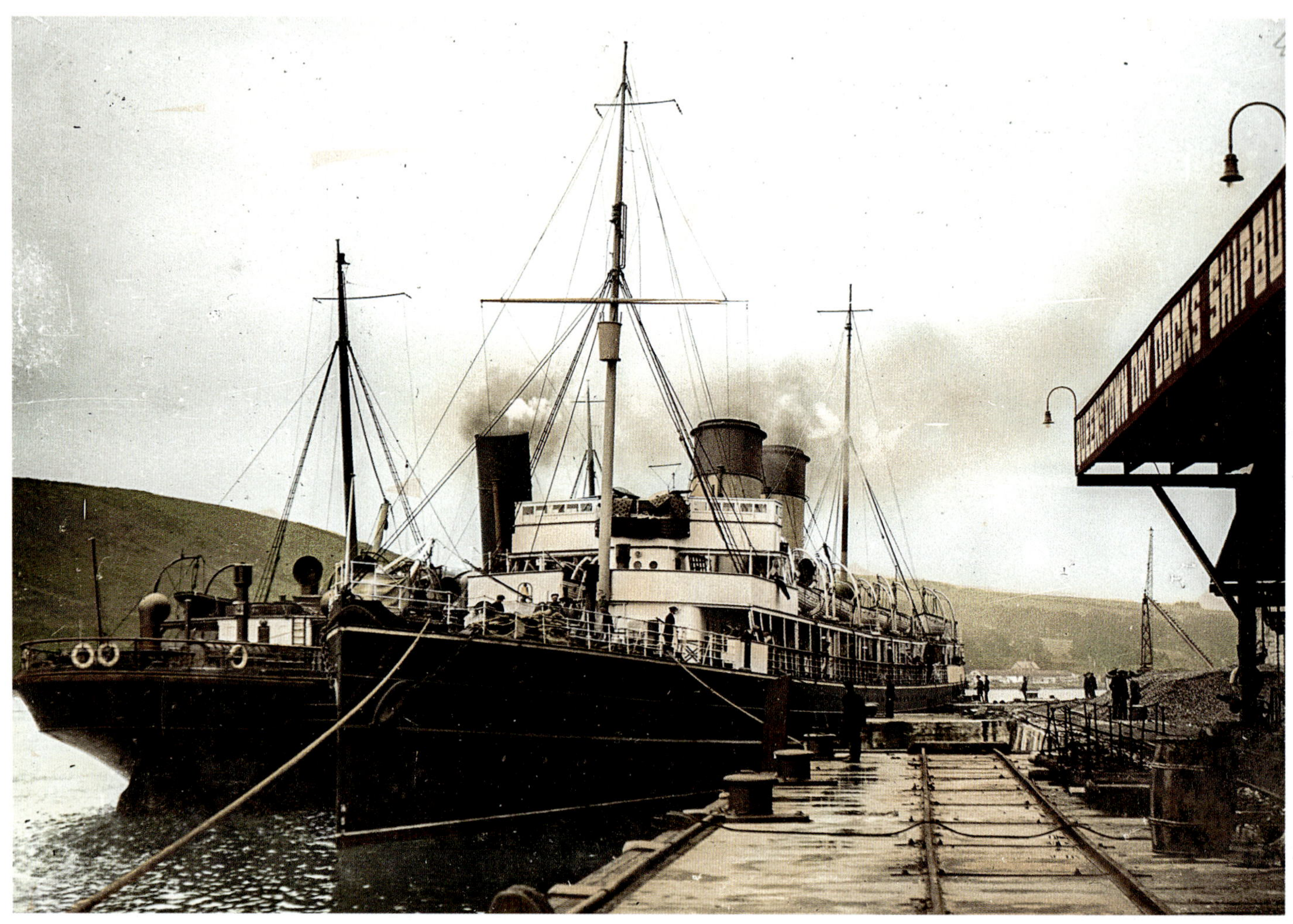

Unable to proceed upriver for fear of mines, the *Arvonia* docked at the Queenstown Dry Docks pier at Passage West at 2.20 a.m. on 8 August. On the left is the steamer *Lady Wicklow*, also commandeered for the expedition.

Right: as the ship's winches were of insufficient lifting capacity, the unloading of the armoured cars and Lancias proved complicated at Passage West. It was necessary to wait until the tide brought the ship to a suitable height. Here, using timber planks and enlisting the aid of the small dock steam crane, the soldiers eventually managed to push the Peerless armoured car (weighing seven tonnes) from the *Arvonia* and manoeuvre it onto the dock.

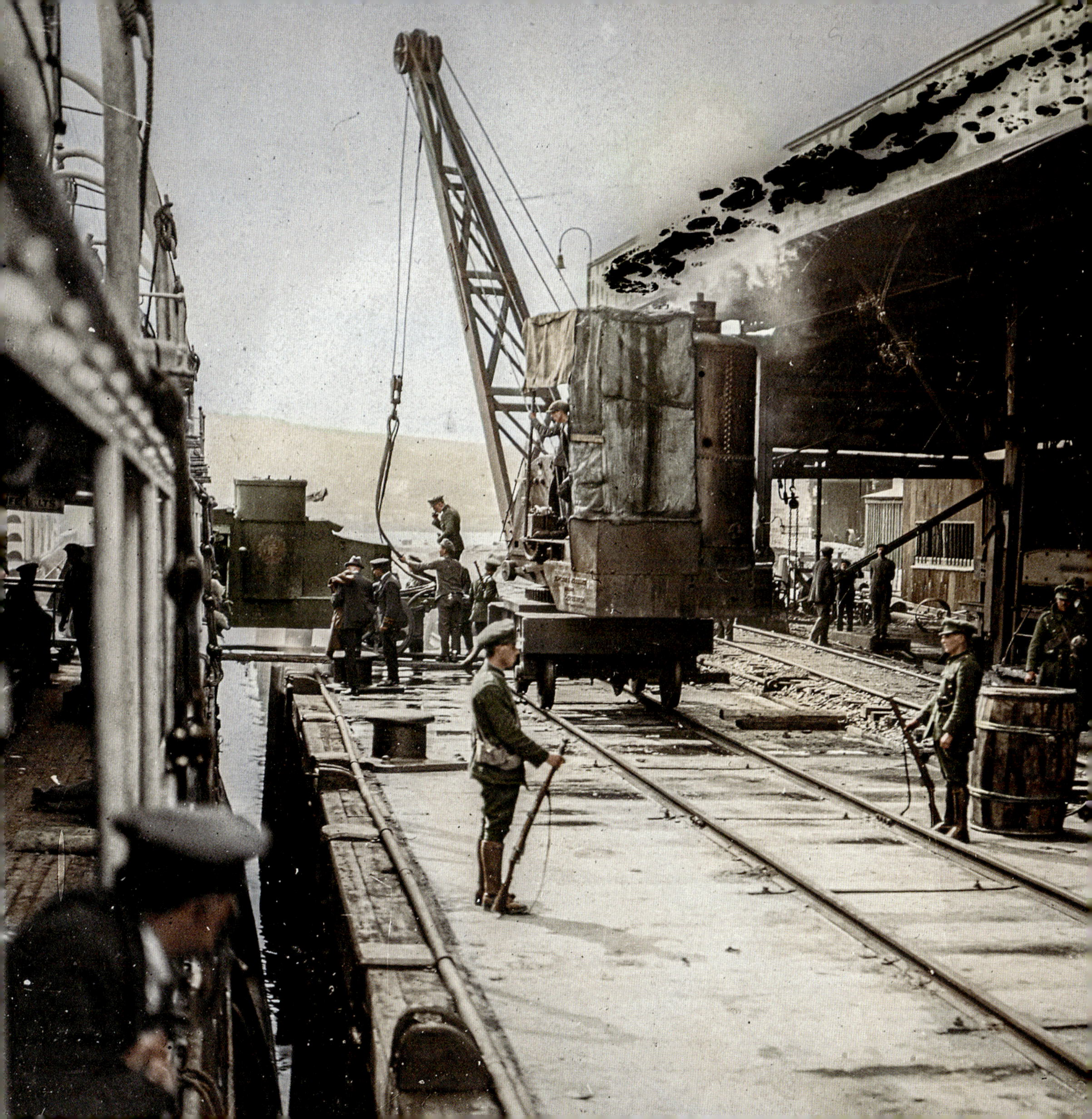

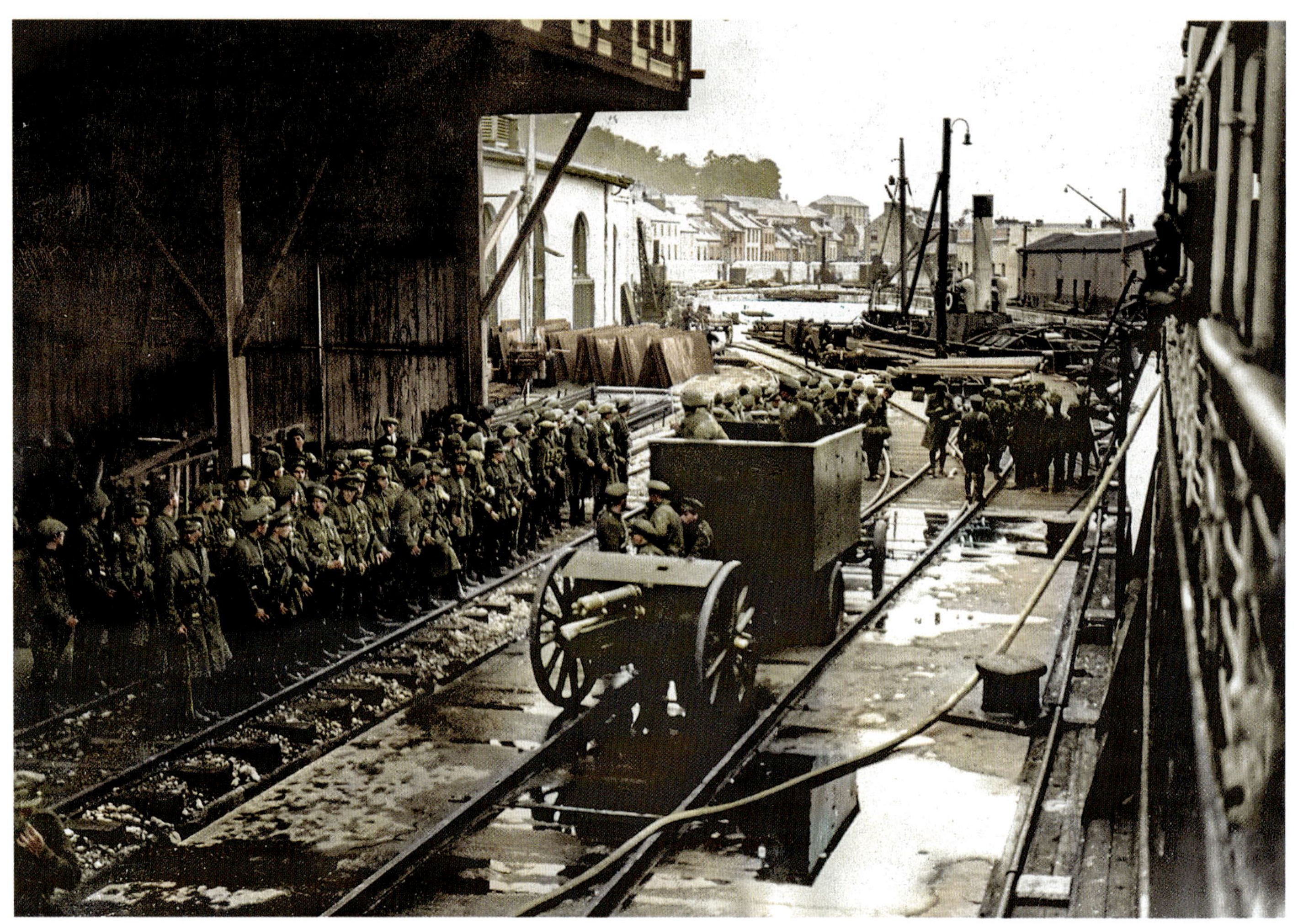

Safely ashore, soldiers assemble at the dockside, about to set off on the journey towards Cork City, around 10km upriver. They were to encounter fierce resistance on the way. The Lancia armoured personnel carrier tows the 18-pounder across the crane tracks towards the dockyard exit.

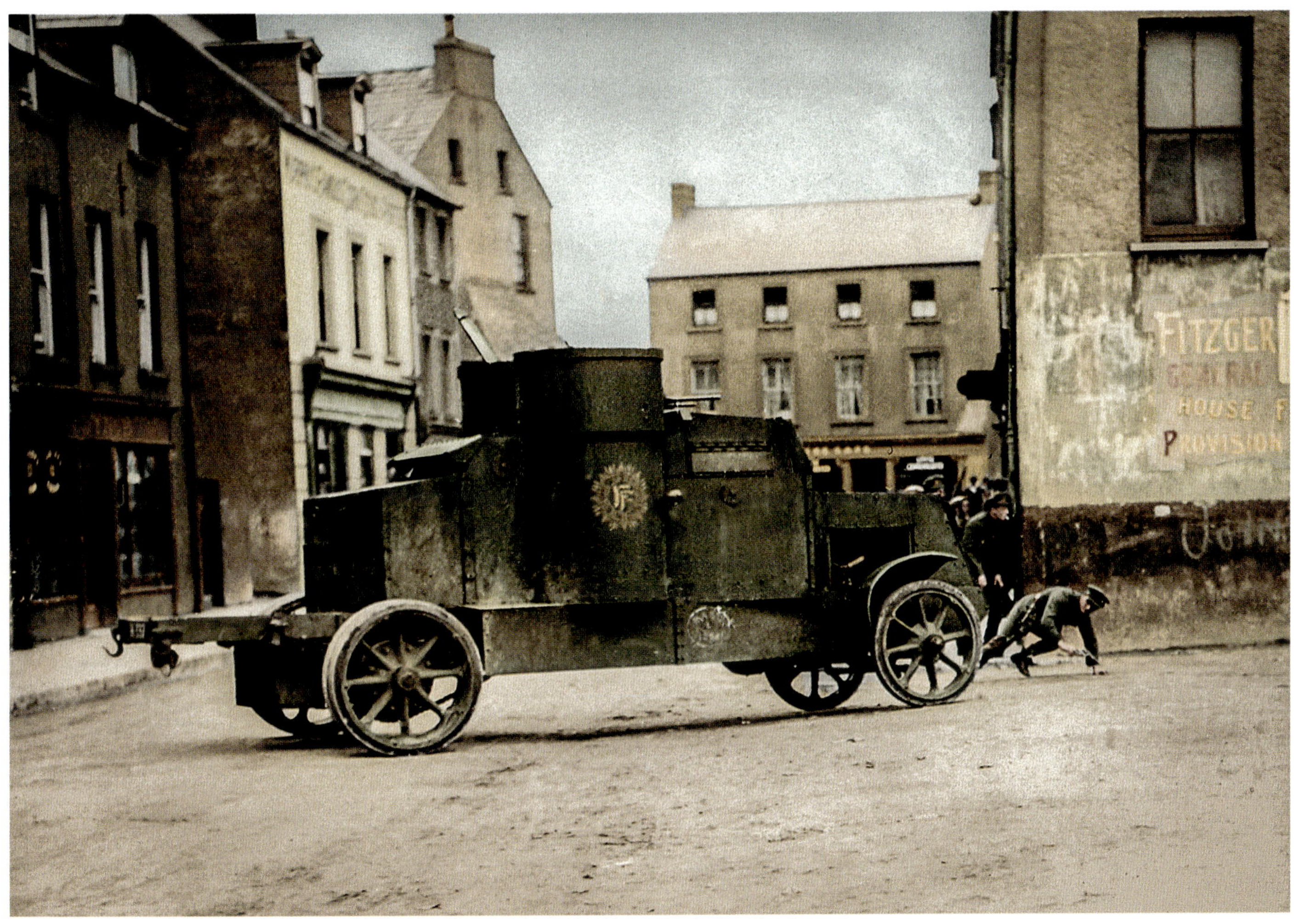

As troops were being disembarked, the *Arvonia* came under fire from positions across the water. The landing party soon came under fire from Republicans ensconced in the heights above Passage West. Here in a street in the town, less than 60m from the waterfront, a pro-Treaty officer, revolver in hand, crouches as his men shelter around the corner. The Peerless armoured car faces up the sloping street, in the direction of opposing fire.

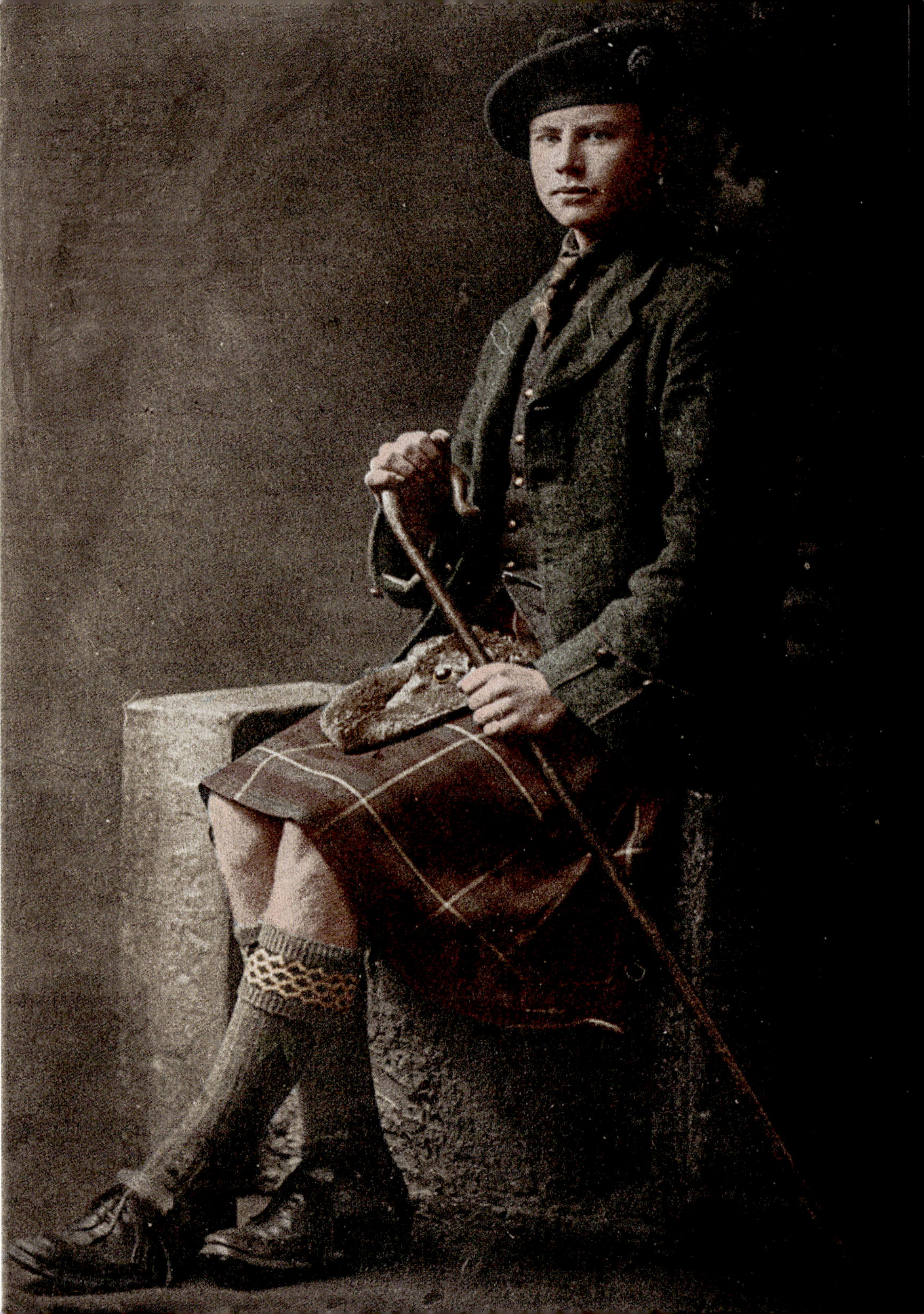

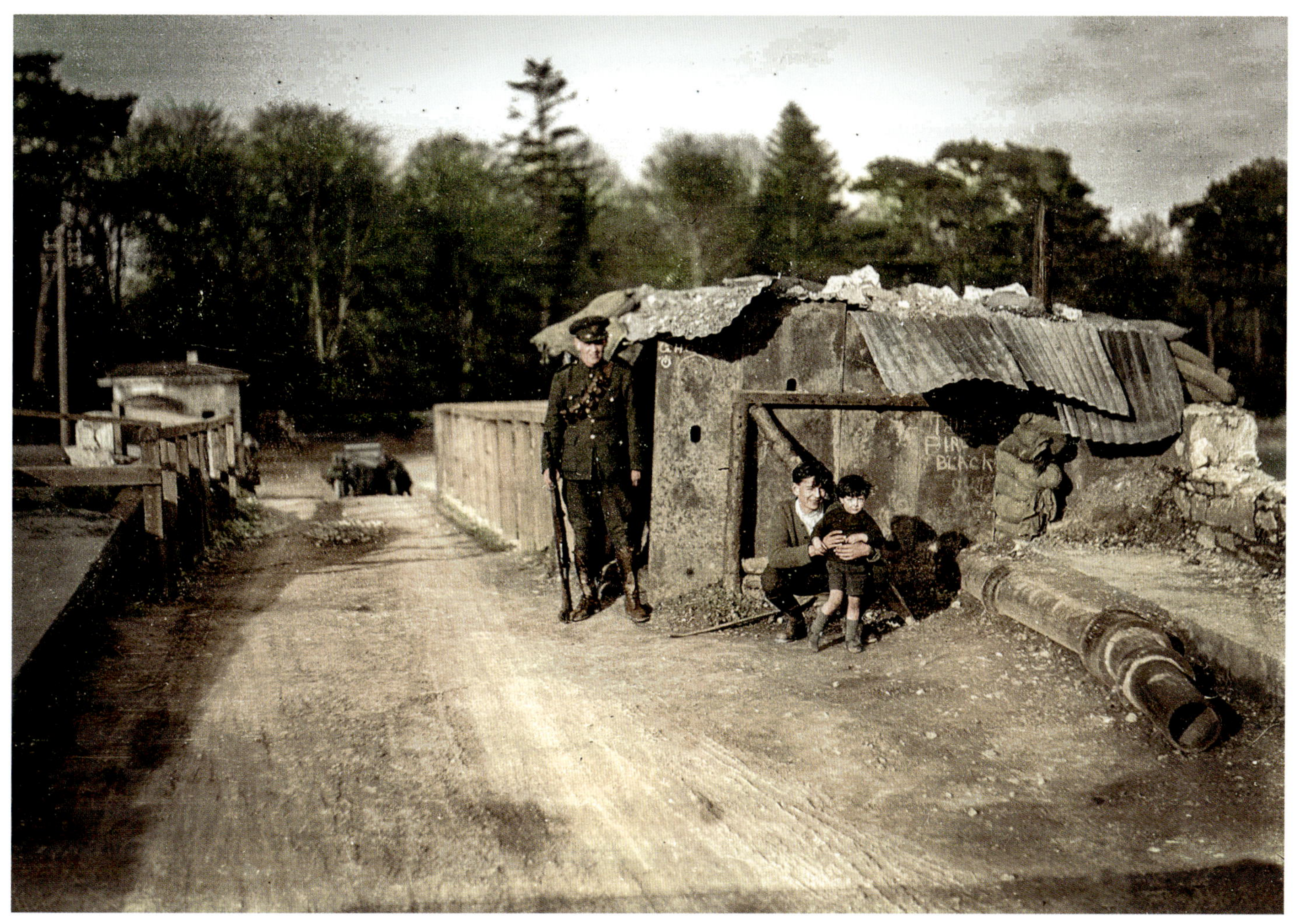

A Provisional Government soldier at a checkpoint at Rochestown, after the location was captured.

Left: Republican forces rushed to resist the incursion. There was heavy fighting amidst the rolling hills, fields and woods between Passage West and Rochestown in the days that followed the August landing. The photograph shows Ian MacKenzie Kennedy, nicknamed 'Scottie'. Born in Scotland, this young man had moved to Ireland in 1916 and went to live in the Ballingeary Gaeltacht, with the objective of learning Irish. In due course this popular youth joined the No. 1 Brigade, Cork IRA. He set out with his comrades to oppose the Provisional Government landing but was killed during the intense fighting at Rochestown on 9 August 1922.

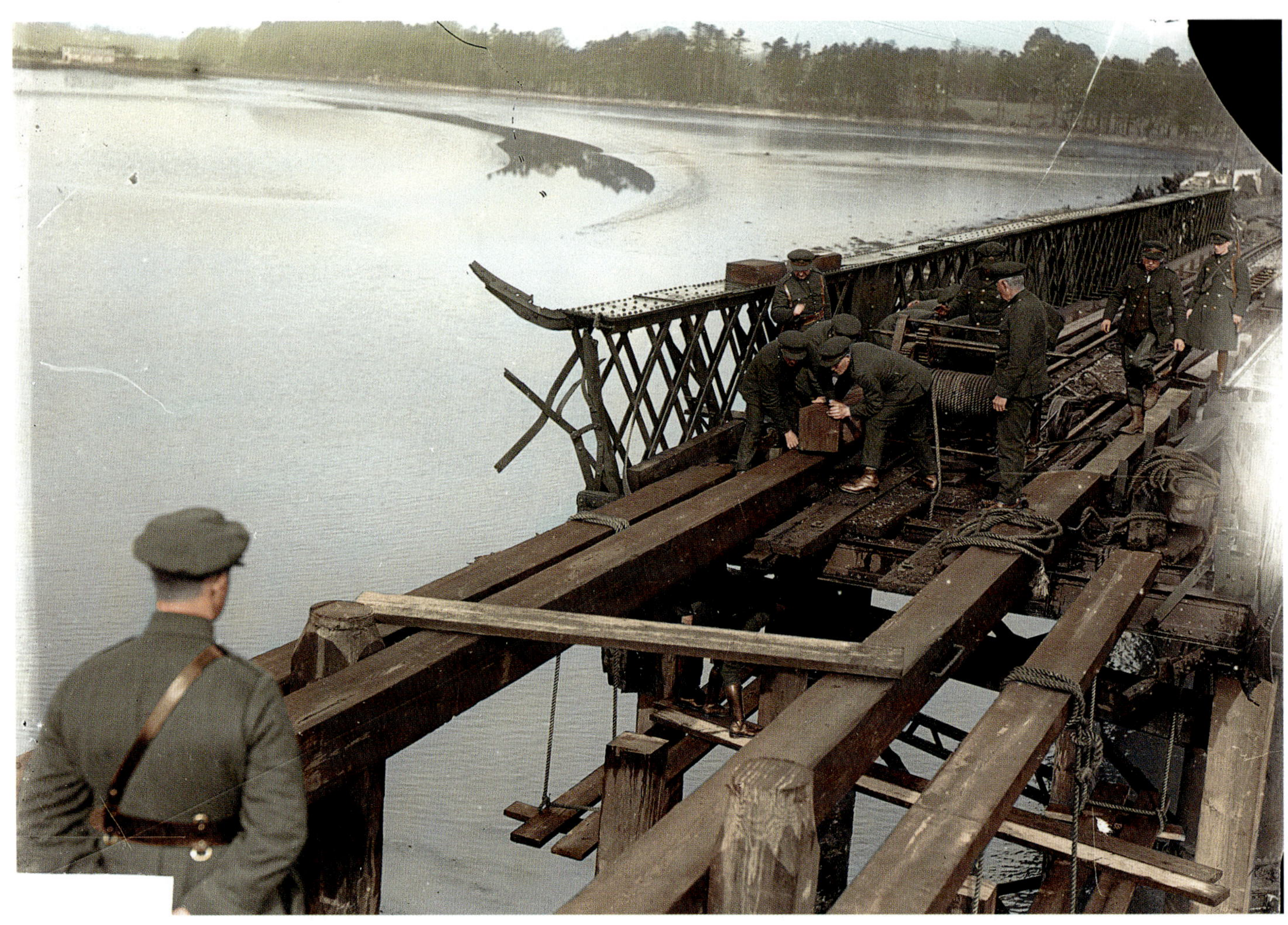

The Douglas Viaduct of the Cork and Blackrock Railway. The Republicans blew up this and other bridges in Cork Harbour to deny transit by rail to the city by the pro-Treaty army. The photograph shows men of the Railway Protection, Repair & Maintenance Corps at work repairing the viaduct in early 1923. This was one of the biggest works they had undertaken.

Right: after fierce fighting on the city's approaches, Cork was taken on the evening of 10 August. During the chaos, Republican forces, using sledgehammers, smashed the linotype machine and printing press of the *Cork Examiner* (seen here). Over the course of the de facto Republican control of the city, the paper was under censorship and obliged to publish anti-Treaty communiqués.

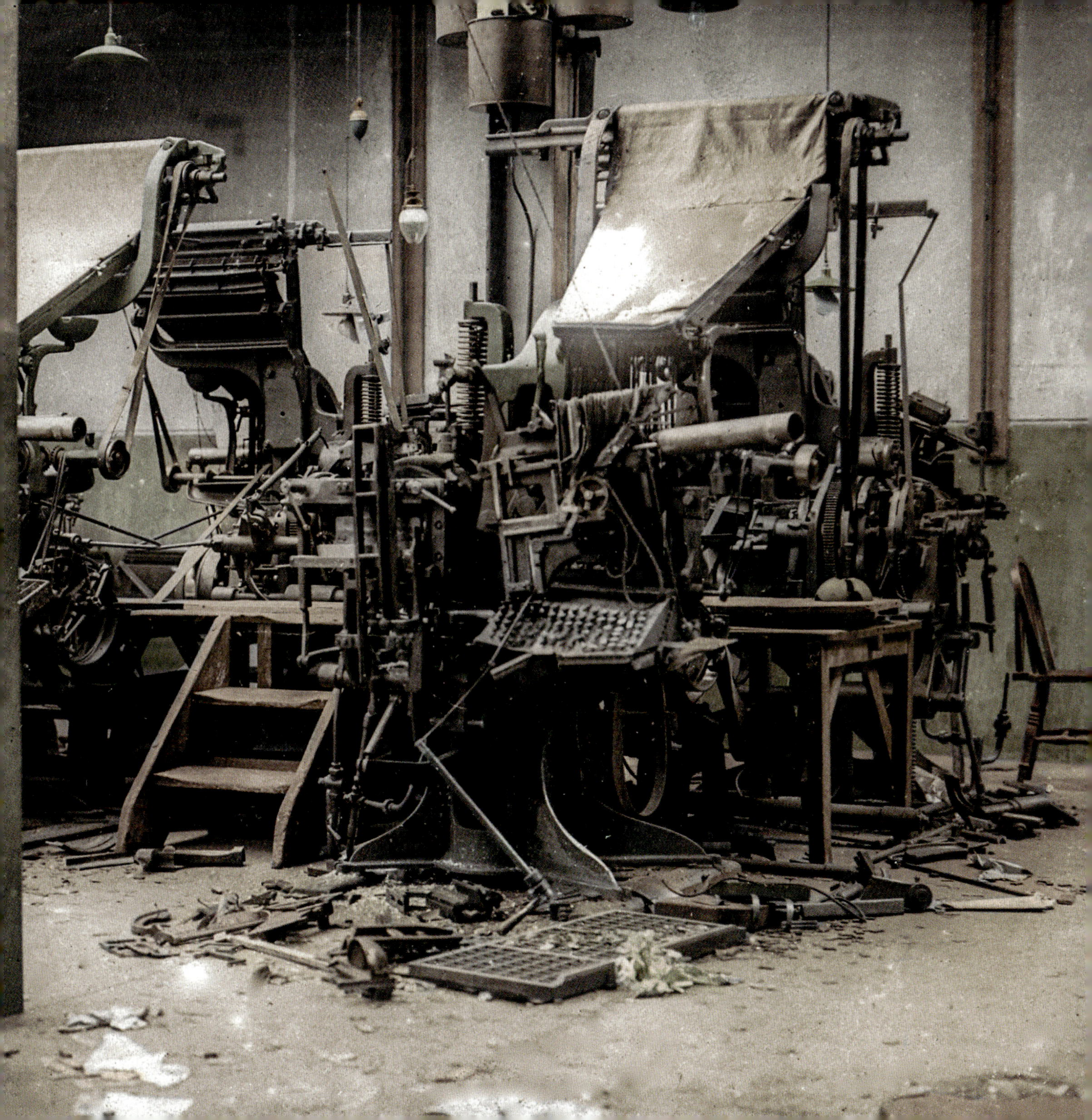

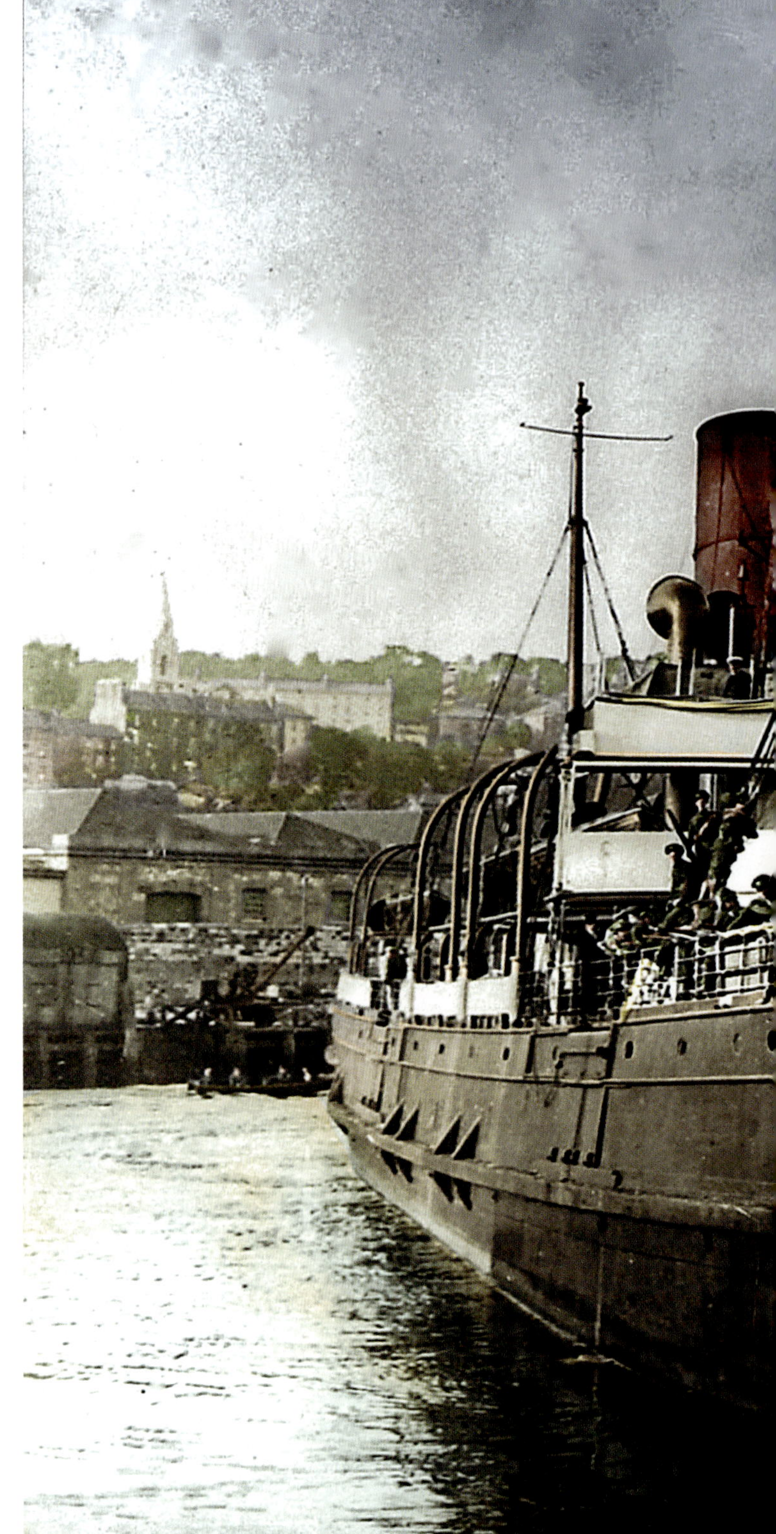

After the taking of the city, ships could sail upriver to berth at the Cork quays. Here is the steamer *Lady Wicklow*, laden with troops, in the upper reaches of Cork Harbour. At 80m in length, it was smaller and slower than the *Arvonia*, which it had accompanied to Passage West. Before its Cork duties, it had carried troops for the Fenit landing on 2 August 1922.

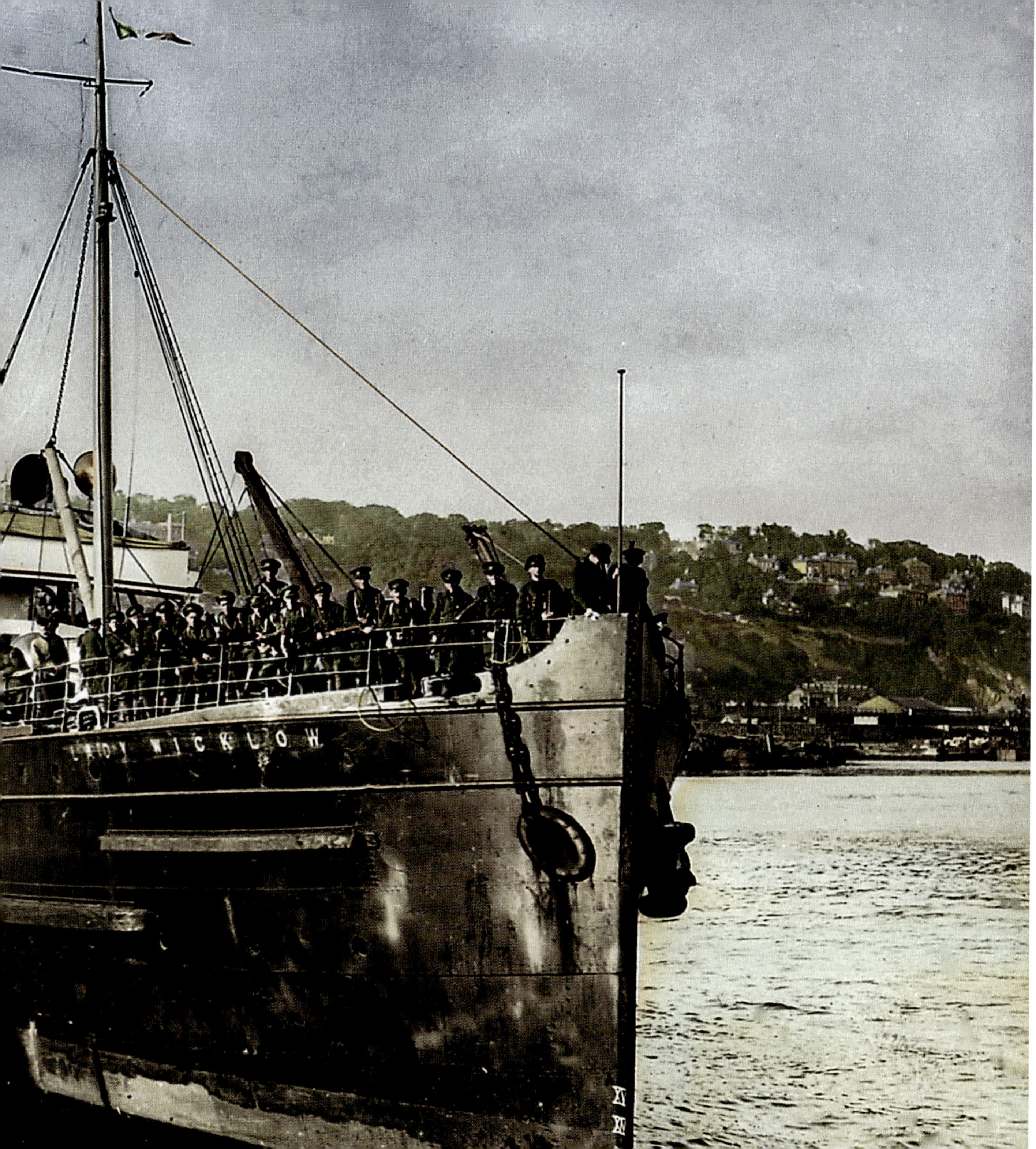

WICKLOW

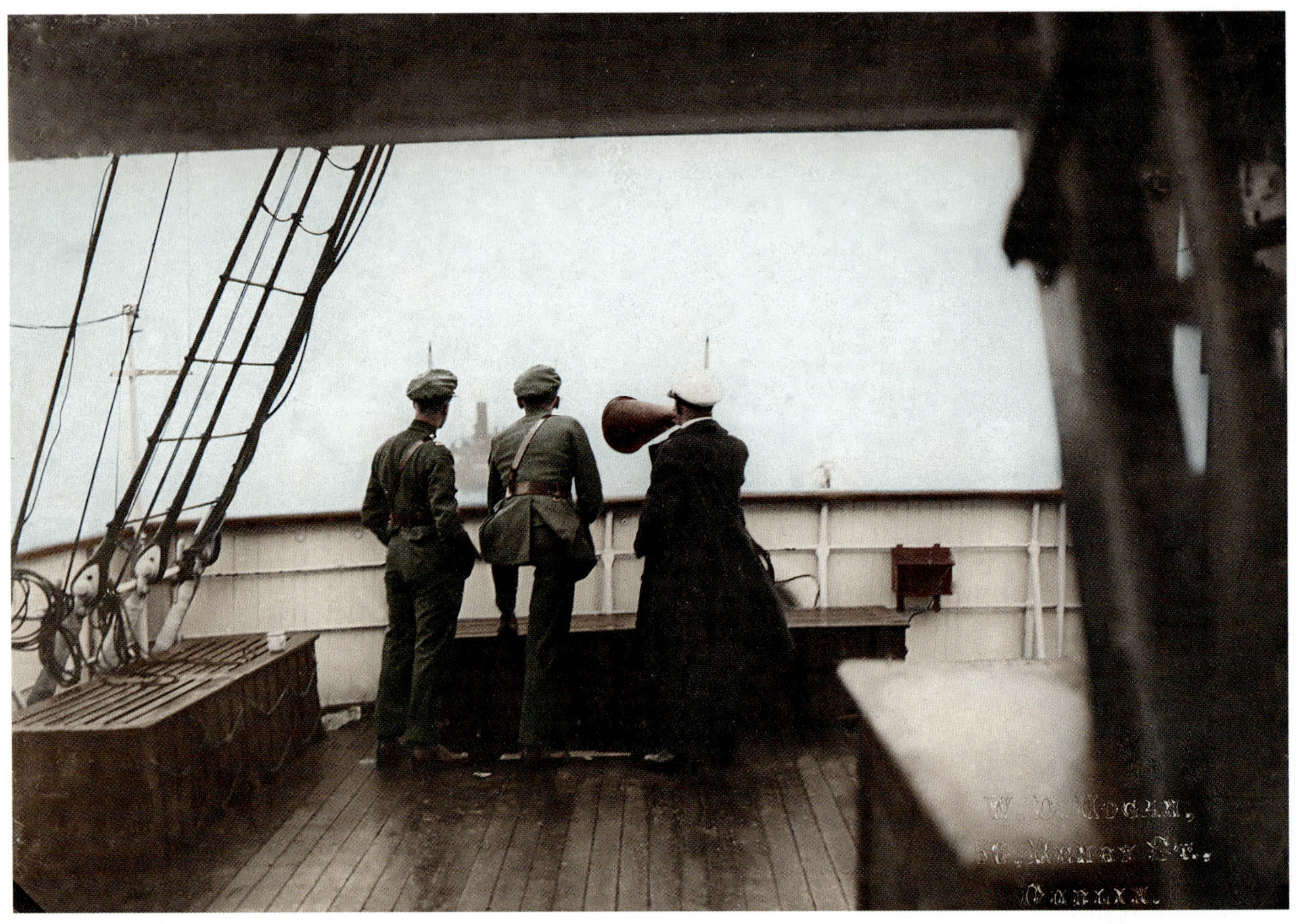

Sailing upriver, the photographer W.D. Hogan captures the scene on the bridge deck of the *Lady Wicklow*. What appears to be Generals Dalton and Ennis look on as the captain of the ship warns a passing vessel of the dangers to navigation.

Right: as the *Lady Wicklow* sails along Lough Mahon in the upper reaches of Cork Harbour, care is taken in navigating past the wrecks of the *Gorilla* (a steamer) in the foreground and, just visible, the *No. 1 Hopper* (a dredging barge). These had been sunk by the Republicans to prevent passage of ships upriver.

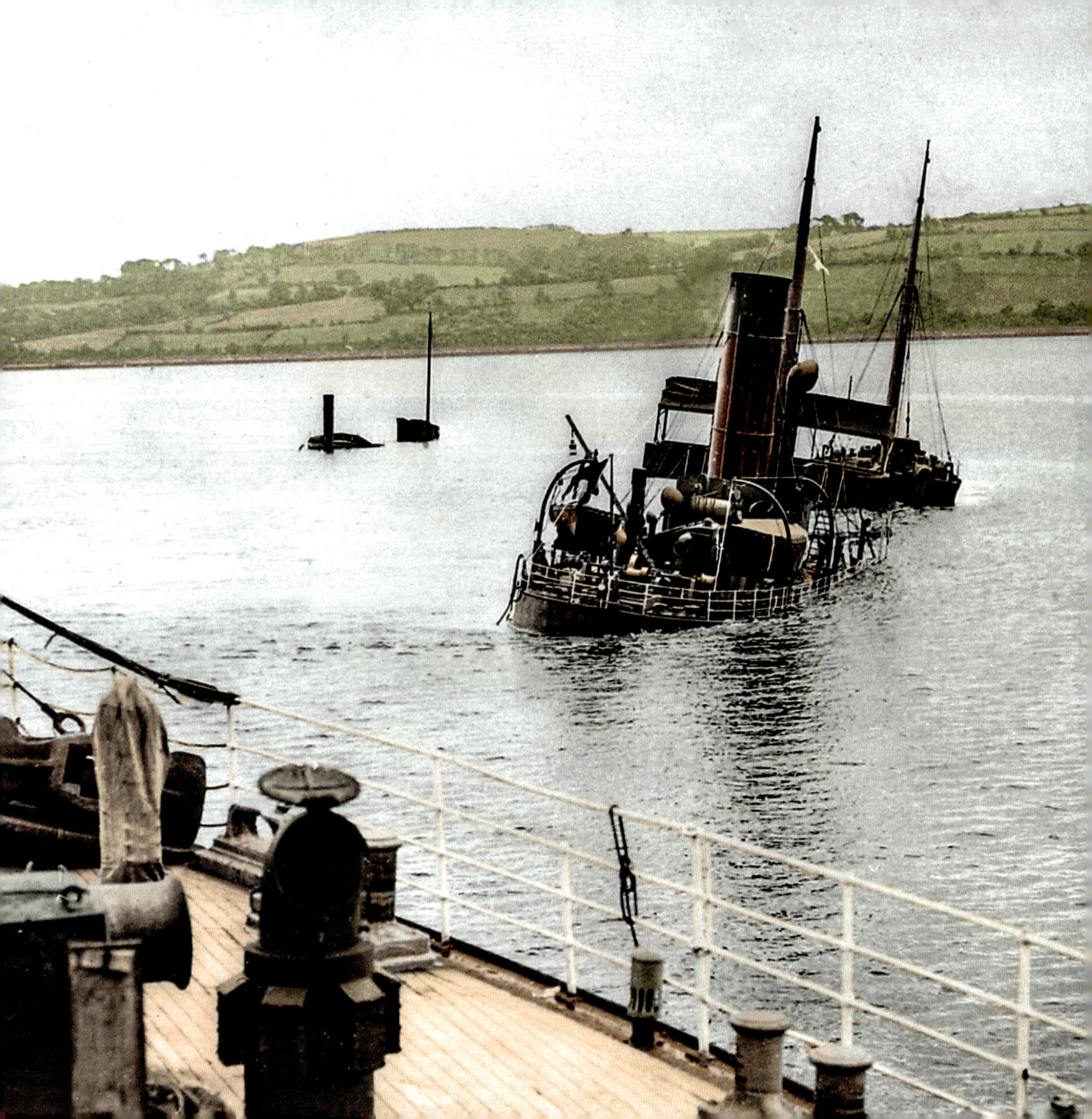

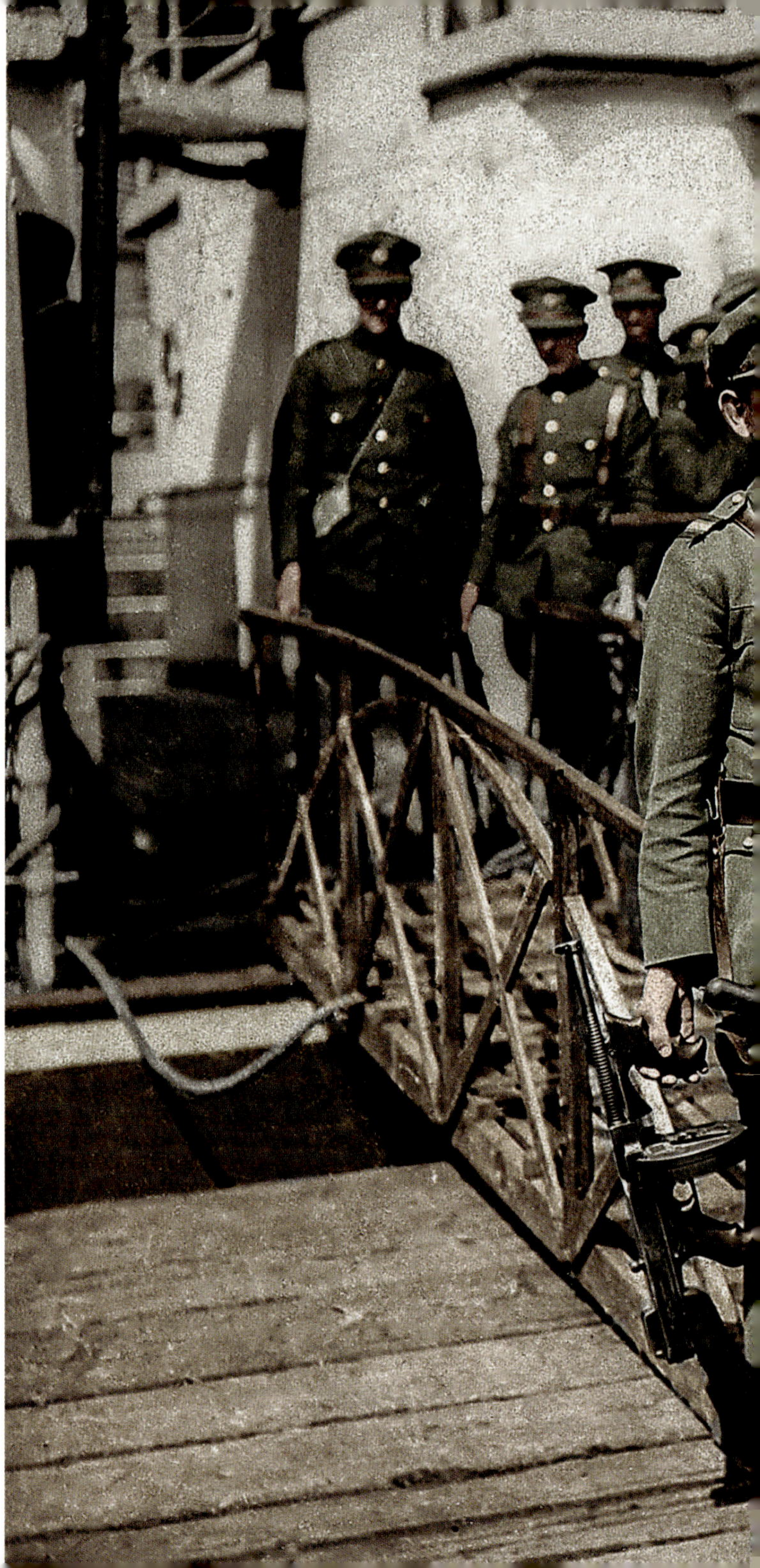

The Provisional Government Army was now in command of Cork City. At the gangplank of the *Lady Wicklow*, is Major-General Tom Ennis, nicknamed the 'Manager' (page 148) who was described by Ernie O'Malley as the 'best officer in Dublin'. He looks relaxed as he carries a Thompson gun. On the right is a more reserved-looking Colonel-Commandant Pat McCrea (another veteran of the War of Independence in Dublin, including such actions as Bloody Sunday and the attempt to free Seán Mac Eoin from Mountjoy Prison).

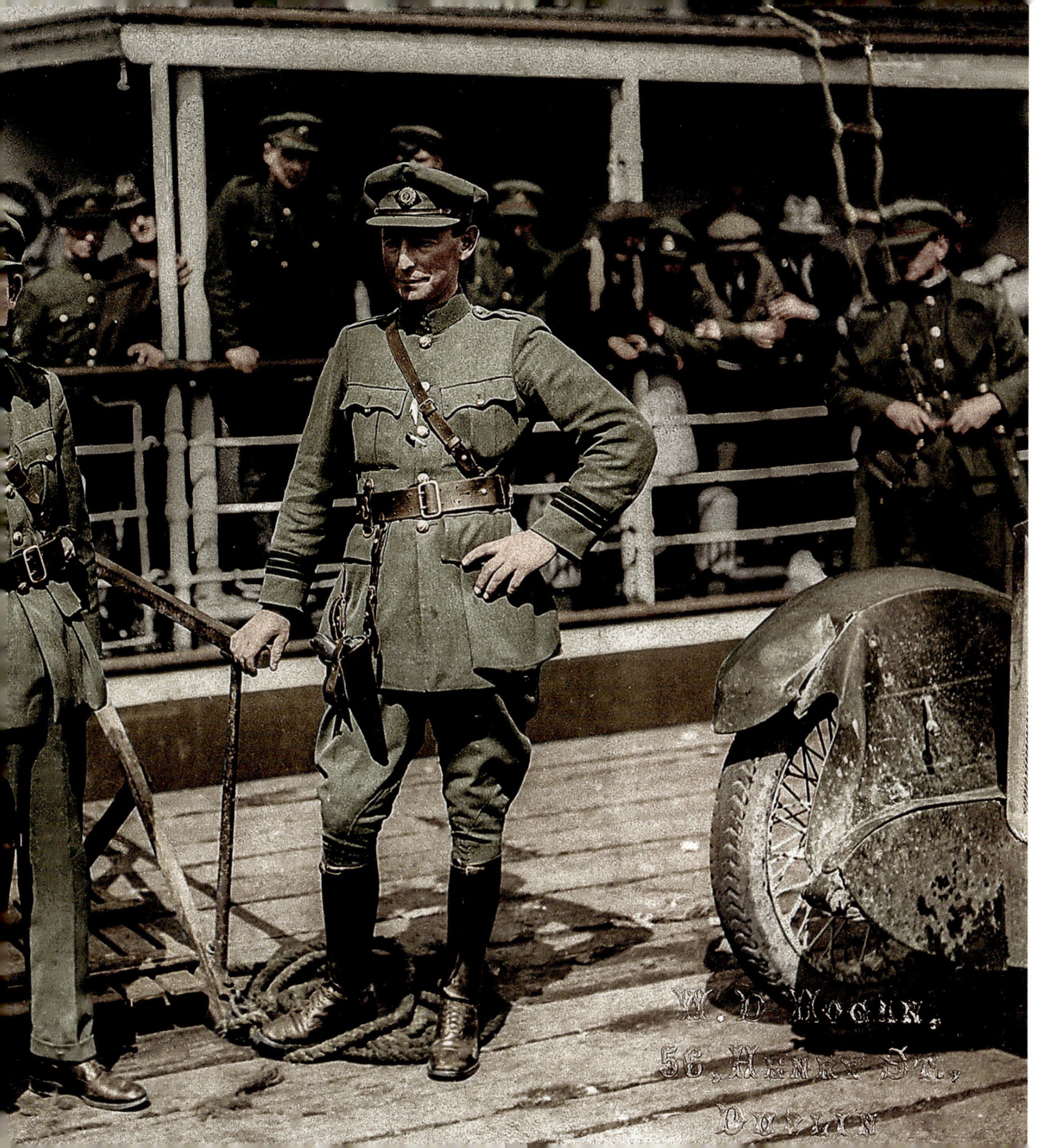

W. D. HOGAN.
56, HENRY ST.,
DUBLIN.

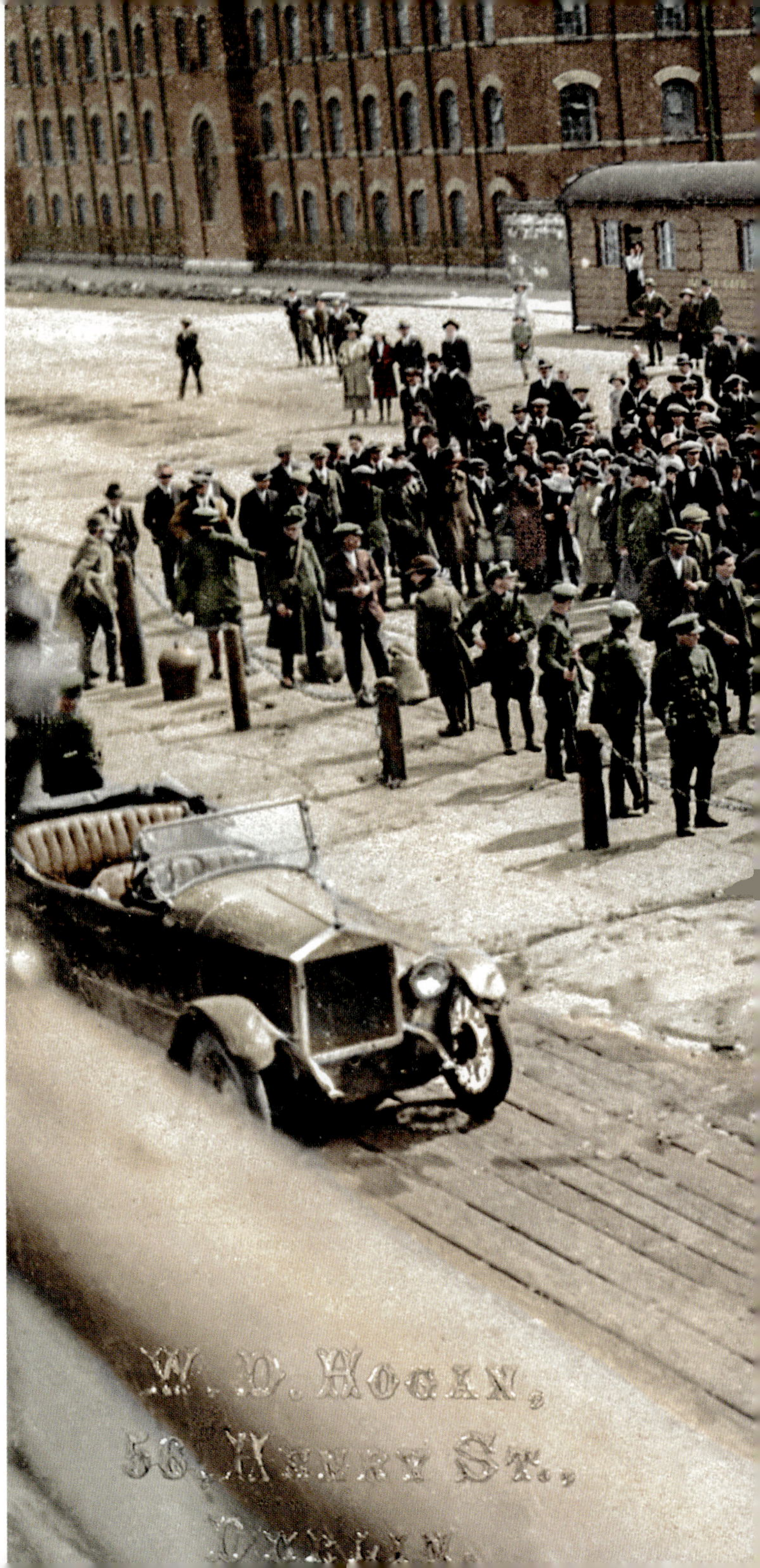

In Cork, observed by a large crowd of curious onlookers, Provisional Government soldiers march captured Republicans off to captivity. As can be seen by the embossing, this is another of the series of images taken by W.D. Hogan, who accompanied the troops on the mission to capture Cork.

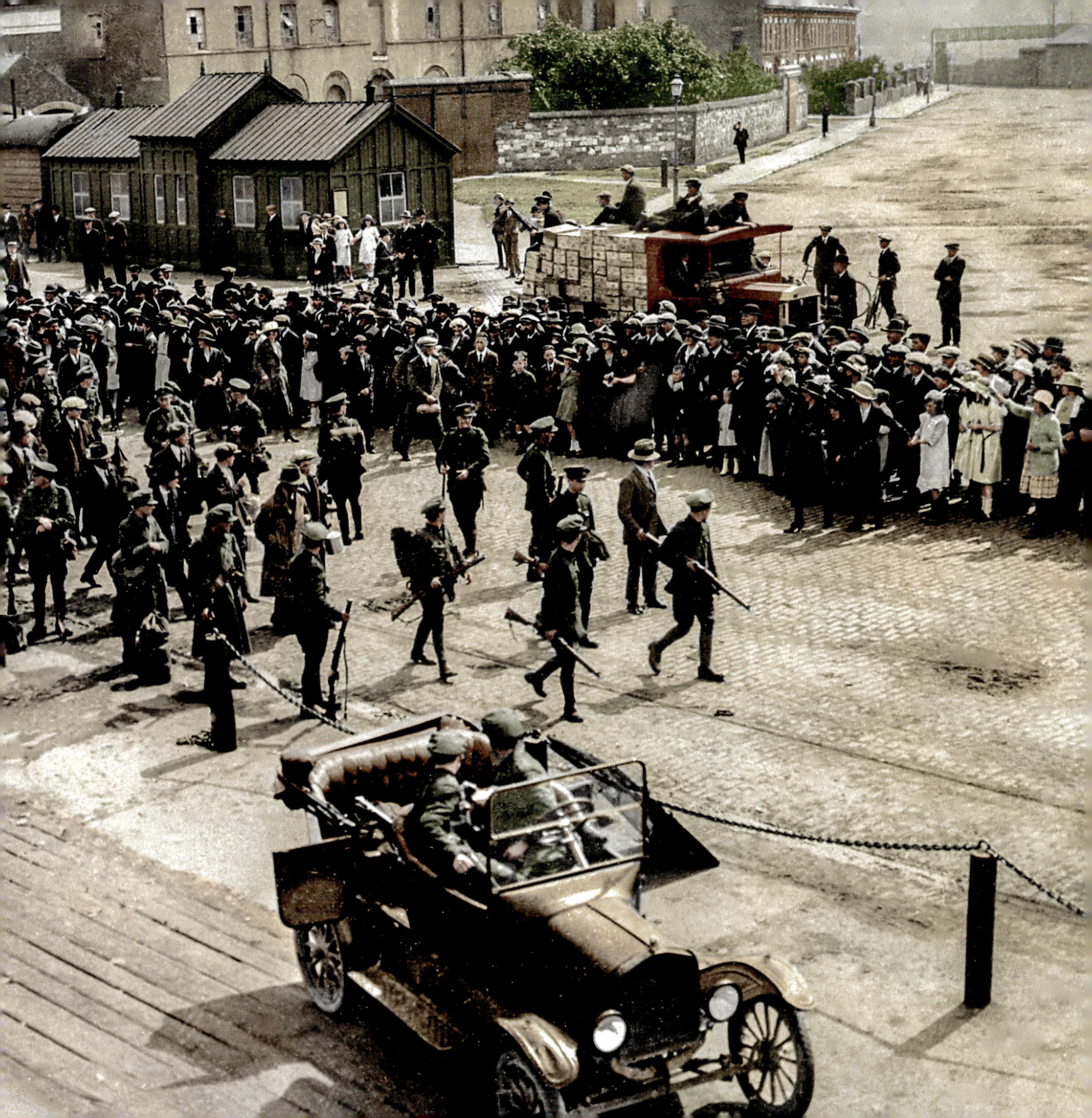

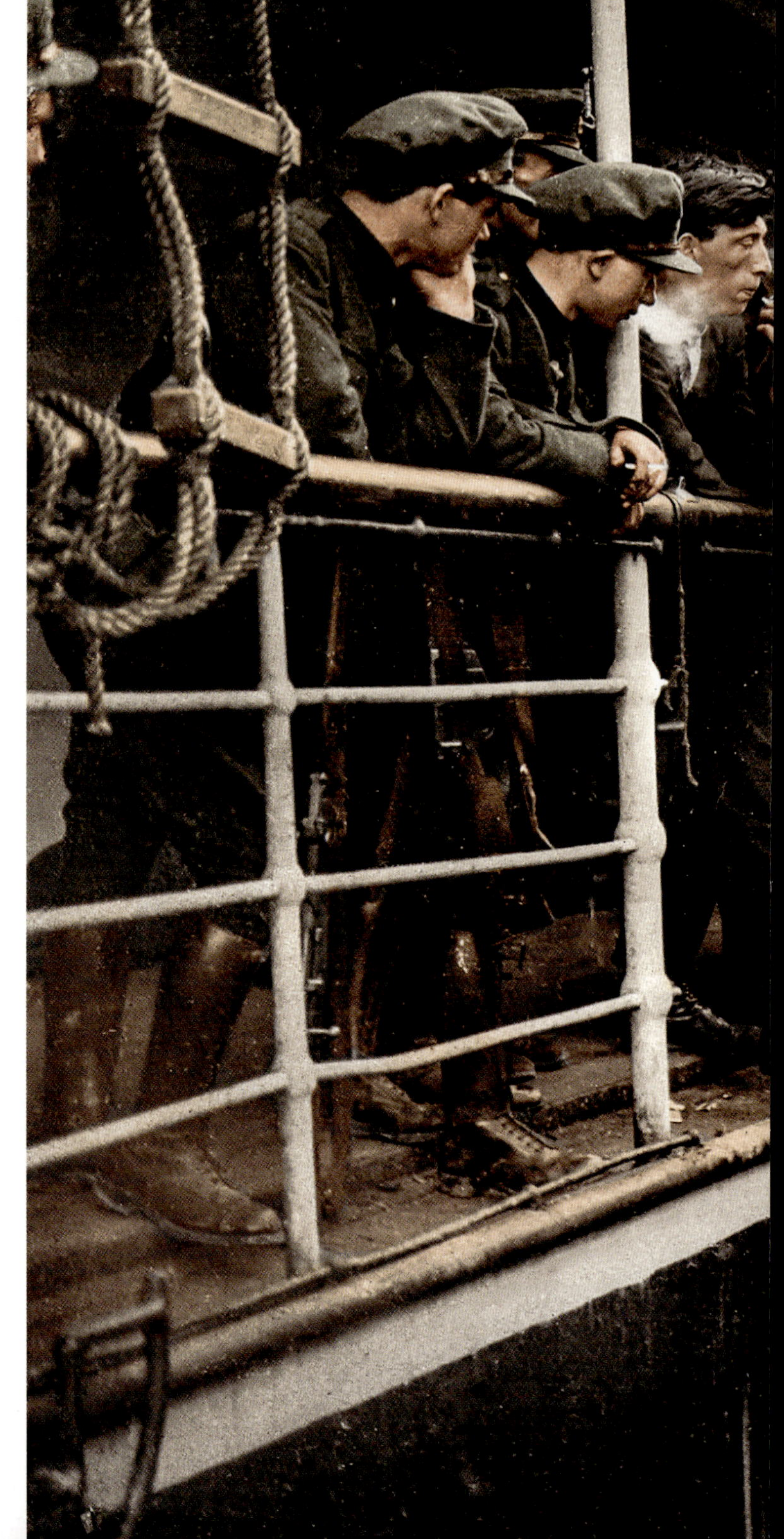

Closely watched by their captors, Republican prisoners say goodbye to their families at the quayside, as they wait to be transported on the *Lady Wicklow* to Dublin for internment. This informal scene is evidence that the war was still in its 'civilised' phase, where captured prisoners were treated relatively leniently.

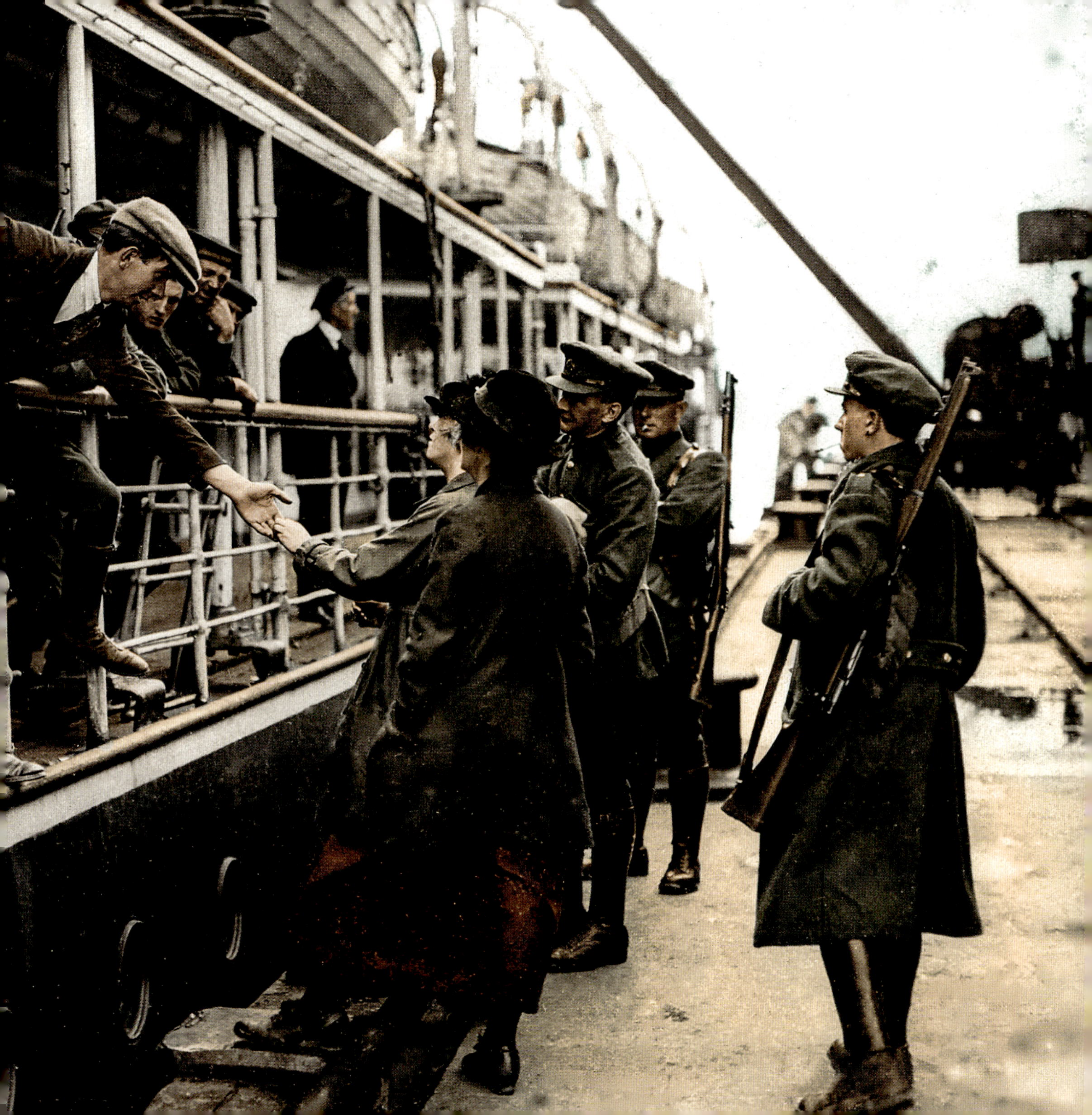

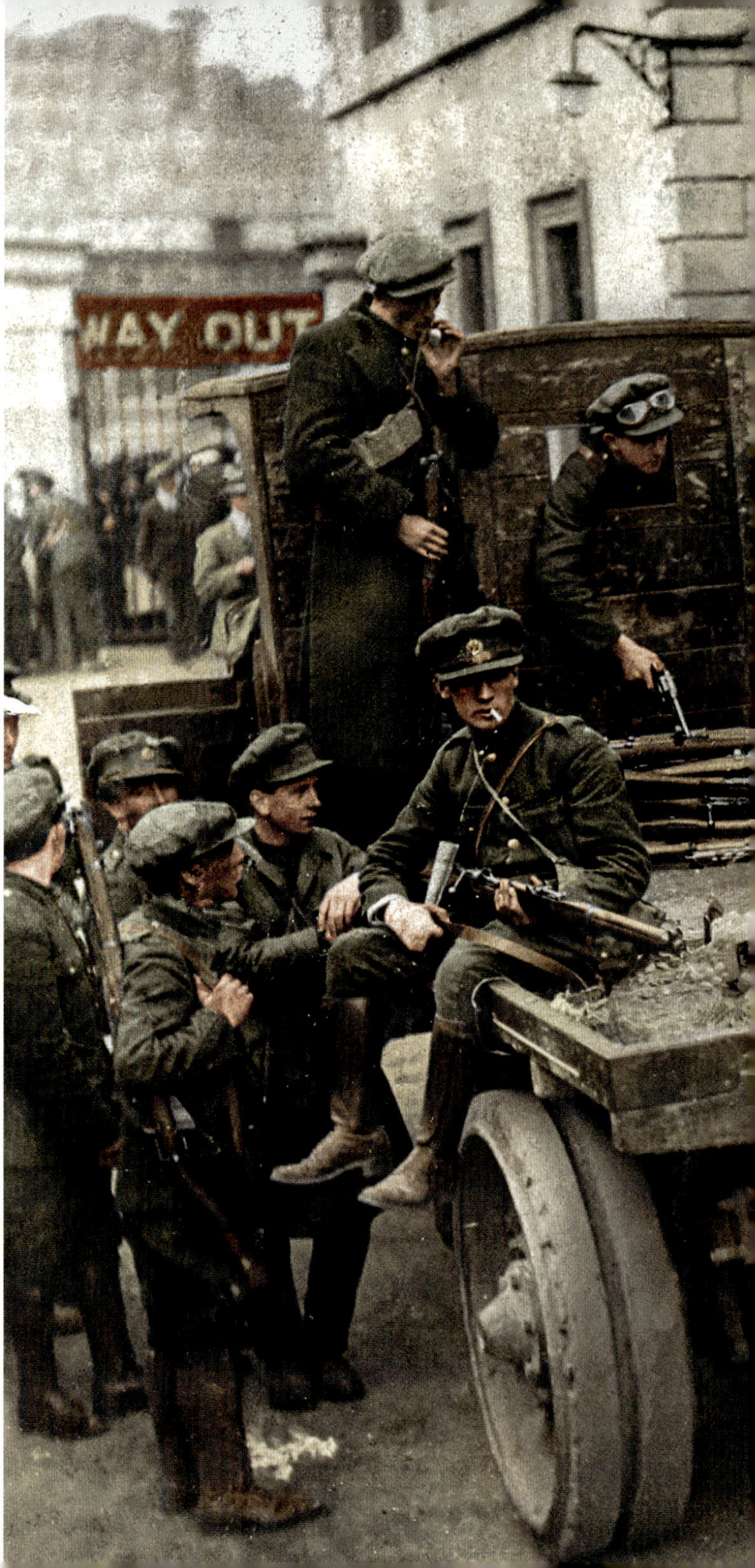

At the Cork, Bandon and South Coast railway station at Albert Quay a soldier, surrounded by his watchful armed comrades, grasps a bundle of Lee-Enfield rifles on the back of a lorry. He is distributing rifles to local pro-Treaty recruits. The *Cork Examiner* (now back in print), in its description of the scene, refers to the rifles as having been captured in the Douglas and Rochestown fighting.

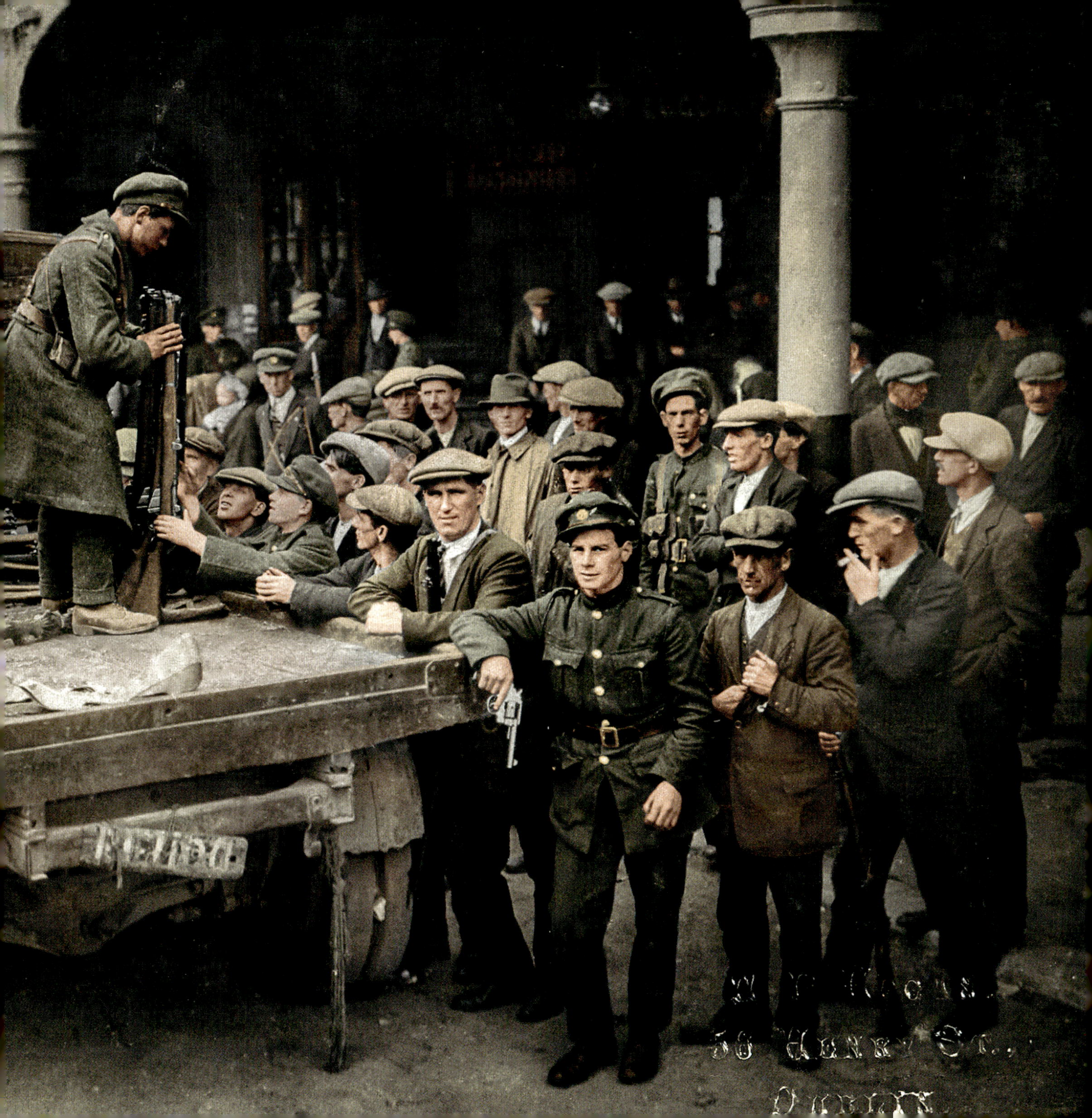
W. D. Hogan.
56 Henry St.,
Dublin.

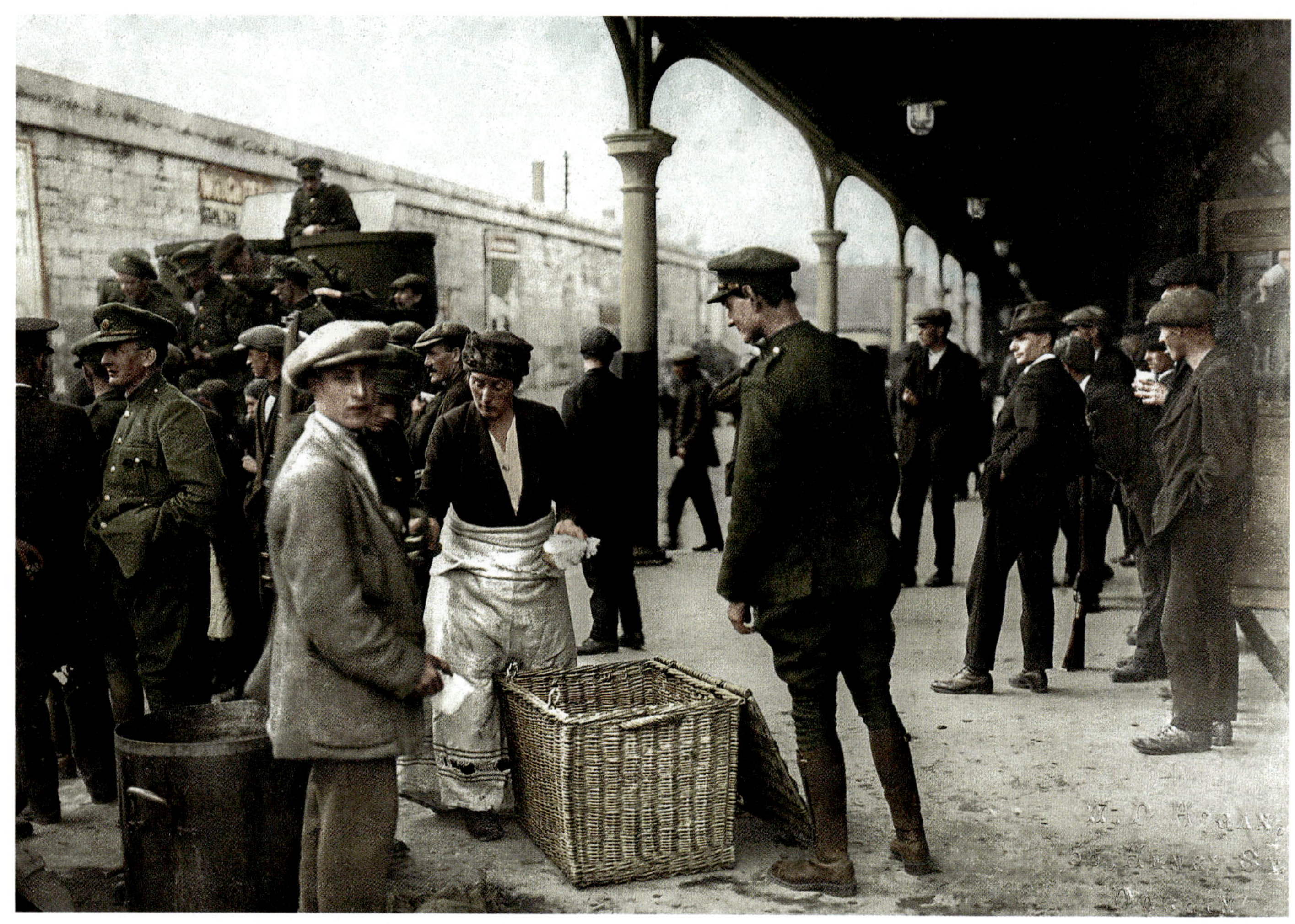

After the taking of Cork, it was a time of rest and recreation for the troops. In this busy scene at Albert Quay Station, soldiers mill around, with the Peerless armoured car in the background. A sandwich vendor finds a ready market for her wares.

Right: No winning of hearts and minds. Many of the pro-Treaty troops had been recruited in Dublin. Here young soldiers cradle their Lewis guns in front of a fortified building in the heart of Cork. Demonstrating some Dublin arrogance towards 'the country', they, without any ambiguity, convey the message 'Up Dublin'. For good measure they add 'Beware of the Free State Sons'.

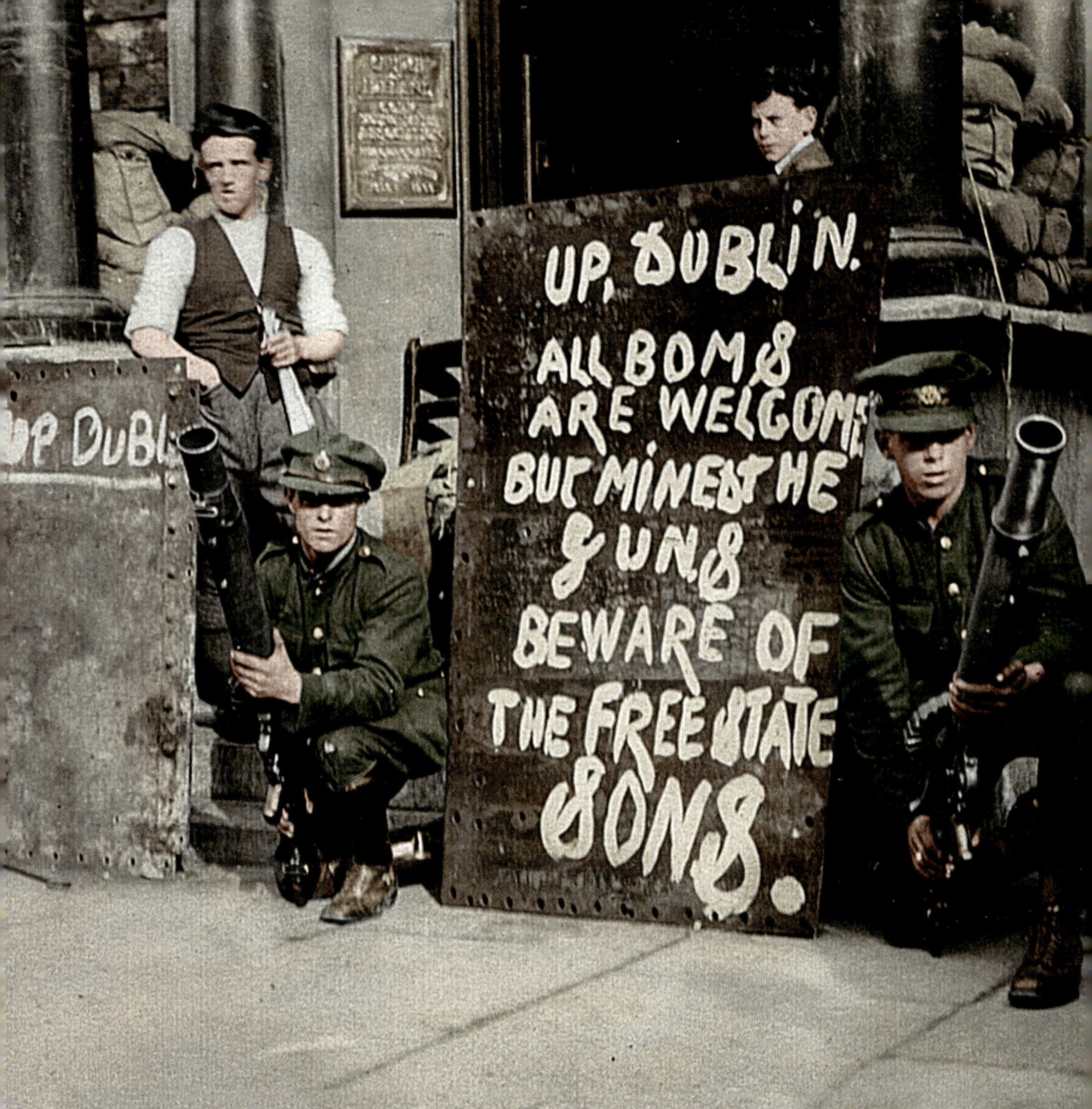
UP, DUBLIN.
ALL BOMS
ARE WELCOME
BUT MINE THE
GUNS
BEWARE OF
THE FREE STATE
SONS.
UP DUBL

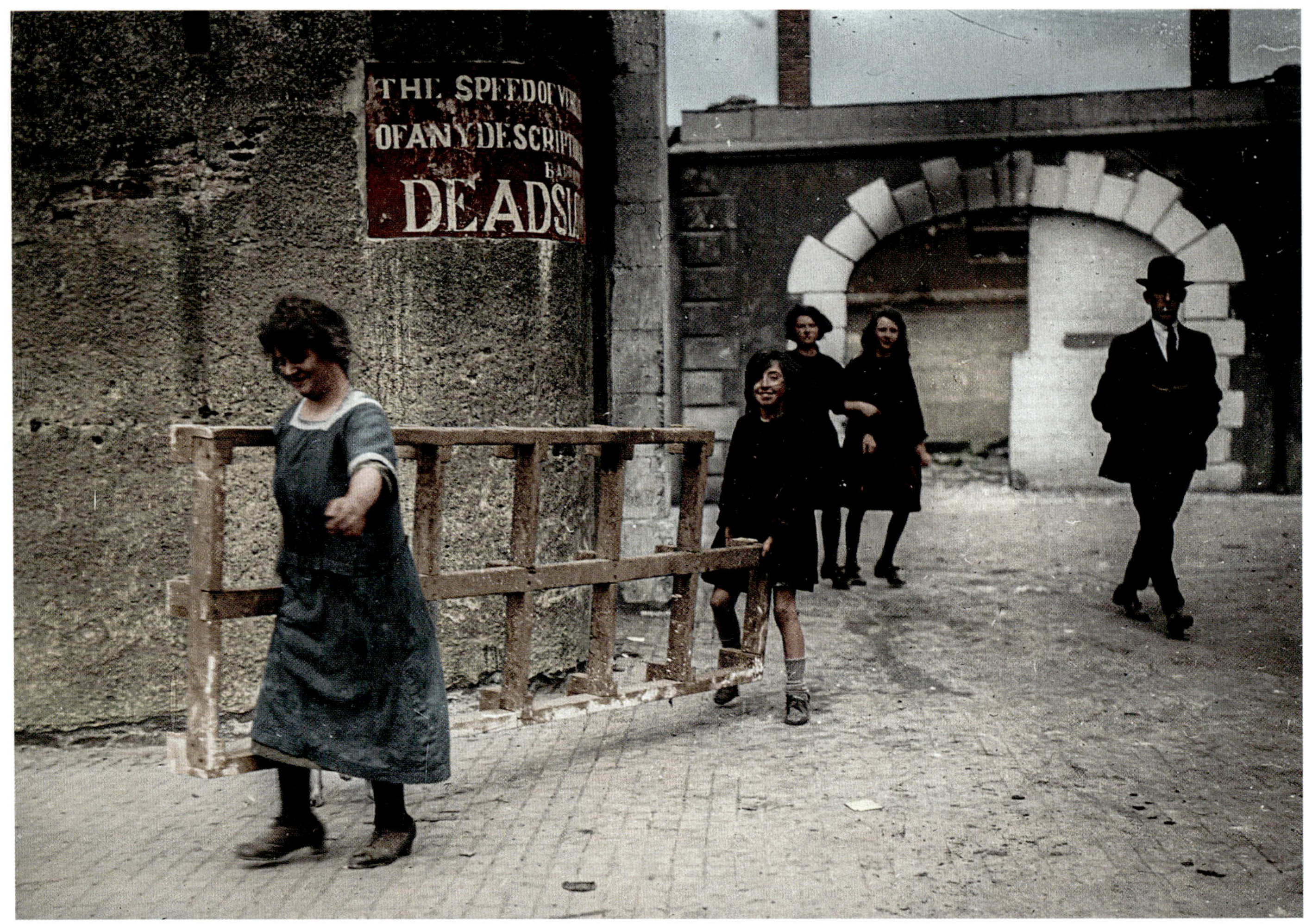

As they departed, the Republicans set Victoria (now Collins) Barracks on fire. Here, in the aftermath, locals salvage what they can from the burnt-out buildings.

Right: a barefoot boy adopts a martial pose, displaying the sword and scabbard that he had discovered in the barracks.

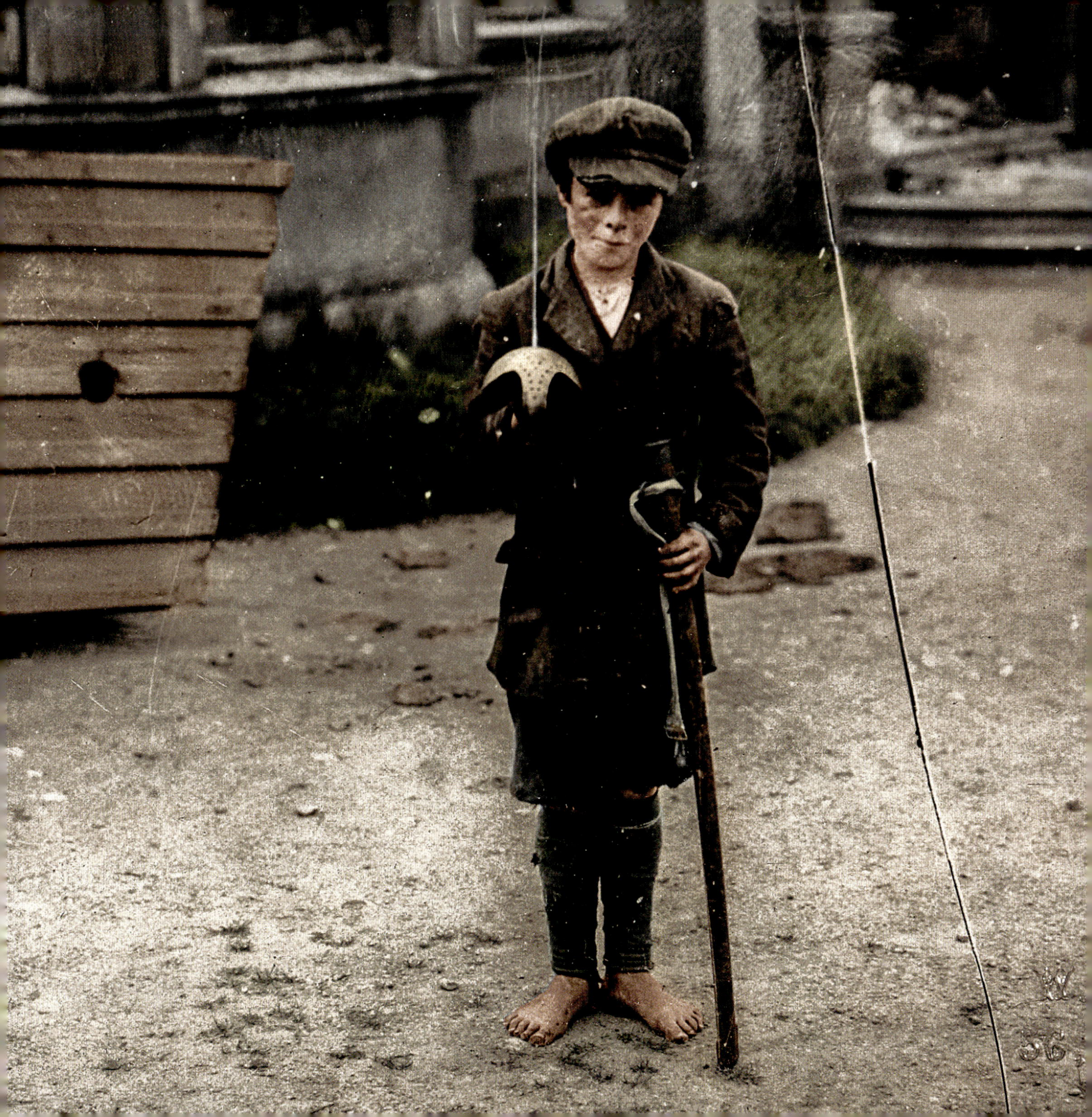

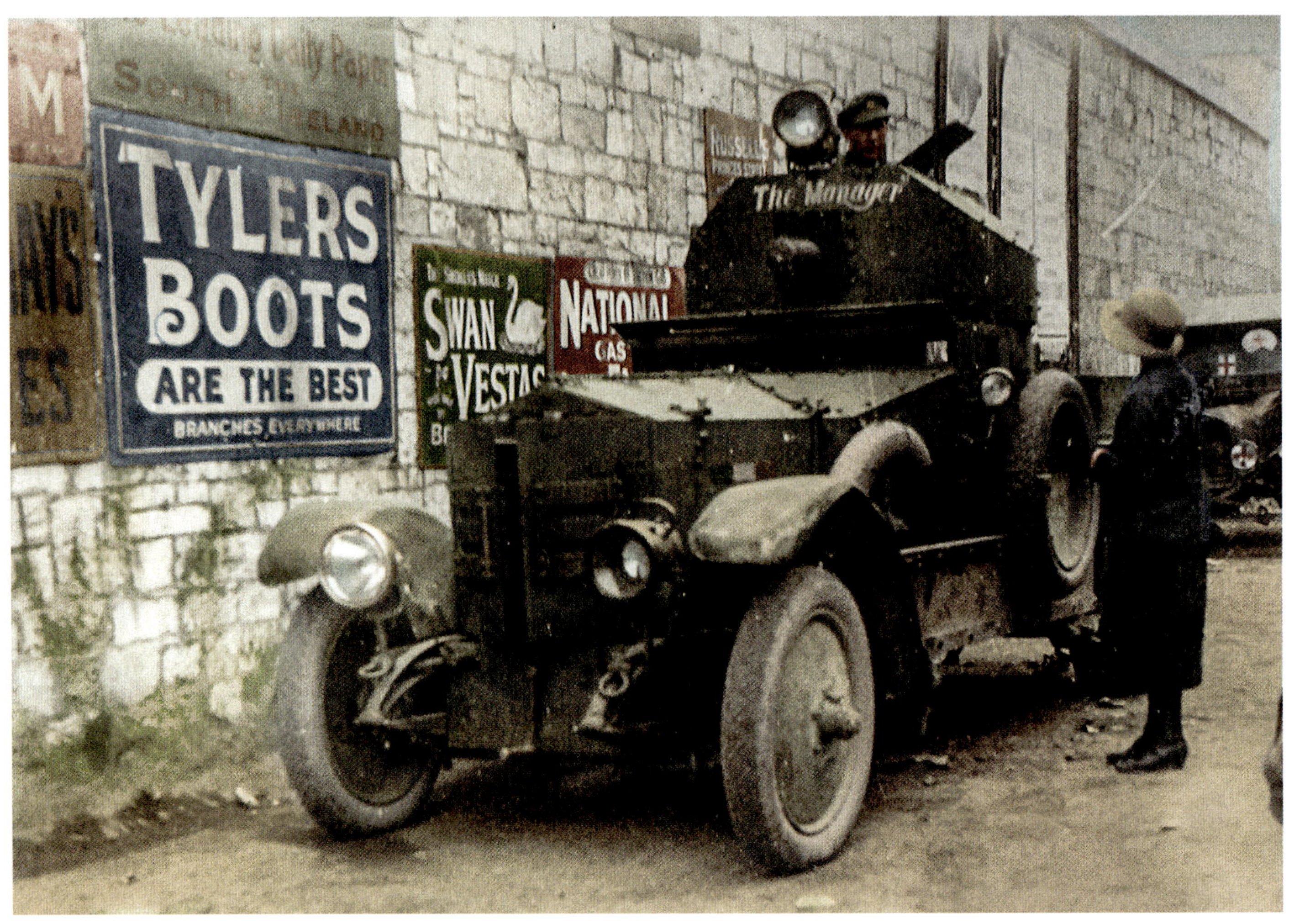

Last seen on board the *Arvonia*, the *Manager* Rolls-Royce armoured car parked in Cork. It demonstrated the superb mobility of its type, as well as the devastating power of its Vickers machine gun, during the fighting between Passage West and Cork City. As the convoy of the Provisional Government forces made its way into the city on the evening of 10 August, Major-General Tom Ennis rode in the vanguard, standing in the turret of this armoured car (named after him, page 148).

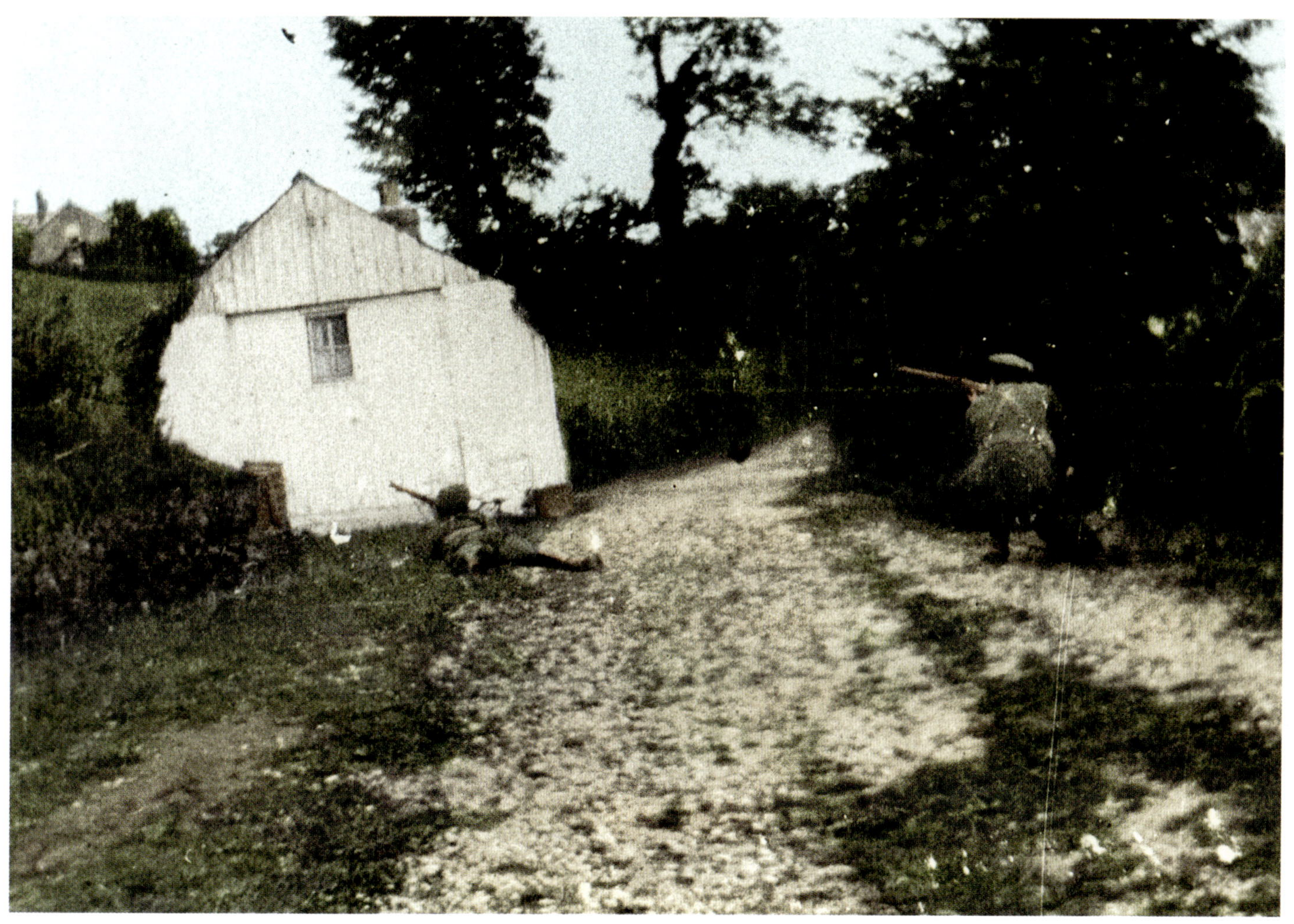

Republican forces regrouped at Macroom Castle and then dispersed. In the course of the following weeks, Major-General Emmet Dalton sent out expeditions which captured the main towns of Co. Cork and some adjacent ones in Waterford and Kerry. However, the Republican forces still roamed and made attacks, being particularly strong in the mountains around Ballyvourney. Here, in an engagement in rural Co. Cork, Provisional Government soldiers make their advance.

Overleaf: at Glanmire Road station, men pose on the locomotive of the first local train to travel after the taking of Cork. It was to take until October 1923 for the railway connection to Dublin to be restored, when the Mallow Viaduct reopened (page 226–227).

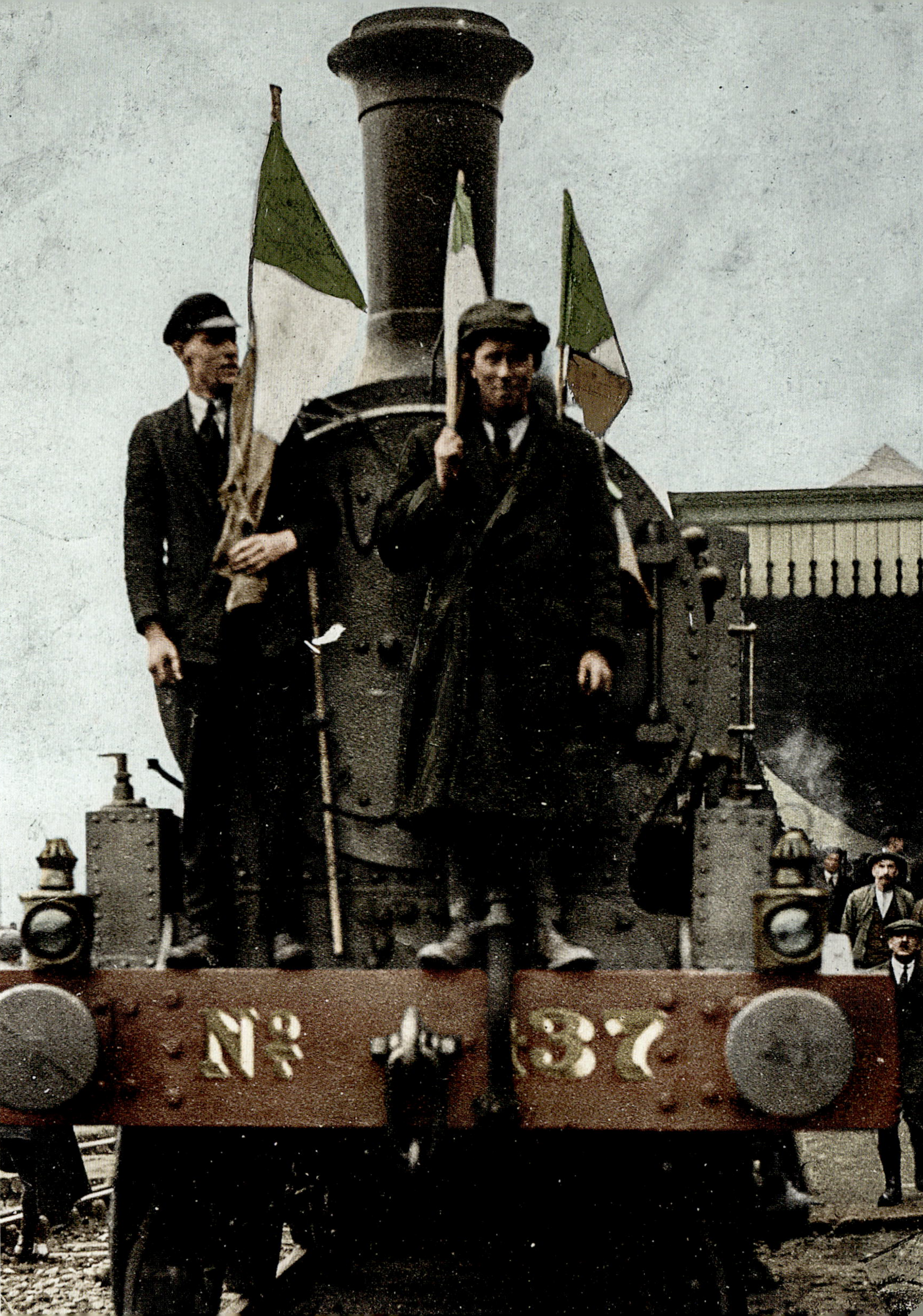

Nº 37

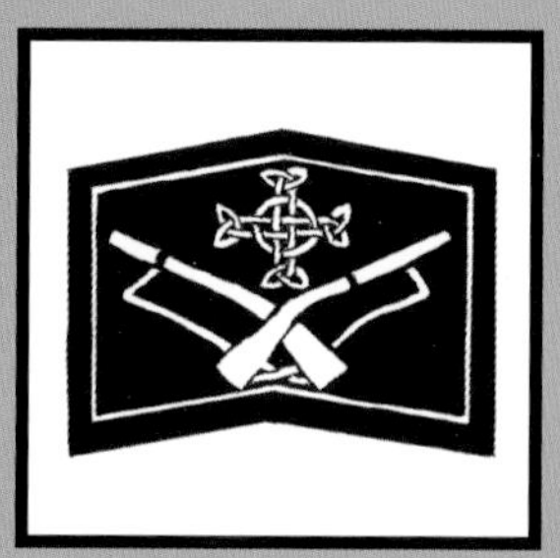

Chapter 4
Deaths of Griffith and Collins

Collins was at the beginning of a tour of the south when the news came of
the death of Arthur Griffith. He returned to Dublin to attend the funeral
on 16 August 1922, unaware that he would meet his death only six days
later. He resumed his tour and, travelling in a convoy through West Cork,
was shot dead in an ambush on 22 August. An enormous State funeral
followed. General Richard Mulcahy issued an order for the Army to stand
firm and that there be no reprisals. However, in the days that followed,
three on the anti-Treaty side were murdered. From August onwards, the
Provisional Government, well armed with artillery, armoured cars and
the fighter planes of its fledgling Air Service, continued to establish its
authority over towns across the State. The Republicans grimly held on.
Enduring poor conditions, they maintained a presence across parts of the
country, particularly the remoter and more mountainous areas.

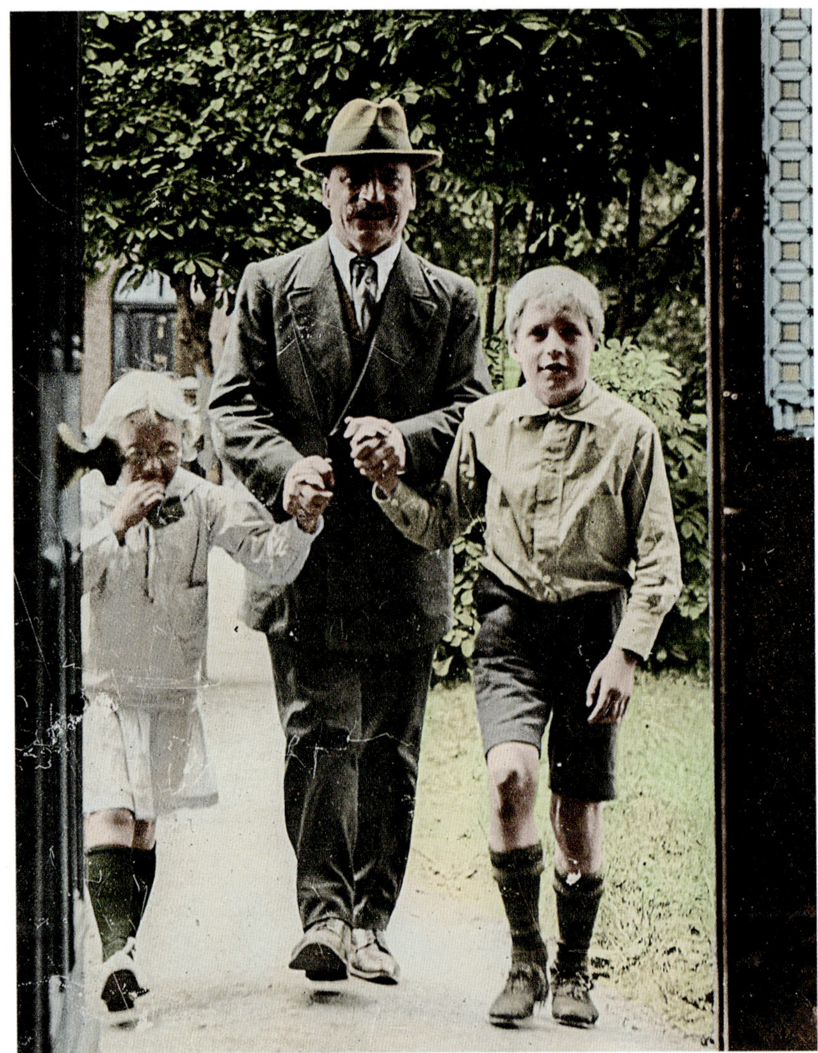

On 12 August 1922, the Provisional Government was dealt a blow when Arthur Griffith, President of Dáil Éireann, died of a cerebral haemorrhage, aged 51. With the cachet of an elder statesman, he had been the most eminent of the pro-Treaty leaders. Here we see Griffith with his children, Ita and Nevin.

Right: Michael Collins, Commander-in-Chief of the Provisional Government Army, had just begun a tour of the south in early August when news came of Griffith's death. Collins returned for the funeral.

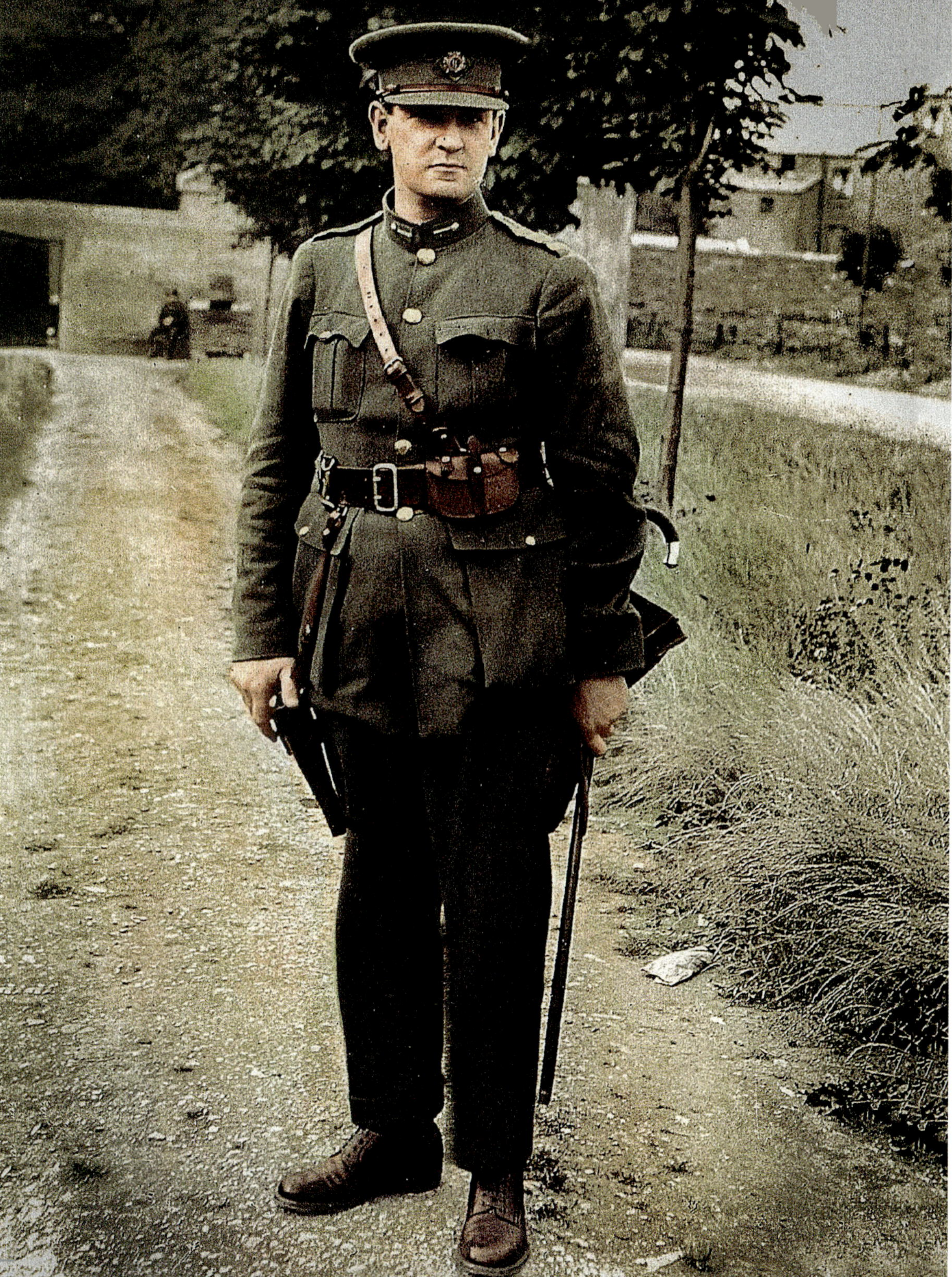

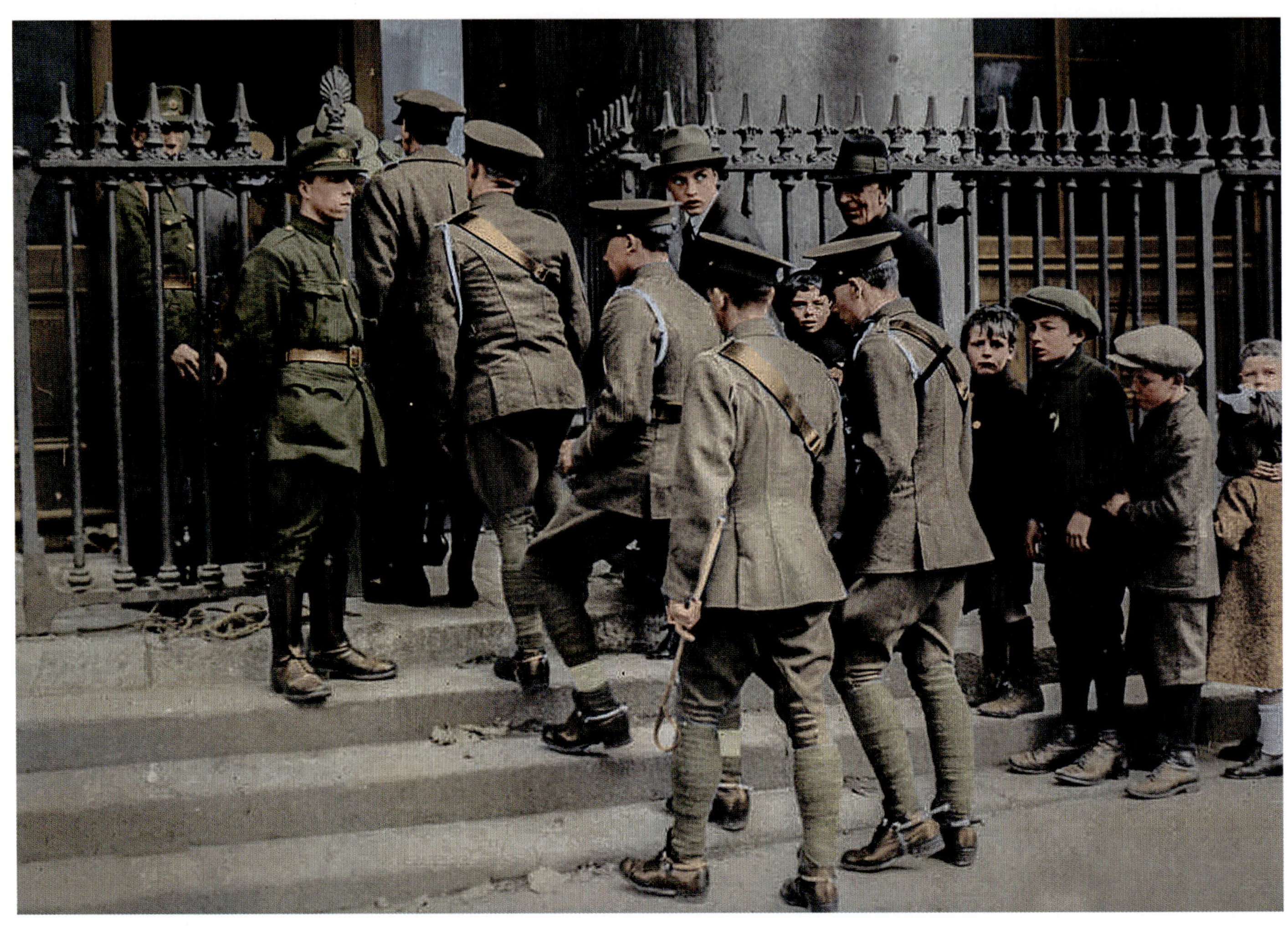

A group of British soldiers (still stationed in barracks around Dublin) enter the Pro-Cathedral at Marlborough Street to pay their respects to Arthur Griffith.

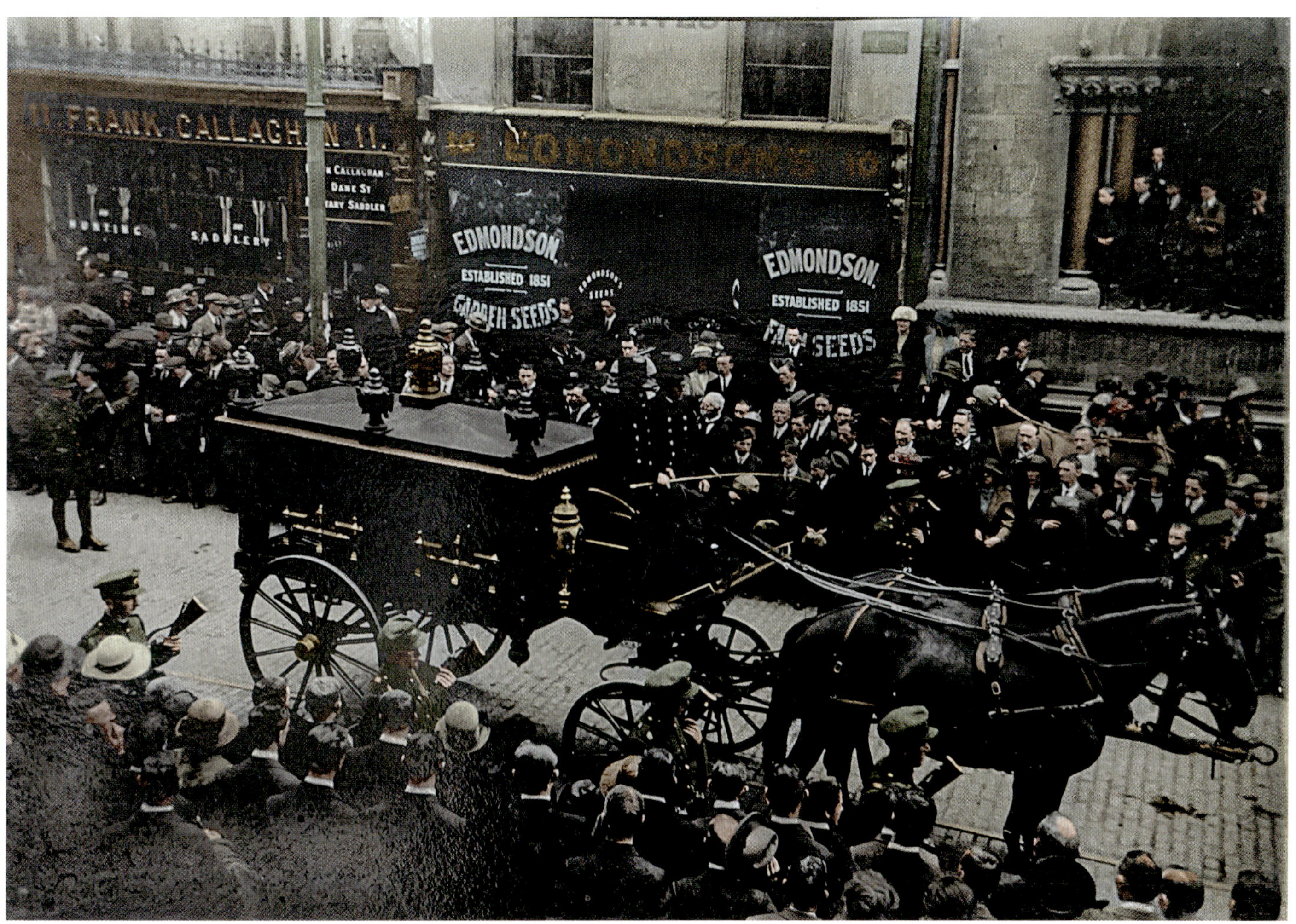

Arthur Griffith's funeral procession travels west along Dame Street on 16 August 1922. Bank staff stand on the window ledge of what was then the Munster and Leinster Bank (designed in Lombardic style in 1872 by Thomas Deane, now an AIB branch). Crowds thronged the streets – a half-million according to Pathé News. Michael Collins and Richard Mulcahy led the procession.

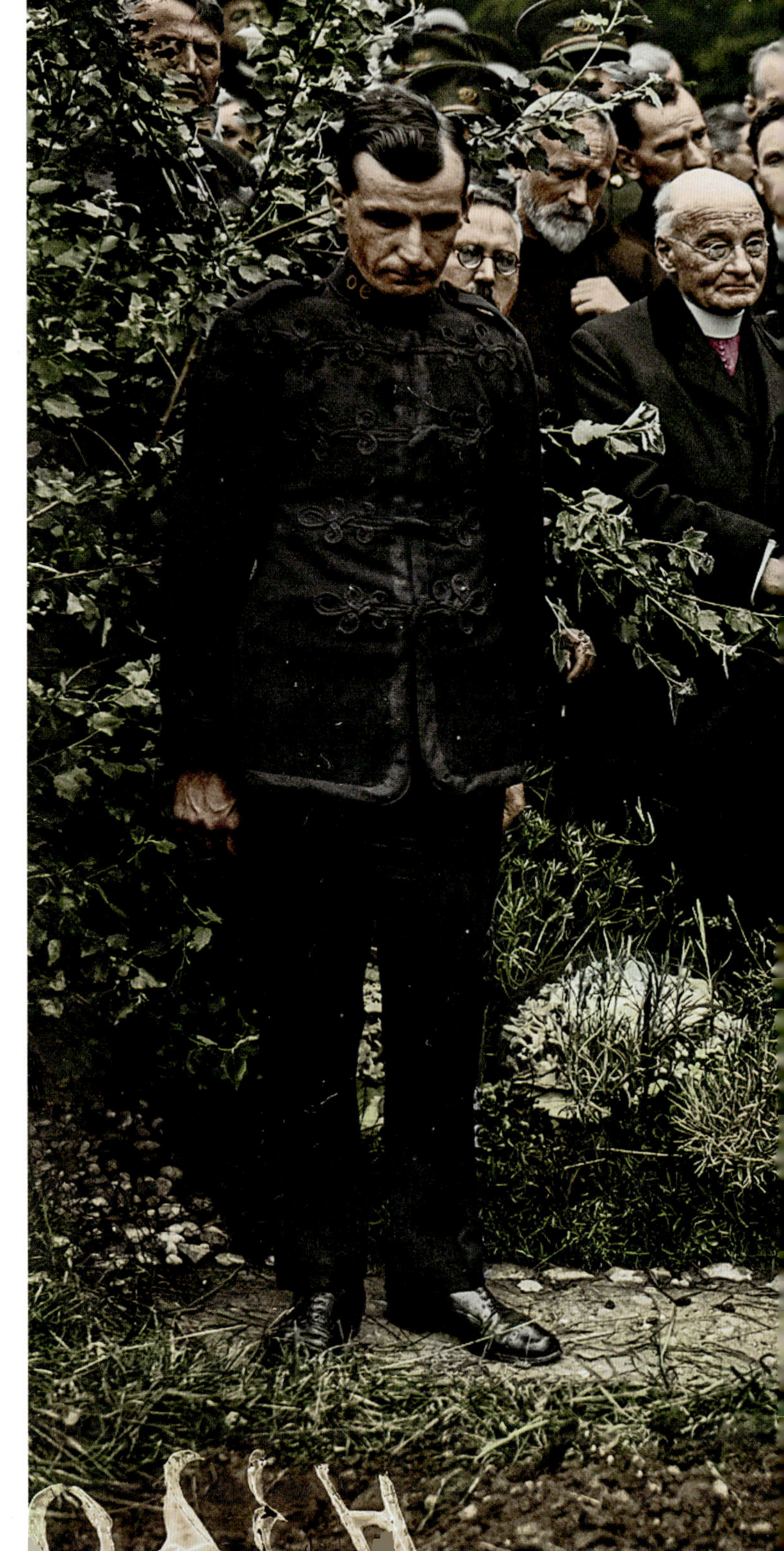

At Arthur Griffith's funeral in Glasnevin Cemetery. W.T. Cosgrave gives the graveside oration. During his speech he took the opportunity to lash out at his anti-Treaty opponents (with de Valera clearly in mind) when he referred to 'those magicians of political metaphysics who say one thing and mean another'.

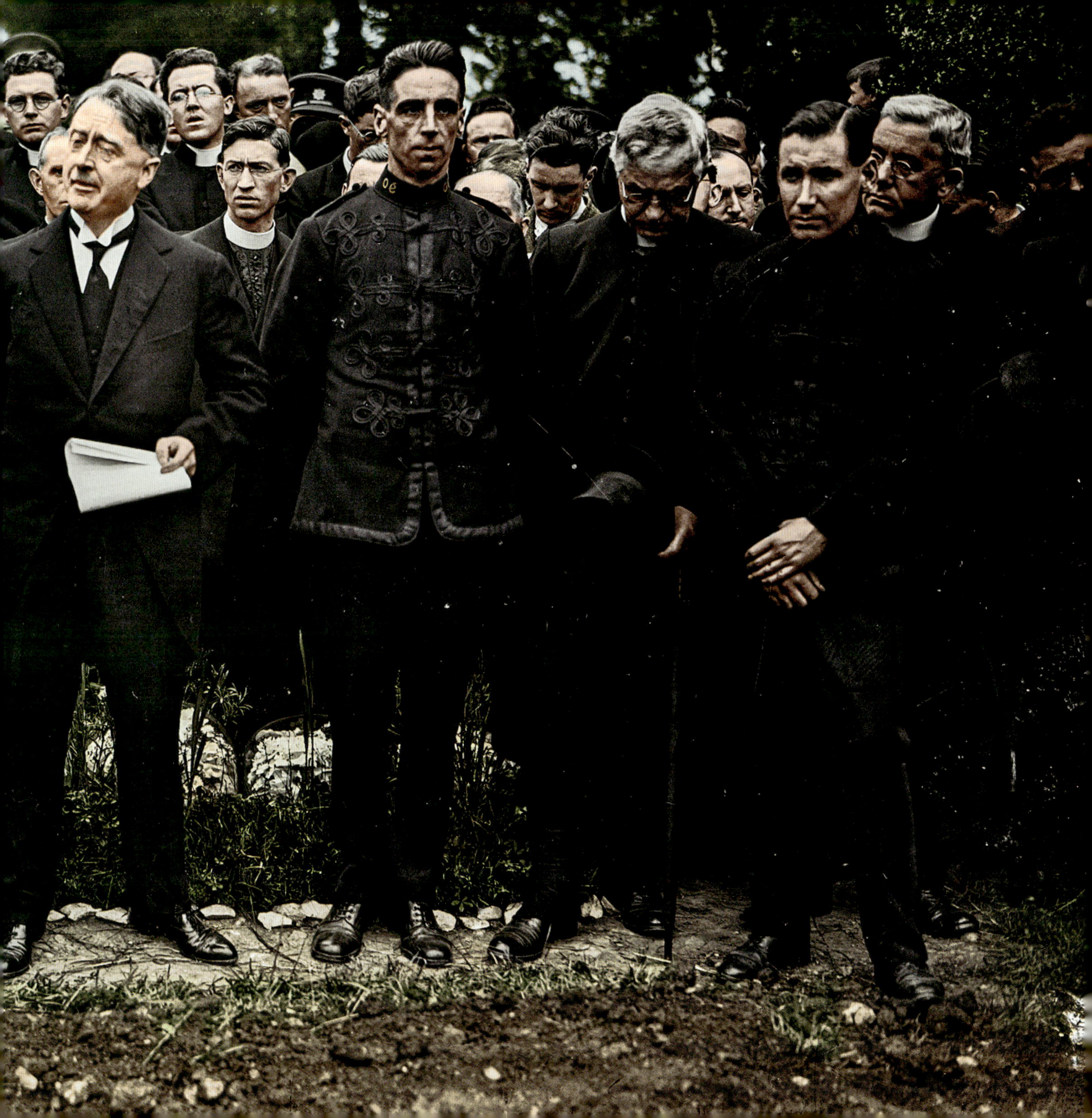

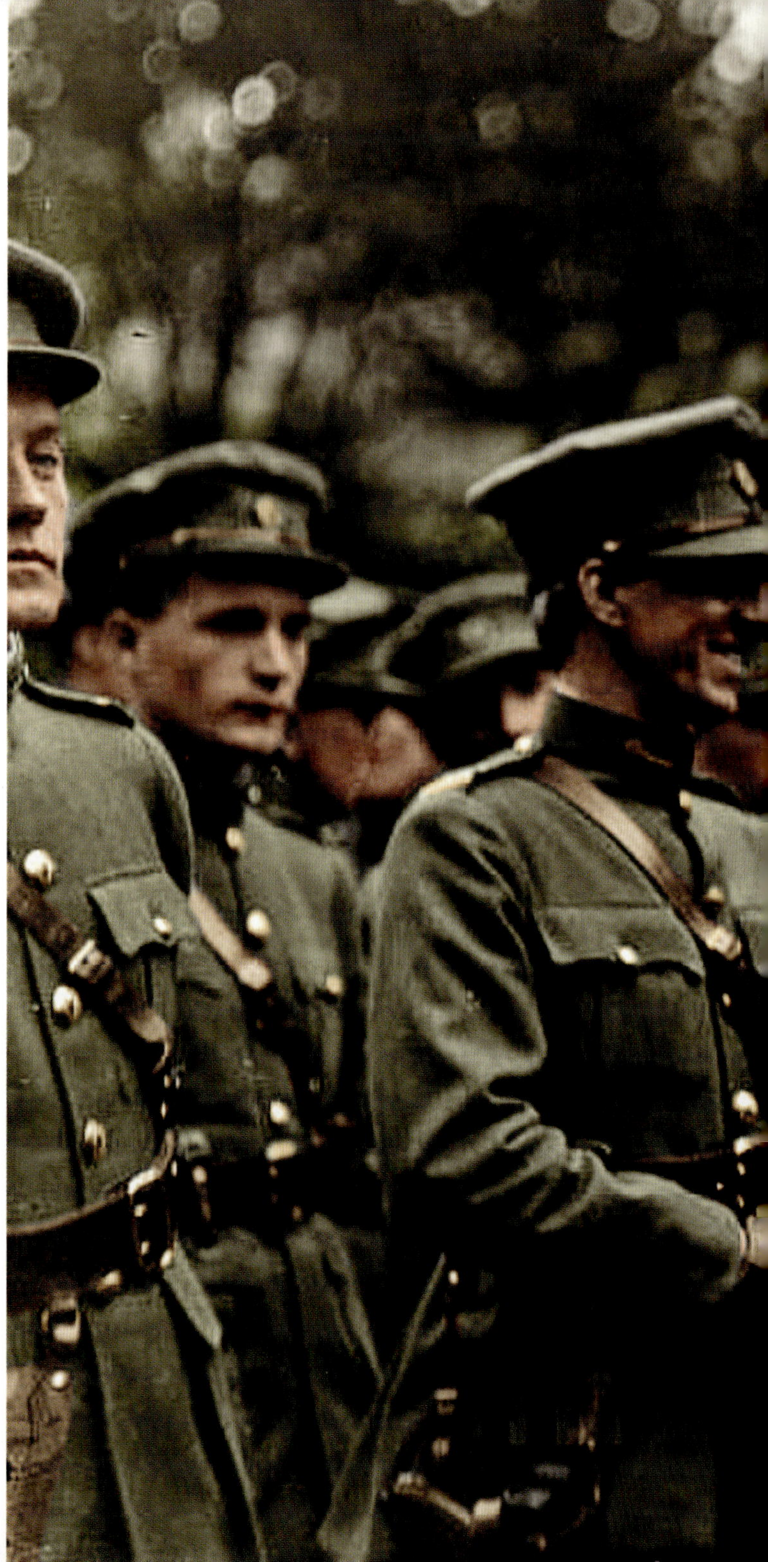

Michael Collins at Griffith's funeral on 16 August 1922. He, himself, had only six days left to live. Even though he was suffering from a bad cold, Collins resumed his southern journey on 20 August and reached Cork City that night. He stayed in the Imperial Hotel which, owing to the complete destruction of the military barracks by the departing Republicans, had been made the Provisional Government military headquarters in the city. He spent the next day trying to trace Republican funds lodged in the city's banks. The ever-active Collins, along with Major-General Emmet Dalton (GOC Cork), also managed to find time to visit Macroom, where he met Florence O'Donoghue, who had founded the 'Neutral' IRA, which argued for compromise. Following a discussion on mediation and how to stop the Civil War, Collins and Dalton returned to Cork in the early evening.

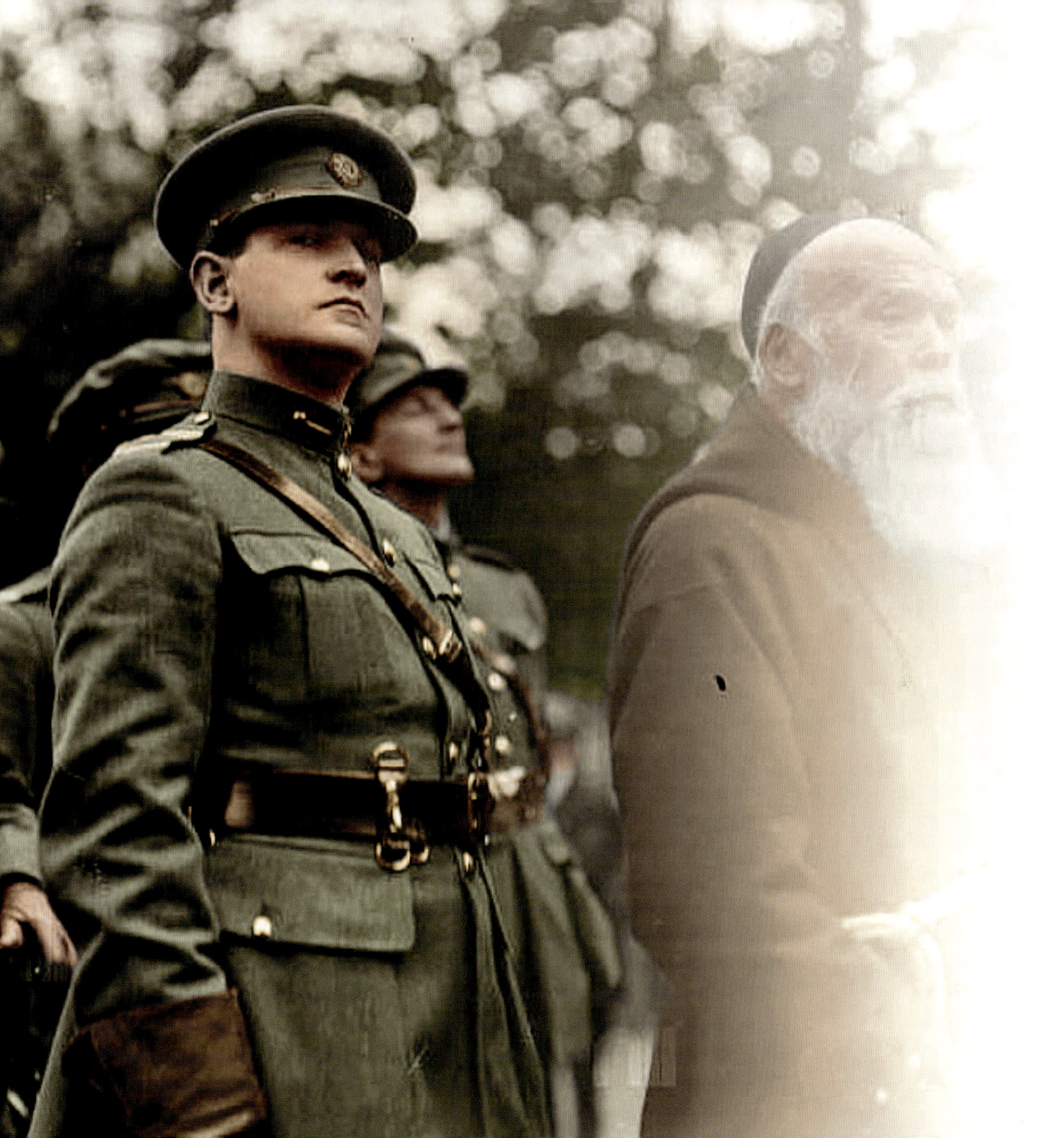

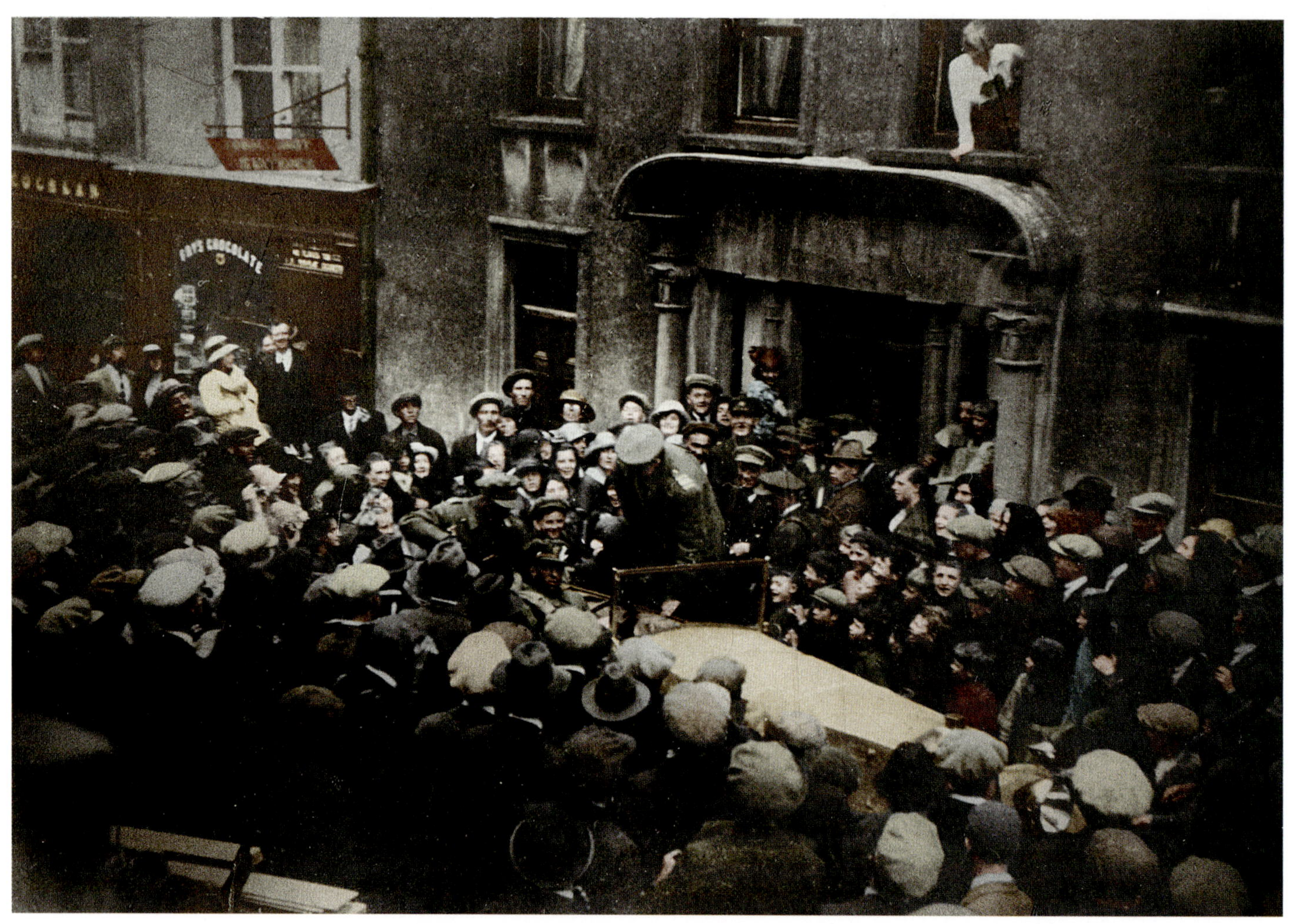

At 6.15 a.m. on 22 August 1922, accompanied by Emmet Dalton, Michael Collins set out from the Imperial Hotel for his tour of West Cork, with the objective of assessing the situation on the ground and meeting old comrades. The convoy consisted of a motorcycle outrider, a Crossley Tender carrying soldiers, a Leyland Eight touring car and, bringing up the rear, the *Sliabh na mBan* Rolls-Royce armoured car. En route, the party stopped at Bealnablath crossroads at around 9 a.m. to ask a man (who happened to be an IRA Volunteer) for directions. In this photo, Collins climbs into his touring car at around 4.30 p.m. for the return journey to Cork. He is leaving the Eldon Hotel in Skibbereen, where he had a meal. This was the furthest point of his journey that day.

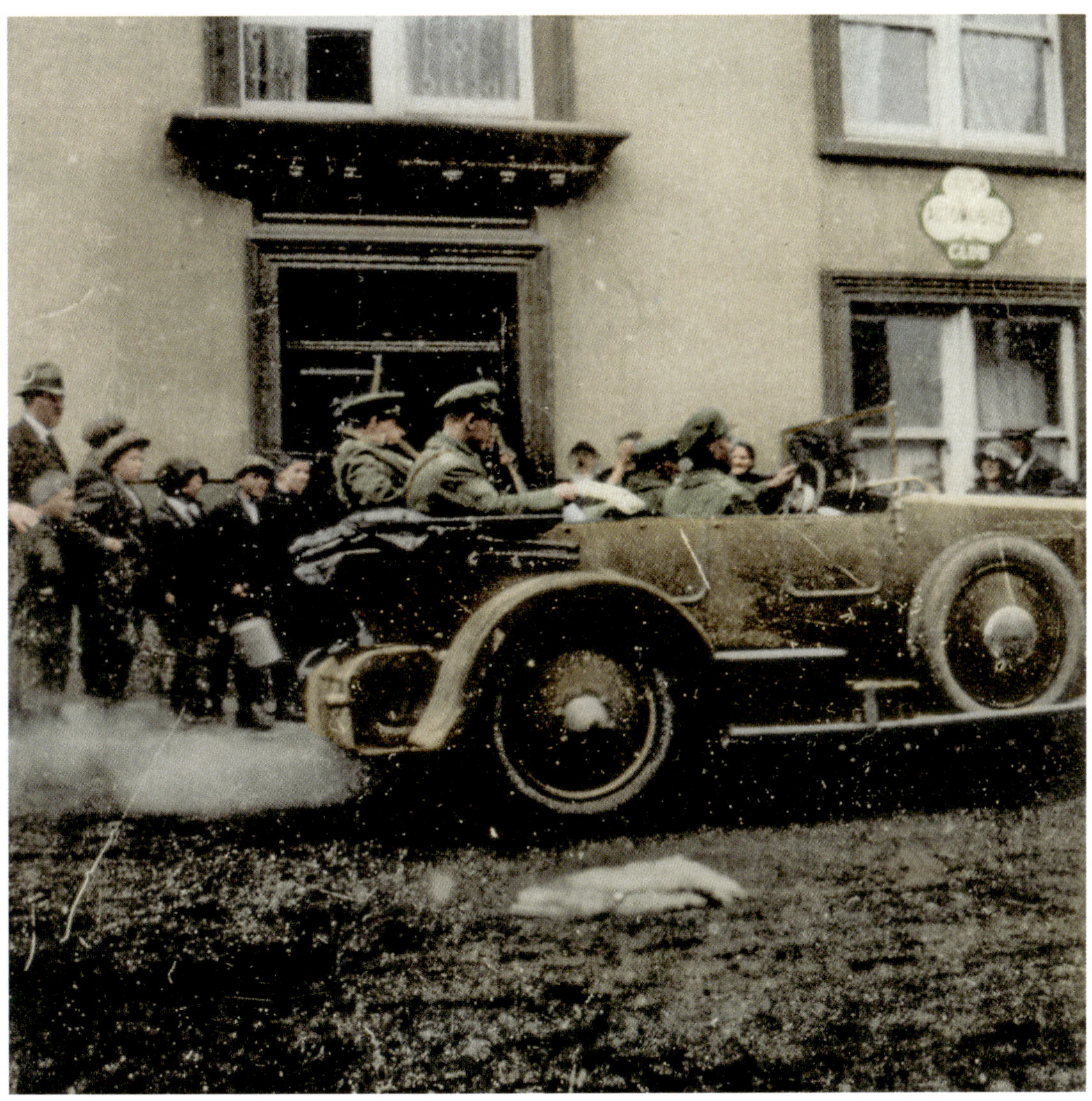

The last photograph of Michael Collins, taken as he passed through Bandon on the return journey. At around 7.15 p.m., in fading light, the convoy approached Bealnablath, where an ambush had been prepared by the anti-Treaty IRA. The ambushers were about to clear away a barricade and a mine when the convoy arrived. There was a heavy exchange of fire. Collins fired at the attackers with his rifle. A shot rang out and Collins fell, mortally wounded, with a gaping hole behind his right ear.

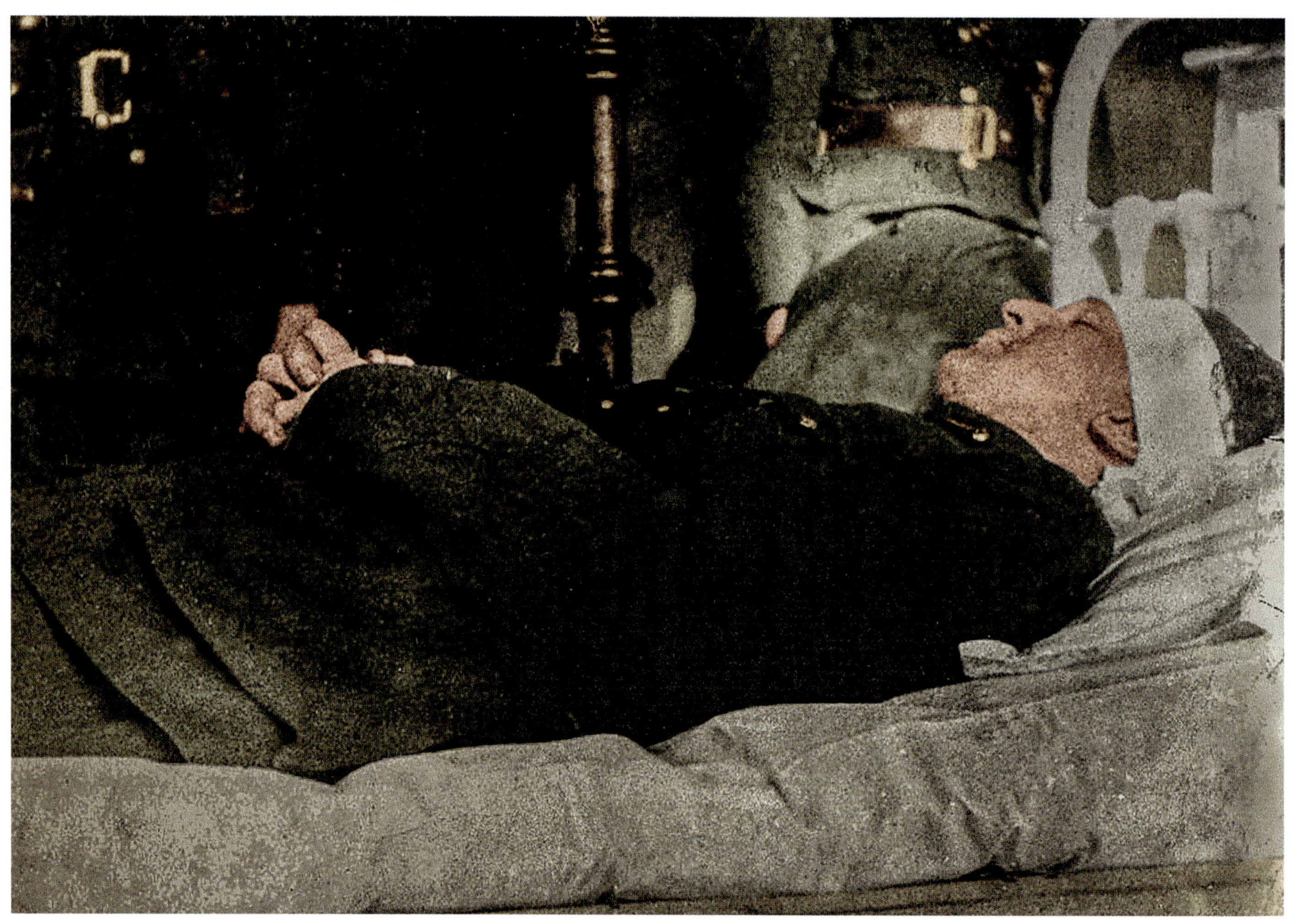

Collins's body was first placed onto the rear of the armoured car and was later transferred to the Leyland Eight tourer. Following a nightmarish journey, the party reached Cork City after midnight. As seen here, his body was laid out in Shanakiel Hospital. Emmet Dalton managed, with difficulty, to send the news of his death back to Army GHQ, Dublin in the early hours of 23 August. The message was relayed by shortwave radio to Waterville, cabled from there to New York, thence by cable via London to Dublin.

Right: at Bealnablath, Michael Collins's sister, Mary Collins Powell, in the course of a ceremony held some time after the ambush. A simple wooden cross marks the spot where he died.

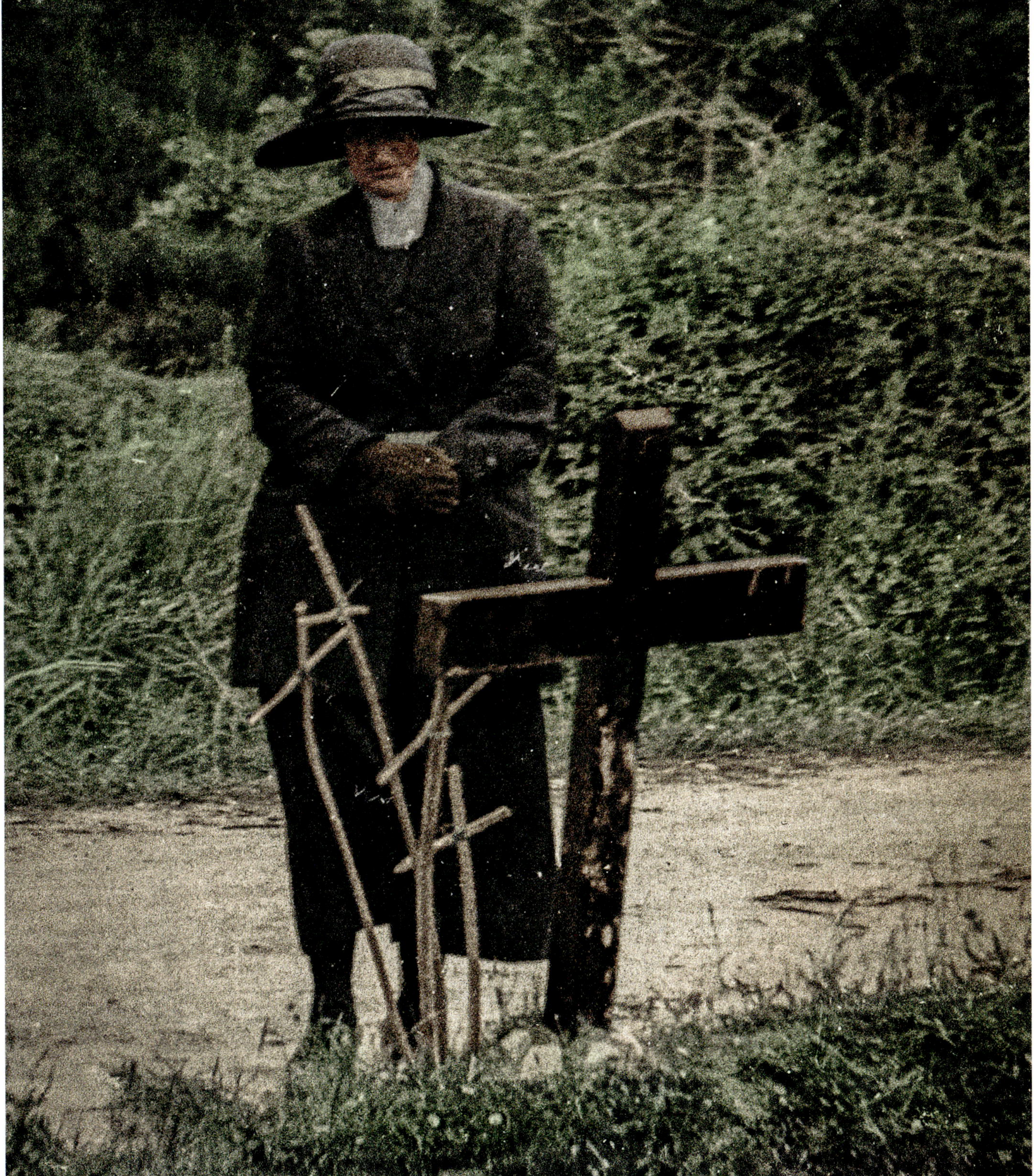

There was immediate grief in Cork City as the news of
Collins's death filtered through. In response, businesses
voluntarily closed. On the evening of 23 August, as citizens
lined the streets, a hearse, escorted by soldiers with reversed
rifles, transferred the remains to the quays. In the scene
here at Penrose Quay, the coffin is being carried onto the
cross-channel steamer *Classic* for the journey to Dublin.
The ship sailed down Cork Harbour and, as it passed the
Royal Navy base at Haulbowline, the crew of the light
cruiser HMS *Castor* saluted and sounded the last post.

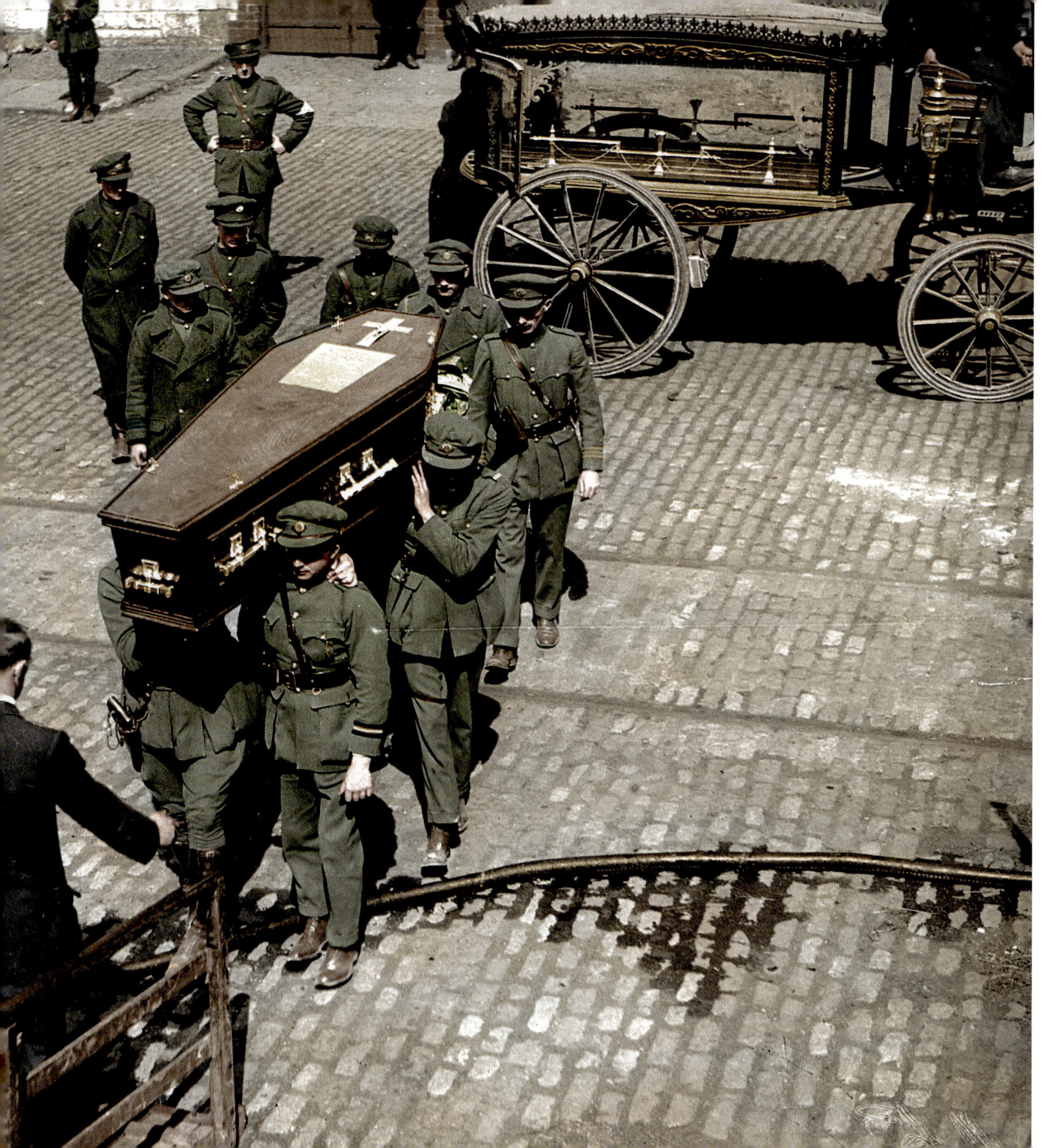

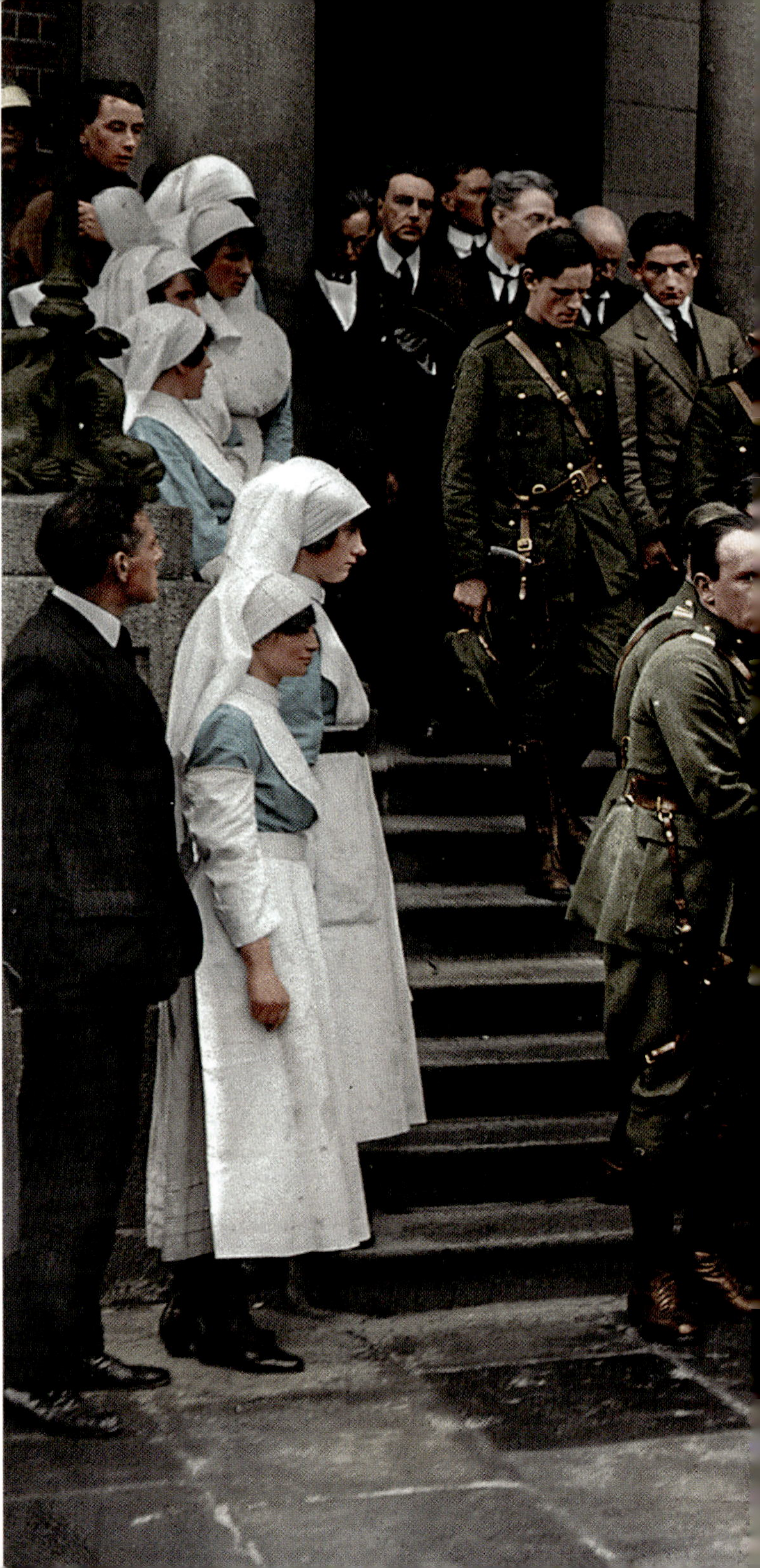

On arrival at Dublin, the remains of Michael Collins were transferred to St Vincent's Hospital (then located on the east side of St Stephen's Green). Oliver St John Gogarty embalmed the body, Sir John Lavery painted a deathbed portrait and Albert Power made a death mask. In turn, the remains were transferred to City Hall. In this scene, nurses form a guard of honour as leading army officers (including, from left at the back, Kevin O'Higgins, Richard Mulcahy, partly obscured, and Gearóid O'Sullivan) carry the coffin down the hospital steps. W.T. Cosgrave, also partly obscured, is at the top of the steps.

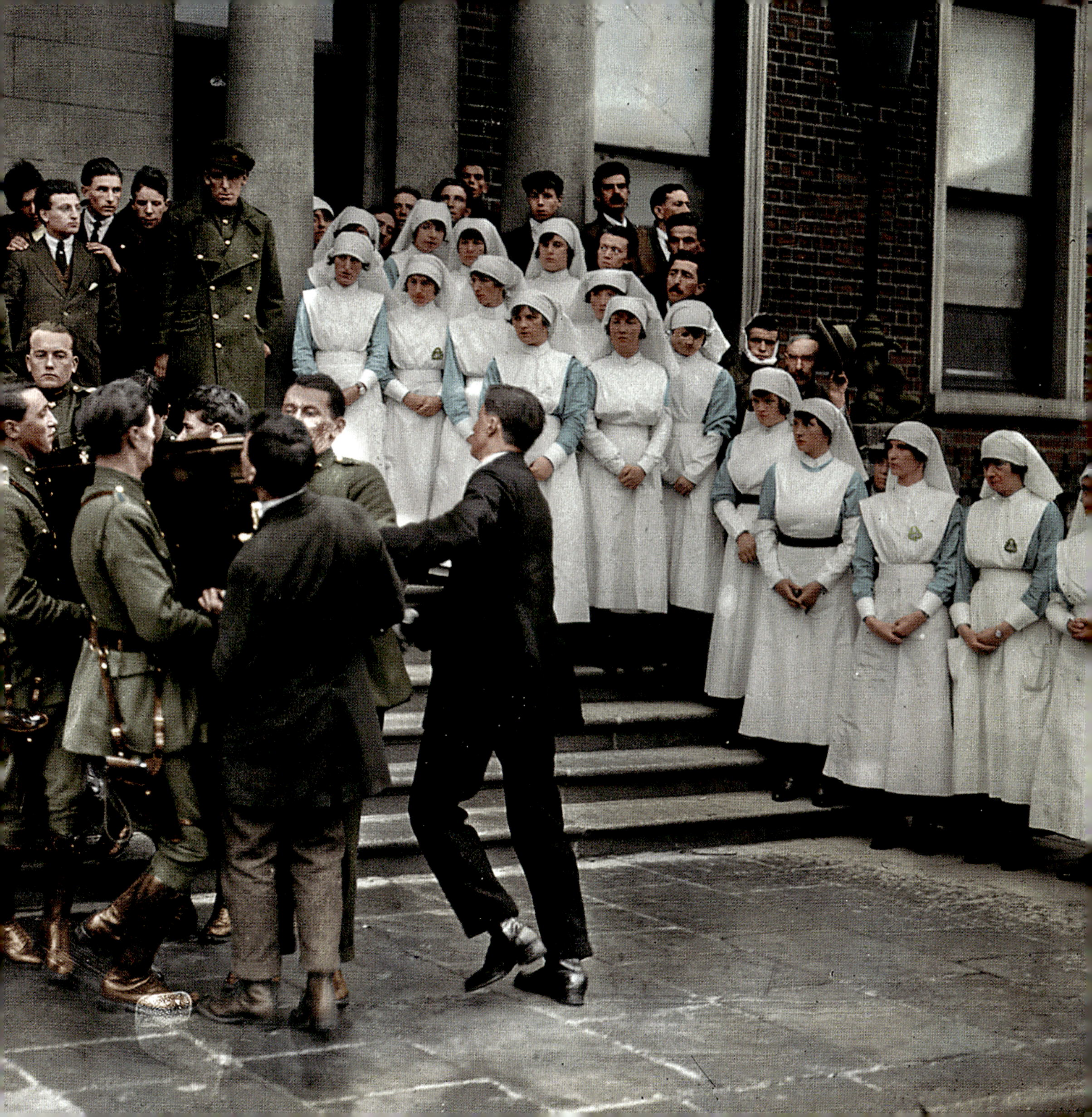

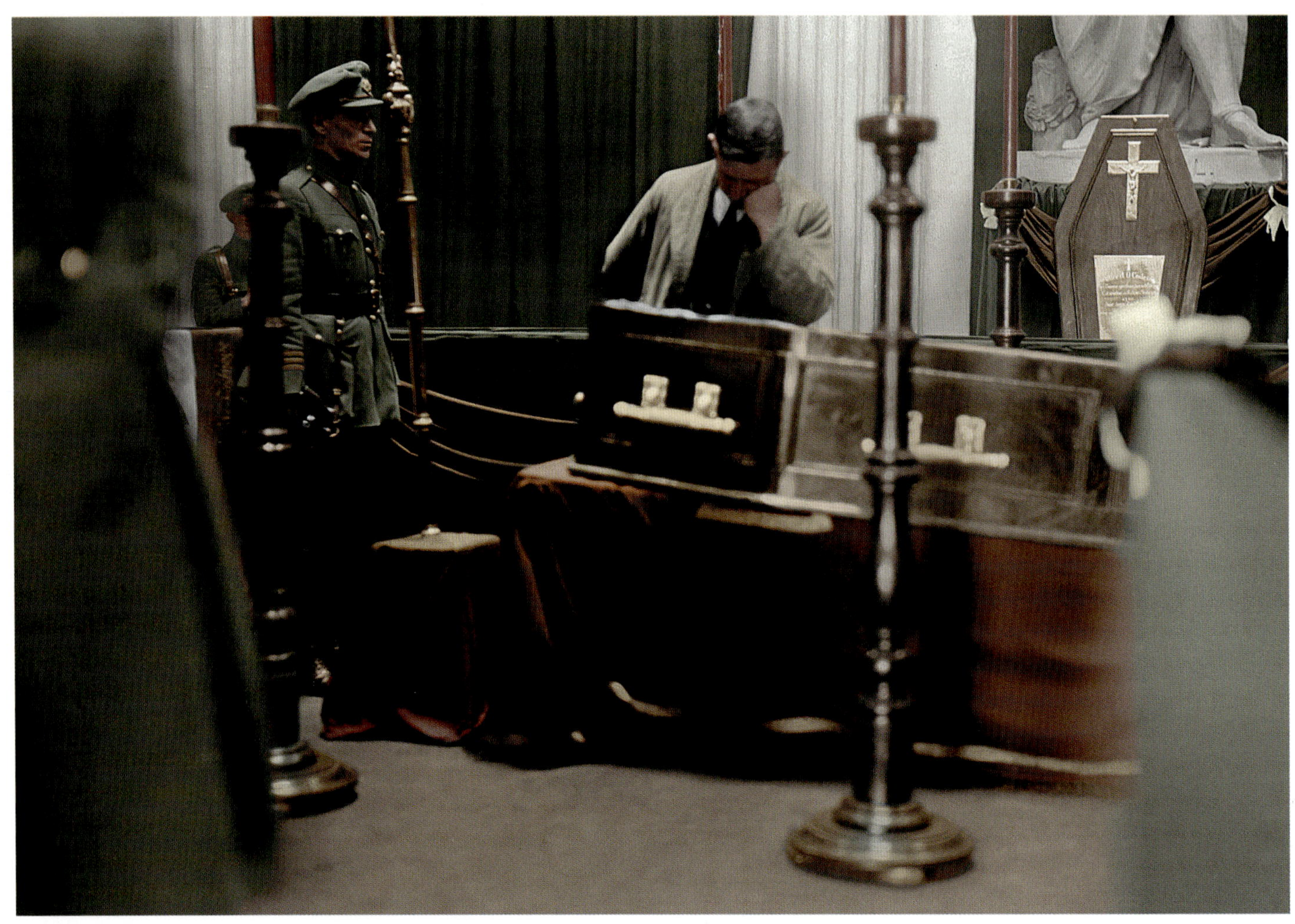

The remains were placed in the Rotunda of the City Hall for a public lying-in-state until Sunday 27 August. Here, Seán Collins (who had last met his brother, Michael, in West Cork on the fatal day, 22 August) mourns.

Right: the remains were removed to the Pro-Cathedral, where a funeral mass was celebrated on 28 August. Next, the coffin was placed on a gun carriage of one of the 18-pounders used for the Four Courts bombardment. For the journey to Glasnevin Cemetery, this was drawn by four artillery horses, specially purchased from the British Army. As seen here, the tricolour over the coffin was mistakenly reversed. (The protocol is that the green should be at the head of the coffin.) The error was soon corrected.

196

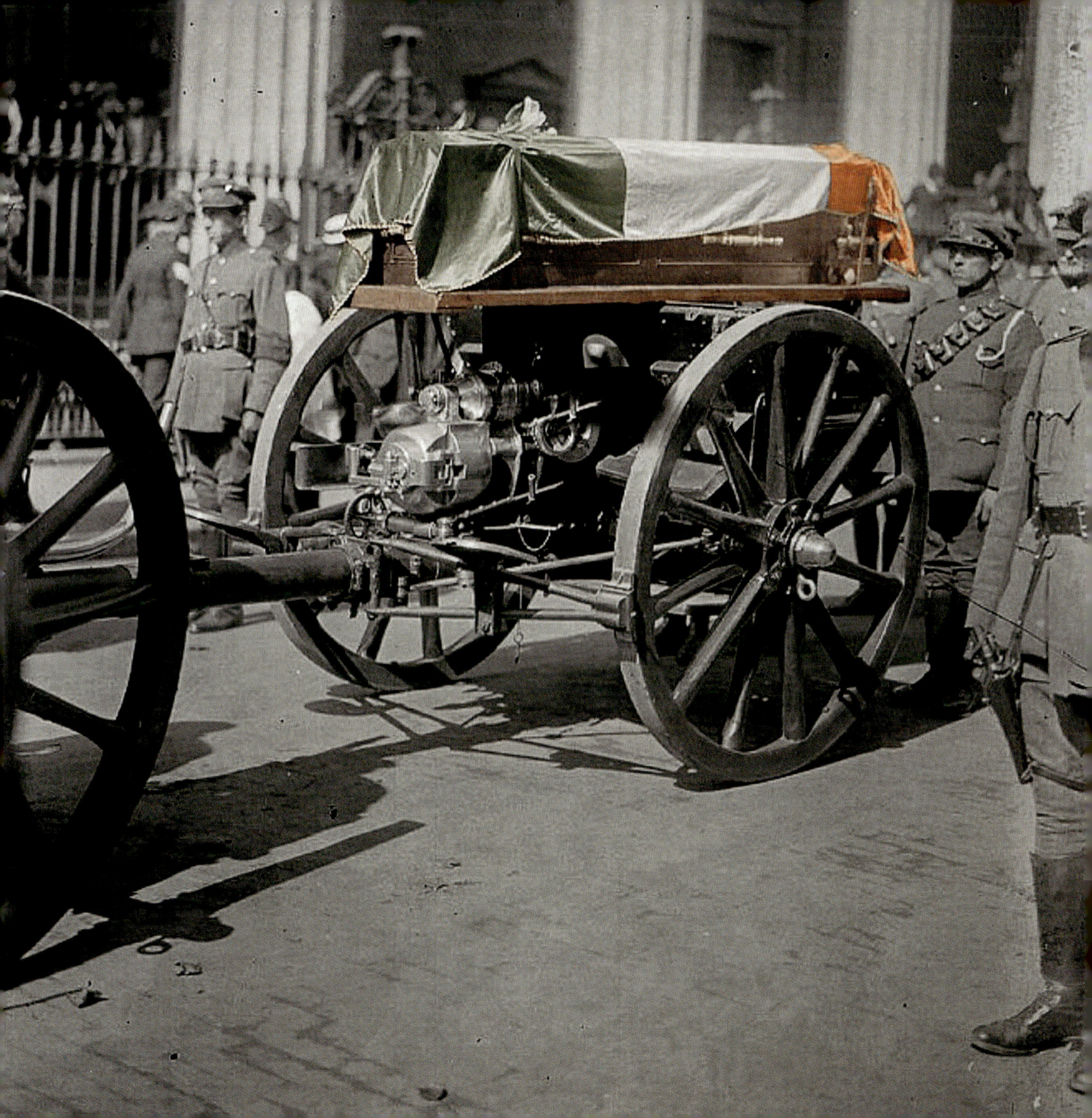

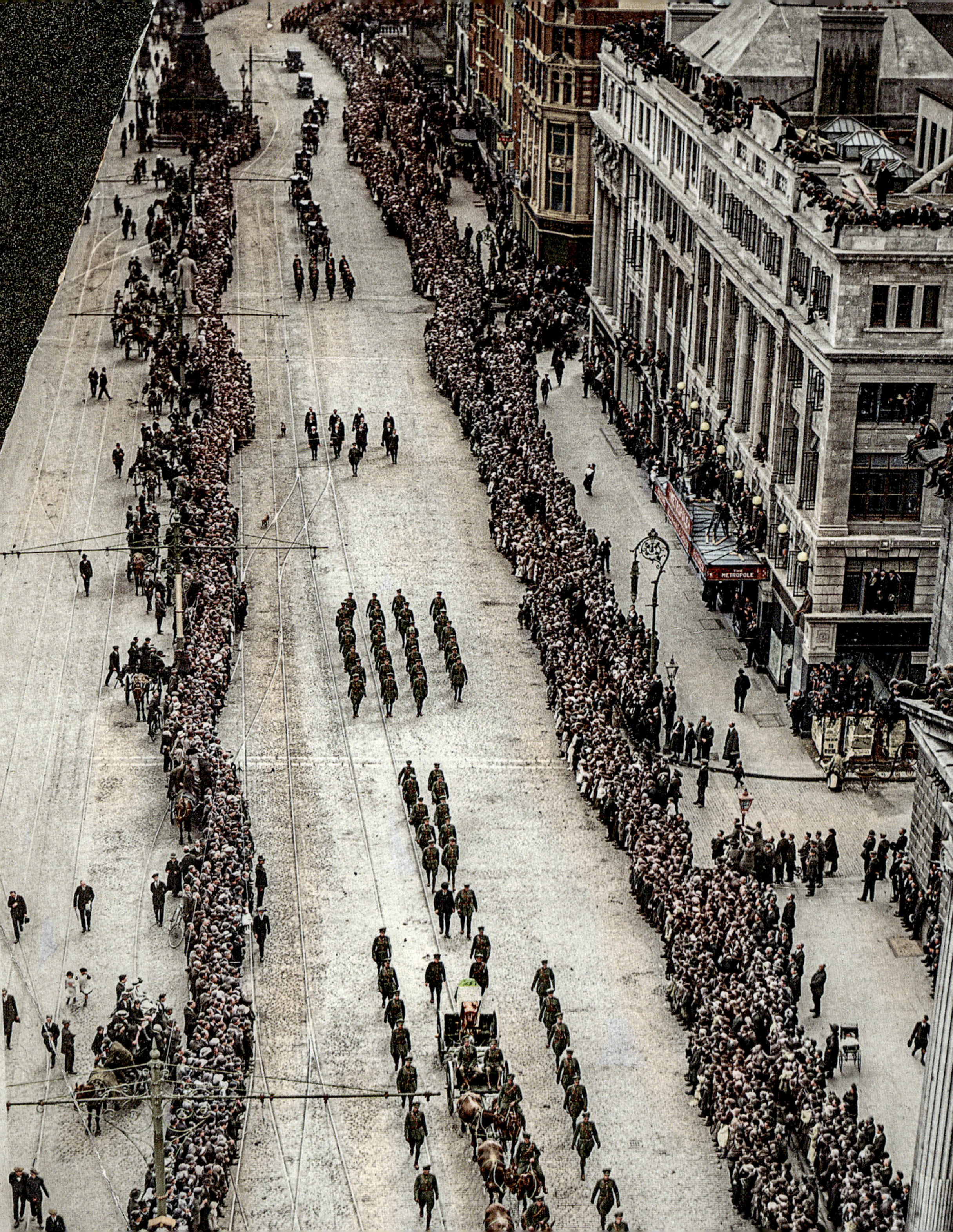
THE METROPOLE

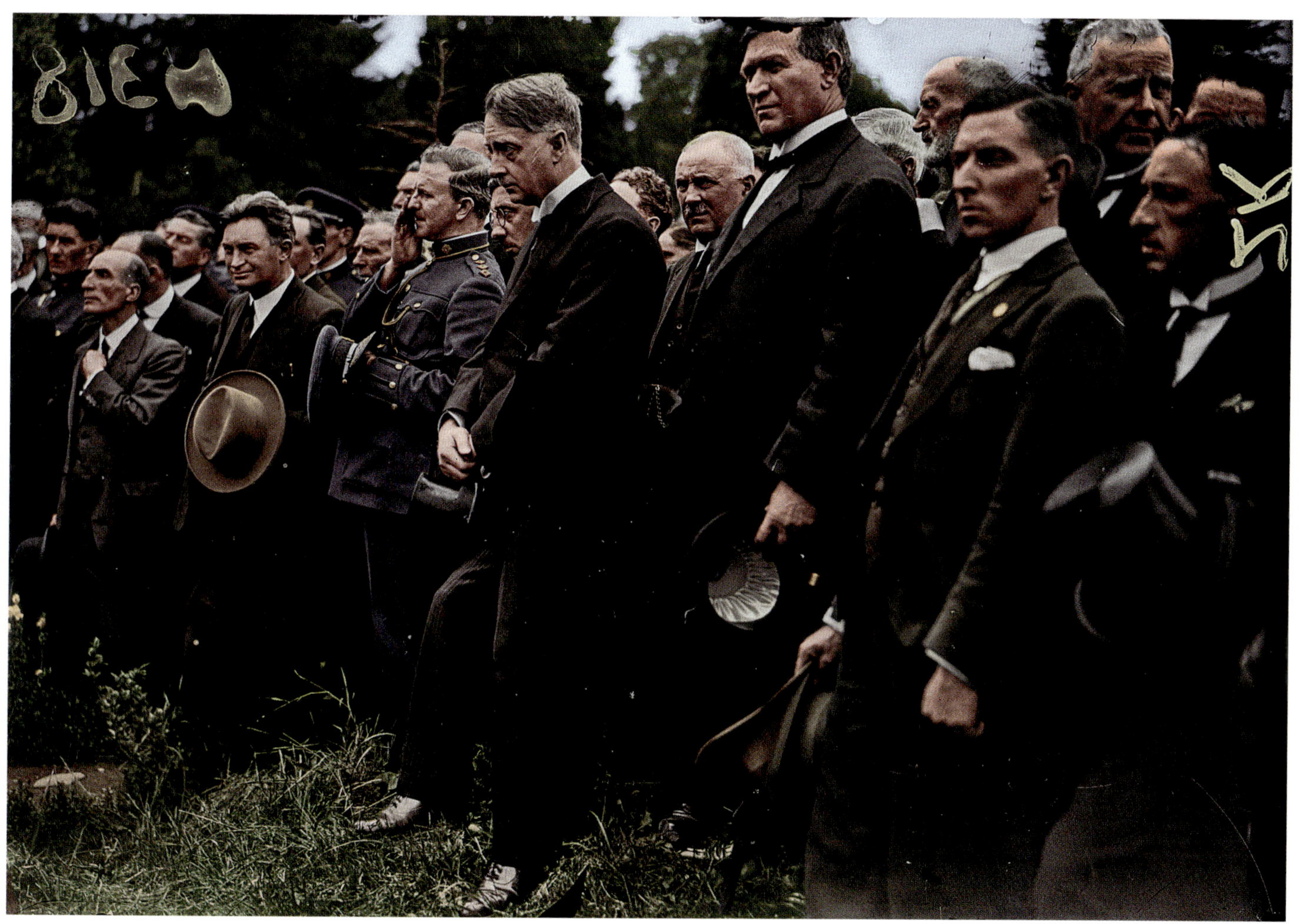

Amongst the personages at the graveside at Glasnevin are, from centre left, General Eoin O'Duffy (in Garda Commissioner's uniform, a post he would take up the following month), W.T. Cosgrave and, standing tall, Michael Collin's brother, Seán. Cosgrave was appointed Chairman of the Provisional Government as a replacement for Collins.

Left: a view from Nelson's Pillar of the funeral cortège on Lower Sackville Street. As the crowds watch, the coffin and gun carriage are escorted by troops of the National Army. In the background, a convoy of cars pass the O'Connell Monument.

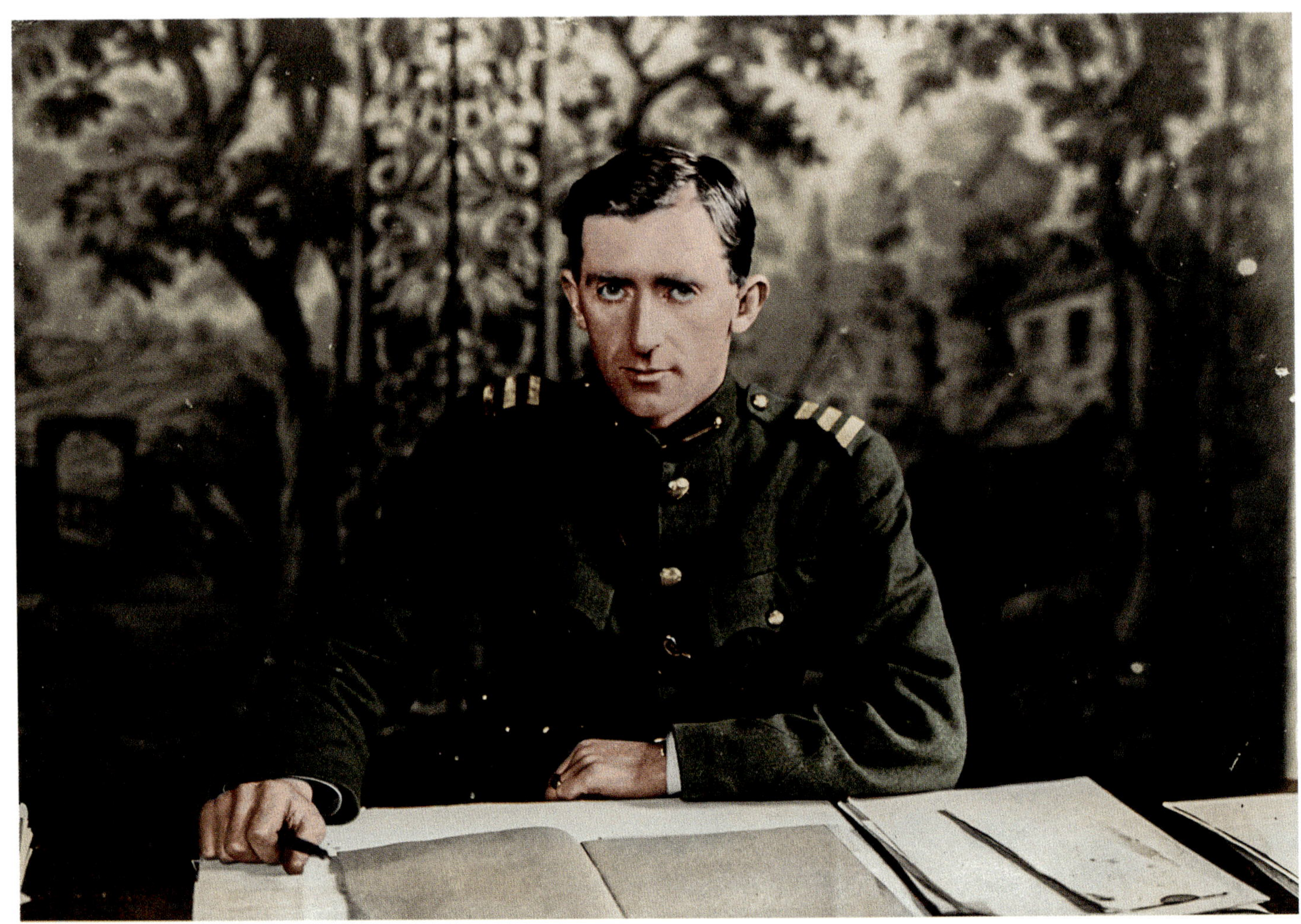

During the early hours of 23 August, after Richard Mulcahy heard of Collins's death, he immediately wrote a message, as Chief of the General Staff, to the 'Men of the Army'. It states: 'Stand calmly by your posts. Bend bravely and undaunted to your work. Let no cruel act of reprisal blemish your bright honour … Ireland! The Army serves – strengthened by its sorrow'.

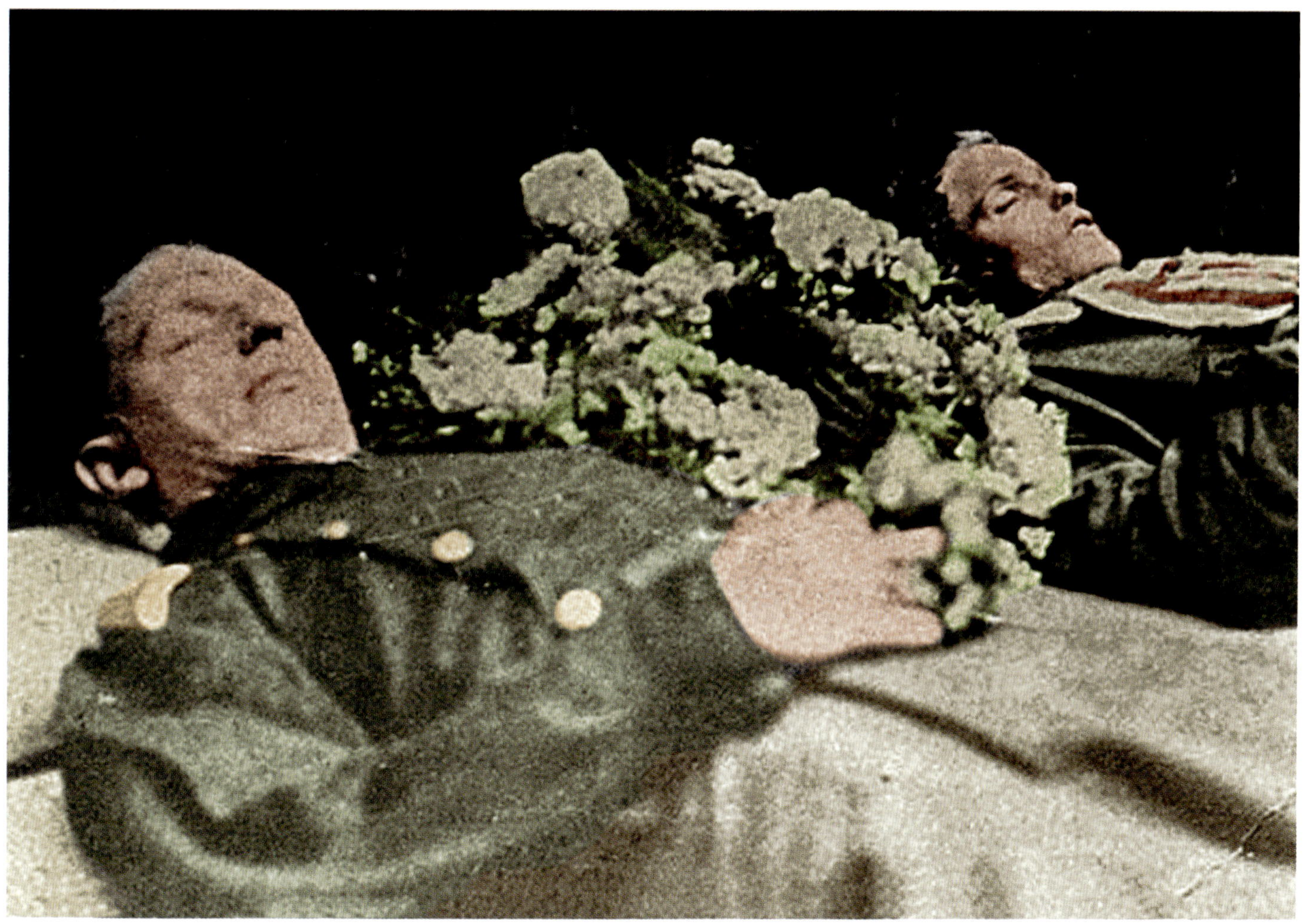

However, despite the fine words, there were immediate reprisals in the Dublin area. The dark shadow of Oriel House (see page 261) was made manifest in Dublin when on 26 August, Bernard Daly, a lieutenant in the anti-Treaty IRA, was detained by armed men at Suffolk Street. That night his body was brought to the city morgue by Provisional Government troops, who claimed to have discovered it. Also on the same day, two anti-Treaty youths, officers of Fianna Éireann, were abducted by armed men at Annesley Bridge near Fairview Park and driven to Whitehall. In full sight of witnesses, Alf Colley (21) and Seán Cole (19) were shot at a gate leading to a field. The killers then drove away. This poor-quality photograph shows the laid-out bodies of Cole and Colley.

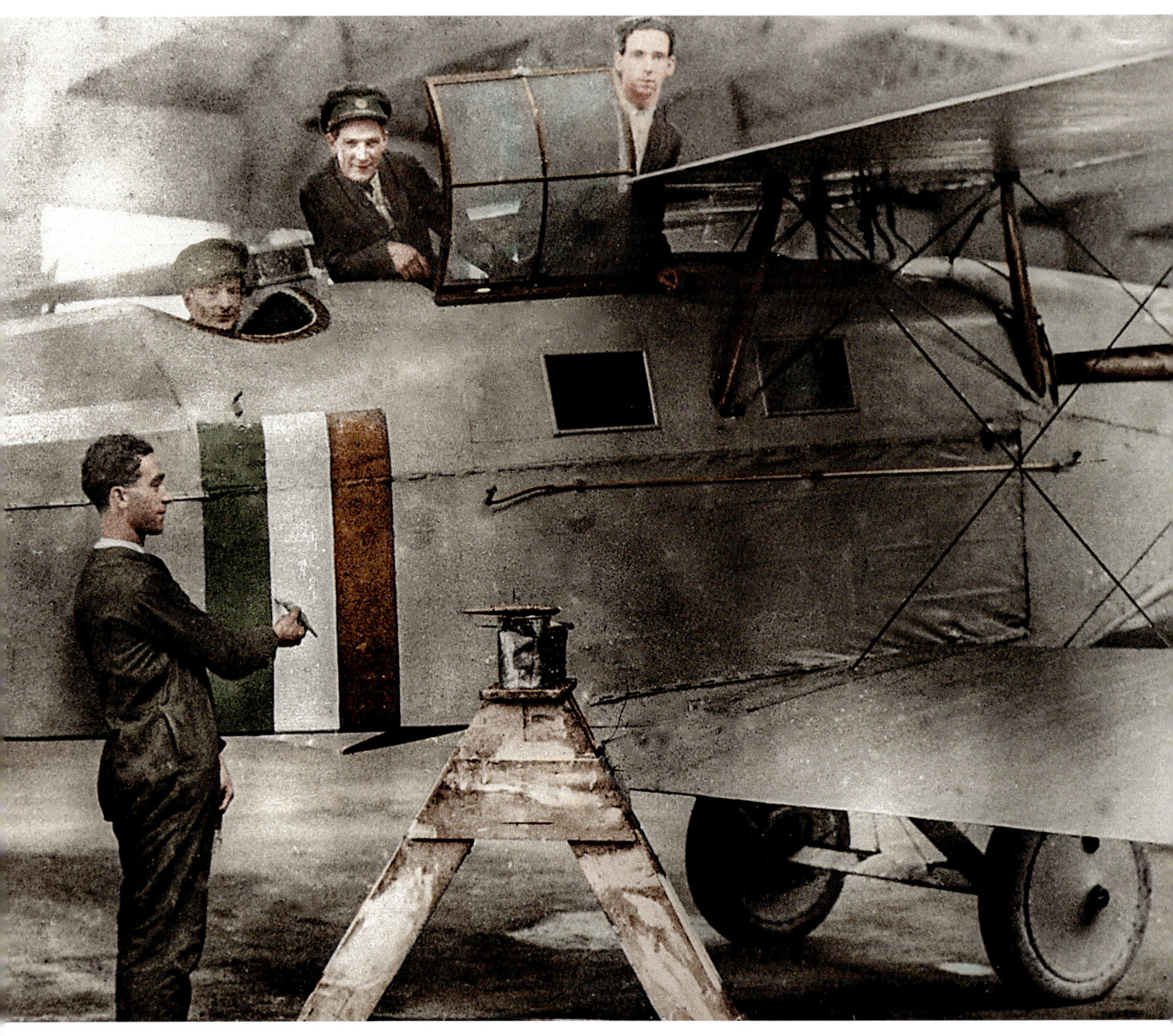

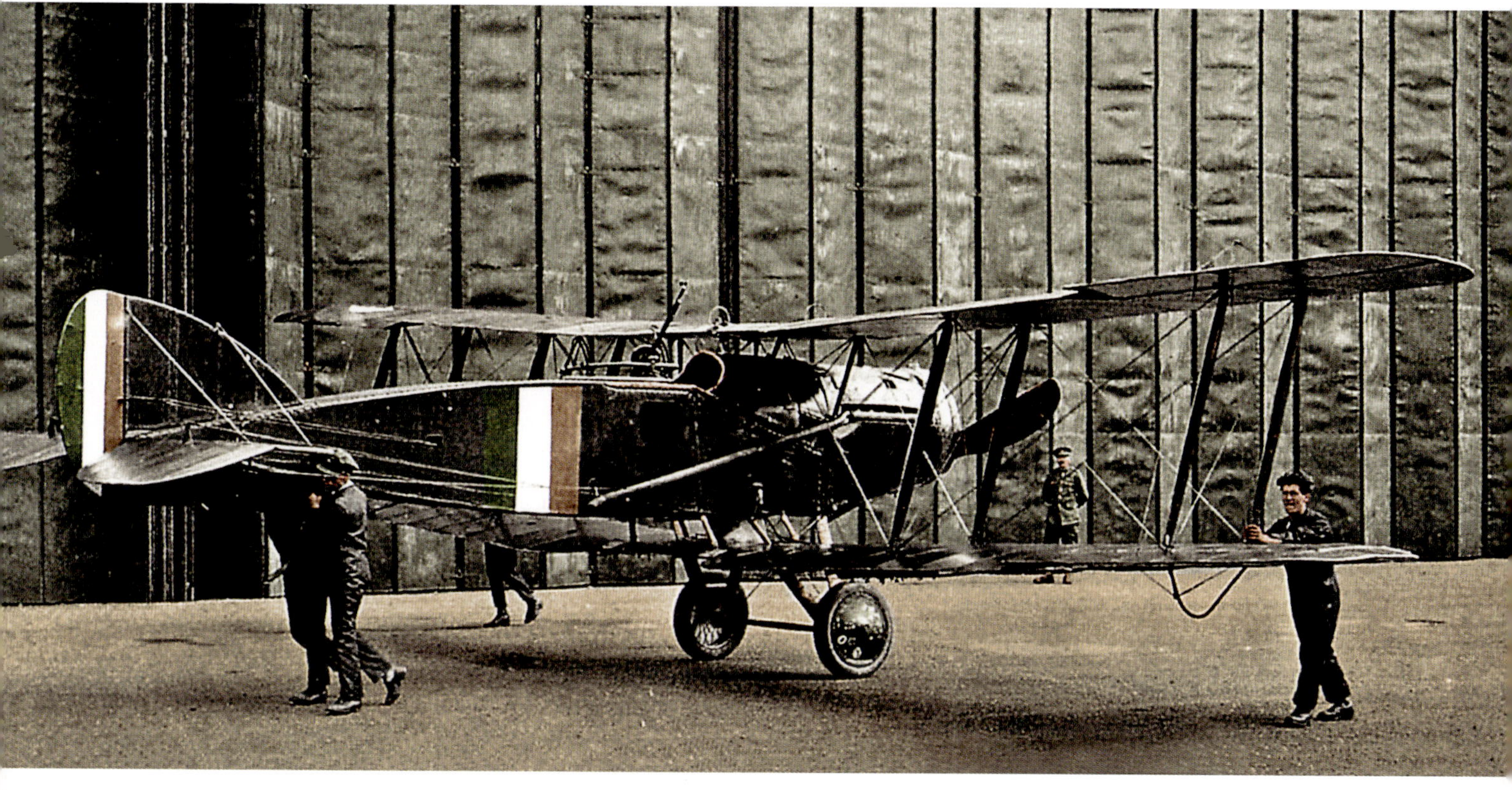

The Army Air Service (later known as the 'Army Air Corps') was established in mid-1922, acquiring its first fighter in early July. By the end of October 1922 there were 15 aircraft in service, of which six were Bristol F.2B fighters (above).

Left: the very first plane, a Martinsyde Type A1 Mk II, purchased during the Treaty negotiations. Seen here at Baldonnell (formerly an RAF base, now the HQ of Irish military aviation), the Irish tricolour is being painted on its fuselage.

Overleaf: a line-up of some of the Air Service fleet: from left, a Martinsyde F.4 Buzzard (one of the fastest fighters of its time); a Bristol F.2B and two DH.9 DII fighters. These Air Service aircraft were extensively used during the campaign in the south-west. As well as strafing Republican positions, duties included reconnaissance, patrolling railway lines and dropping propaganda leaflets.

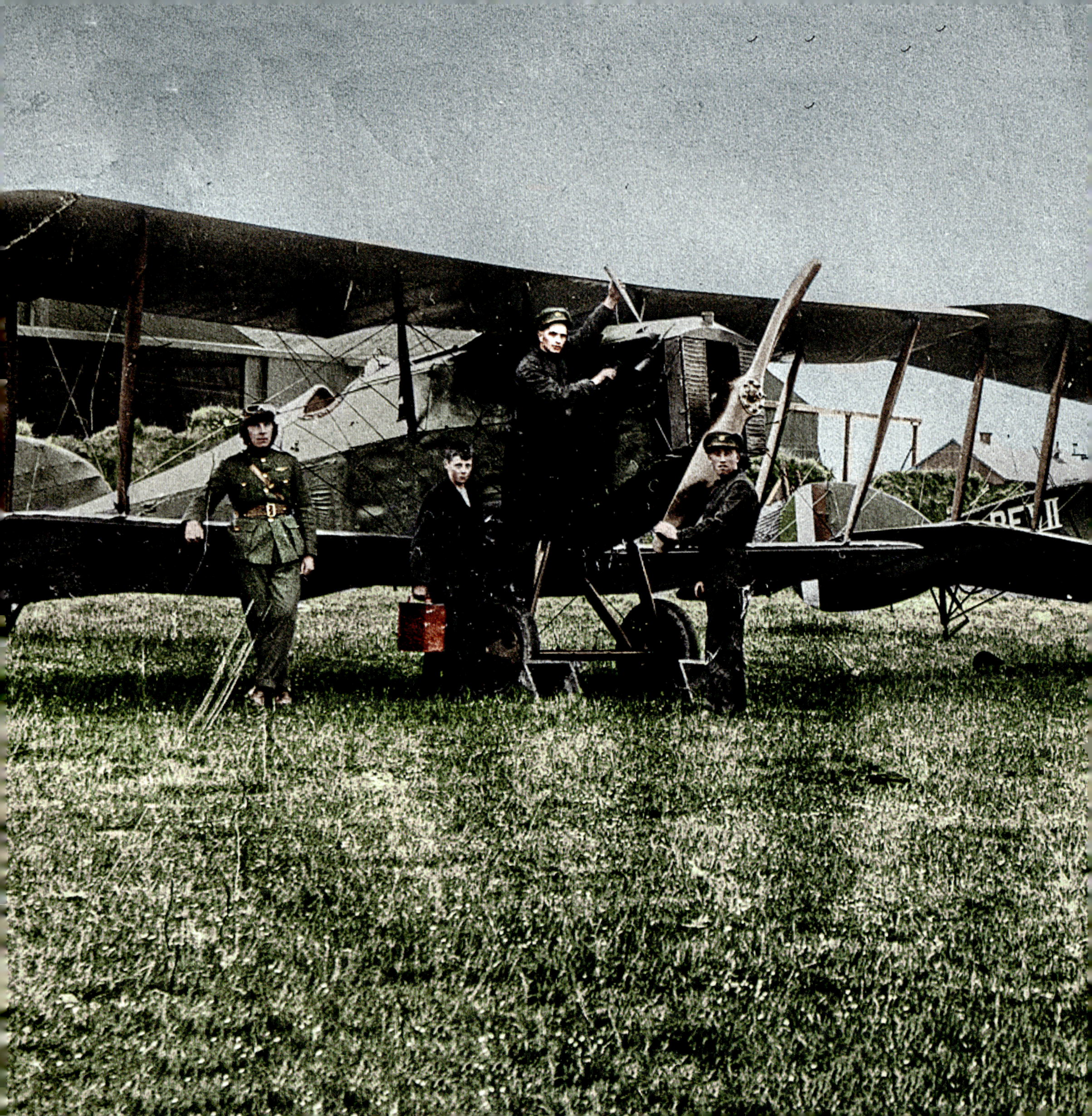
RE II

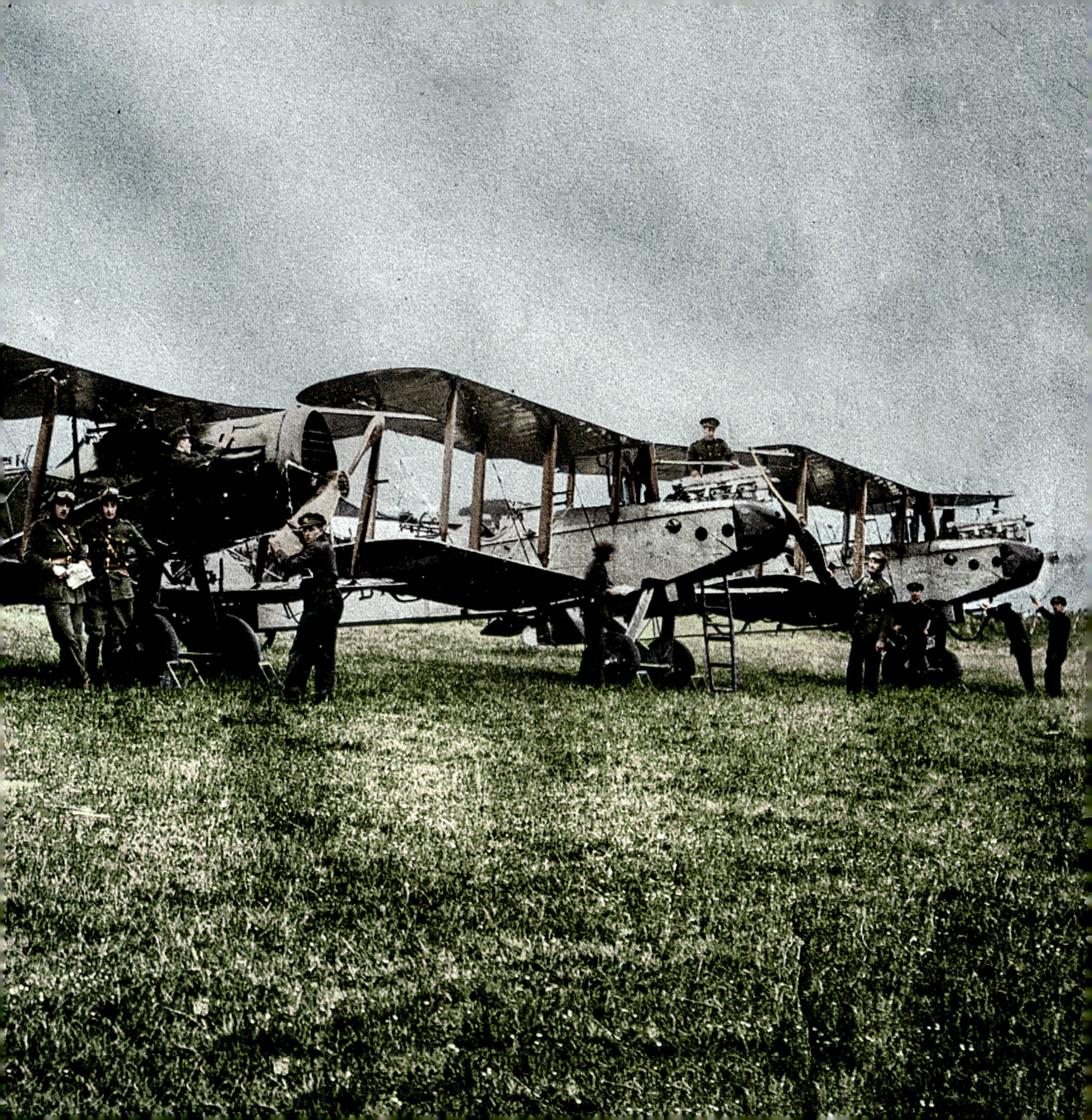

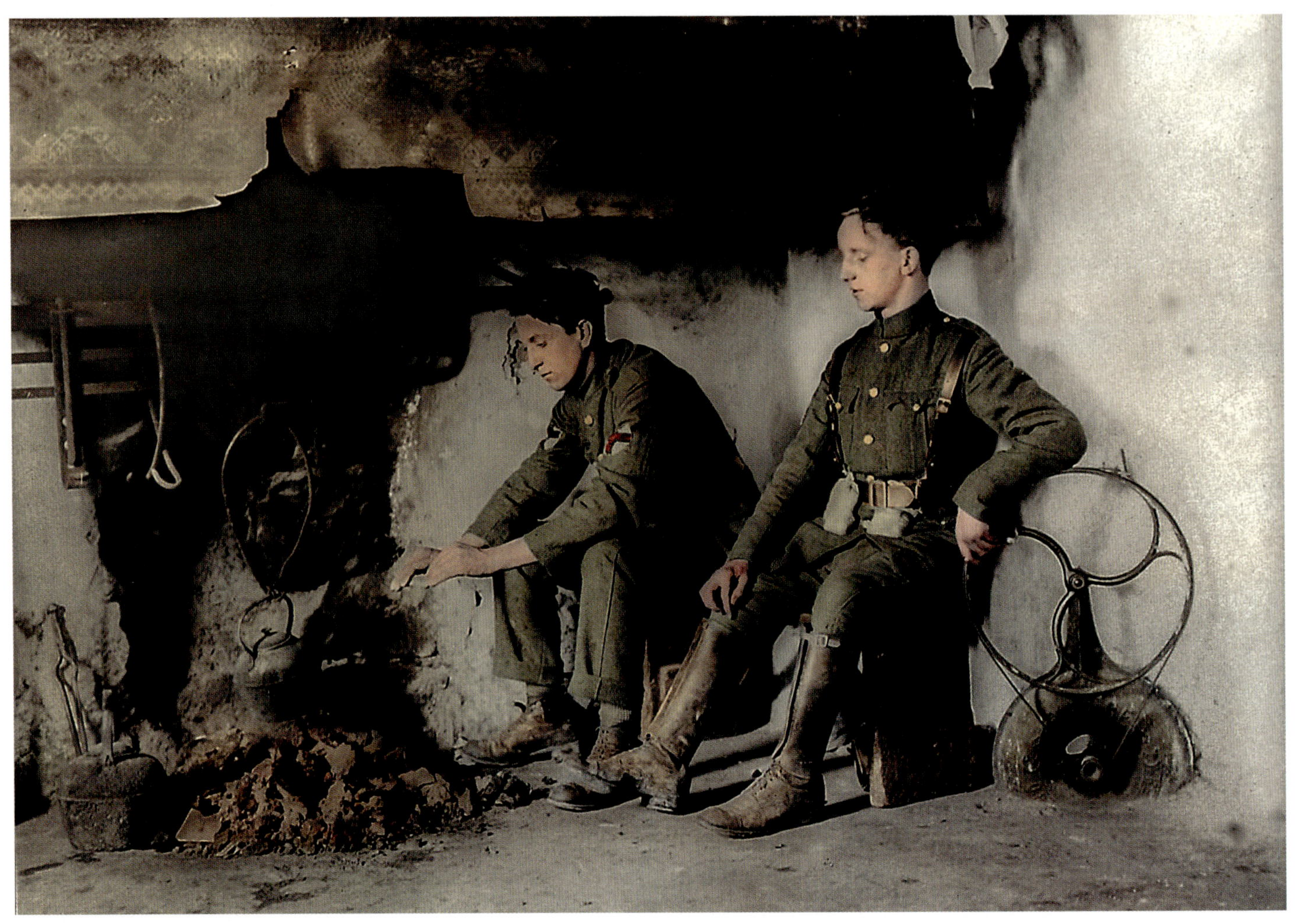

Most of the participants in the Civil War were surprisingly young. In mid-1922, senior leaders such as Major-General Emmet Dalton (GOC Cork) and Ernie O'Malley (Deputy Chief of Staff, IRA), were 24 and 25, respectively. Michael Collins was only 31 when he was killed. In this photograph, these two young National Army soldiers (the soldier on the left is a medic) billeted in the countryside, seem scarcely out of their teens.

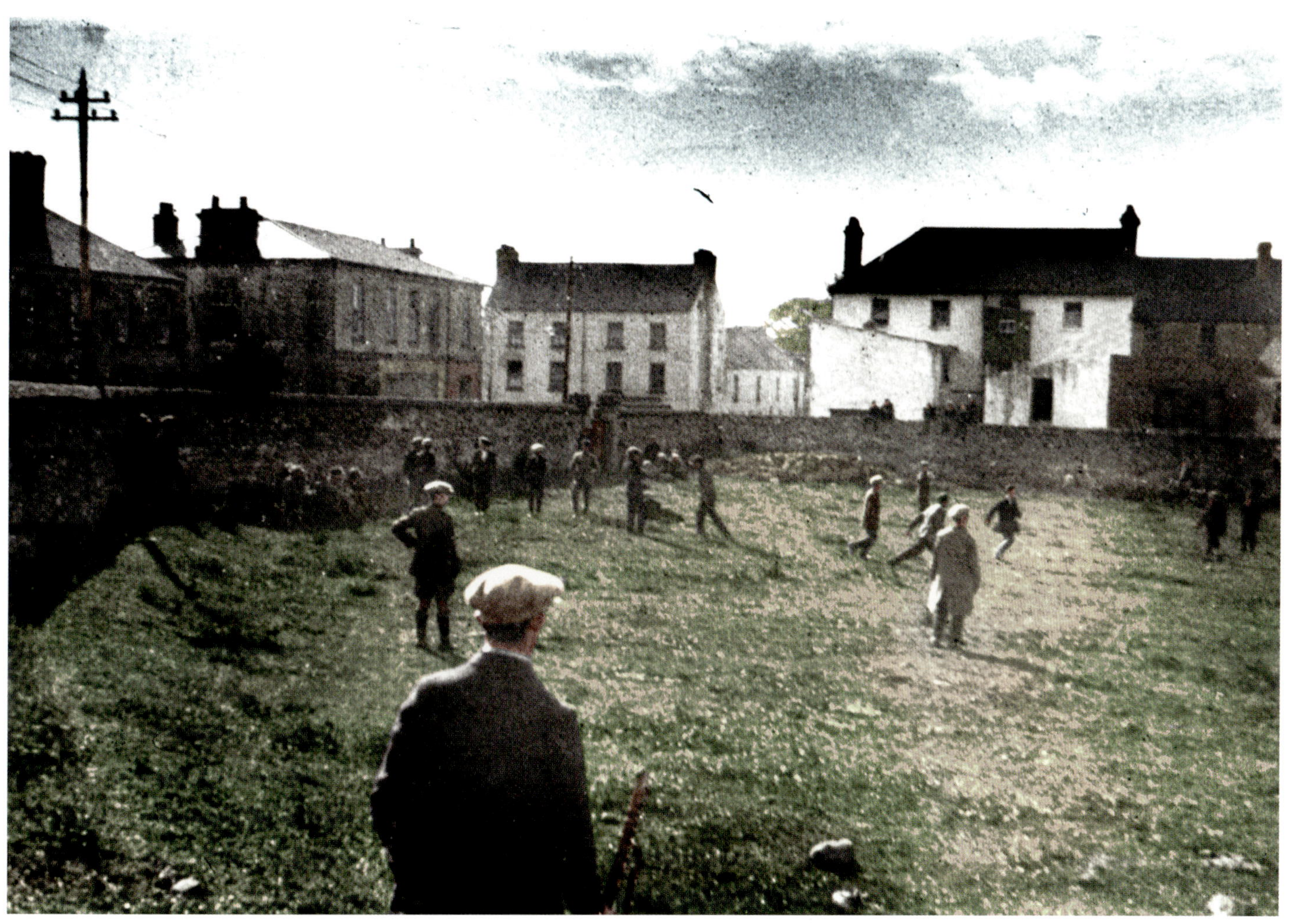

A rare photograph of captured pro-Treaty men, taken during the early stages of the Civil War. Under the eyes of their Republican guards, they play a football match at Swinford, Co. Mayo. As the pro-Treaty forces steadily captured more territory, the number of Republican prisoners in captivity grew. By contrast, the Republican forces, who led a peripatetic guerrilla existence, without barracks to keep their prisoners, tended to let them go on foot of a promise that they would not fight again.

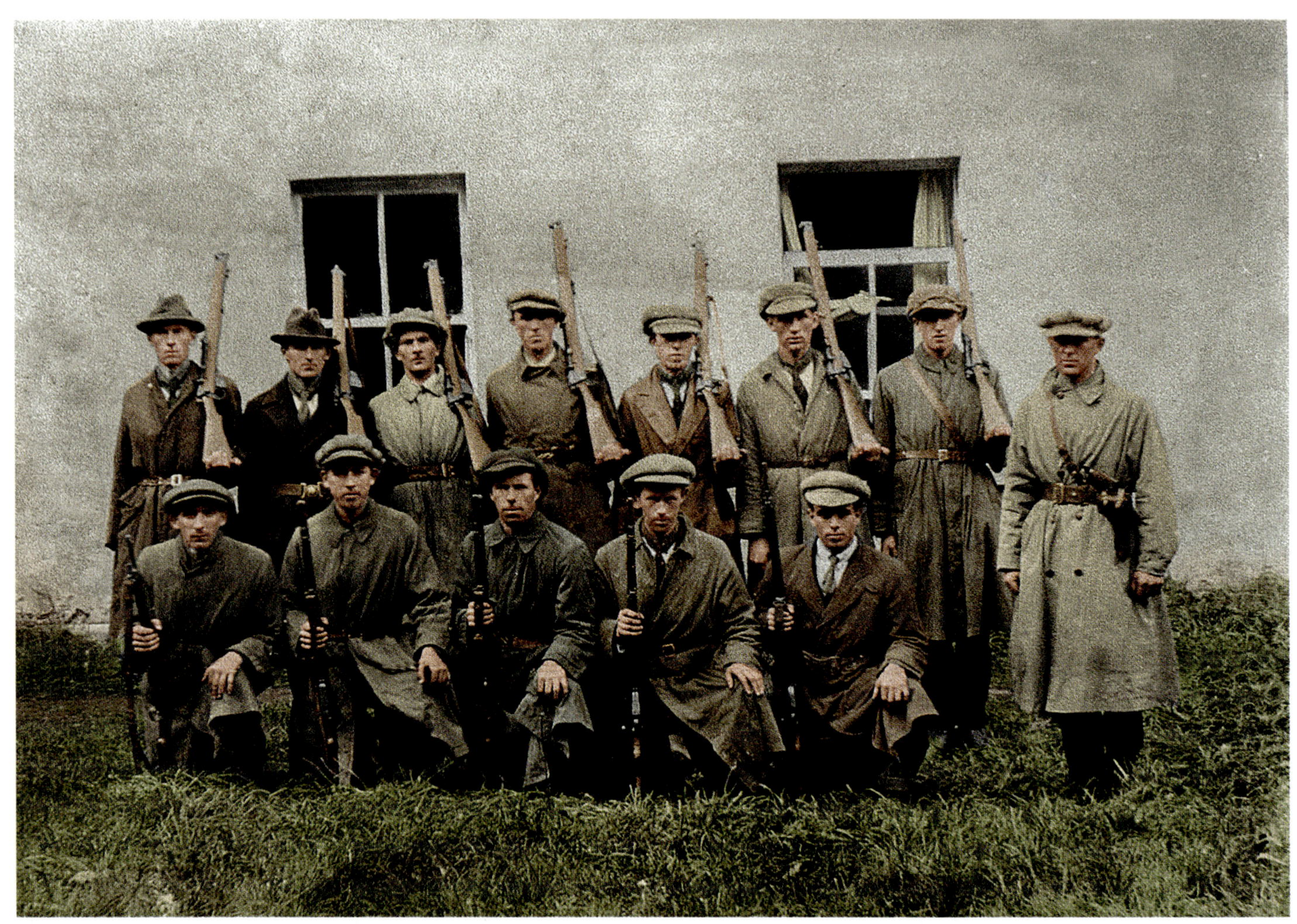

A photograph of an anti-Treaty IRA unit (attributed, in one source, as being from Sligo). On 19 September 1922, pro-Treaty forces mounted a large push in the Sligo area and captured the *Lough Gill* armoured car (page 51). The next morning, fleeing Republicans scrambled up Benbulben mountain. Six of these (including Séamus Devins, TD, and Brian MacNeill, son of Eoin MacNeill) were captured by Provisional Government soldiers and summarily shot – they are now popularly known as the 'Sligo Noble Six'.

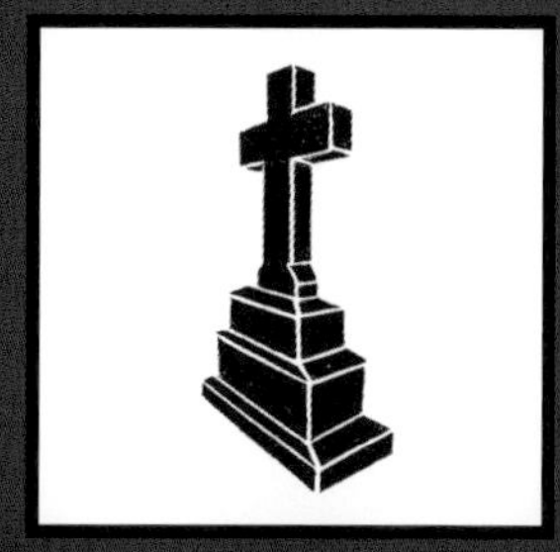

Chapter 5

The Bitter End

Autumn 1922 was the beginning of the end. The Provisional Government had captured the cities and was gaining control of the towns. Anti-Treaty fighters still roamed the mountains, particularly those of Kerry, Cork and Mayo. As the war continued there were waves of destruction on the railway network – derailments and the wrecking of signal cabins, stations and bridges. A cycle of ruthless executions of Republicans started in November 1922, which generated reprisals. After Seán Hales TD, was killed in a Dublin street in December 1922, four prominent Republicans were immediately executed as a reprisal. The nadir came in early 1923 when the slaughter of pro-Treaty troops by a trap mine in Kerry led to the brutal murder of prisoners near Tralee. As the anti-Treaty struggle ebbed away, Liam Lynch was shot on a lonely mountainside. The conflict juddered to an inconclusive end when Frank Aiken issued a ceasefire order to the IRA on 24 May 1923.

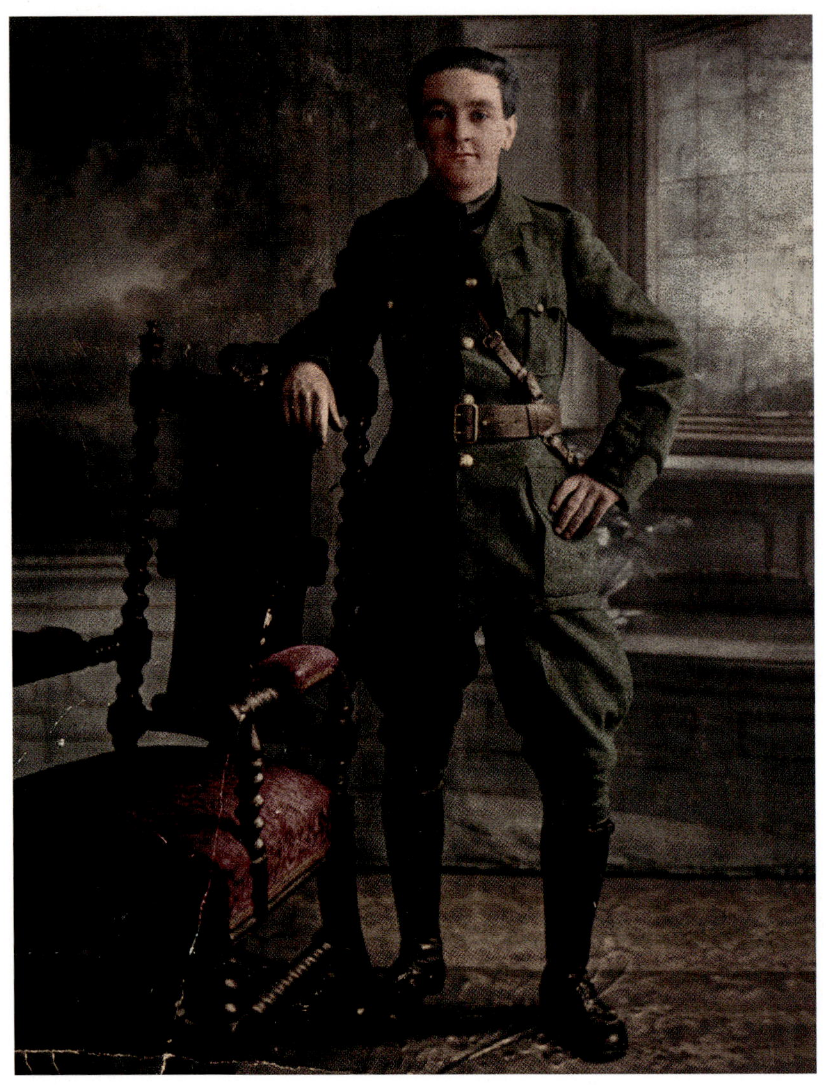

Several IRA men were slain in Cork in September 1922. IRA Captain Timothy Kennefick (pictured) was captured by a convoy (commanded by Emmet Dalton, according to a witness) and shot on 8 September. A coroner's jury declared that he had been 'wilfully murdered … by … Free State troops'.

Right: Major-General Emmet Dalton gets married at Cork on 8 October 1922. Note the Velazquez *Meninas*-like touch – the reflected image in the large mirror on the right.

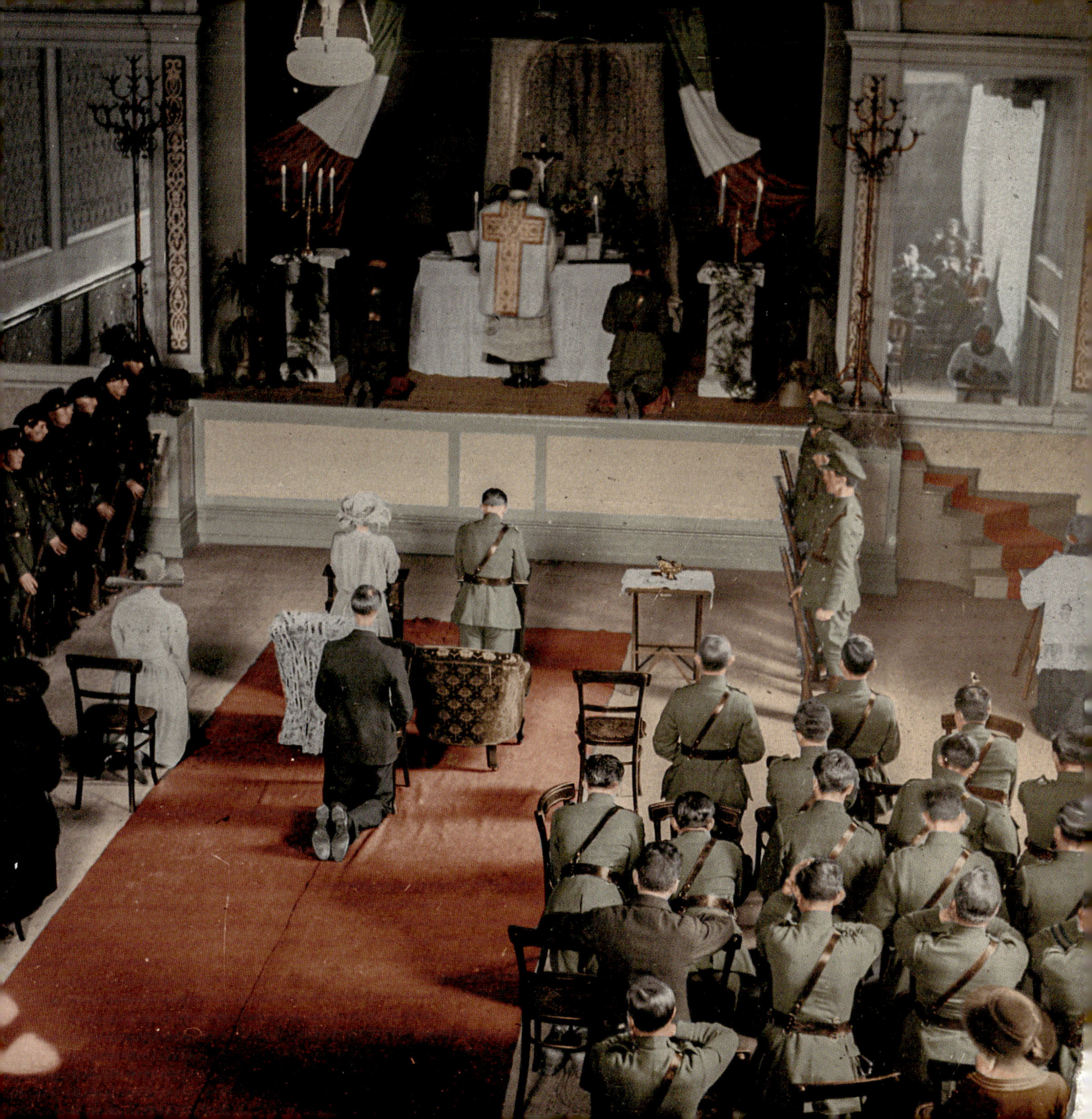

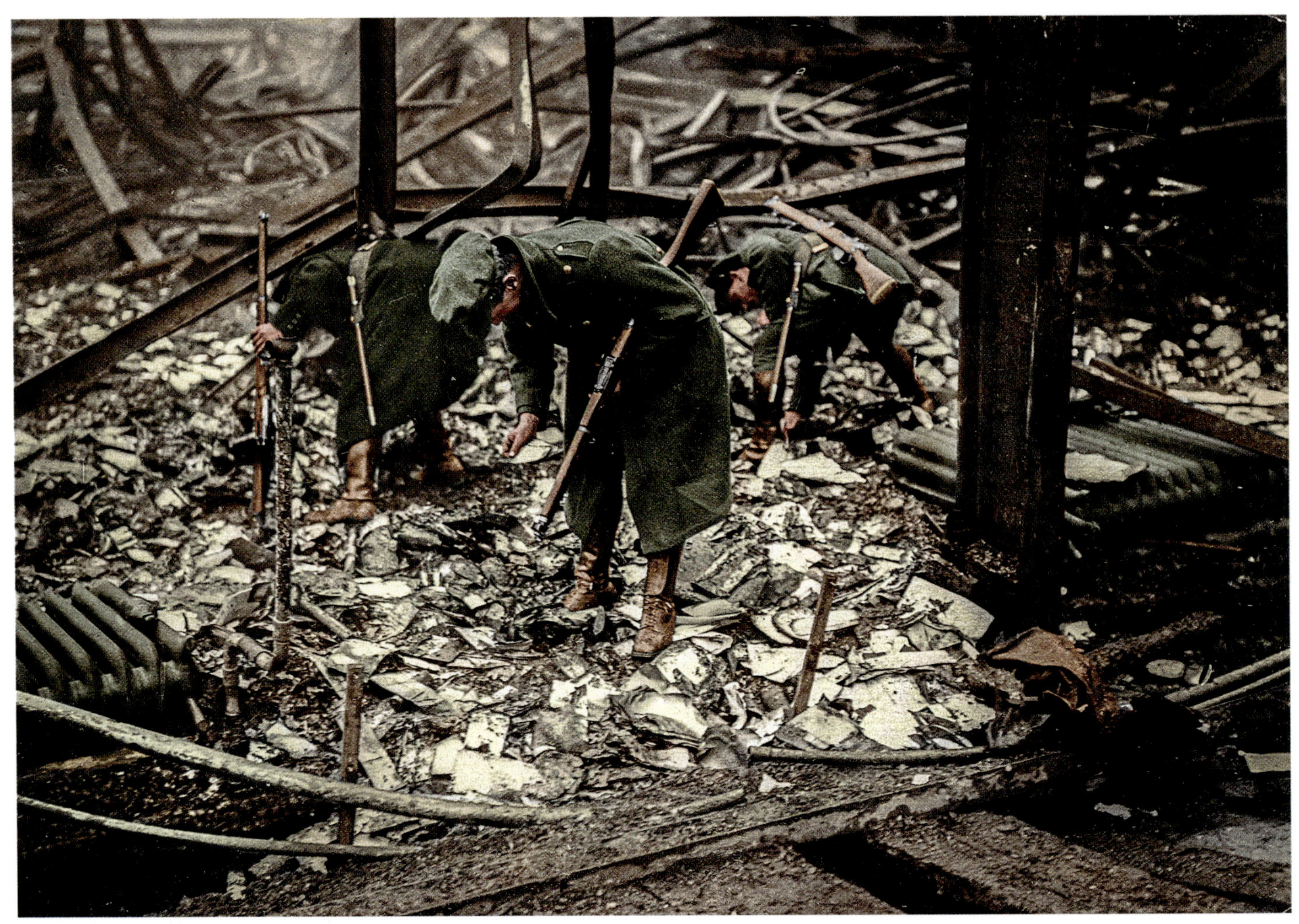

The Rotunda Rink (originally a roller-skating venue) in the Rotunda Gardens, Dublin, was in use as a postal sorting office, when on 5 November 1922, armed men using petrol set it on fire. Here, soldiers rake through ashes and twisted steel.

Right: the draconian Public Safety Act (which included the death penalty for possession of arms) came into force at the end of September 1922. It was first used when four young IRA men were executed on 17 November. Next came Erskine Childers (pictured), captured in Co. Wicklow, in possession of a miniature automatic (a gift from Michael Collins). He was executed at Beggars Bush on 24 November. He shook hands with each member of the firing squad, and met his death bravely and with dignity.

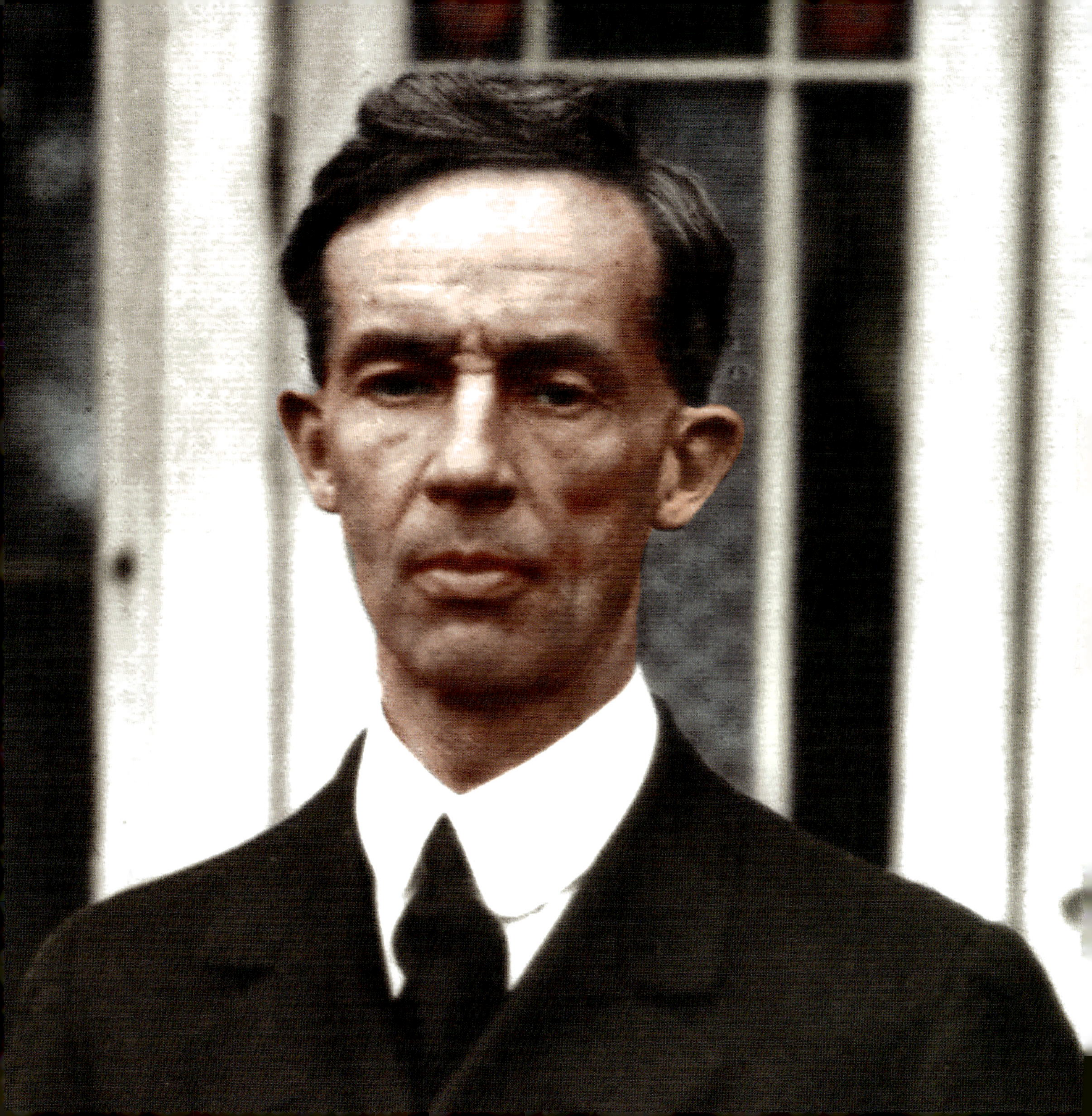

When this photograph came to auction in 2021, it caused
an immediate stir – was this truly a real-life execution
scene? The location has been identified as the Cork Tram-
ways Depot, Albert Road, a strategic location (it had an
electric generating station) which Provisional Government
troops occupied after the taking of Cork in August 1922.
There are many reasons to conclude that this is staged and
probably a barracks jape: the soldiers are not at ninety
degrees to the prisoner; there is what looks like levity
on some soldiers' faces; the relaxed manner of the 'condemned' man, cigarette in hand; the implausibility that
an official photograph would have been allowed for such a
ghastly scene. Indeed this would have been the antithesis
of any kind of staged propaganda.

The first execution in Cork occurred on 1 September
1922 (authorised by Major-General Dalton). A pro-Treaty
private, John Winsley, condemned for selling arms to the
IRA, was shot at Cork County Gaol. The other official
execution in the city took place, also at the Gaol, on 13
March 1923 when an anti-Treaty Volunteer, William
Healy, was shot under the Public Safety Act.

A recent estimate of the number of official executions by
the Free State during the conflict of 1922–23 is 83.

In contrast to what might be considered the flippancy
inherent in this staged photograph, the reality was bloodily
traumatic for all. For example, whiskey had to be specially
purchased for the members of the firing squad at Dundalk
Barracks.

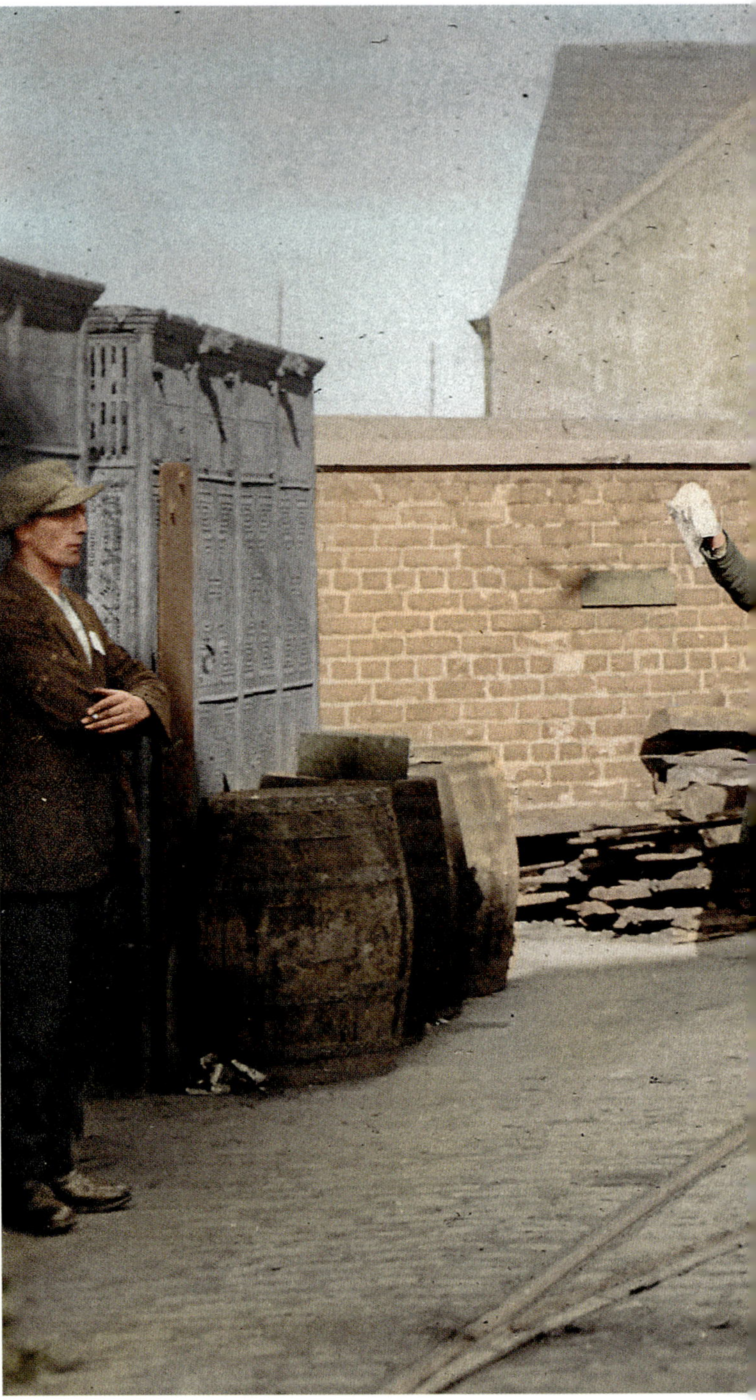

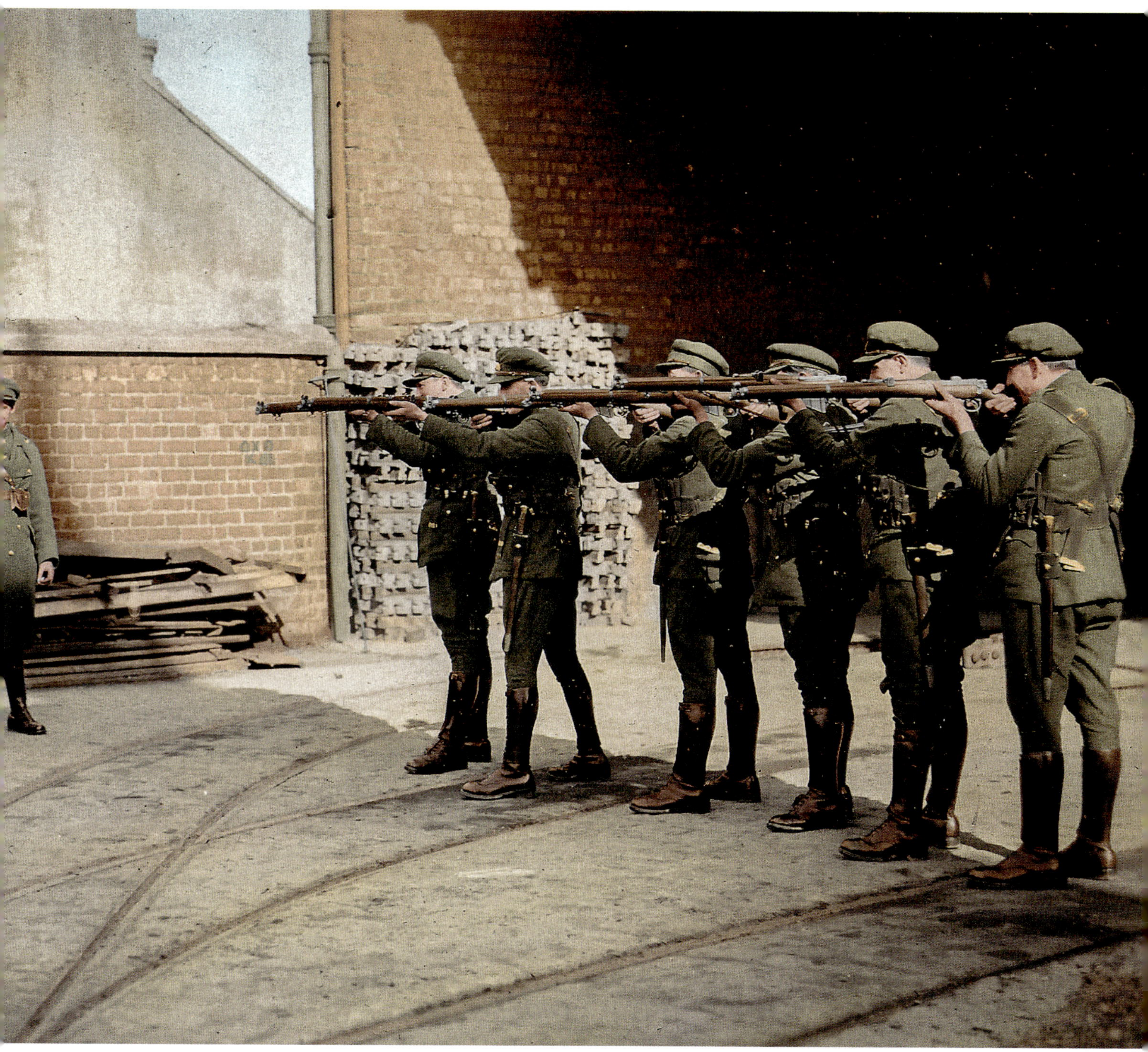

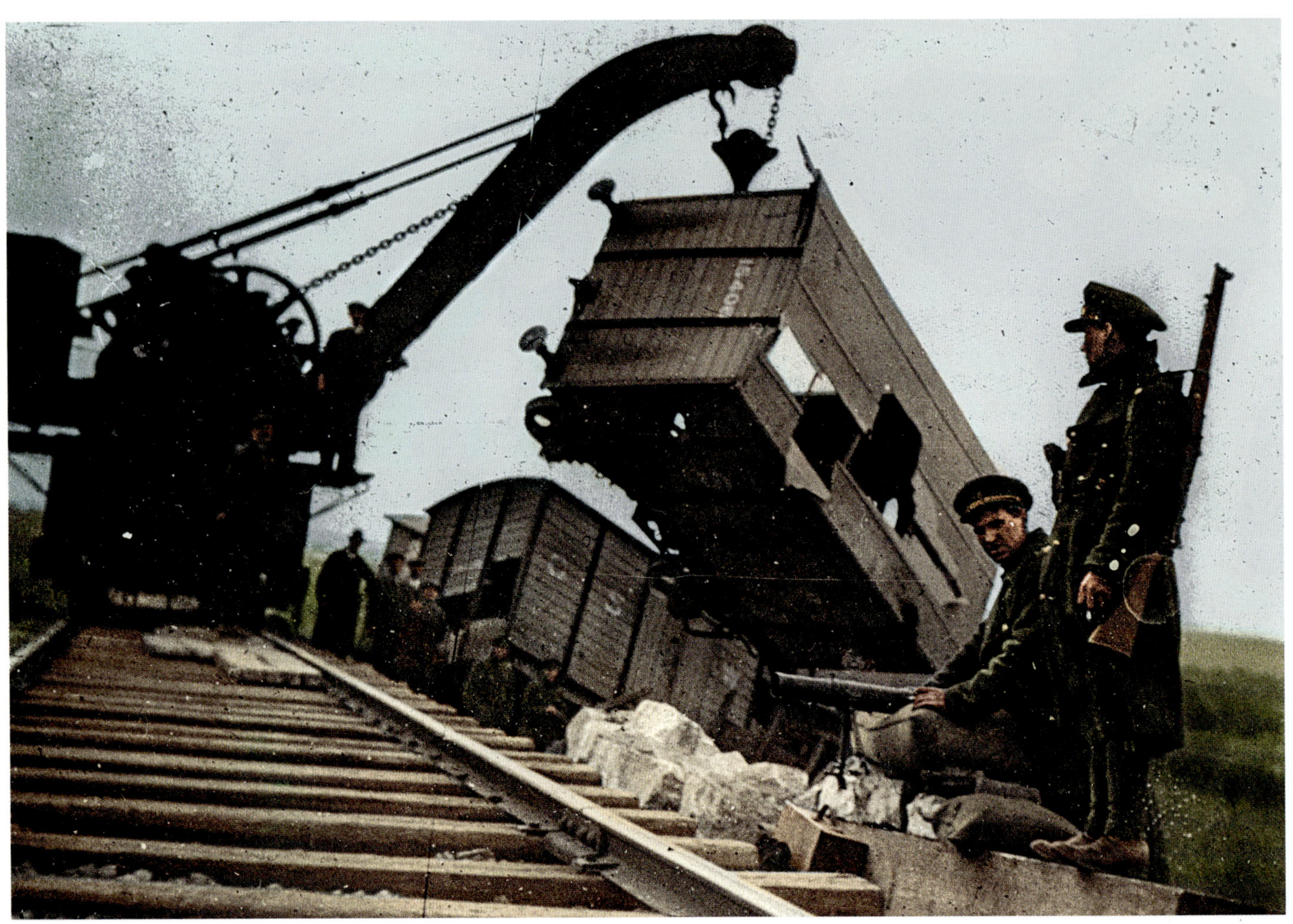

Few people realise the extent of the damage inflicted on the railway system during the Civil War. Initially, the anti-Treaty IRA destroyed railways leading to the south to prevent pro-Treaty troop movements. Later, as the struggle moved to its guerrilla phase, the railways, a soft target, were sabotaged at will. Here, in what became a usual scene, a railway steam crane lifts derailed freight wagons.

Right: at Ballywilliam on 12 January 1923. Derailed locomotive No. 45 lies upside down on the embankment. The rescue crew pose for a photo. The railways had (and still have) effective procedures, equipment and capable trained staff who step in, recover derailed and damaged vehicles and get the track repaired and fit for traffic.

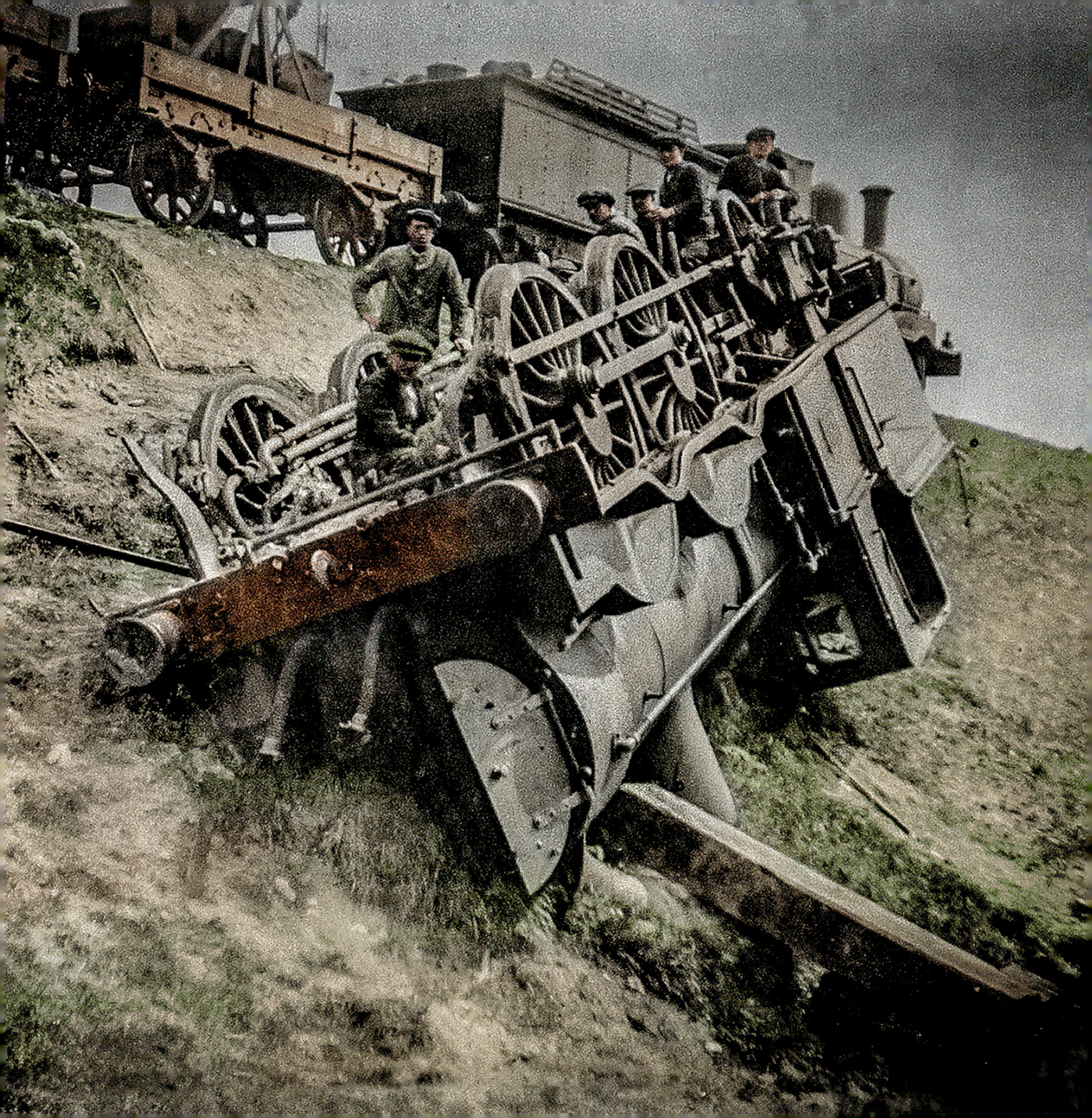

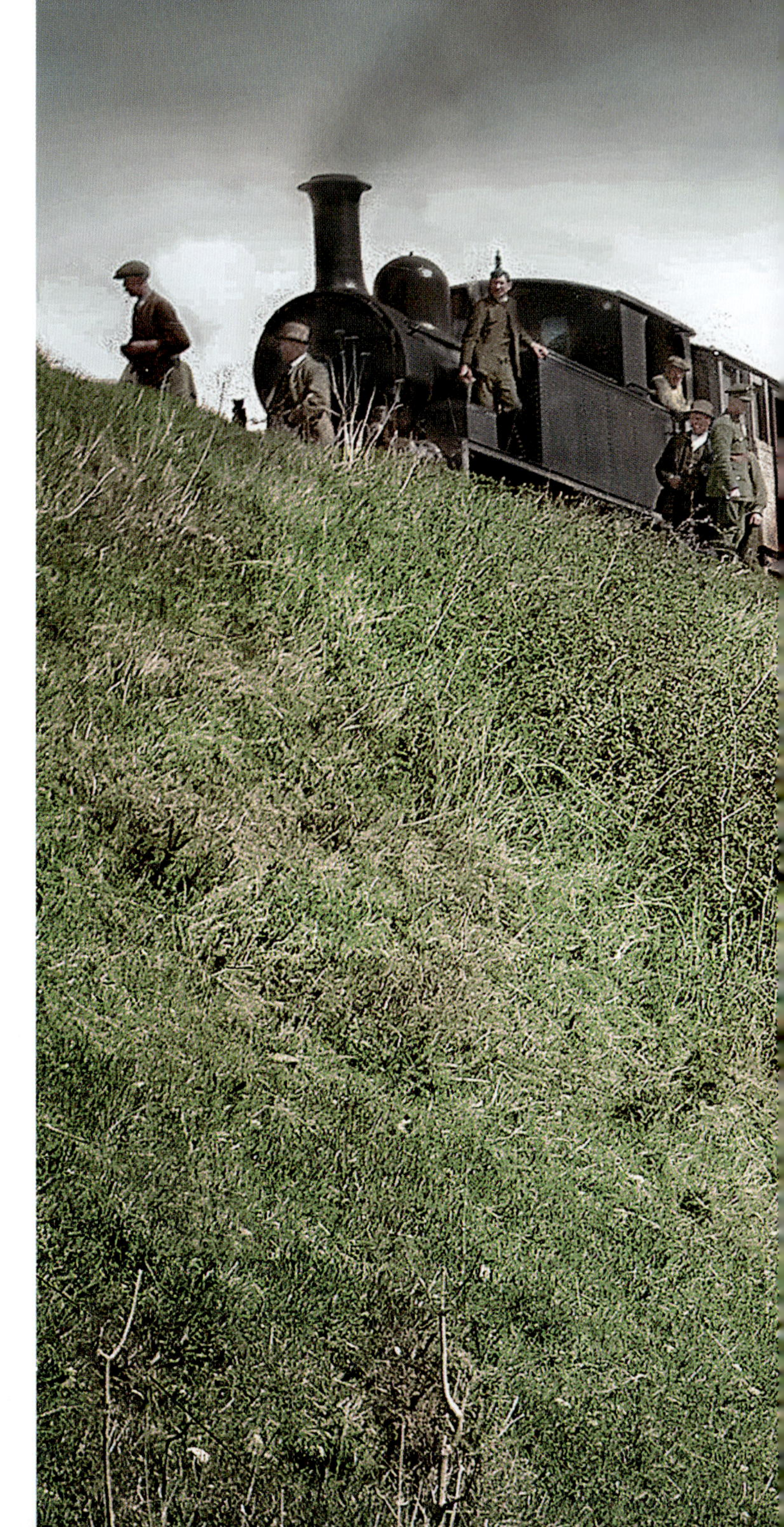

As the locomotive and carriages wait on the embankment, soldiers assist in recovering the mail following a raid in August 1922 by the anti-Treaty IRA on this train of the Cork and Macroom Direct Railway.

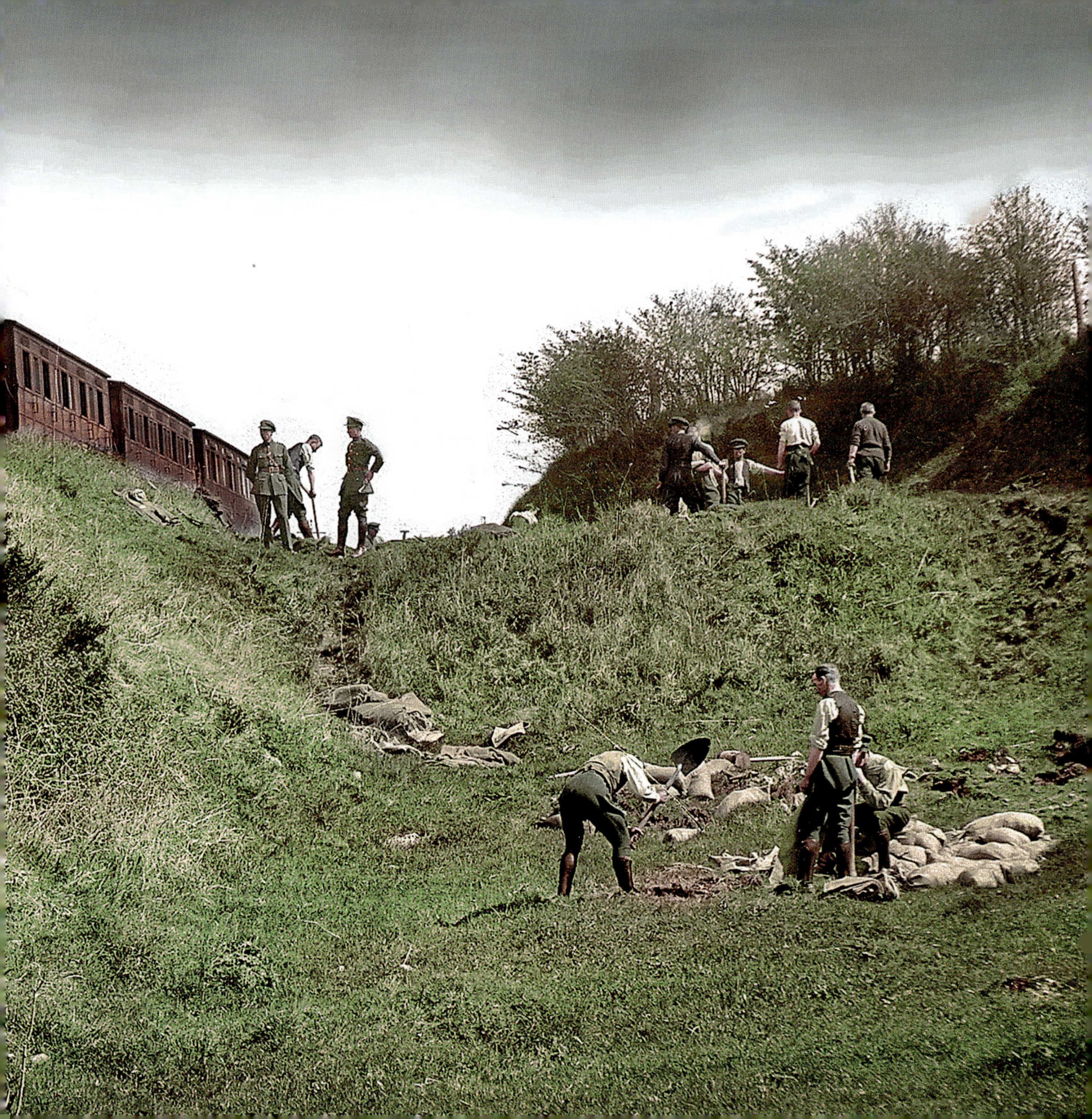

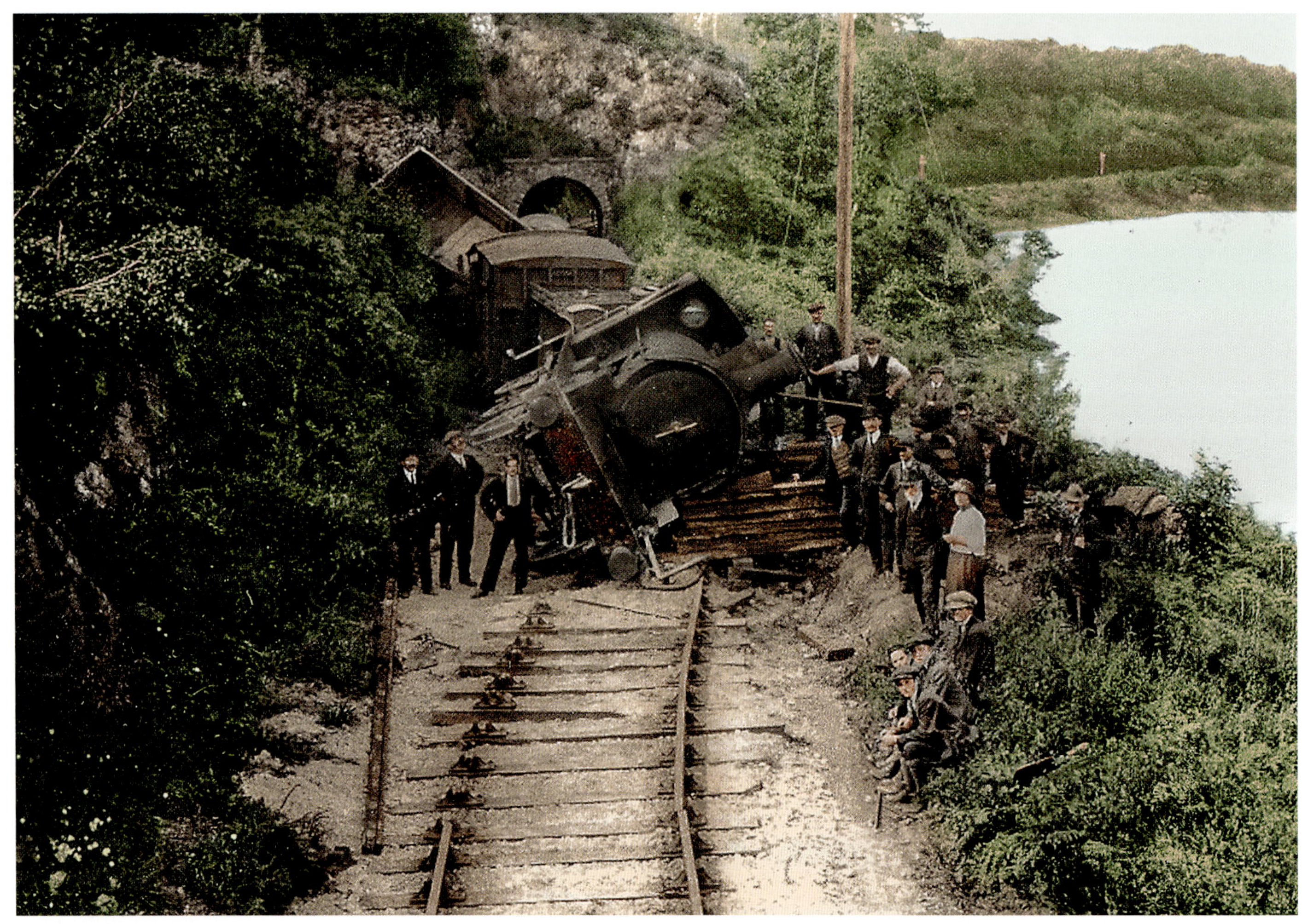

At this derailment on 15 August 1922 on the Dublin & South Eastern Railway in Co. Wexford, two rails had been removed. As it emerged from Killurin tunnel, the locomotive of the down Night Mail ran on the sleepers for over 150 metres before turning over.

Right: in August 1922, the multi-arched Ballyvoyle Viaduct (spanning the River Dalligan) on the Waterford to Mallow line was blown up. This was followed by more destruction the following January when the IRA sent a ballast train backwards over the abyss. Here railway staff are about to winch the derailed tender up a temporary track laid at the side of the abutment.

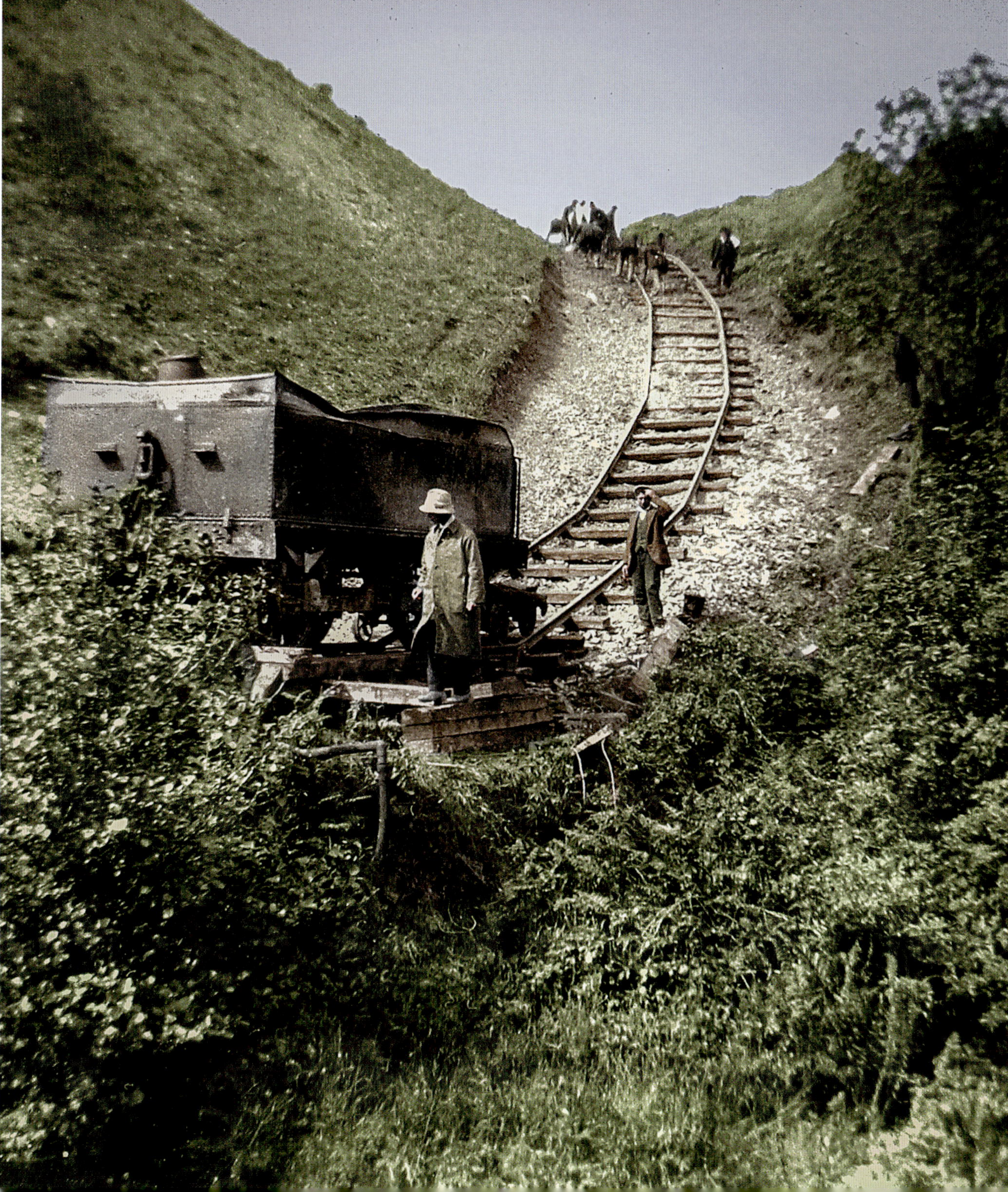

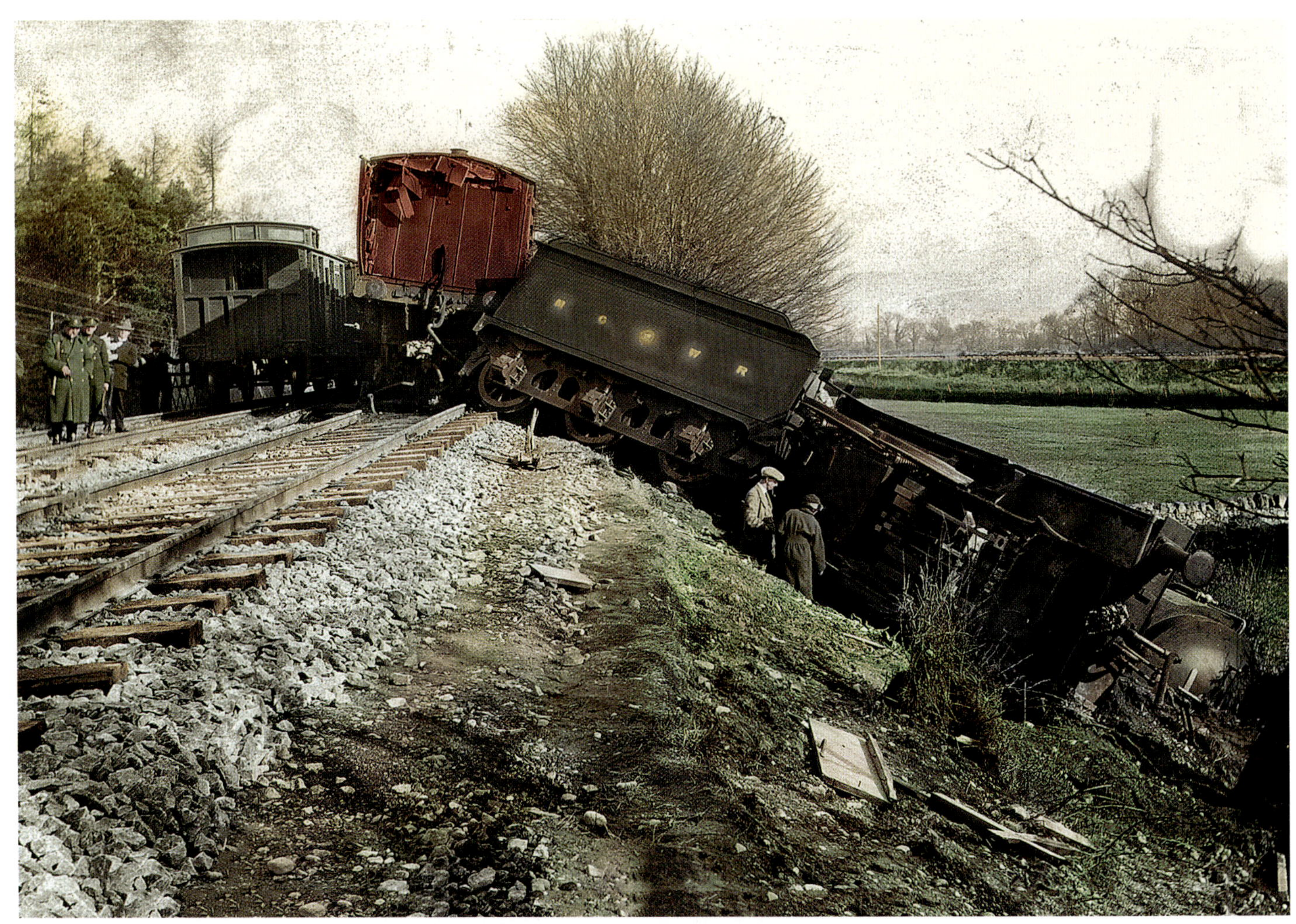

17 February 1923, a winter scene at Edenderry Junction on the Midland Great Western Railway (MGWR). The down Galway Express train has been derailed. The carriages remain on the track, but the tender has spilled onto the embankment and the locomotive is lying on its side in the adjacent field.

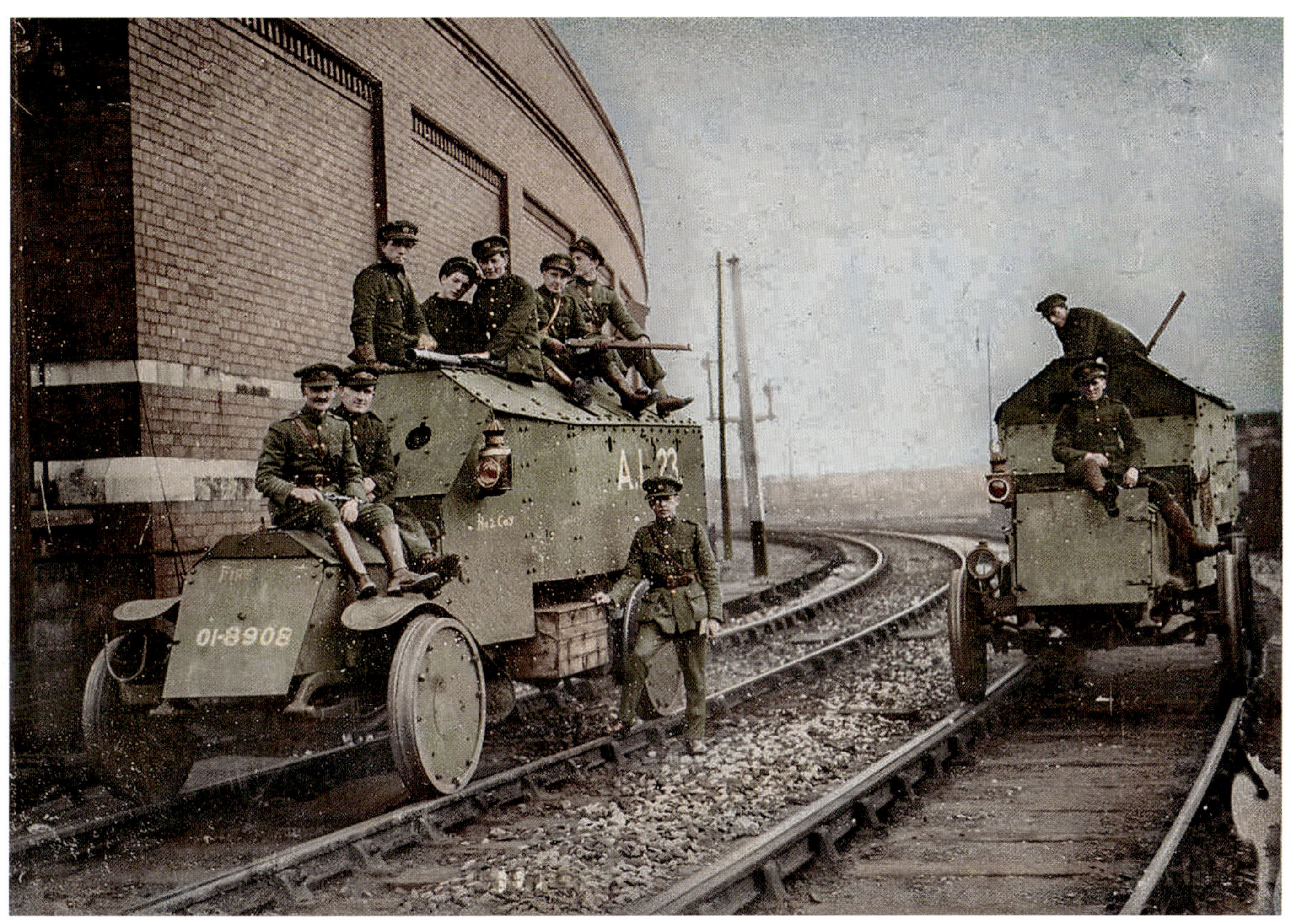

In October 1922, in response to the assault on the railways, the Provisional Government set up the Railway Protection, Repair & Maintenance Corps (RPR&MC) to guard the network and repair damage. It was staffed by a mixture of soldiers and railway workers. Here, at Glanmire (now Kent) Station in Cork, are two specially adapted Lancias, used by the RPR&MC to patrol the railways. A number of these armoured vehicles had been fitted out at the Inchicore Railway Works of the Great Southern & Western Railway and equipped with flanged steel wheels, which allowed travel on the rails (with a top speed of around 70km per hour.)

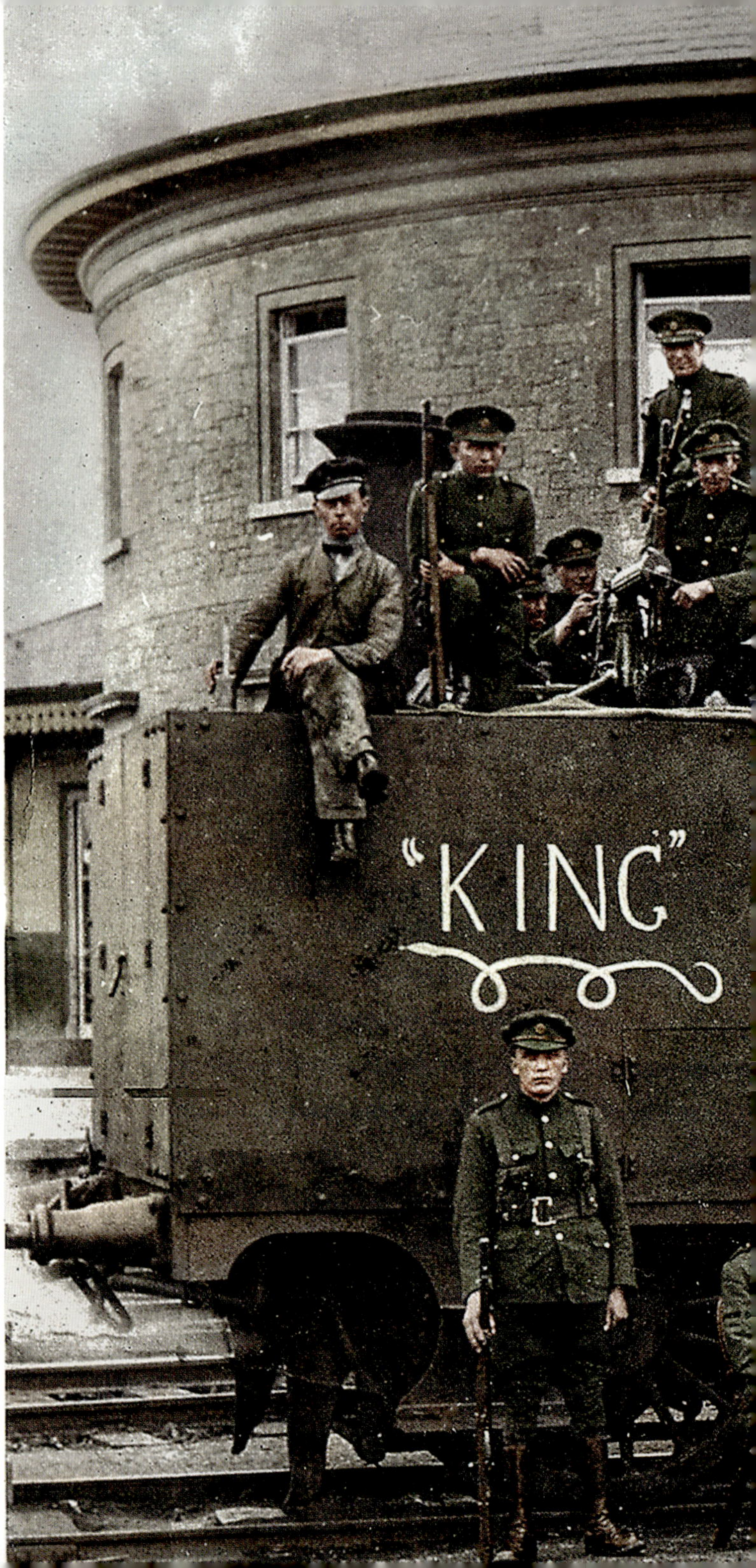

Another MGWR scene – at Mullingar station the armoured train of the RPR&MC, dubbed *King Tutankhamen* (the name reflects the fascination with Egypt after the recent discoveries that had been made there), with soldiers and crew. Note the sheepdog next to the machine gun, on top of the tender.

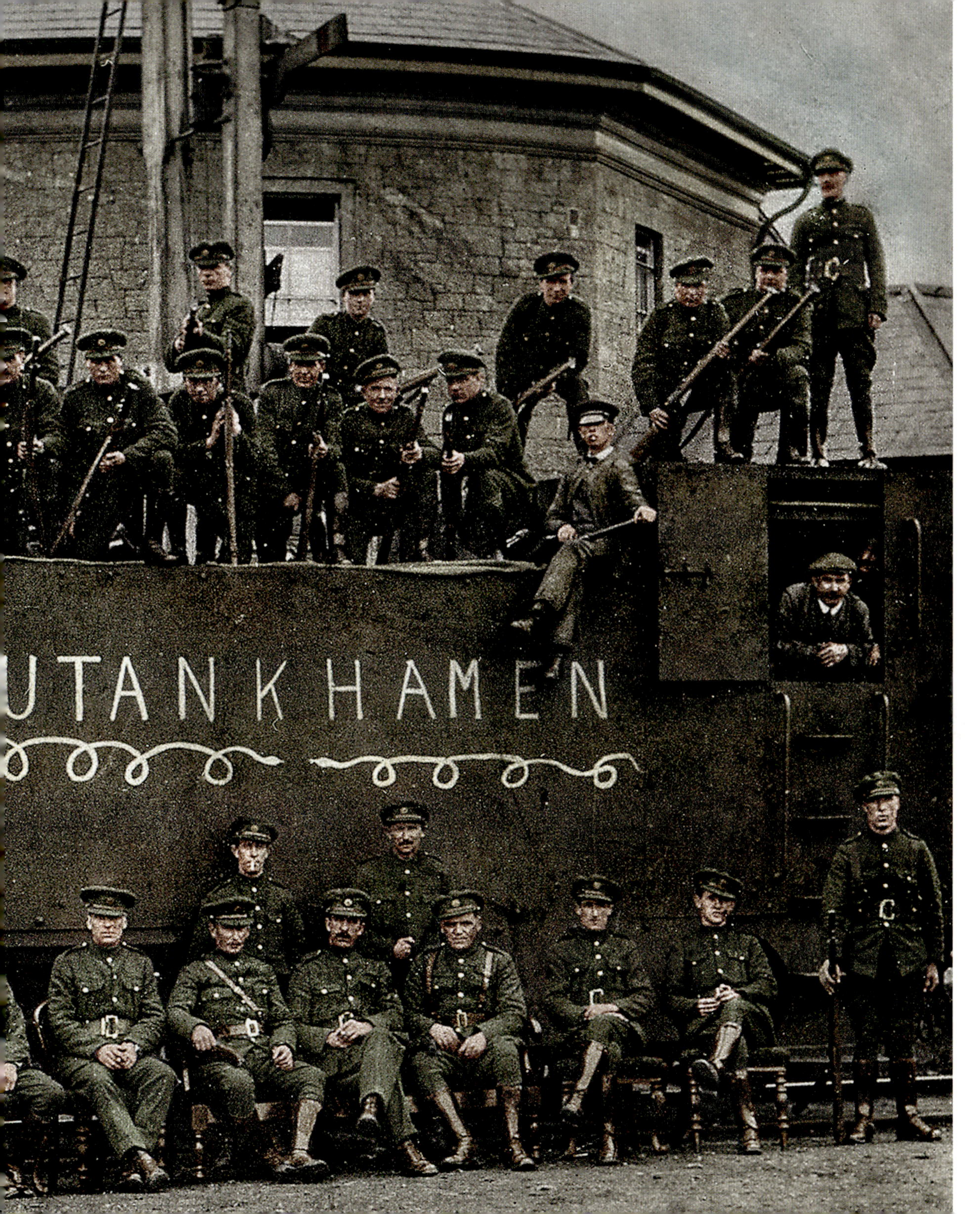

UTANKHAMEN

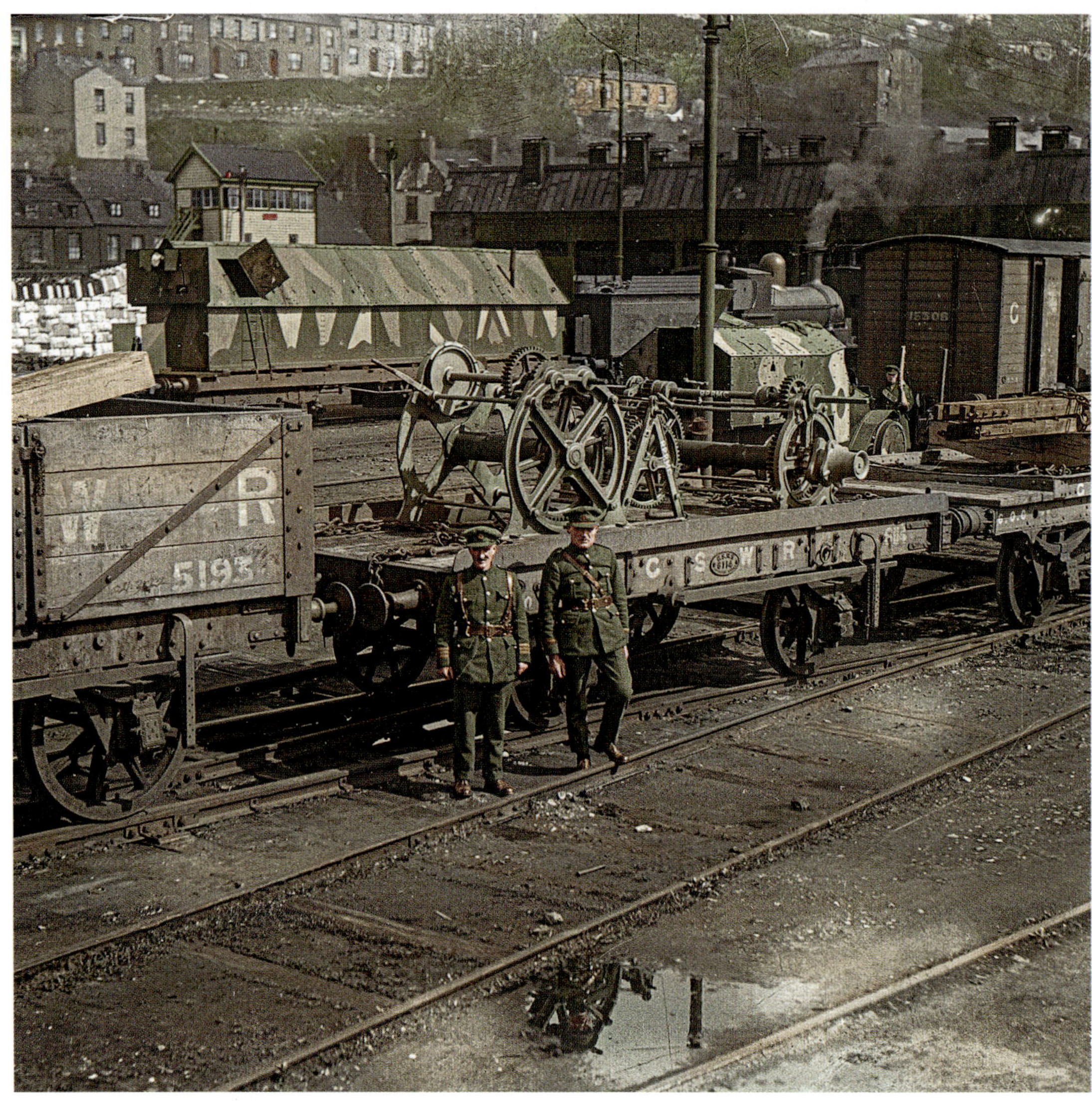

Officers of the RPR&MC at Glanmire Road, Cork. A camouflaged armoured works wagon is at the back and, just visible in front of the locomotive, the camouflaged Lancia, nicknamed the *Grey Ghost*.

Right: work underway rebuilding the strategic bridge at Mallow, which carried the Dublin-Cork main-line over the River Blackwater. The ten-arch masonry viaduct had been blown up in August 1922.

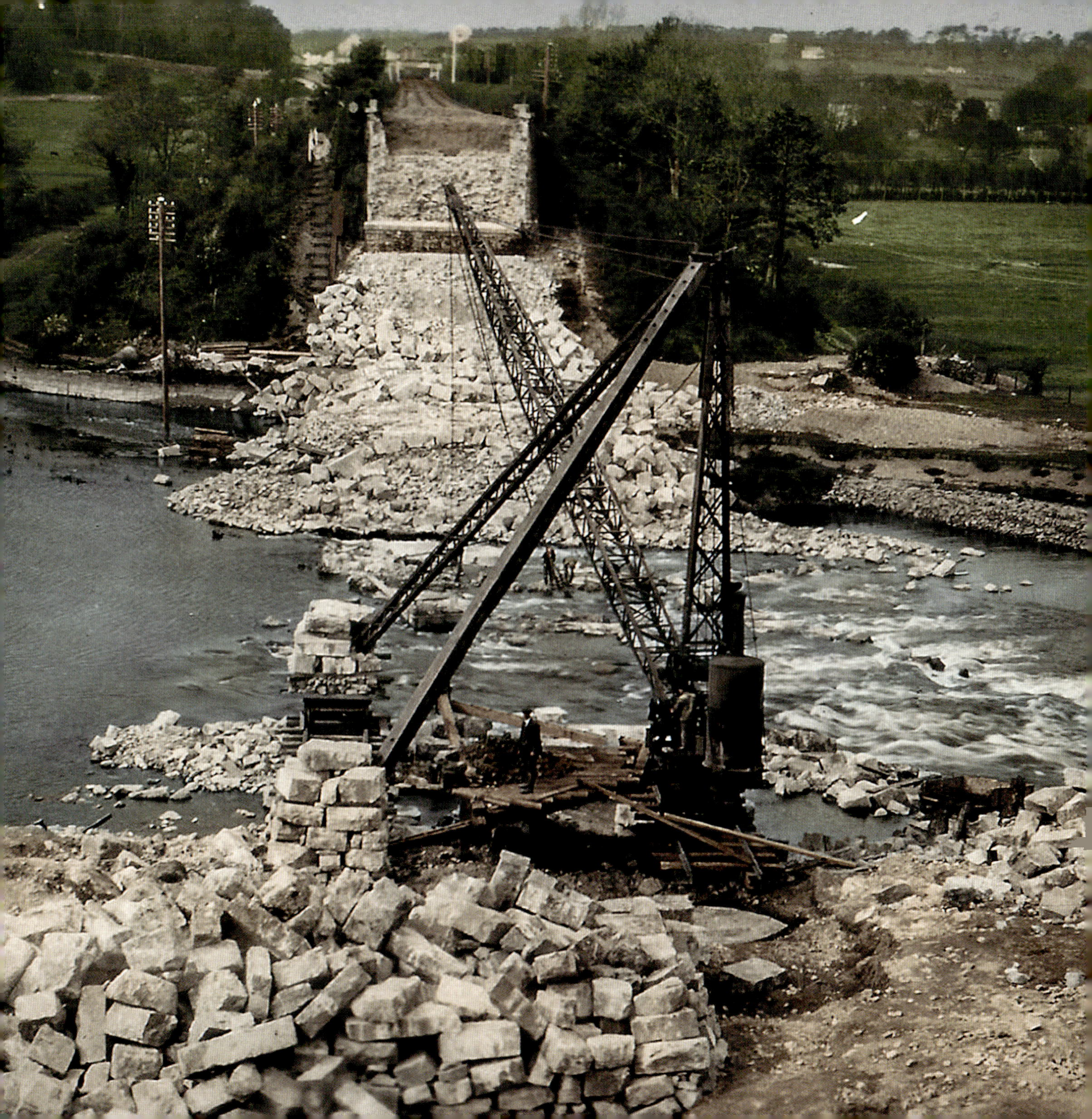

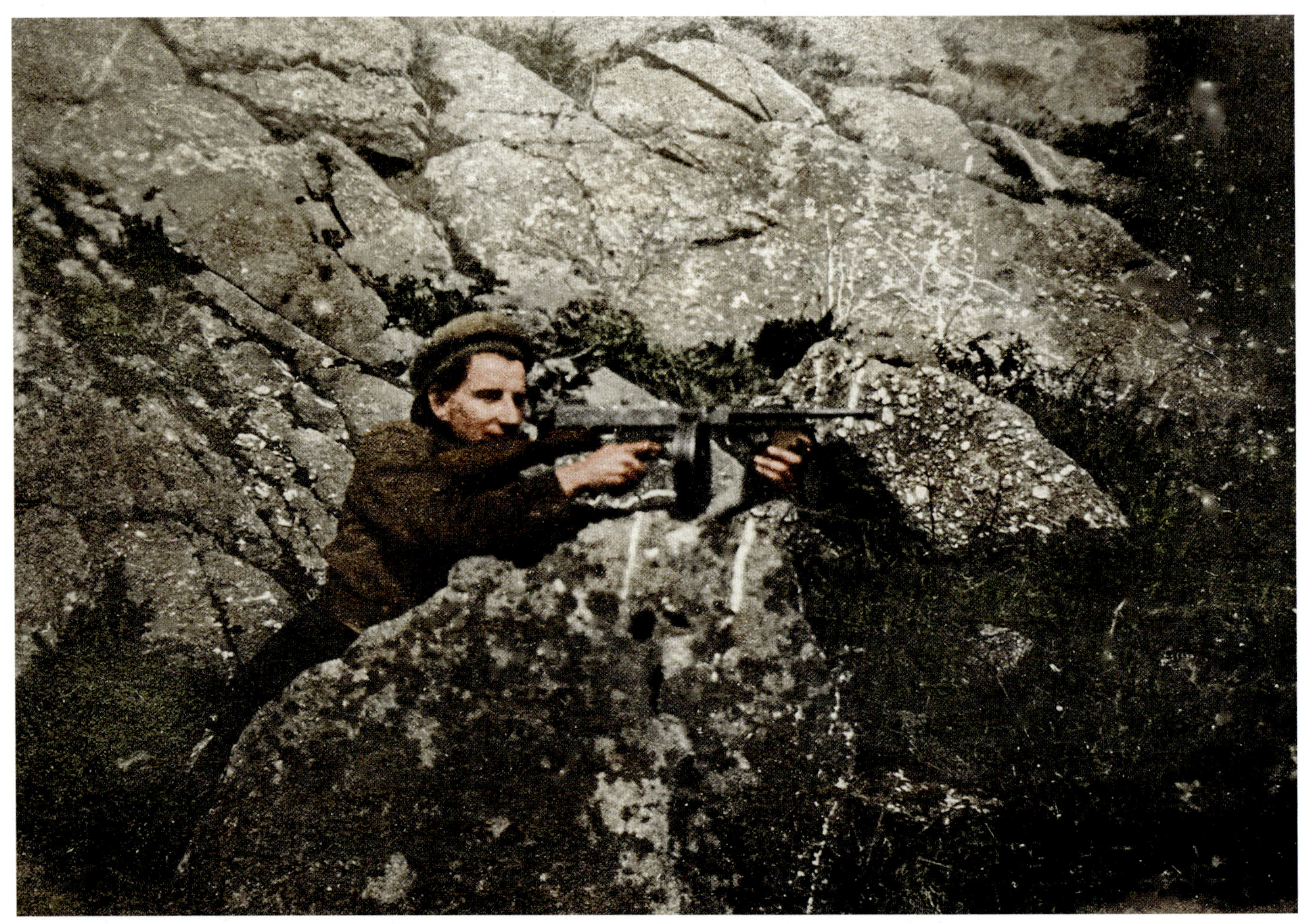

Despite the challenges, the anti-Treaty IRA maintained a semblance of organisation and practice. This included training, as evidenced here in the latter part of 1922, where a Republican practises using a Thompson sub-machine gun at cliffs by the sea near Dungarvan.

Right: the identity of this Volunteer (possibly from the Roscommon area) is unknown, but the photograph is illustrative of the exigencies of guerrilla life that anti-Treaty men had to endure. They were short of supplies; many had to live in rough terrain, sometimes having to commandeer provisions. While they were still able to inflict damage on their enemy, they had lost much territory and local support. The executions from the end of 1922 onwards severely affected morale.

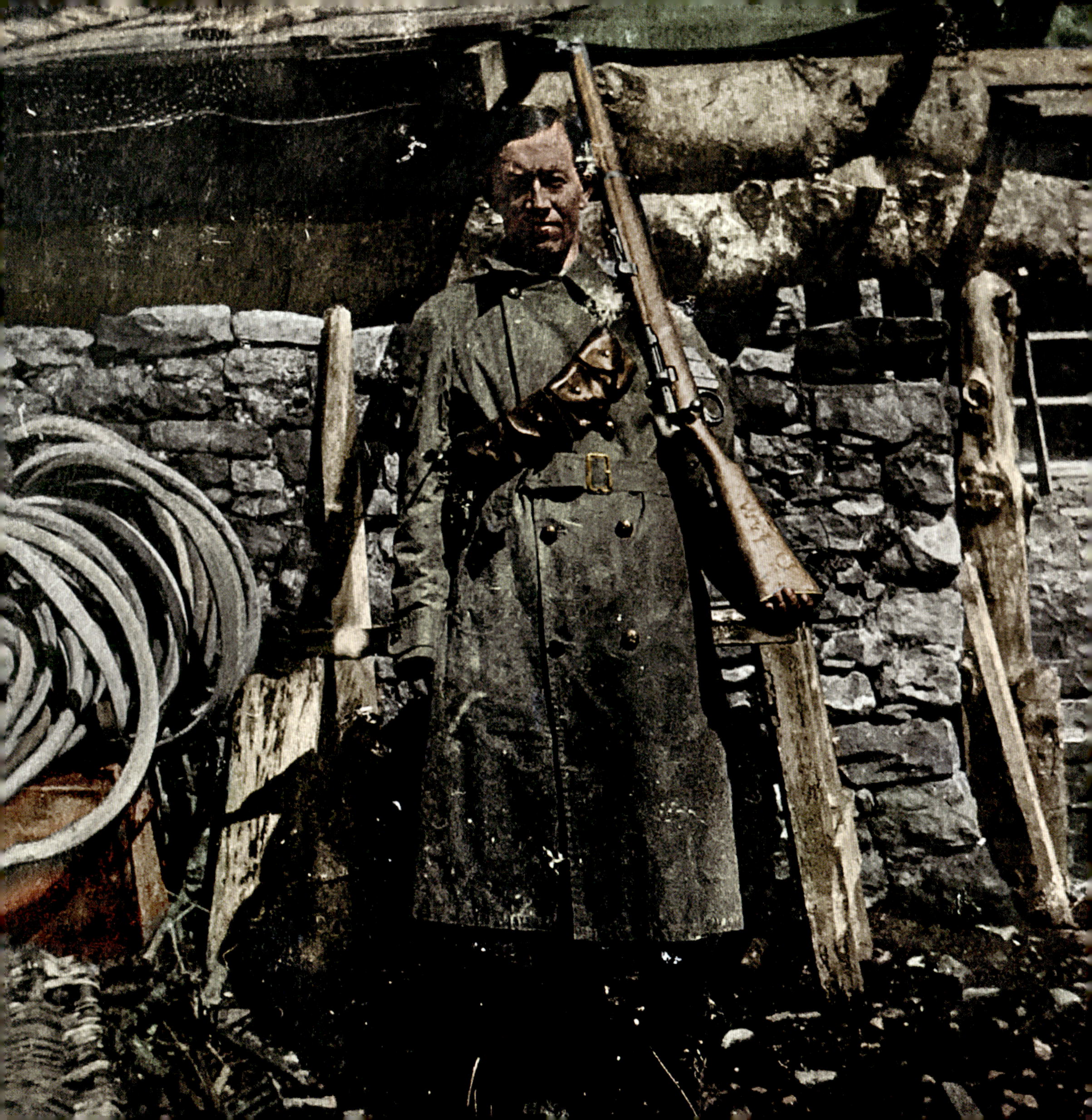

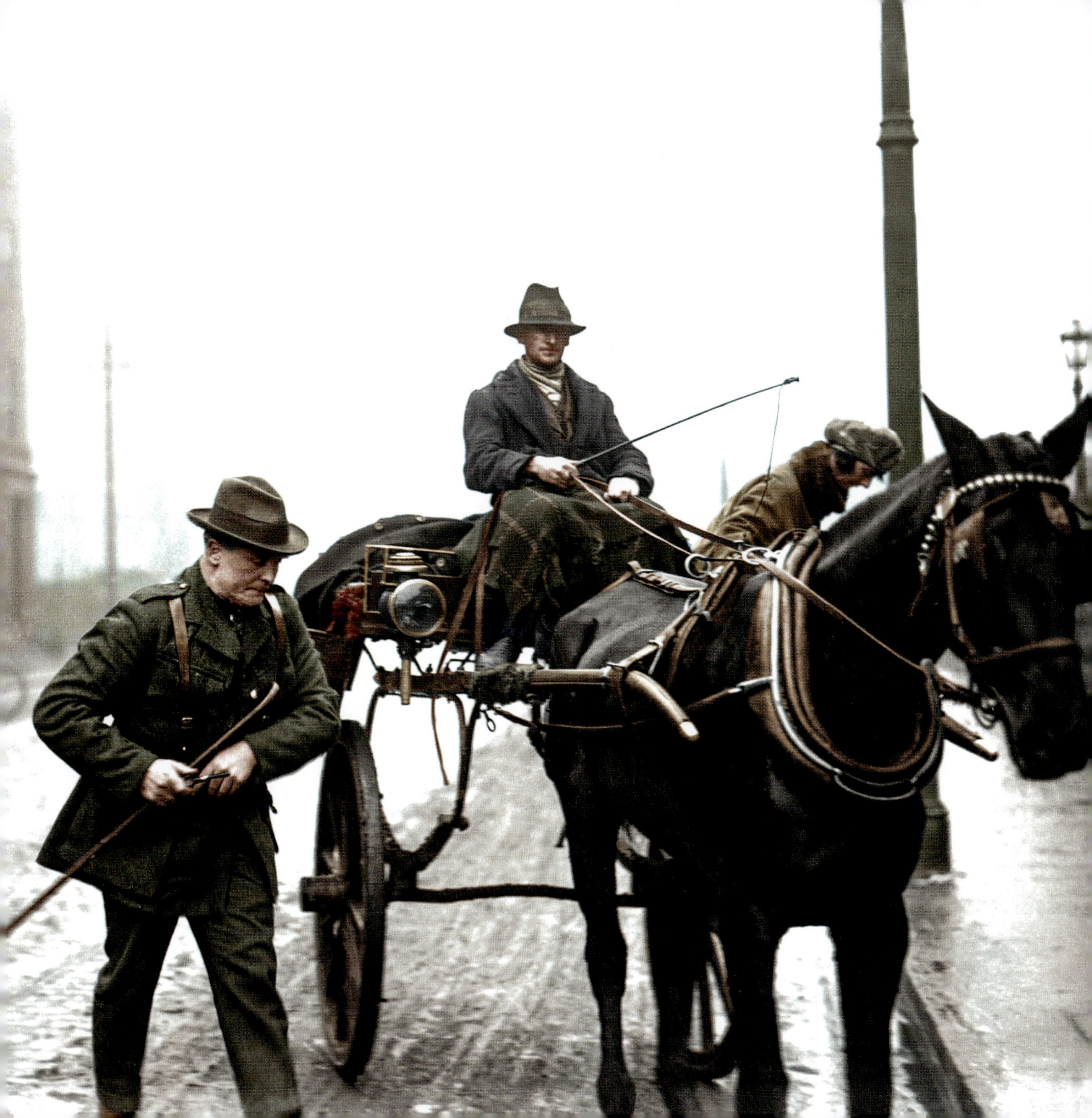

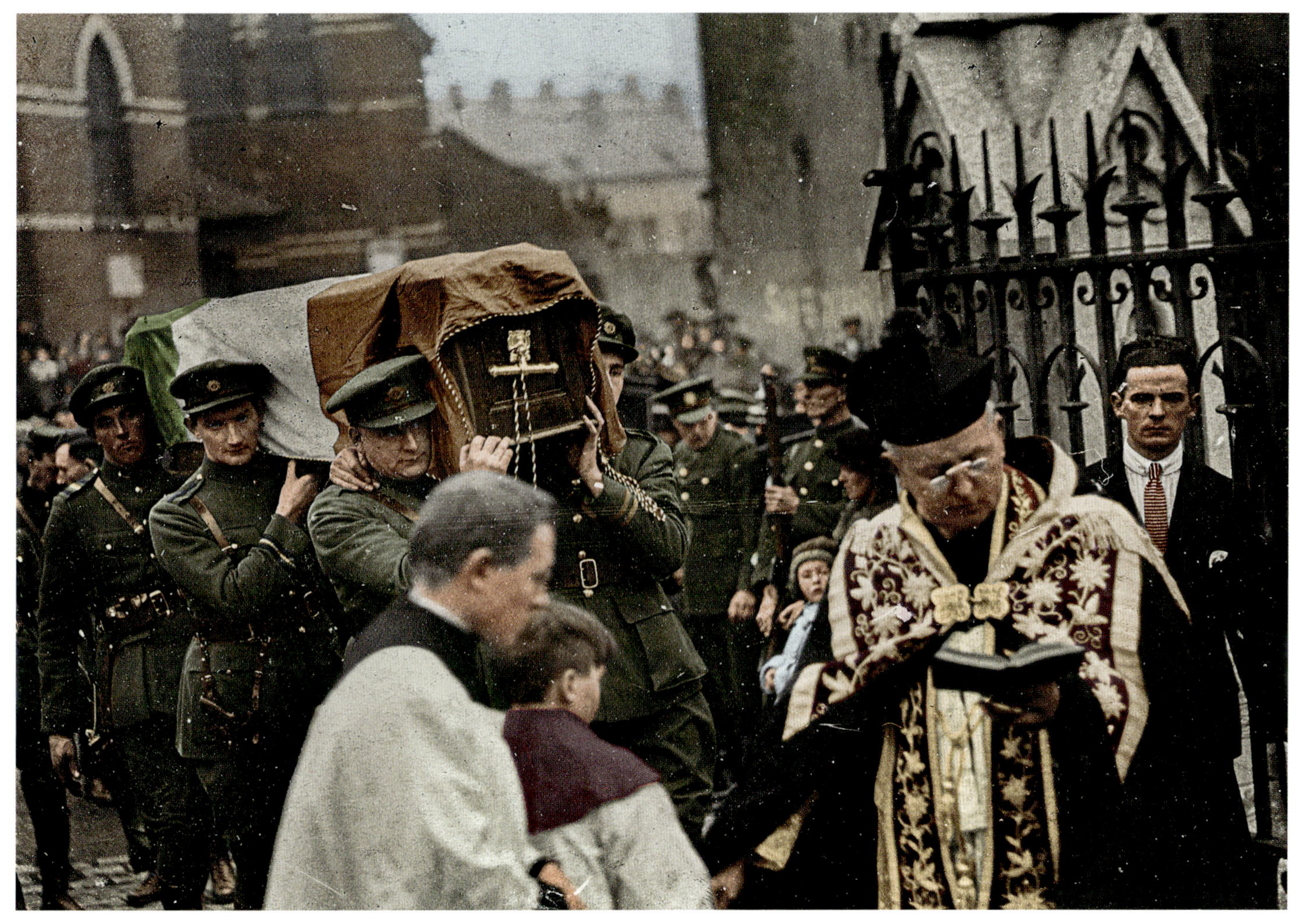

The funeral of Seán Hales, TD and Brigadier-General at Cork Cathedral. He received full military honours.

Left: Seán Hales, who had played a prominent role in the West Cork IRA during the War of Independence. On 30 November 1922, angered by the official executions, Liam Lynch, anti-Treaty IRA Chief of Staff, ordered that all members of the Dáil who had voted for what he called the 'Murder Bill' be shot on sight. On 7 December, this was acted on when a member of the Dublin IRA shot Hales dead and wounded Pádraic Ó Máille, Leas-Cheann Comhairle of the Dáil, as they left a hotel on Lower Ormond Quay.

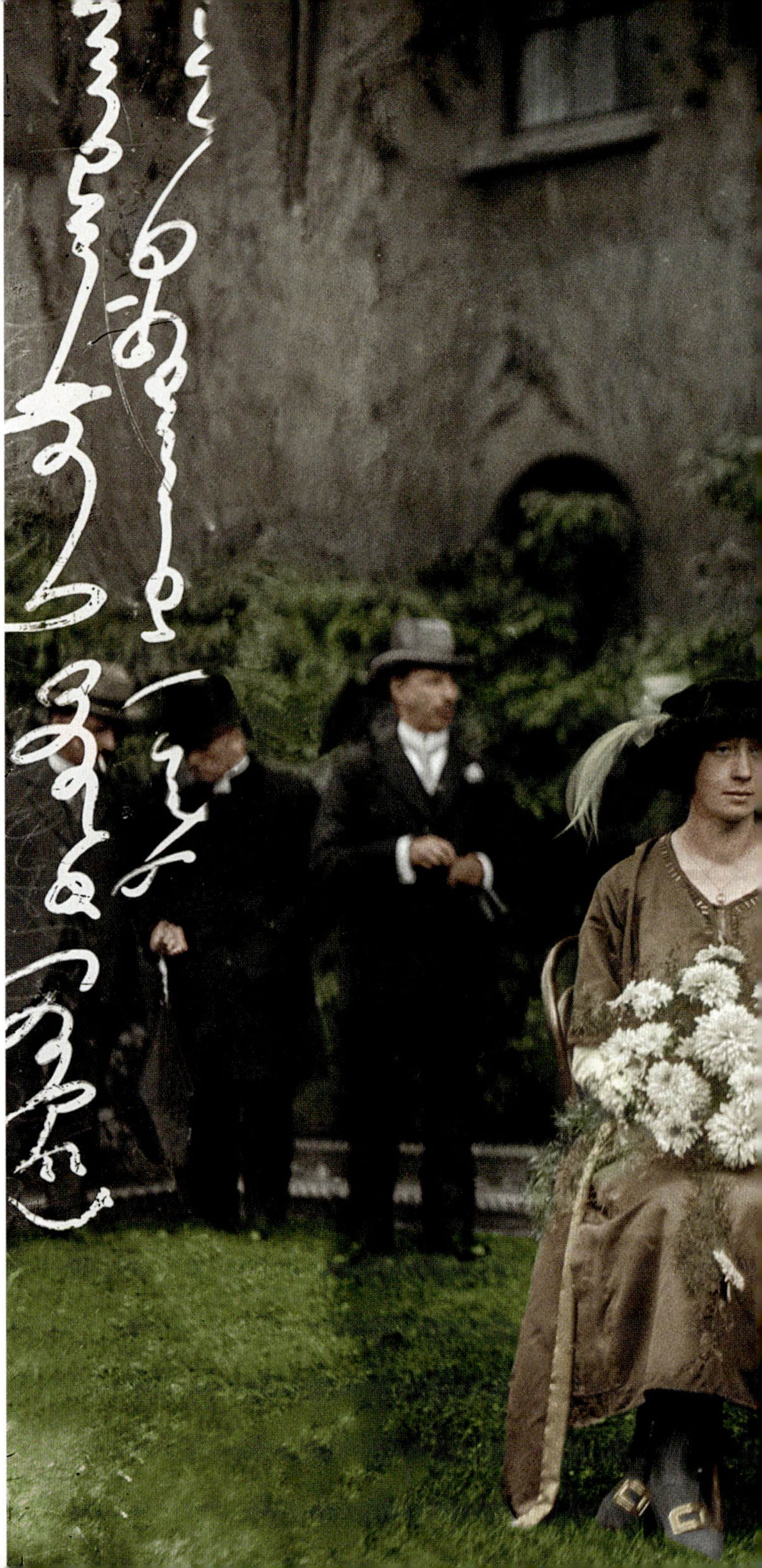

The Irish Free State officially came into being on 6 December 1922 (in accordance with the Treaty signed one year previously). The next day, hours after the assassination of Seán Hales that morning, the Executive Council of the Free State held an emergency meeting. Vengeance was in the air. After some debate, the meeting concluded with an order to execute, the following morning, four prominent Republicans (including Rory O'Connor) incarcerated in Mountjoy Prison.

There is cruel irony in this photograph: Rory O'Connor (on the right) was best man at Kevin O'Higgins's wedding in October 1921. Éamon de Valera is standing on the left. O'Higgins, as Minister for Justice, was one of the Executive Council that approved the executions, although accounts say that he initially hesitated.

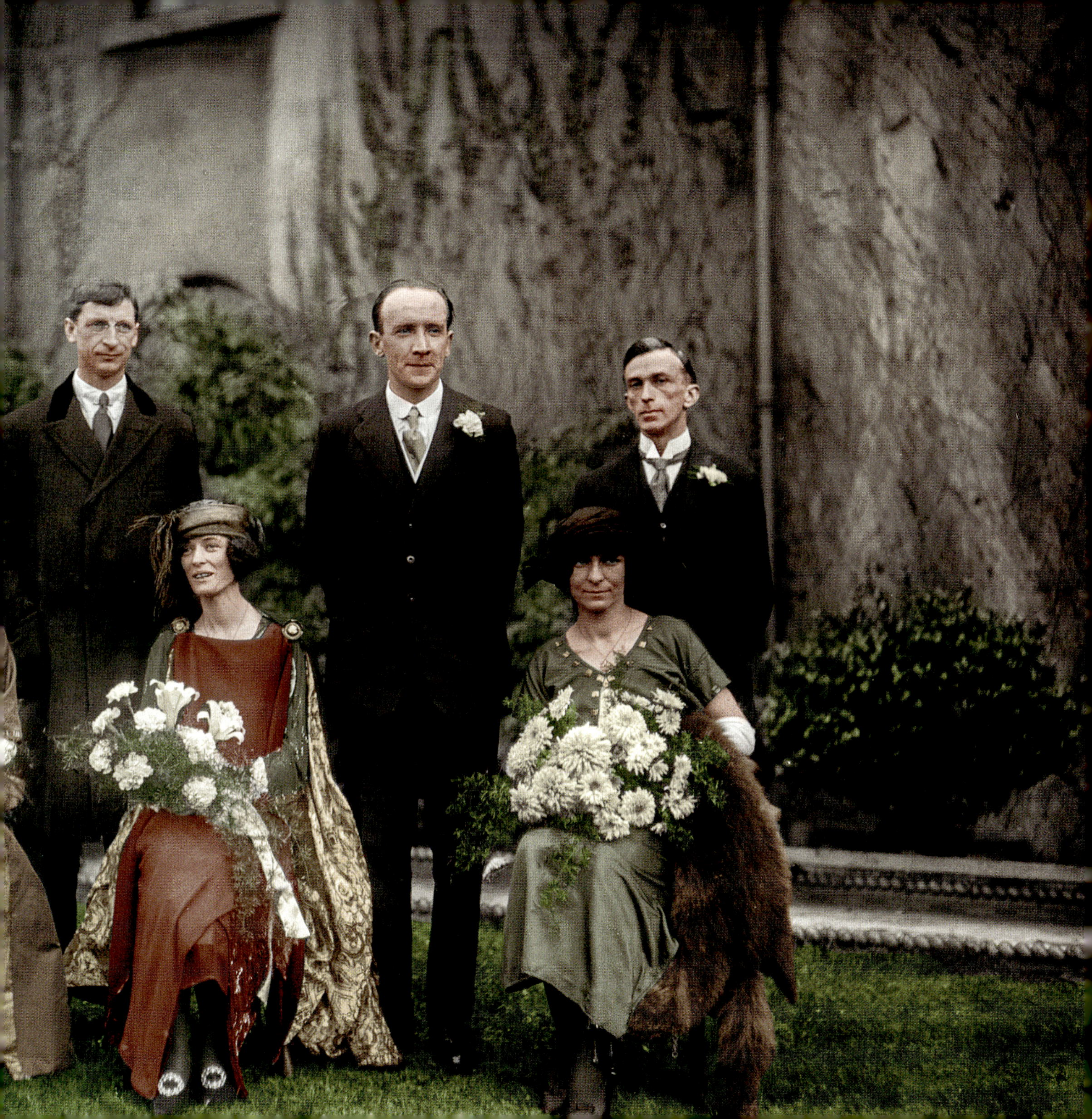

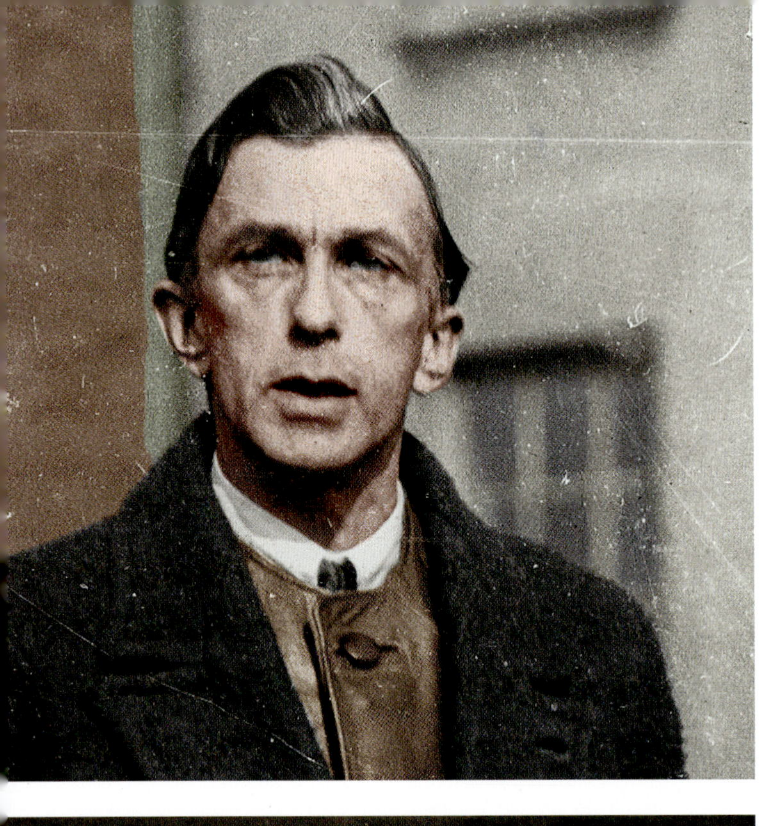
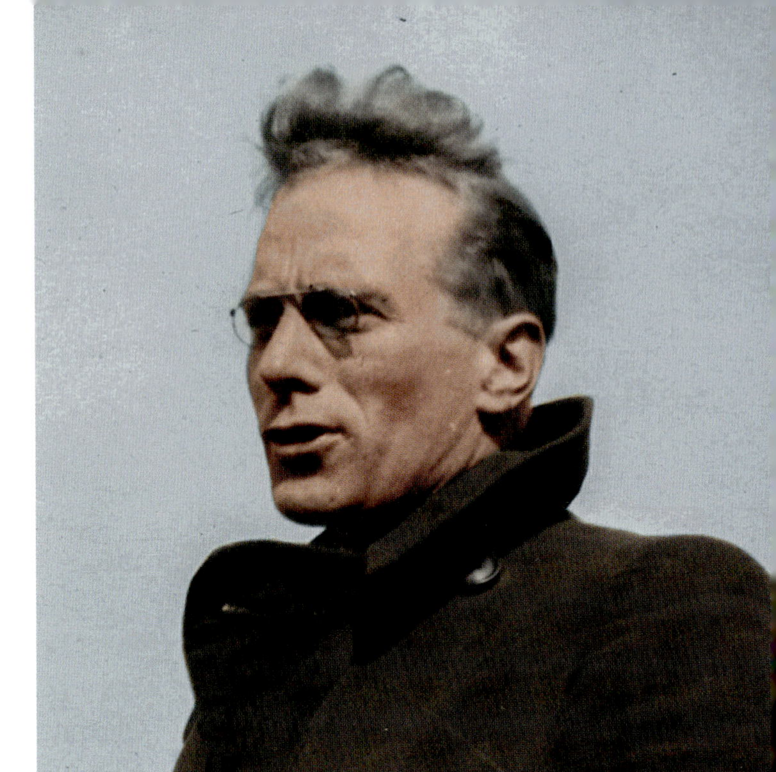
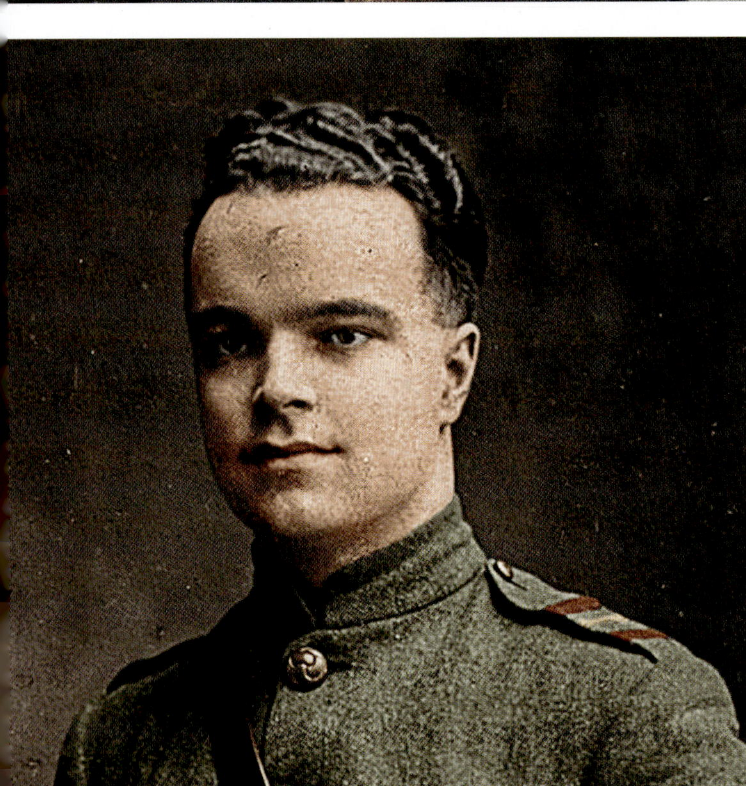
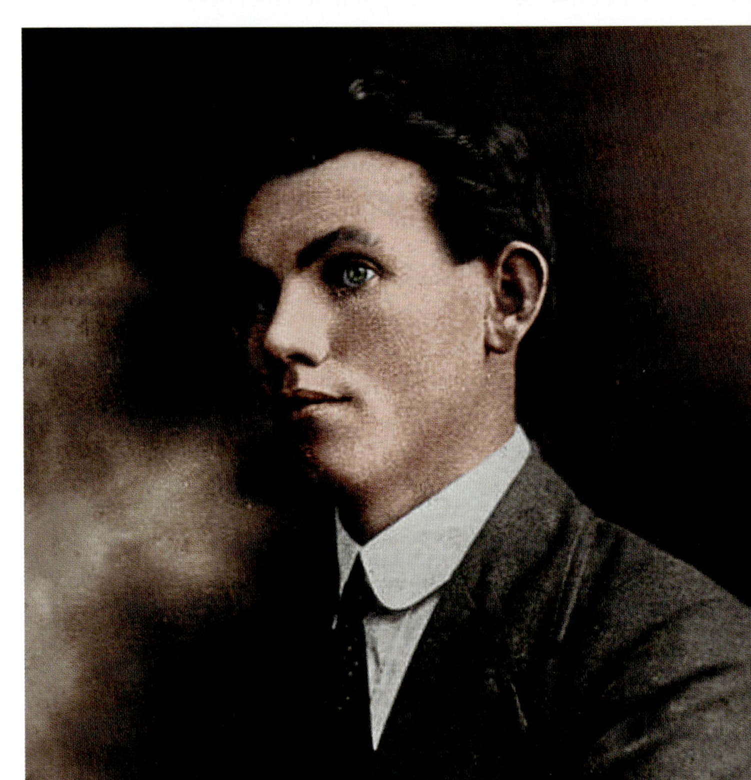

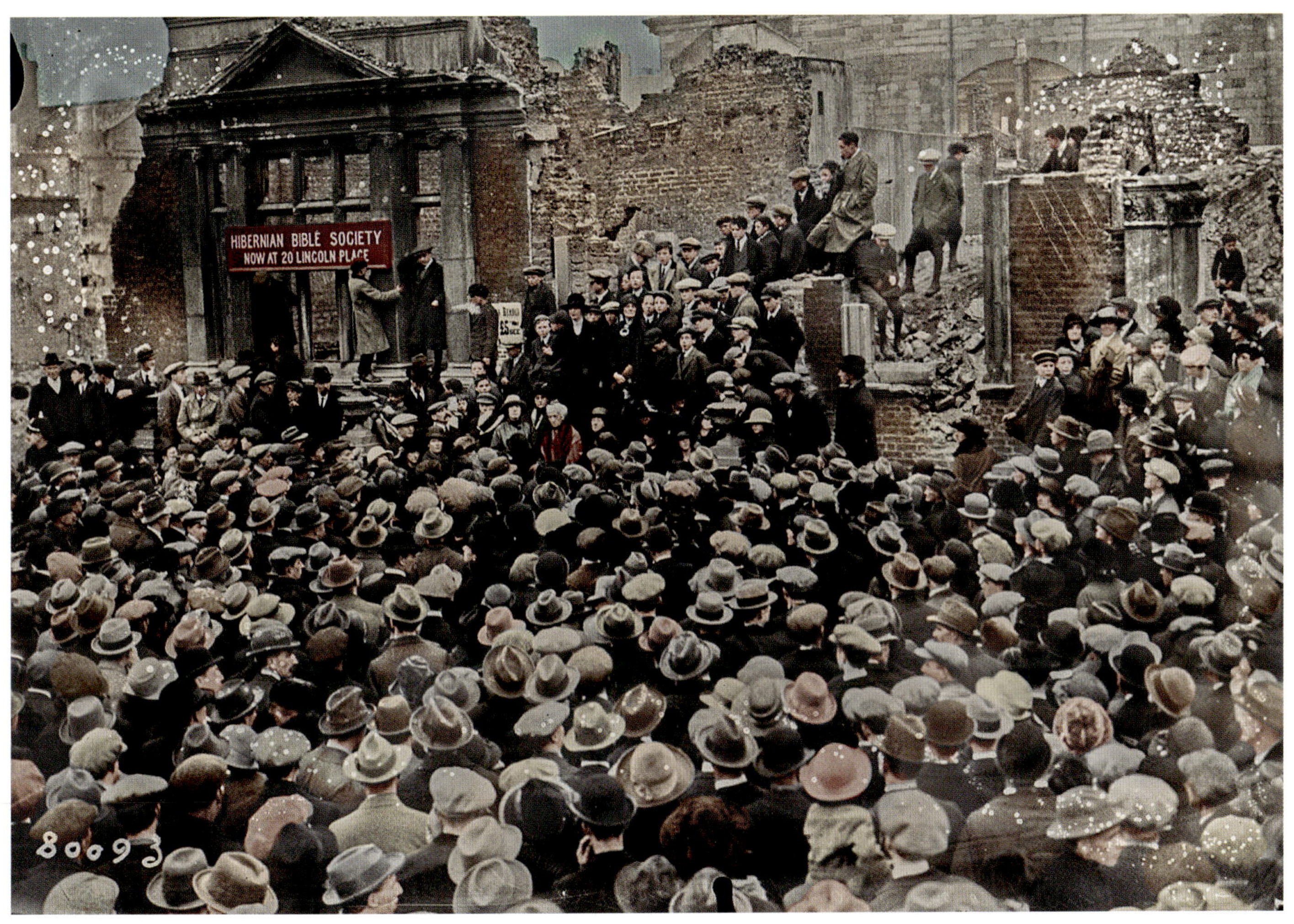

A meeting is held, in front of destroyed buildings on Upper Sackville Street, to protest against the Mountjoy executions.

Left: clockwise from top left, the executed four: Rory O'Connor, Liam Mellows, Dick Barrett and Joe McKelvey. At 3.30 a.m. on 8 December, the prisoners were roused from their cells in Mountjoy Prison and told that they were to be shot, as a reprisal, at 7 a.m. A firing squad shot the four together. The execution was conducted clumsily: nine revolver shots were required as coups de grâce. The prisoners had not been tried and these executions were not based on any law. Ernest Blythe, a Minister who had voted for the executions, later wrote: 'I frankly regarded it as an act of counter-terror, not of vengeance, and … an extreme act of war'.

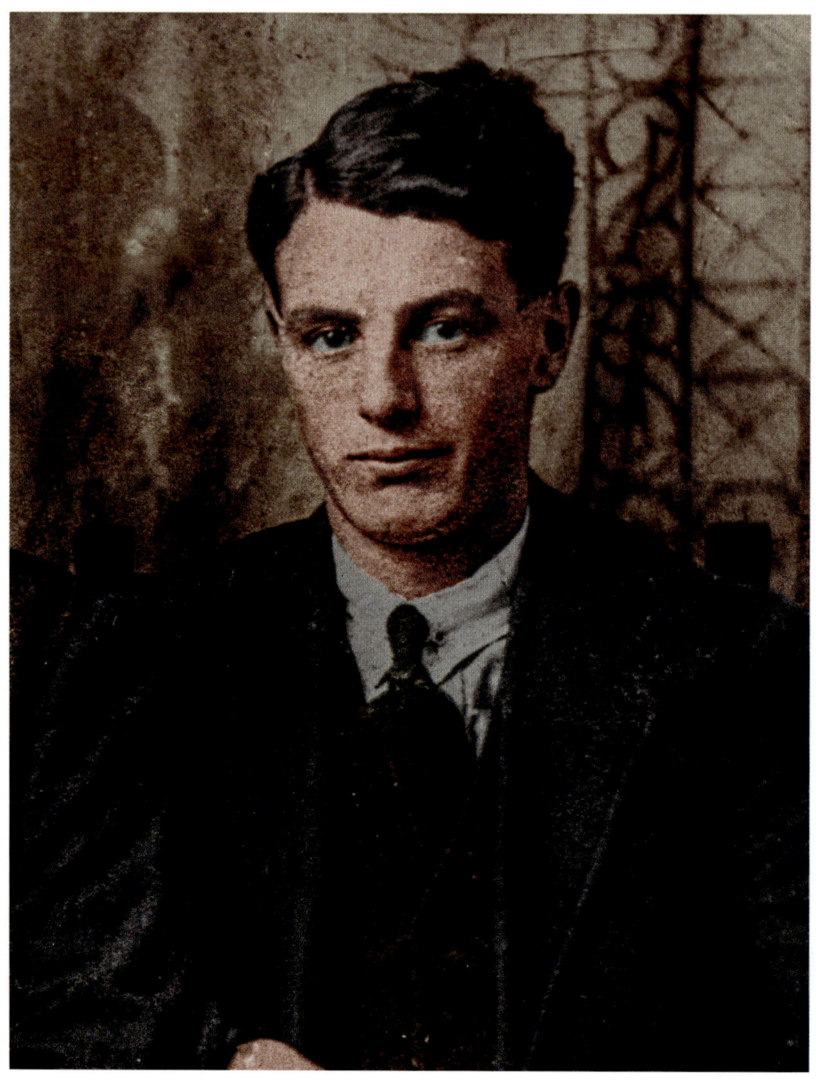

James O'Connor, a railway worker, was among a group of seven Volunteers executed at the Curragh Camp on 19 December 1922. The bodies were buried adjacent to the 'Glasshouse', the military detention prison. In 1924 the remains were exhumed and re-interred in a cemetery near Kildare town. There were 13 executions in December – the number peaked in January 1923, with 34 executions.

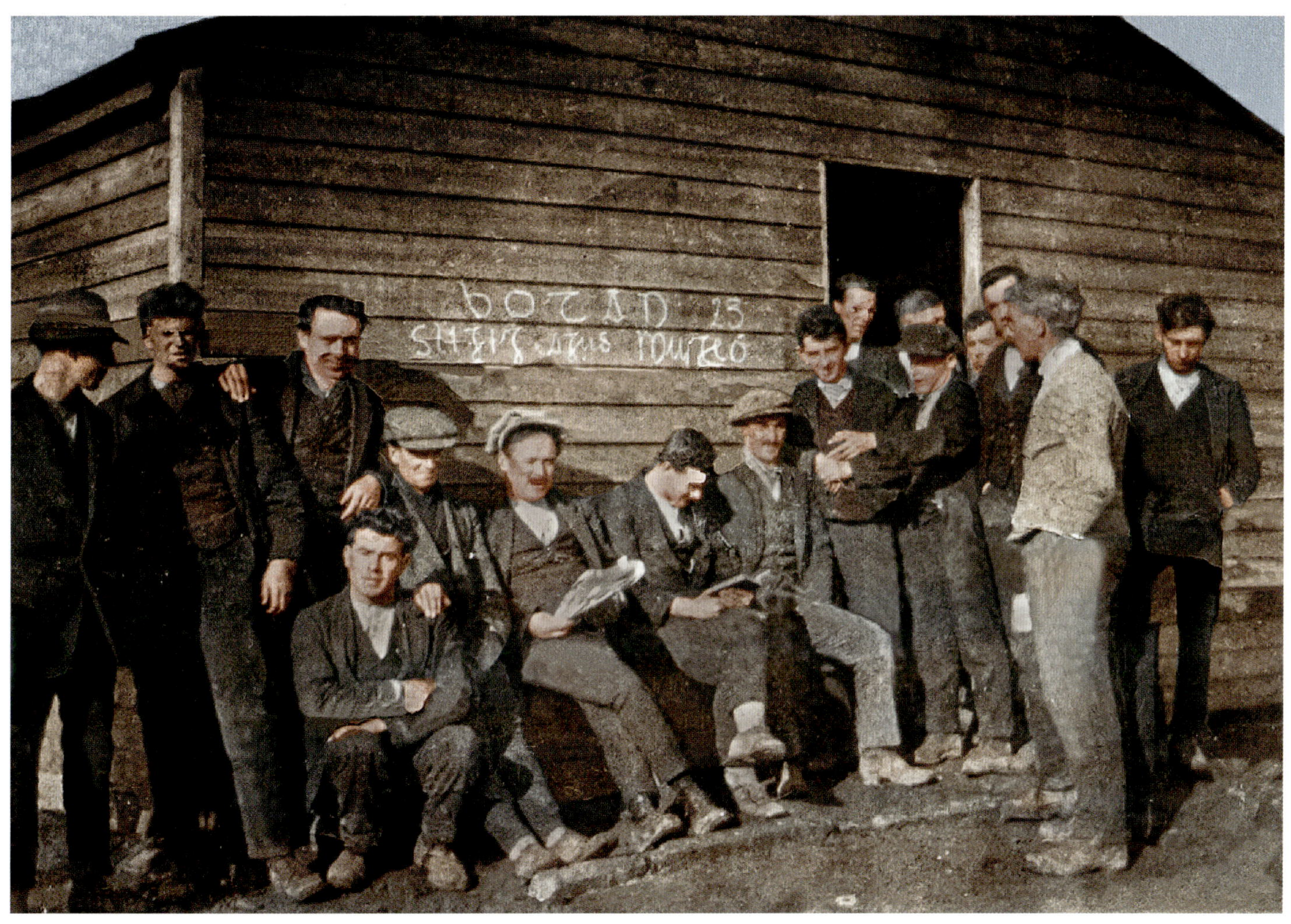

Republican prisoners pose outside the hut, chalked 'Bothán 15 Shligigh agus Mhuigheó' ('Hut 15, Sligo and Mayo') at the 'Tin-town' internment camp in the Curragh. Food was poor, sanitary conditions primitive and life monotonous. Many turned to education, but a few made efforts to tunnel out. Some did exercise, including playing Gaelic football. One account claims that, as most of the Kerry football team happened to be interned in the camp, there were some 'brilliant football matches'.

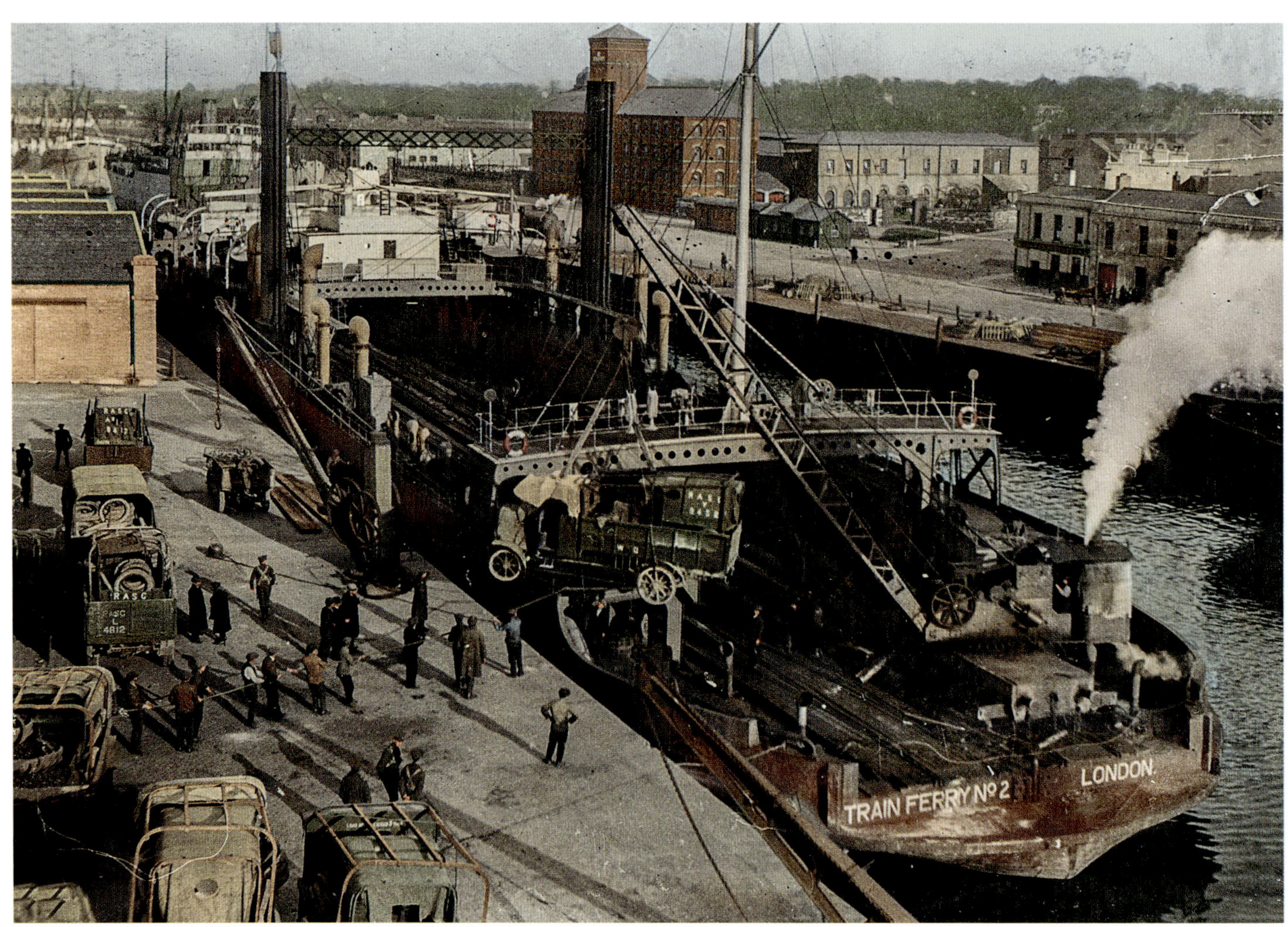

A scene, from earlier in 1922, at the docks in Cork. The steam crane on Train Ferry Number 2 is loading British army trucks. The vessel had been specially designed during WWI for the rapid transport of railway wagons carrying artillery and munitions from Britain to the front in France. By the middle of the year British troops had withdrawn from most of southern Ireland, leaving around 5,000 stationed in the Dublin area. At the end of 1922, confident that the Free State Government would prevail in the Civil War, the British made arrangements to evacuate the last of their troops.

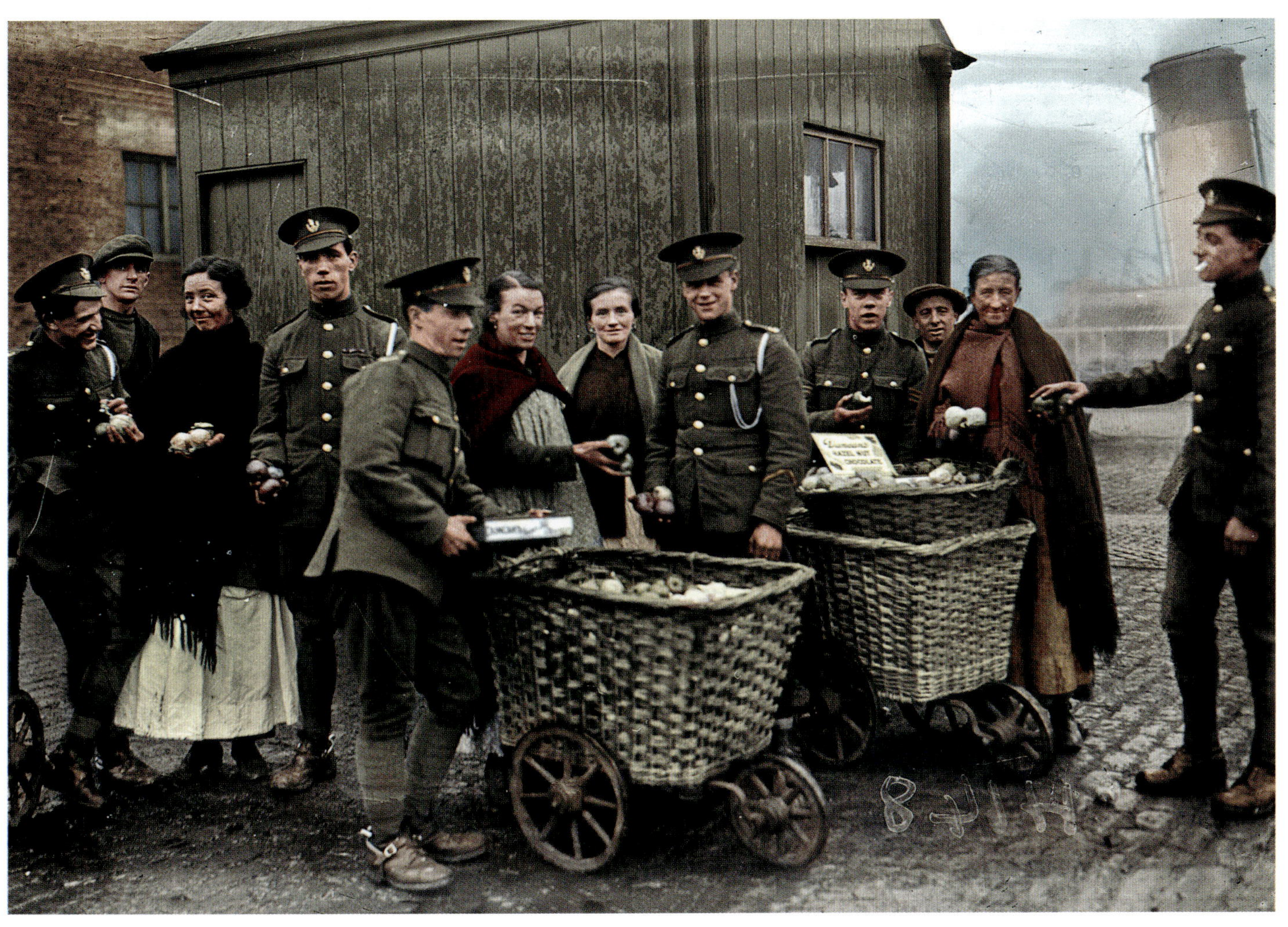
It is December 1922 and there are smiles on the Dublin quays as British troops buy last-minute snacks as they depart from Ireland. The soldier on the left appears to have turned on the charm for the woman vendor, who is proudly displaying her apples. On 13 December a destroyer was sent to Dublin Port to protect the ships carrying troops. National Army patrols were deployed north and south of the Liffey. Cross-channel steamers (including the *Arvonia*) were engaged for the evacuation exercise. On 17 December General Nevil Macready made a last review of the troops and left for Dún Laoghaire (recently renamed from 'Kingstown'), where he received the honour of a 17-gun salute and sailed away on the cruiser HMS *Dragon*.

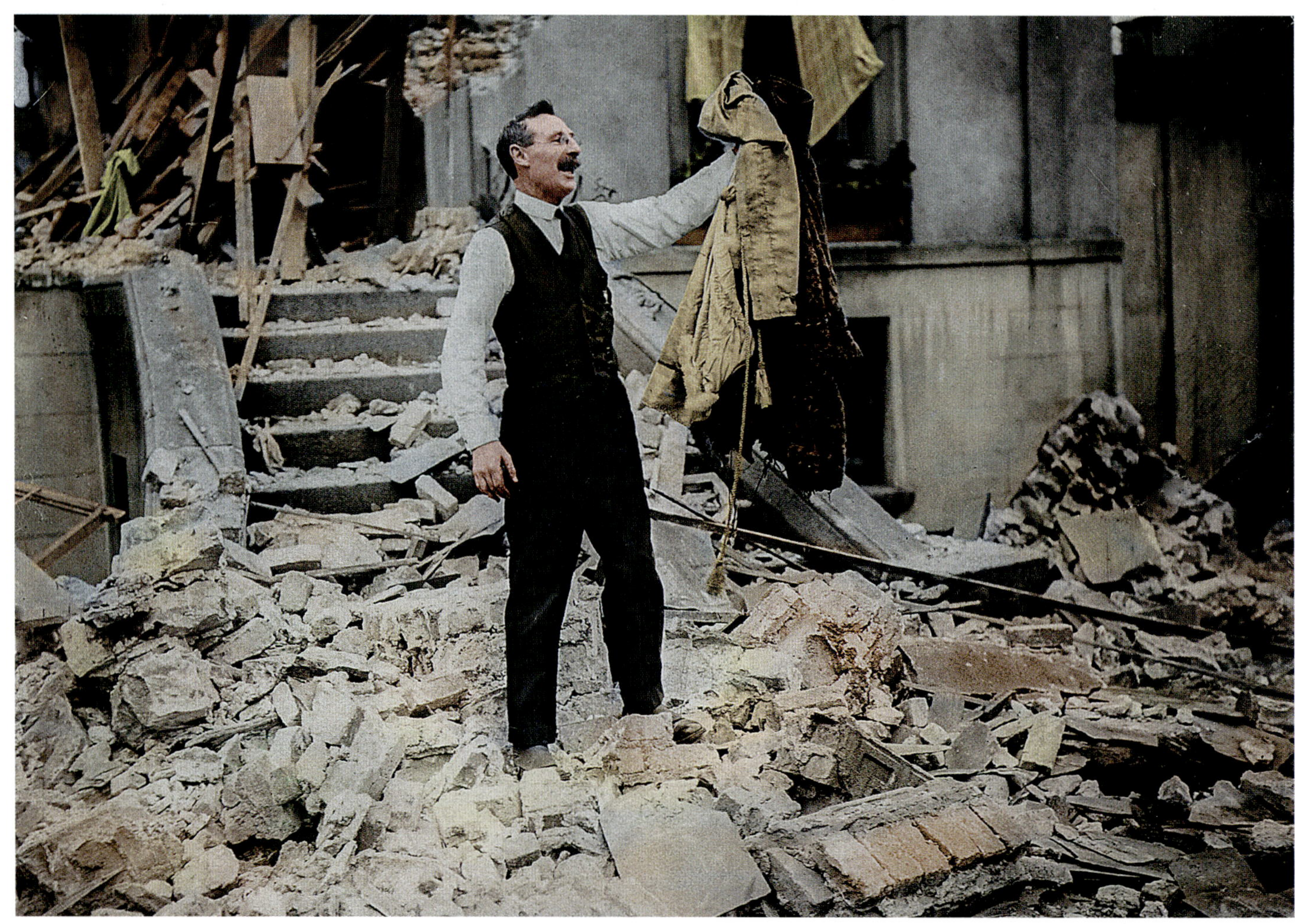

The Rathmines house of the Chief State Solicitor, Michael Corrigan, was blown up on 29 January 1923. The unfortunate gentleman surveys the ruins of his house. By the end of 1922, Free State forces had gained the upper hand and executions of captured Republicans continued. There was a wave of retaliation, like this one, against prominent supporters of the Free State authorities.

Right: the house on Philipsburgh Avenue, in Dublin, of pro-Treaty TD (and former president of the IRB) Seán McGarry was set on fire on 10 December 1922. His seven-year-old son, Emmet, pictured here, died of burns received in the fire.

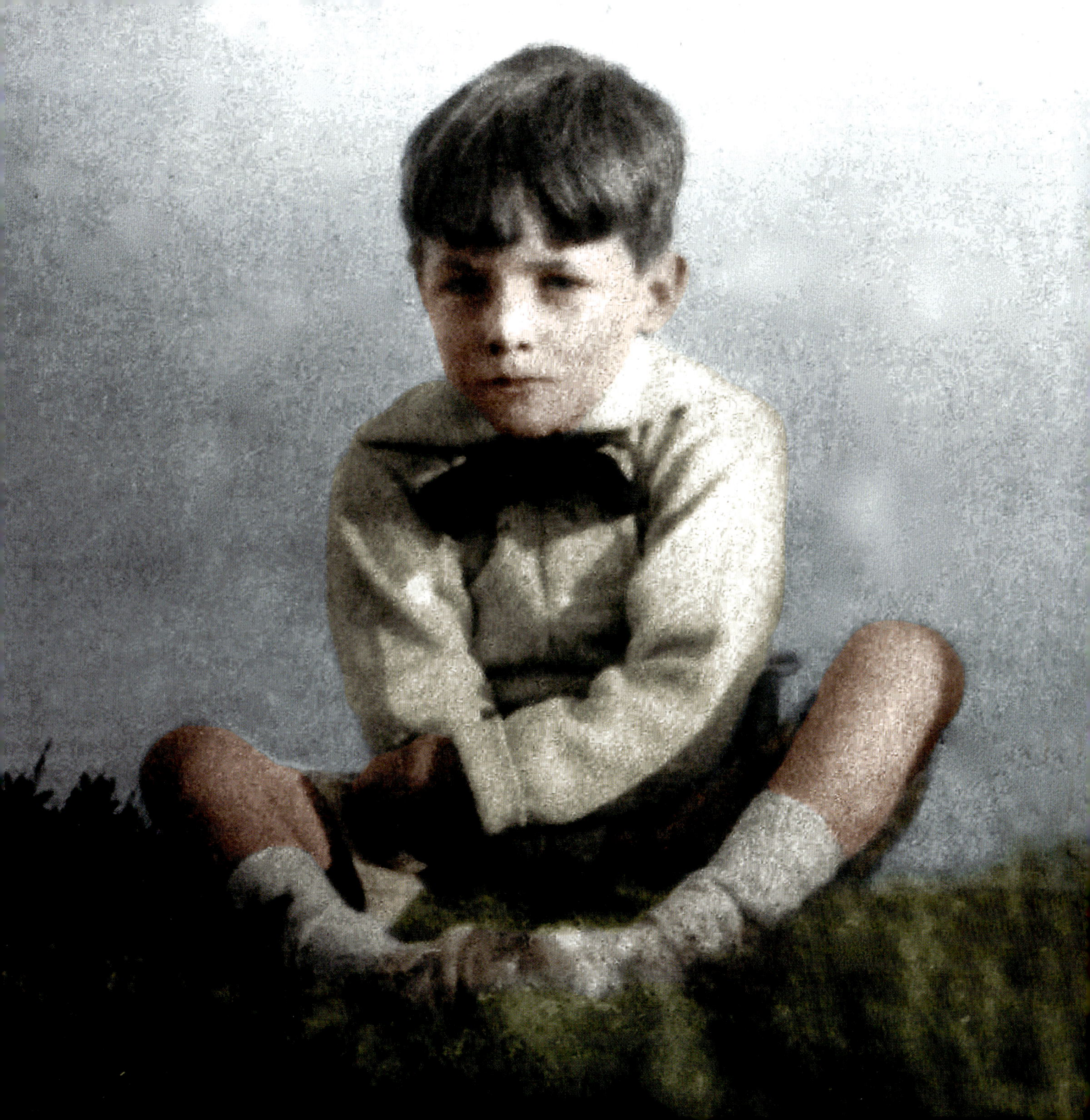

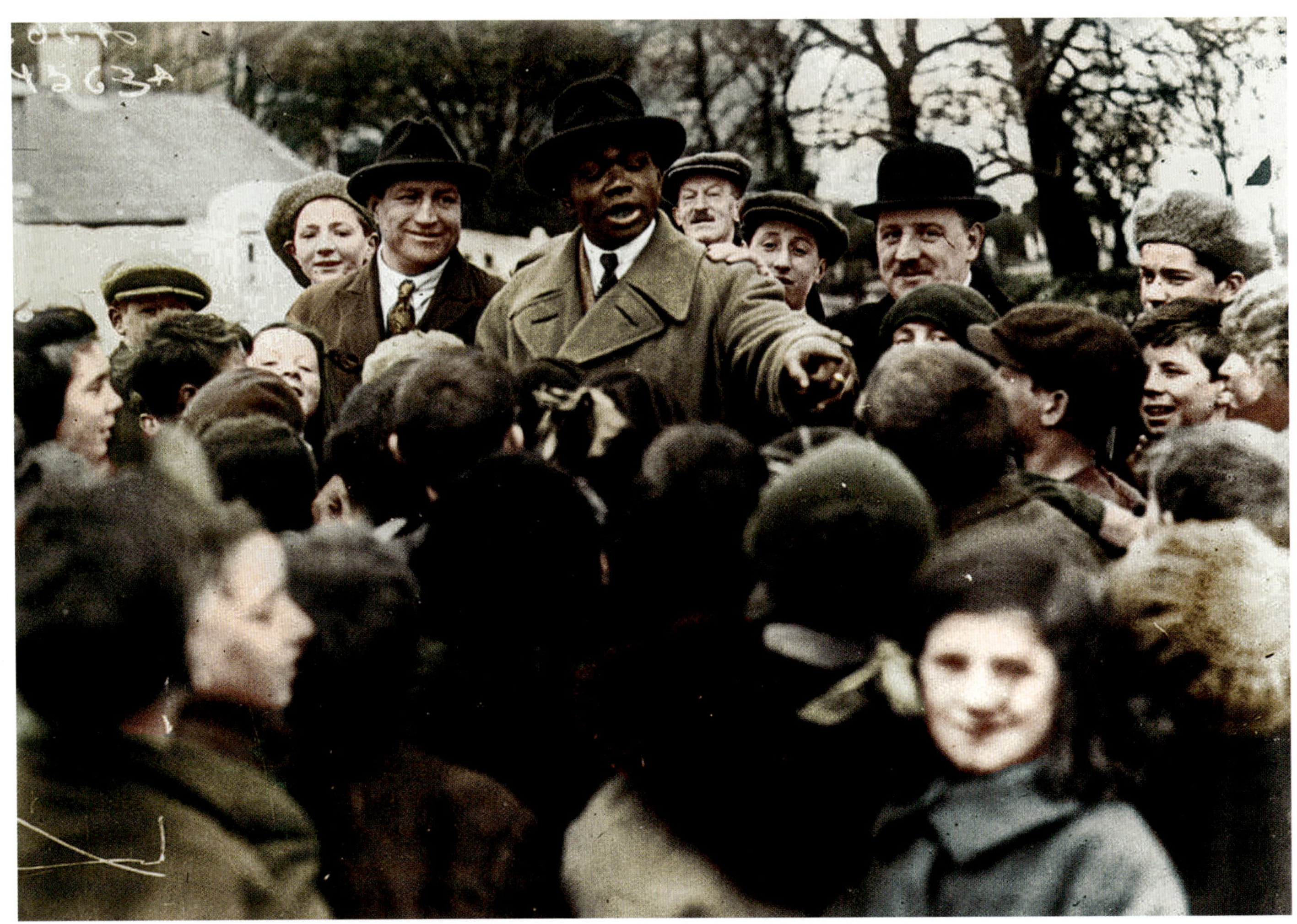

The Senegalese-French boxer Louis M'Barick Fall, better known as 'Battling Siki', goes on a walkabout while in Dublin to fight the Irish boxer Mike McTigue ('The Cyclonic Celt') at the La Scala Theatre. The bout was proscribed by the anti-Treaty IRA but it went ahead on 17 March 1923, heavily guarded by the National Army. McTigue won and became World Light Heavyweight Champion.

Right: in this photograph, Máire Comerford (centre), a veteran of the Four Courts garrison, and other Cumann na mBan members, including, on left, Rosie Hackett and, smiling, top right, Bridie Clyne (who married The O'Rahilly's son, Neill), march at a rally. Cumann na mBan overwhelmingly took the anti-Treaty side in 1922 and were the eyes and ears of the IRA, carrying messages and weapons. Many were imprisoned in Kilmainham and Mountjoy prisons.

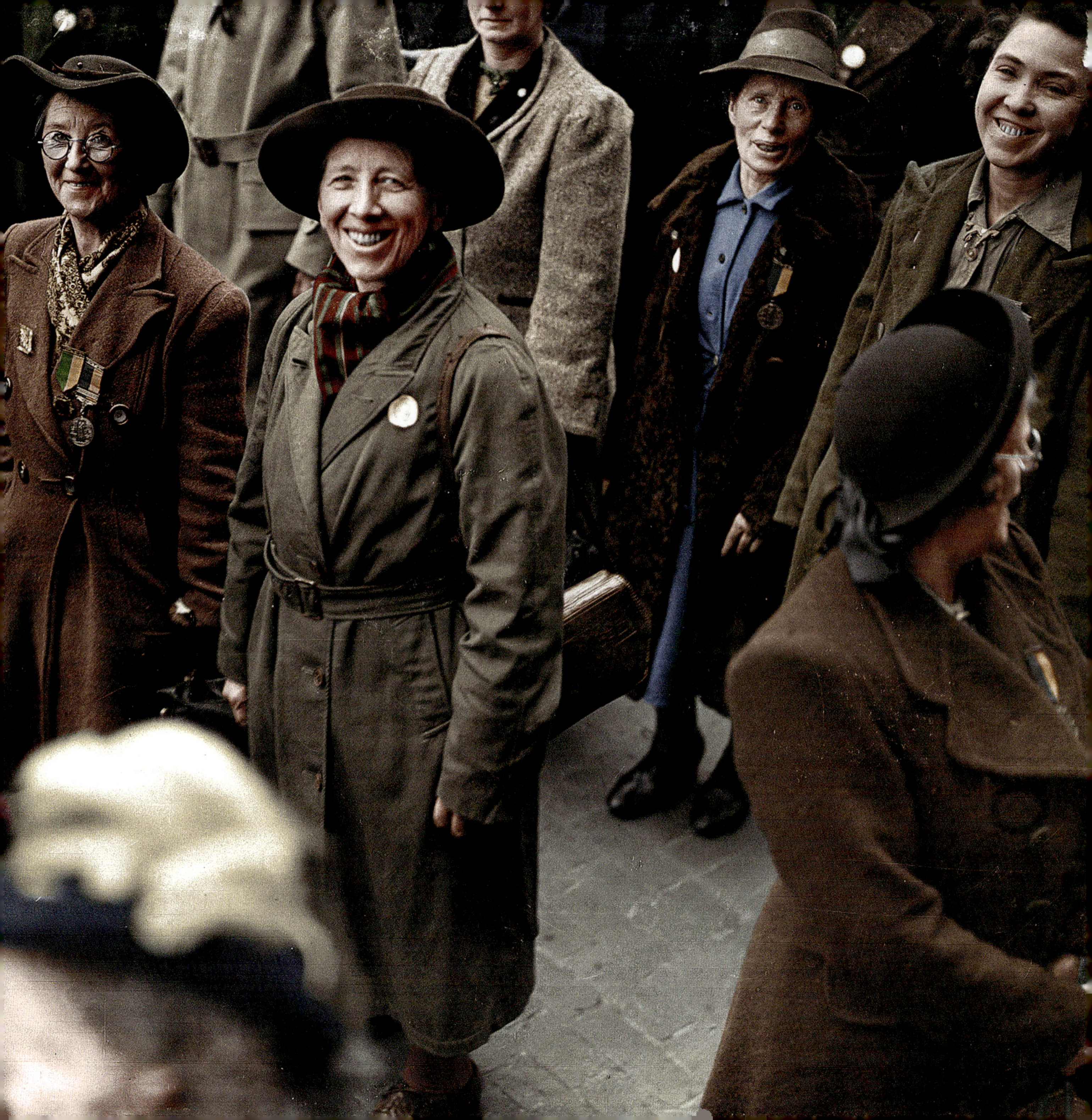

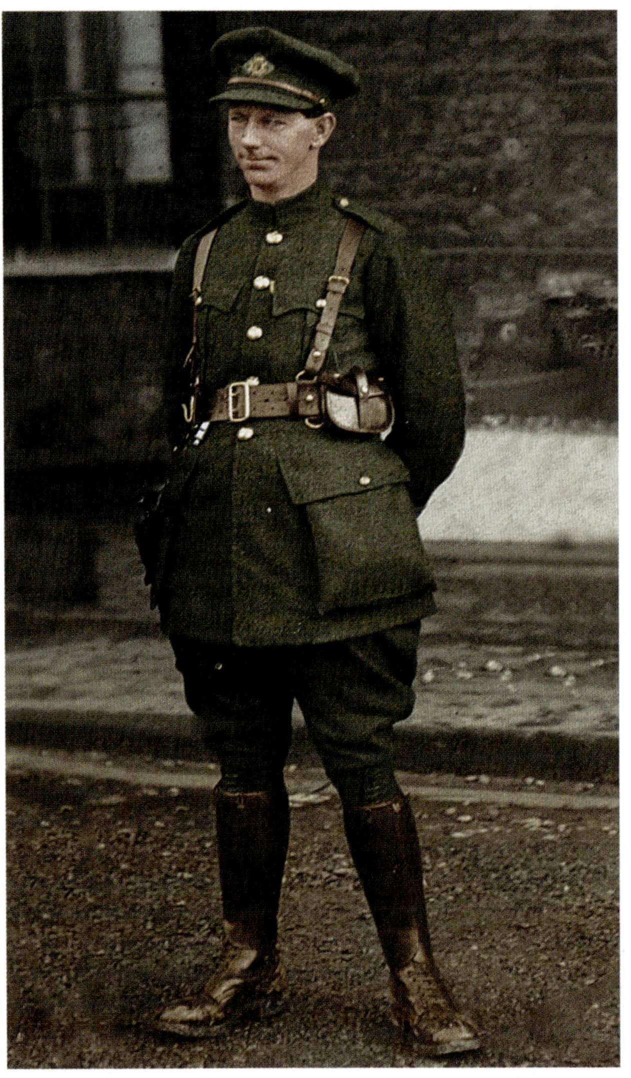

Brigadier-General Paddy O'Daly (pictured), GOC Kerry, was in charge when the cycle of atrocity and reprisal reached a new level of frightfulness. Following the death of five of their comrades by a trap mine at Knocknagoshel on 7 March 1923, the Dublin Guard brought nine Republican prisoners from Ballymullan Barracks to Ballyseedy. They were tied together and blown up by a mine (one survived). Four others were killed near Killarney, and on 12 March five prisoners were blown up by a mine near Caherciveen.

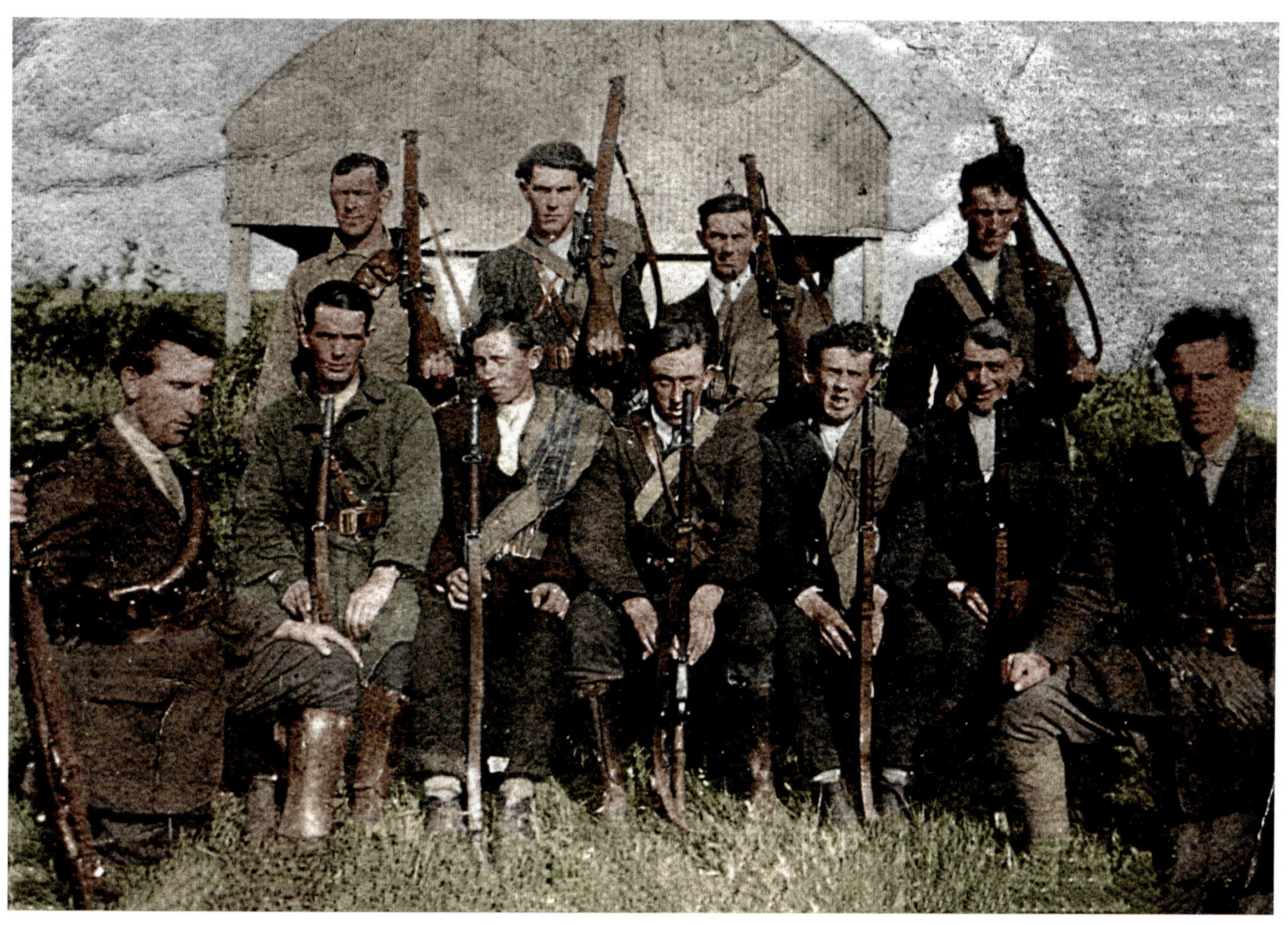

The Kilfynn Flying Column of the IRA, with Timothy 'Aero' Lyons, front row-centre. In the back row, second from the left, is Stephen Fuller (later to be the only survivor of the Ballyseedy massacre). On 16 April 1923, Republicans, in hiding in a cave on the north Kerry coast, were discovered by Free State troops, who tried to flush them out using burning hay and landmines. Eventually 'Aero' Lyons, the leader, surrendered but his rope parted as he climbed up and he was shot dead as he fell on rocks. Another three surrendered. They were brought back to Ballymullan Barracks in Tralee, tried by military court and executed on 25 April.

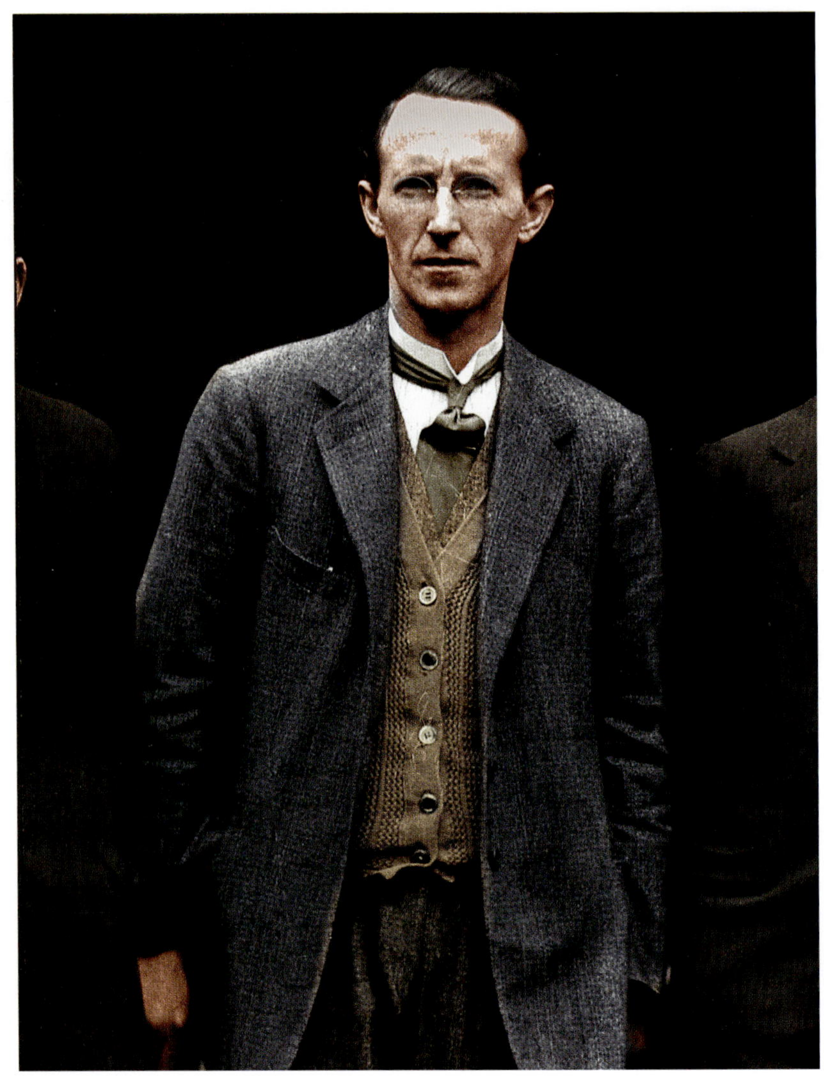

An IRA Executive meeting, held in the isolated Nire Valley in County Waterford, culminated in a vote on 26 March 1923, on a motion that continued resistance would not further the cause of independence. It was defeated by six votes (including that of Liam Lynch, Chief of Staff, pictured here) to five. Due to the diverging opinion, the IRA Executive agreed to meet three weeks later.

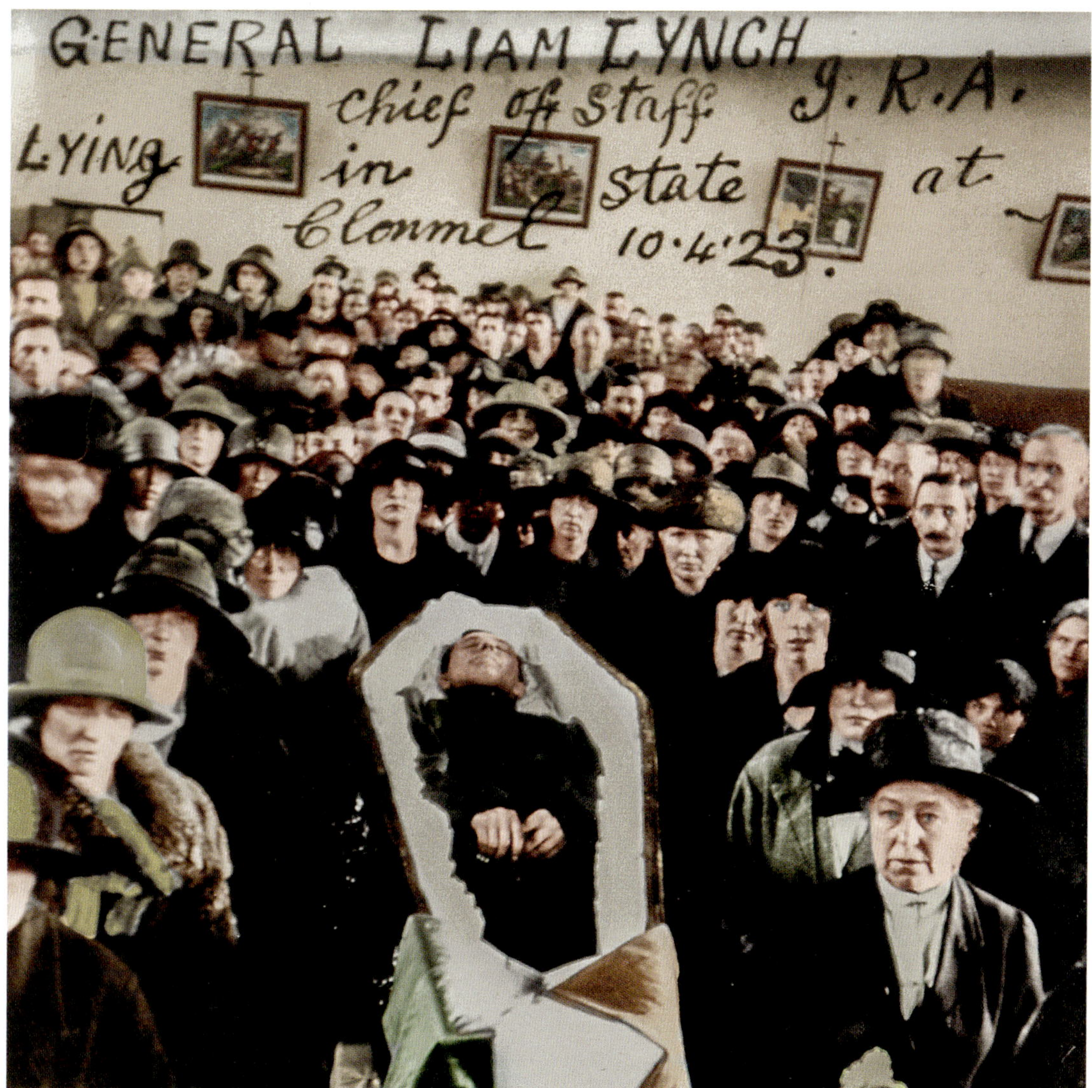

Liam Lynch was en route to the planned IRA Executive meeting to resume discussions on continuation of the war, when he was spotted on 10 April 1923 on the Knockmealdown mountains by National Army troops. Felled by a long-distance shot, he was wounded in the abdomen and carried off the mountain with difficulty. Lynch was eventually transported by ambulance to St Joseph's Hospital, Clonmel, where he died that evening. Here he lies in his coffin.

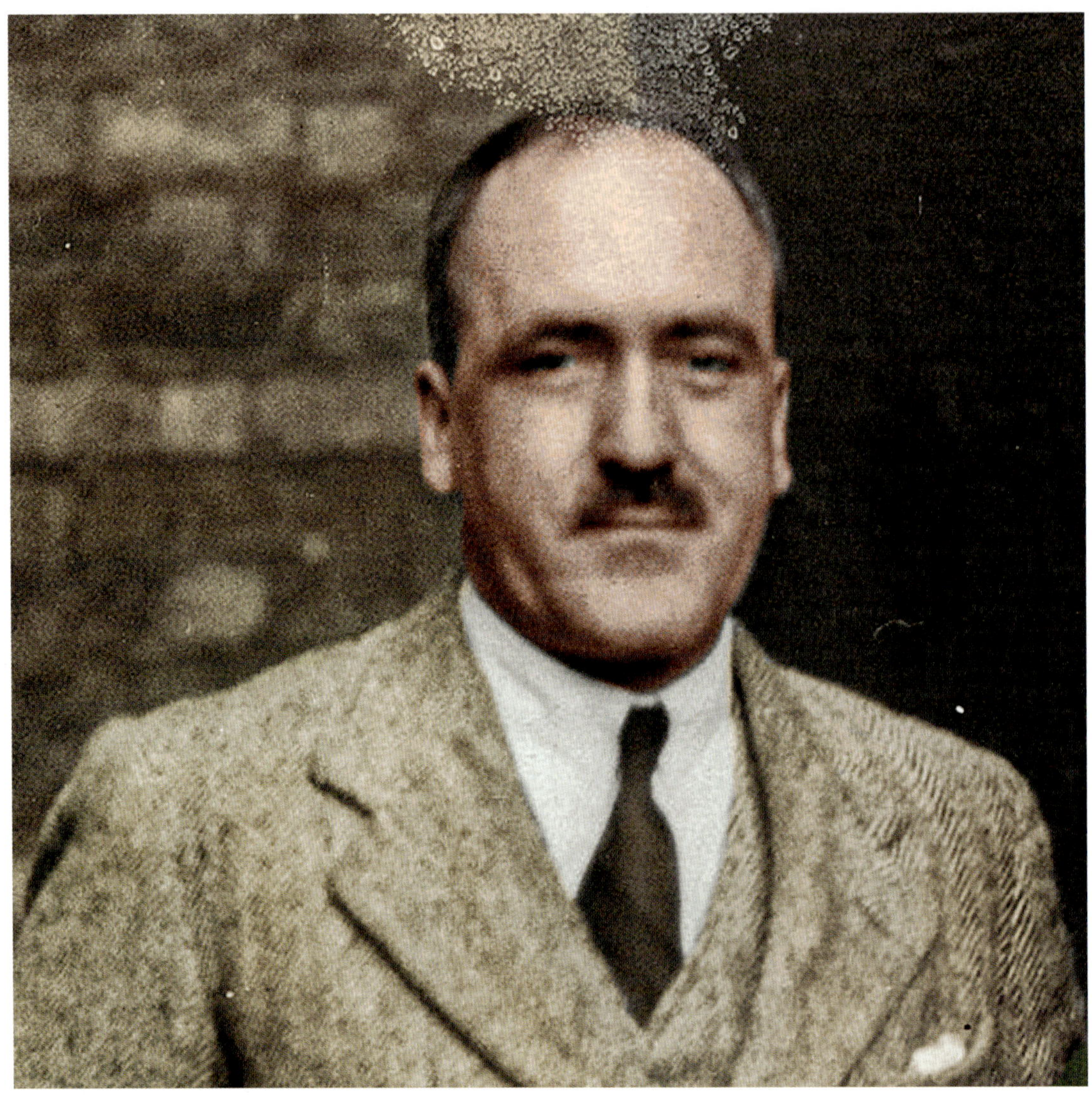

Little over six weeks after Liam Lynch's death, on 24 May 1923, the new IRA Chief of Staff, Frank Aiken (above), sent an order that 'The arms with which we have fought the enemies of our country are to be dumped. The foreign and domestic enemies of the Republic have for the moment prevailed'.

Right: a general election was called for August 1923. Here a man pastes Republican election posters.

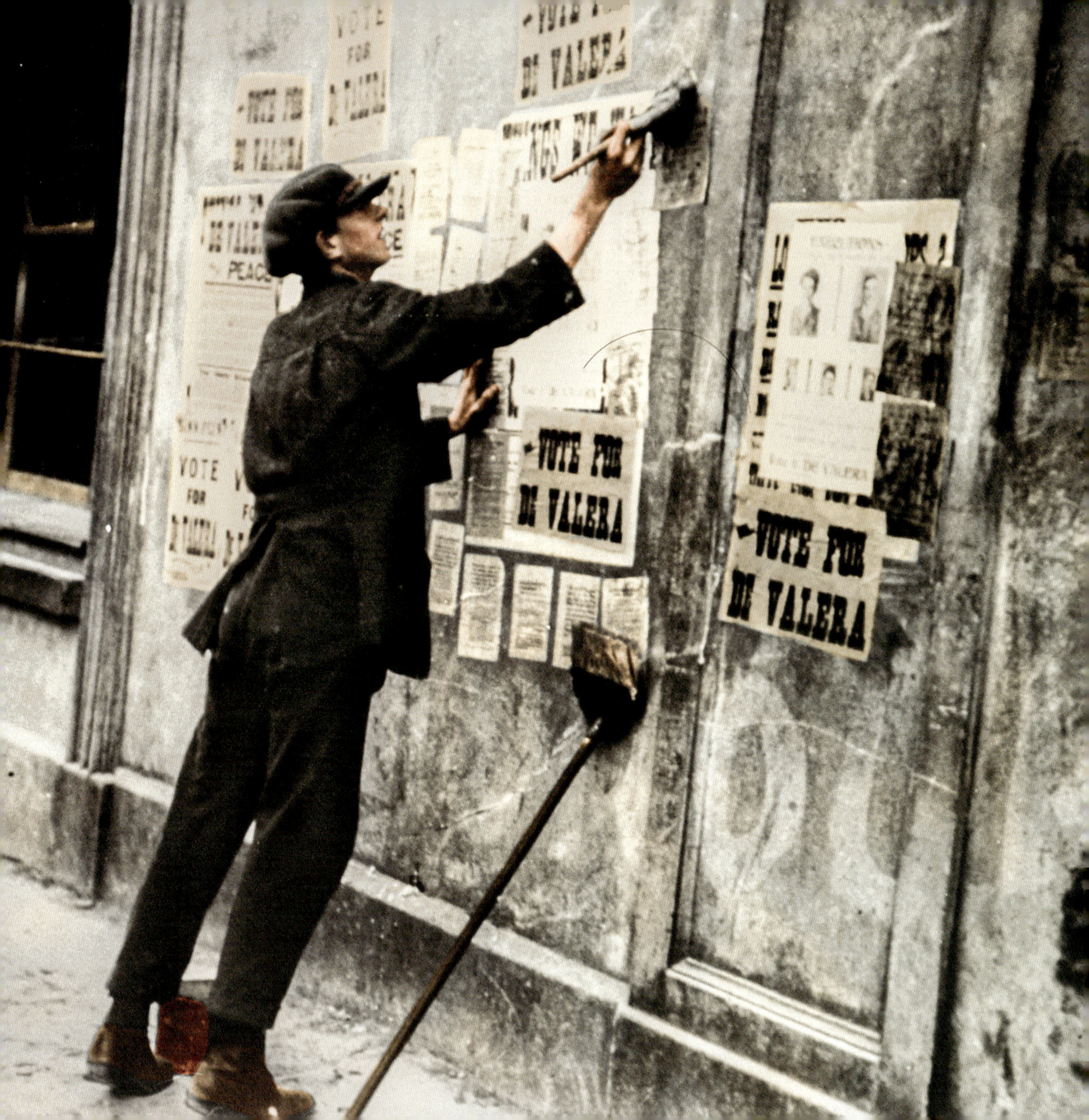
VOTE
FOR
D VALERA
VOTE FOR
DE VALERA
PEACE
VOTE
FOR
DE VALERA
DE VALERA
VOTE FOR
DE VALERA
VOTE FOR
DE VALERA

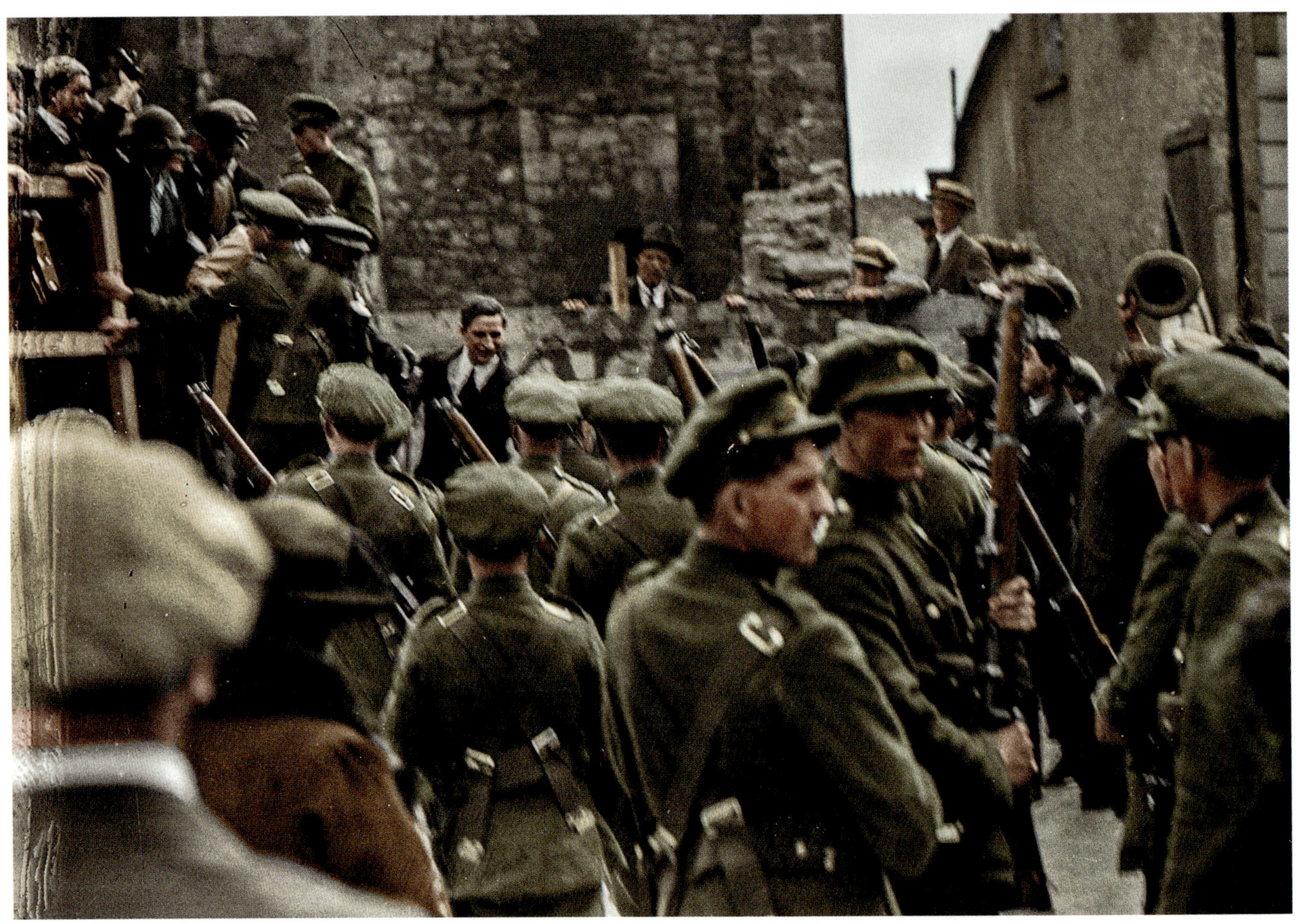

With the IRA weak and exhausted, Éamon de Valera was able to better assert the political aspect of republicanism and proposed participation in the General Election. On 15 August 1923, he emerged from hiding to address a Sinn Féin election meeting at Ennis, Co. Clare. Shots were discharged and scuffles ensued as de Valera (seen in the background, centre left) was seized by Free State troops and dispatched to prison. He was to spend around a year in captivity.

Right: Richard Mulcahy declaims at an election rally, as depicted by a Munich newspaper.

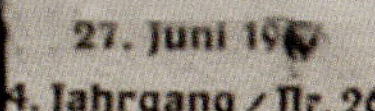

27. Juni 19[..]
4. Jahrgang / Nr. 26

Münchner Illustrierte Presse

Erſcheint wöchentlich
Preis: 20 Pfennig

Knorr & Hirth, G. m. [b. H.,] München

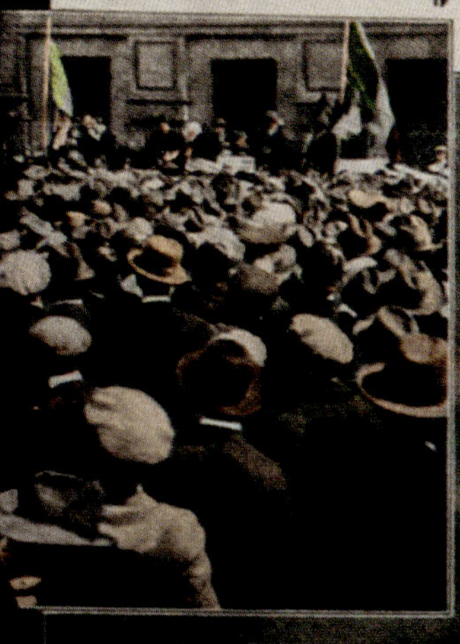

Kampf um die Maſſen

Ein Agi[tations]redner der „Iriſh Independent“-Partei bei einem Mee[tin]g in Dublin (oben: die Menge vor der Rednerbüh[ne])

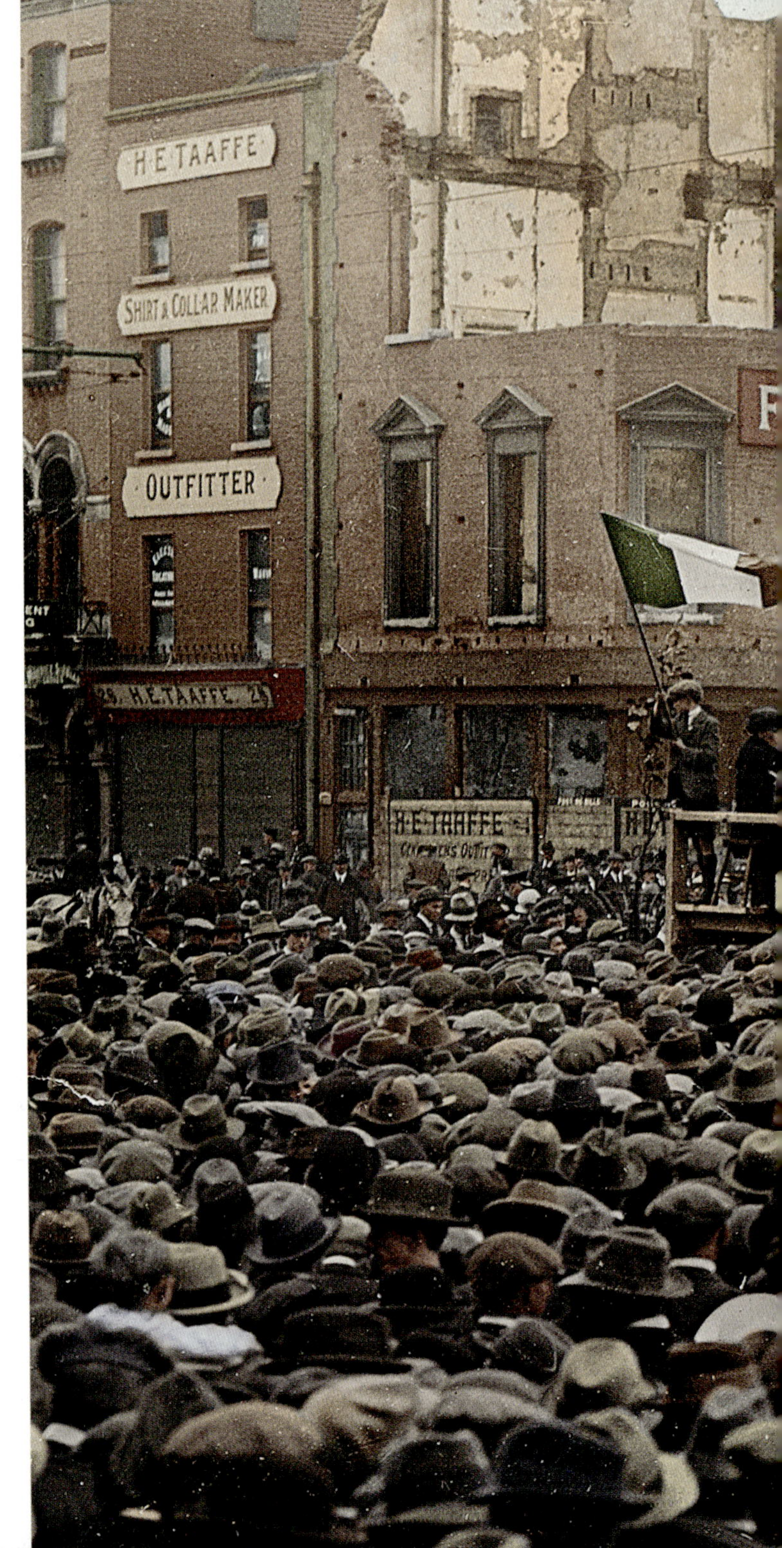

On 19 August 1923, this anti-Treaty election meeting was held at the top of Upper Sackville Street in Dublin. Despite many of their candidates being incarcerated, the election result was surprisingly good for Sinn Féin at 44 seats. The pro-Treaty party in power, Cumann na nGaedheal, gained 63 seats. Labour and others won 46.

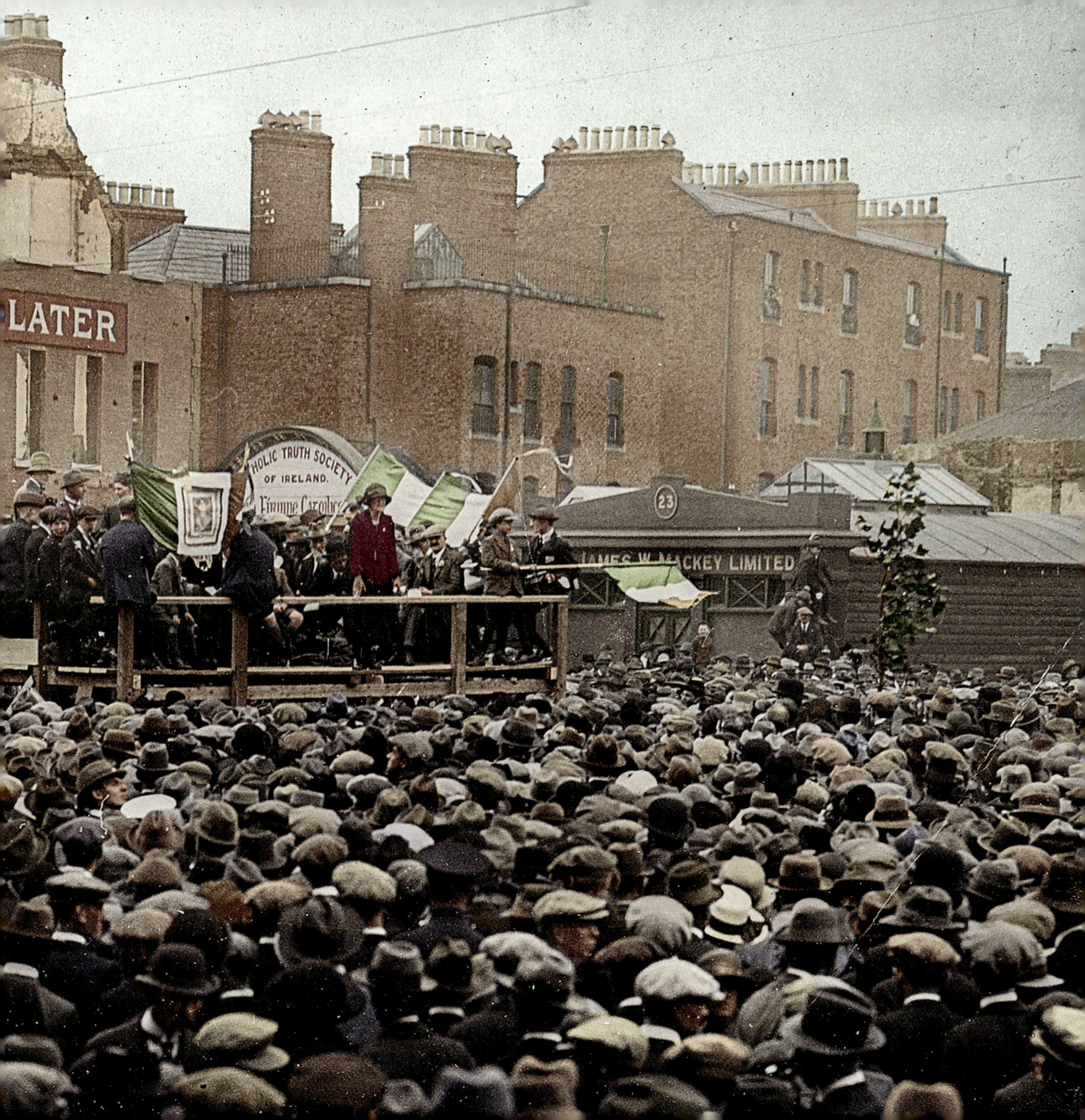
LATER
CATHOLIC TRUTH SOCIETY OF IRELAND.
Fírinne Catoilceach
23
JAMES W. MACKEY LIMITED

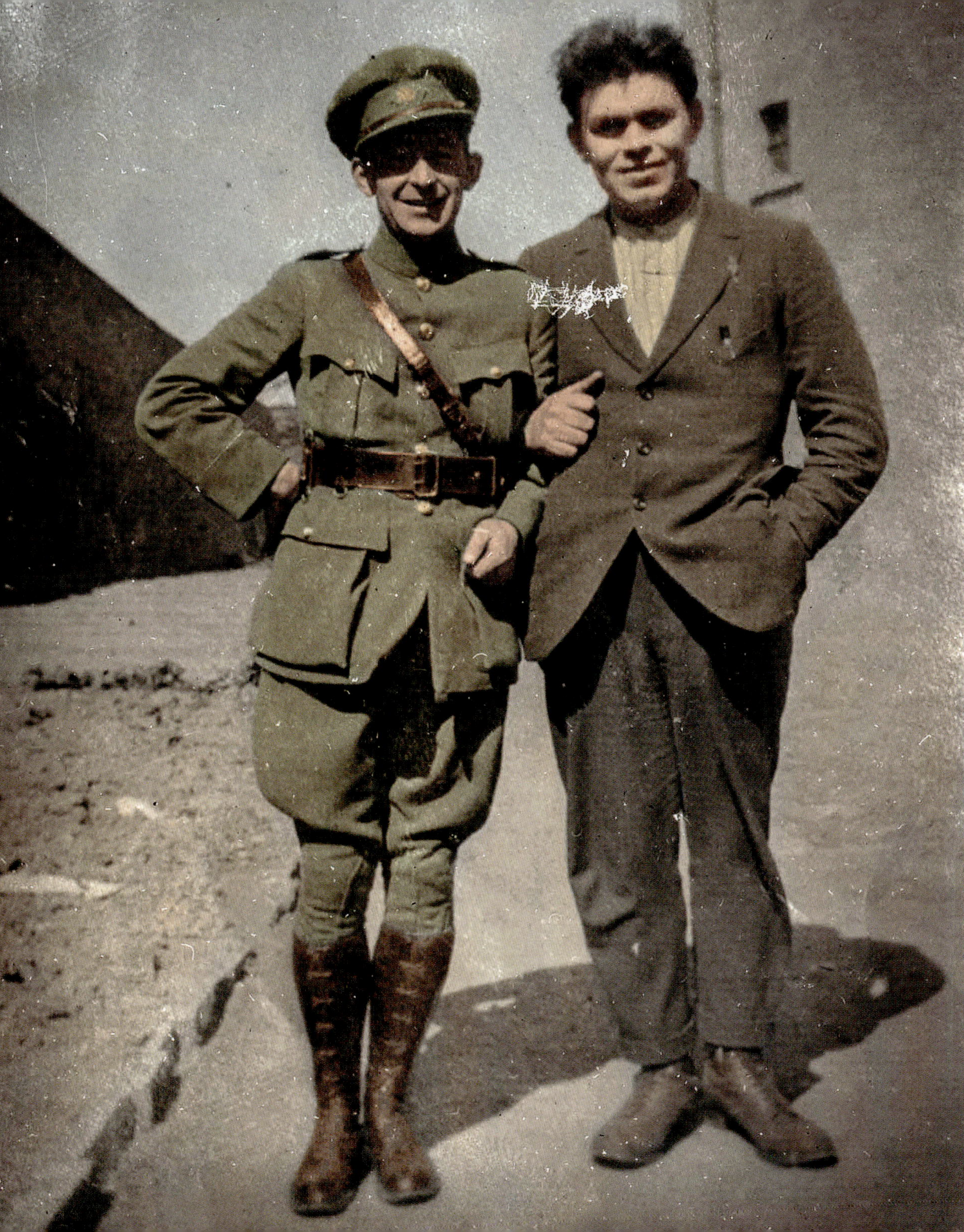

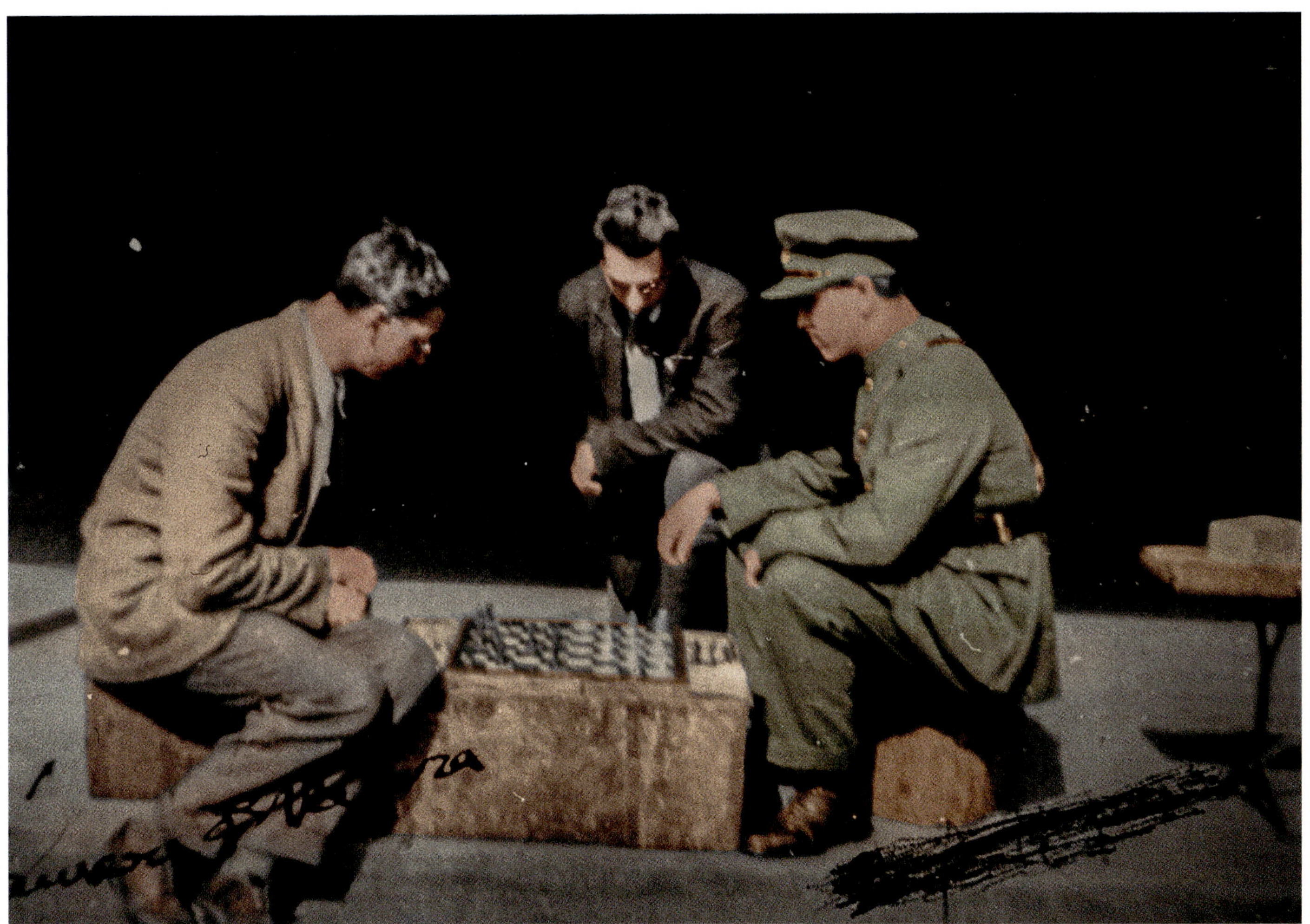

Kilmainham Gaol had been closed when the British left. It was soon re-opened to accommodate Republican prisoners. The last of these, Éamon de Valera (seen here playing chess), was released on 16 July 1924.

Left: Dan Breen with a National Army officer (who had been his driver during the War of Independence) at Limerick Prison. Breen was elected TD in August 1923, while in custody there. At the end of the Civil War there were around 12,000 Republicans in custody. With no negotiated peace and no handover of arms, the Free State authorities were reluctant to release the prisoners. In October 1923, there was a mass hunger strike by the prisoners but it ended in disarray and was called off on 23 November. Over the following months, there was a gradual release of prisoners which was completed in summer 1924.

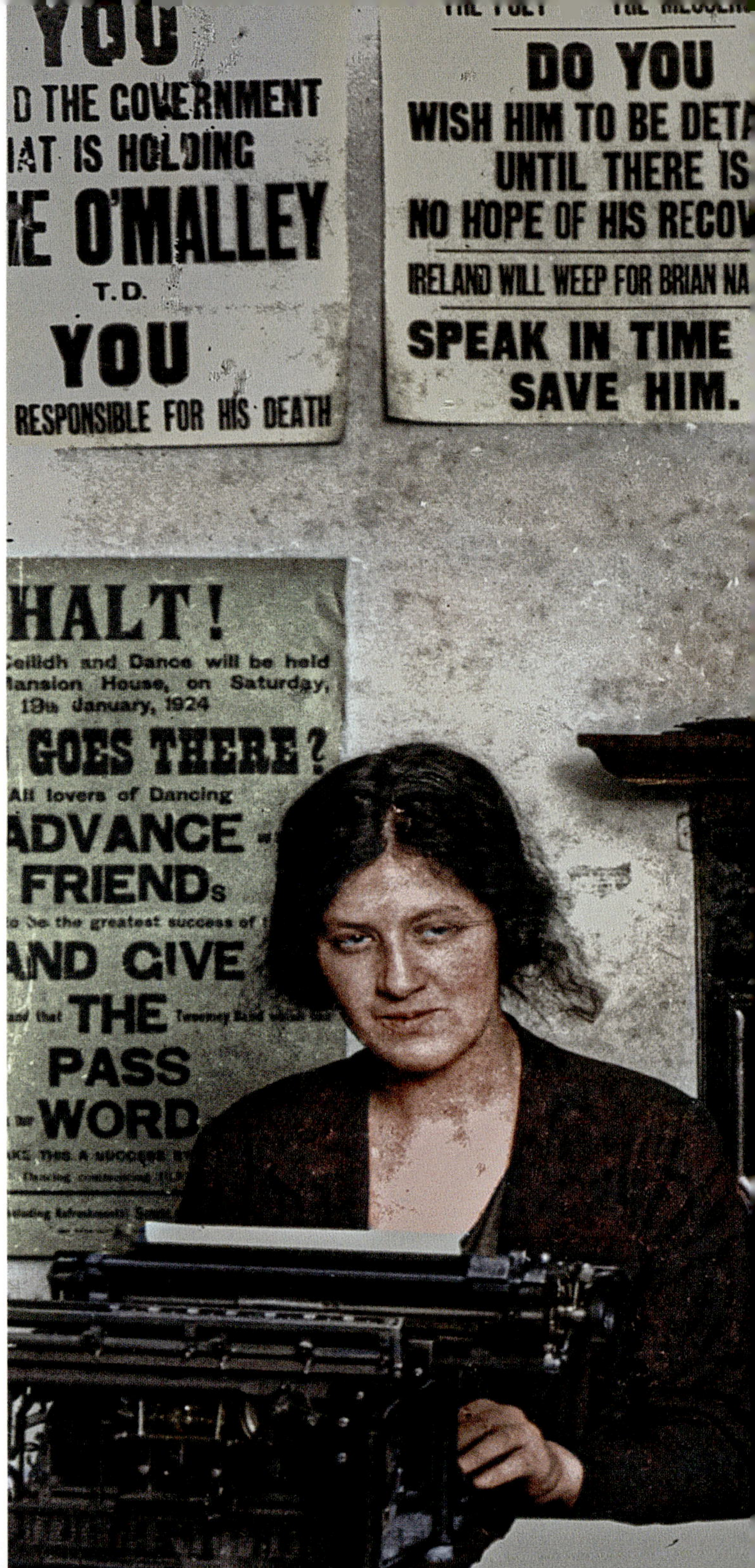

Women at work at the Sinn Féin HQ, 22-23 Suffolk Street, Dublin, towards the end of 1923. Unsurprisingly, the office was the subject of many raids by Free State forces, who arrested several women workers here, imprisoning them in Dublin prisons. Releasing imprisoned Republicans was a constant theme, as the posters on the wall indicate. The central poster, with the strapline 'Do you realise your responsibility?' reproduces the picture (partially seen here), from the Paris *Le Petit Journal*, which sympathetically compares the October 1923 hunger strike with that of Terence MacSwiney three years before.

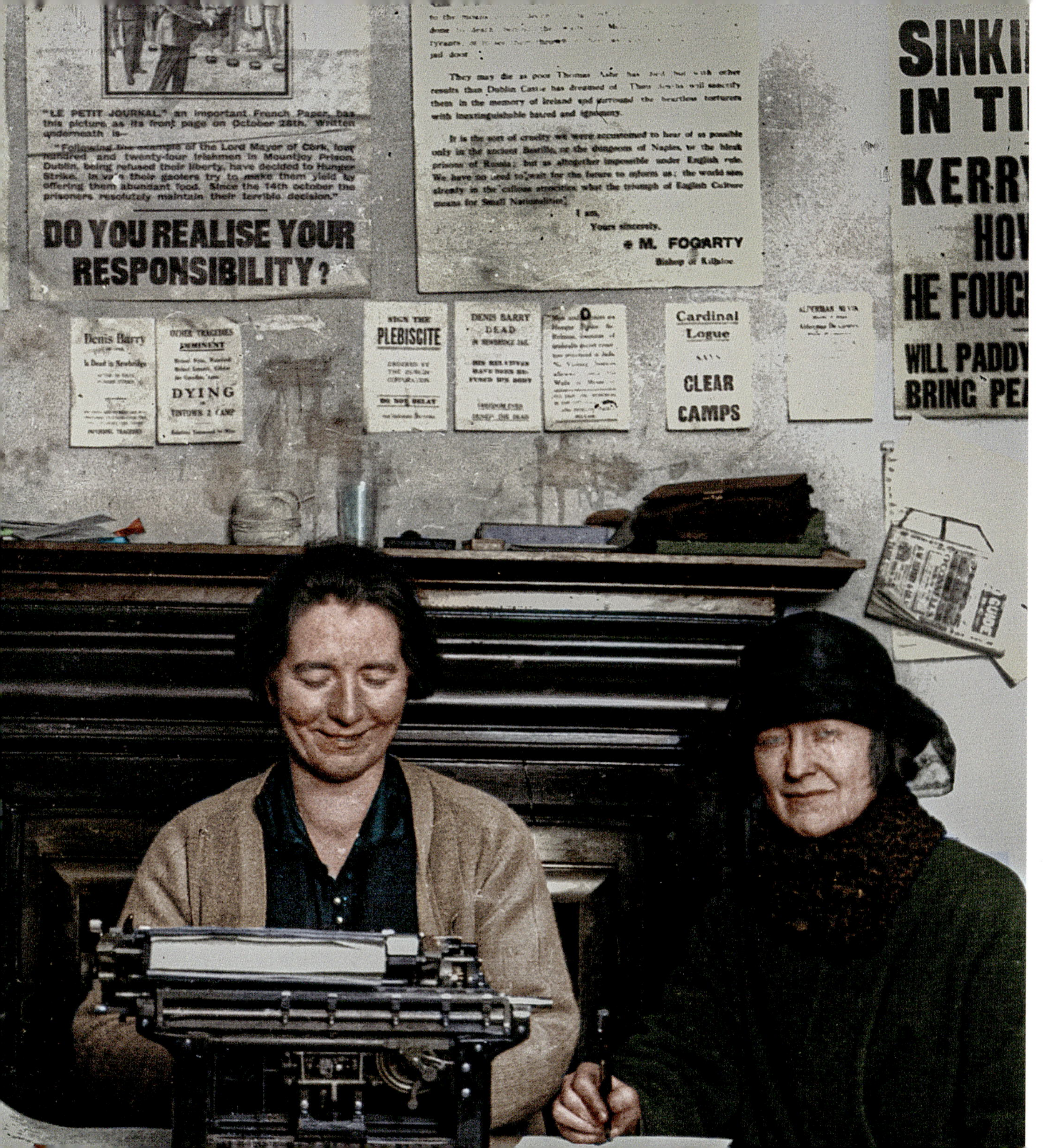
"LE PETIT JOURNAL," an important French Paper, has this picture as its front page on October 28th. Written underneath is:
"Following the example of the Lord Mayor of Cork, four hundred and twenty-four Irishmen in Mountjoy Prison, Dublin, being refused their liberty, have decided to Hunger Strike. In vain their gaolers try to make them yield by offering them abundant food. Since the 14th october the prisoners resolutely maintain their terrible decision."
DO YOU REALISE YOUR RESPONSIBILITY?
They may die as poor Thomas Ashe has died, but with other results than Dublin Castle has dreamed of. Those deaths will sanctify them in the memory of Ireland and surround the heartless tortures with inextinguishable hatred and ignominy.
It is the sort of cruelty we were accustomed to hear of as possible only in the ancient Bastile, or the dungeons of Naples, or the bleak prisons of Russia; but as altogether impossible under English rule. We have no need to wait for the future to inform us; the world sees already in the callous atrocities what the triumph of English Culture means for Small Nationalities.
I am,
Yours sincerely,
✠ M. FOGARTY
Bishop of Killaloe
Denis Barry
SIGN THE PLEBISCITE
DENIS BARRY DEAD
Cardinal Logue
CLEAR CAMPS
DYING
SINKI
IN TI
KERR
HO
HE FOUG
WILL PADDY
BRING PEA

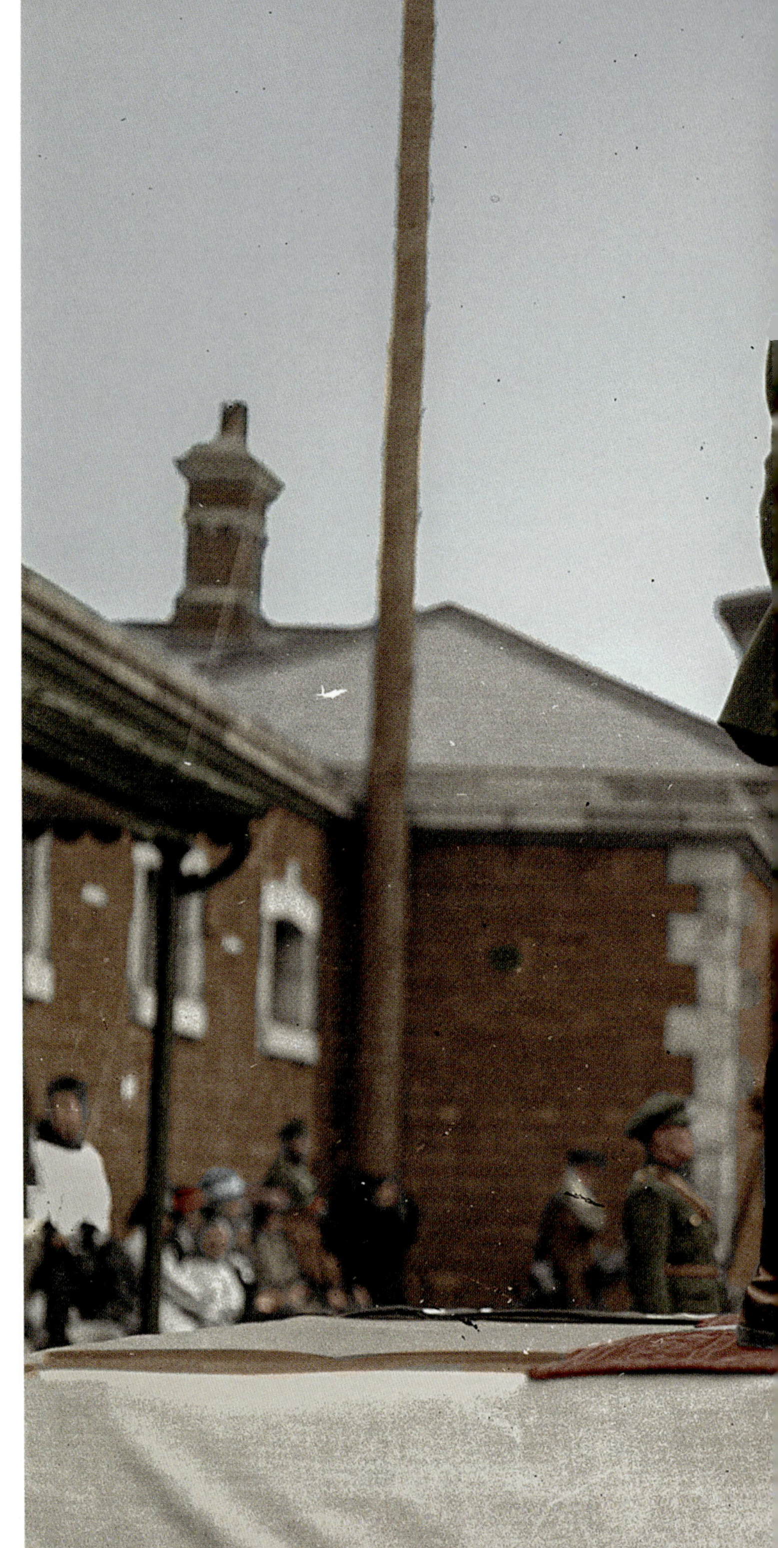

General Richard Mulcahy salutes at the stand-down ceremony, in September 1923, for the Railway Protection, Repair and Maintenance Corps. On disbandment, many of the 5,000-strong unit returned to employment in the railway companies; others joined the Engineering Corps of the National Army, whose size was soon rapidly reduced by the Free State Government, now that the war was won.

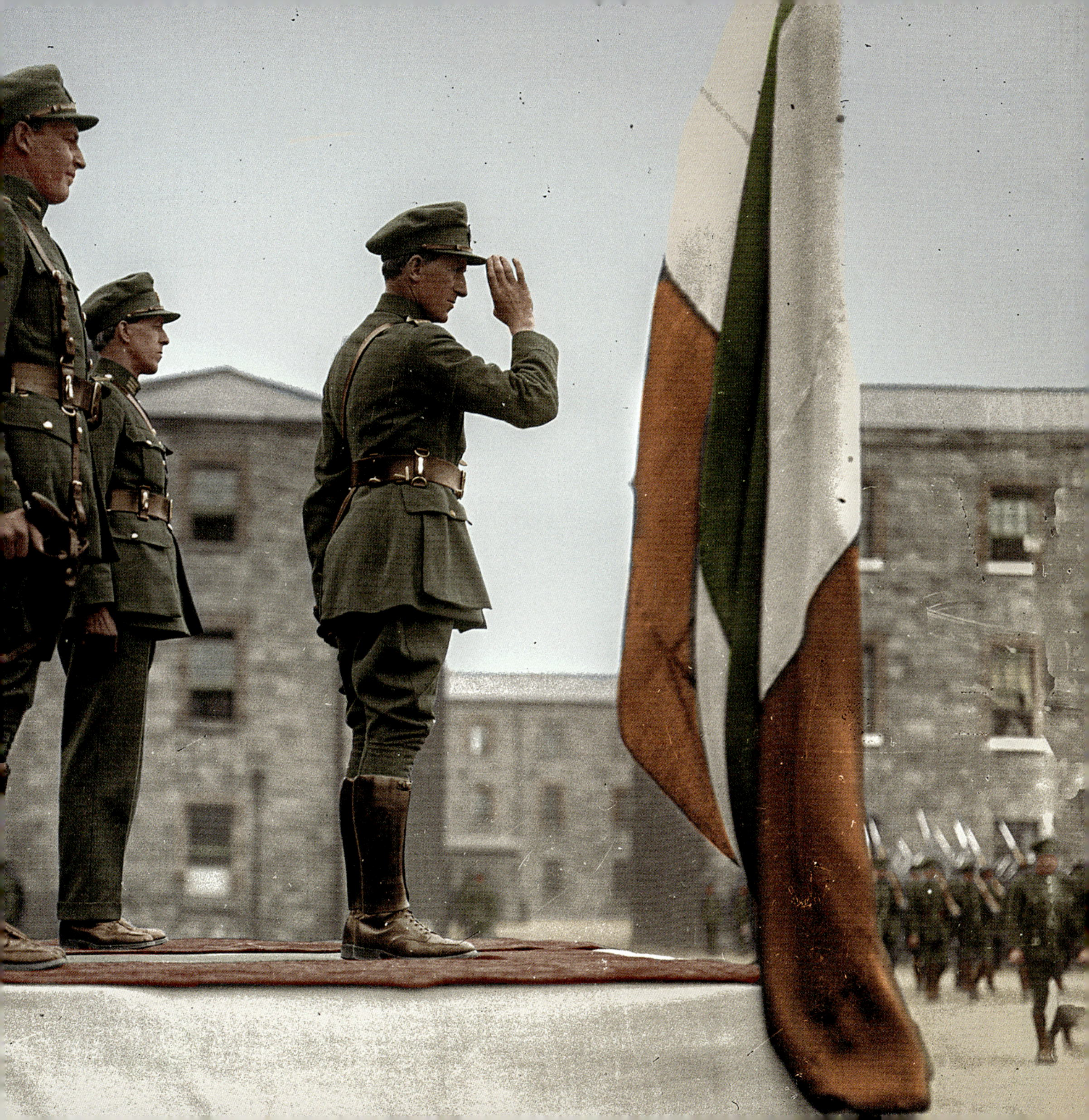

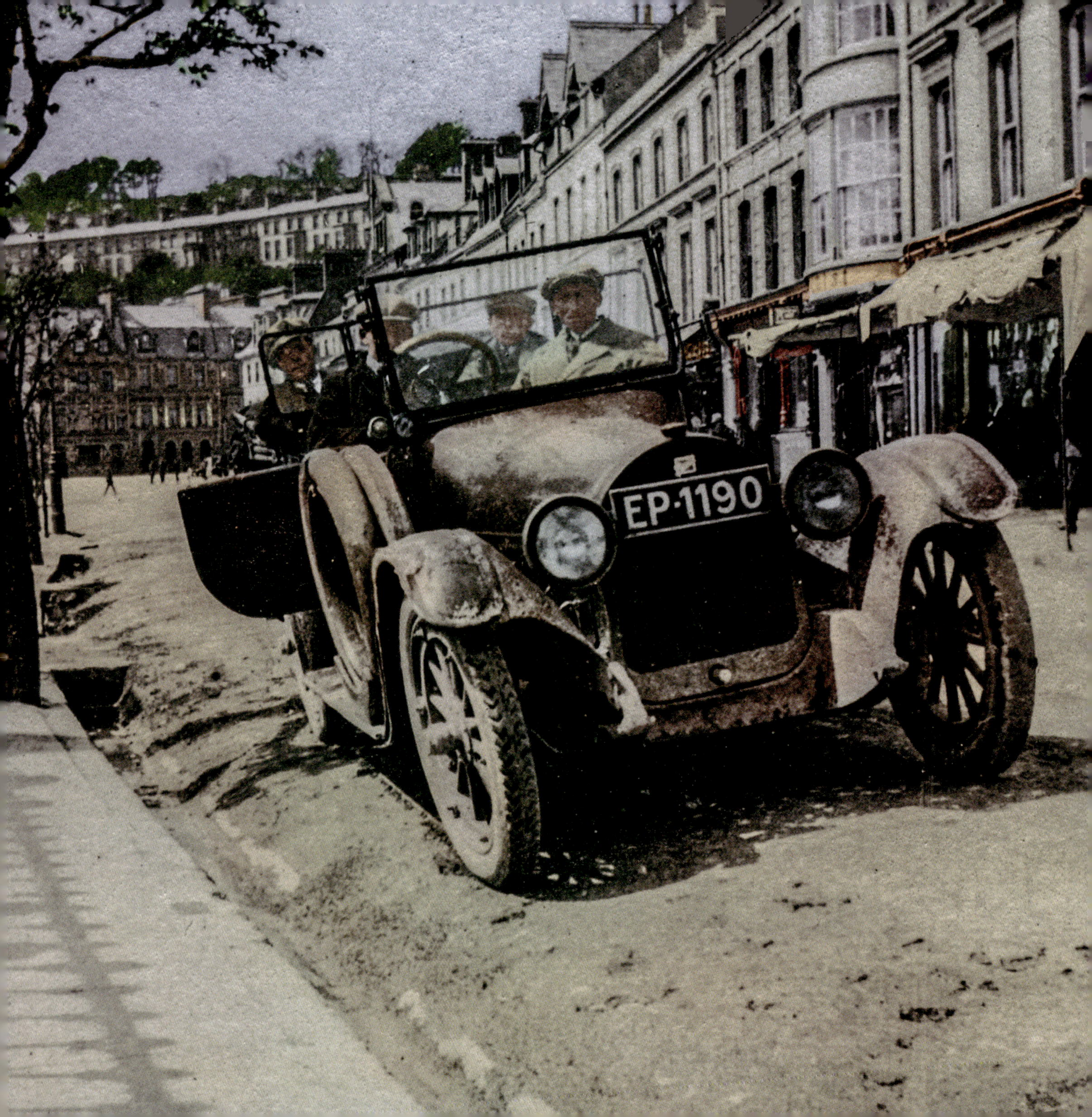

EP·1190

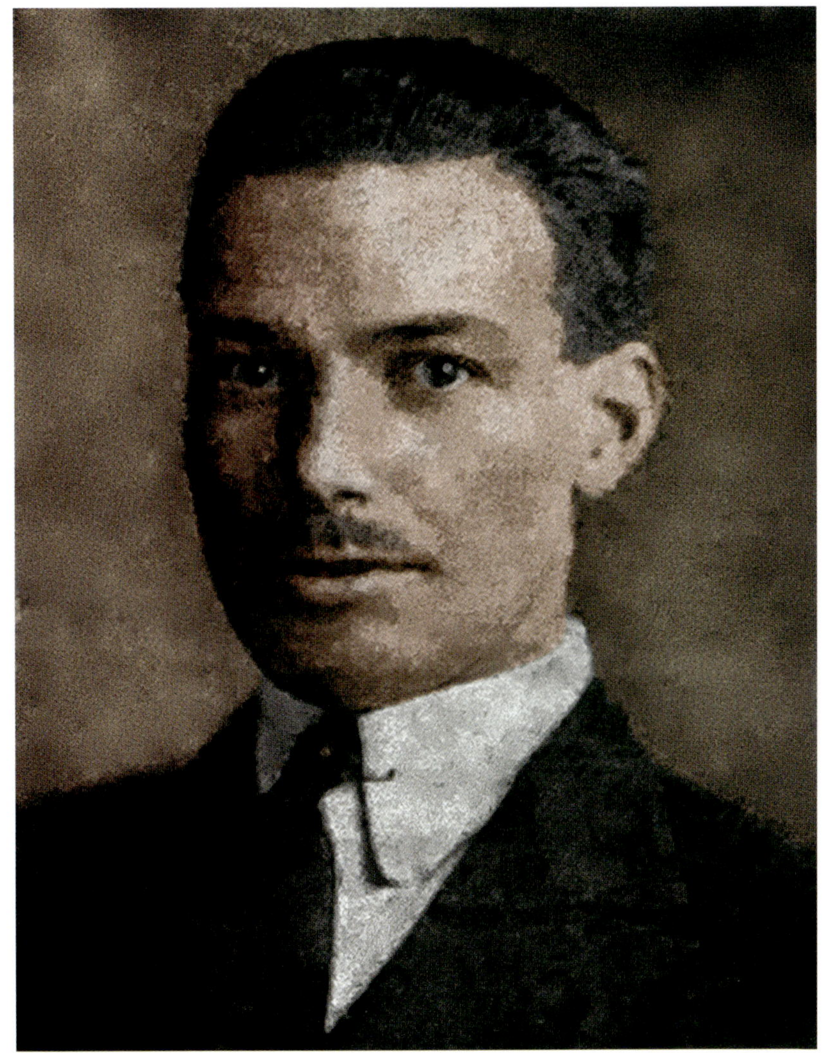

During the Civil War, the CID, based at Oriel House, resorted to a series of extra-judicial killings in Dublin. Noel Lemass (pictured here) was abducted in July 1923, murdered and his body dumped. A coroner's jury stated that it was murder and that 'forces of the State' had been implicated.

Left: for the defeated, there were few options. Emigration was one for these Republicans at Cobh, seen as they head for the harbour to embark on the SS *Ausonia* bound for Canada.

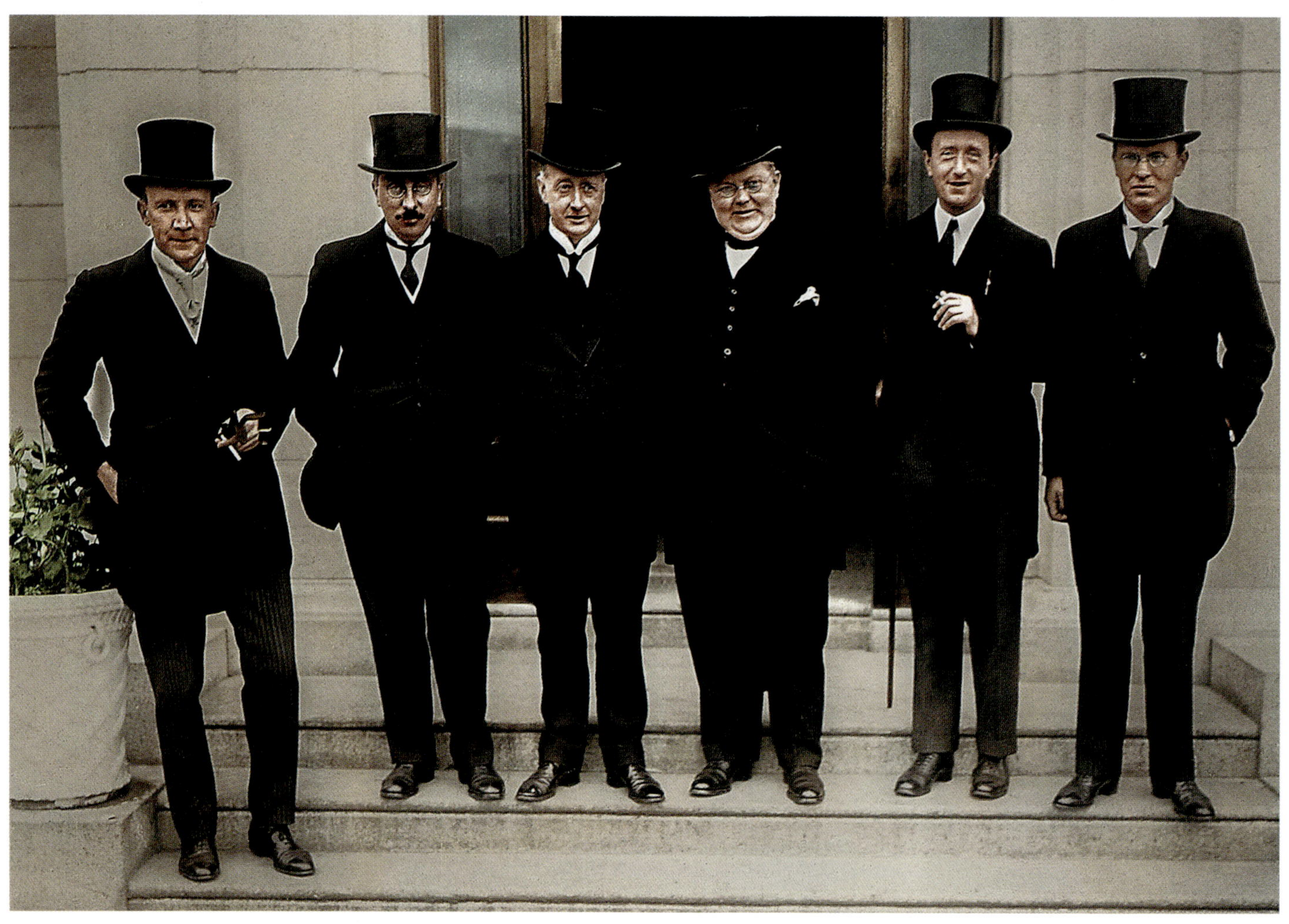

The victors: members of the Free State Government, demonstrating a penchant for formal wear. From left: Kevin O'Higgins, Michael Hayes, W.T. Cosgrave, Hugh Kennedy, Desmond Fitzgerald and Ernest Blythe. This conservative group of men now had to face the task of reducing a swollen army and rebuilding a bankrupt, bitter and divided State.

Right: assessing the damage at the Four Courts. It was rebuilt during the years 1924 to 1931. The State had to reconstruct buildings and infrastructure damaged, not just during the Civil War, but also from the period 1916 to 1921.

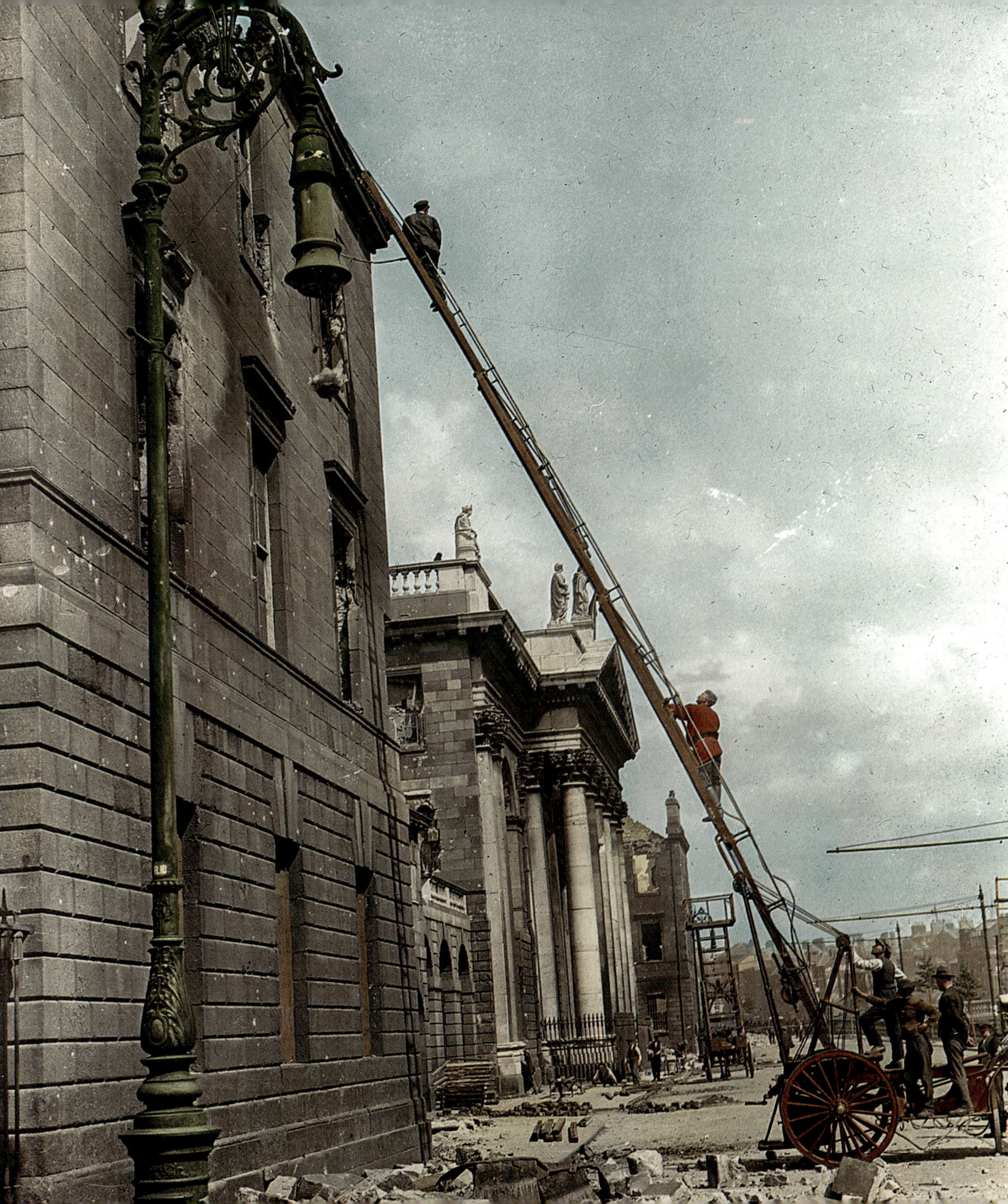

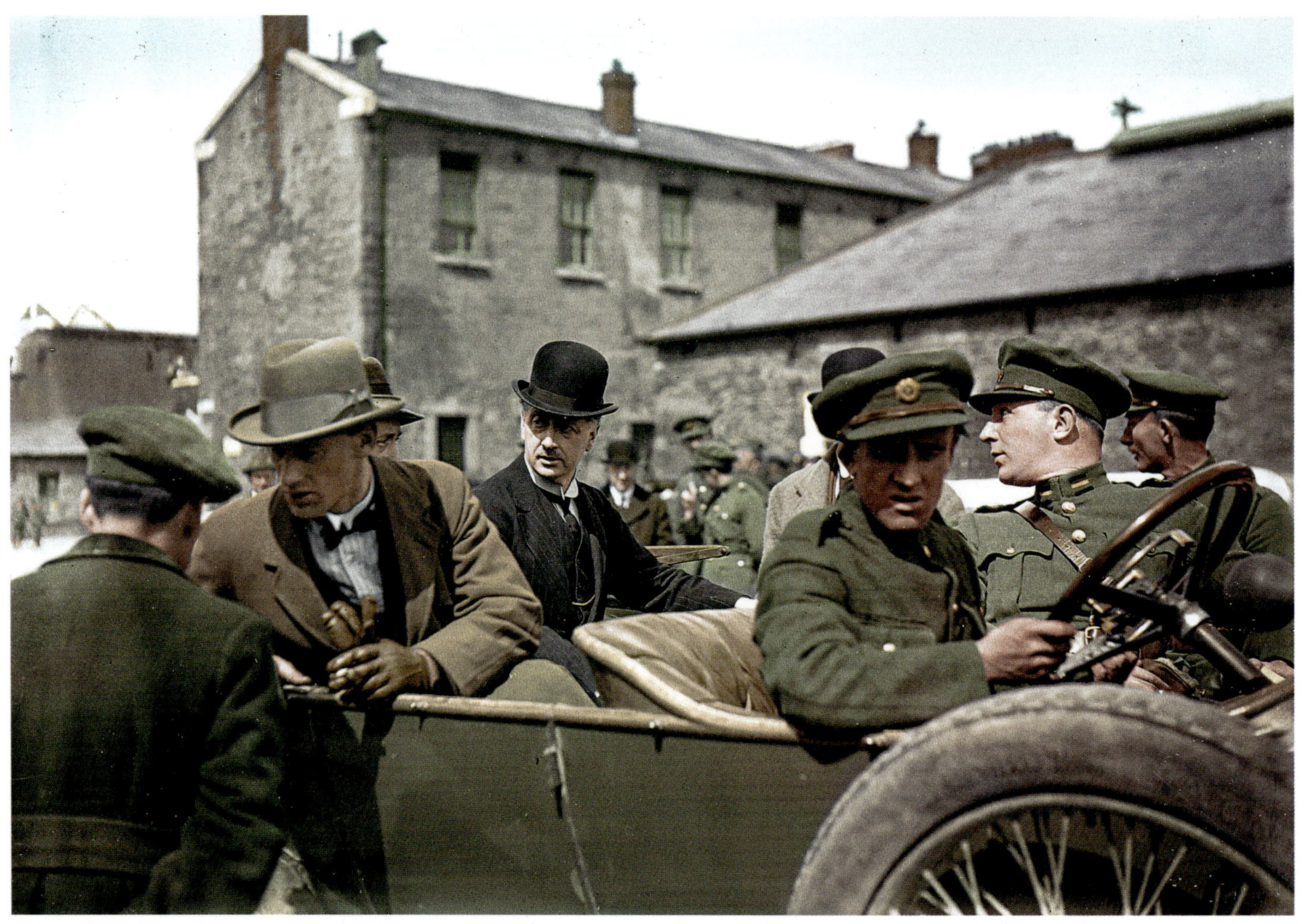

W.T. Cosgrave, President of the Executive Council, tours Cork in 1923. He is seen here at Victoria Barracks, originally named in honour of the British monarch, following her visit to Cork in 1849. After the Civil War it was renamed 'Michael' Barracks after the dead Commander-in-Chief. The name was changed to (the perhaps less clumsy) Collins Barracks in 1924.

Right: Kevin O'Higgins, Minister for Justice, addresses members of the Civic Guard at the Phoenix Park Depot in Dublin. An armed police force had been established in February 1922, but was disbanded by the Provisional Government after a mutiny at the Kildare training barracks in May. A new Civic Guard was constituted in September 1922. As the Civil War ended this new un-armed force was essential in underpinning Government control across the country.

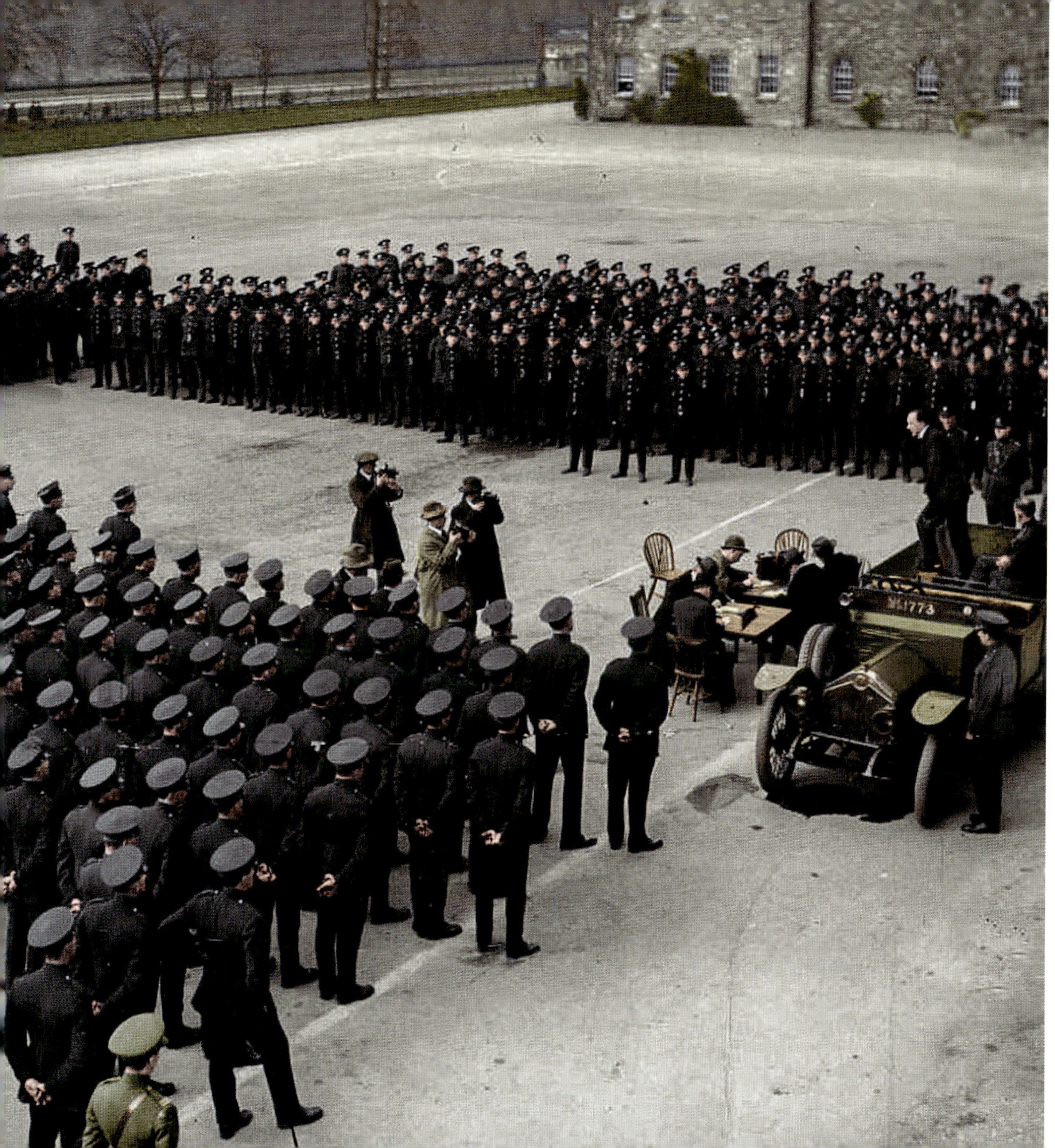

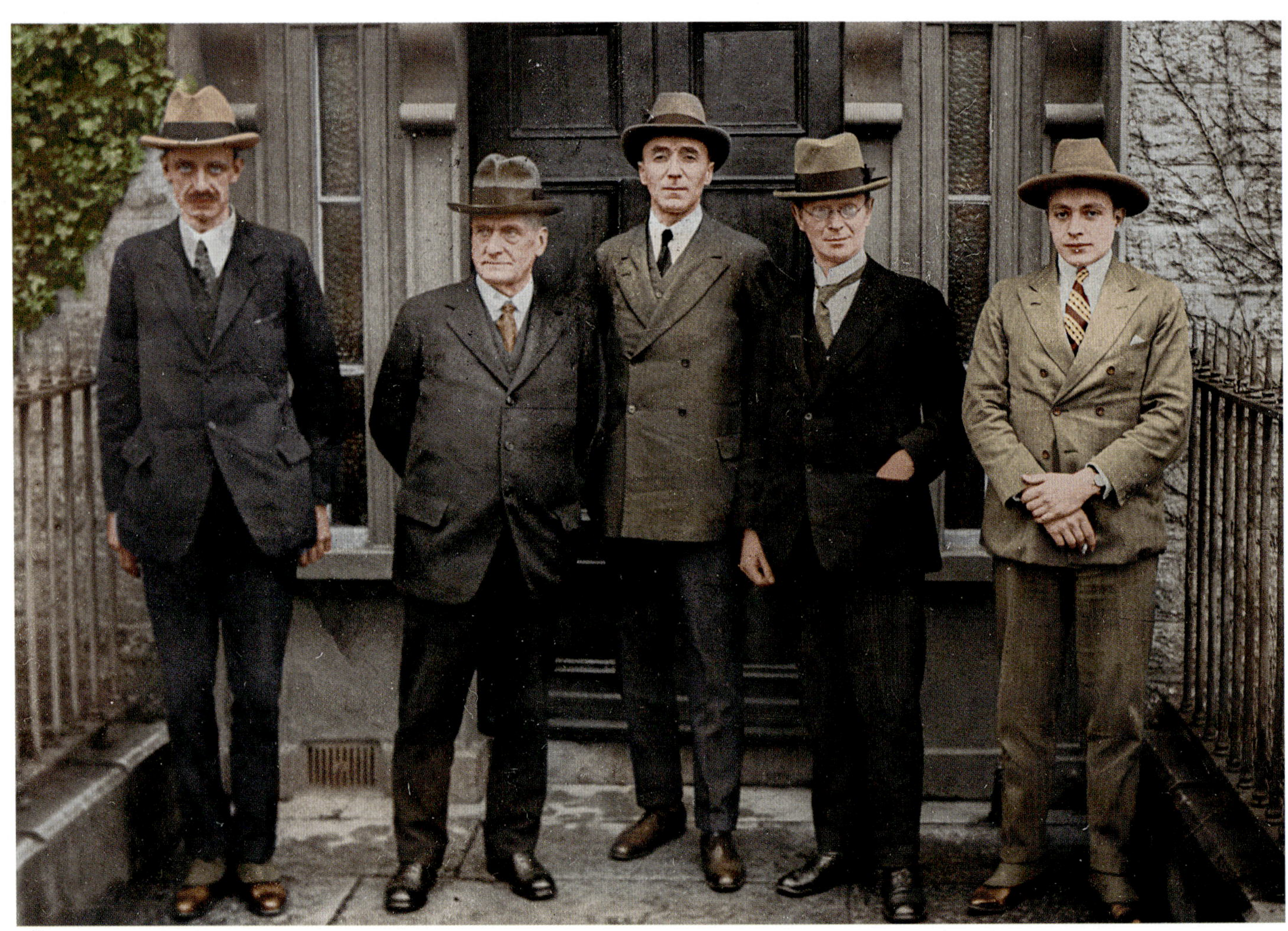

The coda: members of the Boundary Commission at its first sitting in December 1924 (Eoin MacNeill, second from right). During the Treaty negotiations, Lloyd George had implied that setting up such a commission would result in border gains, leading to a reduced and unsustainable Northern Ireland. In the event, with ambiguous terms of reference and the commission format stacked against him, the unassertive MacNeill resigned in November 1925. A month later, the Free State Government agreed to wrap it up, leaving the existing border intact, in effect bribed by the British promise to absolve them from servicing part of the Imperial debt.

Image Credits

Author's collection: 106-107, 137, 197, 201, 220, 261; Bibliothèque nationale de France: 37, 99, 235, 242; Cork Public Museum: 44-45, 70, 188; Dennis Kelly: 245; Derek Jones: 94; Diarmuid O'Connor: 34-35, 76, 86-87, 143, 244; Geraldine McCarthy/Donal King: 261; Getty Images: 52-53; Iarnród Éireann: 216, 221; Irish Railway Record Society: 217, 224-225; Joe Maxwell: 203; Joe Mooney: 68; Kilmainham Gaol Museum: 36, 46, 47, 56-57, 59, 62, 63, 64, 72, 89, 114, 116, 176, 234bl, 234tr, 234br, 234tr; Library of Congress: 14, 74; Limerick Museum: 120, 121, 122-123 (George Imbusch), 124-125 (George Imbusch), 126, 127, 128; Louise Mulcahy: 208, 251; Mediahuis Ireland (Independent News and Media): 10; Mercier Press Archive: 112, 142, 247, 249 (with help from Dún Laoghaire Public Library); Michael Collins Centre, Clonakilty: 189; Michael Fewer: 263; Military Archives, Ireland: 15, 66, 67, 81, 82, 92, 158, 181, 190, 200, 202, 204-205, 226, 254, 255, 258-259; National Library of Ireland: 11, 12-13, 16-17, 18-19, 22, 23, 24-25, 26-27, 28, 30-31, 32, 33, 38, 39, 40-41, 42-43, 48, 49, 50, 51, 69, 71 (George Morrison - GM), 73, 80, 84, 85, 91, 95, 96-97, 98, 102-103, 109, 111, 113, 117, 118 (GM), 129, 132-133, 134 (GM), 135, 136, 138 (GM), 140, 141 (GM), 144-145, 146 (GM), 147, 148, 149, 150-151, 152, 153, 154, 155, 159, 160-161, 162, 163, 164-165, 166-167, 168-169, 170-71, 172, 175, 178, 180, 182, 184-185, 186-187, 191, 194-195, 196, 198, 199, 206, 207 (GM), 211, 212, 213 (GM), 222 (GM), 223, 230, 231, 232-233, 234tl, 237 (GM), 238, 239, 240, 246, 250, 252-253, 256-257, 262, 265, 266; National Museum of Ireland (please note that the NMI was not involved in the colourisation process): 29, 58, 60-61, 177; 236; Pádraig Óg Ó Ruairc: 78-79, 83, 101, 105, 108, 115; Paul Comerford: 54-55; Peadar Collins: 227; Pearse Museum, Rathfarnham: 20-21; RTÉ Stills Library: 243; South Dublin Libraries, courtesy of Janice Broe: 88, 93, 100; Suzanne Buckley:173; Tommy Mooney: 228, 260; Tony McCarthy: 156, 210; UCD Libraries: 75, 90, 104, 130, 131, 174, 248; Veronica Barry (vignettes): 9, 77, 119, 179, 209; Waterford Museum: 139. Copyright © 2022: Irish Examiner: 65, 157, 192-193, 218-219, 264; Conor Dullaghan: 110, 183, 214-215, 229.

Every effort has been made to establish copyright, but if a copyright holder wishes to bring an error or omission to the notice of the publishers, then an appropriate acknowledgement will be made in any subsequent edition.

Glossary

Anglo-Irish Treaty	The Anglo-Irish Treaty signed on 6 December 1921 by Irish plenipotentiaries and representatives of the British Government. It provided for the establishment of an Irish Free State. The six-county entity given the name Northern Ireland was entitled to opt out, which it immediately did.
CID	Criminal Investigation Department, based at Oriel House (at the corner of Westland Row and Fenian Street, Dublin).
Cumann na mBan	Founded in early 1914, this republican women's auxiliary corps supported the objectives of the Irish Volunteers. Cumann na mBan participated strongly during the Rising, War of Independence and Civil War (mostly anti-Treaty) as an active, but non-combatant, support organisation.
Commandant	A military rank used in Ireland, equivalent to 'Major' in some other armies.
Dáil Éireann	The First Dáil (an assembly or parliament) met on 21 January 1919. It was established by Sinn Féin MPs (who won a majority of Irish seats) elected to the UK parliament in the December 1918 UK general election.
D&SER	Dublin & South Eastern Railway.
DMP	Dublin Metropolitan Police. An unarmed urban police force in Dublin, merged into the Garda Síochána in 1925.
Dublin Guard	The first unit in the Provisional Government Army, manned by experienced IRA veterans, including members of the 'Squad'.
Fianna Éireann	Irish nationalist youth organisation founded by Countess Markievicz and Bulmer Hobson in 1909. During the Civil War it took the anti-Treaty side
Free State	The State (known as the Irish Free State or in Irish Saorstát Éireann), a self-governing dominion of the British Empire, established on 6 December 1922 under the terms of the Anglo-Irish Treaty, replacing the Provisional Government established on 16 January 1922. Its remit covered 26 counties of Ireland. It existed until 1937 when, after a referendum, a new constitution, which replaced that of 1922, was approved. Ireland declared itself a republic under the Republic of Ireland Act 1948. This came into effect on 18 April 1949.
GHQ	General Headquarters.
GOC	General officer commanding, a general officer who holds a command appointment.
GNR (I)	Great Northern Railway (Ireland).
Government of Ireland Act (1920)	Also titled 'An Act to provide for the better government of Ireland'. This became law on 23 December 1920. It divided Ireland into two parts. 'Northern Ireland' comprised the six north-eastern counties. 'Southern Ireland' was to comprise the remaining 26 counties. Each entity was to have a bicameral parliament with limited powers. A Northern Ireland parliament was opened on 22 June 1921, in accordance with the Act.
GS&WR	Great Southern & Western Railway.
IRA	Irish Republican Army, which had its origins in the Irish Volunteers established in November 1913. After the split over the Treaty widened in January 1922, the forces on both sides continued to use the terminology 'IRA'. However, in July 1922 newspapers were instructed by the Provisional Government to describe its army as the 'National Army' and the anti-Treaty IRA as 'Irregulars'. The present-day official title in Irish of the Irish Defence Forces is: Óglaigh na hÉireann.
Kingstown	Renamed Dún Laoghaire in 1922.
L&NWR	London and North Western Railway.
MGWR	Midland Great Western Railway.
Northern Ireland	A constituent unit of the United Kingdom of Great Britain and Northern Ireland. It comprises six Irish counties – Antrim, Armagh, Down, Fermanagh, Derry (shired as Londonderry) and Tyrone.
OC	Officer Commanding.
Queenstown	Renamed Cobh in 1922.
RPR&MC	Railway Protection, Repair and Maintenance Corps, established in October 1922, a unit of the National Army.
Sackville Street	Renamed O'Connell Street in 1924.
Sinn Féin	Founded in 1905, under the leadership of Arthur Griffith, who wished to establish a national legislature in Ireland. Griffith and the organisation did not participate in the Rising, despite it being dubbed the 'Sinn Féin Rising' at the time. It was restructured in 1917 to take a more radical nationalist and republican direction.
Squad	A small unit (of tough and resilient Volunteers, who soon gained expertise in assassination) established in 1920 by Michael Collins, to counter British intelligence efforts.
TD	Teachta Dála (member of parliament, Dáil Éireann).
'Trucer'	A derogatory term (sometimes 'Trucileer'). It reflects the pro-Treaty perception that many flocked to join the anti-Treaty IRA after the Truce, having played no part in the War of Independence — hence the slogan 'We have no time for Trucers' chalked on the Lancia during the Sackville Street fighting (page 94). The other side harboured a similar opinion about their pro-Treaty opponents.

Bibliography

Archives Consulted:
Capuchin Archives, Dublin; National Archives, Dublin; Military Archives, Dublin; National Library of Ireland, Dublin; National Museum of Ireland, Dublin; British National Archives, Kew, London; UCD Archives, Dublin.

Periodicals:
General Irish and British newspapers; The Defence Forces Magazine: *An Cosantóir*; *History Ireland*; *Irish Historical Studies*; Journal of the Irish Railway Record Society; *The Irish Sword*.

Books:
Andrews, C. S., *Dublin Made Me*, Lilliput Press, Dublin, 2001.
Barry, M. B., *The Green Divide, an Illustrated History of the Irish Civil War*, Andalus Press, 2014.
Barry, M. B., *An Illustrated History of the Irish Revolution, 1916-1923*, Andalus Press, 2020.
Barry, T., *Guerrilla Days in Ireland*, Mercier Press, Cork, 1955.
Béaslaí, P., *Michael Collins and the Making of the New Ireland*, Phoenix Publishing Company, Dublin, 1926.
Borgonovo, J., *The Battle for Cork*, Mercier Press, Cork, 2011.
Carroll, A., *Seán Moylan: Rebel Leader*, Mercier Press, Cork, 2010.
Connell, J., *Dublin in Rebellion: A Directory 1913-1923*, Lilliput Press, Dublin, 2009.
Connolly, C., *Michael Collins,* Weidenfeld & Nicholson, London, 1996.
Coogan, T. P., *Michael Collins*, Arrow Books, London, 1990.
Coogan, T. P., *De Valera: Long Fellow, Long Shadow*, Hutchinson, London, 1993.
Curran, M., *The Birth of the Irish Free State 1921-1923*, University of Alabama Press, Alabama, 1980.
Deasy, L., *Brother against Brother*, Mercier Press, Cork, 1998.
Dorney, J., *The Civil War in Dublin*, Merrion Press, Dublin 2017.
Doyle, T., *The Civil War in Kerry*, Mercier Press, Cork, 2008.
Doyle, T., *The Summer Campaign in Kerry*, Mercier Press, Cork, 2010.
Durney, J., *The Civil War in Kildare,* Mercier Press, Cork, 2011.
English, R., *Ernie O'Malley: IRA Intellectual*, Oxford University Press, Oxford, 1999.
Enright, S., *The Irish Civil War: Law, Execution and Atrocity*, Irish Academic Press, 2022.
Farry, M., *The Irish Revolution, 1912-23, Sligo*, Four Courts Press, Dublin, 2012.
Farry, M., *The Aftermath of Revolution, Sligo 1921-23*, University College Dublin Press, Dublin, 2000.
Fewer, M., *The Battle of the Four Courts*, Head of Zeus, London, 2018.
Ferriter, D., *Between Two Hells: The Irish Civil War*, Profile Books, London, 2021.
Garvin, T., *1922: The Birth of Irish Democracy*, Gill & Macmillan, Dublin, 1996.
Gillis, L., *Revolution in Dublin: A Photographic History 1913-1923*, Mercier Press, Cork, 2013.
Gillis, L., *The Fall of Dublin*, Mercier Press, Cork, 2011.
Greaves, C. D., *Liam Mellows and the Irish Revolution*, Lawrence & Wishart, London, 1971.
Harrington, M., *The Munster Republic: The Civil War in North Cork*, Mercier Press, Cork, 2009.
Harrington, N. C., *Kerry Landing: August 1922*, Anvil Books, Dublin, 1992.
Hopkinson, M., *Green against Green, The Irish Civil War*, Gill & Macmillan, Dublin, 1988.
Kissane, B., *The Politics of the Civil War*, Oxford University Press, Oxford, 2005.
Lynch, C., ed., *From the GPO to Clashmealcon Caves*, North Kerry Republican Memorial Committee, 2003.
MacCarron, D., *Wings over Ireland: The Story of the Irish Air Corps*, Midland Publishing, 1996.
McCarthy, B., *The Civic Guard Mutiny*, Mercier Press, Cork, 2012.
McCarthy, C., *Cumann na mBan and the Irish Revolution*, The Collins Press, Cork, 2007.
McGarry, F., *Eoin O'Duffy: A Self-Made Hero*, Oxford University Press, Oxford, 2005.
McGowan, J., *In the Shadow of Benbulben*, Aeolus Publications, Manorhamilton, 1993.
Mac Suain, S., *County Wexford's Civil War*, Wexford, 1995.
McIvor, A., *A History of the Irish Naval Service*, Irish Academic Press, 1994.
Macardle, D., *The Irish Republic*, Merlin Publishing, 1999.
Macardle, D., *Tragedies of Kerry 1922-1923*, Irish Freedom Press, 2004.
Macready, N., *Annals of an Active Life*, Hutchinson, London, 1924.

Maxwell, J., Cummins, P. J., *The Irish Air Corps, An Illustrated Guide*, Max Decals Publications, Dublin, 2009.
Mooney, T., *Cry of the Curlew: A History of the Déise Brigade IRA and the War of Independence*, De Paor, Dungarvan, 2012.
Morrison, G., Coogan, T. P., *The Irish Civil War*, Weidenfeld & Nicholson, London, 1998.
Mulcahy, R., *My Father the General: Richard Mulcahy and the Military History of the Revolution*, Liberties Press, Dublin, 2009.
Murphy, G., *The Year of Disappearances: Political Killings in Cork 1921-1922*, Gill & Macmillan, Dublin, 2011.
Murphy, S., *The Comeraghs: Refuge of Rebels*, Kennedy Print, Clonmel, 1980.
National Graves Association, *The Last Post,* Dublin, 1932.
Neeson, E., *The Irish Civil War*, Poolbeg Press, Dublin, 1989.
O'Callaghan, J., *The Battle for Kilmallock*, Mercier Press, Cork, 2011.
Ó Comhraí, C., *Revolution in Connacht: A Photographic History 1913-1923*, Mercier Press, Cork, 2013.
O'Connor, D., Connolly, F., *Sleep Soldier Sleep: The Life and Times of Padraig O'Connor*, Miseab Publications, 2011.
O'Donoghue, F., *No Other Law: The Story of Liam Lynch and the Irish Republican Army, 1916-1923*, Irish Press, 1954.
Ó Drisceoil, D., *Peadar O'Donnell*, Cork University Press, Cork, 2001.
Ó Duibhir, L., *Donegal & the Civil War: The Untold Story,* Mercier Press, Cork, 2011.
O'Dwyer, M., *Seventy Seven of Mine said Ireland*, Deshaoirse, Co. Tipperary, 2006.
O'Farrell, P., *Who's Who in the Irish War of Independence and Civil War, 1916-1923*, Lilliput Press, Dublin, 1997.
Ó Gadhra, N., *Civil War in Connacht*, Mercier Press, Cork, 1999.
O'Malley, C., Martin, H., *Ernie O'Malley: A Life,* Merrion Press, Dublin, 2021
O'Malley, C., Ó Comhraí, C., eds, *The Men Will Talk to Me: Galway Interviews by Ernie O'Malley*, Mercier Press, Cork, 2013.
O'Malley, C., Horgan, T., eds, *The Men Will Talk to Me: Kerry Interviews by Ernie O'Malley*, Mercier Press, Cork, 2012.
O'Malley, E., *On Another Man's Wound*, Anvil Books, Dublin, 1979.
O'Malley, E., *The Singing Flame*, Mercier Press, Cork, 2012.
O'Reilly, T., *Rebel Heart: George Lennon: Flying Column Commander*, Mercier Press, Cork, 2005.
Ó Ruairc, P., *Revolution: A Photographic History of Revolutionary Ireland 1913-1923*, Mercier Press, Cork, 2011.
Ó Ruairc, P., *The Battle for Limerick City*, Mercier Press, Cork, 2010.
Pinkman, J. A., *In the Legion of the Vanguard*, Mercier Press, Cork, 1998.
Quinn, J., *The Story of the Drumboe Martyrs*, McKinney, Letterkenny, 1958.
Regan, J. M., *The Irish Counter-Revolution 1921-1936*, Gill & Macmillan, Dublin, 1999.
Regan, J. M., *Myth and the Irish State*, Irish Academic Press, Kildare, 2013.
Reynolds, B. A., *William T. Cosgrave and the Foundation of the Irish Free State, 1922-23*, Kilkenny, 1999.
Riccio, R., *AFVs in Irish Service since 1922: From the National Army to the Defence Forces*, MMP Books, Petersfield, Hampshire, 2010.
Riccio, R., *Irish Coastal Landings 1922*, Casemate Publishers, 2015.
Ring, J., *Erskine Childers,* Faber & Faber, London, 2011.
Ryan, G., *The Works: Celebrating 150 Years of Inchicore Works,* (n.p.), Dublin, 1996.
Ryan, M., *The Day Michael Collins Was Shot*, Poolbeg Press, Dublin, 1998.
Ryan, M., *The Real Chief: Liam Lynch*, Mercier Press, Cork, 2005.
Ryan, M., *Tom Barry: IRA Freedom Fighter*, Mercier Press, Cork, 2012.
Ryle Dwyer, T., *Michael Collins and the Civil War*, Mercier Press, Cork, 2012.
Ryle Dwyer, T., *Tans, Terror & Troubles: Kerry's Real Fighting Story*, Mercier Press, Cork, 2001.
Share, B., *In Time of Civil War: The Conflict on the Irish Railways 1922-23*, The Collins Press, Cork, 2006.
Townshend, C., *The Partition*, Allen Lane, London, 2021.
Valiulis, M., *Portrait of a Revolutionary: General Richard Mulcahy and the Founding of the Irish Free State*, Irish Academic Press, Dublin, 1992.
Walsh, M., *In Defence of Ireland: Irish Military Intelligence 1918-45*, The Collins Press, Cork, 2010.
Yeates, P., *A City in Civil War: Dublin 1921–1924*, Gill & Macmillan, Dublin, 2015.
Younger, C., *Ireland's Civil War*, Fontana Press, London, 1986.

Index